THE SHIFTING ALLOCATION OF AUTHORITY IN INTERNATIONAL LAW

International law is fragmented and complex, and at the same time increasingly capable of shaping reality in areas as diverse as human rights, trade and investment, and environmental law. The increased influences of international law and its growing institutionalisation and judicialisation invites reconsideration of the question as to how the authority to make and interpret international law should be allocated among states, international organisations and tribunals—or in other words, 'who should decide what?'—in a system that formally lacks a central authority? This is not only a juridical question, but one that lies at the very heart of the political legitimacy of international law as a system of governance, defining the relationship between those who create the law and those who are governed by it in a globalising world.

In this book, leading international legal scholars address a broad range of theoretical and practical aspects of the question of allocation of authority in international law and debate the feasibility of three alternative paradigms for international organisation: sovereignty, supremacy and subsidiarity. The various contributions transcend technical solutions to what is in essence a problem of international constitutional dimensions. They deal, inter alia, with the structure of the international legal system and the tenacity of sovereignty as one of its foundations, assess the role of supremacy in inter-judicial relations, and draw lessons from the experience of the European Union in applying the principle of subsidiarity.

This volume will be of great interest both to scholars and practitioners of international law.

Volume 19: Studies in International Law

Studies in International Law

Volume 1: Between Light and Shadow: The World Bank, the International Monetary Fund and International Human Rights Law
Mac Darrow

Volume 2: Toxics and Transnational Law: International and European Regulation of Toxic Substances as Legal Symbolism
Marc Pallemaerts

Volume 3: The Chapter VII Powers of the United Nations Security Council
Erika de Wet

Volume 4: Enforcing International Law Norms Against Terrorism
Edited by Andrea Bianchi

Volume 5: The Permanent International Criminal Court
Edited by Dominic McGoldrick, Peter Rowe and Eric Donnelly.

Volume 6: Regional Organisations and the Development of Collective Security
Ademola Abass

Volume 7: Islamic State Practices, International Law and the Threat from Terrorism: A Critique of the 'Clash of Civilizations' in the New World Order
Javaid Rehman

Volume 8: Predictablity and Flexibility in the Law of Maritime Delimitation
Yoshifumi Tanaka

Volume 9: Biotechnology and International Law
Edited by Francesco Francioni and Tullio Scovazzi

Volume 10: The Development of Human Rights Law by the Judges of the International Court of Justice
Shiv Bedi

Volume 11: The Environmental Accountability of the World Bank to Third Party Non-State Actors
Alix Gowlland-Gualtieri

Volume 12: Transnational Corporations and Human Rights
Edited by Olivier De Schutter

Volume 13: Biotechnologies and International Human Rights
Edited by Francesco Francioni

Volume 14: Human Security and International Law: Prospects and Problems
Barbara Von Tigerstrom

Volume 15: The Arms Trade and International Law
Zeray Yihdego

Volume 16: Africa: Mapping New Boundaries in International Law
Edited by Jeremy Levitt

Volume 17: Forced Migration, Human Rights and Security
Edited by Jane McAdam

Volume 18: The Use of Nuclear Weapons and the Protection of the Environment during Armed Conflict
Erik Koppe

The Shifting Allocation of Authority in International Law

Considering Sovereignty, Supremacy and Subsidiarity

Essays in honour of
Professor Ruth Lapidoth

Edited by
Tomer Broude and Yuval Shany

·HART·
PUBLISHING

OXFORD AND PORTLAND, OREGON
2008

Published in North America (US and Canada) by

Hart Publishing

c/o International Specialized Book Services
920 NE 58th Avenue, Suite 300
Portland, OR 97213-3786
USA
Tel: +1-503-287-3093 or toll-free: (1)-800-944-6190
Fax: +1 503 280 8832
E-mail: orders@isbs.com
Website: www.isbs.com

Hart Publishing, 16C Worcester Place, Oxford OX1 2JW, UK
Telephone: +44 (0)1865 517530 Fax: +44(0)1865 510710
E-mail: mail@hartpub.co.uk
Website: http://www.hartpub.co.uk

British Library Cataloguing in Publication Data

Data Available

ISBN: 978-1-84113-797-1

Typeset by Forewords, Oxford
Printed and bound in Great Britain by
Lightning Source UK Ltd

Acknowledgements

This collection of essays would not have seen the light of day had it not been for the efforts and support of numerous individuals and institutions to whom we owe a debt of gratitude. First, we thank our fifteen authors for taking the time and care to write thought-provoking and original contributions. It has been an honor and pleasure to work with them all! Second, we thank Ms Efrat Hakak, our dedicated assistant editor, who has provided us invaluable help in editing and proof-reading. Her work has been exemplary in terms of quality and efficiency. Third, we note with appreciation the financial support of the Feinberg Foundation for the advancement of international law research in this publication. Fourth, we are grateful to the Hebrew University, the University's International Law Forum, the Leonard Davis Institute for International Relations, the Jean Monnet Module of the European Community, the Dr Emilio von Hofmansthal Fund and the Hersch Lauterpacht Fund for their generous support of the conference which led to the present publication. In the same vein, we thank Ms Irit Magora-Levy, the Associate Dean of the Hebrew University Law Faculty and her assistant, Ms Mihal Leibel, for their help in organising the aforementioned 2006 conference. Finally, we thank Professor Ruth Lapidoth who provided us with a reason to initiate this publication. Her friendship and words of advice and encouragement have always been for us a major source of support and inspiration.

TB and YS
Reut, Israel

Contents

III
Allocation of Authority among Judicial Bodies

IV
Allocations of Authority in Specific Normative Contexts

Introduction

TOMER BROUDE and YUVAL SHANY

THIS COLLECTION OF essays examines the evolving structure of the allocation of authority in contemporary international law through the prisms of three organising principles: sovereignty, supremacy and subsidiarity. It strives to offer a variety of theoretical, analytical as well as practical responses and approaches to what has become an increasingly complicated and tense situation: an attempt by certain international law-makers, regimes and institutions to exert their authority vis-à-vis states and sub-statal entities, while addressing, at the same time, challenges to their legitimacy and efficacy from other international, national and non-state actors and norms.

THE ORIGINS OF THE BOOK: A TRIBUTE TO PROFESSOR RUTH LAPIDOTH

The essays published in this book were first presented at a conference held in June 2006 at the Hebrew University of Jerusalem, which celebrated the life and work of **Professor Ruth Lapidoth**. Ruth Lapidoth—to whom this book is dedicated—has had a remarkable international law career. After completing her doctoral thesis at the Sorbonne in 1956, she returned to Israel and became a member of the law faculty of the Hebrew University of Jerusalem for a period of almost fifty years. Through these years, Ruth Lapidoth also served Israel in a number of diplomatic and governmental capacities (including serving as the legal adviser to the Israeli Foreign Ministry and participating in the peace negotiations with Egypt) and served as an arbitrator in the famous Taba arbitration.[1] Even after her retirement, Ruth Lapidoth has remained engaged with academic work—she currently chairs the Hebrew University's International Law Forum and teaches at the School of Law of the Israel College of

[1] *Boundary Dispute Concerning the Taba Area* (Egypt/Israel) (1988) 27 ILM 1421.

Management Academic Studies; she also continues to publish on a regular basis on a variety of international law topics. This impressive life's work and record of achievements has received widespread acclaim and Ruth Lapidoth has been granted many prizes and awards, including awards on prominent contributions to law presented by the American Society of International Law and the Israeli Bar Association in 2000 and 2004, respectively. In 2006, she was awarded the Israel Prize—the highest honour and most prestigious award granted to Israeli citizens by the State of Israel.

Large parts of Ruth Lapidoth's scholarship are directly related to the theme of the present book: many of her numerous books and articles—particularly on the topic of autonomy,[2] Jerusalem,[3] the Middle East peace process,[4] the law of the sea,[5] and the relations between national and international law[6]—share a few common threads related to the allocation of authority in international law. First, she has embraced in her work functional arrangements, which deviate, on a pragmatic basis, from traditional models of regulation. Thus, autonomy deviates from long-established notions of statehood and absolute sovereignty; the holy places in Jerusalem ought to be governed by 'functional' not 'formal' sovereignty; and pragmatic harmonisation between national and international law should be developed, at the expense of traditional dualism. Second, in

[2] See, eg, R Lapidoth, *Autonomy: Flexible Solutions to Ethnic Conflicts* (Washington, United States Institute of Peace Press, 1997); R Lapidoth, 'Autonomie, unité et démocratie', in R Le Coadic (ed), *Identités et Démocratie: Diversité Culturelle et Mondialisation—Repenser la Démocratie* (Rennes, Presses universitaires de Rennes, 2003) 263; R Lapidoth, 'Autonomy and Sovereignty: Are They Mutually Exclusive?', in Mala Tabori and Amos Shapira (eds), *New Political Entities in Public and Private International Law* (The Hague, Kluwer, 1999) 3; R Lapidoth, 'Redefining Authority: The Past, Present and Future of Sovereignty' (1995) 17 *Harvard International Review* 8; R Lapidoth, 'Sovereignty in Transition' (1992) 45 *Journal of International Affairs* 325.

[3] See, eg, R Lapidoth, M Hirsch and D Housen-Couriel, *Whither Jerusalem? Proposals and Positions Concerning the Future of Jerusalem* (Dordrecht, Martinus Nijhoff and the Jerusalem Institute for Israel Studies, 1995); R Lapidoth, 'Holy Places' in N Cohen and A Heldrich (eds), *The Three Religions* (Munich, Herbert Utz Verlag, 2002) 19; R Lapidoth, 'Jerusalem—Some Jurisprudential Aspects' (1996) 45 *Catholic University Law Review* 661.

[4] See, eg, R Lapidoth, 'Israel and the Palestinians: Some Legal Issues' (2001) 76 *Die Friedens-Warte* 211; R Lapidoth, 'Security Council Resolution 242 at Twenty Five' (1992) 26 *Israel Law Review* 295; R Lapidoth , 'On the Relation Between the Camp David Frameworks and the Treaty of Peace—Another Dimension' (1980) 15 *Israel Law Review* 191.

[5] See, eg, R Lapidoth, *Les détroits en droit international* (Paris, Pedone, 1972); R Lapidoth, *Freedom of Navigation with Special Reference to International Waterways in the Middle East, Jerusalem* (Jerusalem, The Leonard Davis Institute for International Relations, 1975); R Lapidoth, *The Red Sea and the Gulf of Aden* (The Hague, Martinus Nijhoff, 1982); R Lapidoth, 'The Strait of Tiran, The Gulf of Aqaba, and the 1979 Treaty of Peace between Egypt and Israel' (1983) 77 *American Journal of International Law* 84; R Lapidoth, 'Le passage par le détroit de Tiran' (1969) *Revue Générale de Droit International Public* 30.

[6] See, eg, R Lapidoth, *Les rapports entre le droit international public et le droit interne en Israël* (Paris, Pedone, 1959); R Lapidoth, 'International Law within the Israeli Legal System' (1990) 24 *Israel Law Review* 451; R Lapidoth, 'De la valeur interne des traités internationaux dans le droit israélien' (1959) *Revue Générale de Droit International Public* 65, 221.

her work, Ruth Lapidoth has advocated the creation of distinct solutions specially tailored to accommodate specific problems. Hence, different principles may apply in Jerusalem to the management of municipal issues, on the one hand, and religious affairs, on the other; in the same vein, international straits are governed, according to Lapidoth, by unique rules (which derogate from the rules governing other parts of the sea). Third, Lapidoth's scholarship demonstrates the perforated nature of modern sovereignty—using the latter phrase, really, as an open-ended and loose framework of analysis always subject to overriding international public policy considerations.

THE GOAL OF THE BOOK: FOSTERING DEBATE ON APPROACHES TO ALLOCATION OF AUTHORITY

The present collection of essays builds upon Ruth Lapidoth's intellectual contributions. It represents an attempt by leading international law scholars and experts to systematically examine the tensions between traditional notions of sovereignty and the increasingly frequent allocation of decision-making authority to international organisations, courts and other international actors. This, in turn, facilitates a pragmatic examination of the usefulness of specific power-allocation rules, which may respond to some of the problems of legitimacy, effectiveness, predictability and co-ordination in international law. On a more theoretical level, the book discusses the legal configuration of the structures and meta-structures of international law, as a whole, as choices between (or combinations of) different theories on the allocation of power between international actors. It also assesses the feasibility and desirability of introducing or developing some general legal principles that would govern the allocation of power between the national and the international, as opposed to the case-by-case or regime-by-regime approach advocated by Ruth Lapidoth.

At all events, this book does not offer a single technical or formal solution to what is ultimately a political matter, nor does it argue that such a solution is either desirable or attainable. The book does not even purport to provide a unified theory or complete world view on these 'big' questions. This is partly because the allocation of authority in international law is constantly shifting, and may be in a permanent state of flux. Furthermore, considerable uncertainty and controversy still surround both the descriptive and normative elements of the discourse on the structure of authority.

What this book does seek to achieve, however, is a description and evaluation of important parts of the debate over the allocation of authority in international law, hoping to present a range of ideas on the topic and to foster discussion thereon by a diverse set of outstanding international legal scholars and experts. In other words, it aims to provide a comprehensive set of different approaches and entry points into this difficult debate.

HISTORICAL DEVELOPMENT AND THEORETICAL BACKGROUND

The classical paradigm of international law (commonly known as 'Westphalian') is 'horizontal' in nature. It is based upon the fundamental principle of state *sovereignty*, the formal equality of states and the principle of non-intervention; it also views state consent to international norms and specific regimes of international governance as international law's ultimate legitimising factor. This traditional conceptualisation reflects the lack of central authority in the international political system, and is most commonly contrasted with the centralised character of the state's domestic legal order. Still, this traditional construction does not reflect the complexity of contemporary international relations. The development of sophisticated global and regional institutions for international co-operation, the intensification of international legalisation and the process of judicialisation of international relations (demonstrated, inter alia, by the sharp increase in the number of international courts in recent years and the expansion of their legal authorities) have all contributed to the emergence of a new complex international order—in fact, a multiplicity of legal relationships, with increasingly discernible 'vertical' elements.

First, the gradual strengthening of international norms and institutions seems to have led to a concomitant erosion of national sovereignty and to the subjection of the national to the international in several important contexts. In other words, different degrees of authority have been transferred from the states to the international plane under varying legal and political terms.[7] Second, some international institutions have asserted the supremacy of their powers not only vis-à-vis their member states, but also with regard to other international institutions. Hence, vertical relations may now exist even between international organisations.[8] Third, the increased influence, whether direct or indirect, of sub-state actors—autonomous regions, minority groups, business corporations and the civil society—upon the development of international law and the application thereof[9] introduces another vertical dimension to the classical

[7] The most advanced example, of course, is arguably the European Union.

[8] See, eg, Case T–315/01, *Kadi v Council* [2005] ECR II–3649.

[9] For example, the right of individual petitions to the European Court of Human Rights under Protocol No 11 to the Convention for the Protection of Human Rights and Fundamental Freedoms, ETS 155 (entered into force 1 November 1998).

horizontal paradigm. This is because these new sub-state actors remain subject in many important aspects to the overriding political and legal power of their 'parent' states.

These developments raise a host of practical problems: the uncoordinated nature of the shift in allocation of authority in international law encourages potentially conflicting decision-making processes, resulting in incompatible norm-promulgation, norm-interpretation and dispute-resolution processes. In other words, it raises the questions of *'who decides what?'* and how to settle normative and jurisdictional conflicts, which the present unsatisfactory delineation of authority encourages (eg, how to reconcile incompatible norms or judicial or quasi-judicial pronouncements? Or how to co-ordinate between parallel political or legal proceedings?). Significantly, such conflicts may arise with relation to power interplays subject to either horizontal or vertical configurations (eg, between states and international organisations and among different sets of international organisations). However, the resolution of such conflicts may very well depend on the allocation of power between the competing parties to the political or legal interaction.

In addition, the shifting allocation of authority introduces considerable normative implications. Of course, the classical horizontal paradigm has been fraught with difficulty and the power it confers upon states has often been abused—the result being the de facto insulation of states from effective international supervision and control. In addition, subjecting legal change to state consent has proven a tall obstacle against adjusting the existing status quo to changing realities and needs. The horizontal paradigm has also empowered the central authorities of the state, through granting it exclusive or almost exclusive international standing, at the expense of other domestic constituencies, such as minority groups or federal units.

One conceivable alternative to the classical allocation of authority in international law is a model of *supremacy* (or conversely—*subordination*), representing the predominance of international norms and institutions over state entities. The supremacy paradigm suggests a possible shift of power towards centralised authority created at the global or regional level. Indeed, super-state structures, invested with genuine political and legal power, such as the UN Security Council and the European Union (EU), operate in accordance with this modality.

Still, the movement towards a supremacy-based international system might be limited in its scope in actuality to several specific institutional contexts and projects, and wholesale digression from the horizontal paradigm might be improbable and, moreover, politically unworkable. Furthermore, one might argue that the empowerment of international norms and institutions is also undesirable and flawed from a normative perspective. In particular, such a development might conflict with democratic principles as it moves power from popularly elected national governments to unaccountable international bureaucracies.

An almost contrary organising paradigm that presents itself is based on principles of *subsidiarity*. This notion, which was originally developed in canonic law, is found today in the domestic administrative law of some European states and constitutes one of the basic principles of contemporary EC law. The principle of subsidiarity stands out for the proposition that normative, political and legal decisions should be taken by the competent authority that is closest to where the impact of the decision will be felt. Subsidiarity can thus serve as a bridge between 'Westphalian' state-centrism and the postmodern diversity of actors on the international field.

However, until now, subsidiarity has been mainly understood outside the EC/EU context as an auxiliary concept—eg, a rule of interpretation or decision-making procedure (such as the European Court of Human Right's margin-of-appreciation doctrine) that complements, but does not supplant, either the classic state-centred or modern configurations of power based upon notions of supremacy. Furthermore, application of the principle of subsidiarity might entail difficulties on a number of levels: the empowerment of states (or sub-state actors) under a subsidiarity principle might undermine the effectiveness of international organisations, hinder the development of global legal standards (eg, through customary international law and multilateral legal arrangements), and accelerate the fragmentation of international law

CONTENTS OF THE BOOK

The first of the volume's four parts ('The Structures of International Law'), provides a detailed conceptual overview of different approaches to the tensions that now pervade the structuring of authority in international law and politics, transcending the 'vertical' and 'horizontal' classification.

In the first chapter—'The Centripede and the Centrifuge'—**Professor Thomas Franck** introduces the tensions existing between centralised and decentralised decision-making processes and offers three neutral principles, which serve as guidelines for evaluating different configurations for the allocation of power between the centre and the periphery: (1) 'nearer my law to me'—decisions affecting individuals should be made by persons closest to those directly affected; (2) 'first do no harm'—decisions should be made by those closest to the persons directly affected provided that 'those directly affected' constitute persons similarly situated with respect to the matter being addressed, or, failing this, that persons differently situated had agreed that the imperatives of devising a common solution must take priority over the preservation of existing differences. In other words, decision-making powers which entail redistributive implications must be negotiated with the affected constituencies; and (3) 'responsive governance'—the locus of power needs to be responsive to the preferences, needs and petitions of these individuals towards whom the governance is directed. Franck suggests that these principles, if applied to practical expressions of authority allocation, will allow international law to withstand the powerful strains between the global and the local that arise within the existing 'concentric circles of affinity' in international society.

In 'On the Causes of Uncertainty and Volatility in International Law', **Professor W Michael Reisman** addresses the shifting allocation of authority in international law by exploring the roots and sources of its dynamicism as a legal system. He emphasises that meaningful common interest is the critical political component in the effectiveness of all legal arrangements, and that this is no less true in the area of international law. To Reisman, the power of legal rhetoric is limited in the face of political opposition, and so is the power of historicist primacy. The world is a complex society, inherently volatile as a legal system in the face of shifting political pressures whose expressions are amplified by pervasive global class, religious and cultural diversity and law's dialectical character. Law reflects political arrangements but at the same time generates political opposition, leading especially in international relations to a temporal relativity of the meaning of 'justice', or 'justicial anachronsim'. Reisman notes other sources of volatility in international law, some of them institutional, and focuses on gaps between law's roles as a 'myth system' and as an operational code of international behaviour, creating a volatility that presents significant intellectual challenges to the international lawyer, made even more formidable by the relevance of power. This volatility presents both opportunities and pitfalls to students and practitioners of international law, bringing pause to anyone who would advocate simple structural solutions of authority allocation.

In his essay 'Structural Paradigms of International Law', **Dirk Pulkowski** approaches the overarching concept of a fragmented international legal order from an anthropological perspective of law, complementing the more familiar discussion of conflict between legal regimes as a problem of treaty interpretation to be reconciled through tools such as Article 31(3)(c) of the Vienna Convention on the Law of Treaties (VCLT), *lex specialis*, or general international law. He notes that a plurality of coexisting legal sub-systems is quite a normal state of affairs in any complex society. Building on definitions derived from the general socio-legal work of Boaventura de Sousa Santos,[10] Pulkowski examines three

[10] B de Sousa Santos, *Toward a New Legal Common Sense* (London, Butterworths, 2002).

constitutive components of international legal practice: rhetoric, bureaucracy and power. With regard to each component, he observes a combination of three competing organisational paradigms. International law is simultaneously organised according to (a) 'Westphalian coexistence', a horizontal paradigm in which 'rhetoric' focuses upon sovereignty, 'bureaucracy' upon intergovernmental co-ordinative organizations, and 'violence' upon the obligation to refrain from the use of force, couched in its proper political context; (b) 'hierarchical constitutionalisation', whose rhetoric establishes a formally vertical paradigm, and whose bureaucracy is epitomised by the UN system, but whose main weakness is in the dependence of the use of collective force—violence—upon the will of states; and (c) 'heterarchical network', conglomerating the different visions of Slaughter,[11] Sassen[12] and Hardt and Negri,[13] a web-like concept of the international system, non-vertical or horizontal, whose bureaucracy is diffuse yet organic, whose rhetoric is sophisticated and complex, and whose assertion of violence is difficult to locate. According to Pulkowski, attempts at developing general principles for the allocation of authority in international law will succeed only to the extent that this complex structure of the international order is taken into account.

Dr Gareth Davies offers in 'Subsidiarity as a Method of Policy Centralisation' a sceptical view of the utility of subsidiarity as an organising principle of international decision-making processes—a view informed by the practice of the EU in applying this principle. According to Davies, resort to subsidiarity in the relations between international organisations and their member states might be useful in some limited circumstances, where there is a complete meeting of minds and interests between international institutions and the states comprising them. However, where conflicts of interests between international and national actors exist (especially where the objectives of the policy in question are controversial), application of a principle of subsidiarity can only bring disharmony and confusion. Worse still, Gareth posits that the very structure of subsidiarity actively suppresses these conflicts, making intelligent consideration of how to deal with them harder to attain.

In 'Fragmentation(s) of International Law: On Normative Integration as Authority Allocation', **Dr Tomer Broude** argues that the 'fragmentation' discourse is itself fragmented, with problems of norm fragmentation (eg, conflicting rules) discussed separately from those relating to the fragmentation of authority (eg, competing jurisdiction). However, authority and norms are the warp and weft of international law, with a basic correlation between them: norm integration necessarily leads to

[11] A-M Slaughter, *A New World Order* (Princeton University Press, 2004).

[12] S Sassen, *Losing Control? Sovereignty in an Age of Globalization* (New York, Columbia University Press 1995).

[13] M Hardt and A Negri, *Empire* (Cambridge, MA, Harvard University Press, 2000).

pressures that integrate authority. As a result, some tribunals resist formal norm integration (as advocated with respect to Article 31(3)(c) VCLT) in order to avoid an erosion of their independent authority. It may therefore be necessary to develop methods of norm integration that are less intrusive upon the institutional authority of distinct political and legal actors.

The second part of the book ('International Authority and the State') focuses on conceptions of sovereignty and the tension between international authority and the sovereign state—the bearer of national authority.

In 'State Sovereignty, International Legality and Moral Disagreement', **Professor Brad Roth** defends the moral justification of the concept of state sovereignty, seen by many as an impediment to the global advance of legality. In this article, Roth focuses upon the ideas of self-determination and non-intervention, demonstrating their inherent paradoxes—striving to balance individual rights with collective prerogatives, and universalism with pluralism— through detailed references to contemporary practice and declarations in these areas. He suggests that differences over the depth and breadth of international law's respect for sovereignty are reflective of even deeper differences over the functions of the international legal order. To Roth, the principle of sovereign equality responds to institutional needs by establishing a doctrinal basis for respectful accommodation, or 'bounded pluralism', among international actors beset by persistent disagreement about what constitutes a legitimate and just internal territorial public order. While states may be censured and sanctioned for violating morality-based legal obligations, the practicalities of international relations require that states' core inviolabilities persist, notwithstanding those violations, in all but a narrow range of case. Roth insists that international law, even where prioritising pragmatic over moralistic considerations, generates moral obligations (rebutting Eric Posner's contrary view).[14] He goes on to describe conflicting moral justifications of a pluralistic global order. In contrast to Walzer's[15] or Rawls's[16] culture-based pluralisms, Roth derives a justification of pluralism, and thus of sovereign prerogative, from the nature of political life. In conditions of ethno-national or socio-economic polarisation, informed persons of good faith and sound reason may disagree violently on questions of justice, for reasons bearing no relation to cultural dispositions. Consequently, foreign states need not be agnostic about the wrongfulness of measures invoked in internal political

[14] See particularly EA Posner, 'Do States Have a Moral Obligation to Obey International Law?' (2003) 55 *Stanford Law Review* 1901.

[15] Michael Walzer, *Just and Unjust Wars* (New York, Basic Books, 1977); Michael Walzer, 'The Moral Standing of States' (1980) 9 *Philosophy and Public Affairs* 209.

[16] J Rawls, *The Law of Peoples* (Cambridge, MA, Harvard University Press, 1999).

conflicts, but being untrusted and untrustworthy to act in the name of a global moral order, they must nonetheless refrain, in all but aberrant cases, from imposing their own preferred outcomes to those conflicts. Roth thus defends the Westphalian premise in the face of contemporary dilemmas, concluding that a moral approach to international relations does not require, or even permit, unleashing the strong to impose justice as they understand it.

In 'Democracy without Sovereignty: The Global Vocation of Political Ethics', **Professors Robert Howse** and **Kalypso Nicolaidis** posit that modern governance systems rely on three sources of legitimacy, namely technical and scientific expertise, democratic politics and constitutional settlement, and that global governance really constitutes a series of dynamic and evolving balances between these three sources. Moreover, they argue that legitimate global governance ought to be assessed in light of the degree to which a set of power relations can be justified in terms of people's evolving beliefs, values and expectations. Howse and Nicolaidis then discuss the limitations of standard apolitical architectural responses to legitimacy gaps in international institutions, (expert management or constitutionalisation of the organisation), arguing that if applied exclusively, these strategies provide only partial solutions at best. Recognition of the dynamism and complexity of governance processes is required, premised on the acknowledgement of the contestable nature of the issues at stake, the continuing relevance and mitigability of power relationships, and the political nature of the notion of global justice. Moving on to evaluate the model of governance offered by the now semi-constitutionalised World Trade Organization (WTO), Howse and Nicolaidis argue that when the WTO is compared to its predecessor organisation—the facilitative (but nonetheless norm-generating) General Agreement on Tariffs and Trade (GATT)—it appears that the space for politics in governance of trade relations has diminished, when in fact it should have expanded. The quest for more legitimacy in the WTO thus requires the introduction of political ethics, addressed to the beliefs, values and expectations of participants, and informed by norms such as inclusiveness, mutual respect, transparency, value pluralism, procedural justice and rational deliberation.

In his contribution, entitled 'Subsidiarity, Fragmentation and Democracy: Towards the Demise of General International Law?', **Professor Andreas L Paulus** asks how one can reconcile the role of the state as the main unit of democratic legitimacy, with increasing expressions of international governance. According to Paulus, new international legal regimes are vulnerable because they do not devote sufficient attention to questions of legitimacy. The move from territoriality to functionality should not be accompanied by a shift from democracy to technocracy. As a response to this problem, he develops the argument that in spite of an ever-growing functional differentiation between the national and international spheres, and within international political architecture, issue areas are held together by a minimum of common values and decision-making procedures—indeed, by general international law which bases its legitimacy on decisions of, ideally, democratic national processes of decision-making. Thus, despite the increasing importance of non-state actors and global institutions, states maintain their role as the fundamental legitimiser of governance. Paulus also defends general international law against the democratic deficit critique. While international law is not 'democratic' as such, it is more democratic than any of the alternatives in view of the pluralism of the international community.

The book's third part ('Allocation of Authority among Judicial Bodies') focuses on a particular legal and institutional manifestation of international authority-allocation problems, namely the proliferation of tribunals adjudicating under international law (whether international or domestic), an area in which assertions of normative supremacy abound; the contributions in this part suggest a number of possible alternatives.

In 'Towards a *Solange*-Method between International Courts and Tribunals?', **Dr Nikolaos Lavranos** examines the implications of transposing principles of judicial deference developed by EU Member States—particularly by the German Constitutional Court in the series of so-called *Solange* decisions on the scope of its 'reserve jurisdiction' vis-à-vis decisions of the European Court of Justice (ECJ)—to the relationship between different international courts (in particular, the ECJ and other international courts, such as the European Court of Human Rights (ECHR)). His thoughts on the subject are illustrated through the analysis of the ECHR's *Bosphorus* decision,[17] in which the ECHR was essentially required to review a previous decision by the ECJ, and applied a technique of interjudicial comity similar to the *Solange*-method. Lavranos makes the point that the outcome of these attempts to improve co-ordination between international decisions, important as it is for the maintenance of interjudicial coherence, may be a restriction on access of aggrieved parties to international judicial remedies.

The same important case is then analysed and criticised from a different perspective by **Dr Iris Canor** in her chapter 'Exercise in Constitutional Tolerance? When Public International Law Meets Private International Law—*Bosphorus* Revisited'. Canor takes a critical look at the ECHR–ECJ relationship, and examines the question of whether it is indeed governable by the principle of interjudicial comity, suggesting that this principle is too vague and elastic to be capable of setting clear guidelines to the way international courts and tribunals should treat their counterparts. Having said that, Canor maintains that one way to preserve

[17] *Bosphorus Hava v Ireland* (App No 45036/98) (Judgment) ECHR 30 May 2005.

the pluralistic regime which the ECHR–ECJ relationship constitutes, while safeguarding systemic coherence, is to borrow from equivalent principles of private international law. In particular, in cases such as the one faced by the ECHR in *Bosphorus*, where a prior relevant decision had been rendered by another international court (the ECJ), Canor suggests that recourse to rules concerning the recognition of foreign judgments might be usefully applied.

In 'Domestic Courts and Sovereignty', **Dr Amichai Cohen** examines the potential use of the term 'sovereignty' in order to enhance international regimes of co-operation. Focusing on domestic courts, Cohen argues that courts may employ the characteristics and rights attached to sovereignty to legitimise and internalise international law in national legal systems. Hence, domestic courts which enjoy both national and international legitimacy—an attribute of authority that the notion of sovereignty enhances, rather than undercuts—serve as key participants in the development and enforcement of international law.

The fourth and final part of the book ('Allocations of Authority in Specific Normative Contexts') provides specialised studies of examples of authority allocation principles as they have developed in distinct areas of international law and governance, namely regional trade agreements, investment protection treaties, international humanitarian law and territorial administration.

Dr Guy Harpaz examines in 'Regionalism, Economic Interdependence, Approximation of Laws and their Impact on Sovereignty, National Identity and Legitimacy: The Euro-Med Case' the expansion of European legal influence beyond the borders of the EU. The EU's regional trade arrangements with its neighbours as well as the more comprehensive European Neighbourhood Programme (ENP)[18] call for an approximation or harmonisation of national laws that transcends the needs of trade liberalisation. They reflect the EU's desire to broaden its material and normative influence both regionally and globally. This is a complex exercise that directly threatens to curtail the legislative and regulatory sovereignty of partner states. According to Harpaz, approximation of laws is a one-way process that leaves non-EU states with little or no voice, and so it may raise objections that can only be overcome where a significant degree of historic, social, cultural and economic commonality exists. Harpaz lists many other concerns associated with the idea of approximation of laws as a de jure and de facto mechanism for allocation of authority. As a possible solution, he proposes to temper the process of approximation with a regional principle of subsidiarity that would leave greater decision-making space for partner states.

[18] Communication from the Commission to the Council and the European Parliament, 'Wider Europe-Neighbourhood: A New Framework for Relations with our Eastern and Southern Neighbours' COM(2003) 104 final (2003), 10.

Professor Moshe Hirsch's contribution concerns 'Conflicting Obligations in International Investment Law: Investment Tribunals' Perspective'. He notes that the rapid proliferation in recent years of international investment protection agreements and the considerable rise in investor–state arbitrations increase the prospects of overlap and conflict between investment and non-investment obligations. An analysis of investment tribunals' jurisprudence reveals that while these tribunals often incorporate rules of general international law (eg, on state responsibility and treaty law), they are generally reluctant to accord significant weight to non-investment instruments, such as environmental and human rights treaties. Hirsch analyses the factors leading these tribunals to undertake such a cautious (and even suspicious) approach to non-investment treaties. These factors—which may be seen as de facto determinants of the allocation of authority in difficult cases—include the normative features of investment relations, the institutional characteristics of international investment tribunals and the historic evolution of international investment law. Finally, he examines some on-going processes in investment tribunal proceedings and discusses their likely implications on future jurisprudence of investment tribunals in this sphere.

In 'Multi-level Accountability: A Case Study of Accountability Processes in the Aftermath of the Srebrenica Genocide', **Professor Andre Nollkaemper** proposes to complement the diversification of power allocation in international relations with improved multi-level accountability—a term indicating that accountability processes in regard to one and the same set of events can be spread over multiple responsible actors, multiple forms (legal–political) and across multiple levels (notably domestic–international). Multi-level accountability is a logical consequence of multi-level governance. However, its manifestations, potentials and limitations have rarely been studied. The chapter discusses various aspects of multi-level accountability, notably the question of whether and under what conditions accountability processes at one level can influence or complement processes at another level. Nollkaemper applies the concept of multi-level accountability to the accountability processes in respect of the aftermath of the Srebrenica massacre in 2005, in which thousands of victims have sought relief through a variety of accountability mechanisms. The chapter structures these mechanisms on the basis of party structures: accountability processes for individuals involved in the massacre; accountability processes for collective entities (notably Serbia) involved in the massacre; and accountability processes against 'the international community'. For all three categories, Nollkaemper examines both international and domestic processes and the interplay between them. He identifies how the various procedures can supplement each other, but notably also what gaps they may leave for the persons injured by the events in Srebrenica in 1995

In 'Territorial Administration by Non-territorial Sovereigns', **Professor Malcolm Shaw** examines the emergence of new relationships between sovereignty and effective control resulting from the administration of territories by third states and international institutions. Shaw posits that an examination of this more sophisticated relationship entails a variety of implications for identifying the source of authority and applicable law in the administered territory and designating international accountability. It also places the notion of traditional sovereignty in a broader context than is usual.

SOVEREIGNTY, SUPREMACY, SUBSIDIARITY: LOOKING FORWARD

We hope the articles collected in this volume create, if not a clear picture of the debate over allocation of authority in international law, at least a 'hologram' of the debate: a multi-dimensional vision, which is sufficiently clear, although not in the highest definition; and to some extent, because it only captures the way the assembled authors perceive of the puzzling architecture(s) of international law from their particular viewpoint at a given point in time, it remains an illusory vision. Nonetheless, a better understanding of the past and present terms of the debate over allocation of authority, may help us to predict what the future may hold for the horizontal and vertical allocation of authority in international law.

While it would be foolish to make any firm statements on such a far-reaching question, the 'hologram' that this book provides suggests that the concepts of sovereignty, supremacy and subsidiarity will all form a part of the shape of things to come. Several of the chapters forcefully argue that the news of the death of sovereignty might have been somewhat exaggerated: sovereignty may have shrunk, indeed it has become much more 'functional' than formal, as Prof Lapidoth herself has surmised in several different contexts, but it is far from gone; and there are significant reasons to retain it as an organising principle in the face of globalising pressures, not least of which is the need for political legitimacy of national and international governance measures.

At the same time, we see that international legal systems continue to make bids for supremacy, whether through pressures to approximate laws, constructions of 'reserve' jurisdiction or overt reluctance to apply certain areas of substantive international law. And yet subsidiarity and subsidiarity-like principles of authority (and accountability) allocation can be found in many instances that essentially cover the entire spectrum of contemporary international law, from international economic law to international criminal law and beyond. While the final balance between these competing tendencies has yet to be struck (if ever it will), sovereignty, supremacy and subsidiarity will continue to be the mainstays of the vocabulary of authority allocation in international law in the foreseeable future.

I
The Structures of International Law

1

The Centripede and the Centrifuge: Principles for the Centralisation and Decentralisation of Governance

THOMAS M FRANCK*

I. INTRODUCTION

EACH TIME I type this essay's title—'The Centripede and the Centrifuge'—on my computer, the word 'centripede' comes out, disagreeably underlined in red to indicate that there is no such word. Apparently, I invented a new word (and also, as I will shortly explain, a new machine) just for the purpose of this essay.

But am I being entirely whimsical? Not at all! There certainly is such a thing as a centrifuge. It is a machine that exerts centrifugal force on a field, forcing matter outward, to the periphery of the field. And there most assuredly is such a thing as centripetal force, which forces matter inward, towards the centre of the field. So why shouldn't there be a machine to exert centripetal force, which, in some contexts, we could call gravity? Let us call this machine, which exerts a pull towards the centre, a centripede.

The centripede I have invented should not, of course, be confused with a centipede, without an 'r', a creature defined by Webster, rather unhelpfully, as 'any predaceous segmented anthropod of the class Chilopoda, with a pair of legs on each segment, the first pair being modified into poison fangs'. The correct adjectival reference to the species is 'centipedal' as in: 'you're my centipedal baby'. All this has nothing whatsoever to do with my centripede (with an 'r') and the centripetal force it exerts.

Perhaps it would make things easier if I mentioned that the centrifuge,

* Murry and Ida Becker Professor of Law Emeritus, New York University. This essay was written in honour of my lifelong friend Ruth Lapidoth.

by pushing things towards the periphery of a field, is exercising an efferent pull—that is, a pull away from the centre. And, of course, there is a countervailing afferent pull, which is a tendency towards the centre. The centripede, in other words, exercises an afferent pull that is centripetal: it pulls towards the centre. This, to the international lawyer, is a useful concept, as in:

> *The United Nations Security Council is sort of a centripede,*

or:

> *If the European Commission cannot curb its centripetal proclivities, it will provoke an efferent reaction from the latent centrifugal force of European petty nationalisms.*

So in my surreal world, there is a centrifuge that exerts centrifugal force by directing energy outward from the centre of a field and, of course, there is a centripede that exerts the well-known centripetal force by directing energy inward towards the centre from the periphery of the field

And here is the payoff for letting me indulge in this bit of surreal whimsy. We know from our study of the dynamics of physics that, for there to be stability in a field, the centrifugal and centripetal forces must be in balance. One way to think of international law scholarship and practice is as an all-consuming quest for this very sort of organic stability: a stability that can only come when the great centripede and the great centrifuge of the law have devised an institutional and operational equilibrium between the pull to the centre and the pull to the periphery.

Hans Kelsen proposed a monist theory in which all national law—sovereignty—was legitimated by its conformity to the fundamental norms of international law.[1] This is the ultimate triumph of the centre over the periphery. Nowadays, we tend to regard this monist theory as being contradicted by the current vogue for triumphal nationalism, the pull away from the centre. In any event, we recognise that most exertions of a pull towards the centre are now likely to be met by a strong, sometimes violent, pull in the other direction. In the early twenty-first century, the centrifuge, the force against the centralising efforts of international law, is working overtime. And yet, one of the most frequently remarked upon paradoxes of this age of paradox is that the world has never been so interdependent—so globalised, so intertwined in the mesh

[1] See, eg, H Kelsen, *General Theory of Law and State* (A Wedberg trans, Cambridge, MA, Harvard University Press, 1949) 369; H Kelsen, *Pure Theory of Law* (M Knight trans, Berkeley, University of California Press, 1967) 337–8; H Kelsen, *Introduction to the Problems of Legal Theory* (BL Paulson and SL Paulson trans, Oxford University Press, 1992) 61–2.

of international law—as now, even as nationalism and assertive manifestations of state sovereignty have become so rampant.

Professor Lapidoth—the *raison d'être* of this collection of essays—has tried to modulate this cacophonous clash between the centripede and the centrifuge by bringing them into a stable balance, situation by situation, conflict by conflict. In particular, she has tried to deconstruct some of the elements of these countervailing forces to bring some balance to some parts of a specific clash. For example, if the centrifugal force of nationalism can be detached from the traditional international legal concept of territorial sovereignty; if sovereignty over land can be detached from rights of passage; if surface territorial rights can be separated from subterranean rights; if territorial jurisdiction over some matters can be separated from personal jurisdiction over other matters; and if international and national regimes can exercise defined sectoral jurisdiction over common territory, then, in any particular place of conflict, the centripede and the centrifuge might achieve a sustainable balance.[2]

If this sort of rethinking of sovereignty seems far-fetched, it might be worth reminding ourselves that it is the very thing that made possible the Law of the Seas regime, which has transformed the globe's largest area, the seas, from one of constant conflict to one of comparative peaceability. Such creative rethinking of old legal categories is the inevitable way of the future, if we are to have one. Sovereignty is not obsolete, but it needs to be re-examined carefully.

As international trade, once the rapacious harbinger of nationalism and imperialism, is channelled—by the centripede—into the pacific rabbit-warrens of legalism and rule-regimes—the likes of the World Trade Organization, the General Agreement on Tariffs and Trade, the NAFTAs and CAFTAs with their mandatory arbitrations—even as the fragile federalisms of the former Yugoslavia and the former Soviet Union unravel and descend into the most militant assertions of ethnic and religious *amour propre*—it is necessary to rethink not only the concept of sovereignty but also that of globalisation.

I recently spent a week in Ottawa and Toronto, where I heard a great deal about the resistance of the province of Alberta to Canada's implementation of the mandates of the Kyoto Protocol: the centrifuge's revenge against the centralising force of the centripede. But, while Alberta may not much like mandatory pollution controls imposed from the global centre, it surely craves the protection it gets from the global trading regime against nationalist US tariffs

So, there is a paradox and, as always with a paradox, there is an incipient clash. But let us try to be precise as to what the clash is about. It

2 See R Lapidoth, *Autonomy: Flexible Solutions to Ethnic Conflicts* (Washington, DC, United States Institute of Peace Press, 1997).

is about finding a stabilising balance between the pulls of two dynamic forces. It is not a clash between the forces of light and darkness, but between differing claims to legitimation put forward in the name of centralisation and of decentralisation, of nationalism and internationalism.

As Karl Popper observed in *The Open Society and Its Enemies*:

> Nationalism appeals to our tribal instincts, to passion and to prejudice, and to our nostalgic desire to be relieved from the strain of individual responsibility which it attempts to replace by a group or collective responsibility.[3]

But that is not the whole story of nationalism. It is also about direct participation of persons in the process of governance. It is about a preference for governance that is closer to the governed than are the shadowy and distant transnational regimes: the Gnomes of Geneva, the Bureaucrats of Brussels, the overlords and Under-Secretaries in the United Nations Headquarters on the East River.

Internationalism too has its bright and darker sides. Sure, it tends to manifest itself in governance that is far from the governed. It often lacks direct accountability. Like nationalism, it also appeals to our instincts: in this case, not tribal but survival instincts. We sense that global warming, which threatens our survival, is not a problem that can often be dealt with state by state, tribe by tribe. But internationalism tends to advance its ideas of utilitarian governance at some cost to democratic legitimacy.

The clash, then, is not one between forces of darkness: between the tribe as manifestation of the primitive autonomy of our imagined genetic code, and—on the other hand—remote, faceless international bureaucracies that aim to rob us of our identity in order to pursue agenda to which we never agreed. Neither should it be seen as a collision between nationalism or sovereignty and internationalism and global regimes. In rethinking sovereignty and globalisation, we should follow Ruth Lapidoth's example and rethink the configuration and accommodation between levels of governance, and we should do so subject by subject, law by law, regime by regime, until we bring the centripede and the centrifuge into sectoral balance.

The first step in such rethinking is to stop assigning superior value to either centripetal or centrifugal forces. Inherent in all governance—local, national, regional and global—is the threat of abuse. In one situation, the state or the tribe may be the source of that danger, and the supranational regimes established by international law may be the protectors of individual rights. In another situation, it may be the faceless bureaucrats and diplomats of regional and global regimes who threaten the democratic

[3] KR Popper, *The Open Society and Its Enemies*, vol II (5th edn, London, Routledge, 1973) 49.

accountability so hard-won in our local and national governments. There will always be the ever-ongoing struggle between persons or groups asserting their human and participatory rights and any level of governance that may seek to infringe those rights for some real or imagined greater good. There is no automatic correlation between dangers to the rights of persons and the level at which governance is practised. In theory, a village council can be more threatening to one's personal freedom than the Secretary General of the United Nations.

Yet we may think we see such a correlation. We may simply assume that the further away from individuals the level of governance, the greater the threat to individual liberty. Our tribal instincts may propel us to the conclusion that persons are better protected in their freedoms when governance is local. This may or may not be true depending on a large number of variables, but there certainly is no trace of an actual correlation. It would help our thinking if we could get that false notion out of our heads.

II. SOVEREIGNTY INSTINCT, SURVIVAL INSTINCT

Fortunately, our tribal instincts may be confronted by another instinct, that for survival. Our survival instinct tells us that if the avian flu is not to become the Black Death of the twenty-first century, there must be internationally imposed health standards that inevitably impinge on those sovereign prerogatives that are the bureaucratic-political manifestations of our tribal instincts. Some of our local governance may have to defer to rules worked out farther away with persons not quite like us. Put another way: our desire to be governed only by our peers will have to be reconciled with the inconvenient fact that we, with our peers, sometimes cannot ensure that we get what we want: our survival, for example. We want the right to be close to governance and yet we also want governance that can get the result we need. Those results sometimes can be got only when national sovereignty defers to some other level of governance. Indeed, the very utilities sovereignty seeks to preserve may sometimes be preserved only by its yielding to international governance. Thus it is that international health standards make it possible for nations to survive in an era when travel, transport and communications make every disease anywhere a potential pandemic.

Furthermore, it is international rules of trade that make it possible for national economies, most of which are not economies of scale, to survive and grow in a global market. So it may be said that, sometimes, the centripede empowers the centrifuge, and vice versa, and that this happens when they are in balance.

Nevertheless, this synergy between international and local governance is not endemic. Sometimes it works, at other times it does not. Consider the subject of human rights. At the national level, the rights to speak, to worship and to be left alone are packaged not as 'human rights' but rather as 'civil liberties'. Some nations have them and others do not. Some nations have codified them and others not. Some nations enforce them through their courts, others through their parliaments, and still others enforce them only through ritual and lip-service. But 'human rights'—which look to the naked eye like the twin of civil rights—are a different thing altogether, even though the codex of human rights reads a great deal like the civil rights laws of certain countries.

The difference between civil rights and human rights is that the former rest firmly on the socio-political foundations of the state and manifest the national (or tribal) ethos of its people, while the latter rest on the emerging sense of global socio-political solidarity manifest in treaties that purport to make national governments—and, thus, the peoples—subservient to international standards.

However, even if the general objectives of civil rights and human rights regimes are similar—to protect the dignity, integrity and freedom of persons—it is not true that they operate interchangeably. In each instance of challenge to personal rights, their protection may be achieved by one rights regime and denied by the other. While French law provides extensive protections for persons, even in cutting-edge matters such as same-sex partnerships, French law has long sharply restricted the right to choose, or to alter, one's name. It has done this in the pursuit of the value of social cohesion: that is, the very French notion of social cohesion that is rooted in the French Revolution and its political and social heritage. And French (and English) law upholds dress codes in schools that are intended to integrate young people socially and culturally by denying the student the right to make dissenting cultural or religious statements sartorially.

By way of contrast, European human rights law has been declared, by the European Court of Human Rights, to include the right to choose and change one's name in pursuit of the right to one's identity.[4] This new European human rights regime is also rooted in history: in the European history of centuries of cultural and religious warfare and the oppression of minorities. It has grown out of a revulsion against claims of racial, ethnic and religious supremacy and the enforcement of social conformism by governments. And it may yet be that the English or French student claiming the right to deviate from dress codes will be upheld by the United Nations Human Rights Committee.

[4] See, eg, *Burghartz v Switzerland*, ECHR, Series A, no 280-B (1994); *Stjerna v Finland*, ECHR Series A, no 299-B (1994); *Guillot v France*, ECHR (1996-V) 48.

Thus, the French system, when it emphasises equality and social solidarity in the name of civil rights, may not be in synch with a European or United Nations system of human rights that emphasises the accommodation of social exceptionalism. Two rights regimes, exercising their writs in the same constituency, but pulling in different directions and reflecting different social and cultural values: both with strong claims to authenticity. This indicates what is at stake in seeking a set of neutral principles for the allocation of jurisdictions between the local and the global—and everything in between those polarities. The choice of forum will determine the policy outcome in many instances of genuine disputation.

When it comes to the rights of persons, then, which system of rights is right to regulate which rights? Inevitably, this is a contentious matter in which politics, values and other variables will play their role. This is as it must, and should, be. Nevertheless, those making this critical choice should also take into account basic principles of good governance that are neutral as to outcomes. Where disputes are deadlocked between competing assertions of right, the decisive discourse may have to focus less on outcomes than on principles of good governance that may dictate the choice of forum. That discourse will need to focus less on claims of right and more on neutral principles of good governance.

An example of such a principled approach might be to permit a nation to opt in to a global regime, presumably to maximise a desired utility, but to opt out of some provisions of the regime for a period of years, perhaps renewable. Such opting in and selective opting out could not be tolerated by the other parties to the regime to the extent that the opting out seriously affected the utilities they expected to maximise by joining the regime. The best example, again, is the mutual trade system. The accommodations would have to be mutual, insofar as necessary to preserve reciprocity. But if one nation had a powerful cultural or religious objection to all television, why not permit it to opt out of the obligation to permit free importation of television programmes which no one in the country wants to watch, providing it was obliged to reconsider its opt-out periodically? The same might be said about changes of names. The test would be whether the opt-out would inflict significant damage on the reasonable expectations of the other parties to the multilateral regime. In international law, something of this sort appears to be evolving in the law pertaining to reservations to multilateral treaties.[5] If this succeeds, it will be one more example of neutral principles bringing into balance the centrifuge and the centripede.

It is in quest of such neutral principles that I will now venture. To get the good governance discourse moving, I propose three such neutral principles.

[5] See, eg, ET Swaine, 'Reserving' (2006) 31 *Yale Journal of International Law* 307.

1. Nearer My Law to Me

It is a sound principle for the allocation of power within a multi-layered community that decisions affecting individuals should be made by persons closest to those directly affected. By 'multi-layered community' I mean any system in which loci of power are arranged so as to create foci of governance at varying distances from those being governed. In our everyday experience, that might suggest a system in which decisions affecting oneself were made by local block associations, district councils, city, state and federal governments, regional intergovernmental assemblies and global institutions. Which layer of government is empowered to make what decisions affecting the same individual should, according to this principle, depend upon the extent to which the problem being addressed inherently requires, as a matter of effective management, a uniform approach, and how broadly uniform the approach has to be.

For example, it might be a functional necessity that water conservation rules be mandated for all those regions in which annual rainfall fell below a replenishment level, but not for other regions with a higher incidence of rainfall, and not for regions in which replenishment occurred through other natural phenomena, such as mountain run-off. On the other hand, such a localised water management regime might not be sufficient to resolve the needs of the most drought-impacted regions, in which case some more regional or universal approach would seem necessary through which those with ample water would be required to conserve in order to alleviate the condition of others.

Note, however, that such a utilitarian approach, while having much to commend it, rests on an assumption that everyone wants every problem solved in the most grossly efficient possible way. It is not necessarily true, however, that everyone in the state of California shares such a utilitarian-efficient approach with the people of Colorado or Nevada when it comes to water use. Much less is it certain that the people of the United States are ready to adopt such an equalisation of burdens and benefits approach with the rest of the world.

The 'nearer my law to me' principle thus needs a second principle to accompany it in the making of decisions about the most appropriate loci of governance.

2. First Do No Harm

Regulation or governance is not always—perhaps, even, not often—purely a matter of achieving gross utilitarian efficiency. Or, more accurately, it is almost always also about burden sharing as a prerequisite for achieving an optimally efficient result. However, the way burdens are shared, as, indeed, the choice of problems to be addressed, is a political decision. It is, however, a decision that can be affected or distorted by the selection of the locus of governance at which it is to be made. If the choice of locus is dictated not by the nature of the problem to be regulated but, instead, by a preference for certain redistributive outcomes, then the choice may not be instrumentally effective for dealing with the problem.

An example is the continuing effort by poorer nations to make the World Bank (or more precisely the International Bank for Reconstruction and Development (IBRD)) subject to the closer supervision of the United Nations General Assembly, as echoed in policy recommendations on global governance.[6] The effect, predictably, would be that the borrowers would dictate the terms on which they borrow and repay loans. That this transfer of jurisdiction would be inefficient is suggested by the fact that almost all the Bank's loan capital originates from the richer lenders. If the shift of governance prevents the recapitalisation of the Bank's reserves, the borrowers will be unable to obtain the loans they want.

Obviously, if the power to set income tax laws were to be located in the locus most able to deal with global poverty by redistributing it, the best place to develop the rules and mechanisms for such a poverty-alleviating regime would be the General Assembly of the United Nations. That such a redistribution of regulatory power would lead to a radical redistribution of goods is, to say the least, probable. But, it is even more probable that the citizens of developed countries would not agree to participate in a system that is conduced to such radical results, one that would operate to their fiscal detriment. And, even if compliance could be obtained, a mere redistribution of the world's poverty would, arguably, have a negative effect on poverty alleviation. A neutral principle for determining the best—ie, the most efficient—loci of governance should, first of all, avoid falling prey to such obvious self-disqualification.

The second proposed principle—first do no harm—seeks to address this concern by stipulating that decisions should be made by those closest to the persons directly affected provided 'those directly affected' constituted persons similarly situated with respect to the matter being addressed or, failing this, that persons differently situated had agreed that the imperatives of devising a common solution must take priority over the preservation of existing differences. In effect, the location of the locus of governance should not be determined by, and indeed should not facilitate, the taking of goods: something that, even when desirable, should be pursued by other means such as negotiation. In other words, in a world of states, global redistribution needs to be negotiated.

This is not to say that redistributive principles have no merit. Thus,

[6] See, eg, *Our Global Neighborhood, Report of the Commission on Global Governance* (Oxford University Press, 1995) 149–62.

there may be good reason to establish a regime to redistribute riparian water resources among upstream and downstream users, but it is one that would have to be negotiated among them, politically, using incentives and trade-offs as well as appeals to moral sensibilities. Quite different, however, is the case for a conservation regime in which everyone understood that, without seasonal rationing, there would be drought that would affect everyone and that the proposed rationing regime is one based on an equal reduction of customary use. Such a regime, imposed by governance responsive to both upstream and downstream users—even if there were twice as many of the latter as the former—is justified on the ground that, but for such regulation, first, all would be seriously impacted and, second, the effect of conservation would be to conserve rather than redistribute.

A third relevant principle is suggested by the term used in the preceding paragraph: 'governance responsive' to all those affected.

3. Responsive Governance

The third and final principle for determining the appropriate locus for a specific authority for governance is that such locus be responsive to those towards whom the governance is directed.

While it is no small matter to attempt to define 'responsiveness', the principle is nevertheless of considerable significance. At its heart is one of the most important shared precepts of civil rights and human rights: both are about the rights of individuals. To the extent that all governance implicates the autonomy of individuals, the exercise of governance attains its legitimacy through the governors' demonstrable responsiveness to individuals, their preferences, needs and petitions.

There are many ways in which such responsiveness can be promoted institutionally, just as unresponsiveness can assume many institutional forms and disguises. Whatever the difficulties of applying the principle in practice, it is hardly open to doubt that the claim of a potential locus of governance will be affected by the degree it is perceived to be responsive to its potential constituents.

It also needs to be emphasised that responsiveness is not the same as plebiscitary, or even parliamentary, government. Responsiveness may entail counter-majoritarian principles. It may entail guarantees that minority and dissident points of view are given adequate opportunity to be heard.

With that caveat, however, it is essential that we understand that global governance, at least as presently constituted, is extraordinarily unresponsive. In admitting to this, however, a distinction must be made between human rights and most other subjects of governance.

When it comes to regulating terms of trade, for example, the turn to global governance in the form of global treaties and institutions has been almost complete. That this should have happened does not offend the 'nearer my law to me' principle because the universally accepted objective of increased free trade could not be accomplished at the national level. Moreover, the GATT–WTO system permits regions to move more quickly towards the implementation of that goal and also permits special regimes favouring the less-developed states that were not subject to the overall requirement of symmetry. As for the 'first do no harm' principle, the global regime has no obvious redistributive implications except to the extent that both sides to redistribution agree to it among themselves by extending preferences selectively.

As for the principle of 'responsive governance', while it cannot be argued that the institutions of the world's trading regime are democratic, it may be that the system of diplomatic representation affords those most directly affected by it a reasonable way to present their views through their participation in the politics of their individual countries, whose representatives will reflect those views in international negotiations.[7] Thus, in the global governance of trade there is at least a degree of accountability. The same cannot be said of human rights.

As indicated earlier in this discourse, human rights are the enemy of sovereignty in a way free trade cannot be said to be directly the enemy of sovereignty. True, the requisites of free trade do impinge on the power of government to act to the detriment of other governments. However, the consequences of doing so are so evident, and so severe, that few states actually want a trade war. The global trading system functions because almost every nation, almost all the time, prefers a regime, even if it sometimes interferes with its sovereignty, to the chaos that would ensue without it.

None of this is true of the human rights regime. Most states, much of the time, see it to their advantage to abridge certain of the human rights to which they had agreed in principle when they ratified the relevant treaties. More important, most states have no national interest in offending the violating government merely because it is doing prohibited things to some persons in its own country.[8]

To the extent some states have allowed their own citizens to petition the Human Rights Committee[9]—a group of experts elected by the parties to the International Covenant on Civil and Political Rights—it may be

[7] For discussion and criticism of this statist perspective, see, eg, S Charnovitz, 'Opening the WTO to Nongovernmental Interests' (2000) 24 *Fordham International Law Journal* 173, 197–202.

[8] See, eg, DH Moore, 'Agency Costs in International Human Rights' (2004) 42 *Columbia Journal of Transnational Law* 491.

[9] Optional Protocol to the International Covenant on Civil and Political Rights (adopted 16 December 1966, entered into force 23 March 1976) 999 UNTS 302.

said that a small, but significant, start has been made in the direction of responsive governance, but it has a long way to go.

Nevertheless, human rights should be developed because, as a matter of utilitarian efficiency, the subject matter often cannot be addressed optimally at the purely national level. This has been demonstrated over and over again by the tendency of even the most democratic regimes, states with the best civil rights laws, to cut corners in times of national crisis or aroused passion. The global human rights regime also permits some corners to be cut in what is called 'states of exception',[10] but it does not permit the regime committed to a corner-cutting policy to be the last word as to whether a crisis requiring draconian measures actually exists, and whether the measures taken are reasonable in the circumstances. It also prohibits some extreme measures under any circumstances.

What is lacking, then, in the human rights regime is a rational and effective system of monitoring and implementation, comparable to that which already exists in the trade field. I believe that this can be devised for the global regime, but not by simply utilising the existing institutions of interstate diplomacy. A global system of human rights must seek its compliance-pull through its legitimacy: through relating the regime more directly to the persons, everywhere, it is designed to protect. So far, it is accountable primarily to states, which, in at least some instances, are the very ones against which the human rights regime is designed to protect the individual.

What is needed is some creative thinking about ways to reduce the responsive governance deficit of the human rights regime. If that can be achieved, the global human rights regime, like some other global regimes, can be expected to play an effective role in the peaceful adjustment of problems, before they become armed conflicts between, or within, states.

To summarize: in the twenty-first century, the notion of sovereignty, which has been evolving constantly from the days of the Greek city-state to the present, will change even more. Sovereignty will become ever more layered. Persons will have more rights and duties that are protected by, and owed to, the city, province, nation, region and global system. The task of allocating the new layers of protections and governance must be addressed by balancing concern for efficiency, fairness and transparency or accountability.

This is not a task for Kelsenian monism. It must be addressed in a way that responds to our evolving, increasingly complex and multi-layered sense of personal identity. We are all becoming bearers of multi-layered identities: citizens of a town, nation, multinational affinity groups—religious, commercial, ideational—and citizens of a region and

[10] See, eg, International Covenant on Civil and Political Rights (adopted 16 December 1966, entered into force 23 March 1976) 999 UNTS 171, Art 4.

of the world.[11] This does not mean that our loyalty, our identity, is like a piece of cake being divided into slices, but, rather, that our consciousness is expanding to encompass a sense of entitlement and of reciprocal responsibility towards concentric circles of affinity. This expansion of personal consciousness has its resonance in concentric circles of governance.

It is hardly surprising that these concentric circles of identity and governance set up powerful strains between the local and the global. Ruth Lapidoth has challenged us, as scholars and social architects, to seek the balance: the equilibrium that brings stability, between the pulls of the centripede and the centrifuge. She has made important strides both theoretical and practical, towards that equilibrium, and she has 'pied-pipered' many of us to join her quest.

[11] See, eg, JHH Weiler, *The Constitution of Europe* (Cambridge University Press, 1999) 344–7.

2

On the Causes of Uncertainty and Volatility in International Law

W MICHAEL REISMAN*

LAW IS FREQUENTLY conceived of as fixed and stable, and, of course, the principles of natural law are assumed to be permanent. But law is actually a dynamic process and its components are far less certain than popularly supposed. As for international law, it is particularly volatile, presenting especially daunting intellectual and moral challenges to the lawyers who practise it.

I

At any level of any social organisation, law is most comprehensively understood as the processes by which persons, who are politically relevant with respect to each other, establish and maintain arrangements for securing order, allocating the opportunities and the benefits and burdens of life, and providing for modes of resolving differences—all in ways that serve what they believe to be their interests. These arrangements may not be explicit; indeed, they may operate at levels of consciousness so deep that many of the persons involved are unaware of them, or are taught, or simply assume, that they are part of a natural order of things. The arrangements necessarily include agreements about the performance of critical parts of decision making, in particular about how these legal arrangements themselves are to be amended and applied (constitutive arrangements); and agreements about the content of specific legal arrangements in all of the areas of concern to the politically relevant

* Myres S McDougal Professor of International Law, Yale Law School. Parts of this paper will appear in the 2007 General Course of the Hague Academy of International Law, 'International Law in the Twenty-First Century.'

actors: power, wealth, enlightenment, skill, well-being, affection, respect and rectitude.[1]

'Agreement', it should be said, is a term covering a spectrum of consensus. Rather than the result of happy and spontaneous or carefully negotiated consensus of all the persons to be affected by them, some arrangements may be based on 'offers that cannot be refused'. Other arrangements may be the result of real agreements but only between some persons who are then able to impose them on others who are handicapped by having less knowledge and information, influence, access, manipulative skill, organisation or the tools of violence and the aptitude and appetite for using them.

Mainstream contemporary legal theory emphasises the state as the centrepiece of a legal system and 'state' and 'law' as two parts of the same identity. In this view, law means only those written arrangements that have been prescribed and applied by specific organs of the state. In some territories, the most critical legal arrangements may, in fact, be made and applied by the apparatus of the state. As a matter of preference, one might well posit that arrangements made in highly organised and explicit rather than informal processes are better, both in their content and in the procedures by which they were made. But any attempt to identify, understand, predict or influence these types of decisions in the myriad exchanges that take place continuously *between* groups and individuals around the world will fail if the framework of inquiry is built upon a premise of state/law identity. There is no extant 'global state' nor is there an incipient one. Pretending that the Security Council is the embryonic Executive Branch or Executive Committee of a World State, that the General Assembly is its embryonic legislature and that the International Court is its embryonic Supreme Court may serve some unifying mythic purposes.[2] But this attitude disserves inquiry if it directs attention away from the processes by which law is actually made and applied in international politics; to the extent that it does so, faulty theory undermines those trying to perform legal functions.

In every type of interaction, arrangements, at both the constitutive and specific levels, are characterised by distinctive modes of communication—the language or dialects of the law. As a semantic matter, legal statements are expressed in the imperative or subjunctive mood: 'do or refrain from doing something' or 'do something in a particular way and secure a certain benefit or suffer a certain loss'. But it is not their linguistic form that makes these statements law. Legal communications are distinguished from the daily bombardment of 'you-shoulds' and 'you-oughts'

[1] HD Lasswell and MS McDougal, *Jurisprudence for a Free Society* (New Haven, CT, New Haven Press, 1992).

[2] On the functions of myth systems in international law, see discussion below at pp 42–7.

by the symbols of authority and commitments of control that attend them; both serve to mark them as legal communications and render them effective.

Symbols of authority are designed to indicate to their intended audiences that the arrangements which they attend are 'law' and so enhance respect for, and a predisposition to comply with, these arrangements. Symbols of authority are also a factor in compliance. (So is the content of an arrangement; the more the content is perceived as in an actor's interest, the more that actor will support the arrangement without symbolic authorisation or external compulsion.) What will constitute symbols of authority will vary with the culture of the audience; the symbols may import, for example, invocations of divine authorisation or approval, derivations from utterances attributed to a charismatic leader or his successor or from a sacred text, or supposed emanations of the popular will.

The effectiveness of symbols of authority in legal arrangements frequently depends upon the culture, class and religious cohesiveness of the audience. If all of its members do not share in the same authority or belief system, the symbolic component for sustaining the arrangements will be less effective and may even be a negative factor among particular strata or groups. The use of the word 'crusade' to characterise a legal arrangement may have a powerful authoritising force for an audience of Catholics and some other Christian denominations, evoking at deep levels of consciousness images of heroism and self-sacrifice *ad majorem dei gloriam*; it will have exactly the opposite effect for an audience of Muslims. In parallel fashion, the ascription of the word 'jihad' to a legal arrangement may evoke a powerful positive emotion for Muslims and exactly the converse effect for Christians. The selection or crafting of symbols of authority has obvious implications for those multi-ethnic conglomerations in which there are few or only incipient and weak trans-ethnic identifications. It is an especially daunting task in the extraordinarily diverse international community. One of the challenges of governance in such environments is the cultivation of common authority symbols.

Legal arrangements must also include credible commitments to apply the resources necessary to make them effective. The expectation that there are meaningful commitments is an important factor in compliance. The less advantageous to politically relevant actors the content of an arrangement is, and the less compelling its symbolic component, the more the arrangement must depend upon the credible commitment of those who are effective actors to uphold it. Where formal and effective institutions, endowed with sufficient resources and adequately skilled personnel, are charged with implementing arrangements, those affected by the arrangements will expect, with a probability commensurate with their confidence in the institutions, that the arrangements will be sustained. Such an expectation may be self-fulfilling in that the very expectation of effectiveness is likely to lead to adjustments in behaviour to conform to those arrangements.

Where, however, there are no institutions able to sustain the arrangements, those arrangements will depend, for their effectiveness, on one of two factors: (i) on the self-interest of those to whom the arrangements are addressed, leading to voluntary compliance; or (ii) on the resources of other participants and their interest in and willingness to deploy them. Effective institutional arrangements are plainly to be preferred over ad hoc coalitions of the willing. The readiness and ability of other participants to continue to invest their own resources may decline: they may decline because of a change in interest; a willingness to see the arrangement, which they had theretofore supported, adjust, change or terminate; or a diversion of resources to other interests that have come to be deemed more important.

Here we encounter one of the critical problems of contemporary international law. At the constitutive level, institutional arrangements have been established, but they have not been given sufficient resources and adequately skilled personnel to accomplish the tasks assigned to them. Nor is this the result of accident or oversight: many actors in international law are ambivalent about establishing highly effective international institutions. Yet, paradoxically, reliance on other participants to make specific arrangements effective when the institutions that were created to do this cannot runs counter to a widely affirmed constitutive policy: prohibiting unilateral initiatives by confining the exclusive right of forceful implementation to the most inclusive institutions. When other participants with sufficient resources decide to apply them in a specific instance, their actions may implement that arrangement but at the cost of undermining the more general constitutive arrangement.

II

No legal arrangement is self-sustaining. At any level of social organisation, people will defend constitutive or structural legal arrangements against those who would prefer to replace them with other arrangements as long as the existing arrangements are believed to serve their interests. People who do not believe or cease to believe that the conception and institutional expression of common interest satisfies their own interests will be disinclined to support those arrangements, and indeed may actively agitate and struggle against them. Hence the mobilisation—as opposed to the coercion—of diverse actors in support of a legal arrangement requires crafting or adjusting that arrangement so that a sufficient number of the relevant actors see it as in their *common* interest.

It is easy to lose sight of the fact that meaningful common interest is the critical political component in the effectiveness of legal arrangements. Attractive moral arguments may be marshalled in favour of arrangements that encompass the interests of all relevant actors. But designing arrangements in the common interest is, ultimately, an imperative of political efficiency rather than morality. This political imperative is sometimes forgotten by those who are the momentary beneficiaries of an indulgent and apparently stable legal system whose arrangements generally work in their favour. Such beneficiaries are prone (as long as they benefit) to mythologise the arrangements as 'The Law', ascribing to them a majestic, enduring and self-sustaining neutrality. In their view, obedience is universally owed to 'The Law' simply because it is 'The Law', without regard to its content and distribution of benefits.

Expressions such as 'the pillars of the law', 'the grandeur of the law', 'the majesty of the law', and so on, which are endlessly repeated in post-prandial Bar Association speeches and international discussions of the rule of law, import an inherent permanence and self-enforcement to legal arrangements simply because they are 'legal' arrangements. By contrast, those who view themselves as excluded from, or insufficiently indulged or victimised by, legal arrangements tend to view and often wittily to characterise 'the law' and the institutional practices it supports as an artefact of alien power and oppression. The locus classicus is surely Anatole France's observation that 'the law, in its majestic equality, forbids the rich as well as the poor to beg in the streets, steal bread or sleep under a bridge'. Yet as soon as those who had been excluded gain sufficient power to share in redefining what will henceforth constitute the common interest, they undergo conversion to the law and become apostles of its 'majesty', 'grandeur' and 'permanence'—and, of course, of the 'universal' duty of obedience to it.

The function of such rhetoric is to reinforce respect for, and obedience to, legal arrangements, whatever their content. For some audiences and for some time, such rhetoric and the symbols that resonate to it may contribute to the fulfilment of this function. But it is the perception by actors that arrangements are also in their interest that accounts for their compliance and their willingness to support and to contribute resources for the implementation of legal arrangements. Participants who succeed in getting everything they want in a specific arrangement to the exclusion of their competitors thus win pyrrhic victories because the arrangement generates opposition and is unstable and will always require excessive resources for 'enforcement'.

III

Historicist theories would have us believe that institutions and practices perpetuate themselves automatically from generation to generation. They do not. No matter how skilfully the rhetoric of legal grandeur is deployed, both the content and procedures of legal arrangements in complex societies—and the world community is *the* complex society—are inherently volatile even when they seek to express and implement an interest common to all participants. By volatile or unstable, I do not refer to the contention of deconstructionists that language is inherently imprecise. That is a view I do not share. I mean, rather, that the *content* of both constitutive and specific arrangements is constantly under political stress to change, and that changes in the context of the arrangements will be registered in adjustments in the content and procedures of those arrangements. This volatility is the result of a number of factors.

The first is pervasive class, religious and cultural diversity. If all politically relevant actors shared the same perspectives, the same identifications, the same images of the past and the future, and the same demands, the common interests of all of these actors, once identified and expressed in a legal arrangement, would be universally shared, stable and enduring. Even if some discord crept in, the fact that all the participants in such a process resonated to the same symbols of authority would act to support the arrangements. Even if actors' perspectives did not coincide, but they believed their interests were served by a common constitutive arrangement, in accordance with which each and every actor agreed on and believed in his or her place in an interlocking set of subordinations and superordinations, the legal arrangements produced in this constitutive context would be stable.

Such arrangements, which may have achieved their most refined philosophical endorsement in Confucianism, are commonly espoused in regimes that invoke a divinity as one of the bases of authority. This is by no means an exclusively Asian value. In a nineteenth-century version of the Anglican Book of Common Prayer, the catechist undertakes to

> submit myself to all my governours, teachers, spiritual pastors and masters: To order myself lowly and reverently to all my betters: . . . and to do my duty in that state of life, unto which it shall please God to call me.[3]

This is, obviously, a most beneficial pledge for those at or near the apex of the social pyramid.

[3] *The Book of Common Prayer, and Administration of The Sacraments, and Other Rites and Ceremonies of The Church, According to the Use of The United Church of England and Ireland: Together with The Psalter or Psalms of David, Pointed as they are to be sung or said in Churches* (Church of England, 1815) 214.

Other than in charismatic political systems (which can last only as long as the charismatic leader), congruence of perspectives and effective deference to a single symbol of authority is ephemeral. This is especially so in the global community. The international political system is comprised of peoples with radically different conceptions of past and future and of assumptions about human and divine agency. They belong to different religions, classes and cultures and are distributed in territorial communities at different levels of development. Their communities or the parts or strata of those communities that they inhabit exhibit different levels of minimum order and different levels of expectation of violence.

Nor are all of the relevant communities to which people owe loyalty territorial. Some are non-governmental, ranging from corporate entities devoted to the maximisation of wealth, to religious entities, to private armies and to transnational criminal organisations. All of these entities generate their own symbols of authority and, indeed, their own 'legal' systems;[4] those symbols and legal systems need not recognise the superiority of another authority even if their members take it into account as an occupational hazard. Many of these groups now operate effectively transnationally and can insist on participating in the definition of the common interest.

There have always been some actors *within* the international system who aspire and actually seek to transform the world according to their own idiosyncratic vision, whether it be secular and materialistic—eg, a world of liberal democracies or a world of capitalism or of communism—or divine—eg, a world of a particular Christian sect or of a particular denomination of Islam.

The pursuit of these diverse visions puts stress on existing legal arrangements, increasing the volatility of international law. Were any one of these visions to be realised, it would, at least for the short term, reduce the volatility of international law. But no single dogma of universal ambition has yet prevailed. Even the contemporary international human rights movement which describes itself as 'universal' is not. To be sure, its code is *universalisable*, in the sense of being capable of application to everyone, without regard to race, religion, ethnicity or gender. But it is not universally accepted. In sum, in a world of diverse images of past and future, of radically different demands, of sharply demarked identities and of jagged distributions of political power, it is difficult to agree upon or to establish and maintain stable arrangements.

A second factor causing instability in all legal arrangements relates to law's dialectical character. Every specific legal arrangement is born of political bargains and compromises, and each arrangement, reflecting the prevailing allocation of power and calculus of fairness or justice, discrim-

[4] L Pospisil, *Anthropology of Law: A Comparative Theory* (New York, Harper and Row, 1971).

inates, perforce in varying degree, in favour of some and against others. So the moment a legal arrangement is struck, it generates opponents demanding its adjustment, amendment or replacement, whether by formal amendment within the system or by non-compliant behaviour that tests and stresses the particular arrangements if not the constitutive arrangement itself. This is the dynamic dialectic of law that gives it its vitality and its volatility—what Rudolf von Jhering called its struggle.[5]

This dialectical dynamic means that at every moment the arrangements that comprise the corpus of any body of law and especially international law include (i) some inherited arrangements whose support is declining, while other inherited arrangements overcome or accommodate challenges; (ii) new arrangements which are displacing existing ones; and (iii) surviving arrangements, usually described as historical or path-dependent, that continue, thanks to a common interest or disinterest in them. The arrangements in this last group may seem natural and inevitable but their duration, too, is uncertain. In this respect, Francis Fukuyama was profoundly wrong:[6] as long as there are human beings, there will be neither an 'end of history' nor an end to law's volatility.

A related reason for the volatility of all law, but especially of international law, is to be found in the phenomenon of 'justicial anachronism', ie, the changing content of the term 'justice', accompanied by a demand for the retroactive application of the newer conception.[7] In the kaleidoscope of the international process, self-selected leaders of groups that were hitherto unorganised or ineffective try to raise in others a consciousness of their shared identity and of the deprivations that they believe they have suffered as members of that group. As soon as they can organise and mobilise a constituency, they agitate for adjustments in legal arrangements to ameliorate their situation. Thus, they may seek compensation for deprivations that may have been lawful in the past, but would be unlawful by reference to the newly demanded or newly installed arrangements. The new arrangements they seek are not only *pro futuro;* they often demand retroactive adjustment.

This is a world-wide phenomenon. Whether we speak of Asian 'comfort women' of the Second World War, Germans expelled from Upper Silesia or Sudetenland, African-Americans seeking compensation for the deprivations of slavery, indigenous peoples demanding restitution of land that had been legally alienated (ie, in terms of the legal system of the then dominant group), 'decolonisation', or Palestinians seeking to return to lands from which they were expelled or fled more than half a century ago, we are encountering the same phenomenon: the insistence, on the

5 R Von Jhering, *The Struggle for Law* (John Lalor trans, Whitefish, MT, Kessinger Publishing, 2007).

6 F Fukuyama, *The End of History and the Last Man* (New York, Simon and Schuster, 2006).

7 I am grateful to Megumi Kayaki-Taniguchi for helping me to understand this concept.

basis of the application of contemporary or evolving notions of justice, that past practices which violated them but were accomplished under arrangements then lawful, be recharacterised *nunc pro tunc* as unlawful and requited by a significant remedy.

Justicial anachronism has become a recurring feature of contemporary law, both because of the dialectical dynamic we considered earlier and because of sociological changes in the agitational professions. Of particular importance is the catalytic role of specialist groups of lawyers, moral entrepreneurs and other agents of change, who see opportunities for moral satisfaction, profit and personal power in the installation of new notions of collective social responsibility.

The phenomenon of justicial anachronism is not limited to international law. Yet even when apparently internal to a particular territory, it is likely to invoke whatever international legal symbols promise to be useful as one of the bases of its demands. When justicial anachronism transcends the boundaries of an efficiently organised state, it becomes particularly complex and conflictive because the remedies may then entail adjustments in other states, yet the international legal arrangements for the orderly and fair termination of existing arrangements remain undeveloped.

Some reasons for the volatility of international law are shared with other intellectual disciplines. Although history as a discipline may seem to be concerned only with the verification and assembly of objective facts from the past, history, as a narrative or meditation on the past, is actually a palimpsest. Narratives of past events are constantly being rewritten and reinterpreted upon that palimpsest as a function of the perspectives and values of the culture, class, gender and crisis experience of each successive historian. Major events or leaders who might have been viewed affirmatively or neutrally or even ignored by one generation may be appraised negatively by a subsequent generation, whose evaluation will be shaped by its own perspectives. In some cases, successive reinterpretations are quite rapid.[8]

Comparable revisions occur in international law. In its heyday, imperialism and colonialism and their ostensible *mission civilisatrice* were glorified. On the basis of their fundamental legal arrangements, long-term private rights and duties were established. In current international

[8] Thus, to cite an acute international legal example, when Israel, in a lightning aerial raid, destroyed the Osiraq reactor in Iraq in 1981, its action was roundly condemned as unlawful by the Security Council and by much of the media. Ten years later, with the Saddam regime condemned for its effort to seize and annex Kuwait, the Israeli action was re-evaluated and viewed quite differently, indeed viewed by some with retrospective relief. Fifteen years later, as Iran persisted in developing the wherewithal for a nuclear arsenal and the United States and Israel were reported to have begun to consider pre-emptive actions akin to the destruction of Osiraq, fears of the consequences of such a prospective action in a new context forced a further re-evaluation of the Osiraq incident.

law, imperialism and colonialism are viewed as irredeemably evil and many (but not all) of the institutional arrangements and, in particular, private rights that were established and have been transmitted through time on the basis of law in that era are now subject to demands for their termination or adaptation to new values.

Instability in judgments about international events is also caused by incomplete knowledge of events. Assessments of lawfulness in international law, as in all law, are, in the first instance, fact-determined. In some critical cases, facts that could have a major impact on the assessment of lawfulness will become known only many years later. While the policies underlying the principle of *res judicata* may insulate judicial decisions from revision in the light of new information, no comparable principle insulates general assessments of the lawfulness of other legal events after authoritative decision about them.

Our civilisation of science and technology introduces a further factor that causes volatility in the law. For better or worse, participants in a civilisation of science and technology are locked in a relentless process of research and a frenzied, competitive drive to apply the results wherever they promise enhanced productivity and profit. Each innovation stimulates further innovations which stimulate still further innovations. As for the installation of legal arrangements that would regulate it all, thanks to legislation's characteristic deliberative and measured methods, this often lags behind the innovations. As a result, there are legal gaps during which the relevance or applicability of putatively lawful arrangements becomes uncertain.

IV

Until now, we have considered reasons for the volatility of the content of international law. Those reasons arise mostly from conflicts between groups with different perspectives and demands and distinctive symbols of authority. There is yet another factor that contributes to the uncertainty and volatility of international law and which makes the role of the international lawyer challenging and, in some circumstances, perilous. This factor has to do with the phenomenon of the multiplicity of images or versions of law of varying authority and control and the cathexis, as if it were a type of secular religion, to some manifestly inoperative versions.

Drawing upon the seminal work of Eugen Ehrlich, Roscoe Pound usefully distinguished between the 'law-in-the-books' and the 'law-in-action'. The law-in-the-books, according to Pound, presents a very complete picture of apparently authorised arrangements including how disputes about them should be processed. But that lovely picture does not always correspond, point for point, with the actual flow of decisions taken by the various authoritative institutions. Pound called the latter flow the 'law-in-action'.

Some jurists might assume that whatever is not consistent with the law-in-the-books is, indeed must be, unlawful. Pound's genius was to appreciate that what was *actually* done might well be lawful, even if it were inconsistent with the law-in-the-books. That is not to say that Pound was content with the inconsistency of the 'law-in-action' departing from the 'law-in-the-books'. At heart, he too believed that the 'law-in-the-books' should be the exclusive law; the discrepancy between the 'law-in-the-books' and the 'law-in-action' was a remediable pathology, if only law-makers would be disciplined and realistic in enacting legislation.

Discipline and realism are certainly desirable traits for legislators, but the reasons for the discrepancy between the 'law-in-the-books' and the 'law-in-action' are not always attributable to legislative incontinence or fecklessness. In every legal system, some legislation is enacted simply to affirm a value or placate a constituency without any intention or expectation of making it effective. The exercise is apparently legislative but the product is simulated law or *lex simulata*: the process is a simulation of law-making in which the key actors appreciate that they neither intend nor are installing an operative prescription. In some circumstances, political mediation between contending groups produces legislation that vindicates one group's claims but is designed to be unenforceable because it is inconsistent with other legislation demanded by other equally powerful or more powerful groups. In different circumstances, a law is enacted without a specified or sufficient sanction or is rendered unenforceable by under-budgeting or under-staffing. The exercise is legislative or, one might better say, 'legislatistic', but the product of the exercise is and was intended to be genetically ineffective, the so-called *lex imperfecta*.

Jurists who have not grasped the function of *lex simulata* and *lex imperfecta* assume, like Dean Pound and his notion of 'law-in-action', that an imperative juridical task is to correct the failure of a presumed feckless legislator by making simulated and imperfect law effective. But they miss the point; paradoxically, the intention and function of this type of inoperative legislation is to be inoperable!

Be that as it may, the net result of *lex imperfecta and simulata* is persisting discrepancies between certain parts of the formal legal system and the way decisions are actually taken. Those persistent discrepancies do not mean that there is no 'law' in the sectors in which practice deviates from formal law. Some of the discrepancies may indeed be violations, but some may conform to a different code, based on another set of expectations and demands. These latter are distinctive in that they are effectively, though usually informally, sanctioned. Thus actors who must actually make and contend with decisions encounter two 'relevant' normative systems: one that is *supposed* to apply, continues to enjoy public deference among elites and is presented to the relevant community at large as the law, and another that is *actually* applied. To complicate matters further, different arenas or application agencies may apply one or the other of the codes in question: there are jurisdictions which apply the myth system and jurisdictions which apply the operational code.

In other work,[9] I have called the norms of the official picture the 'myth system' of the group. Parts of it may be operational and may indeed provide the appropriate code of conduct for many group members; for all those members of a community who are not actually or actively engaged in the decision process, most of the myth system is their normative guide. But there are enough discrepancies between this myth system and the way things are actually done by key official or effective actors to warrant reserving another name, the 'operational code', for the unofficial but nonetheless effective code of behaviour in those discrepant sectors.

Myth systems are different from 'legal fictions'. The latter are authoritative statements the patent falseness of which is, by convention, scrupulously ignored. They occur in legal systems in which veneration for existing prescriptions is great or formal amendment procedures are cumbersome and expensive or easily blocked by a small minority. The device of the fiction enables those charged with making decisions to abrogate existing law without formally changing it, a function usually beyond their formal competence. Virtually all who resort to a particular legal fiction know it for what it is: a device for circumventing a norm that is obsolete but the costs of whose formal abrogation would exceed the benefit.[10] By contrast, the myth system is *not* widely appreciated as consciously false. It does not express values that are obsolete. On the contrary: it affirms values that continue to be important socially and personally. Although not applied in the 'jurisdiction' of the operational code, the myth system may yet influence decision-making.

Precisely because discrepancies between myth system and operational code can erode the credibility of the myth system, maintenance of belief in the myth system is a dynamic process requiring ongoing contributions

[9] WM Reisman, *Folded Lies: Bribery, Crusades and Reforms* (New York, Free Press, 1979).

[10] A classic example is to be found in the Common Law's invention of the 'Doe-Roe' writ in which, as Jenks tells us 'every action of Ejectment was between fictitious or, at least, nominal parties'. Jenks explains that 'Clumsy as it seems to modern eyes, this curious procedure appears to have been the universal method of trying title to land from the close of the present period, until the great reforms of 1833 and subsequent years; in other words, for a period of nearly two centuries. Not only did it take complete possession of the Courts in England; but, as we are informed, the name, at least, of the action of Ejectment passed, with other institutions of more value, to the English colonies in America, where, however, the necessities of practical life, combined with the stern Puritan dislike of fictions, soon caused great modification in the forms used.' E Jenks, *A Short History of English Law: From the Earliest Times to the End of the Year 1911* (Boston, MA, Adamant Media Corporation, 2002) 179.

from many. By contrast, those who practise the operational code try to obscure it from the general public. But there is an almost symbiotic relationship between myth system and operational code, with the latter providing a degree of suppleness and practicality that the myth system could not achieve without changing much of its content and procedure of application.

Members of the community who are not privy to its operational code may, at one level, view operational code activities as unlawful. Yet there may also be a certain uneasy toleration or even a desire for ignorance. A fascinating recent example of this double-thinking may be found in the reaction to NATO's bombardment of Serbia over its human rights violations in Kosovo. The bombardment was clearly against international law's myth system, yet NATO nonetheless felt that it was the right thing to do. A number of sociologists have studied 'dirty work' in society—things which a community requires to be done in order for it to function efficiently but which cannot be done in accordance with the community's law—and have noted the way that ignorance about it is cultivated.[11]

The concept of operational code does not mean that nothing is ever unlawful. Much will remain unlawful and even be effectively condemned. Operators know that some discrepancies from the myth system are licit, ie, are part of the operational code, and will be tolerated; others will not or will not in certain circumstances. In other words, determining the socially proper course of behaviour in a particular setting necessitates a much wider inquiry than the simple consultation of a single black-letter rule or the authoritative processes of formal law. But there is also uncertainty in relying on the operational code, for its is never certain that the best judgment, which is exercised at a critical moment and even acknowledged as the right thing to do then, will not later be reconsidered in terms of the myth system and penalised in its name.

When there are myth system purges of operational code practices, the 'operators' or practitioners of the operational code will often stand together and try to thwart the effort. Even if sanctions are imposed and new prescriptions are made to prevent the practices, indeed even if the old operators are purged and replaced by new operators, it is likely that many of these practices will continue if those who control them conclude that they are necessary for the operation of the collective enterprise or, exploiting that justification, convenient for the new operators. We need only reflect on the sad case of 'Oil-for-Food', a programme rife with self-dealing by scores of governments who were involved in it. Multiple investigations and reports have produced a handful of prosecutions but

[11] See, eg, E Hughes, 'Good People and Dirty Work' (1962) 10 *Social Problems* 3; J Bensman and I Gerver, 'Crime and Punishment in the Factory: The Function of Deviancy in Maintaining the Social System' (1963) 28 *American Sociological Review* 588.

no change in the essential arrangements that made such a scandal possible.

One reason operational codes persist is because those who apply and benefit from them have a continuing interest in sustaining them and keeping them confidential. Although they provide a certain flexibility or suppleness to that component of the myth system which is unworkable in critical situations, many parts of an operational code, if not the code itself, are not necessarily good for the community at large. Every norm of the operational code need not contribute to group weal. Indeed, in terms of the goals expressed in the myth system, much of the operational code may be profoundly dysfunctional, serving only to protect the entrenched position of elites or particular groups, eg, allowing rewards to be granted on the basis of 'old-boy' connections or class, caste, tribal or ethnic ties rather than on the basis of merit prescribed by the myth system.

The distinction between myth system and operational code is important for the lawyer and, in particular, the international lawyer for a number of reasons. The advice and guidance the lawyer gives is vital to those making decisions and those affected by them because expectations of authority are a critical variable in effectiveness. But those who are risking life or treasure appreciate the difference between what *is likely* to happen and what *should* happen and are entitled to be informed of the spread between them. It is important to have a framework of inquiry that permits the identification of the full range of those expectations of authority which are *actually operative*. Many legal formulations in international law establish prescriptions that express aspiration, but those who understand the decision processes know that they are not likely to be implemented. Those who seek advice and will then risk their treasure, and possibly their lives, relying on certain apparent legal arrangements should be advised as to whether those arrangements are truly effective or are aspirational statements: whether they are law-in-the-books, without the resource commitments to make them effective.

But, as noted, even when operators are privy to the operational code, there are always perils in following—or not following it. It will always be possible for reformers, some political opponents, or counter-elites to belatedly prosecute actions that were consonant with the operational code as defections from the myth system, either in response to popular outcry about deviations or in order to provoke such an outcry and then to demonstrate their own courage and skill in protecting the integrity of the myth system. The defence of compliance with the operational code will not prevail against these deferred prosecutions.

None of this is to say that the myth system is irrelevant and that only the operational code counts. Many of the key values of a community are expressed in the myth system and one of the *goals* of an enlightened jurisprudence may be to secure greater and greater realisation of that system.

But before that goal is ever achieved, responsible lawyers must advise those who repose trust in them, as to the law in the operational code.

The cultivation and elaboration of the myth system is particularly fascinating in international law. Consider the United Nations Security Council, a body formally endowed with apparently unlimited competence and with the theoretical capacity to compel United Nations Member (and non-member) States to comply with its decisions, even if their compliance in a particular case might require their violating existing treaty obligations. Merely open the UN Charter and you must conclude that international law is an effective system. But every international lawyer reading these pages knows that the Council, as a practical matter, can rarely act in precisely those critical events for which it was created. On the celebrated occasions when it proves itself capable of securing internal agreement and of acting, its decisions are often so anodyne as to amount to exercises in *lex simulata*. Even permanent members pressing for a meaningful decision may ultimately accept a compromise that is anodyne, thereby elevating the illusion that the Council is making a meaningful decision over the reality that it is not and maintaining the myth that this part of international law is effective. Yet there may be times when the Council can and does make a meaningful decision or at least may act in such a way as to render itself a significant factor in effecting an arrangement.

The very transposition of key concepts of organised domestic legal systems to international law embroiders the latter's myth system. Many of the domestic concepts presuppose an omnipresent hierarchical enforcement mechanism. Indeed positivism insists that such a structure is the essential indicator of law. Consider the concept of 'duty' in a developed legal system. It rests on the presumption that there are effective institutions to compel performance of that duty. Thus a 'duty' in a domestic legal system not to cause harm to the environment may be made meaningful. The willy-nilly transposition of such terms to international law, whose context and institutional articulation are radically different, creates an idealised image of a legal system that may bear little correspondence to the processes of decision which actually obtain. This is not to say that international law 'is not law', that it cannot be enforced or that it is a negligible factor in international politics. But those who would be effective in understanding and shaping international law must distinguish between its myth system and its operational code.

The myth system and operational code of international law, along with the factors causing its volatility, present formidable intellectual challenges to the international lawyer. These challenges are made even more formidable by the relevance of power, a factor to which we now turn.

V

Power is the capacity of one party to a relationship to influence the behaviour of another party to that relationship. Power is authoritative when it is applied in accordance with expectations of authority and for the achievement of authoritative objectives. When power is not used in this fashion, it is naked power. Authoritative power is an indispensable component of any effective legal arrangement. Naked power, in contrast to authoritative power, is used without regard to, or against, legal arrangements.

Power in the service of legal arrangements must be planned and built into those arrangements. Purported legal arrangements without power remain semantic exercises, whether they were only intended to be struts of the myth system with no expectation that power could sustain them or originated in real efforts to install an arrangement which then failed of its purpose because it could not mobilise sufficient power. The need for sufficient power to make arrangements effective also affects the content of the arrangements; mobilising power may require adjustments in their content in order to win sufficient support. The point of emphasis is that it is a mistake to assume that law and power are elements which are inherently and always opposed and incompatible.

For many students of international law, power is not simply a professionally irrelevant word; it is an obscene word: the 'P' word. The scholar who dares mention it is immediately viewed as cynically denying meaningful law or serving as the agent of a powerful state, usually seeking to justify that state's disregard for the legal arrangements demanded by others.

For many of their professional roles, international lawyers require a way of mapping and then mobilising or neutralising the power process. Consider, again, law-making or prescription. Normative arrangements require power to support and implement them. In a legally developed state with an effective political and legal system, formal institutions may usually (but not always) be relied upon for implementation. In international law, that is not the case, so the would-be international law-maker must either adjust the normative content of a prescription to win support and/or assemble coalitions to support the preferred normative content. Similarly, in application, one of the requisites of *effective* decisions is that they be crafted to win the support necessary to make them meaningful. Thus the international lawyer, in many roles, must understand the variable of power and be adept in using it.

That said, there are no simple and easy metrics for assessing power because it is always *relational* and *contextual*. The statement that 'A is powerful' is meaningless. A is not a weightlifter admiring his physique in a mirror. The statement 'A is powerful' can be made meaningful only in the sense that A is powerful in relation to some B in a particular context and with respect to particular matters. If B associates with C and D in that same context, A might cease to be 'powerful' with respect to those matters. If B should devise or acquire ways of counteracting A's power, A ceases to be powerful; the power relationship is reversed and B is powerful in relation to A for those contexts and matters. If A is a composite actor, some of whose components are ill-disposed to permit the exercise the influence of A vis-à-vis B, preferring it to be applied, for example, against C or D or preferring it to be reserved or directed to the achievement of internal goals, A is not powerful with respect to B.

Thus power is not a fixed factor but a variable one, always subject to possible adjustment and manipulation by other actors—if the actors' frame of reference includes ways of identifying and influencing power constellations. The statement that A, the weightlifter, is powerful is meaningful only insofar as others allow it to be self-fulfilling, ie, that others, unequipped with a way of thinking about and influencing power relationships or unable to shape the power variable and fearing A's bulging biceps, yield to him. For such actors, the jungle may be full of terrifying 'paper tigers'.

In international politics, power preponderance is not usefully measured by the number of missiles, bombs, tanks, or men and women under arms. Nor can power be assessed by a measure such as gross domestic product, the number of people in a population, the number of universities, and so on. Consider 'trophy' indicators of power, such as nuclear weapons, or the enormous ballistic missiles of the Soviet era, those great phallic symbols which were traditionally hauled through Red Square each May Day. Moreover, such prestige weapons are frequently neutralised by an adversary's comparable arsenal whose ready deployability ensures that the initiation of the use of these particular weapons would be self-destructive. They may also be rendered obsolete by the refinement of new asymmetrical weapons that adversaries are constantly trying to invent.

Even in situations in which such weapons are not available to an actual or latent adversary, a distinction must be drawn between what sociologists call 'fate control' and 'behaviour control'. Many of the weapons commonly assumed to indicate ultimate power enable an actor to annihilate its adversary, but do not necessarily enable it to control the adversary's behaviour. Insofar as annihilation has ceased to be a legitimate, beneficial or practicable objective, the critical issue has become behaviour control.

In the myriad networks of which modern international politics is composed, there are many shifting power relationships. The bases of a power relationship may be any of the values that serve as the resources of different parties or of the community as a whole. Which of those resources will prove effective and serve as means of influence in a particular situation will depend on many factors: the context, the interrelated dependencies of the participants concerned, and the relative abilities of each of the participants to understand and to mobilise internal resources for that particular relationship. Since, as noted earlier, the techniques of our science-based and technological civilisation are constantly changing or being adapted to new purposes, what will constitute a useful instrument or value for the exercise of power in a particular setting will be changing constantly.[12]

The fluidity of power and the ineluctable relationship between legal arrangements and power in international politics contributes to and exacerbates the volatility and uncertainty of the international legal system. It is, in itself, a source of conflict because at any moment there may be contending symbol systems, through whose respective prisms those who are subject to them view the same events as either exercises in naked power or exercises of power in defence of public order.

VI

Law in any system is unstable. International law is particularly volatile; its content and mode of application to new events are always more uncertain than in the domestic law of organised states. Moreover, assessments of lawfulness made within it are frequently adjusted retroactively. This volatility presents opportunities to would-be reformers for constructively shaping international law in better ways. However, it poses special challenges to the lawyer who would responsibly advise any of the participants in the international process as to which arrangements in international law are operative at particular moments and for particular events to enable them to assess the lawfulness of prospective actions.

[12] See above at p 42.

3

Structural Paradigms of International Law

DIRK PULKOWSKI*

I. INTRODUCTION

The practice of international law is not what it used to be. Classical doctrine portrayed the international system as a loose body of norms, focused on key aspects of inter-state relations and administered by '"generalist" lawyer-diplomats'.[1] Contemporary international law, by contrast, resembles a dense web of detailed prescriptions in almost any conceivable subject area. Formerly the language of diplomats, international law is now routinely used by a variety of actors, including administrators in national bureaucracies, international functionaries, human rights activists and environmentalists. This radical transformation of international law has prompted three related questions for legal theorists: first, does it still make sense to conceive of international law as a system based on state sovereignty; or should the 'S word'[2] (Louis Henkin) be banished? Second, how can the increasing involvement in international decision making of non-state actors and actors at the sub-national level be accounted for? And third, how can the relationship between various functional sub-systems of regulation that have evolved at the global level—international regimes—be theorised? All three questions are central to the theme of this collection of essays: the allocation of authority in international law. In the present contribution, I

* Attorney, International Trade/Arbitration team, Sidley Austin LLP, Brussels, doctoral candidate, Ludwig-Maximilians-Universität (München); LLM, Yale Law School (New Haven); Ass jur (München). I am particularly grateful for the helpful comments by Professors Robert Howse, Kalypso Nicolaidis, Andreas Paulus, Michael Reisman and Brad Roth following the presentation of an earlier version of this paper at the Conference.

[1] M Koskenniemi and P Leino, 'Fragmentation of International Law? Postmodern Anxieties' (2002) 15 *Leiden Journal of International Law* 553, 562.

[2] L Henkin, 'That "S" Word: Sovereignty, and Globalization, and Human Rights, etc' (1999) 68 *Fordham Law Review* 1.

will mainly be concerned with the last question, the differentiation of international law into multiple regimes.

In over 50,000 international treaties (6,000 of which are of the multilateral type), states have submitted themselves to international regulation in almost every conceivable area. Trade relations, monetary policy, environmental and technical standards, and the domestic treatment of a country's citizens are only some of the areas that are subject to the logic of international law. A good part of such 'new' international law is administered by robust bureaucratic arrangements. Think of the Dispute Settlement Body of the World Trade Organization (WTO), the World Heritage Center of the United Nations Educational, Scientific and Cultural Organization (UNESCO), the World Health Organization's various, disease-specific programmes (such as the Global Malaria Programme or the Polio Eradication Initiative), or the 'ad-hoc bureaucracies' of the dozens of arbitral tribunals formed every year to adjudicate disputes over foreign investment agreements.[3] Theorists of international relations have thus observed the emergence of distinct, subject-matter-specific 'regimes'.[4] International lawyers have mostly preferred to speak of the 'fragmentation of international law' into various 'sub-systems'.[5]

How do these regimes or sub-systems relate to one another? Most scholarly treatments of the fragmentation of international law proceed along the following familiar lines:

1. At the outset, the problem is framed in terms of potential rule conflicts. As more and more international law is being made, there is a heightened risk that rules of different sub-systems contain irreconcilable

[3] The practice of international investment law is so lively that tribunals currently hand down about one significant award per week. For a helpful tool for monitoring these developments, see the website http://www.investmentclaims.com/.

[4] Recent studies in regime theory include OS Stokke, 'The Interplay of International Regimes: Putting Effectiveness Theory to Work' *FNI Report* (14/2001); H Loewen, 'Towards a Dynamic Model of the Interplay between International Institutions' *GIGA Working Papers* (17/2006); GK Rosendal, 'Impact of Overlapping International Regimes: The Case of Biodiversity' (2001) 7 *Global Governance* 95, 100; S Blau, 'The Relationship between the Climate Change and the World Trade Regimes: A Case Study of Regime Interplay' available through Climate Action Network Europe (CAN-E) at http://www.climnet.org/pubs/WTO%20 Kyoto.pdf; G Teubner and A Fischer-Lescano, *Regimekollisionen: Zur Fragmentierung des globalen Rechts* (Frankfurt am Main, Suhrkamp, 2006) 128; GJ Ratto-Nielsen, *The International Telecommunications Regime: Domestic Preferences and Regime Change* (Spain, Lulu Press, 2006).

[5] See first and foremost the study by the International Law Commission, 'Fragmentation of International Law: Difficulties Arising from the Diversification and Expansion of International Law—Report of the Study Group of the International Law Commission' 13 April 2006, A/CN.4/L.682. Important scholarly discussions in the field include P-M Dupuy, 'L'unité de L'ordre Juridique International' (2002) 297 *Recueil des Cours* 1; the symposia in the (1999) 31 *NYU Journal of International Law and Politics* 679–933 and the (2004) 25 *Michigan Journal of International Law* 845–1375; and E Benvenisti and GW Downs, 'The Empire's New Clothes: Political Economy and the Fragmentation of International Law' (2007) 60 *Stanford Law Review*, 595.

prescriptions.[6] One and the same situation may be subject to the rules of Sub-system A (designed, for example, to impose stricter sanitary standards) and Sub-system B (designed to remove anticompetitive trade barriers). As '[t]he world community still has no legislature',[7] the task of finding out which rule applies falls to international lawyers, acting as government advisers, members of governing bodies in international organisations, or adjudicators.

2. The relationship between two different treaty regimes is governed by the Vienna Convention on the Law of Treaties[8] and such principles of customary international law as may be applicable. Among the Vienna Convention rules, Article 31(3)(c) stands out as a general principle of systemic integration (as demonstrated by the International Court's Oil Platforms judgment).[9] As to customary rules, the *lex specialis* principle has recently received particular attention.[10] In Joost Pauwelyn's view, for example, the maxim can help clarify the relationship of a functional regime with other branches of international law. Thus, non-WTO treaties may prevail over WTO law as *leges speciales* or vice versa.[11]
3. To the extent that a functional regime does not contain a specific rule, the focus shifts to general international law. Without the 'omnipresence of "general law"'[12] a special legal sub-system may, as Georges Abi-Saab has put it, mutate into 'a legal Frankenstein' that 'no longer partakes in the same basis of legitimacy and formal standards of pertinence'.[13] General international law, it is said, automatically fills up lacunae that remain in the regulatory scope of special regimes.[14]

[6] When exactly rules are in conflict with one another is an intricate question that is hotly disputed among legal theorists. For an excellent discussion, see E Wiederin, 'Was ist und welche Konsequenzen hat ein Normkonflikt' (1990) 21 *Rechtstheorie* 311.

[7] W Jenks, 'Conflict of Law-Making Treaties' (1953) 30 *British Yearbook of International Law* 401.

[8] Vienna Convention on the Law of Treaties (adopted 23 May 1969, entered into force 27 January 1980) 1155 UNTS 331.

[9] *Oil Platforms (Iran v United States)* (Merits) [2003] ICJ Rep 161, especially at para 41. For a more general discussion, see C McLachlan, 'The Principle of Systemic Integration and Article 31(3)(c) of the Vienna Convention' (2005) 54 *International and Comparative Law Quarterly* 279.

[10] See eg the International Law Commission's deliberation of the notion of *lex specialis*, M Koskenniemi, 'Study on the 'Function and Scope of the *lex specialis* Rule and the Question of "Self-Contained Regimes"' Preliminary Report by the Chairman of the Study Group submitted for consideration during the 2004 session of the International Law Commission, unpublished (on file with the author); International Law Commission, above n 5, paras 46ff.

[11] According to Pauwelyn, environmental considerations (to take one example) can thus be relevant in two ways: first (and more conventionally), panels need to take account of environmental matters in the context of Article XX GATT. In addition, panels must determine in each case whether parties have effectively contracted out of a standard required by WTO law by concluding an *inter se* environmental agreement. J Pauwelyn, *Conflict of Norms in Public International Law: How WTO Law Relates to other Rules of International Law* (Cambridge University Press, 2003) 388 (in particular).

[12] Koskenniemi, above n 10.

[13] G Abi-Saab, 'Fragmentation or Unification: Some Concluding Remarks' (1999) 31 *NYU Journal of International Law and Politics* 919, 926.

[14] Classically, B Simma, 'Self-Contained Regimes' (1985) XVI *Netherlands Yearbook* 111. For a

The scholarly debate along these lines rests on one central presupposition: the idea that international law is an organised system of rules. 'L'unité de l'ordre juridique', as Pierre-Marie Dupuy has entitled his General Course at the Hague Academy,[15] is more than a catchword for the sum total of disconnected should-statements. It denominates an organised whole, a system. Now, it is certainly possible to *construe* international law as a single unified system from what HLA Hart has famously called the 'internal point of view',[16] and Dupuy's treatise is a particularly sophisticated example of such an exercise.[17] The present collection of essays, however, is intended to explore a different direction. Under the heading *The Allocation of Authority in International Law*, we are challenged to investigate the neural points of the contemporary international system in which legal authority is actually situated; and to develop legal techniques for shifting such authority in appropriate ways (in particular, the principles of sovereignty, supremacy, subsidiarity). To set the stage for this debate, the present contribution will attempt to identify the organisational paradigms that underlie the contemporary international legal order.

To that end, I will proceed from a working definition of law borrowed from cultural anthropology. A brief *tour d'horizon* of legal anthropology illustrates that a plurality of coexisting legal sub-systems is quite a normal state of affairs in any complex society. On the basis of this working definition I will take a close look at three constitutive components of international legal practice: rhetoric, bureaucracy and power. With regard to each component, a mélange of three competing organisational paradigms can be observed. International law is simultaneously organised according to the Westphalian paradigm of coexistence, the hierarchical paradigm of constitutionalisation and the heterarchical

more recent exposition of this view, albeit one that questions the 'automatism' of the fallback on general international law, See B Simma and D Pulkowski, 'Of Planets and the Universe: Self-contained Regimes in International Law' (2006) 17 *European Journal of International Law* 483.

[15] Dupuy, above n 5.

[16] K Zemanek, 'The Legal Foundations of the International System' (1997) 266 *Recueil des Cours* 62, has suggested in this vein that '[t]he "unity" of international law in the sense of its homogeneity is therefore a construct.'

[17] Pierre-Marie Dupuy's unity of the international legal order rests on three interlocking arguments. Firstly, the concept of general international law constitutes a non-negotiable and virtually uncontested expression of common legality. At the heart of this core legal order is a set of imperative norms (jus cogens) that represent an international '*ordre public*'. Secondly, the unity of the international legal order is based on the recognition of the notion of 'international community' in positive law. Dupuy introduces *La communauté internationale* as a constitutive legal fiction, which, rather than implying the negation of the reality of an international community, serves as a convenient shorthand for its demonstration ('*l'économie de sa démonstration*'). This fiction of an international community works as a counterpart to another, more traditional legal fiction, namely the principle of sovereign equality. Thirdly, this legal fiction of international community is normatively grounded on a Kantian concept of international community as a categorical imperative. Universal solidarity must be assumed a priori in order to encourage states to act as if it actually existed.

network paradigm. Attempts at developing general principles for the allocation of authority in international law—the theme of this volume—can only be successful to the extent that the complex structure of the international order is taken into account.

I. LEGAL PLURALITY, DOMESTICALLY AND GLOBALLY

A. Anthropological Readings of the Law

Let us take a contemporary anthropological definition of law as a starting point. Sociologist Boaventura de Sousa Santos identifies three components that are present, with varying degrees and with different articulations, in the operation of all legal systems: rhetoric, bureaucracy and violence. The higher the level of bureaucratic institutionalisation of juridical production and the more powerful the instruments of violence in the service of juridical production, the smaller is the rhetorical space for legal discourse. Based on these structural characteristics, Santos adopts a working definition of law as

> a body of regularized procedures and normative standards that is considered justiciable—ie, susceptible of being enforced by a judicial authority—in a given group and contributes to the creation and prevention of disputes, as well as their settlement through an argumentative discourse coupled with the threat of force.[18]

Santos's definition falls squarely in a tradition of legal anthropology that combines a procedural and a substantive element. As to substance, the community must consider a prescription to be judiciable.[19] As to procedure, a prescription is law only if it is applied to concrete incidents through a specific argumentative discourse that is backed by some form of sanction. Contrast Santos with a classical definition by Leopold Pospisil, which is similar in its key aspects.[20] Pospisil identifies the following elements that turn prescriptions into law: Prescriptions

[18] B de Sousa Santos, *Toward a New Legal Common Sense* (London, Butterworths, 2002) 86.

[19] It should be noted that this is, again in the anthropological tradition, an empirical standard, not a theoretical concept. Judiciability does not necessarily require the presence of courts in any formal sense. Rather, the idea is that appropriate standards of conduct can be formulated *a priori* and with a view to universal application—a precondition of authoritative decision making by a designated third party.

[20] L Pospisil, 'Legal Levels and Multiplicity of Legal Systems in Human Societies' (1967) XI *Conflict Resolution* 2, 8–9. One could add other names to the list, such as Sally Falk Moore who, in her seminal article 'Law and Social Change: The Semi-autonomous Social Field as an Appropriate Subject of Study', defines her field of inquiry 'by a processual characteristic, the fact that it can generate rules and coerce or induce compliance to them.' (1973) *Law and Society Review* 719, 722.

- must emanate from a authority recognised as such in their community;
- must be intended to apply universally;
- must be provided with some kind of sanction;
- must be capable of leading, in third-party settlement, to obligating one of the parties to a particular conduct.

In international law literature, the New Haven School has adopted an even more concise definition along the same lines. Prescriptions qualify as law provided that they derive from an authoritative decision, in which authority and control are combined. Authority requires that the decision be taken 'in accordance with community perspectives about who is to make what decisions and by what criteria'.[21] The requirement that control intention be communicated sets law apart from mere pretence or normative expectation. Recent constructivist scholarship in international relations theory has made an interesting attempt to recast the New Haven approach so as to align it with more orthodox theories of law as a system of rules. According to Anthony Clark Arend, rules qualify as legal if decision-making elites perceive the rule to be authoritative (a requirement akin to *opinio juris*[22]) and the norm is sufficiently controlling of social conduct.[23]

B. Legal Plurality at the Domestic Level

Applying the anthropological perspective to domestic societies, legal anthropologists have found that the Roman maxim *ubi societas ibi ius* captures a profound truth: even at the national or local level a variety of systems of rule coexist. The rule of the nation-state arguably constitutes the most elaborate legal system. By virtue of its superior resources in all three constitutive categories—rhetoric, bureaucracy and violence—it has a strong potential to overpower local or community-based systems of

[21] HD Lasswell and MS McDougal, 'Criteria for a Theory about Law' (1971) 44 *Southern California Law Review* 362, 384.

[22] It is doubtful whether Arend's borrowing of the customary international law terminology of *opinio juris* is fortunate. The authority of a prescription, according to the New Haven School, is first and foremost determined by whether community expectations of legitimate *authorship and procedure* are met. *Opinio juris*, by contrast, is first of all a criterion for distinguishing *behaviour* that is legally required from mere habit, courtesy, or moral imperatives (I Brownlie, *Principles of Public International Law* (4th edn, Oxford, Clarendon Press, 1990) 7). Thus, the claim that 'states hold an *opinio juris* that *p*' says that relevant elites consider *p* to be legally required according to whatever theory of law that they may hold, no matter how the prescription has come into being. By contrast, the claim that 'states hold *p* to be an authoritative prescription' says that the prescription has come into being through law-making procedures that are recognised by the relevant elites as appropriate.

[23] AC Arend, *Legal Rules and International Society* (Oxford University Press, 1999) 87.

rule.[24] The nation-state has thus established itself 'in a relation of superior power to other systems of regulation as the ultimate source of coercive power'.[25]

Yet, the law of the state does not have a legal monopoly and it is not always effective in and by itself: macrolegal changes might require adjustments in lower-level systems of normativity to produce effects on the ground. No society is 'monolithic' in the sense that it consists merely of individuals who interact to form a single, greater whole (such as in the famous cover illustration of Hobbes's *Leviathan*). Complex societies are composed of different subgroups of varying membership inclusivities, structures of decision-making and sanctioning. Some of these decision-making processes qualify as law. In Pospisil's words, 'Any human society . . . does not possess a single consistent legal system, but as many such systems as there are functional subgroups.'[26] Each functional legal system thus identified, as simple as it may be, is constituted by a set of decision-making institutions, distributive criteria and cultural traditions.[27]

Hence, the coexistence of multiple systems—a state of legal plurality defined as 'a situation in which two or more legal systems co-exist in the same social field'[28]—is a perfectly normal feature of every complex society. In Santos's terms, interests, values and policies confront each other in 'multiple sites and idioms of social struggles, constellating around forms of power, forms of law and forms of knowledge'.[29] However, this is not to conjure up a romantic image of peaceful coexistence.[30] Rather, to borrow Santos's words again,

24 See G Massell, 'Law as an Instrument of Revolutionary Change in a Traditional Milieu: The Case of Soviet Central Asia' (1968) 2 *Law and Society Review* 179; S Diamond, 'The Rule of Law versus the Order of Custom' in D Black and M Mileski (eds), *The Social Organization Law* (New York, Academic Press, 1973) 318; S Burman and BE Harrell-Bond (eds), *The Imposition of Law* (New York, Academic Press, 1979).

25 SE Merry, 'Legal Pluralism' (1988) 22 *Law and Society Review* 869, 874.

26 Pospisil, above n 20, 3.

27 See on this point, RA Macdonald, 'Metaphors of Multiplicity: Civil Society, Regimes and Legal Pluralism' (1998) 15 *Arizona Journal of International and Comparative Law* 69, 77. A potential point of critique is of course that these systems should not be denoted as 'law proper', but rather be called 'rule systems' or the like. Applying the term 'law' to social phenomena not related to the nation state may cause confusion outside the community of anthropologists and sociologists. However, this should not distract from the central point: there is a plurality of different systems of normativity operating at every level of social organisation that, with the exception of their source of authority, have characteristics equivalent to the law of the nation state.

28 Thus a consensual definition by Sally Merry, above n 25, 870.

29 Santos, above n 18, 418.

30 Indeed, there is nothing inherently positive or emancipatory about non-state systems of law in the first place. Such systems have a repressive potential as much as an emancipatory potential. The centralisation of legal power by the nation-state, for example, often seen in a critical light by legal pluralists, has made major contributions to the emancipation of disenfranchised groups often discriminated against on the basis of race, gender or sexual orientation by 'traditional' rule systems. See also W Twining, *Globalisation and Legal Theory*

> As far as laws are concerned, . . . irrespective of the plurality of normative orders circulating in society, each one of them, taken separately, aspires to be exclusive, to have the monopoly of regulation and control of social action within its legal territory.[31]

Der Kampf ums Recht[32] (the struggle for the law) involves, last but not least, a competition of various normative systems to authoritatively govern a particular subject matter.

What kind of decision-making procedures do anthropologists qualify as 'legal'? As early as 1868 Otto von Gierke recognised that the internal orderings of *Genossenschaften* (co-operatives) were vested with the essential characteristics of law.[33] In his path-breaking *Soziologie des Rechts*, Eugen Ehrlich identified *Verbände* (associations), defined as 'a plurality of human beings who recognise in their relationships among each other certain rules as determinative of their action and who, at least in general, in fact conduct themselves accordingly',[34] as legally organised entities within a society. Early twentieth-century studies in anthropology then focused on colonial societies; they demonstrated the coexistence of indigenous legal systems—the rule of the lineage, the band or the band faction—alongside the codified legal system imposed by colonial administrators. In the second half of the twentieth century, anthropologists turned their attention to systems of normativity in industrialised societies. The rule of the family, the rule of the workplace, the rule of the market and the rule of particular identity-based communities came into focus. The best-known examples are perhaps Sally Moore's study of the New York garment industry,[35] Otto Weyrauch and Maureen Bell's analysis of the autonomous legal system of Roma communities,[36] and

(London, Butterworths, 2000) 86–7; Santos, above n 18, 91; Reisman, above n 36. See for an exposition of the repressive potential of non-state systems in the Roma context, J Timmerman, 'When Her Feet Touch the Ground: Conflict Between the Roma Familistic Custom of Arranged Juvenile Marriage and Enforcement of International Human Rights Treaties' (2004) 13 *Journal of Transnational Law and Policy* 475. For this reason, the more neutral term 'legal plurality' should be preferred to the term 'legal pluralism' with its inherently positive connotations.

[31] Santos, above n 18, 419. See also P Bourdieu, 'The Force of Law: Toward a Sociology of the Juridical Field' (1987) 38 *Hastings Law Journal* 805, 819: 'The juridical field is the site of a competition for monopoly to determine the law.'

[32] Thus the title of Rudolf von Jhering's famous lecture at Vienna University in 1868.

[33] O von Gierke, *Das deutsche Genossenschaftsrecht* (1868).

[34] E Ehrlich, *Grundlegung der Soziologie des Rechts* (4th edn, M Rehbinder, 1989) 45: 'Ein gesellschaftlicher Verband ist eine Mehrheit von Menschen, die im Verhältnisse zueinander gewisse Regeln als für ihr Handeln bestimmend anerkennen und wenigstens im allgemeinen tatsächlich danach handeln.'

[35] Moore, above n 20, 719.

[36] OW Weyrauch and MA Bell, 'Autonomous Law Making: the Case of the Gypsies' (1993) 103 *Yale Law Journal* 323; See also the critique by WM Reisman, 'Autonomy, Interdependence and Responsibility' (1993) 103 *Yale Law Journal* 401. The Amish or Hasidic sects would be other examples of religion-based membership groups that have a strongly developed system of rule. See eg C Carmichael, 'Gypsy Law and Jewish Law' (1997) 45 *American Journal of Comparative Law* 269.

Santos's discovery of systems of dispute prevention and settlement in the Brazilian *favelas*.[37] Michael Reisman even identifies rule-governed procedures of decision in simple everyday operations such as looking, glaring and staring, or lining up. As evidenced by such 'microlegal systems', to Reisman, law is quite simply 'a property of interaction'.[38]

Most recently, anthropologists have questioned the unity of the 'official' legal system of the nation-state. Examining how laws are made and applied by courts, pressure groups, and institutions at the national and global level, anthropologists emphasise that the law of the state has itself emerged as a site for 'internal legal pluralism', which is characterised by the 'coexistence of different logics of regulation, carried out by different state institutions with very little communication between them'.[39] As we shall see in more detail below, similar conclusions may well be warranted with respect to contemporary international law, shaped by transnational processes of law-making at the global level.

C. The Multiplication of International Norms and Institutions

Seen through the anthropological lens, the *domestic* sphere emerges as an arena of intense competition between multiple normative systems. Somewhat counter-intuitively, at the *international* level the situation used to be much simpler. Law above the state level had long been a rather clearly arranged system, removed from the legal plurality that existed at the state level. Only few actors were able to interact at a supranational or even global level and establish normative systems with a distinct mode of rhetoric and a certain degree of bureaucracy and violence. For centuries, the principal actors on the global plane were nation-states and traders.[40] International law and the *lex mercatoria,* respectively, were their systems of rule.

The birth of medieval law among merchants is generally associated with the flourishing of the newly independent *repubbliche marinare*—the city-states of Genoa, Pisa, Venice and Amalfi—as Byzantine power waned in the eleventh and twelfth centuries. These city-states soon established themselves as centres of transnational commerce. The decay of the Roman roads had resulted in long-distance commerce shifting almost entirely to the Mediterranean Sea, favouring the Italian coastal cities.[41]

37 B de Sousa Santos, 'The Law of the Oppressed: The Construction and Reproduction of Legality in Pasargada' (1977) 12 *Law and Society Review* 5.

38 WM Reisman, *Law in Brief Encounters* (New Haven, CT, Yale University Press, 1999) 2.

39 Santos, above n 18, 95. See also K Günter and S Randeria, *Recht, Kultur und Gesellschaft im Prozeß der Globalisierung* (Werner Reimer Stiftung, Bad Homburg, 2001) 86.

40 Another actor with a truly global reach was (and still is) the Catholic Church.

41 The Brenner Pass, one of the most important remaining land roads across Europe, fell into the hands of Venice in 1178.

The *repubbliche* also offered a legal environment favourable to merchants. At the time, the feudal laws of much of Europe were either silent about trading relations or outright hostile towards the merchants' order—the *pied poudreux* (dusty feet) as the feudal lords would derogatorily label profit-seeking merchant bands.[42] In the new city-states, by contrast, mercantile families made up much of the ruling class.[43] The *repubbliche* permitted traders to fashion their own legal system that would apply with a considerable degree of homogeneity to their 'transnational' transactions. The system's defining characteristics were a strong emphasis on *pacta sunt servanda*, flexible debt financing and impartial mechanisms for prompt adjudication *ex aequo et bono* (so-called piepowder courts[44]).

The demise of the *lex mercatoria* coincided with the advent of modernity. As trade expanded to include an increasing number of cultural communities, the merchants' law proved less capable of providing a satisfactory framework for ordering diverse trade customs. At the same time, the emerging modern nation-state gained effective control over its territory and claimed exclusive regulatory power. As a consequence, merchantile law was either assimilated into the newly evolving national court systems or repressed by the competing systems of the nation-states. Diverging business customs were henceforth co-ordinated through a decentralised system of private international laws, coupled with harmonising international conventions. At the global level, the law among nation-states—international law—remained the only significant system of rule.[45] Empirically, three observations underscore the special status of international law: to date, no other global system of rule has been able to weave such an elaborate and dense web of normativity, in diverse subject areas, administered by comparable bureaucratic resources.

Since 1945, over 50,000 treaties have been registered with the United Nations Secretariat pursuant to Article 102(1) of the UN Charter, many of which have been concluded during the past 15 years.[46] In the twentieth century, about 6,000 multilateral treaties were concluded, almost one-third of which are open to accession by any state.[47] But it is not so much the mere number of treaties, but their content that has brought

[42] See ME Tigar (with MR Levy), *Law and the Rise of Capitalism* (New York, Monthly Review Press, 1977) 4–5; Santos, above n 18, 209.

[43] H Hansmann et al, 'Law and the Rise of the Firm' (2006) 119 *Harvard Law Review* 1333, 1364.

[44] C Gross, 'The Court of Piepowder' (1906) 20 *Quarterly Journal of Economics* 231.

[45] Besides the demise of the *lex mercatoria*, one may add the diminishing importance of the law of the Catholic Church as a consequence of secularisation.

[46] Presentation by B Smith, Office of Legal Affairs, 'International Treaty Law: The Role of the Office of Legal Affairs, the Sixth Committee and the International Law Commission', slides 15–6 (on file with the author).

[47] See C Ku, 'Global Governance and the Changing Face of International Law' ACUNS Keynote Paper 2001–2, 45.

about the most fundamental changes to the legal system. As Joseph Weiler has observed, early twentieth-century treaties were predominantly of a bilateral, 'contractual' character, often concerned with the preservation of the status quo. In the mid-century, multilateral treaties emerged, which 'privileg[ed] change and transformation and in which both treaty and "custom" often prized the communal and universal over the particularistic'.[48] In the past two decades, a third treaty paradigm has gained ground: detailed agreements of a regulatory character have addressed issues such as regional trade integration, financial co-operation or environmental standard-setting.

According to a classification by the office of the Secretary General the following broad issue areas are subject to multilateral treaties:[49] pacific settlement of international disputes; privileges and immunities (diplomatic, consular, etc); human rights; refugees and stateless persons; narcotic drugs and psychotropic substances; traffic in persons; obscene publications; health; international trade and development; transport and communications; navigation; economic statistics; educational and cultural matters; declarations of death of missing persons; status of women; freedom of information; penal matters; commodities; maintenance obligations; law of the sea; commercial arbitration; law of treaties; outer space; telecommunications; disarmament; environment; and fiscal matters. It can be easily imagined that this 'web' of treaty obligations that enmeshes states today reduces dramatically the *domaine reservé* that classical international law had ascribed to states. The price for adaptation to a variety of social contexts has been a decline of the *völkerrechtsfreien Raum,* the space that international law still accords to exclusive domestic regulation.

Institutionally, contemporary international law is a far cry from the legal order of the seventeenth to nineteenth centuries. Classical international law was almost exclusively administered by the governmental administrations of the nation-state. As Inis Claude has observed, it was not until the nineteenth century that the conditions for the 'birth' of the modern international organisation were satisfied:

> The first two [requirements] relate to the existence of objective facts or conditions: the world [was] divided into a number of states which function as independent political units, and a substantial measure of contact must exist between these subdivisions. The other requirements are subjective in nature: the states must develop an awareness of the problems which arise out of their coexistence, and, on this basis, come to recognize the need for creation of insti-

[48] JHH Weiler, 'The Geology of International Law—Governance, Democracy and Legitimacy' (2004) 64 *Zeitschrift für Ausländisches. Recht und Völkerrecht* 547, 549.

[49] List of Multilateral Treaties Deposited with the Secretary-General, available at http://www.un.org/millennium/law/titles.htm.

> tutional devices and systematic methods for regulating their relations with each other.[50]

'Coexistence' is the emblematic word at this stage of international organisation. The few international organisations that came into existence then would essentially resolve nonpolitical functions. They were creatures of necessity, not of grand ideals. The trend towards 'public international unions' represented 'adaptation, not innovation; it was less the work of idealists with schemes to advance than of realists with problems to handle'.[51] The International Telegraphic Union (1865) or the Universal Postal Union (1874) resolved simple co-ordination problems in what could be referred to as non-zero-sum games: every participating state gained from participation. Other examples include the various river commissions set up across Europe to cope with unprecedented ship traffic in the wake of European industrialisation.[52]

Public international unions set the stage for more robust international institutions. Contemporary international organisation is characterized by a standing bureaucratic structure of secretariat, council and general conference. Nevertheless, back in the nineteenth century, states discovered the multilateral convention as an innovative law-making tool for enacting rules with a universal reach.[53]

> The treaty, traditionally an agreement negotiated by the representatives of two or a few states for the establishment of particular legal rights and duties pertaining to themselves, was given the form of the multilateral convention, hammered out in committee and conference of many states, voted upon as if it were a legislative bill, and adopted to serve as a joint legislative enactment.[54]

Interestingly, the international conference also marked the debut of expert representation (as opposed to the representation of governments by its diplomatic corps). Subject-matter specialists from appropriate departments were entrusted with negotiating the often technical multilateral conventions (telecommunications, industrial property, copyright, etc).

[50] IL Claude, *Swords into Plowshares: The Problems and Progress of International Organization* (3rd edn, New York, Random House, 1964) 17.

[51] *Ibid*, 30.

[52] The Danube Commission, established through the 1856 Treaty of Paris, is the classical example. River commissions continue to exist as institutions for inter-state co-ordination. Besides the Rhine and Danube commissions, recent creations are the Mekong River Commission (MRC), the Organisation pour la Mise en Valeur du Fleuve Sénégal (OMVS), the Niger Basin Authority (NBA), the Comisión Mixta Argentino-Paraguaya del Río Paraná (COMIP) and the Amazon Cooperation Treaty Organization (ACTO). See FB Sayre, *Experiments in International Administration* (New York, Harpers, 1919) for a discussion of many historical river commissions.

[53] Universal, of course, understood in the now questionable sense of operating within the exclusive 'community of civilised nations' of the nineteenth century.

[54] Claude, above n 50, 32.

In 2006, the Union of International Associations (UIA) counted an impressive 7,350 intergovernmental arrangements. Of these, 246 qualify as formal conventional bodies, with 34 organizations being open to universal membership; 1,440 organizations are dependent arrangements related to other international or national bodies; and 2,473 arrangements are listed as 'organisational substitutes', a category that includes autonomous conference series and bodies established by multilateral agreements that fall short of the status of an international organisation.[55] A novelty of the past few decades is the creation of numerous judicial or quasi-judicial institutions for the settlement of disputes. The Project on International Courts and Tribunals (PICT) has identified 23 standing international judicial bodies (a number that excludes extinct, dormant or proposed institutions). More than twice as many quasi-judicial bodies (most notably the 'committees' in the field of human rights, including labour law, torture and racial discrimination) and special courts and tribunals complement the PICT's comprehensive picture of the 'International Judiciary'.[56]

Not surprisingly, the growth of norms and institutions has made it increasingly difficult to understand the role of international law in international relations. In classical lawyerly accounts, international law was essentially a tool for achieving inter-state co-ordination ('realist' colleagues in the departments of international relations even denied the significance of law altogether). The 'law of nations' established certain generally acceptable ground rules for intercourse and transactions, which would permit states to develop relationships ranging from 'co-existence' to 'co-operation'.[57] This model has proved unsatisfactory. Rather than merely co-ordinating action, contemporary international law is also expressive of certain communal values. Rather than a mere tool for states, international law is increasingly being used by international organisations, civil society movements and even private actors with a view to defining what constitutes appropriate international conduct. In the following section, Boaventura de Sousa Santos's definition of law provides a convenient lens for observing the radical structural transformation of the international legal order. All three 'structural components' that Santos identifies—bureaucracy, violence and rhetoric—are affected by this transformation.

[55] *Yearbook of International Organizations* (2005/2006), vol V, Appendix 3, 2966–7, available at http://www.uia.org/statistics/organizations/types-2004.pdf.

[56] 'The International Judiciary in Context', Synoptic Chart, available at http://www.pict-pcti.org/publications/synoptic_chart/synoptic_chart2.pdf.

[57] Thus the categories by W Friedmann, *The Changing Structure of International Law* (New York, Columbia University Press, 1964). For recent assessments, see P-M Dupuy, 'International Law: Torn between Coexistence, Cooperation and Globalization' (1998) 9 *European Journal of Iinternational Law* 278; S Yee, *Towards an International Law of Co-progressiveness* (Leiden, Martinus Nijhoff Publishers, 2004) 1–26.

II. THREE PARADIGMS OF INTERNATIONAL ORGANISATION

A. The Westphalian Paradigm

Consider, first, the model that underlies classical theories of international law—widely been termed the Westphalian model. In the *Lotus* case, the Permanent Court of International Justice (PCIJ) famously gave expression to a conception of international relations as state-to-state co-ordination: International law

> leaves [states] a wide measure of discretion which is only limited in certain cases by prohibitive rules; as regards other cases, every state remains free to adopt the principles which it regards as best and most suitable.[58]

While some authors have questioned the pertinence of the denomination 'Westphalian', and have proposed to speak of a Vattelian model instead,[59] there appears to be considerable merit in retaining the reference to Westphalia, not so much as a historical claim but as a professional 'code word' whose core is largely undisputed.[60] Under the Westphalian model, the international system is conceived as a purely horizontal arrangement for the co-ordination of sovereign states. States—perceived as opaque and unitary actors ('billiard balls')[61]—would act in ways largely unconstrained by legal norms. As François Ost and Michel van de Kerchhove put it,

> Il s'agissait d'un ordre de simple coexistence ou juxtaposition de puissances souveraines formant ce qu'on appellerait plus tard la 'famille' des nations. Sur

[58] *SS Lotus (France v Turkey)* 1927 PCIJ Series A, No 10, 19.

[59] SD Krasner, *Sovereignty: Organized Hypocrisy* (Princeton University Press, 1999) 3ff. See also the interview with Krasner by Harry Kreisler, Conversations with History: Institute of International Studies, UC Berkeley, available at http://globetrotter.berkeley.edu/people3/Krasner/krasner-con3.html.

[60] See, eg, the use of the term 'Westphalian sovereignty' by A-M Slaughter and W Burke-White, 'The Future of International Law is Domestic (or, the European Way of Law)' (2006) 47 *Harvard International Law Journal* 327, 328: 'This foundation of international law reflects the principles of Westphalian sovereignty, often seemingly made up of equal parts myth and rhetoric. In this conception, the state is a defined physical territory 'within which domestic political authorities are the sole arbiters of legitimate behavior.' [footnote omitted] States can be part of the international legal system to the degree they choose by consenting to particular rules. Likewise, they can choose to remain apart, asserting their own sovereignty and eschewing international involvement. Formally, Westphalian sovereignty is the right to be left alone, to exclude, to be free from any external meddling or interference. But it is also the right to be recognized as an autonomous agent in the international system, capable of interacting with other states and entering into international agreements. With these background understandings of sovereignty, an international legal system, consisting of states and limited by the principle of state consent, emerged.'

[61] The metaphor is attributed to Arnold Wolfers. A Wolfers, *Discord and Collaboration: Essays on International Politics* (Baltimore, MD, Johns Hopkins University Press, 1962) 19–24.

> la base de relations pour la plupart bilatérales, les Etats poursuivaient des objectifs essentiellement privés, dont le seul point commun était la sauvegarde de l'indépendance de chacun (principe de non-ingérence). Dans cet ordre juridique décentralisé, dépourvu d'autorité suprême, l'Etat s'érige comme unique personne juridique à part entière: personnifiant la nation, il parle au nom des personnes qui le composent ; c'est lui aussi qui impose sa volonté aux futures organisations internationales qui ne sont jamais que des entités inter-étatiques.[62]

The bureaucratic backup support for the Westphalian system was mainly constituted by the governmental administrations of the nation-state. International organisations (or 'public international unions', in Inis Claude's terminology), according to the Westphalian paradigm, would essentially resolve co-ordination problems. Characteristically, international bureaucracy remained removed from the heat of everyday political controversy. As Claude had it,

> domestically, the agencies of expanded territorial and functional jurisdiction were instruments of authoritative government; internationally, the corresponding agencies were instruments of voluntary cooperation among states. Public international unions were not segments of governmental apparatus, drawing power from the circuits of a pre-established dynamo of sovereignty, but rudimentary pieces of a system of intergovernmental collaboration, dependent for their operation upon such power as could be generated in the new and drastically incomplete plant of international authority.[63]

Violence in the Westphalian system would be bilateral. In its bluntest sense, violence is military force. Although formally outlawed by Article 2 of the UN Charter (allegedly 'the basic rule of contemporary public international law'[64]), the latent threat of military intervention continues to contribute, as a matter of fact, to the enforcement of international obligations.[65] Compliance with disarmament obligations may even depend on credible, reciprocal threats of force.[66] At the same time, other

[62] F Ost, M van de Kerchove, *De la pyramide au réseau? Pour une théorie dialectique du droit* (Bruxelles, Facultés Universitaires Saint Louis, 2002) 162. 'It was an order of simple coexistence or juxtaposition of sovereign powers, which formed what one would later call the "family" of nations. On the basis of mostly bilateral relations, states pursued essentially private goals, of which the sole common point of reference was to safeguard the independence of each of them (principle of non-interference). In this decentralised legal order, deprived of supreme authority, the state stands out as the only full juridical person: personifying the nation, it speaks on behalf of the people that make it up; it is the state that imposes its will on future international organisations, which are never more than inter-state entities' (translation by the author).

[63] Claude, above n 50, 31.

[64] E Jiménez de Aréchaga, *El derecho internacional contemporáneo* (Madrid, Editorial Tecnos, 1980) 108.

[65] N Stürchler, *The Threat of Force in International Law* (Cambridge University Press, 2007).

[66] The (then) US Deputy Secretary of Defense, J Wolfowitz, suggested that '[o]ur only

forms of bilateral coercion, such as economic sanctions or ideological warfare, have supplemented the military instrument. Reprisals—or in the politically correct terminology of the International Law Commission (ILC), countermeasures—constitute the classical enforcement device in international law. Immediately, coercive reprisals may cause the target state to discontinue unlawful conduct. In the long run, countermeasures contribute to creating future expectations of effective enforcement. As Michael Reisman has noted, 'the expectation of the effectiveness of enforcement mechanisms is a factor inducing compliance. Enforcement becomes a "self-fulfilling prophecy".'[67] Once countermeasures have contributed to the peaceful resolution of a particular incident of non-compliance, 'expectations of effectiveness are generated, permitting enforcement machinery subsequently to fulfil its function by symbolic presence rather than by active intervention.'[68]

The rhetoric of the Westphalian model was centred on the notion of sovereignty. Residues of that rhetoric pervade contemporary international law: sovereignty over natural resources or non-intervention into the *domaine réservé* are typical *topoi* of the Westphalian-style discourse. The interpretive maxim *in dubio mitius*—mandating that among several plausible constructions that meaning is to be preferred which is less restrictive of sovereign prerogatives—is still routinely invoked in international litigation, albeit rarely with success. *Oppenheim's International Law* continues to list the maxim as a valid principle of treaty interpretation. Yet, in the rich body of case law created by the WTO, only a single ruling by the Appellate Body, *EC—Hormones*, was specifically based on *in dubio mitius*:

> We cannot lightly assume that sovereign states intended to impose upon themselves the more onerous, rather than the less burdensome, obligation by mandating conformity or compliance with such standards, guidelines and recommendations.[69]

In the remainder of cases, repeated efforts by defendant Member States (and scholars)[70] to commend to the WTO's Dispute Settlement Body an

hope . . . of achieving the peaceful disarmament of Iraqi weapons of mass destruction is by having a credible threat of force behind our diplomacy. To be effective, the two must be part of a single policy.' Speech of 28 October 2002, available at http://www.globalsecurity.org/wmd/library/news/iraq/2002/iraq-021030-usia03.htm.

[67] WM Reisman, 'The Enforcement of International Judgments' (1969) 63 *American Journal of International Law* 1, 7 (footnote omitted).

[68] *Ibid.*

[69] *EC—Measures Concerning Meat and Meat Products*, Report of the Appellate Body, WT/DS26/AB/R, para 165 and n 154.

[70] RE Hudec, 'The New WTO Dispute Settlement Procedure: An Overview of the First Three Years' (1999) 8 *Minnesota Journal of Global Trade* 1, 30–31. For a critical view, see L Hughes, 'Limiting the Jurisdiction of Dispute Settlement Panels: The WTO Appellate Body Beef Hormone Decision' (1998) 10 *Georgetown International Environmental Law Review* 915.

attitude deferential to sovereignty proved unsuccessful.[71] In the foreign investment law context, arguments from state sovereignty appear to be even less successful: the Eureko tribunal noted polemically that

> reliance . . . on the maxim *in dubio mitius* so as effectively to presume that sovereign rights override the rights of a foreign investor could be seen as a reversion to a doctrine that has been displaced by contemporary customary international law, particularly as that law has been reshaped by the conclusion of more than 2,000 essentially concordant bilateral investment treaties.[72]

In light of such stark rebuttals of sovereignty-based defences, John Jackson has concluded that, nowadays, 'the principle "in dubio mitius", or certain applications of standards of review or deference toward nation state determinations' constituted an 'absurdity'.[73] The rhetoric of the co-ordination paradigm is definitely on the decline.

B. The Hierarchical Paradigm

Yet, to the extent that Westphalia no longer adequately describes international practice, what has come to replace the classical international law of co-ordination? A partial response is hierarchisation. In terms of bureaucracy, the League of Nations, a brainchild of Wilsonian idealism, and later the United Nations were decisive steps towards a hierarchically 'constituted life' (as David Kennedy put it).[74] The historical predecessor

[71] In one further panel report, *US—Safeguard Measures on Imports of Fresh, Chilled or Frozen Lamb Meat from New Zealand and Australia*, Report of the Panel, 21 December 2000 WT/DS177/R, n 59, the panel cited the Appellate Body report in *EC—Hormones* in support of its conclusions (although the ruling did not strictly speaking turn on that argument). In one other case, *US—Anti-Dumping Act of 1916*, Report of the Panel, 31 March 2000 WT/DS136/R, the panel provided an express justification as to why the maxim *in dubio mitius* should not apply. In the remainder of cases, the panels or the Appellate Body took note of the argument from sovereignty in the section summarising the position of the parties but never expressly addressed *in dubio mitius* in its own reasoning: *EC—Export Subsidies on Sugar*, Report of the Panel, 15 October 2004 WT/DS265/R, WT/DS266/R, WT/DS283/R; *US—Subsidies on Upland Cotton*, Report of the Panel, 8 September 2004 WT/DS267/R/Add.1; *Chile—Price Band System and Safeguard Measures Relating to Certain Agricultural Products*, Report of the Appellate Body, 23 September 2002 WT/DS207/AB/R; *Chile—Price Band System and Safeguard Measures Relating to Certain Agricultural Products*, Report of the Panel, 3 May 2002 WT/DS207/R; *US—Definitive Safeguard Measures on Imports of Circular Welded Carbon Quality Line Pipe from Korea*, Report of the Appellate Body, 15 February 2002 WT/DS202/AB/R; *US—Sections 301–310 of the Trade Act of 1974*, Report of the Panel, 22 December 1999 WT/DS152/R; *Canada—Measures Affecting the Importation of Milk and the Exportation of Dairy Products*, Report of the Panel, 17 May 1999 WT/DS103/R; *Korea—Taxes on Alcoholic Beverages*, Report of the Appellate Body, 18 January 1999 WT/DS75/AB/R.

[72] *Eureko BV v Republic of Poland*, partial award, 19 August 2005 (on file with the author).

[73] JH Jackson, 'The Changing Fundamentals of International Law and Ten Years of the WTO' (2005) 8 *Journal of International Economic Law* 3, n 35.

[74] D Kennedy, 'The Move to Institutions' (1986) 8 *Cardozo Law Review* 841, 979.

of the League was the Concert of Europe, which had been initiated in 1815 as a mechanism to enforce the decisions of the Congress of Vienna.[75] Compared to the Concert of Europe, which provided for a series of successive inter-governmental conferences, the Council of the League was a significant step forward in terms of permanent institutionalisation,

> incorporating the principles of legal definition of authority and terms of reference, institutional continuity, regularity of session, and balanced composition of great and small power representatives.[76]

Moreover, the League's Assembly was a blueprint for a periodical general conference of nations; the PCIJ (whose Statute entered into force in 1921) was a step towards institutionalised judicial review (as opposed to the possibility of occasional arbitration).

The League's substantive competence remained a sectorally restricted one: motivated by the spectre of the 'Accidental War',[77] the League's own powers extended to the maintenance of peace and the peaceful settlement of disputes. Article 24 of the Covenant compensated to some extent the League's limited substantive competences by an element of procedural centralisation. Institutionally, paragraph 1 provided that

> There shall be placed under the direction of the League all international bureaux already established by general treaties if the parties to such treaties consent. All such international bureaux and all commissions for the regulation of matters of international interest hereafter constituted shall be placed under the direction of the League.

Moreover, paragraph 2 contained a mechanism that would allow the League to become the 'super bureau' of multilateral agreements enacted independently of the League system:

> In all matters of international interest which are regulated by general convention but which are not placed under the control of international bureaux or commissions, the Secretariat of the League shall, subject to the consent of the Council and if desired by the parties, collect and distribute all relevant information and shall render any other assistance which may be necessary or desirable.

[75] The Concert of Europe was constituted by the Quadruple Alliance of Russia, Prussia, Austria, and Great Britain. Its focus was on establishing a balance of power, the preservation of the territorial status quo and the protection of 'legitimate' governments.

[76] Claude, above n 50, 38.

[77] Arthur Sweetser captured the spirit of the negotiations of the Covenant as follows: 'the war came into being largely by default, because the forces of negotiation and peaceful settlement marshaled against it suddenly collapsed . . . the world in 1914 got itself into a blind alley where all doors were closed except to the war.' *The League of Nations at Work* (New York, Macmillan, 1920) 5.

While Article 24 offered the potential for bureaucratic centralisation, it did so under the reservation of the consent of the Council and/or the parties. The voluntary character of centralisation of powers may have been one reason, among many others, why Jan Christiaan Smut's promise that the League would 'become part and parcel of the common international life of states' and 'an ever visible, living, working organ of the polity of civilization'[78] remained largely unfulfilled.

At least in aspiration, the United Nations represents a new type of international organisation that overcomes this shortcoming. The UN Charter conceives of the United Nations as 'the organisation of organisations', demonstrated by a positive obligation on its members to integrate the numerous sectoral agencies into the UN system as 'specialised agencies'. Article 57 of the Charter[79] represents a model of bureaucratic hierarchisation rather than centralisation. At the same time, the United Nations is the first organisation that can itself claim a quasi-universal subject-matter competence, ranging from the League's concern with international security to human rights, economic co-operation, development and the environment. Through its organs and specialised agencies, the United Nations monitors and polices the nation-state—often ineffectively, but in almost any conceivable domain. The United Nations has, thus, justly been called 'an agency of the world community at large'.[80]

Yet it would be too simple to focus exclusively on the United Nations as the sole engine of hierarchisation—even constitutionalisation[81]—of the international order. In *A New World Order*, Anne-Marie Slaughter has perceptively pointed out another dimension of the bureaucratic hierarchisation of the international system: the phenomenon of so-called vertical networks. In vertical networks, international bodies entertain direct hierarchical relations with functionally equivalent bodies at the national level. So far, the European legal system provides the most developed vertical enforcement mechanisms. In the context of the European Competition Network, for example, national authorities effectively function as lower-level European authorities.

[78] Cited in FP Walters, *A History of the League of Nations*, vol I (London, Oxford University Press, 1952) 59.

[79] Article 57(1) of the Charter provides: 'The various specialized agencies, established by intergovernmental agreement and having wide international responsibilities, as defined in their basic instruments, in economic, social, cultural, educational, health, and related fields, shall be brought into relationship with the United Nations in accordance with the provisions of Article 63.'

[80] Claude, above n 50, 59.

[81] B Fassbender, 'The United Nations Charter as Constitution of the International Community' (1998) 36 *Columbia Journal of Transnational Law* 529.

> Together the [National Competition Authorities] and the Commission form a network of public authorities: they act in the public interest and co-operate closely in order to protect competition. The network is a forum for discussion and co-operation in the application and enforcement of EC competition policy.[82]

The subordination of national courts for all practical purposes under the European Court of Justice, often euphemistically called a 'relationship of co-operation',[83] is another case in point.

The weakness of any hierarchical model of the international system lies in Santos's second criterion: violence. To deploy armed force, the stability of the international system remains dependent on the willingness of individual states. This is particularly true in light of the absence of agreements by Member States pursuant to Article 43 to permanently make available military troops to the Council. Nevertheless, it would be short-sighted to stop here with the simple conclusion that the regime of violence in contemporary international law still entirely follows the Westphalian logic. To do so would block out other forms of coercion, in particular at the economic level. For example, the WTO (with the instrument of trade sanctions/suspension of concessions) and the World Bank (with the instrument of loan conditionality) have enforcement mechanisms at their disposal that may even surpass the effectiveness of bilateral violence.

Most visibly, however, the hierarchical paradigm has colonised the field of professional rhetoric, transforming our conception of what constitutes an acceptable argument in legal discourse. Numerous formal and informal hierarchies pervade contemporary legal reasoning. The key examples of formal hierarchies are of course *jus cogens* and Article 103 of the UN Charter. In the Lockerbie case, the International Court of Justice ruled that,

> in accordance with Article 103 of the Charter, the obligations of the Parties in that respect prevail over their obligations under any other international agreement, including the Montreal Convention.[84]

The Court consequently declined to order provisional measures on the grounds

[82] Commission Notice on cooperation within the Network of Competition Authorities, 2004/C 101/03. The European Competition Network was established by Council Regulation (EC) No 1/2003 of 16 December 2002 on the implementation of the rules on competition laid down in Arts 81 and 82 of the Treaty.

[83] The term *Kooperationsverhältnis* was coined by the German Constitutional Court in its landmark *Maastricht* judgment, *BVerfGE* 89, 155 at 156, 175 and 178. P Rüffert, *Das Kooperationsverhältnis von EuGH und BVerfG* (Tübingen, Mohr Siebeck, 1997).

[84] *Questions of Interpretation and Application of the 1971 Montreal Convention Arising from the Aerial Incident at Lockerbie (Libya v US)*, Order, [1992] ICJ Rep 114, 126, para 42.

> that . . . the rights claimed by Libya under the Montreal Convention cannot now be regarded as appropriate for protection by the indication of provisional measures.[85]

Recently, the Court of First Instance of the European Communities, in its *Yusuf* judgment, decided quite unequivocally that the EC Treaty was displaced by a Resolution of the Security Council. The Court ruled that, as a consequence of Article 103 of the Charter,

> 'Member States may, and indeed must, leave unapplied any provision of Community law, whether a provision of primary law or a general principle of that law, that raises any impediment to the proper performance of their obligations under the Charter of the United Nations.[86]

In the *Al-Adsani*[87] and *Pinochet*[88] cases, *jus cogens* has come into focus. The European Court of Human Rights and the House of Lords, respectively, confronted the question as to whether peremptory norms can, in certain cases, displace a whole complex of traditional international norms, namely the law on state immunity.

Such formal hierarchies are supplemented by a range of informal quasi-hierarchical distinctions: counsel in various recent cases before the International Court have advocated that certain 'fundamental human rights' cannot be suspended in times of armed conflict (this group of rights may or may not correspond to the norms that enjoy jus cogens status). In the Wall and *Armed Activities (Congo v Uganda)* cases, the Court has started taking up this rhetorical figure, albeit without specifying which human rights should count as more 'fundamental' than others.[89] Perhaps the most important quasi-hierarchical distinction is of a seemingly technical nature. International legal doctrine places great emphasis on the concept of general international law, denoting a body of

[85] *Ibid*, 126–7, para 43.

[86] *Yusuf and Al Barakaat International Foundation*, Case T–306/01, Judgment of the Court of First Instance, [2005] ECR II–03533, para 240.

[87] In this case, the Court recognised the hierarchical superiority of *jus cogens* norms in principle but declined to attach far-reaching legal consequences to such norms. *Al-Adsani v United Kingdom* (Judgment) 21 November 2001, available at http://hudoc.echr.coe.int.

[88] *Regina v Bow Street Metropolitan Stipendiary Magistrate and others, Ex parte Pinochet Ugarte (No 3)* (1999) 2 WLR 827.

[89] See the numerous references to fundamental human rights in the pleadings of the Congo, many of which are cited in the Court's judgment in *Armed Activities on the Territory of the Congo (Democratic Republic of the Congo v Uganda)*, [2005] ICJ Rep 1. The Court has taken up the notion of fundamental human rights as its own in its order of 1 July 2000, in which it indicated provisional measures, *Armed Activities on the Territory of the Congo (Democratic Republic of the Congo v Uganda)*, (Provisional Measures) Order of 1 July 2000, [2000] ICJ Rep 111. In the *Wall* case, the separate opinions of Judge Elaraby makes reference to the concept of fundamental human rights, *Legal Consequences of the Construction of a Wall in the Occupied Palestinian Territory*, Sep op Elaraby, [2004] ICJ Rep 246, 256.

norms that apply automatically and in which all 'special' law is embedded.[90]

C. The Heterarchical Paradigm

While the hierarchical paradigm pervades all three 'constitutive components' of contemporary international law, one should not too easily jump to the conclusion that international law is transforming, on a straight path, from a horizontal to a vertically integrated order. Simultaneously, the past decades have lead to a stunning diversification of international law—often occurring outside the UN system. This development fits neither the Westphalian nor the hierarchical paradigm. In contrast to the Westphalian model, many recent international conventions impose a dense web of detailed prescriptions that deeply intrude on states' sovereignty. In contrast to the hierarchical model, many recent treaties do not aspire to superior constitutional status. They contain detailed regulatory regimes that pretend to be of a purely technical nature. In light of such transformations, political and legal theorists have discovered heterarchisation as a third structural paradigm of the legal order. Anne-Marie Slaughter has described international law as a network of government officials, legislators and judges;[91] Saskia Sassen speaks of a deterritorialised 'system of rule', in which states are both embedded and subject to transformation;[92] and Michael Hardt and Antonio Negri depict global law as a flexible, horizontal structure of production of legitimacy spread out over world space[93] operating as a 'self-organizing network of plural sub-systems, each of which organizes the norms of numerous private (or, really, singular) regimes'.[94]

In attempts to structure heterarchical regime relationships, international lawyers have increasingly resorted to the *lex specialis* maxim—a classical tool in the legal rhetoric box. In a WTO context, litigants have objected to the appropriateness of subjecting an issue to the disciplines of the world trading system by arguing that other regimes contained a 'more special' rule for a given situation. Such objections have been raised frequently, but with mixed success. In response to a WTO complaint by the US and Canada with respect to its admissions practice of genetically

[90] For a far-reaching exposition of this view, T Schilling, 'On the Constitutionalization of General International Law' (2005) 6 *Jean Monnet Working Paper*, available at http://www.jeanmonnetprogram.org/papers/05/050601.pdf.

[91] A-M Slaughter, *A New World Order* (Princeton University Press, 2004).

[92] S Sassen, *Losing Control? Sovereignty in an Age of Globalization* (New York, Columbia University Press, 1995) xv, 25.

[93] M Hardt and A Negri, *Empire* (Cambridge, MA, Harvard University Press, 2000) 13.

[94] M Hardt and A Negri, *Multitude: War and Democracy in the Age of Empire* (New York, Penguin Press, 2004) 204.

modified organisms (GMOs), the European Community argued that complainants failed to refer to 'the relevant rules of public international law (*lex specialis*) which have been adopted to regulate the concerns and requirements which arise from the particular characteristics of GMOs'.[95] More particularly, the EC continued, '[t]he Biosafety Protocol is the international agreement which is most directly relevant to the matters raised by the present proceedings.'[96] The EC added that 'the international Community has, through the Biosafety Protocol, recognised that GM products are such that they require their own, distinct authorisation procedure'.[97] The panel declined to look at the Protocol, let alone to consider it 'more special' than the WTO's SPS Agreement.[98]

In the *US–Shrimp* case, the US had argued, albeit less emphatically, that the Convention on International Trade in Endangered Species (CITES) contained a special legal regime for such species that were listed in the Appendix; that CITES 'required parties to take action to protect animals in other jurisdictions';[99] and that CITES could be read as a 'derogation to GATT rights'.[100] The Appellate Body did not go so far as to refrain from the application of WTO law altogether. It did, however, confirm the special character of multilateral environmental agreements in environmental matters. In the Appellate Body's view, 'modern international conventions'[101] in the environmental sector must be deemed to contain an authoritative interpretation of the term 'exhaustible natural resources', which must be taken into account in the application of WTO law.

The interpretation of the law of one regime 'in the light of' the law of another regime, as famously propagated by the Appellate Body in the *US–Shrimp* case, is probably the most promising tool for heterarchical regime co-ordination. One of the earliest expositions of this technique is

[95] *EC—Measures Affecting the Approval and Marketing of Biotech Products*, DS291, DS292, DS293, First Written Submission by the European Communities, available at http://trade-info.cec.eu.int/wtodispute/show.cfm?id=188&code=2, para 353.

[96] *Ibid*, para 357.

[97] *Ibid*, para 535.

[98] The panel did not discuss whether the Cartagena Protocol could derogate WTO law, because the complainants, the United States, Canada, and Argentina, were not parties to the Protocol. More strikingly, however, and in contrast to the Appellate Body's approach in the *US–Shrimp* case, the Panel also refused to consider that the Cartagena Protocol as a specific agreement relating to biosafety might inform the interpretation of WTO law. In para 7.71 of its report, the Panel explained that 'it is not apparent why a sovereign State would agree to a mandatory rule of treaty interpretation which could have as a consequence that the interpretation of a treaty to which that State is a party is affected by other rules of international law which that State has decided not to accept.' *EC—Measures Affecting the Approval and Marketing of Biotech Products*, Report of the Panel, 29 September 2006, WT/DS291/R, WT/DS292/R, WT/DS/293/R.

[99] *US—Import Prohibition on Shrimp and Certain Shrimp Products*, Report of the Panel, WT/DS58/R, 15 May 1998, para 3.105.

[100] *Ibid*, at paras 3.105 and 3.171.

[101] *US—Import Prohibition of Certain Shrimp and Shrimp Products*, Report of the Appellate Body, 6 November 1998, WT/DS58/AB/R, para 130.

the *Namibia* advisory opinion of the International Court of Justice. In the Court's view,

> interpretation cannot remain unaffected by the subsequent development of law. . . . Moreover, an international instrument has to be interpreted and applied within the framework of the entire legal system prevailing at the time of the interpretation.[102]

A less noted, more recent example of heterarchical co-ordination is the *Al-Adsani* case in the European Court of Human Rights. The case is well known for the applicant's attempt to use *jus cogens* to pierce the shield of state immunity in civil matters (see the discussion in the previous section). What is less known is that the Court was also confronted with the task of reconciling two bodies of norms of equal rank: the right to fair trial and the customary law of state immunity. The European Court decided to interpret the right to fair trial in the light of the state immunity regime. It concluded that measures

> which reflect generally recognized rules of public international law on state immunity cannot in principle be regarded as imposing a disproportionate restriction on the right of access to court as embodied in Article 6(1).[103]

In a heterarchical network of international regulation, the prescriptive force of a regulatory regime is also a function of its bureaucratic resources. As Martti Koskenniemi and Päivi Leino have suggested, each regime must strive to create 'a workable structure of tectonic counter-weight'[104] against other regimes. Take the example of commercial cultural content, such as motion pictures, music or books. Trade in cultural products may be subject to the law of the WTO, which will favour far-reaching deregulation. The recent UNESCO Convention on Cultural Diversity,[105] by contrast, entitles (and, arguably, obliges) states to adopt such cultural policy measures as are necessary to safeguard and promote a diversity of cultural products on their territory. From a human rights perspective, the right to take part in cultural life[106] (a special case of the right to cultural development)[107] and the freedom of expression[108] must

[102] *Legal Consequences for States of the Continued Presence of South Africa in Namibia (South West Africa) Notwithstanding Security Council Resolution 276 (1970)*, Advisory Opinion, [1971] ICJ Rep 16, 31.

[103] *Al-Adsani v United Kingdom*, above n 87, para 56.

[104] Koskenniemi and Leino, above n 1, 574.

[105] Convention on the Protection and Promotion of the Diversity of Cultural Expressions, 20 October 2005, available at http://unesdoc.unesco.org/images/0014/001429/142919e.pdf.

[106] International Covenant on Economic, Social and Cultural Rights (adopted 19 December 1966, entered into force 3 January 1976) 993 UNTS 3 (hereafter 'ICESCR') Art 15.

[107] Art 1(1) of both UN Covenants, the International Covenant on Civil and Political Rights (adopted 16 December 1966, entered into force 23 March 1976) 999 UNTS 171 (hereafter 'ICCPR'), and the ICESCR.

[108] ICCPR, Art 19(2).

be taken into account. Characteristically, no institutional hierarchy operates between the regimes of global trade, international cultural policy and human rights. Rather, each system attempts to maximise the rationality it stands for through its own bureaucracy. The WTO's organs operate at both the political and the judicial level. The human rights regime might in fact have the most elaborate bureaucratic structure, including, at the global level, the Human Rights Council and the various treaty bodies and, at the regional level, various commissions and courts. UNESCO has recently beefed up its resources in the field by creating a new Intergovernmental Committee for the Protection and the Promotion of the Diversity of Cultural Expressions and a (non-permanent) Conciliation Commission for the settlement of disputes.

Analytically, the hardest question is how power—violence—is exercised in such a bureaucratic network structure. One suggestion, although framed in rather vague terms, comes from Michael Hardt and Antonio Negri. These two theorists attempt to complement a quasi-Luhmannian systems perspective with a quasi-Foucaultian power analysis. 'Empire' (as Hardt and Negri term the current global system) is a diffuse and anonymous network of all-encompassing power: power in the Hardt–Negri sense is 'structural power', located in the worldwide network of elite relations itself.[109] The crucial take-away point of their analysis may be the following: in a network model, actors do not necessarily require coercive power themselves—as in the hierarchical model of a chain of subordination. Instead, actors may choose to become parasitical of the coercive capacity of other actors. The effectiveness of the contemporary transnational regime for the protection of foreign investment, for example, is almost entirely premised on the latent coercive force of the state.[110] Some scholars have suggested that the environmental regime or the human rights regime (in particular the system of labour rights) should creatively use the WTO, so as to have its values indirectly enforced against Member States by the Dispute Settlement Body.[111] These

[109] The key to Empire's authority is neither sheer economic nor military force: 'Empire is formed not on the basis of force itself but on the basis of the capacity to present force as being in the service of right and peace' (Hardt and Negri, above n 93, 15). What is central to the power of Empire is its capacity to resolve global conflicts. To the extent that Empire is capable of such conflict resolution, it 'envelop[s] all power relations within its world order' (*ibid*, 20). By equating power with conflict resolution, Hardt and Negri conflate to some extent violence and rhetoric. While this theoretical move is attractive, the theorists may overestimate 'Empire's' capacity of settling what are often highly divisive antagonisms.

[110] In the New York Convention (United Nations Convention on the Recognition and Enforcement of Foreign Arbitral Awards of 10 June 1958), contracting states have obliged themselves to have their courts enforce arbitral awards issued in other states within their domestic legal orders, subject only to limited exceptions.

[111] E-U Petersmann, 'Time for a United Nations "Global Compact" for Integrating Human Rights into the Law of Worldwide Organizations: Lessons from European Integration' (2002) 13 *European Journal of International Law* 621.

examples may be first signs of a heterarchisation of legitimate violence at the global level.

III. CONCLUSION

A brief look at contemporary international legal practice along the vectors of bureaucracy, violence and rhetoric reveals that contemporary international law fits neither the Westphalian model nor the hierarchical or heterarchical models in their pure form. International law constructs a complex mélange of relationships of co-ordination, hierarchical subordination and heterarchical competition. It is premature to refer to the Westphalian system as the 'model of the past' (as indeed many theorists have done). In reality, important residues of the Westphalian system continue to constitute the underpinnings of international relations. This is most obvious with respect to the vector of violence. While the use of force is of course outlawed as a formal matter by Article 2(4) of the UN Charter, it is hard to deny that the operation of the international system is still backed by latent force on the part of its powerful members. Elements of hierachisation, by contrast, have effectively found their way into the rhetoric of international law (*jus cogens*, Article 103 of the UN Charter, but also the 'informal hierarchy' of general international law). Finally, the heterarchical model appears to best describe the structure of international bureaucracy. While the integration of 'specialised agencies' under the roof of the UN has added an element of bureaucratic hierarchy, the default rule is that international organisations are not accountable to any institution of higher rank.

Westphalian bilateralism, hierarchy and heterarchy—or to use Joseph Weiler's terms: structures of transaction, community and governance—are multiple 'layers'[112] that persist and thrive concurrently in contemporary international law. Legal authority is being located in largely heterarchical bureaucracies, largely bilateral enforcement mechanisms and a complex rhetoric with many hierarchical elements. What follows, then, from this observation for 'shifting' the legal authority among various regimes of international law, as the editors of this volume have asked us to consider? Many proposals for allocating authority are conceivable; but only some will actually work to co-ordinate regimes in concrete cases. Those that work will reflect, and play creatively with, the structures of the international system as it is today. We need authority-allocating principles that are attractive for decision-makers in the decentralised network of international bureaucracies. Tools that follow a 'heterarchical logic', such as the *lex specialis* principle or the subsidiarity

[112] Weiler, above n 48, 551.

principle, may be better suited for regime co-ordination than grand communitarian designs following the logic of hierarchical supremacy. On the other hand, the international system remains dependent on the ultimate enforcement power of states. Not everything that seems attractive to decision-makers within international regimes will be enforceable. As a consequence, the 'S-word' inevitably remains in the equation. Some deference to state sovereignty will be a necessary element of any workable proposal for the allocation of legal authority.

The 'space for manoeuvre' for allocating authority in international law is a constricted one. It is with these limitations in mind that creative thinking about *The Allocation of Authority in International Law* can make a difference.

4

Subsidiarity as a Method of Policy Centralisation

GARETH DAVIES*

I. INTRODUCTION

SUBSIDIARITY, AT LEAST as defined within the European Union, provides that the centre will only act where the goals of the proposed action cannot, or cannot adequately, be met by decentralised action.[1] It therefore assumes an agreed goal, unsurprising given its Catholic roots, and is a principle concerning who should take measures to achieve this. This exposes two limits to the value of subsidiarity in the EU or other international organisations:

1. Many conflicts between levels do not concern who is best placed to pursue an agreed goal, but are conflicts over the relationship between the goals of the lower and higher levels; which should prevail, or to what extent. To this situation, subsidiarity has no relevance.
2. As a rhetorical device subsidiarity is intellectually centralising. It places the central policy goal beyond dispute, while denying any voice to the potentially diverging policy goals of the states. It translates the complex relationship between levels into the single question of who can best implement the policies of the centre.

* Professor of European Law, Vrije Universiteit, Amsterdam. This chapter draws on G Davies, 'Subsidiarity: The Wrong Idea, In the Wrong Place, At the Wrong Time' (2006) 43 *Common Market Law Review* 63.

[1] Art 5 EC: 'In areas which do not fall within its exclusive competence, the Community shall take action, in accordance with the principle of subsidiarity, only if and insofar as the objectives of the proposed action cannot be sufficiently achieved by the Member States and can therefore, by reason of the scale or effects of the proposed action, be better achieved by the Community.' See, for an expanded version of this definition, providing clues on what 'sufficiently achieved' and 'by reason of the scale or effects' may mean, the Protocol (No 30) to the Treaty of Amsterdam, on the Application of the Principles of Subsidiarity and Proportionality, [1997] OJ 1997 C340/105.

Indeed, its talk of the 'goals of the proposed action' indicates a certain linguistic sneakiness. Actions have all the purposes possessed by those supporting them, which may be multiple, contradictory and even paradoxical. Speaking of the goal as if this was a simple and uncontested attribute suggests either that all participants have a level of unity and agreement which does not exist in the real world, or is a rhetorical trick to avoid thinking about real people and purposes at all, and elevate the action to a status of self-evident singularity of purpose which can only stifle discussion.

These intellectual deficits are translated into concrete problems as a result of the relatively imprecise delimitation of Community competences,[2] and the Community law principle of supremacy. The first of these means that there are many areas where Community and national policies meet and potentially conflict, and that is it not possible to say with any satisfying degree of precision what the limits to Community activities are.[3] In the internal market, in particular, the Community's powers to harmonise all national law obstructing movement or affecting competition touch on many areas of activity.[4] Supremacy then makes these problems more immediate by requiring that where national and Community rules do conflict, all national judges and authorities immediately disapply the national rule in favour of the Community one.[5] This directly effective and widely enforced principle means that states can hardly avoid or delay conflicts, or indulge in the luxury of limited or late compliance with directly effective Community law.[6] If states attempt to sideline Community law in favour of other policies, then in general their own judges will call them to order.[7]

By embracing subsidiarity as a central idea in choice-of-level decisions states therefore emasculate themselves. They back the wrong horse,

[2] See A Von Bogdandy and J Bast, 'The European Union's Vertical Order of Competences: The Current Law and Proposals for its Reform' (2002) 39 *Common Market Law Review* 227.

[3] A Dashwood, 'The Limits of European Community Powers' (1996) 21 *European Law Review* 113; R Barents, 'The Internal Market Unlimited: Some Observations on the Legal Basis of Community Legislation' (1993) 30 *Common Market Law Review* 85.

[4] See Articles 94 and 95 EC; Barents, above n 3; J Usher, 'Annotation of Case C-376/98' (2001) 38 *Common Market Law Review* 1519.

[5] See Case 6/64 *Costa v Enel* [1964] ECR 585; Case 106/77 *Simmenthal* [1978] ECR 629; PP Craig and G De Burca, *EU Law* (4th edn, Oxford University Press, 2007) 344–78.

[6] Direct effect is the Community law rule providing that measures to which it applies (generally those that are sufficiently clear to be justiciable, probably the majority of legislation and Treaty texts) must be applied not only by Community courts and institutions but all national courts and authorities too. See Craig and De Burca, above n 5, 268–304.

[7] Litigants are able to pursue delinquent states and authorities in national courts, and Community law provides procedural as well as substantive safeguards for these trials. See, eg, J Komarek, 'Federal Elements in the Community Judicial System: Building Coherence in the Community Legal Order' (2005) 42 *Common Market Law Review* 9; M Accetto and S Zleptnig, 'The Principle of Effectiveness: Rethinking its Role in Community Law' (2005) 11 *European Public Law* 375.

focusing on a principle that does not in fact protect their powers, with direct and visible domestic legal consequences. This chapter suggests that instead of concentrating on subsidiarity, which simply defends their right to act as the delegates of the higher level and its stated objectives, states should be calling for Community law to explicitly apply a balancing process between the autonomous and conflicting goals of different levels.[8] The target of Member State ire should be the dominance of subsidiarity, and its implicit presumption that all lower policies, however important, must always give way before all higher policies, however marginal.

The interpretative mistake that the states make, and which is often made in popular discourse, is reading subsidiarity as no more than a cipher for 'which level should do what'. It is suggested here that it is a more precise and technocratic concept than this. Ignoring its internal structure in favour of broad policy arguments results in miscommunication with the Commission,[9] failed lawsuits and an inability to deal with competence disputes in a legal way. By mislabelling conflicts between national and Community objectives as subsidiarity issues, states are in fact saying, although it is not what they mean to say, 'the problem here is deciding who can achieve Community goals best'. The Commission and European and national judges therefore look at this issue alone, ignoring the national goals. The very matter that states wished to draw attention to, the conflicting of objectives, is therefore missed in the judgments and decisions, no doubt to the great frustration of national authorities.[10] This chapter argues that if they used legal principles more carefully they could avoid this misunderstanding.

II. CONFLICTS BETWEEN LEVELS

There are two kinds of fundamental problems that international organisations face. One is how to achieve their goals most effectively and efficiently. There is a tendency for institutions and bureaucracies to give up control reluctantly, to delegate too little and to over-centralise. Yet often, much of the work of achieving practical ends is best done by those familiar with local circumstances—state or sub-state governments.

The other problem is how to balance the goals of the organisation against the interests and goals of the states with which they may conflict.

8 On this balancing see J Snell, 'True Proportionality' (2000) 11 *European Business Law Review* 50.

9 Particularly in the context of consultations on subsidiarity: see below n 51.

10 This is precisely what occurred in: Case C–154/04 *Alliance for Natural Health* (Judgment) 12 July 2005; Case C–491/01 *British American Tobacco* [2002] ECR I–11453; Case C–84/94 *UK v Council (Working Time Directive)* [1996] ECR I–5755; Case C–377/98 *Netherlands v Parliament and Council (Biotechnology Directive)* [2001] ECR I–7079.

In principle, one would think that states would not delegate powers to an organisation that might conflict with their own interests. In practice, the compromises necessary to reach international agreements mean that international (and European) law are riddled with over-absolute, over-simple, over-broad statements of law, which have the potential to conflict with many other policies.

It is this latter kind of problem that has caused the greatest stress within international organisations in recent years. In particular, the relatively stark principles of free trade found in the World Trade Organization (WTO) and the EU can conflict with national policies concerning environment, culture, consumer protection, morality and social solidarity.[11] One solution is to encourage international dispute resolution bodies to balance these interests in their decision-making, but this entails a transfer of power over such sensitive matters to the centre, which is controversial for at least two reasons. On the one hand, there is resistance to centralisation in itself, while on the other, this form of centralisation will stimulate, and perhaps result from, increased judicial activism, which is viewed with particular suspicion when it takes place in an international forum. For both reasons, many are unhappy with the WTO Appellate Body or European Court of Justice having the final word on state standards of morality or environmental protection.[12] The alternative is to soften the requirements of the trade law, which is of course resisted on many other grounds.

Both of these kinds of problems are conflict-of-level problems, where the essential question is which level gets to decide on some disputed point, or which level gets to exercise the power in a certain area. Subsidiarity is therefore often thought to be of help. It appears to call for the greatest decentralisation possible, and so should provide a framework for ensuring that sensitive and nationally variable matters are not taken over by centralised bureaucracies or courts.[13] The argument of this chapter is that subsidiarity is no use here. It helps with the first kind of problem, the efficiency type, but does not address the issue which presents the more serious threat, that of the conflict of interests. Moreover, the argumentative structure of subsidiarity actively suppresses and denies these conflicts, making intelligent consideration of how to deal with them

[11] The literature is vast. An introduction to the issues can be found in, eg, B De Witte, 'Non-market Values in Internal Market Legislation' in NN Shuibhne (ed), *Regulating the Internal Market* (Cheltenham, Edward Elgar, 2006) 61; J Scott, 'International Trade and Environmental Governance' (2004) 15 *European Journal of International Law* 307; JP Trachtman, 'Trade and . . . Problems, Cost–Benefit Analysis and Subsidiarity' (1998) 9 *European Journal of International Law* 32.

[12] See Trachtman, above n 11.

[13] See LC Backer, 'Harmonization, Subsidiarity and Cultural Difference: An Essay on the Dynamics of Opposition Within Federative and International Legal Systems' (Nov 1997) 4 *Tulsa Journal of Comparative and International Law* 185.

harder to attain. The argument is made with reference to the EU, where subsidiarity has a history, and cases and concrete examples are used. However, it is relevant to any multi-level organisation which thinks that it may preserve the autonomy of its lower levels by building subsidiarity into its rules.

III. SUBSIDIARITY IN THE EU

Subsidiarity in the EU requires that the Community only act where 'the objectives of the proposed action cannot be achieved sufficiently by the Member States'.[14] The point of the principle, clearly, and conventionally, is to ensure that functions are delegated to the lowest level capable of performing them effectively.[15]

Subsidiarity has therefore been embraced as an intellectual and legal framework for protecting the competences of the Member States from unnecessary annexation by Brussels.[16] Whatever the Member States can adequately do themselves, they should. Of course, subsidiarity offers no protection for states who wish to do things that they cannot adequately do, but the desire to exercise competences beyond their capacity is something that politicians tend to keep to themselves. In public at least, subsidiarity is accepted as an appropriate guide to deciding who gets to do what.

That is far from saying that it is unproblematic, or widely praised; the criticisms of its vagueness are ubiquitous,[17] and it is possible to debate what level of achievement is 'sufficient'.[18] Supposing Member States could perform a function, but just not quite as well as the EU—that 'by reason of the scale or effects of the proposed action' there were advan-

[14] See above n 1.

[15] See generally: GA Bermann, 'Taking Subsidiarity Seriously: Federalism in the European Community and the United States' (1994) *Columbia Law Review* 331; R Van den Bergh, 'Economic Criteria for Applying the Subsidiarity Principle in the European Community: The Case of Competition Policy' (1996) 16 *International Review of Law and Economics* 363; N Bernard, 'The Future of European Economic Law in the Light of the Principle of Subsidiarity' (1996) 33 *Common Market Law Review* 633; NW Barber, 'Subsidiarity in the Draft Constitution' (2002) 11 *European Public Law* 197.

[16] See DZ Cass, 'The Word that Saves Maastricht? The Principle of Subsidiarity and the Division of Powers within the European Community' (1992) 29 *Common Market Law Review* 1107.

[17] See AG Toth, 'Is Subsidiarity Justiciable?' (1994) 19 *European Law Review* 268; K van Kersbergen and B Verbeek, 'The Politics of International Norms: Subsidiarity and the Imperfect Competence Regime of the European Union' (2007) 13 *European Journal of International Relations* 217; D Wyatt, 'Subsidiarity: Is it Too Vague to be Effective as a Legal Principle?' in K Nicolaidis and S Weatherill (eds), *Whose Europe? National Models and the Constitution of the European Union*, Oxford University European Studies, available at http://www.europeanstudies.ox.ac.uk/WhoseEurope.pdf, 86.

[18] See below n 51, for documents outlining the Commission's approach to this question.

tages to centralisation.[19] Who would get to do it then? That would depend on the meaning of 'sufficiently', about which there are some comments in the relevant protocol, but nothing very concrete.[20] So subsidiarity does not answer the question—but at least it provides an agreed framework, if a loose one, for finding the answer.

But is it the right question? Member States are often upset about the Community invading their turf, but how often is their claim that they could have achieved the goal sufficiently themselves? Actually they quite often do make this claim, but usually because they have misunderstood the law. In most situations their argument should be that the Community action just is not worth doing because the costs for the states—various kinds of costs—are so high.[21] A highly quantifiable example is the impact of free movement of services on healthcare. By requiring patients and healthcare providers to be able to cross borders, healthcare costs are likely to rise. Given that states do not have unlimited funds, some balancing of interests may be necessary. More abstractly, one may consider the effect of a measure harmonising education or language use, as discussed below in this chapter. While having great value to the internal market, its costs in national culture might be astronomical. Again, sensible policy requires a balance to be made. In both cases, this balancing process is an application of proportionality, not subsidiarity.[22]

IV. SUBSIDIARITY AND SHARED COMPETENCES

Looking at the various kinds of competences that the Community has—and any other international or higher-level governance body might have—makes these abstract statements a bit clearer, and more convincing. Those competences can be categorised or described in many ways, but a conventional division is between the exclusive and the shared.[23] The first are things that only the Community can do, like determining the amount of tax to be collected on imports from outside the Community. Clearly this should not vary from state to state, since the borders between states are open. It would be the equivalent of having different customs duties at different harbours within a state, which would quickly put some out of business. Therefore, Member States can no longer make any decisions about levels of duties, or at least they can only make

[19] EC, Art 5.

[20] Protocol on the Application of the Principles of Subsidiarity and Proportionality, above n 1.

[21] Bermann, above n 15, 339–44.

[22] G De Burca, 'The Principle of Proportionality and its Application in EC Law' (1993) 13 *Yearbook of European Law* 105; J Jans, 'Proportionality Revisited' (2000) 27 *Legal Issues of Economic Integration* 239; Snell, above n 8.

[23] See D Chalmers et al, *European Union Law* (Cambridge University Press, 2006) 188–93.

their decisions collectively via the Community law-making processes.[24] Then there are shared competences, which are found where both the Community and Member States have the power to act in a field. An example of this might be regulating product composition, the way sausages and chairs are made, and so on. In the absence of Community rules it is for the Member States to decide about things like this. On the other hand, if every state has different rules, this could make it difficult to import and export between them, which would hinder the free movement of goods. For this reason, the Community has the power to harmonise such product rules, which it exercises from time to time, when it thinks that the problems arising are serious enough.[25]

Now, as is well known, subsidiarity does not apply to exclusive competences.[26] It makes no sense to ask whether the Community should be leaving things to the Member States if the Treaty says that these states no longer have the power to act. Subsidiarity is only relevant where action could come from either side, the shared situation. So, let us imagine that sausage exporters are complaining bitterly about the costs and problems of doing business with 27 different national sets of rules (I expect sausages were harmonised long ago, but it could be some other product, or indeed service), and the Community thinks it would be a good idea to harmonise. On the other hand, several Member States—but not enough to be a blocking majority, otherwise the point might be moot—really do not want this to happen. They do not want interference with national rules that are established and which the states claim reflect local traditions and preferences.[27] Isn't this what subsidiarity is all about? Who should be making the rules on sausages?

Before answering that, one more example: there are many directives dealing with recognition of qualifications, helping Europeans to move from state to state and overcome the national tendencies to regard all foreign degrees as suspect, inadequate, or both.[28] These directives rely on

[24] *Ibid.*

[25] EC, Art 95. For further discussion see G Davies, 'Can Selling Arrangements be Harmonized?' (2005) 30 *European Law Review* 370.

[26] EC, Art 5.

[27] I am grateful to the reviewer of this chapter for pointing out that such rules could also reflect local sausage producers' interests and government capture. This observation captures the tension in harmonisation perfectly. The Community will take the view that it is helping the local consumer by freeing him from such capture and opening up national markets. But it may be that in fact the rules are genuine reflections of local preferences. Indeed, it may not be an either/or choice: capture may have helped form those preferences. Put another way, there may be consumer capture by the sausage manufacturers too! Which view of the value and nature of the rules is correct is controversial, variable and unlikely to be 'objectively' determinable. The temptation is to think that subsidiarity leads to deference to the states' interpretation. They can decide on their own what local preferences are and how to protect them. The text above argues that where Community free movement rules are involved, subsidiarity has no such conclusion.

[28] A great deal of information is available on the Commission's web pages at http://ec.europa.eu/education/policies/rec_qual/rec_qual_en.html.

the competence that the Community has to harmonise to remove obstacles to the free movement of persons.[29] They might have gone further. Moving between educational systems or transferring qualifications continues to be a tricky matter, and there would have been a good argument for harmonising the length, and at least to some extent the content, of the different phases of education. In fact, something like this is happening informally, as regards universities, via the so-called Bologna process.[30] In any case, it would not be difficult to make the case that such measures would be effective and useful contributions to the goal of free movement, and so prima facie within Community competence. But of course, the Member States would never agree to such far-reaching measures, which is why the more limited ones on mutual recognition are what we in fact have.[31] Yet supposing a proposal had been made for broader harmonisation; would this not be another subsidiarity case study, all about making sure that competences do not get taken away from the states?

Yet subsidiarity would have nothing to do with these situations.[32] In both cases the Community wants to act in order to facilitate free movement. By contrast, the Member States want their own rules on sausages and education because they care about these things, and have strong feelings about what they should consist of. The objective of Community rules would be free movement, but the objective of the national ones is the preservation of national standards, values, culture, history and autonomy. In other words, there is a conflict of objectives or interests.[33] However, asking which interests should take precedence, or how they should be balanced against each other, is quite different from asking, as subsidiarity does, whether the objective of the Community action can be sufficiently achieved by the states.[34]

[29] The legal basis for EC and EU legislation is found in the preamble. For references to legislation, see *ibid*.

[30] This is a process of gradual voluntary harmonisation of aspects of higher education. The Council of Europe has an excellent guide, 'Bologna for Pedestrians' in its higher education section (www.coe.int) (choose education, then higher education, then Bologna process). The current official Bologna Process website is also useful: http://www.ond.vlaanderen.be/hogeronderwijs/bologna.

[31] There is much literature on mutual recognition as a response to the desire to limit competence transfer. See eg SK Schmidt, 'Mutual Recognition as a New Mode of Governance' (2007) 14 *Journal of European Public Policy* 667; K Nicolaidis, 'Trusting the Poles? Constructing Europe through Mutual Recognition (2007) 14 *Journal of European Public Policy* 682; G Davies, 'Is Mutual Recognition an Alternative to Harmonization?' in L Bartels and F Ortino (eds), *Regional Trade Agreements and the WTO Legal System* (Oxford University Press, 2006) 265.

[32] AG Toth, 'The Principle of Subsidiarity in the Maastricht Treaty' (1992) 29 *Common Market Law Review* 1079.

[33] Bermann, above n 15, 339–44.

[34] It is of course true that in signing the Treaty states implicitly adopted free movement as a goal of their own. However, states have multiple and overlapping goals, so the balancing issue does not go away. It is also true that state measure may ostensibly serve legitimate goals

It might be possible for the states to try and bring their objections within this. They could say that by having some flexibility in their national rules, and allowing foreign products to deviate from national standards, they can achieve 'sufficient' free movement, while still preserving a degree of diversity. Then we would come back to the argument about what 'sufficient' means. Here it is worth listing the criteria that the protocol on subsidiarity provides for deciding whether Community action should be taken or Member State action is sufficient:

- whether the issue has transnational aspects that cannot be sufficiently regulated by action of the Member States;
- whether action by Member States alone or a lack of action by the Community would conflict with the requirements of the Treaty or would otherwise significantly damage Member State interests;
- whether actions at Community level would produce clear benefits by reason of scale or effects.

It is clear from these that the focus is on achieving the goals of the Community—in this case free movement—and the methodology is this: first decide how much free movement the Community needs, and then decide whether the Member States can achieve this alone. That means that the reasons that the Member States might have for not wanting harmonisation—autonomy and culture and so on—are not relevant to determining what is sufficient. They have no place in subsidiarity.

One might think that this is just an oddity of the way the EU uses subsidiarity. 'Sufficiently' could be used in a broad way that allowed all kinds of factors to be taken into account. However, this would change the nature of subsidiarity, and go against the rest of its wording.[35] The essence of subsidiarity is to ask who can reach a given goal best, whether the higher level needs to intervene. It assumes that agreed goal. Consider the classic religious formulation:

but in fact be disguised protectionism. However, this is a matter for judicial review, at least within the EU, and does not remove the balancing need when the goals *are* legitimate. In an international trading system judicial determination of the true character of a measure may be more controversial, leading to other problems. It is the particular and accepted legalisation of the EU system which makes legal principles such as subsidiarity so important.

[35] Subsidiarity in the EU is used in a way broadly consistent with that in other jurisdictions and contexts, ie Germany and Catholic dogma. See I Pernice, 'The Framework Revisited: Constitutional, Federal and Subsidiarity Issues' (1996) 2 *Columbia Journal of European Law* 403; G Taylor, 'Germany: The Subsidiarity Principle' (2006) 4 *International Journal of Constitutional Law* 115; NW Barber, 'The Limited Modesty of Subsidiarity' (2005) 11 *European Law Journal* 308; Cass, above n 16; T Schilling, 'A New Dimension of Subsidiarity: Subsidiarity as a Rule and a Principle' (1994) 4 *Yearbook of European Law* 203.

[36] Pope Pius XI, *Quadragisimo Anno*, para 79 (1931).

> So also it is an injustice and at the same time a grave evil and disturbance of right order to assign to a greater and higher association what lesser and subordinate organisations can do.[36]

The principle does not address, is not intended to address, the situation where the different levels are actually trying to do different things. Without a common goal, it is 'nonsense'.[37]

V. SUBSIDIARITY AND PURPOSIVE COMPETENCES

Even if subsidiarity does not encompass the situations above, perhaps it can nevertheless be seen as a useful tool, preventing competence creep in other, still significant ways. A closer examination suggests not. Here it is helpful to consider another way in which competences can be described, dividing them into purposive and categorical powers. A purposive power is one whose scope is defined by its goal—such as the power to harmonise in order to achieve free movement, or perhaps to achieve security and prevent crime—while a categorical power (I may be inventing the phrase here, but it is useful) is one that is defined by a given activity or function—such as the power to determine which level of customs duties will be levied on imported goods, or the power to determine what level of pollutants cars may be permitted to emit.

If an inter-state, or higher-level, body is attributed categorical powers, then subsidiarity will not have much use at all. Such powers are likely to be exclusive, for the reason that it hardly makes sense to attribute a specific role to another body while retaining power to fulfil that role oneself. If the Community is the body deciding acceptable levels of contaminants in drinking water, then it follows as a matter of coherent policy that Member States are no longer doing the same thing.

On the other hand, where purposive powers are attributed, then this is often likely to be because the particular goals entrusted to the higher level are ones that lower bodies acting alone cannot achieve. Hence the Community is given the objectives of ensuring that inter-state trade and movement work well because this goal requires co-ordination and harmonisation of different national laws which manifestly individual states cannot achieve. Hence subsidiarity has no relevance to such purposive powers.[38] Note that this is precisely the sausages and education

[37] 'In relation to levels with no common purpose, talk of subsidiarity is nonsense', G Heraud, *Les principes de Fédéralisme et la Fédération Européene* (Paris, Presses d'Europe, 1965) quoted in V Constaninesco, 'Who's Afraid of Subsidiarity' (1991) 11 *Yearbook of European Law* 33.

[38] Toth, above n 32.

example; the Community there was pursuing goals that were beyond the capacity of the Member States alone to achieve.

So if subsidiarity has any relevance to higher bodies it will be where they are attributed the power to achieve an objective that lower bodies also continue to pursue, where there is a shared goal in which contributions from both sides are necessary. Examples of this might be combating international crime or preventing epidemics or dealing with migration of persons. Here there is clearly a role for a co-ordinating and legislating central body, because of the international element, but much of the actual work done will be local and does not need to be done in the same way everywhere.[39]

In this context subsidiarity compensates for clumsy attribution. One might hope that the powers of the higher body would be defined in a sufficiently precise way that in fact there was little or no overlap with the lower ones—as categorically as possible, one might say. Those writing the treaties would consider which actions need to be taken at the centre—which would usually be the co-ordinating and harmonising ones that Member States cannot do, and to which subsidiarity has no relevance—and only attribute powers to do these. Still, there may be ambiguity or simply bad drafting, and there may even be times when it is necessary to have potential power on both levels, perhaps for reasons of flexibility. Then—and only then—does subsidiarity actually have a potential role to play.[40]

However, that potential probably will not be realised. If there is a genuinely shared goal, then disagreements about which level can achieve it best are likely to be relatively technocratic.[41] That is not to say that the issue will not be hugely political, but the political aspects are likely to result from the interaction with other objectives, which subsidiarity will not consider. For example, if the Community decides that it is necessary to ensure that Member States provide each other with evidence concerning international crimes, then the question whether this is best achieved via a central clearing house and standard formats and definitions of evidence, or via a network of bilateral agreements with minimum standards, is essentially technical. Member States may have strong

[39] Backer, above n 13.

[40] Notably in the allocation of roles in the enforcement of rules. See B Rodger and S Wylie, 'Taking the Community Interest Line: Decentralisation and Subsidiarity in Competition Law Enforcement' (1997) 18 *European Competition Law Review* 485; K Lenaerts, 'The Principle of Subsidiarity and the Environment in the European Union: Keeping the Balance of Federalism' (1994) *Fordham International Law Journal* 846; N Farnsworth, 'Subsidiarity—A Conventional Industry Defence. Is the Directive on Environmental Liability with Regard to Prevention and Remedying of Environmental Damage Justified under the Subsidiarity Principle?' (2004) 13 *European Environmental Law Review* 176.

[41] Farnsworth, above n 40, for examples.

feelings concerning other, non-technical aspects, of the measures, such as the implications for rights and freedoms, but here they will be bringing in other interests not strictly relevant to the question of whether bilateral agreements sufficiently ensure the effective exchange of evidence.

Thus such measures will involve two sorts of disagreement: technical disagreements about which measures are most effective, to which subsidiarity is theoretically relevant but as a general principle is likely to be sidelined in favour of the concrete specifics of the issue; and policy disagreements about whether such action is a good thing in the broader context, to which subsidiarity has nothing to add.

In order to make subsidiarity really important in these shared-purpose contexts the objectives of the Community would have to be defined broadly. If, for example, the Community was given the power to take measures 'to create an area of freedom, security and justice', then this would entail not just combating crime but also protecting rights, and the question would then become whether individual Member States or the Community could create the best balance, a subsidiarity argument with real substance. However, attributing such a power to the Community would also entail that it had prima facie competence to more or less take over all aspects of criminal and constitutional law. Thus in order to make subsidiarity exciting, one has to create a higher body with hugely open or broad powers, which is neither in the interests of the lower body—unless it has political ambitions to transfer its powers—or likely to be effective or efficient. One could say here that subsidiarity is a compensation for over-attribution, but one could also say that it provides an inducement to it: the more that is shared, the more can be controlled by subsidiarity. Thus seeking to make subsidiarity central to competence control entails imagining Community powers as broadly as possible. Subsidiarity implicitly encourages centralisation.

VI. SUBSIDIARITY AND INSTITUTIONAL DYNAMICS

Perhaps more important than any of the above is the simple question of whether higher bodies are really likely to run out of control in these shared-purpose contexts.[42] Is this really the problem? From the point of view of their attributed objectives, there is no motivation to do so. Acting where their purposes could be achieved by the Member States is simply a waste of resources.

If there is a motivation to act even where it is unnecessary it is

[42] A question ultimately requiring empirical research. The text here can do no more than provide a framework for thinking about the issue.

therefore not from the attributed goals but out of institutional motives—the desire to grow and expand the higher apparatus and its powers. The self-maximising urge is certainly common in institutions and we may expect it to exist in the Community. Here subsidiarity provides a policy and efficiency argument against a natural but unhealthy institutional dynamic. It argues against the higher level on its own terms; it says don't do this, because someone else could do it better. Save your resources.

But it is open to question how often higher bodies, and the Community in particular, actually get the opportunity to engage in ineffective measures that are not necessary for their stated goals but are simply self-aggrandising. Community measures do, after all, require the assent of the Member States in the Council.[43] That may only be by majority,[44] but is it likely that there would be a majority of states interested in unnecessarily transferring powers to the Community?

This could happen if states wished to centralise for other reasons. One possibility would be political ambition for Europe, the desire to build a bigger, more 'prestigious' EU. However, while often mentioned in various countries—at least until recently—it is suggested, tentatively since this is really a matter for the political scientists, that when it comes to concrete measures Member States are usually reluctant to give up their own powers for such a woolly reason. This is particularly so since shared-purpose contexts tend to be politically sensitive. They are, of their essence, matters that are too important for states to let go, and yet where their capacity to act autonomously is threatened by externalities, requiring them to co-operate. In such contexts states are usually reluctant to give up power, and will not rush to do so.

The other reason why they might vote for apparently unnecessary measures is where there is genuine disagreement about the technocratic question of which level is most effective. But then they are, in their own eyes, not voting against subsidiarity at all. Thus this is not a situation where subsidiarity will add anything to the analysis. While the minority may cry that it has been violated, others will genuinely feel that it has not, and the Court, assuming that it is a matter where expert arguments for both views exist, will be unlikely to second-guess the majority.

By contrast, where one does get real fierce disagreement between Member States is when it comes to the balancing of interests and goals. Should privacy be sacrificed to fight crime? Is trade more important than the quality of sausages? Such value questions are the traditional stuff of politics, that is to say they are unanswerable definitively, and there will be great differences of view. In particular, the Community is likely to

43 See Craig and De Burca, above n 5, 108–25.
44 *Ibid*.

value its goals more highly than those of the states, and vice versa, but it may, to some extent, be able to influence some states towards its point of view. In the situations where Member States feel that the Community has taken its competences too far, the legislation in question invariably embodies a value-balance that the majority are comfortable with, but which the minority abhor. Then there is a really important question to be answered: should the majority be able to impose their value choices like this? Clearly they must be able to sometimes, because a choice has been made to allow the Community to legislate in the given area. However, there is no need to interpret that to mean that measures which, from the point of view of the Community, are not particularly important should be allowed when the value-violence that they do to some states, or the autonomy cost they impose, is considerable. In other words, there is a proportionality argument to be had. Subsidiarity, however, will not be involved.

Even where subsidiarity does apply to a measure, and actually bites, it is not clear that this has a meaningful autonomy-preserving effect. If a measure fails the subsidiarity test, then this is because its goals could have been achieved sufficiently by the Member States. Thus, under subsidiarity, the alternative to Community action is Community-instructed Member State action to achieve the same end.

In practice this means that either the Community can issue very detailed legislation, or perhaps create a new Community organ or agency, or it can issue general instructions to Member States to achieve certain goals themselves.[45] This effectively makes them Community agents, and when they are achieving these goals—by legislating or creating agencies or spending or whatever—they will be acting within the sphere of the Community instructions and constrained by these and all the other principles of Community law. Subsidiarity thus offers the choice between centralisation or co-option.[46]

This choice may have efficiency implications which could lead in either direction. Sometimes it is better to act centrally, and sometimes not. However, its implications for national autonomy are equally open. There are times when requiring national ministries to devote themselves to preparing laws and measures to implement Community goals will entail a greater loss of national policy freedom than creating a Community

[45] The so-called 'new approach' to harmonisation. See Chalmers, above n 23, 474–505. See on agencies Case C–217/04 *UK v Parliament and Council* [2006] ECR I–3771; Case C–436/03 *ECS* [2006] ECR I–3733; both annotated by V Randazzo at (2007) 44 *Common Market Law Review* 155.

[46] See N Emiliou, 'Subsidiarity: An Effective Barrier against the Enterprises of Ambition?' (1992) 17 *European Law Review* 383; Schilling, above n 35; Barber, above n 15; MP Maduro, 'So Close and Yet So Far: the Paradoxes of Mutual Recognition' (2007) 14 *Journal of European Public Policy* 814; Davies, above n 31.

agency to do the same, or passing very detailed Community legislation which can be mindlessly adopted into national law. The issues here are institutional. When national authorities are working full time in the service of Community goals they have less time and resources left over for other national matters. Moreover, they way they think and work becomes structured by Community ways of doing things, with knock-on effects for other matters.[47] There is a good argument that the move from regulations to directives, which was embraced as subsidiarity at work, and a way of giving Member States more autonomy within the sphere of Community law, has backfired.[48] The coherence of national legal systems is superficially protected by allowing Community law to be translated into national legislation, but the political autonomy of Member States is threatened. Many governmental departments have become little more than outsourced units of the EU, devoting themselves full time to questions of implementation—of how to achieve the Community's goals—when once they had energy to develop national policy too. Co-option is here more centralising than centralisation, which at least leaves the periphery intellectual freedom.[49]

What subsidiarity does not at all offer is a leave-well-alone option, a reason for the Community to simply back off from an issue and let the states occupy that field as they wish. That could only happen if the goal of the Community measure was rejected as well, thus preventing the obligation to reach that goal from being transferred unto the states. Implicitly such a rejection is outside of subsidiarity itself. Subsidiarity assumes the validity of the goal and asks who should meet it. In the Community context the goal in question is usually lifted directly from the Treaty, and so its validity is hardly an issue. It only becomes one where the real goal of the measure is clearly something other than the goal attributed to it. However, in that case the measure is annulled for lack of legal base, or an incorrect legal base, and the subsidiarity question is never reached.[50]

[47] See S Weatherill, 'Harmonisation. How Much, How Little?' (2005) 16 *European Business Law Review* 533.

[48] The fact that it is since the birth of the new approach, in the late 1980s, that concerns over spreading Community competence have come to the fore—culminating in the proposed constitution—indicates that the new approach has above all functioned as a mechanism to enable the Community to legislate more broadly, and thus occupy more territory that was previously that of the Member States, at the relatively minor cost of sacrificing some legislative detail.

[49] See JHH Weiler, 'The Transformation of Europe' (1991) 100 *Yale Law Journal* 2403, 2476–8.

[50] See Chalmers, above n 23, 140–44.

VII. THE EUROPEAN EXPERIENCE

Subsidiarity has been widely used as a political and rhetorical device: it is used as a procedural guide at the pre-legislative stage,[51] and can be invoked before the Court of Justice. In every case where it has been before the Court, the Member States have lost because they have, as in the sausages and education examples, invoked other interests that are legally irrelevant.[52] The Community was generally seeking to harmonise in order to create the uniformity that allows easy movement and fair competition, and the state claims that they were capable of regulating the particular sector in question were irrelevant. Perhaps they were, but they were not capable of ensuring that all states regulated in the same way. This uniformity of regulation was, however, the Community's goal, and so the goal relevant to subsidiarity. In each case this inability of the states to ensure uniformity between states was precisely the argument of the Court in rebutting the Member State arguments.

Politically the story is similar. No body has pushed subsidiarity as hard as the German Länder, which were familiar with the concept from German law and wished to see it acquire teeth in the Community context.[53] It seemed to them that Community law enabled the German domestic division of powers to be bypassed. While certain matters were reserved, under German law, for the regions, nevertheless the Federal Government acting in Brussels seemed to have the capacity to pass measures that touched on these regional competences, for example education. Yet as with the lawsuits, the kinds of measures that offended the Länder were the internal market ones, the ones whose aim was harmonisation for the sake of uniformity, the goal that only the centre can achieve and to which subsidiarity provides no answer.[54]

It seems as if subsidiarity confuses. Each level looks at a measure in terms of its own objectives. Thus Member States and their constituent parts look at measures concerning sausages and education and ask whether they can regulate these things sufficiently. Of course they can! They have more expertise in sausages and education than the Community does, and much more knowledge of the particular factors relevant

[51] Protocol to the Treaty of Amsterdam on the Application of the Principles of Subsidiarity and Proportionality, above n 1; Impact Assessment Guidelines, 15 June 2005, SEC(2005)791; Communication from the Commission on Impact Assessment, 5 June 2002, COM(2002)276 Final (expanding on the principles behind the guidelines).

[52] See cases: *Alliance for Natural Health; British American Tobacco; Working Time Directive; Biotechnology Directive*, above n 12.

[53] C Jeffery, 'Regions and the Constitution for Europe: German and British Impacts' (2004) 13 *German Politics* 605; FC Mayer, 'Competences—Reloaded? The Vertical Division of Powers in the EU and the New European Constitution' (2005) 3 *International Journal of Constitutional Law* 493.

[54] Mayer, above n 53.

to their own state. From this point of view it looks as if subsidiarity is on their side. However, as a matter of law they are wrong in thinking that protecting national preferences and culture, or the quality of sausages and degrees, is the 'objective' of the Community measure which must be sufficiently achieved. Subsidiarity is only concerned with the objectives that the higher level is pursuing. In order to understand subsidiarity Member States have to look from the Community's perspective, and set aside their autonomous national interests.

Clearly—given their failure to do so in lawsuits—this is asking quite a lot from the Member States, and it is also silencing the most important arguments that they have.[55] Of course in principle there is nothing to stop them from bringing an additional proportionality argument to the effect that the Community progress in free movement does not justify the high national costs.[56] However, the pervasiveness of subsidiarity as the framework for competence issues seems to blind them to this possibility.

One may expect something similar to be happening at the pre-legislative stage. The Commission has lots of subsidiarity checklists which it goes through when developing measures, and no doubt if the measure passes all the tests, then it is put forward with a clear conscience and a light heart.[57] Yet this should not be the case. The really important competence issues will be still unconsidered, and again the dominance of the principle may be elbowing more important arguments out of the way. A linguistic comment may be appropriate: the structure of subsidiarity and its focus on the object of the measure encourage a blinkered approach to thinking about these issues.

On the whole, subsidiarity may at the moment be doing more harm than good. At some points, and in some contexts, there may be important arguments to be had about who can best achieve given goals. However, the issue that continues to confront the Community is one of substantive conflict of goals between levels, and emphasising subsidiarity is not making it easier to address this openly and sensibly. As a result, important national goals do not carry the weight in decision-making that they deserve, while hostility to the Community is cultivated at national level as a result of apparent disrespect for national priorities.[58]

An example of subsidiarity not helping may be found in the procedure embodied in a protocol to the ill-fated EU constitution,[59] for subsidiarity

[55] Schilling, above n 35.

[56] Above n 22.

[57] Impact Assessment Guidelines; Communication from the Commission on Impact Assessment, above n 52.

[58] See Von Bogdandy and Bast, above n 2; G De Burca and B De Witte, 'The Delimitation of Powers Between the EU and its Member States' in A Arnull and D Wincott (eds), *Accountability and Legitimacy in the European Union* (Oxford University Press, 2002) 213.

[59] Treaty Establishing a Constitution for Europe OJC 2004/310/01. At time of writing the

consultation with national parliaments.[60] Each proposal for legislation would be sent out to them and they would have the chance to submit opinions on its compatibility with the principle. If more than a certain number did so, the Commission would be obliged to respond with a reasoned opinion, and if the parliaments were still not satisfied there would still be the possibility of legal action on the question.[61]

This involvement of national parliaments has a certain logic to it; if the competences of the lower level are to be protected, then it makes more sense to ask them if the higher-level measure is justified than it would be to ask the higher level itself, eg, the European Parliament. Moreover, national parliaments remain the primary democratic organs in Europe, so the democratic legitimacy of measures would be given a boost by their assent. For these reasons—who dares be against democracy and subsidiarity?—the protocols instituting this procedure formed one of the few aspects of the constitution that had widespread support, and they have been transferred almost unchanged to the Treaty of Lisbon, the amending treaty which replaces the constitution and which seems likely to come into force in 2009.

Yet how much sense does it make to ask national parliaments whether they are capable of achieving the goals that the Community is trying to reach? Firstly, parliaments are bad on technical questions—it would make more sense for the Commission to consult with national administrative agencies—and secondly, is there any chance at all that parliaments will actually answer this question?[62] It is in the nature of politicians that the question which will capture them is whether or not the measure is one that the Community ought to take, a far more open and political question than subsidiarity contains. They will object, saying that sausages and universities should be for the Member States to regulate, and face a technical rebuff because their arguments are legally beside the point. The dynamic of the lawsuits will be re-enacted at a political level.

The only way this process can make sense is if all parties accept subsidiarity as no more than a cipher for the desirability of Community action, a question to be decided by elected representatives.[63] But if that is the case, and the internal structure and logic of subsidiarity is stripped

constitution has been abandoned under that name following embarrassing negative referenda in France and the Netherlands, but most of its content, including the protocol referred to, has been reformulated as an amending treaty, the Treaty of Lisbon, which is currently being ratified by the Member States.

60 Protocol to the Treaty establishing a Constitution for Europe, on the role of national parliaments in the European Union; Protocol to the Treaty establishing a Constitution for Europe, on the application of the principles of subsidiarity and proportionality.

61 See G Davies, 'The Post-Laeken Division of Competences' (2003) 28 *European Law Review* 686.

62 *Ibid*.

63 See Emiliou, above n 46; Toth, above n 17; Bermann, above n 15, 393–4.

out, then appeal to the Court of Justice will be a damp squib; no court will second guess the purely political desirability of a measure. Thus the process will be one without teeth.[64]

The writers of the protocols reflect the same confusion about what subsidiarity is that we see in the lawsuits and the political rhetoric. Yet it does have a meaning, and one that the Court and Commission use. Better to accept this, and with it to accept that subsidiarity cannot do everything that everyone wants it to do.

VIII. CONTEXT IS EVERYTHING

The difference is perhaps between autonomy of organisation and of policy. Subsidiarity protects, to some extent, the right of states to carry out missions in their own way. It does not protect their right to formulate their own mission or make substantive choices about values and policy.

Subsidiarity would therefore be useful within a corporation, or an organisation where strategy is formulated at the top, and where the lower levels are expected to be serving the same goals as the higher, and to have no independent goals outside the scope of the higher purpose. Then it would ensure that implementation took place at the most efficient level.

International organisations are not like this. Policy trickles up at least as much as it trickles down, and there is substantive and important and independent policy-making at each level, with conflicts inevitably arising. The challenge is how to deal with this. Until recently scholars of the EU were enthusiastic about models of participation and multi-level governance, in which the impossibility of clear division of competences was addressed via communication between levels and representation of all interests in all decision making places. While the perception that there can never be a clear line between Community and national activities seems quite right, it is increasingly clear that participatory responses are not enough. Even if everyone is heard, there will not always be a consensus; there is no single policy which satisfies all.

This means that conflict management is needed, which in turn entails an open acceptance by Courts and Community organs of the fact that not everyone can achieve all their goals. Member States have long accepted this, and are used to redesigning their national policies to comply with Community law. However, the Community, encouraged by far-reaching judgments on the nature of Community law from the Court of Justice, tends to adhere to a fundamentalist approach. Its goals cannot be compromised—there is no space for that in the Treaty. Therefore it is hardly

[64] See Toth, *ibid;* Snell, above n 8.

surprising that the Community can embrace subsidiarity without too much trouble. While it may occasionally result in the reallocation of an activity from the Community to Member States, its greater importance lies in the fact that it assumes the inevitability of fully achieving Community goals, and denies a discursive place to any of the good reasons not to do this.

IX. CONCLUSIONS

Legislative measures typically have a whole bunch of effects, and the objectives of those who support them will differ too. Any attempt to look at them in the light of just one purpose, or the purposes of just one involved party, is stifling of discussion and will hinder intelligent discussion about their value and importance. There really should be no role for a principle which pretends that what the Community wants is the only goal that matters.

More aesthetically, one should be suspicious of a principle that refers to the objectives of a measure. Measures do not have objectives; people do. Embedding the psychological in the inanimate is a factually implausible rhetorical trick that serves to privilege certain goals and elevate them beyond discussion or compromise. Suppose subsidiarity were rephrased this way, which I do not think changes the meaning:

> Wherever the Community wishes to achieve something it will make the maximum possible use of national authorities and bodies to do this.

Would it have such a good press?

5

Fragmentation(s) of International Law: On Normative Integration as Authority Allocation

TOMER BROUDE*

I. INTRODUCTION

> International law is a legal system. Its rules and principles (ie its norms) act in relation to and should be interpreted against the background of other rules and principles. As a legal system, international law is not a random collection of such norms. There are meaningful relationships between them.

THUS BEGIN THE 2006 conclusions of the Study Group of the International Law Commission (ILC) on fragmentation in international law.[1] How could any international lawyer contest these premises? To argue that international law is not at all a legal system (as some 'antagonists' seem to argue),[2] or to accept that international law is not just an inherently problem-ridden anarchical society but a chaotic one,[3] comprising a random collection of norms devoid of 'meaningful interrelationships', would be self-defeating. It would also render the work of the Study Group useless. Might an international jurist reasonably

* Lecturer, Faculty of Law and Department of International Relations, Hebrew University of Jerusalem.

1 See M Koskenniemi, 'Report of the Study Group of the International Law Commission, Fragmentation of International Law: Difficulties Arising from the Diversification and Expansion of International Law' (13 April 2006) UN Doc A/CN.4/L.682 (hereafter 'the ILC Study Group Report').

2 See JL Goldsmith and EA Posner, 'A Theory of Customary International Law' (1999) 66 *University of Chicago Law Review* 1113; and JL Goldsmith and EA Posner, *The Limits of International Law* (Oxford University Press, 2005).

3 'Anarchy' (literally, the absence of authority) is not synonymous with 'chaos' (the absence of order), as cogently argued by the 'English School' of international relations; see H Bull, *The Anarchical Society* (New York, Columbia University Press, 1977); and AC Cutler, 'The "Grotian Tradition" in International Relations' (1991) 17 *Review of International Studies* 41.

prefer a system of fragmented norms for any reason based in law? This seems unlikely. Why, then, are the conclusions of the ILC Study Group Report so controversial at this point in time, lacking even the full support of the members of the group itself?[4]

The ILC Study Group Report is an important document, for several reasons, even if only because it transparently transfers some ideas on integration in international law[5] from what has been until now an essentially academic discourse to a more official plane from which constructive international law-making might follow. 'Integration in international law' refers in the present context to a deliberate process of countering the 'difficulties arising from the diversification and expansion of international law'[6] by reconciling formally disparate elements of international law through normative hierarchy, inter-institutional comity, margins of appreciation, *lex posterior, lex specialis*, subsidiarity, and other such principles and conceivable methods. Yet the ILC Study Group Report is easily faulted, like other treatments of the problems of integration, because it focuses on only one dimension of fragmentation (and corresponding remedial responses), ie, upon the fragmentation of international *norms*. The Report is, on its face, entirely silent on questions relating directly to the fragmentation of international *authority*. This article argues that the structure of international law is such that one cannot effectively (or, indeed, even legitimately) address one form of fragmentation—norm fragmentation or authority fragmentation—without addressing the other, as the ILC Study Group Report, for one, has attempted to do. It is the difficulty (if not intractability) of accepting the integration of authority in international law that sustains the controversy over the integration of norms.

In the second section below, I will set out the difference between problems of norm fragmentation, on one hand, and questions of authority fragmentation, on the other, demonstrating how the discourse of fragmentation has itself been bifurcated and 'fragmented' between them, amid many particular debates relating to specific issue areas and legal regimes and their interrelationships. In the subsequent third section, I will posit that there exist in fact important linkages between the fragmentation of norms and the fragmentation of authority, suggesting some cross-cutting observations on the basic correlation between these expres-

[4] The draft conclusions of the ILC Study Group Report, above n 1, are circumscribed as 'finalized by Martti Koskenniemi'; as the Report specifies (para 4), only draft conclusions 1–23 had been 'provisionally agreed' to by the group members, while draft conclusions 24–43 had not yet ripened in the group's process of deliberation.

[5] Particularly those of J Pauwelyn, *Conflict of Norms in Public International Law: How WTO Law Relates to Other Rules of International* Law (Cambridge University Press, 2003); and C MacLachlan, 'The Principle of Systemic Integration and Article 31(3)(c) of the Vienna Convention' (2005) 54 *International and Comparative Law Quarterly* 279.

[6] As per the title of the ILC Study Group Report.

sions of fragmentation. On this basis, in the fourth section, I will pursue the claim that normative integration in international law (whether or not it is in itself an attractive goal as a juridical matter) creates pressures that are strongly associated with more integrated international authority—a significantly more political and problematic proposition. In the fifth section I will briefly show that as a result of this relationship between norm integration and authority integration, some international tribunals and institutions are deterred from pursuing the former, in order to avoid complications in the latter. In conclusion I will suggest that qualitatively different models of norm integration—such as Article 31(3)(c) of the Vienna Convention on the Law of Treaties (VCLT)[7] and Paragraph 4 of the 1992 United Nations (UN) Rio Declaration on Environment and Development ('the Rio Declaration')[8]—should be evaluated according to their different levels of intrusiveness into the problem area of international authority allocation; the model of normative integration that less creates less pressures towards authority integration has better chances of attaining its goals.

II. THE WARP AND WEFT OF FRAGMENTED INTERNATIONAL LAW: SUBSTANTIVE NORMS AND AUTHORITY ALLOCATION

The 'fragmentation' of international law is itself a fragmented concept. Analytically, the problems associated with the fragmentation of international law fall into two broad categories, reflecting two distinct points of entry.

One of these categories deals with the fragmentation of *substantive norms*, ie, the complex interactions caused by the existence of a staggering variety of substantive sources of international law,[9] made up of tens of thousands of international treaties in addition to customary rules. In this puzzle, the concern is how to determine which rules are relevant and applicable to a given issue, and most importantly, how to reconcile conflicts between such rules as they arise.[10] The 'trade and . . .' debate is illustrative in this respect. International trade disciplines promote economic liberalisation. However, non-economic values and concerns, enshrined in international legal conventions, may in some cases seek to

[7] Vienna Convention on the Law of Treaties (adopted 23 May 1969, entered into force 27 January 1980) 1155 UNTS 331.

[8] See UN Doc A/CONF.151/26 (Vol I), 'Report of the United Nations Conference on Environment and Development, Rio de Janeiro' 3–14 June 1992, Annex I, Rio Declaration on Environment and Development, (1992) 31 ILM 874.

[9] Here I refer of course to normative 'sources' of international law in the sense specified in Art 38(1) of the ICJ Statute, not in the sense of law-making institutions.

[10] The leading treatise on this subject is currently Pauwelyn, above n 5.

restrict it.[11] It thus becomes necessary to regulate the relationship between these norms. Structurally similar problems arise with respect to 'investment and . . .',[12] the relationship between international humanitarian law and international human rights law,[13] multilateral rules and regional rules—given the diversity of international law today, there is an abundance of possible conflicts and combinations.

Moreover, norm fragmentation raises problems even when normative conflicts do not exist overtly—ie, in cases where different legal sources contain the same obligations and imperatives (or substantially similar ones), but produce potentially different results. For instance, the legality of the use of force in self-defence is based on both international customary law and treaty law—Article 51 of the UN Charter; despite the substantive similarity between the two norms, their (fragmented) independent existence gave rise to significant legal controversy before the International Court of Justice (ICJ) in the Nicaragua case.[14] This is but one of many examples of 'multi-sourced obligations' or 'parallel regimes' that raise problems due to norm fragmentation, even in the absence of normative conflict.

The other category of problems relates to the fragmentation of international *authority*. Here we are concerned not with the interrelationship between rules, as such, but rather with the distribution of power (in the legal sense of the word) among the plethora of international and national institutions and organisations who produce, interpret and apply international law. We ask who has the authority to make a determination on a particular question arising under international law? And if more than one body has such authority, whose determination should prevail? This problem has attracted considerable attention in the area of international dispute settlement, as similar or even identical legal and factual questions are brought before different tribunals.[15] But clearly this dimension of

[11] For example, the 'trade and . . .' problem is expressed in conflicts between trade rules and environmental norms (see, eg, S Shaw and R Schwartz, 'Trade and Environment in the WTO: State of Play' (2002) 36 *Journal of World Trade* 129), or between trade rules and agreements relating to cultural diversity (see T Broude, 'Taking "Trade and Culture" Seriously: Geographical Indications and Cultural Protection in WTO Law' (2005) 26 *University of Pennsylvania Journal of International Economic Law* 623; and T Voon, 'UNESCO and the WTO: A Clash of Cultures' (2006) 55 *International and Comparative Law Quarterly* 635).

[12] See M Hirsch, 'Conflicting Obligations in International Investment Law: Investment Tribunals' Perspective', elsewhere in this volume (p 323).

[13] See C Droege, 'The Interplay between International Humanitarian Law and International Human Rights Law in Situations of Armed Conflict' (2007) 40(2) *Israel Law Review* 310; and A Gross, 'Human Proportions: Are Human Rights the Emperor's New Clothes of the International Law of Occupation?' (2007) 18 *European Journal of International Law* 1.

[14] See *Military and Paramilitary Activities in and against Nicaragua (Nicaragua v US), Merits*, (Judgment of 27 June 1986) [1986] ICJ Rep 14.

[15] The leading treatise on this subject is Y Shany, *The Competing Jurisdiction of International Courts and Tribunals* (Oxford University Press, 2003); See also N Lavranos, 'Concurrence of Jurisdiction between the ECJ and other International Courts and Tribunals' (2005) *European Environmental Law Review*, part I, September, 213–25, and contributions by N Lavranos, I Canor and A Cohen elsewhere in this volume (on pp 217, 237 and 265, respectively).

fragmentation exists among political bodies as well. For example, the Kimberly Process Certification Scheme relating to 'blood diamonds' was sanctioned by the UN Security Council, and yet its participants requested (and received) a waiver from the World Trade Organization (WTO) Goods Council for the operation of some of its elements, implying that UN approval was not sufficient for this purpose. Had the WTO waiver not been forthcoming, the fragmentation of political authority between the UN and the WTO would have been acute, because an ostensible clash between UN and WTO authorities would have arisen.[16] The fragmentation of authority in international law also manifests itself in unsettled relationships between judicial and political international institutions, even organs of the same international organisation, as cases of international 'constitutional' crisis have appeared in the UN, the WTO and the EU,[17] amid concerns over international 'judicial activism' and problems of separation of powers.[18]

This book, as its title implies, is dedicated to an exploration of the ways authority is allocated in international law. In other words, its focus is on the second of the two above-mentioned categories: the fragmentation of international authority. It may thus seem odd that this chapter lingers on the first category, the fragmentation of substantive norms, even culminating in a brief discussion of two principles—Article 31(3)(c) VCLT and Paragraph 4 of the Rio Declaration—whose operation would apparently relate primarily, if not exclusively, to that fragmentation category. Article 31(3)(c) VCLT is part of the general rule of interpretation of treaties, clearly an instrument of normative integration,[19] particularly as a judicial reasoning tool. Paragraph 4 of the Rio Declaration certainly seeks to inform the process of decision-making, requiring environmental protection to be considered as 'an integral part of the development process', but seemingly this requirement tells us nothing about *who* should be making such integrated decisions. The Rio principle of integration is formally agnostic as to the locus of decision-making authority, as long as environmental protection is considered in substance and sustainable

16 See J Pauwelyn, 'WTO Compassion or Superiority Complex? What to Make of the WTO Waiver for "Conflict Diamonds"?' (2003) 24 *Michigan Journal of International Law* 1177.

17 For a comparative analysis of such problems, see T Broude, *International Governance in the World Trade Organization: Judicial Boundaries and Political Capitulation* (London, Cameron and May, 2004).

18 See eg P Mahoney, 'Judicial Activism and Judicial Self-Restraint in the European Court of Human Rights' (1990) 11 *Human Rights Law Journal* 57; L Bartels, 'The Separation of Powers in the WTO: How to Avoid Judicial Activism' (2004) 53(4) *International and Comparative Law Quarterly* 861; and P Kooijmans, 'The ICJ in the 21st Century: Judicial Restraint, Judicial Activism, or Proactive Judicial Policy' (2007) 56(4) *International and Comparative Law Quarterly* 741.

19 Both McLachlan above n 5, and the ILC Study Group Report above n 1 (at 8–10) refer to Art 31(3)(c) VCLT in terms of 'systemic integration', but this is not in the sense of integration between institutional systems of authority but rather in the sense of integration between different systems of norms.

development is achieved.[20] Why should such legal principles bearing directly on normative integration be discussed here in the context of the structure of authority in international law?

The response to this question underscores the fundamental point I would like to elucidate and discuss in this chapter. The problems of substantive norm fragmentation, on one hand, and the problems of authority fragmentation, on the other, are bound at the hip, two sides of the same coin. It is indeed at times convenient for lawyers to analyse them in isolation from each other, and there is no doubt that they do pose discrete problems in the technical or doctrinal legal senses. Still, even the few examples presented above show that norm fragmentation and authority fragmentation are inseparable. Substantive conflicts between trade and environmental norms arise because rules are made in multilateral and particular treaties between different (but overlapping) groups of states, or in international institutions, each endowed with the authority to make law(s); and these conflicts manifest themselves most clearly when different tribunals address them differentially, each within its own mandate—a mandate that is itself derived from agreed upon but fragmented norms. Multi-sourced obligations are similarly problematic because they are the consequences of fragmented authority, and may lend themselves to dissimilar application by differently authorised institutions. Conversely, the fragmentation of authority is most challenging when it results in fragmented normative determinations, such as conflicting judicial decisions made by different courts.

Authority fragmentation (together with the authority allocation rules that govern it) and norm fragmentation (along with the principles regulating the relations between substantive norms) are the warp and weft of the complex fabric that is international law. There are many interactions between fragmented authority and fragmented norms worthy of exploration, but here I will dwell only on two such interactions: first, the general link between these two 'fragmentations', according to which changes in one will lead to corresponding changes in the other; and second, the way in which the pursuit of norm integration leads to pressures towards an integrative allocation of authority.

[20] However, it should be noted that the Committee on the International Law of Sustainable Development of the International Law Association (ILA) has opined that para 4 of the Rio Declaration prescribes integration not only in systemic, legal, normative and judicial reasoning dimensions, but also in the institutional realm; see International Law Association, 'Report of the 72nd Conference' Toronto, June 2006, 475–83. See also JC Dernbach, 'Achieving Sustainable Development: The Centrality and Multiple Facets of Integrated Decisionmaking' (2003) 10 *Indiana Journal of Global Legal Studies* 247, 252, stating that para 4 of the Rio Declaration 'asserts that environmental protection and development must be considered together, which would require integration of decisionmaking'.

III. THE BASIC CORRELATION BETWEEN NORM FRAGMENTATION AND AUTHORITY FRAGMENTATION

There is an under-explored correlation between norm fragmentation and authority fragmentation.[21] Put simply, the significance of authority fragmentation and the seriousness of the problems it presents largely depend upon the degree of norm fragmentation, and vice versa. Where substantive norms are integrated or harmonised rather than fragmented, identifying the proper forum for producing them or for making determinations based upon them is of less importance, because the room available to different fora for manoeuvring between different and potentially conflicting decisions is reduced. The normative commonality overcomes institutional differences. Thus, for example, the rapidly growing area of international criminal law is enforced nowadays by many different tribunals, both national and international. Although differences of opinion and interpretation exist among these judicial bodies, the body of law they apply is essentially the same, turning these disparate and loosely linked institutions into a 'community of courts around the world, engaged in a common endeavor'.[22] The 'common law' of international criminal norms becomes the tie that binds formally independent institutions together.

Similarly, if decision-making authority were formally more integrated, the fragmentation of norms would be naturally mitigated and, in any case, would not be as problematic. This is because institutionally integrated decisions would reconcile fragmented norms in a consistent manner. Consider, for example, the debate over the need to establish an 'appellate mechanism' in the area of investment treaty arbitration.[23] Such

[21] But see JP Trachtman, 'Trade and . . . Problems, Cost–Benefit Analysis and Subsidiarity' (1998) 9 *European Journal of International Law* 32; and JP Trachtman, 'Institutional Linkage: Transcending "Trade and . . ."' (2002) 96 *American Journal of International Law* 77. In these articles (especially in the second) Trachtman astutely reflects upon issue linkages (ie, interactions between different international normative regimes) as problems of allocation of regulatory jurisdiction between states, between national and international decision-makers and among international organisations. Trachtman suggests that the solutions to fragmented norms are to be found in institutional (ie, authority-allocating) devices. The present article is a partial mirror image of this analysis: where Trachtman traces the effects of institutions on norm fragmentation, here I probe the impact of normative integration on institutional structures. See also JP Trachtman, 'The Domain of WTO Dispute Resolution' (1999) 40 *Harvard International Law Journal* 333, discussing normative linkages with WTO law in terms relating to the authority of the WTO.

[22] See LR Helfer and A-M Slaughter, 'Toward a Theory of Effective Supranational Adjudication' (1997) 107 *Yale Law Journal* 273, 372; and W Burke-White, 'A Community of Courts: Toward a System of International Criminal Law Enforcement' (2002) 24 *Michigan Journal of International Law* 1.

[23] See DA Gantz, 'An Appellate Mechanism for Review of Arbitral Decisions in Investor–State Disputes: Prospects and Challenges' (2006) 39 *Vanderbilt Journal of Transnational Law* 39; several contributions in F Ortino, A Sheppard and H Warner (eds), *Investment Treaty Law: Current Issues*, vol I (London, British Institute of International and Comparative Law, 2006);

authority integration in the form of a 'supreme' court of investment appeals would surely remedy the acute case of authority fragmentation found in the investment protection arena, where tribunals are established ad hoc on a case-by-case basis, deriving their jurisdiction from many different sources, and employing different procedural rules (mainly International Centre for Settlement of Investment Disputes (ICSID) or United Nations Commission on International Trade Law (UNCITRAL)). An extreme example of authority fragmentation, and, indeed, of the 'forum shopping' that thrives upon it, can be found in the circumstances of the celebrated 'Lauder' cases, which involved the issuance of conflicting awards in two separate actions relating to essentially the same events brought by the same investor against the same host state (one brought directly to an investment tribunal established in London under the US–Czech Bilateral Investment Treaty (BIT), and a second brought indirectly, through a holding company, to an investment tribunal established in Stockholm under the Netherlands–Czech BIT).[24] Clearly, an appellate mechanism would have reduced the severity of this conflict of authority, and perhaps even pre-empted the problem entirely, as the investor would have had less of an incentive to file in two different proceedings with the knowledge that ultimately they would both reach the same higher authority. However, an appellate mechanism for international investment law would do much more than achieve authority integration; in fact, the proponents of an appellate system seem more concerned with normative fragmentation, arguing that it would prevent inconsistent rulings.[25] There are literally thousands of investment protection treaties, which are similarly constructed, though concluded between different parties. Although the considerable degree of similarity between investment protection treaties means that the actual normative fragmentation is reduced from the outset, non-integrated investment arbitration tribunals issue conflicting interpretations of the same literal clauses in investment protection treaties.[26] An appellate investment mechanism would overcome this by creating consistent jurisprudence, achieving greater normative

and A Qureshi, 'A Possible Appellate System' in P Muchlinski, F Ortino and C Schreuer (eds), *The Oxford Handbook of International Investment Law* (Oxford University Press, 2008, forthcoming).

[24] For more details and analysis of the Lauder cases, see SD Franck, 'The Legitimacy Crisis in Investment Treaty Arbitration: Privatizing Public International Law Through Inconsistent Decisions' (2005) 73 *Fordham Law Review* 1521; and Y Shany 'Similarity in the Eye of the Beholder: Revisiting the Application of Rules Governing Jurisdictional Conflicts in the Lauder/CME cases', in A Rovine (ed), *International Arbitration and Mediation* (The Hague, Martinus Nijhoff, 2008, forthcoming).

[25] See, eg, Frank, above n 24.

[26] See Y Shany, 'Contract Claims vs Treaty Claims: Mapping Conflicts between ICSID Decisions on Multisourced Investment Claims' (2005) 99 *American Journal of International Law* 835.

integration. A 'supreme court' of investment disputes would become the tie that binds together the similar distinct norms.[27]

This scenario in the field of investment is somewhat analogous to the effect of the consolidation of dispute settlement procedures in the multilateral trading system and the establishment of the WTO Appellate Body by the Uruguay Round Agreements in 1995. Prior to this development, many of the 1979 Tokyo Round Agreements had included separate dispute settlement procedures.[28] Under both the general General Agreement on Tariffs and Trade (GATT) procedures and the separate procedures relating to areas such as anti-dumping and government procurement, dispute settlement panels were established ad hoc, and although efforts were made to produce consistent jurisprudence, they did not always succeed. The normative integration achieved by the 'single undertaking' of the Uruguay Round agreements was significantly augmented by the unified Dispute Settlement Understanding (DSU) and even more so by the creation of an Appellate Body.

It would be taking the argument too far to say that the question of authority allocation only matters if there are differences in questions of substance, and/or that fragmentation among substantive norms only matters if they inform fragmented authority; but surely there is a strong link between the fragmentation of both authority and norms, if only because one produces and feeds upon the other. So, in logical terms, norm integration or authority integration, appear to constitute sufficient conditions for countering fragmentation in international law. That is, it may not be necessary to integrate both norms and authority; the integration of one has a tempering effect on the fragmentation of the other.

A specific example should prove illuminating in this regard. Think, for instance, about the *Swordfish* dispute between the European Union (EU) and Chile.[29] Chile had taken conservation measures with respect to swordfish fishing in the South Pacific, with which the EU declined to comply. The EU initiated dispute settlement proceedings at the WTO, arguing that measures taken by Chile to enforce its conservation regime violated Articles V and XI of the GATT 1947—two clauses relating to the commercial movement of goods, either in transit, or in access to the local

[27] The opposite is also possible: effecting a normative change that will promote authority integration, eg, changing the status of investors so that they are treated as third-party beneficiaries to investment treaties rather than owners of derivative rights, allowing greater co-ordination between competing tribunals; see AK Bjorklund, 'Private Rights and Public International Law: Why Competition Among International Economic Tribunals is Not Working' 59 *Hastings Law Journal* (2008, forthcoming).

[28] See E-U Petersmann, *The GATT/WTO Dispute Settlement System: International Law, International Organizations and Dispute Settlement* (The Hague, Martinus Nijhoff, 1997) 271–84.

[29] See M Orellana, 'The EU and Chile Suspend the Swordfish Case Proceedings at the WTO and the International Tribunal of the Law of the Sea' *ASIL Insights*, February 2001, available at http://www.asil.org/insights/insigh60.htm; M Orellana, 'The Swordfish Dispute between the EU and Chile at the ITLOS and the WTO' (2002) 71 *Nordic Journal of International Law* 55.

Chilean market.[30] Since the Chilean measures in question were conservation measures, had a dispute been litigated at the WTO, it would have additionally raised the question of the applicability of the general exception relating to 'exhaustible natural resources' in Article XX(g) GATT, and perhaps the applicability of other exceptions.[31] In parallel, Chile charged the EU with violations of the UN Convention on the Law of the Sea (UNCLOS) before a chamber of the International Tribunal for the Law of the Sea (ITLOS). Chile argued that the EU had violated conservation-related obligations under Articles 64 and 116–9 UNCLOS, and also dispute settlement obligations under Articles 297 and 300 UNCLOS. The EU countercharged that Chile had itself violated these (and other) UNCLOS provisions by unilaterally applying its conservation regime.

This dispute was ultimately settled by mutual arrangement between the EU and Chile.[32] Moreover, was the way it developed an outcome or expression of fragmented authority or fragmented norms? Clearly, it was a bit of both: WTO versus ITLOS, as well as GATT versus UNCLOS. But consider this perspective: the parallel invocation of the jurisdiction of two international tribunals over disputes derived from what was essentially the same set of facts was troubling not because of the institutional idiosyncrasies of the different tribunals, but rather mainly because the *law* that would have been applied by each tribunal was substantively different. Whereas the WTO would have tended to apply GATT rules, ITLOS would have applied UNCLOS provisions. Counterfactually, if GATT and UNCLOS rules had been fully integrated, equally applicable in both tribunals and subject to the same conflict rules, a WTO Panel and an ITLOS chamber should have reached substantially the same decisions, subject to reasonable differences of opinion and interpretation among decision-makers. These differences would then be akin to the regular 'fragmentation' that arises when different national courts or benches of the same national court with different personal composition adjudicate cases in which similar questions arise. On the national level, such instances of fragmentation are often overcome by the intervention of a supreme judicial authority, an institutional harmoniser in the form of a

[30] See WTO, WT/DS193/1, G/L/367 *Chile—Measures Affecting the Transit and Importation of Swordfish—Request for Consultations by the EC*, 26 April 2000.

[31] Art XX(b) ('necessary to protect human, animal and plant life') or Art XX(d) ('necessary to secure compliance with laws and regulations which are not inconsistent with the provisions of this Agreement') might also have applied.

[32] Both WTO and ITLOS proceedings were not, however, terminated, but have been continuously suspended through agreement of the parties (see WTO, WT/DS193/3, *Chile—Measures Affecting the Transit and Importation of Swordfish—Arrangement between the EC and Chile—Communication from the EC*, 6 April 2001) and the approval of the Special Chamber of the ITLOS (see, most recently, ITLOS, Case No 7, *Case Concerning the Conservation and Sustainable Exploitation of Swordfish Stocks in the South-Eastern Pacific Ocean (Chile/European Community)*, Order 2007/3, 30 November, 2007). In both tribunals, complaining parties have reserved the right to revive the proceedings at any time.

'high' court that has the final integrating word. But in the *Swordfish* case, the starting point was an uncertain, unintegrated relationship between GATT obligations, on one hand, and UNCLOS obligations, on the other. Also, there was no unified judicial decision-maker for both trade and law of the sea disputes, no international *supreme* court of international justice with jurisdiction over the disputes, and in the alternative, no agreed rules on the choice of forum. Thus, the diversity of norms accentuated the problem of fragmented authority, and the existence of parallel authority exacerbated the problem of non-integrated substantive norms. Integration of either sort, of norms or of authority, would have eliminated the awkwardness of the *Swordfish* case.

The authority–norm fragmentation correlation is quite clear in dispute settlement issues that involve both jurisdictional competition and fragmented norms, but it manifests itself in international law-making as well. Lawrence Helfer has assiduously explored the idea of 'regime shifting',[33] which is relevant in the present context. The fragmentation of international law-making authority in issues that even peripherally relate to international intellectual property rights has resulted in a fragmented spectrum of international norms on the subject, permitting interest groups and states to pursue what is essentially a form of legislative 'forum shopping': if their goals are not met by the norms produced in one forum such as the WTO, they seek them elsewhere, in other international fora. Had law-making authority been institutionally integrated, regime shifting would have been neither attractive nor indeed possible to those who would pursue it, and fragmented norms would not have arisen. Conversely, had norm integration been the standard, there would be little point in taking advantage of authority fragmentation through attempts at regime shifting in law-making, whose results would ultimately be integrated in substance. Consider also the interplay between multilateral and regional systems of trade regulation. The stalling of the Doha Round of multilateral negotiations at the WTO has been viewed by some as one of main reasons for the proliferation of parallel regional and bilateral agreements that enable trading parties to achieve their negotiating goals on a differential and fragmented basis.[34] Dispute settlement in trade agreements is currently fragmented, with each agreement establishing its own dispute settlement arrangement. Hypothetically, however, had the settlement of trade disputes been institutionally integrated so that disputes based upon either regional agreements or the WTO would be ultimately settled by the same dispute settlement mechanism, perhaps

[33] See LR Helfer, 'Regime Shifting: The TRIPS Agreement and New Dynamics of International Intellectual Property Lawmaking' (2004) 29 *Yale Journal of International Law* 26.

[34] See, eg, RV Fiorentino, L Verdeja and C Toqueboeuf, *The Changing Landscape of Regional Trade Agreements: 2006 Update*, WTO Discussion Paper No 12 (2007), available at http://www.wto.org/english/res_e/booksp_e/discussion_papers12a_e.pdf, at 1.

the attraction of multilateral/regional norm fragmentation would be reduced.

There is, therefore, a basic general correlation between norm fragmentation and authority fragmentation, between norm integration and authority integration. The decrease or increase of one results in a corresponding effect in the other. I will now focus on one vector of this correlation: the way normative integration can effectively act as a catalyst for authority integration.

IV. NORMATIVE INTEGRATION AS INDIRECT AUTHORITY INTEGRATION: LAW'S EFFECTS ON INTER-INSTITUTIONAL POLITICS

That on the descriptive, almost mechanical, level there exists a basic correlation between norm fragmentation and authority fragmentation is not, I believe, an overly controversial proposition. Although the second type of connection between the two expressions of fragmentation, which I address here, can be derived from the first, it is less obvious and has more nuanced political implications.

Stated abstractly, my second claim is as follows: if in a fragmented system of law, as international law surely is, the integration of norms generally results in a correlative reduction in the fragmentation of authority (or at least a reduction in its significance), then the quest for normative integration is by default associated with a drive for a more integrated authority. Viewed this way, legal principles of normative integration are not merely technical, lawyerly methods for producing consistent legal outcomes. They have a political meaning for the entire international system's structure of authority and governance. Their result (if not their goal) is not only normative coherence and regularity, but also a trend towards greater centralisation and/or harmonisation of authority. It would be unnecessarily tenuous to delimit and dichotomise norms and authority as legal 'outputs' or 'inputs', respectively (or otherwise), since there is a virtuous (or vicious) circle between them. However, there is certainly an interaction between norms and authority that makes it difficult, if not impossible, to integrate one without simultaneously influencing the integration of the other.

This claim can be illustrated and refined, if instead of a systemic viewpoint we adopt the perspective of an international decision-maker (for various reasons[35] it is convenient to think first of a judicial decision-

[35] Not least among these are the impartiality and independence expected of international judicial decision-makers. Rules of ethical judicial conduct, written (eg, Art 2(3), WTO, WT/AB/WP/5 *Working Procedures for Appellate Review*, 4 January 2005) and unwritten, require international judges to ignore personal interests as well as the interests of their home

maker, but the same logic should apply to other forms of authority in international law) faced with a broad range of fragmented international norms that might inform its decision. As a working example, let us return to the pre-suspension *Swordfish* dispute.[36] In a counterfactual fully integrated legal system (both normatively and institutionally), a single, central tribunal would have full authority to consider all relevant claims, defences and counterclaims on the basis of all valid normative sources. The relationship between GATT/WTO market access and transit rules, on one hand, with UNCLOS rules on conservation measures, on the other hand, would then have to be examined under both general conflict rules (eg, *lex specialis*) and particular ones (eg, the provisions of Article XX GATT).[37] The situation of a decision-making body established under a certain section of a fragmented legal system—namely, in this case, a hypothetical WTO panel—would be, however, quite different. Normative integration would not necessarily be taken for granted, if only because its jurisdiction were specific, not general. The panel would need to consider the question of integrating UNCLOS rules on conservation measures into its GATT/WTO-focused normative deliberation. Crucially, such a panel would have to be sensitive not only to the (not inconsiderable) questions of *normative* integration, but also to the dynamic ramifications of its findings in this respect for *authority* integration. These fall under the following consecutive headings.

First, *to integrate the norms of another system is to acknowledge the authority of that system to produce pertinent norms*. As a question of norm integration, a panel in the *Swordfish* dispute would have to consider whether rules derived from outside its normative sub-system may apply,

state. To the extent that this is complied with, this should allow us to focus on the interpretation of the law as influenced by inter-institutional considerations, and neutralise some of the international and national political considerations that otherwise affect decision making in non-judicial institutions. On impartiality in international tribunals see EA Posner and M de Figueiredo, 'Is the International Court of Justice Biased?' (2005) 34 *Journal of Legal Affairs* 599; EA Posner and JC Yoo, 'Judicial Independence in International Tribunals' (2004) 93 *California Law Review* 37 (suggesting that ICJ judges are nationally biased on the basis of empirical research); and *contra*, E Voeten, 'What Motivates International Judges: Evidence from the European Court of Human Rights', available at http://papers.ssrn.com/sol3/papers.cfm?abstract_id=705363 (suggesting that the impartiality of international depends upon the legal culture of their home state; counterintuitively, judges from countries with low levels of domestic judicial independence tend to find against their own state's positions more often).

[36] See text accompanying n 29 *et seq*. I deliberately wish to address a case in which the problems discussed did not reach actual judicial determination, as well as one that displays both forms of fragmentation.

[37] This is in fact the situation that would exist if the case had been brought to a tribunal of general jurisdiction, such as the ICJ. Proponents of full norm integration in international law, such as Pauwelyn, above n 5, and the ILC Study Group Report, above n 1, would argue in accordance with a generally formal normative perspective that the same situation should apply in tribunals of specific jurisdiction, ie, both in the WTO dispute settlement system and in the Special Chamber of the ITLOS.

or perhaps must apply, in the case at hand, before even debating the possible relationships between the different applicable rules. Otherwise they would simply be irrelevant to its work. The formal integration of disparate rules into a normative decision-making process requires an at least minimal acknowledgement of the normative force of each such rule. So the normative integration of UNCLOS provisions with those of the GATT/WTO would require a finding by a WTO panel, implicit or explicit, that UNCLOS norms are valid, binding and with legal effect in the WTO, even if possibly subordinate to WTO rules when their interrelationship were to be subsequently examined. In a shift from questions of normative integration to questions of authority, however, such a finding would in itself suggest recognition by a WTO body of the authority of a non-WTO international law-making collective—the states parties to the UNCLOS (whose membership does not fully overlap with the membership of the WTO)—to produce norms that influence decisions taken in the WTO. This would be even more obviously the case if the integration of UNCLOS norms included, for example, reference to interpretations of UNCLOS by the ITLOS or other tribunals. In any event, the significant point here is that the recognition of norms implies recognition of authority.

Second, *to integrate the norms of another system is to assert authority over them*. Formal integration of UNCLOS rules into the WTO adjudicative process of a case would necessarily imply that the WTO dispute settlement system possesses judicial authority to apply UNCLOS rules and disputes.[38] Thus, the question of normative integration is in fact, if indirectly, one that is determinative of the boundaries of the WTO's authority. At this stage I refer to the determination by the panel, as an international decision-making body, of the scope of its own authority looked at from within its jurisdiction as an autonomous matter, *irrespective* of its relationship with other authorities. The important issue here is that the integration of norms becomes a statement of positive authority. To press the point, even had the parties to the *Swordfish* dispute expressly agreed among themselves to settle their UNCLOS differences in the WTO (a scenario that would indeed be possible under UNCLOS rules),[39] thus entirely setting aside the problem of competing or conflicting jurisdiction, the panel would still have to consider whether it at all had the competence to entertain such an agreement in the first place, which would entail subjecting UNCLOS provisions to WTO authority. In the WTO, such a

[38] I deliberately eschew the term 'jurisdiction' here: this would be a question of applicable law, not jurisdiction (the latter meaning the authority to adjudicate actions brought under non-WTO law).

[39] Art 280 UNCLOS states that 'Nothing in this Part [Part XV UNLOS—Settlement of Disputes] impairs the right of any States Parties to agree at any time to settle a dispute between them concerning the interpretation or application of this Convention by any peaceful means of their own choice'; see also Arts 281–2 UNCLOS.

question would relate to the interpretation of various articles in the WTO DSU that suggest that panels and the Appellate Body may apply only provisions of the WTO 'Covered Agreements', eg, Articles 1:1, 3:2, 7:1 and 7:2 DSU. This formal question is a key element in the debate over normative integration in the WTO.[40] I do not wish to revisit this debate here, but only to point out that while it focuses on normative integration, at the same time it distinctly affects the autonomous delimitation of authority.

Third, *to integrate the norms of another system is to introduce the problems of overlapping authority*. The integration of UNCLOS norms and the statement of panel authority that comes with it would inevitably lead to an overlap between WTO authority and ITLOS jurisdiction. As noted in the previous section, the *Swordfish* dispute was a case of both norm fragmentation and authority fragmentation. The crucial point for present purposes, however, is that it would be the integration of norms (the acceptance of UNCLOS rules on conservation measures as valid in the WTO) that would perfect the competition of authority between the WTO and ITLOS. If the applicability of UNCLOS rules in the WTO were denied by the panel, both norm fragmentation and authority fragmentation would be maintained. If applicability were accepted, however, the two tribunals would be applying the same law.

Fourth, *problems of overlapping authority agitate towards authority-integrating solutions*. In the circumstances described here, the panel would have to consider its inter-institutional relationship with the ITLOS chamber. Having integrated the norms of UNCLOS, and thereby accepted the authority of UNCLOS rule-making processes, the panel would be pressed to act in ways that reduce inter-institutional tension. The result would, in a number of scenarios, be authority-integrating or at least fragmentation-mitigating. The panel might decide to defer, formally or in practice, to the ITLOS; or await a signal of deference from the ITLOS. The commonality of legal sources applied, if the path of norm integration were followed, would probably lead, as argued above, to a convergence of decisions in any case, reducing the risks of fragmentation. To be sure, this would not always be the result. Conflicting decisions and interpretations might arise. However, the pressure would be to reach authority-integrating solutions.

Importantly, this pressure would have been lower if the norms had not been integrated; although the facts of the WTO dispute would essentially be the same as the one in ITLOS, the law applied would be different and

40 Compare Trachtman, above n 21, 342–3; and J Pauwelyn, 'The Role of Public International Law in the WTO: How Far Can We Go?' (2001) 95 *American Journal of International Law* 535, 541; and also JP Trachtman, 'Book Review: 'Conflict of Norms in Public International Law: How WTO Law Relates to Other Rules of International Law' by Joost Pauwelyn' (2004) 98 *American Journal of International Law* 855.

each tribunal would be free to act within its own 'territory' of authority. This can be thought of as a result that relates to decision-making legitimacy. In the non-integrated norms scenario, it is legitimate for each tribunal to apply the rules of its own system to the facts of the case, even if the results of each dispute are inconsistent in practice, eg, a WTO finding that Chile had violated GATT, versus an ITLOS decision that the EC had violated its UNCLOS obligations. If the same law is applied, however, the burden of legitimating inconsistent decisions is much higher.[41] Put simply, when the law is the same, conflicting rulings necessarily mean that one of the tribunals has made a mistaken decision.

Note that these observations accumulate into a dialectic situation: the decision to integrate 'external' norms with those of one's 'own' system simultaneously entails a recognition of the authority of the other (an integrative element) *and* an assertion of one's own authority (a potentially fragmenting element), leading to authority parallelism (a problem of fragmentation) that must ultimately be resolved through authority integrating means.

The combined result is that the decision to integrate norms leads to an integration of authority. One might even say that it leads to a sharing of authority, which in some cases is tantamount to a loss of authority (eg, if the path of deference is followed). As will be discussed in the next section, international decision-making bodies (and again the focus will be mainly on tribunals, although similar considerations apply to other international organs and institutions) who are sensitive to the maintenance and preservation of their authority may be deterred from integrating norms, leading to the continued state of both norm and authority fragmentation.

V. AUTHORITY INTEGRATION AS A DETERRENT OF NORMATIVE INTEGRATION

I have postulated that international decision-makers may be deterred from pursuing normative integration, despite its juridical value in terms of systemic coherence and consistency, because it necessarily requires complex authority-integrating solutions, some of which may even bring

[41] As an example, consider the efforts made by Chief Justice Aharon Barak of the Israeli Supreme Court in HCJ 7957/04 *Mara'abe v Prime Minister of Israel* (Judgment) 15 September 2005, to legitimate the Supreme Court's findings with respect to the legality of the separation barrier, because they were different from those of the ICJ in *Legal Consequences of the Construction of a Wall in the Occupied Palestinian Territory*, Advisory Opinion (2004) 43 ILM 1009 (9 July 2004). Barak's main contention is that although the law applied by both tribunals is essentially the same, the Israeli court's access to facts and ability to analyse them in detail is superior. See also Y Shany, 'Capacities and Inadequacies: A Look at the Two Separation Barrier Cases' (2005) 38 *Israel Law Review* 230.

about a loss of authority. The discussion of a few examples—not comprehensive, but indicative—demonstrates that this is not merely a theoretical conclusion. The most instructive, in this regard, is the *Mexico—Soft Drinks* dispute.[42]

In *Mexico—Soft Drinks*, the relationship between the WTO and regional trade agreements (as non-WTO rules) arose acutely, in terms of both authority and norms. *Mexico—Soft Drinks* was a complaint by the United States against a discriminatory taxation scheme imposed by Mexico. In its defence, Mexico as respondent had first requested that the WTO dispute settlement system decline to exercise jurisdiction over the dispute in favour of an Arbitral Panel under Chapter 20 of the North American Free Trade Agreement (NAFTA).[43] In the terms of this article this was, most overtly, an authority-integrating proposition, a jurisdictional question in which a party proposed deference to NAFTA tribunal jurisdiction while suspending that of the WTO's—truly a political 'hot potato' for the WTO Appellate Body (AB) to handle.

Mexico's second important argument on appeal was that the measures complained against were justified under the general exception in Article XX(d) GATT, which excuses (under the terms of the *chapeau* of Article XX GATT) measures 'necessary to secure compliance with laws or regulations which are not inconsistent' with the GATT. This exception applied, according to Mexico, because its taxation measures were taken in order to secure compliance by the US with its obligations under the NAFTA. This second argument was, in the parlance of Article XX, quite simply a bold norm-integrating one, asking the WTO to consider the rules of the NAFTA, not on the basis of a general principle of integration, but on that of a GATT-specific exception.

Thus, *Mexico—Soft Drinks* involved both norm-integrating and authority-integrating claims. Now, had the dispute been adjudicated in a counterfactual system of integrated authority, it would have been purely a case of norm integration, and arguably the integration of WTO and NAFTA norms would not have been especially difficult. That is, the challenges of authority integration and norm integration were (at least technically) severable. In the case itself, the AB could have conceivably declined Mexico's authority-integrating, jurisdictional request (ie, no deference to the NAFTA process),[44] and still have accepted Mexico's norm-integrating article XX(d) GATT claim (ie, allow measures taken specifically under NAFTA to override GATT obligations), and vice versa.

[42] See WTO, WT/DS308/AB/R, *Mexico—Tax Measures on Soft Drinks and Other Beverages* (Appellate Body Report) 6 March 2006.

[43] *Ibid*, 15. The reasons for Mexico's request, involving a complaint by Mexico against the US through NAFTA channels (including the fact that a Chapter 20 tribunal had not been established in fact), are briefly noted by the WTO Appellate Body, *ibid*, 22, n 106.

[44] A separate substantive question I will not deal with here is whether the AB *should* have accepted Mexico's jurisdictional argument.

Yet ultimately, the AB rejected both of Mexico's claims, jurisdictional and substantive. Surely there are many possible legal bases for this result, but it is the AB's reasoning that is illuminating here, because it emphasises both the norm–authority integration linkage, and the way a tribunal might avoid norm integration because of its disdain of authority integration.

In terms of authority, the AB upheld the general *Kompetenz–Kompetenz* of WTO panels, the overall right of an (indeed, of any) international judicial body to determine the scope of its own authority,[45] a finding that ostensibly left the field open to siding with Mexico's request for authority-integration and inter-institutional consideration. However, in its reasoning the AB did not examine the policy considerations[46] or even the textual imperatives[47] that might inform its decision regarding the scope of its own competence, but instead soon turned to a discourse of norms, not authority, relying on previous WTO jurisprudence[48] in order to find that a panel's discretion to determine its own authority could not in itself modify the rules, rights and obligations contained in the WTO's 'covered agreements'. This was an explicit example of the norm–authority linkage, under which the AB found that the impermeability of WTO norms (a counter-integrative normative force) overrode the request by Mexico to decline WTO jurisdiction (a pro-integrating force). It was the AB's reluctance to face the far-reaching political implications of authority integration within its discretion—including both an *assertion* of authority over regional trade agreements and also a discretionary, comity-based *surrender* of authority to a NAFTA tribunal, well in accordance with the dialectics noted in the previous sections—that led it to harden the normative segregation of WTO norms, as a justifying factor for the limitation of its own discretion.

To be sure, there is an optical judicial illusion involved in this part of the *Mexico—Soft Drinks* AB Report. It might appear that the cause of the decision to reject authority integration was norm fragmentation (the incapacity to modify WTO rules, etc), but it is actually the AB's reluctance to partake of authority integration—that was self-admittedly within the discretion of the AB—that caused it to rely on the fragmentation of norms

[45] WTO Appellate Body, above n 42, 18: 'Notably, panels have the right to determine whether they have jurisdiction in a given case, as well as to determine the scope of their jurisdiction.'

[46] This is not, in itself, very surprising. The WTO dispute settlement system is notorious for its textual, even decontextualised interpretations. See F Ortino, 'Treaty Interpretation and the WTO Appellate Body Report in *US—Gambling*: A Critique' (2006) 9 *Journal of International Economic Law* 117; and T Broude, 'Genetically Modified Rules: The Awkward Rule–Exception–Right Distinction in *EC—Biotech*' (2007) *World Trade Review* 6, 215.

[47] Eg, Art XXIV GATT relating to regional trade agreements and their substantive relationship with the other rules of the GATT.

[48] WTO, WT/DS50/AB/R, *India—Patent Protection for Pharmaceutical and Agricultural Chemical Products* (Appellate Body Report), adopted 16 January 1998, para 92.

as the basis for its decision. In any case, the AB's logic appears tautological, even vacuous, when read in the present context. Surely *any* decision by a tribunal not to exercise authority might result in a modification of the rights of parties, even in a diminishment thereof?[49] In the AB's reading, any tribunal's *Kompetenz–Kompetenz* (as a matter of authority) is empty, because it is ultimately limited by the bounds of parties' (segregated) rights.

In considering Mexico's request to decline jurisdiction, the AB further noted that Mexico 'could not identify a legal basis that would allow it to raise, in a WTO dispute settlement proceeding, the market access claims it is pursuing under the NAFTA'.[50] Was this a problem of norm integration or of authority integration? Taken together, it was an expression of the WTO's splendid normative isolation—the AB essentially asking what its authority was to consider these 'other' norms, after it had already consolidated its authority to determine its own authority, and although the substantive relationship between the NAFTA and the WTO was not problematic in itself. This, again, is an optical illusion, the minor, legalistic *problematique* of norm-integration overtaken by the jurisdictional problem so subdued in the phrases 'legal basis' and 'in a WTO dispute settlement proceeding'. For present purposes, what is important is that the real problem of inter-jurisdictional relations is scantily clad in the clothing of normative conflict. The substantive, normative gap between WTO and NAFTA claims, however small, was relied upon as a basis for the AB's unwillingness to accommodate authority-integration in the form of deference to NAFTA jurisdiction.

The AB also discounted Mexico's claims regarding jurisdiction as such that would 'imply that the WTO dispute settlement system could be used to determine rights and obligations outside the covered agreements'.[51] This is a key sentence in the AB's logic, perhaps the clearest expression of this chapter's thesis. The AB fundamentally deflected the very idea of integrating NAFTA rules with those of the WTO by voicing abhorrence towards the possibility that it would then have to exercise its jurisdiction over NAFTA rules. It declined the application—read integration—of non-WTO norms because this would have implied jurisdiction over them, creating the problem of overlapping authority with NAFTA, agitating towards authority integration. These were problems the WTO AB did not wish to deal with; it was far easier to exclude them by relying on a limited normative basis—the 'covered agreements'.

[49] Consider, for example, the normative impact of ICJ jurisdictional decisions—a considerable part of ICJ jurisprudence. Should it not be said that they impart upon parties' rights? This would seem self-evident, but see T Broude, 'The Legitimacy of the ICJ's Advisory Competence in the Shadow of the *Wall*' (2005) 38 *Israel Law Review* 189 and sources cited therein.

[50] *Mexico—Soft Drinks*, above n 42, para 54.

[51] *Ibid*, para 56.

With respect to Mexico's other major claim, that its measures were necessary to enforce NAFTA obligations, the AB made two additional findings. First, NAFTA obligations were not 'laws and regulations' within the meaning of Article XX(d) GATT because they were not part of the domestic legal order;[52] and second, even if this were not the case, the AB 'would have to assess whether the relevant international agreement [NAFTA] has been violated' in order to examine the applicability of Article XX(d), and 'this is not the function of panels and the Appellate Body as intended by the DSU'.[53] Thus, the AB deflected Mexico's second norm-integrating claim in terms of both normative fragmentation (ie, NAFTA rules are not domestic) and authority fragmentation (ie, the WTO dispute settlement system cannot judge NAFTA compliance). The AB was deterred from norm integration because it would require an institutional integration it could not risk.

The *Mexico—Soft Drinks* case shows not only that normative and authority integration are intertwined, but also that norm-integrating decisions (such as the prospect of examining NAFTA norms in the context of the WTO) might be scuttled due to authority-fragmenting considerations (such as the rejection of international rules as 'laws and regulations' whose enforceability might be of interest in the WTO).

Overall, the *Mexico—Soft Drinks* case is an exceptionally vivid instance with respect to concurrent authority and norm integration concerns. These do appear, however, in other contexts as well.

Inter-institutional reflexity in international law is evidently such that parties involved in cases in which norm integration is a sensitive issue simply refrain from authority-integrating claims. This is apparent, *sotto voce*, in the *Mexico—Soft Drinks* case: Mexico was very careful not to argue that the WTO did not hold any jurisdiction over the case,[54] arguing instead that jurisdiction should be declined. Returning to the *Swordfish* case, this is apparent as well. Chile's UNCLOS request made no explicit reference to the WTO;[55] and the EC's requests to the WTO made no reference to the ITLOS.[56] In this perhaps most explicit case of combined

[52] *Ibid*, para 69ff.

[53] See *Ibid*, para 78.

[54] Mexico did not question that the Panel has jurisdiction to hear the United States' claims. *Ibid*, para. 44.

[55] See ITLOS, Case No 7, *Case Concerning the Conservation and Sustainable Exploitation of Swordfish Stocks in the South-Eastern Pacific Ocean (Chile/European Community—Constitution of Chamber)*, 20 December 2000); the WTO was not mentioned, but Chile trod very lightly in its assertion that the EC had 'challenged the sovereign right and duty of Chile, as a coastal State, to prescribe measures within its national jurisdiction for the conservation of swordfish and to ensure their implementation in its ports, in a non-discriminatory manner, as well as the measures themselves, and whether such challenge would be compatible with the Convention.' This wording might refer to the EC's unilateral acts, but also to its complaint in the WTO.

[56] See above n 30.

authority/norm fragmentation, it would have done no good to either party to cite at so early a stage in the process that inter-institutional problems were involved. Indeed, it is perhaps the case that this dispute reached settlement because of its authority-fragmentation implications.

From another example, not from the WTO field—the *Lauder* investment cases[57]—it is also evident that international tribunals opt for technical, norm-fragmenting techniques (such as strict interpretations of the 'same proceedings' requirement)[58] in order to avoid authority integration: had the investment tribunals involved considered the cases before them as same proceedings, they would also have had to confront their concurrent jurisdiction.

Finally, the same phenomenon—the norm–authority integration correlation and a reluctance to integrate norms because of authority-integrating implications—can be found in the interaction between political decision-making fora (ie, international norm-making actors that do not serve as dispute settlement actors and have a more legislative role). In the Kimberley process mentioned above,[59] it is perhaps not coincidental that the relevant UN Kimberley Resolutions made no operative reference to the possible need for a WTO waiver; and, conversely, that the WTO waiver made no operative reference to UN authority, only mentioning in preambulary form the prior existence of the UN Resolutions, as semi-historical context but not as a normatively influencing element.

VI. CONCLUSIONS: WHICH NORMATIVE INTEGRATION?

I return now to the first questions asked in the introduction above. Why (rather than how) would one argue with the conclusions of the ILC Study Group and claim that international norms should not be integrated? I suggest that reluctance to accept normative integration, or rather the resistance to accept binding normative integration, is the result of the structure of international law, in which substantive norms forms the warp on which the allocation of authority is woven. One cannot pull at any of the threads of the warp without unravelling some of the weft. To integrate norms necessarily has implications for the authority of allocation, and so it may be resisted by any institution that prefers the status quo.

However, while this may serve as a general rule, there are exceptions and modifications to be explored. Different principles and methods of norm integration may have different degrees of effects on authority. Their

57 See above n 24.

58 See Shany, above n 24.

59 See text accompanying n 16 above.

political and institutional implications may be weaker, making it possible to pursue normative integration without integrating authority. It is the challenge of the master weaver to find those methods of integration that will be least intrusive and least threatening to authority as it is freely structured in international law.

On this background, it is worth considering that the application of the method of normative integration most strongly advocated by the ILC Study Group Report and by others, Article 31(3)(c) VCLT,[60] has been (controversially) reduced to almost meaninglessness by a WTO dispute panel interpreting it as applying only to non-WTO treaties to which all WTO members are party.[61] This can be explained by the system's fear of authority sharing, as can a string of other interpretations pursued by panels and the AB that insulate, if not isolate, the WTO from the full legal force of non-WTO norms. And yet, at the same time, the WTO AB has displayed considerable de facto willingness to pursue substantive integration that recalls the loose, even fluid structure of the Principle of Integration in paragraph 4 of the Rio Declaration, [62] most notably in the *US—Shrimp* cases.[63] This is neither contradiction nor coincidence:[64] the path of normative integration is easier to follow when it is chosen by decision-makers, not forced upon them, and so does not lead to a threatening integration of authority.

60 See above n 19.

61 See WTO, WT/DS291/R, WT/DS292/R, WT/DS293/R *EC—Measures Affecting the Approval and Marketing of Biotech Products*, Panel Report, 29 September 2006, at paras 7.67–7.71.

62 See T Broude, 'Elements of the Principle of Integration in WTO Jurisprudence: Another Look at the Shrimp Cases' in ILA Report, above n 20.

63 See WTO, WT/DS58/AB/R *US—Import Prohibition of Certain Shrimp and Shrimp Products*, Appellate Body Report, 6 November 1998.

64 For a detailed analysis of WTO AB decisions as essentially integrative, highly critical of the interpretation of Art 31(3) VCLT by the *Biotech* panel, see R Howse, 'The Use and Abuse of "Other Relevant Rules of International Law" in Treaty Interpretation: Insights from WTO Trade/Environment Litigation' Institute for International Law and Justice, NYU School of Law, Working Paper 2007/1, available at http://www.iilj.org/working%20papers/documents/2007-1.Howse.web.pdf.

II
International Authority and the State

6

State Sovereignty, International Legality and Moral Disagreement

BRAD R ROTH*

I. INTRODUCTION

REALLOCATIONS OF AUTHORITY from the domestic to the international level are a natural preoccupation of international legal scholarship. These reallocations, increasingly prominent though they are, should not lead scholars to neglect an important aspect of international law's mission: to protect an inner core of state authority against external encroachments. Although sometimes cast as the antithesis of international legality, the principle of state sovereignty remains deeply embedded within international legal doctrine, in ways that, though surely controvertible, are substantially defensible as a matter of political morality. This essay will first outline, and will then seek in some respects to justify, sovereignty's contemporary role within the project of international legality.

The foundational principle of the international legal order is the 'sovereign equality' of states. 'Sovereignty' in this sense refers, not to authority altogether beyond the reach of law, but to the reciprocal terms of the recognition that the members of an international legal order confer on one another.[1] Although the predication of international order on

* Associate Professor of Political Science and Law, Wayne State University. JD, Harvard University, 1987; LLM, Columbia University, 1992; PhD, University of California, Berkeley, 1996. The author wishes to thank Yuval Shany, Tomer Broude, Stephen Macedo, James Chalmers, Daniel Bodansky, Peter Spiro, and especially Jamie Mayerfeld for their helpful comments and criticisms.

[1] Much confusion arises from the use of the term 'sovereignty' to refer, not merely to different conceptions, but to wholly different concepts, pertinent to different conversations. I have elsewhere distinguished the international-juridical sense of sovereignty (the terms of the reciprocal recognition that states accord one another in the international order) from the domestic-juridical sense (the ultimate source of authority within a particular domestic legal regime), the empirical political science sense (the effective capacity to exercise unilateral

respect for the sovereignty of each member entity is traceable to the 1648 Peace of Westphalia—a point frequently highlighted by those seeking to portray the notion as outmoded—the legal implications of this sovereignty have varied markedly from era to era.

The current understanding of sovereign equality is owing in part to the 1945 United Nations Charter, which exalts the concept,[2] but even more to the geopolitical realities of the period from the late 1950s to the late 1980s. As Western and Socialist blocs turned from open confrontation to espousal of 'containment' and 'peaceful coexistence' (respectively), and as a Non-Aligned bloc emerged from decolonisation to assert distinctive interests and values in the name of a 'Third World', the United Nations system became a platform for accommodation among international actors who recognised few common principles of legitimate and just internal public order. The resulting normative formula, stressing non-intervention in the internal affairs of states, achieved its most authoritative expression in the General Assembly's 1970 statement of legal principles known as the Friendly Relations Declaration.[3]

Sovereign equality, so understood, has all the while drawn moral and political criticism from nearly every quarter—from liberal cosmopolitans, from conservative realists, from neoconservative unilateralists, and from advocates for groups marginalised by the international system. The changed material and ideational conditions of the early twenty-first century have further called into question the continued viability of sovereign equality as the foundational principle of the international legal order. Long-term structural changes inevitably will—and indeed, should—result in modifications to normative constructs developed in a bygone era.

Nonetheless, calls for sweeping reform need to confront an accurate unifying account, and a properly qualified moral and political defence, of the existing legal framework. It is by no means clear that the core elements of that pluralistic framework are outmoded or dysfunctional. The foundations of the United Nations system reflect persistent, albeit bounded, disagreement within its membership as to fundamental principles of political morality. While the boundaries of the system's pluralism have narrowed progressively in the course of the United Nations era—excluding conquest and genocide from the outset, colonialism and apartheid in the 1960s and 1970s, and 'ethnic cleansing' and

control over a field of activity, or to set policies unilaterally in a particular field of activity), and the policy sense (a supposed imperative to maintain or reassert unilateral control over a field of activity). BR Roth, 'The Enduring Significance of State Sovereignty' (2004) 56 *Florida Law Review* 1017, 1018–23.

[2] UN Charter, Art 2(1).

[3] Declaration on Principles of International Law Concerning Friendly Relations and Co-operation Among States in Accordance with the Charter of the United Nations (hereafter 'Friendly Relations Declaration'), UNGA Res 2625 (XXV) (24 October 1970).

peculiarly unpopular and violent seizures of state power in the 1990s—accommodation of diversity in modes of internal political organisation remains a durable theme of the international order. This accommodation of diversity underlies the international system's commitment to preserve states' territorial integrity and political independence, often at the expense of other values.

The persistence of sovereign prerogative within international legal doctrine is especially unpopular with certain human rights-oriented scholars—advocates for expansive assertions of *jus cogens*, universal jurisdiction and humanitarian intervention—for whom international legality represents the promise of a global justice that transcends territorial limitations as well as political, ideological and cultural differences. Yet one can posit, *contra* this 'transcendent justice' approach, a more modest project of international legality, based on a recognition that fundamental disagreement about principles of just public order constitutes, at least for the time being, an ineradicable aspect of the human condition. An alternative jurisprudence of 'bounded pluralism' may vindicate the essence of the currently prevalent doctrinal structure, even if not each and every victory of state prerogative.[4] Moreover, because international obligations on matters of internal public order and international strictures on (even righteous) cross-border exercises of power operate on separate legal planes, one can concede the inviolability of illiberal systems of internal public order without withholding judgment on the duly incurred legal obligations—let alone the moral duties—that states owe to their own nationals.

Contemporary normative political theory has given little systematic attention to the distinctive problems of international legal order.[5] Theorists of human rights have typically sought to derive universally applicable standards of internal public order from first principles, without much regard to the implications for the international system of the empirical reality of conflicting political moralities.[6] Theorists of 'ethics

[4] Gerry Simpson has elaborated a similar contrast between 'Charter liberalism', as he (controvertibly) terms the pluralist vision associated with the Charter, and the 'liberal anti-pluralism' of a set of leading US-based international law scholars (ie, Thomas M Franck, Anne-Marie Slaughter, W Michael Reisman and Fernando Tesón). G Simpson, 'Two Liberalisms' (2001) 12 *European Journal of International Law* 537. For related defences of sovereign prerogative grounded in a qualified pluralism, see JL Cohen, 'Whose Sovereignty? Empire Versus International Law' (2004) 18 *Ethics & International Affairs* 1; B Kingsbury, 'Sovereignty and Inequality' (1998) 9 *European Journal of International Law* 599.

[5] Allen Buchanan's recent book, *Justice, Legitimacy and Self-Determination: Moral Foundations for International Law* (Oxford University Press, 2004), points out and seeks to remedy this deficit. Some other significant recent efforts to bring normative political theory to bear on the foundations of the international legal system include SR Ratner, 'Is International Law Impartial?' (2005) 11 *Legal Theory* 39; D Held, 'Law of States, Law of Peoples: Three Models of Sovereignty' (2002) 8 *Legal Theory* 1.

[6] Much literature has, of course, addressed the philosophical validity of the cultural relativist challenge to the assertion of universally applicable moral rights, but less has focused

and international affairs' have been more concerned to develop moral standards for a given state's external behaviour in discrete subject areas (eg, the criteria of 'just war')[7] than to formulate a legal framework for coexistence and co-operation among non-like-minded states. Even John Rawls's path-breaking late work on a liberal *ethos* of relations with non-liberal political communities did not purport to provide a blueprint for an international public order; whatever implications Rawls expected his 'law of peoples' to have for international law, he understood his enterprise as the development of moral rather than strictly legal standards, recognising that the latter would need to take account of practical considerations beyond the scope of his project.[8] It is one project to develop guidelines for unilateral action in the absence of a positive legal order, and quite another to prescribe reforms to the standards and processes that govern an existing (even if only partially efficacious) multilateral order, or to establish thresholds for unilateral ad hoc flouting of applicable positive norms that impede morally desirable action in particular instances.

The moral justification for a pluralist international order is frequently assumed to rest on a claim that human beings' very identities are shaped by the communities in which they are 'radically situated',[9] and that, consequently, political values can be assessed only within the framework of a given community's distinctive character and traditions. This claim, however, is not only highly questionable on its merits, but also a poor fit with the pluralism that the international system actually embodies. Moreover, cultural difference, so frequently discussed in this context, is neither a necessary nor sufficient condition for radically conflicting conceptions of legitimate and just public order. The relevant challenge is not, as Rawls imagined, the existence of inherently 'non-liberal peoples', but the existence of highly unfavourable social conditions that give rise to a multiplicity of plausible, but sharply clashing, political solutions. Harsh circumstances call forth harsh measures, frequently adopted (often mistakenly, to be sure) by informed persons of good faith and sound reason. A focus on the immutable rather than the contingent—on the collective past rather than on the present collective projects that call for

on evaluating institutional responses to the fact of moral discord. Important exceptions are Michael Walzer's brief defence of non-intervention doctrine in *Just and Unjust Wars* (New York, Basic Books, 1977) and his more elaborate response to critics of that defence, M Walzer, 'The Moral Standing of States' (1980) 9 *Philosophy & Public Affairs* 209.

[7] Walzer's *Just and Unjust Wars*, above n 6, is, of course, a classic in this respect.

[8] J Rawls, *The Law of Peoples* (Cambridge, MA, Harvard University Press, 1999).

[9] This notion reflects the most extreme version of the 'communitarian' approach to political morality, embraced in a moderate form by contemporary theorists such as Michael Sandel. See M Sandel, *Liberalism and the Limits of Justice* (Cambridge University Press, 1982), 144 (staking out a middle position on the extent to which one's community is 'constitutive' of the self).

distinctively political decisions—distorts the understanding of fundamental political disagreement and the consequent need for accommodation among such political entities as have adopted, for the time being, incompatible conceptions of public order.

Sovereign equality is an unromantic foundational principle, designed for an unromantic social reality. Its moral and pragmatic justifications are intertwined. The next section will summarise the unifying account of the principle's manifestations in international law.[10] Section III will defend the principle as a morally sound response to persistent and profound disagreement within the international community as to the requirements of legitimate and just internal public order.

II. SOVEREIGN EQUALITY IN THE INTERNATIONAL SYSTEM

A. The Nature and Content of Sovereignty in International Law

The term 'sovereign equality' might well be deemed semantically inept, as on its face it demands a reciprocal renunciation of the same unlimited authority that it nominally invokes. The international system affirms and bolsters only such assertions of state prerogative as are consistent with the system's animating purposes; it therefore necessarily qualifies the nature and scope of state prerogative. Yet the paradox and tension inherent in the term are appropriate to describing a complex, contested, and not strictly hierarchical relationship between international and internal legal orders.

The sovereign equality of states is best understood to establish three strong, but not irrebuttable, legal presumptions: (1) a state is presumed to be obligated only to the extent of its actual or constructive consent; (2) a state's obligations, while fully binding internationally on the state as a corporative entity, are presumed to have legal effect within the state only to the extent that domestic law has incorporated them; and (3) the inviolability of a state's territorial integrity and political independence, as against the threat or use of force or 'extreme economic or political

[10] For a more elaborate account, see BR Roth, 'The Enduring Significance of State Sovereignty', above n 1, 1026–37. That article articulates in more general terms an approach developed in earlier writings on collective non-recognition of governments, armed intervention, and international criminal justice. See, eg, BR Roth, *Governmental Illegitimacy in International Law* (Oxford, Clarendon Press, 1999); BR Roth, 'Bending the Law, Breaking It, or Developing It? The United States and the Humanitarian Use of Force in the Post-Cold War Era' in M Byers and G Nolte, (eds), *United States Hegemony and the Foundations of International Law* (Cambridge University Press, 2003) 232; BR Roth, 'Anti-Sovereigntism, Liberal Messianism, and Excesses in the Drive against Impunity' (2001) 12 *Finnish Yearbook of International Law* 17; BR Roth, 'Retrospective Justice or Retroactive Standards? Human Rights as a Sword in the East German Leaders Case' (2004) 50 *Wayne Law Review* 37.

coercion', is presumed to withstand even the state's violation of international legal norms.[11] Thus, however paradoxically, international law demands respect for state prerogative, even at the risk of impeding, not only the establishment of new legal norms, but also the implementation of existing legal norms.

Consequently, states are, at once, legally bound by obligations pertaining to the character of internal public order (ie, human rights norms) and legally protected from the very coercion that may be required to assure their compliance. Human rights norms do not, in and of themselves, vitiate the legal constraints on the application of power across territorial boundaries.[12]

Yet respect for sovereignty in no way excludes judgmental scrutiny of, or international ostracism for, internal practices. Even to the extent that such respect renders international standards of internal public order effectively non-compulsory, it renders them no less obligatory.[13]

Moreover, the barriers that sovereignty poses to international regulation of internal public order are somewhat less formidable than they may initially appear. International norm-formation is in many respects only superficially consensual: states can become bound to customary international human rights norms collectively and implicitly, as a result of their acquiescence in (largely rhetorical) patterns of practice. Although 'persistent objection' would in principle exempt a state from an emergent norm's coverage, there is no way to 'opt out' after the customary norm is deemed to have been fully established (even if the state in question came into being only after the norm's formation). Moreover, certain norms, such as the prohibition of genocide, are so fundamental that 'the international community of States as a whole' is said to have recognised them

[11] See Roth, 'The Enduring Significance of State Sovereignty', above n 1, 1026.

[12] Frustrated by such legal constraints, W Michael Reisman has complained that '[b]ecause rights without remedies are not rights at all, prohibiting the unilateral vindication of clear violations of rights when multilateral possibilities do not obtain is virtually to terminate those rights.' WM Reisman, 'Sovereignty and Human Rights in Contemporary International Law' (1990) 84 *American Journal of International Law* 866, 875. As Reisman himself acknowledges, however, routine circumvention of those constraints would erode the underpinnings of the system that makes those rights possible. WM Reisman, 'Why Regime Change Is (Almost Always) a Bad Idea' (2004) 98 *American Journal of International Law* 516, 516–17 ('Our international legal system is scarcely imaginable without' territorial communities having the right to govern themselves 'without interference'; 'state sovereignty prevails in all but the most egregious instances of widespread human rights violations').

[13] Although in lay parlance, 'obligatory' and 'compulsory' are generally taken to be synonyms, the two terms can be distinguished in a juridically useful way. A legal obligation entails legal consequences in the event of breach, but those consequences do not necessarily include legal susceptibility to measures adequate to compel one's fulfilment of the obligation. The obligor may possess legal protections that withstand the breach and that thereby preclude particular enforcement measures. For example, a prohibition of involuntary servitude may preclude a court from compelling specific performance of a personal service contract, or immunity may preclude a court from exacting redress for certain categories of wrongful action by a public entity or official.

as 'peremptory' norms (*jus cogens*), subject neither to persistent objection nor to 'derogation' (ie, justification or excuse for non-performance).[14]

In addition, although international obligations are ordinarily addressed to states and not to individuals, certain norms (most prominently, the core standards of the humanitarian laws of war) are understood to entail personal criminal (as well as civil) liability, even where they are unreflected in or contradicted by the domestic legal order in force at the time and place of the offending act's commission. Notwithstanding extensive jurisdictional limitations, personal and functional immunities, and safeguards against retroactive criminalisation of conduct, individuals—including state officials carrying out putatively official functions—may under certain conditions be prosecuted in Security Council-authorised ad hoc international criminal tribunals, in the newly created International Criminal Court, or in foreign state courts asserting extraterritorial jurisdiction.

Finally, the Security Council (operating on the basis of nine out of fifteen affirmative votes, and in the absence of a veto from one of the five Permanent Members) has unreviewable discretion under Chapter VII of the Charter to find even purely internal crises (such as Somalia in 1992) a threat to international peace, and pursuant to that finding, to authorise coercive measures, both short of and including the use of military force.[15] Furthermore, in certain instances in which the Security Council has issued no such authorisation, forcible responses to perceived threats of imminent humanitarian catastrophe have proceeded without international condemnation and even have received, in the cases of interventions by the Economic Community of West African States (ECOWAS) in Liberia and Sierra Leone, a post hoc Security Council imprimatur.[16]

Thus, the international system's deference to sovereign prerogative is by no means absolute. Nevertheless, non-consensual norms, personal

[14] See Vienna Convention on the Law of Treaties (adopted 23 May 1969, entered into force 27 January 1980) 1155 UNTS 331, Art 53; M Byers, *Custom, Power, and the Power of Rules* (Cambridge University Press, 1999) 186 (*jus cogens* norms considered to bind states notwithstanding any effort at 'persistent objection'); J Charney, 'Universal International Law' (1993) 87 *American Journal of International Law* 529, 538–42 (outlining the relationship between consent, persistent objection and *jus cogens* norms).

[15] See UN Charter, Arts 39, 41, and 42. Although a nexus, however tenuous, to external effects was formerly a rhetorical requisite to the use of this power, the Security Council is now clearly understood to have authority—indeed, the 'responsibility'—to invoke its extraordinary powers where 'national authorities are manifestly failing to protect their populations from genocide, war crimes, ethnic cleansing, and crimes against humanity.' UNGA Res 60/1 (24 October 2005) (adopted without a vote) para 139; UNSC Res 1674 (28 April 2006) (reaffirming same).

[16] UN Doc S/22133 (22 January 1991) (Security Council statement commending ECOWAS efforts 'to restore peace and normalcy in Liberia'); UNSC Res 788 (19 November 1992) (imposing an arms embargo against Liberian factions resisting ECOWAS); UNSC Res 1132 (8 October 1997) (imposing an arms embargo against the Sierra Leonean *de facto* government in support of ECOWAS military efforts to restore the elected government).

legal accountability for state-sponsored conduct in breach of international obligations, and coercive intervention to enforce breached obligations are exceptional, not routine. Efforts to extend, let alone to generalise, these exceptions occasion principled confrontations between those committed to maintaining, and those committed to transcending, the pluralistic framework of the international legal order.

B. Self-Determination and Non-Intervention

The central normative idea underpinning the existing sovereign equality framework is the right of 'peoples' to self-determination:

> All peoples have the right to self-determination; by virtue of that right they freely determine their political status and freely pursue their economic, social and cultural development.[17]

Yet contrary to common belief and a torrent of wishful scholarly rhetoric, the authoritative interpretation of the self-determination right that emerges from United Nations pronouncement and practice reduces almost entirely to a prohibition on coercive interference in the internal affairs of existing states. The right's bearers are territorially defined political communities—conforming to the recognised borders of either existing states or overseas colonial territories—not ethno-national groups or other affective communities.[18] Those accredited to assert the right in

[17] Declaration on the Granting of Independence to Colonial Countries and Peoples, UNGA Res 1514 (XV) (14 December 1960) (89–0–9), para 2. The Security Council reaffirmed the statement in UNSC Res 183 (11 December 1963), para 4, and the language is repeated verbatim in Common Article 1 of the 1966 Human Rights Covenants. International Covenant on Civil and Political Rights (adopted 16 December 1966, entered into force 23 March 1976) 999 UNTS 171 Art 1 (hereafter ICCPR); International Covenant on Economic, Social and Cultural Rights (adopted 19 December 1966, entered into force 3 January 1976) 993 UNTS 3 Art 1. Moreover, one of the enumerated purposes of the United Nations is to 'develop friendly relations based on respect for the principle of equal rights and self-determination of peoples', UN Charter, Art 1(2), and the Charter itself speaks in the name of 'We the Peoples of the United Nations', *ibid*, preamble.

[18] Although the definition of the term 'people' for the purposes of the self-determination right is not so limited in principle, the international community has never authoritatively designated a bearer of this right outside of the context of colonialism and its vestiges. Even 'indigenous peoples', the sub-national groups to which the self-determination right might most naturally apply, were long denied this status. See Convention Concerning Indigenous and Tribal Peoples in Independent Countries (adopted 27 June 1989, entered into force 5 Sept 1991) (ILO No 169) 72 ILO Official Bulletin 59 Art 1(3) ('The use of the term 'peoples' in this Convention shall not be construed as having any implications as regards the rights which may attach to the term under international law'). The 2007 United Nations Declaration on the Rights of Indigenous Peoples, UN Doc A/61.L.67 (12 September 2007) (143–4–11), passed over dissenting votes of the United States, Canada, Australia and New Zealand, finally ascribed to indigenous peoples the right to self-determination, nominally including the right to 'freely determine their political status', *ibid*, Art 3, but pointedly excluding any impairment of

the name of its bearers earn their standing by achieving, not popular approval by democratic means, but popular acquiescence by whatever means (with the exception of undue interference from abroad). The right can be summarised, with much irony but little exaggeration, as a right of territorial populations to be ruled by their own thugs, and to fight their civil wars in peace.

(1) Popular Sovereignty and Effective Control

The conceptual relationship between sovereignty and self-determination in the contemporary international order is frequently obscured by the tendency, in common parlance, to identify 'the state' with a set of governmental institutions. For the purposes of international law, however, sovereignty belongs not to any governmental apparatus, but to 'the state' in the abstract. Sovereignty is a legal attribute of a territorially bounded political community enjoying full membership in the international system. Recognised exercises of sovereignty are acts legally attributed to the will of the designated territory's permanent population as a whole. Irrespective of changes in government, however sweeping or violent, the state's legal identity remains unaltered, and obligations incurred under former governments remain binding. From international law's external standpoint, sovereignty itself lies not in a given political or constitutional order (*pouvoir constitué*), but in the underlying constituency (*pouvoir constituant*) to whose will that order and its international undertakings are attributed—by whatever processes and substantive criteria the international system may employ.

Nonetheless, where a governmental apparatus exercises 'effective control through internal processes', the international system generally accords that apparatus presumptive standing to assert rights, incur obligations and confer immunities on behalf of the sovereign entity.[19] According to the system's prevalent wisdom, empirical investigation to

existing states' 'territorial integrity or political unity', *ibid*, Art 46. This qualification apparently assuaged African states that had theretofore insisted that the 'principle of self-determination applies only to peoples under colonial and/or foreign occupation'. African Group, Draft Aide Memoire on United Nations Declaration on the Rights of Indigenous Peoples, 9 Nov 2006, available at http://www.ipacc.org.za/uploads/docs/Africanaidememoire.pdf.

[19] A concise statement of the effective control doctrine can be found in a 1950 British proposal, not then accepted but eventually achieving prevalence, for resolving UN credentials contests: '[W]here the question of the representation of a Member State arises in consequence of internal processes or changes which have taken place in that State, the right of a government to represent the Member State concerned in the United Nations should be recognized if that government exercises effective control and authority over all or nearly all the national territory, and has the obedience of the bulk of the population of that territory, in such a way that this control, authority and obedience appear to be of a permanent character.' 5 GAOR, Annexes, Agenda Item 61, at 8, UN Doc A/AC38/L21/Rev 1 (1950).

ascertain public opinion in a foreign state is most often impracticable, 'popular will' itself is a complex and normatively loaded concept, and any imposition from abroad of procedures calculated to measure 'popular will' is presumptuous at best, and a usurpation at worst.[20] The Friendly Relations Declaration accordingly transforms the language of the right of peoples to self-determination into the right of states to non-intervention:

> Every State has an inalienable right to choose its own political, economic, social and cultural systems, without interference in any form by another State.[21]

Lacking shared normative criteria for governmental legitimacy, the international community has most frequently taken popular acquiescence as an indicator of—or proxy for—sovereign will, provided only that such acquiescence be secured without undue external interference.[22] There thus follows a presumptive duty, on the part of each of the entities bearing equal juridical status, to respect the outcome of political processes—that is to say, civil wars, insurrections and coups no less than free and fair elections—internal to the others.[23]

[20] See generally: Roth, *Governmental Illegitimacy*, above n 10, 136–49, 160–71, 253–364.

[21] See Friendly Relations Declaration, above n 3. The document elaborates as follows:

> No State or group of States has the right to intervene, directly or indirectly, for any reason whatever, in the internal or external affairs of any other State. Consequently, armed intervention and all other forms of interference or attempted threats against the personality of the State or against its political, economic and cultural elements, are in violation of international law.
>
> No State may use or encourage the use of economic, political or any other type of measures to coerce another State in order to obtain from it the subordination of the exercise of its sovereign rights and to secure from it advantages of any kind. Also, no State shall organize, assist, foment, finance, incite or tolerate subversive, terrorist or armed activities directed towards the violent overthrow of the regime of another State, or interfere in civil strife in another State.

[22] See Roth, *Governmental Illegitimacy*, above n 10, 136–49, 160–71, 253–364.

[23] The non-intervention norm was most famously elaborated by the International Court of Justice in condemning US military support for Nicaraguan '*contra*' insurgents. *Military and Paramilitary Activities (Nicaragua v US)* [1986] ICJ Rep 14, paras 257–68. The Court reached beyond the pleadings to address the claim of the US Congress that the Government of Nicaragua had breached 'solemn commitments to the Nicaraguan people, the United States, and the Organization of American States' regarding the character of its internal public order. The Court examined 'whether there is anything in the conduct of Nicaragua which might legally warrant counter-measures by the United States'. The Court pointed out that even had there been a legal commitment (which there had not been) and standing on the part of the United States to enforce the commitment unilaterally on behalf of the OAS (which there would not have been), the US could hardly make use for [that] purpose of methods which the Organization could not use itself; in particular, it could not be authorized to use force in that event. Of its nature, *a commitment like this is one of a category which, if violated, cannot justify the use of force against a sovereign State.' Ibid*, para 262 (emphasis added).

The Court went on to note that to hold a state's adherence to any particular governmental doctrine a violation of customary international law 'would make nonsense of the *fundamental principle of State sovereignty, on which the whole of international law rests*, and the freedom of

Throughout most of the history of the current system, internal armed conflict was widely perceived, not as an anomaly or as evidence of 'state failure', but as a legitimate way for questions of public order to be worked out within states. Most governments through most of that period, after all, traced their origins more or less directly to a *coup d'état*, insurrection or decisive civil war. The warring factions typically succeeded in presenting internal armed conflicts (often inaccurately) as struggles between ideologically motivated factions allegedly speaking for the undivided population, rather than as ethno-nationalist bloodletting or as the simple thuggery of armed gangs. Since foreign intervention has generally been assumed to be predatory, and to be perceived internally as such, even a tyrannical government would figure to be a more authentic representative of the polity's interests and views than foreign powers announcing benevolent intentions. Thus, the decision of the bulk of the population to acquiesce, however grudgingly, in the winning faction's project of public order has been taken as a decision to have that faction speak for the political community in international affairs.

In recent years, these assumptions about political life have eroded considerably, and for good reason. Nonetheless, effective governments have been denied legal standing only in rare instances—as following coups against overwhelming winners of internationally sponsored elections in Haiti in 1991 and Sierra Leone in 1997—where popular repudiation of the effective regime has been so manifest as to be perceived in common across the international community's spectrum of political, ideological and cultural perspectives. Pluralism remains the rule, and exceptions must meet a high threshold of justification.

(2) Peoples and Territorial Units

Cultural and ethnic affinities do not establish political communities for the purposes of international law. Apart from the peculiar context of the struggle to eradicate the international system's original sin, Western European colonial domination of overseas territories, the self-determination right has operated in support of the territorial integrity and non-fragmentation of existing states—conceptualised as consummations

choice of the political, social, economic and cultural system of a State'. *Ibid*, para 263 (emphasis added). The Court further pointed out that the Friendly Relations Declaration and related documents 'envisage the relations among States having different political, economic and social systems on the basis of coexistence among their various ideologies; the United States not only voiced no objection to their adoption, but took an active part in bringing it about'. *Ibid*, para 264.

of the self-determination of their territorial populations—at the expense of the secessionist aspirations of territorial sub-communities.[24]

It is no accident that the most vociferous advocates of the right to self-determination, the new states emerging from decolonisation, were also the most determined to limit its application. The new states perceived most keenly their vulnerability to territorial fragmentation and to threats to their political independence posed by neocolonialist penetration. Just as the long-established states were concerned to contain secessionism, so too were new states just as eager to close the door on the recognition of new 'peoples' within established self-determination units.

The new states were furthermore determined to assert in the most extravagant terms the *absolute* inadmissibility of *any form* of foreign interference, *for any reason whatsoever*, with the right of their political communities—now presumptively represented, like the rest, by a ruling apparatus in effective control—to determine their own systems of internal public order.[25] Self-determination, by light of this notion, entails a people's right to maintain its cohesion by whatever means it (or the effective authority that speaks on its behalf) sees fit, and to resist all efforts (including advocacy of any conception of internal rights not harmonious with the state's purposes) to subvert its unity and independence.[26] The General Assembly's increasingly aggressive approach to

[24] The Declaration on the Inadmissibility of Intervention and Interference in the Internal Affairs of States, UNGA Res 36/103 (9 December 1981) (hereafter '1981 Non-Intervention Declaration') (passed 120–22–6 over the opposition of many Western liberal states) emphasised, inter alia, '[t]he duty of a state to refrain from the promotion, encouragement, or support, direct or indirect, of rebellious or secessionist activities within other States, *under any pretext whatsoever*, or any action which seems to disrupt the unity or to undermine or subvert the political order of other States'. Annex, Art 2(f) (emphasis added).

[25] See especially the contested 1981 Non-Intervention Declaration, *ibid*, asserting, inter alia, '[t]he duty of a State to refrain from the exploitation and the distortion of human rights issues as a means of interference in the internal affairs of States'; see also Friendly Relations Declaration, above n 3; Declaration on the Inadmissibility of Intervention in the Domestic Affairs of States and the Protection of Their Independence and Sovereignty, UNGA Res 2131 (XX) (21 December 1965) (109–0–1).

[26] In order to fully appreciate the point, one must understand the fear of neo-colonialism (often manipulated for partisan advantage, of course) that played so central a role in the era's politics. In the words of Ghana's founding President and Third World icon Kwame Nkrumah, the colonial power that grants independence '[b]y its very next act . . . seeks without grace to neutralize this same independence by fomenting discontent and disunity; and finally, by arrogant ingratiation and wheedling it attempts to disinherit the people and constitute itself their conscience and their will, if not their voice and their arm. Political decisions, just as they were before independence was won, lose their reference to the welfare of the people, and serve once again the well-being and security of the erstwhile colonial power and the clique of self-centered politicians.' K Nkrumah, *Consciencism: Philosophy and Ideology for Decolonization* [1964] (New York, Monthly Review Press, 1970) 101–2. The new African states faced danger, Nkrumah believed, from internal forces seeking 'to promote those political ties by which a colonialist country binds its [former] colonies to itself with the primary object of furthering her economic advantage'. The colonial power's local clients are 'the political wolf masquerading in sheep's clothing'; 'like a wasting disease they seek from the inside to infest, corrupt, pervert and thwart the aspirations of the people'. *Ibid.* Thus, the imperative of self-determination was hardly antithetical to, but actually a justification of, repressive dictatorship.

self-determination beginning in the 1960s thus coincided with a stream of maximalist articulations of the non-intervention norm.[27]

The Friendly Relations Declaration 'squares the circle' in an instructive way. It follows its elaboration of the right to self-determination with the following 'safeguard clause':

> Nothing in the foregoing paragraphs shall be construed as authorizing or encouraging any action which would dismember or impair, totally or in part, the territorial integrity or political unity of sovereign and independent States *conducting themselves in compliance with the principle of equal rights and self-determination of peoples as described above and thus possessed of a government representing the whole people belonging to the territory without distinction as to race, creed or colour.*[28]

Subsequent iterations have broadened the last clause of the qualifier to speak of 'a government representing the whole people . . . without distinction of any kind'.[29]

This supple and nuanced provision is best read, in light of its historical and political context, to reflect the animating principles of a global legal order marked by pronounced ideological pluralism (in 1970, it should be remembered, only a minority of states espoused liberal-democratic political principles) and extraordinary deference to states' choices of 'political, economic, social, and cultural systems' (including, on the basis of sovereign equality, one-party regimes that tolerate no organised opposition). The above italicised qualification to the imperatives of territorial integrity and political unity seems to have been designed to function, not as an ongoing operative exception to the sovereign prerogative of existing states, but as a moral rationalisation for singling out 'colonial domination, foreign occupation and racist [ie, apartheid] regimes' as special cases of derogation from the otherwise-fiercely-reaffirmed non-intervention norm.

In this reading, each existing state is the presumed manifestation of the self-determination of 'the whole people belonging to the territory'. This presumption allows the Declaration to justify attributing to the state the people's 'inalienable right to choose its political, economic, social and

[27] Michael Walzer's 1980 exaltation of the self-determination right as the collective right on which all individual rights depend was, if a bit overly exuberant, consistent with the spirit of the times: '[T]he distinction of state rights and individual rights is simplistic and wrongheaded. Against foreigners, individuals have a right to a state of their own. Against state officials, they have a right to political and civil liberty. Without the first of these rights, the second is meaningless: as individuals need a home, so rights require a location.' Walzer, 'The Moral Standing of States', above n 6, 228.

[28] See Friendly Relations Declaration, above n 3 (emphasis added).

[29] See UNGA Res 50/6 (24 October 1995); United Nations World Conference on Human Rights, Vienna Declaration and Programme of Action (adopted 25 June 1993) 32 ILM 1661, 1665 (1993).

cultural systems, without interference in any form', a choice that the state's effective government (even where objectively tyrannical) is further presumed to embody. Thus, the qualification, which appears to open a door, is best understood as an ingenious effort to keep that very door closed, while at the same time rendering a moral rationale for the disparate treatment of Western European colonialism and its vestiges.

Still, having articulated the principle, the fraternity of sovereign states cannot blunt its edge entirely.[30] Where a government manifestly fails to 'represent the whole people belonging to the territory without distinction', as by the conduct of ethnic cleansing, the imperatives of 'territorial integrity' and 'political unity' lose their rationale. Arguably, being subjected to gross and systematic discrimination reveals a minority group (whether marked by ethnic or other characteristics) to be a 'people' with its own right to self-determination—though no minority group in the non-colonial context has ever been authoritatively declared to be a 'people'.[31] More likely, patterns of extreme discrimination are now seen

[30] Despite overwhelming international resistance to a right to secession outside the colonial context, self-determination continues to be presented as a right of general applicability. Thus, when India attached to its ratification of the ICCPR a declaration interpreting the right of self-determination to 'apply only to the peoples under foreign domination and [not] to sovereign independent States or to a section of a people or a nation', invoking in support of this interpretation 'the essence of national integrity', it drew objections from the Netherlands, France and the Federal Republic of Germany. J Crawford, 'The Right of Self-Determination in International Law: Its Development and Future', in P Alston (ed), *People's Rights* (Oxford University Press, 2001) 7, 28.

Some international jurists have sought to reconcile self-determination with non-fragmentation by speaking of a 'right to internal self-determination'. This language is, however, misleading insofar as it suggests an international legal mandate for any of the consociational devices that certain domestic systems have employed to empower sub-national groups—such as territorial autonomy, representational quotas in governmental and other institutions, super-majority legislative voting rules for group-sensitive subject matter, and so on. See, eg, Ruth Lapidoth, *Autonomy: Flexible Solutions to Ethnic Conflicts* (Washington, DC, United States Institute of Peace Press, 1997). Except for 'indigenous and tribal peoples' (additional victims of the Western European colonialism that represents the 'original sin' for which the international system seeks to atone), sub-national groups, whether or not territorially coherent, have no established standing in international law. Individuals, however, may have special rights in consideration of their group membership. See, eg, ICCPR, above n 17, Art 27 (cultural rights of 'persons belonging to national or ethnic, religious and linguistic minorities').

[31] Instructive on this point is the domestic court decision dealing most elaborately with the international law of self-determination, the Canadian Supreme Court's advisory opinion in *Reference re Secession of Quebec* [1998] 1 SCR 217, available at www.scc-csc.gc.ca/reference/rea.htm. In deciding that the right, though applicable in the non-colonial context, did not justify unilateral secession, the court managed to sidestep the elemental question of whether the 'people' entitled to self-determination was comprised of (a) the entire Quebec population, (b) the entire Quebec population minus the indigenous communities; (c) Francophone Quebecois, or (d) all Francophone Canadians. *Ibid*, para 125. It stressed merely that none of these groups is blocked from the meaningful exercise of self-determination, since Canada is 'possessed of a government representing the whole people belonging to the territory without distinction'. *Ibid*, para 136. But see Crawford, above n 30, 59–60 (construing the court's position as consistent with 'both the view that self-determination applies to peoples in the ordinary sense of the term, and is not confined to the whole population of existing states, and the view that several peoples may co-exist in relation to a particular territory').

as justifying the international community—especially collectively, through Security Council action under Chapter VII of the Charter—in derogating from the system's ordinary respect for territorial integrity and political unity, as in the case of the international trusteeship that has supplanted Serbian rule over Kosovo.[32]

On the whole, an understanding of the self-determination right as it has operated in the existing international system requires a flair for the counterintuitive and the paradoxical, not to say the Orwellian. But contrary to the inferences that may be drawn by political theorists not steeped in the intricacies of international law, the right's paradoxical elements entail only a rebuttable presumption of certain core inviolabilities. The collective right does not pre-empt individual rights maintained against the collectivity. It operates primarily on a different plane, limiting, not the content of a state's duties toward its citizens, but cross-border exertions of power undertaken in the name of implementing those duties. Pluralism is not moral relativism, either in rationale or in effect.[33]

III. A MORAL JUSTIFICATION FOR THE SOVEREIGN EQUALITY FRAMEWORK

A. International Ethics and International Law

Sovereign equality is an institutional response to persistent disagreement about what constitutes a just and legitimate territorial public order. The persistence of sovereign prerogative as a barrier to recognition and implementation of international norms is not a mere inconvenience or failure of political will. It is the basis for respectful accommodation, based

[32] See UNSC Res 1244 (10 June 1999) (paying lip service to the sovereignty and territorial integrity of the Federal Republic of Yugoslavia while setting up an international administration to hold those norms in abeyance, at least temporarily); see also UNSC Res 1160 (31 March 1998), UNSC Res 1199 (23 September 1998), UNSC Res 1203 (24 October 1998) (all invoking Chapter VII powers in addressing the Kosovo situation prior to the NATO intervention).

[33] The duty of foreign states to respect core inviolabilities does not preclude states from giving effect to moral judgements within the confines of the discretionary aspects of their foreign policy, eg: declaring objectionable political figures *persona non grata*; providing peaceful refuge for militant opponents of objectionable regimes; severing diplomatic relations with, cutting off economic assistance to, and effecting a direct economic boycott of a state that engages in objectionable internal practices (but not a 'secondary' boycott of the target state's trading partners, which is a form of economic sabotage likely constituting unlawful coercion). What the doctrine limits is the authority of individual (more powerful) states—themselves both untrusted and untrustworthy—to employ extraordinary measures of compulsion in the service of their controversial moral judgements. And as noted above, even these limitations, while strongly presumptive, are subject to exceptions, both express and tacit.

on a 'bounded pluralism' in regard to clashing political moralities. It is morally irresponsible to eschew respectful accommodation, not because the truth of political morality is culturally relative or because moral truth is unachievable on ontological or epistemological grounds, but because pluralism is needed to satisfy an objective moral interest in coexistence and co-operation. The fact that human beings systematically and profoundly disagree has morally significant consequences, irrespective of how gravely mistaken the holders of a controverted position may be.

(1) Moral and Practical Considerations in the Crafting of Legal Standards

In lamenting the lack of systematic theorising about international legal order, Allen Buchanan has observed as follows:

> [I]t is often said that humanitarian intervention is justified only to stop gross and large-scale violations of the most fundamental human rights, in particular the right against genocide, not to stop 'lesser' human rights violations. What remains obscure is whether this constrained view on intervention is (1) grounded on a belief that a wider range of interventions is in principle morally justifiable, tempered by an appreciation of the fallibility and abuse that a less constrained rule would risk, (2) a concession to feasibility (on the assumption that states would not agree to a more permissive rule), (3) an implication of a particular theoretical tenet about the moral right of self-determination, according to which this right provides a fundamental moral barrier to intervention, or (4) a combination of all the preceding. Only a self-consciously systematic approach—an attempt to develop a moral theory of international law that distinguishes between basic moral principles and practical prescriptions responsive to the constraints of feasibility—can sort these matters out.[34]

Buchanan is surely correct that clarification is necessary, but the promise of a 'sorting out' is misleading. Where one takes unilateral ad hoc decisions in a legal vacuum, one treats considerations of moral justification separately from those of feasibility and diplomacy; once one articulates a persuasive moral standard under which one's own measures are properly subsumed, one can move on to the discrete practical questions of whether one's well-intentioned measures will miscarry or whether they will so anger others as to produce bad overall consequences. The crafting of legal norms, however, entails additional moral responsibilities.

First, whereas the above-hypothesised proponent of a moral norm will also determine its application, and so can trust that the norm's application will be marked by the same judgment and integrity brought to bear on its articulation, the proponent of a legal norm must take care that

[34] Buchanan, above n 5, 29.

the norm not license the kinds of decisions that tend, for systematic reasons, to be made badly. Legal standards are designed to impose accountability on not-fully-trusted implementers; a rule-of-law *ethos* militates against broadly licensing 'totality-of-the-circumstances' judgments, since such judgments, even if potentially the most sound, also have potential to be radically unsound. The contours of a legal right to self-determination need to reflect not only the political community's moral interest in immunity from even enlightened coercive interference in its internal affairs, but also the community's moral interest in immunity from an undue risk of self-interested, arrogant or sophomoric interference.

Second, in authoring standards for a 'basic structure' of international legal order, one must take appropriate account of the moral interest in peaceful coexistence and co-operation among bearers of conflicting conceptions of legitimate and just public order. This moral interest should not be confused with any supposed moral duty to respect non-like-minded human beings' capacity to exercise reason on matters of political morality,[35] nor with a supposed moral duty to accept as valid for culturally different societies such home-grown ordering principles as are minimally 'decent'.[36] One might, indeed, accept the proposition that a single-minded effort to eradicate unjust public order everywhere would be morally desirable if it could be undertaken at an acceptable human cost. But insofar as the projected human costs of forsaking peaceful coexistence and co-operation render such an effort morally irresponsible, a designer of international legal order must offer good-faith terms for respectful accommodation among such polities as one has decided—based on a calculation of the human costs and benefits of toleration and confrontation—to include. The resulting *modus vivendi* will contain elements of both overlapping consensus and compromise among bearers of differing conceptions of just public order, and fidelity to that *modus vivendi*, even at the expense of optimally just outcomes, will henceforth be a presumptive moral obligation, as a matter of *honour* (in the sense that one 'honours' one's word in upholding even a dissatisfying agreement).

Consequently, in the crafting of international legal standards, moral and pragmatic rationales are intertwined. This observation is important to an appreciation of paradoxical aspects of the enterprise: a stricture that

[35] Such an argument might arise as an extrapolation—albeit probably not a very good one—from Jeremy Waldron's respect-based argument against judicial usurpation of the political participation rights of those who might not be trusted to reason correctly about substantive rights. See J Waldron, *Law and Disagreement* (Oxford, Clarendon Press, 1999) 250–51. Though inspired in part by Waldron's focus on disagreement about justice, I do not accept the proposition that equal respect for persons requires allowing the supporters of substantive injustice an equal say in political decisions.

[36] See Rawls, *The Law of Peoples*, above n 8, 59–61.

requires objective injustice to be left undisturbed may nonetheless be a product of moral, rather than 'merely' practical, considerations.

(2) Moral Obligations to Comply with Existing International Law

In a provocative essay, Eric A Posner has called into question whether international law, as such, is ever morally binding, and thus whether breaches of existing legal norms should be evaluated entirely on the basis of prudential considerations. He concludes as follows:

> It can be useful for international-law scholars to point out that an act of the United States or some other country 'violates international law' as long as we understand what this phrase means. It means that the United States is not acting consistently with a treaty or a customary international-law norm, and as a result the expectations of other states might be disappointed (or not), and these states might retaliate (or not), or adjust their expectations in ways that may not be to the advantage of the United States. These are all reasons not to violate international law, but they are prudential reasons, and they are reasons to be taken into account even when international law is not at issue. The phrase does not mean that the United States has a moral obligation to bring its behavior within the requirements of the treaty or customary international-law norm, or that its citizens or leaders have a moral obligation to cause the United States to do this.[37]

Although Posner's is a realist perspective, many moralists display a parallel resistance to regarding international law as a source of moral obligation; the latter selectively regard particular positive norms (especially human rights norms) as a reflection of moral duties binding on independent grounds (just as Posner regards particular positive norms as supported by prudential considerations), but do not ascribe moral significance to positive norms that impede, rather than further, their moralistic designs. Thus, whatever may be thought of Posner's politics,[38] his scepticism is hardly parochial.

[37] EA Posner, 'Do States Have a Moral Obligation to Obey International Law?'(2003) 55 *Stanford Law Review* 1901, 1919. In arguing against international law's advocates, Posner's article tends to conflate support for obedience to existing legal standards with support for expansion of international legal commitments. International law's advocates contend, he says, 'that if states entered treaties with more precise and stronger obligations, gave up more sovereign powers to independent international institutions, used transparent and fair procedures when negotiating treaties, and eschewed unilateralism and bilateralism for multilateralism, then a greater level of international co-operation would be achieved than is currently observed'. *Ibid.* Support for obedience to existing legal standards, however, in no way depends on, or commits one to, this optimistic view.

[38] Posner is generally associated with unilateralist thinking within the current Bush Administration, and has come to the defence of the highly controversial positions on international humanitarian law developed by John Yoo and other Justice Department officials. See EA Posner and A Vermeule, 'A "Torture" Memo and Its Tortuous Critics' *Wall Street Journal*, 6 July 2004; Posner and Vermeule, 'Should Coercive Interrogation Be Legal?' (2006) 104 *Michigan Law Review* 671.

Posner's contention rests essentially on two points. The first is that the supposed consensual basis of international legal norms is illusory. Posner has chosen to emphasise in this regard the difficulty of establishing a moral obligation on the part of individual citizens—the sole bearers, he believes, of moral personality—to shoulder the burden of a past government's commitment.[39] He might equally have focused on the methodological finesses by which consent is imputed to states, on the power imbalances that mark international negotiation processes, or on the problematic relationship between a government's consent and the collective will of the underlying political community—all of which constitute on the facially plausible objections.

Second, Posner argues, the international legal order is inefficacious. Although admitting that state behaviour most frequently conforms to the standards of international law, Posner concludes that it does so principally for reasons of convenience and confluence of interests, not because the standards have the authority of law. International law does not, according to his empirical assessment, prevail upon states to do what they are disinclined to do.[40]

The illusoriness of consent is a familiar point, but the objection is troubling only if a moral obligation can be predicated on nothing short of a genuine voluntary undertaking. However artificial, what passes for 'consent' is the common theme of the international legal system's 'secondary rules' (to use HLA Hart's term for those rules that govern the recognition, legislation and adjudication of the 'primary rules' regulating conduct).[41] These secondary rules are established and accepted within a system that brings a modicum of decent regulation to what otherwise would be a severely chaotic state of affairs, with bad consequences not only for governments but also for their constituents, jointly and severally. Just as Rawls, following Kant, ascribed to individuals 'a natural duty . . . to support and to comply with just institutions that exist and apply us',[42]

[39] Posner complains that unlike shareholders, who are free 'not to join the corporation if they prefer to avoid the corporation's liabilities', citizens cannot avoid the supposed obligation, even if they had been powerless under the political system that undertook the commitment, or had not yet been born. Posner, above n 37, 1905, 1907. But as EH Carr wryly observed, the idea of a state as a 'group person' with moral responsibilities 'seems to present more difficulty to the philosopher than to the ordinary man'. 'The question whether the Belgian Guarantee Treaty of 1839 imposed an obligation on Great Britain to assist Belgium in 1914 raised both legal and moral issues. But it cannot be intelligently discussed except by assuming that the obligation rested neither personally on Palmerston who signed the treaty of 1839, nor personally on Asquith and Grey who had to decide the issue in 1914, neither on all individual Englishmen alive in 1839, nor on all individual Englishmen alive in 1914, but on that fictitious group-person "Great Britain", which was capable of moral or immoral behaviour in honouring or dishonouring an obligation.' EH Carr, *The Twenty Years' Crisis* [1940] (New York, Harper & Row, 1964) 150.

[40] Posner, above n 37, 1914.

[41] HLA Hart, *The Concept of Law* (Oxford, Clarendon Press, 1961) 91–6.

[42] J Rawls, *A Theory of Justice* (Cambridge, MA, Harvard University Press, 1971) 115 (requiring only that the institutions be 'as just as it is reasonable to expect in the circumstances'); see

so, too, one can attribute to collectivities and their constituents a natural duty to support and comply with international institutions that, even if not 'just' in any thoroughgoing sense, facilitate co-ordination and militate against predation to a greater extent than any available alternative. Moreover, while the 'consent' that the system's secondary rules represent is concededly far too thin to be a self-sufficient source of moral obligation, the secondary rules, in deferring to the internal processes of territorial political communities, at least draw on such vehicles for stakeholder participation as are available. In the absence of a more legitimate and just alternative system that might feasibly be implemented, there is a fully plausible obligation to uphold rather than to undermine the existing international legal order.

This rationale presupposes, of course, that Posner's second objection cannot be sustained. If, as an empirical matter, international law does not meaningfully contribute to peaceful coexistence and co-operation, then it cannot be morally binding. The empirical controversy cannot be resolved in this space, but it is worth noting that the best evidence for international law's efficacy may be only indirectly observable. A world without international law would be a world without the baselines that are partly constitutive of international actors' very understanding of the issues at stake. To speak of a state is already to have in mind a package of legal attributes, rights and responsibilities; a world without these could be imagined, but it would require rethinking much that is currently taken for granted, and pondering measures that are currently almost never considered. It is true that breaches are frequent in those few areas of international law (eg, the use of force and human rights) where parties have enough of a stake in their momentary ends to risk destabilising long-term accommodations, but even in those instances, there is a commonly recognised basis for mobilising opposition to the breaching acts, and breach entails a real, even if not a decisive, cost.[43] A world in which this were not the case would be a very different, and even far more troubled, world.

also J Ladd (trans), I Kant, *The Metaphysical Elements of Justice* (Indianapolis, Bobbs-Merrill, 1965), para 42, 71 ('If you are so situated as to be unavoidably side by side with others, you ought to abandon the state of nature and enter, with all others, a juridical state of affairs . . .'); see generally: J Waldron, 'Special Ties and Natural Duties' (1993) 22 *Philosophy & Public Affairs* 3, 4–5, 14–15.

[43] It is instructive, for example, that Israelis and Palestinians of virtually all stripes, for all of the parochialism that frequently characterises their respective positions regarding the conflict, find themselves impelled to justify their positions to external audiences by reference to norms of the international legal order. Even when they dismiss that order as rank idealism, they often find themselves invoking one of its norms in the next breath. They do this, I contend, because the legal validity *vel non* of their positions, even though not in itself determinative of outcomes, is not politically irrelevant.

Although Posner and his frequent co-author, Jack L Goldsmith, have sought (quite controversially) to denigrate invocations of legal norms as 'cheap talk' (JL Goldsmith and EA Posner, 'Moral and Legal Rhetoric in International Relations: A Rational Choice Perspective' (2002) 31 *Journal of Legal Studies* S115), their primary aim is to deny the rhetoric's relevance to

In the absence of commonalities of short-term material interest and substantive moral principle, efficacious actors need to find common ground on a different plane. A shared sense of honour fills this need, transcending differences of material and moral ends through a common commitment to keep faith with whatever accommodations are concluded. The duty to honour agreements—and other forms of accommodation on which others are led to rely—in part reflects a pragmatic concern of the 'repeat player' to maintain a reputation that will enable her to obtain co-operation on subsequent 'plays', but it is also a matter of integrity and of respect for the other.

Of course, considerations of justice, even unilaterally conceived, may override considerations of honour in particular cases,[44] but they do not automatically do so. For instance, one ordinarily upholds guarantees of safe passage given to criminals and terrorists, not merely because it is irresponsible to do otherwise when morally important interests depend on maintaining the ability to trade on one's word in similar future contexts, but also because there is something deeply unvirtuous about perfidy, even when employed against actors who are themselves immoral.

International law is thus capable of generating moral obligations. Such obligations may be binding not only where they demand compromise of material interests, but also where they demand forbearance from the single-minded pursuit of one's unilateral moral ends.[45]

the speaker's motivation to comply with international norms. They contend that such talk is costless and that failure to engage in it would gratuitously 'convey information that the speaker is not cooperative' (*ibid* at S124). Be this as it may (and there is reason to question whether rhetorical acceptance of legal constraint is as costless as the authors assert), those authors do not deny the need to appeal to internationally efficacious political constituencies that are motivated by moral considerations (*ibid* at S136), denying only that such constituencies regard international law as relevant to those considerations (*ibid* at S131). In making the latter assertion (for which they cite little evidence), the authors fail to recognise that international law frequently furnishes the only ostensibly impartial baseline by which external constituencies can judge the moral merits of competing claims that are otherwise steeped in hopelessly parochial fixations (eg, biblical claims to Judea and Samaria or the legacy for the Serb nation of the 1389 Battle of Kosovo Polje).

44 In such cases, it is important that the norm be breached in the name of an alternative norm that most of the international community could plausibly embrace. I have made this argument at length in regard to the NATO intervention to prevent the Serb campaign of 'ethnic cleansing' in Kosovo. Roth, above n 10, 232.

45 Michael Reisman argues that because the international legal system is partially inefficacious, vindication of certain—ie, human rights-oriented—norms requires reliance on extralegal modes of enforcement. WM Reisman, 'Unilateral Actions and the Transformations of the World Constitutive Process: The Special Problem of Humanitarian Intervention' (2000) 11 *European Journal of International Law* 3, 14–17. His argument begs the question, though, of whether sovereignty-oriented obstacles to lawful implementation represent the system's dysfunction rather than its deliberate adoption of a particular balance of considerations that Reisman finds objectionable. If the latter is true, extralegal enforcement, whatever its other merits, cannot be regarded as a vindication of the legal order.

B Conflicting Political Moralities in the International Arena

(1) The Elusive Consensus on Universal Norms

Moral criticism of the sovereign equality framework typically cites universal norms that purportedly transcend territorial and other boundaries. Invocations of universality often contain an ambiguity about whether the norm in question is asserted to be *universally espoused* as well as *universally applicable*. The claim that a norm is universally applicable need not rest on, but frequently trades on (and would always benefit from), a claim that the standard is universally espoused. Moreover, whereas philosophical truth alone is sufficient to establish the authority of moral norms, bare invocations of natural law are a problematic basis for the assertion of legal norms.

Assertions of universally espoused norms in real-life disputes amount to the rather curious contention that empirical discord has a solution rooted in empirical consensus. Whereas consent can, without contradiction, bind someone to standards with which she does not presently agree, the same cannot be true of consensus unless a peculiar condition holds, such as (a) the relevant community that is the referent of consensus does not include the dissident, or (b) all informed persons of good faith and sound reason can deduce from an uncontested consensus a conclusion that the dissident, for lack of one or more of these attributes, rejects.

The real problem with condition (a) is not the debater's point that the condition becomes tautological where dissidence itself suffices to expel the dissident from the relevant community. One can, without doing too much violence to the concept, redefine 'consensus' as an insistent near-consensus, as in the authoritative definition of a peremptory (or *jus cogens*) norm as one 'accepted and recognized by the international community of States as a whole as a norm from which no derogation is permitted'.[46] More seriously problematic are efforts to redefine the lawmaking community so as systematically to exclude the non-like-minded. Thus, 'global civil society' may be cited as an alternative source of lawmaking authority. '[W]orld social and decision processes' may be said to include the participation of,

> [b]esides the traditional nation-state, . . . intergovernmental organizations, non-self-governing territories, autonomous regions, and indigenous and other peoples, as well as private entities such as multinational corporations, media, nongovernmental organizations, private armies, gangs, and individuals.[47]

[46] Vienna Convention on the Law of Treaties, above n 14, Art 53.

[47] S Weissner and AR Willard, 'Policy-Oriented Jurisprudence and Human Rights Abuses in Internal Conflict: Toward a World Public Order of Human Dignity' (1999) 93 *American Journal of International Law* 316, 323; see also Reisman, 'Unilateral Actions', above n 45, 13.

In the absence of a formally structured account of their supposed juridical authority, the views of any such actors can be invoked or ignored, as expediency dictates. The 'international community' can thus become a pseudo-empirical category, membership of which is ascribed on the basis of cosmopolitan characteristics that correlate with liberal views.

The more frequent and significant problem, however, is posed by condition (b) above, which rests on the assumption that consensus on an abstract norm can be unproblematically projected forward to a determinate application. The scope of consensus is easily exaggerated. We often imagine that the matters of which we feel the most certain and to which we assign the greatest importance are matters about which human beings share a common intuition, and that genuine differences pertain only to the peripheral questions, concerning which we can plainly perceive room for disagreement. It is not easy to accept that informed persons of good faith and sound reason can find themselves on opposite sides of violent confrontations, that they may apply characterisations such as tyranny and freedom, hero and murderer, in opposite ways.

The beginnings of wisdom about political conflict lie in recognising that informed persons of good faith and sound reason,[48] while subscribing to familiar moral principles in the abstract, can disagree fundamentally on questions of public order, including on whether to support ruthless measures such as dictatorship, repression and terrorism. If this is so, a substantial incidence of harsh political methods is endemic to the human condition, even if most human beings are basically good.[49]

[48] The criteria of the three characteristics—'informed', 'good faith' and 'sound reason'—are intended to be as independent of normative judgement as possible (though the criteria for empirical categories are never really free of the influence of normative perspectives). Thus, by 'informed' I mean being neither ignorant of nor deceived about the basic facts of the situation, rather than being possessed of the insights about the situation that we would like for persons to have (so that they see it our way); by 'good faith' I mean that they take seriously some general duty to 'do right by' all other human beings (even if their conception of that duty is objectively inadequate), and genuinely believe that their support of particular measures observes that duty (even if they are objectively mistaken); by 'sound reason' I mean that they process information in a fairly sophisticated and non-pathological way.

The goal of this formulation is to avoid the question-begging that results from conflating principled disagreement (a descriptive characterisation) with 'reasonable' disagreement (a normative characterisation). I cannot exclude the possibility that, for example, some Nazis fulfilled the criteria of the above categories (even though Nazism *per se* seems to have entailed a general repudiation of moral duties to non-Aryans). Rather than to blur the distinction, I would prefer to say that there is some objective threshold of aberrational injustice beyond which possession of the three characteristics is, for thoroughly practical reasons, irrelevant to the question of toleration (ie, we cannot reach a morally worthwhile *modus vivendi* with such persons).

[49] It is worth recalling, as Jeremy Waldron frequently points out, that Kant attributed the perils of the state of nature not to selfishness, but to moral vehemence. 'Even if we imagine men to be ever so good natured and righteous before a public lawful state of society is established, individual men, nations, and states can never be certain that they are secure against violence from one another, because each will have his own right to do what *seems just and good to him*, entirely independent of the opinion of the others'. Kant, above n 42, s 44, 76.

However much of the world's illiberal coercion, force and violence may be attributed to human evil, much would withstand even the eradication of that evil. Global conflict management thus requires a pluralistic framework.

(2) Culture-Based Pluralisms: Walzer and Rawls

Michael Walzer and John Rawls have both offered pluralistic approaches to international ethics. Both approaches, in different ways, predicate international pluralism on the cultural differences thought to be reflected in political communities' varying systems of public order.

Walzer posits a 'morally necessary', though rebuttable, presumption to govern relations with foreign states: 'that there exists a certain "fit" between the community and its government', such that the community is 'governed in accordance with its own traditions'.[50] This presumption is overcome in extreme cases, as where governments engage in 'massacre or enslavement'.[51] But the presumption holds in the case of 'a military dictatorship and a religious "republic", without civil and political liberties, and brutally repressive', under which women are subjected to 'their traditional religious subordination to patriarchal authority', in keeping with the locality's 'political and religious culture' and the regime's 'deep roots' in the community's history.[52] Walzer does not deny that a foreign community's principles of internal public order 'may be wrong or badly conceived'. Still, he maintains:

> [I]t is not the sign of some collective derangement or radical incapacity for a political community to produce an authoritarian regime. Indeed, the history, culture, and religion of the community may be such that authoritarian regimes come, as it were, naturally, reflecting a widely shared world view or way of life.[53]

Given a hypothetical opportunity to transform the situation by drugging the community's elites and masses with a 'wondrous chemical' that 'would wipe out of their minds their own political and religious culture' and turn them into Swedish-style social democrats, he would refuse do so on the ground that this would deprive them of 'the only kind of state that they are likely to call their own'.[54]

Rawls's pluralism is not nearly as broad as Walzer's, but it is every bit as deep—coming close to accepting foreigners' illiberal practices as 'right

[50] Walzer, 'The Moral Standing of States', above n 6, 212.
[51] *Ibid*, 217.
[52] *Ibid*, 225.
[53] *Ibid*, 224–5.
[54] *Ibid*, 225–6.

for them', rather than merely as immune from coercive interference—and just as reliant on cultural difference as a justification. In regard to 'decent, non-liberal peoples', Rawls posits a duty 'not only to refrain from exercising political sanctions—military, economic, *or diplomatic*—to make a people change its ways', but also 'to recognize these non-liberal societies as equal participating members in good standing of the Society of Peoples'.[55] He stresses 'the great importance of all decent peoples' maintaining their self-respect and having the respect of other liberal or decent peoples',[56] in consideration of which an international system should not even 'offer incentives for its member peoples to become more liberal'.[57] Rawls does not elaborately account for the rejection of liberalism by peoples that are nonetheless 'decent', but he assumes that a 'people' is the kind of entity that can properly be characterised as liberal or non-liberal, and that a non-liberal people's self-respect is somehow invested in its non-liberal principles of public order. From these assumptions, and from his choice of a hypothesised Islamic republic ('Kazanistan') as his illustration of a decent non-liberal order,[58] one must deduce that Rawls, like Walzer, regards principles of public order as, at least potentially, embedded in a community's history, traditions, religion and culture, and worthy of presumptive respect on this basis.

Rawls's toleration is deep, but for just that reason, necessarily narrow. The 'decent' non-liberalism that he posits reflects only such deviation from liberal norms as a liberal sensibility, straining for open-mindedness, can abide. Decency ends up as a near-liberal requirement that the non-liberal authority structure be (a) reasonably close to just (oriented toward a plausible conception of a common good and not in violation of a truncated set of core human rights) and (b) reasonably close to legitimate (participatory, even if through a merely consultative process and subject to hierarchical premises). Informed persons of good faith and sound reason are supposed to agree, it would seem, on the normative points that liberals deem most central and certain, but may differ on more peripheral details. Relations with non-decent systems of public order—outlaw states, burdened peoples, and even benevolent dictatorships—are not to be governed by the terms of reciprocity that Rawls sketches out, but are left to be governed in accordance with what amount to standard 'cosmopolitan liberal' principles—the 'transcendent justice' approach, as defined herein.

Since real-world decent non-liberal regimes, by Rawls's criteria, comprise almost a null set (Singapore, for one, might qualify), Rawls's *Law of Peoples* makes little practical contribution to the present discussion,

[55] Rawls, *The Law of Peoples*, above n 8, 59 (emphasis added).
[56] *Ibid*, 62.
[57] *Ibid*, 84.
[58] *Ibid*, 75–8.

except as an alternative, and more attractively broad-minded, rationale for the international pursuit of liberal justice.[59] In setting conditions for inclusion appropriate to an overlapping international consensus among liberal and (almost exclusively hypothetical) 'decent non-liberal' communities—conditions for a deep respect—Rawls's text forgoes devising a useable platform for a real-world *modus vivendi* based on a more shallow respect among political communities.

(3) Rejecting Culture-Based Pluralism

Walzer and Rawls join many other less systematic thinkers in predicating their calls for an international pluralism on cultural difference. This emphasis has several troubling implications. First, as noted above, if respect for persons is understood to demand respect for cultural characteristics as constitutive of personhood, and the culture is understood to include principles of public order, then respect precludes even such measured responses to foreign public-order practices as condemnations or boycotts. Second, cultural difference is privileged over mere ideological difference: traditional-hierarchical non-liberalism has this special immunity, whereas revolutionary-egalitarian non-liberalism, being mere ideology, does not. Third, culture-based pluralism is naturally disposed to accept convenient claims of illiberal factions about the authoritative interpretation of cultural norms, while dismissing local liberal dissidents in non-Western societies as culturally inauthentic, thereby potentially rendering aid and comfort to repression. Fourth, the association of public-order practices with a social phenomenon as intractable as 'culture' tends to encourage ordinarily justice-minded actors to write off whole societies—and their most vulnerable members—as a lost cause.

None of these consequences seems justified on the merits. Liberalism has supporters and opponents in all parts of the world. The level of support depends on many variables, including the compatibility of liberal ideas with local traditions, but liberalism's following has gradually increased even in parts of the world where it had been thought unpromising. The success of liberal ideas seems to depend less on cultural norms than on the presence of the economic, political and social circumstances of liberalism—conditions that produce questions to which liberalism is a plausible answer. These circumstances attend economic development. Of course, resistance to liberalism, whether from the Right (traditional-

[59] This is not to say that Rawls—or any of the more standard cosmopolitan theorists—denies the importance of the general pragmatic and humanitarian considerations that frequently weigh against cross-border impositions. It is to say that the restraints specific to Rawls's pluralism apply to interactions only with regimes that he regards as within the realm of 'decency', whereas interactions with regimes that fail, for one reason or another, to meet this standard are governed by straightforward applications of liberal political morality.

hierarchical) or the Left (revolutionary-egalitarian), remains viable in developing societies to varying extents, but it also remains viable to varying extents in the developed Western societies in which liberalism was born.

Moreover, 'globalisation', which actually started centuries ago, has long since done away with any possibility of hermetically sealed 'cultures'. Many local representatives of supposed non-Western interests and values have been either directly or indirectly Western-educated, and many postcolonial ideologies would have been impossible without influences from Western thought. Efforts to reach back in time for a purer, more 'authentic' approach are not traditionalist but revivalist, applying venerable ideas to conditions never imagined in, say, the days of the Qu'ran. Whatever else may be said for or against these ideas, they are ideology, pure and simple, not culture.

A culture, as such, does not entail a distinctive conception of public order, unless the former is tendentiously defined so as to make the point tautological. Indeed, whereas territorial political communities have boundaries that more or less identify a permanent population as a fixed membership to which political judgments can somehow—whether or not by popular vote—be imputed, cultures have no established boundaries; who is and who is not a member is frequently a contested question, and it is impossible for a culture, even metaphorically, to take a decision.

To be sure, culture influences subjective perceptions of the essential nature of the relationship between the individual and the community. Such perceptions affect the popularity of liberal thought, and especially of the rhetoric by which liberals habitually express themselves. But it is important not to conflate the individual's relationships to three separate entities: (a) a community of attachment—whether it be a local village, a geographically coherent or dispersed ethnic group or clan, or a notional community of coreligionists living anywhere in the world—that may be regarded, subjectively or even objectively, as constitutive of the individual's identity and ends; (b) the notional political community associated with the state, which is unlikely to be coextensive with any community 'constitutive' of the individual's identity or ends; (c) the governmental apparatus that rules in the name of, and may or may not be accountable to, that notional political community. Although some human rights issues authentically concern the relationship between the individual and a local community's traditional structures of authority (eg, female genital mutilation and honour killings), most—including the almost all of the ones that occasion proposals for cross-border exertions of power—concern the conduct of an at least quasi-modern governmental apparatus that is usually unaccountable to, and often directly at odds with, such traditional and/or local structures.

In general, there is no reason to presume that the patterns of coercion, force and violence being inflicted on individuals reflect the authentic ordering principles of some community to which these individuals are organically attached.[60] Indeed, the most seriously illiberal practices are less likely to be a product of coherent cultural communities than of intra- and inter-communal clashes that exceed institutional capacities for conflict management.[61]

None of this is to deny that cultural difference is one of the main forces driving deep political disagreement. But in this regard, culture is not worthy of special standing, analytically independent of and morally privileged over garden-variety ideological difference. The proper focus is on ideological difference, irrespective of its (always-contested) relationship to cultural difference.

Beyond this, cultural difference may present practical considerations that affect human rights implementation. Liberal institutions and processes, designed for a Western setting, may produce perversely illiberal results if implanted without adaptation in a society where conditions, including but not limited to culture and tradition, are different. But this calls into question merely the familiar institutional implementations of liberal principles, not the applicability of liberal moral criteria. Moreover, in any political context, local sensibilities determine what kinds of measures and arguments will be effective, and these sensibilities, of course, depend partly on cultural factors. Such sensibilities will affect strategy and tactics, and may impose practical limitations on what can be achieved, but these are not matters of normative principle.

Liberal cosmopolitans are thus correct in rejecting cultural difference as a basis for a pluralistic approach to international order.[62] Yet they are

[60] Allen Buchanan makes a similar point. See Buchanan, above n 5, 179.

[61] Almost without exception, the kinds of events that have prompted calls for international criminal justice and humanitarian intervention—such as gross and systematic recourse to killings and torture—have been occasioned by a perceived urgent need to suppress internal challenges to a social order (eg, the Latin American dirty wars of the 1970s and 1980s) or by a perceived dire threat from a rival community (eg, the former Yugoslavia and Rwanda in the 1990s). Of course, suppressions of freedom, denials of gender equality, oppression of homosexual persons, and cruel and unusual punishments are frequently rooted in cultural tendencies, but however often condemned as human rights violations, these illiberal practices almost never call into question a state's ultimate authority within its territory. Moreover, these latter practices tend to manifest themselves most dramatically when traditionalists within a culture feel that they are losing their grip, prompting a neo-traditionalist revival that is both far harsher than the community's historical norm and of highly contested cultural authenticity (eg, in Iran and Afghanistan).

[62] See, eg, J Donnelly, *Universal Human Rights in Theory and Practice* (Ithaca, NY, Cornell University Press, 1989) 118 ('We must not be misled by complaints of the inappropriateness of "Western" human rights made by repressive regimes whose practices have at best only the most tenuous connection to the indigenous culture; communitarian rhetoric too often cloaks the depredations of corrupt and often Westernized or deracinated elites'); FR Tesón, 'The Rawlsian Theory of International Law' (1995) 9 *Ethics & International Affairs* 79, 98 (complaining that Rawls's later work has 'embraced a more relativistic, context-based conception of justice and political morality, in which rights and liberties no longer had a foundation in higher principles or liberal views of human nature').

wrong in rejecting global pluralism on the whole, for completely different reasons.

(4) The Justification of a Non-Culture-Based Pluralism

The problem of deep political disagreement is rooted, not in the immutable cultural characteristics of holders of conflicting views, but in the nature of political life. The quest for an international justice that transcends territorial and political divisions comes to grief because that quest operates, at least implicitly, from an unrealistic premise: that informed persons of good faith and sound reason, notwithstanding such disagreements as are conceded to be inevitable among human beings, can be expected to reach an overlapping consensus on a core set of morally imperative political norms.

The quest finds encouragement in an empirical consensus that can be found to exist on abstract norms, such as those found in international human rights instruments. But such consensus too often ends up being illusory. First, apparent consensus on abstractions frequently dissolves at the level of application, because in the face of concrete circumstances, adherents of competing 'comprehensive doctrines', who endorsed the abstractions for differing reasons, will interpret the same abstract norms in conflicting ways, or assign them conflicting priorities. Second, consensus as to the presumptive wrongfulness of particular conduct often gives way to discord about under which adverse conditions the presumption is overcome; agreement as to inadmissible means typically fails to hold in the face of sufficiently grave threats to what some see as morally imperative ends.

The fact of political life that necessitates a pluralistic solution can be summarised as follows: *Under sufficiently adverse conditions, such as extreme ethno-national or socio-economic polarisation, the interaction of these two problems—the inability to agree on a fair basic structure of public order, and the inability to exclude recourse to extraordinary means in the struggle to install or maintain a basic structure of public order that comports with one's own conception of fairness—leads informed persons of good faith and sound reason to support ruthless measures against one another.* Where the gap between competing conceptions of fairness is sufficiently great, and the perceived moral stakes of political conflict sufficiently high, efforts to forge a mutually acceptable institutional solution will fail, prompting recourse to an unmediated clash of social forces. The result is a principled recourse to measures, such as dictatorship, repression and terrorism, that would be rejected in the abstract.

This unhappy tendency is not something that is true of some discrete, culturally different, 'them'. It is true of 'us'. What follows is a schematic account of why politics, even when driven by wisdom and good intentions, is universally a 'contact sport' that, under the right (or more properly, the wrong) social conditions, will lead to harshly incompatible moral stands on vital issues.

Universal principles demand political action to secure to all the conditions of a dignified human existence. It is for this very reason that the contemporary human rights movement posits not merely state duties to avoid violating human dignity by discrete and direct acts of violence, but further state duties to affirmatively protect the right-bearer from violence and from analogous inflictions with similarly dehumanising effects. Beyond those lie duties to take all necessary measures to secure for all right-bearers (within the limits of what is materially feasible) the conditions that permit human potentialities to be realised. The proliferation of internationally certified human rights—now encompassing 'first-generation' civil and political rights well beyond inviolability of the physical integrity of the person, 'second-generation' economic and social rights, and 'third-generation' collective rights to the minimal conditions of societal flourishing—represents a series of efforts to correct for the manifest inadequacy of simple negative imperatives.

The more holistically rights claims address human dignity, however, the more inexorably and expansively do they appropriate the space of politics. Invocation of the term 'human rights' altogether fails to pre-empt political contestation because competing views of how to prioritise and how to accomplish the posited ends constitute the very core of politics.

By all accounts, individual pursuit of the good life requires the existence of certain non-divisible public goods. The creation of these public goods is burdened by collective action problems, the solution to which frequently requires collective decisions authorising coercive implementation. Social life, by its nature, presents myriad co-ordination problems. However much one may wish to exalt the self-actualising individual, individual aspirations cannot be realised—or often even conceived—without others' co-ordinate actions and forbearances that combine to establish the infrastructure for that realisation (just as a career as a cellist presupposes compositions, instruments, orchestras and orchestra halls, which themselves presuppose complex social institutions, and so on in regression). The co-ordination of actions and forbearances depends, in turn, on decisions attributable to and binding on some collectivity, backed by a capacity for compulsion that militates against free riders and other spoilers.

Human flourishing therefore demands decisions of particular political communities about the nature of the good society wherein the good life is pursued. These decisions pertain, not merely to distributive justice, but to the moral environment that lays the foundation for the fulfilment of the civic responsibilities indispensable to the good society. If, in the inevitable trade-offs that such decisions entail, fundamental interests of end-choosing human subjects turn out to be rival, the political community has little choice but to establish priorities by comparatively evaluating, in light of preferred conceptions of the good life, the ends that those subjects might choose.[63]

The main current of contemporary liberal thought—reflected in Rawls's *Political Liberalism*[64]—seeks to establish that a basic constitutional framework for such a society can be specified independent of a collective adoption, not simply of a particular 'comprehensive doctrine of human flourishing', but of a particular accommodation among some such doctrines to the disparagement or exclusion of others. This variant of liberal theory resists regarding the basic structure as a site of ineluctable conflict among bearers of common-good-oriented but mutually incompatible world views, a conflict that will necessarily result in, if not outright victory for bearers of one conception, a bargain reflective of the comparative political leverage of the factions, with some factions disadvantaged and others excluded altogether. Rather, the theory imagines, as an achievable ideal, a basic structure that reflects an overlapping consensus among all 'reasonable' world views.

This notion has spawned a debate far beyond the scope of the present work. Suffice it to say here, though, that the losers in this formula would scarcely accept the 'persuasive redefinition' of reasonableness that Rawls devised to effect their delegitimation, and not for lack of knowledge, intelligence or public-spiritedness. Informed persons of good faith and sound reason will inevitably struggle over the terms of the basic structure.

This inevitable struggle does not, in itself, necessarily augur severe strife or harsh measures. Constitutional compromises often secure social peace, not because they are universally fair or engender universal satisfaction, but because no faction that is sufficiently efficacious in destabilising the institutional framework has sufficient motive to do so, based on a comparative assessment of the attendant risks and benefits. Moreover, even where the constitutional order's specifications are in tension with international standards, the very context of social peace will probably persuade international agencies and jurists to find the deviations to fall within a 'margin of appreciation'.

Nonetheless, in polities sharply polarised on socioeconomic, ethnonational or other bases, efficacious factions who regard their material interests and moral principles as unfairly subordinated or marginalised may have insufficient motive to remain loyal to the prevailing processes of decision. The potential for an unmediated clash of social forces augurs

[63] For an elaboration of the argument that liberalism's core encompasses rival freedoms that cannot be prioritised by deduction, see J Gray, *Two Faces of Liberalism* (New York, New Press, 2000) 69–104.

[64] J Rawls, *Political Liberalism* (Cambridge, MA, Harvard University Press, 1993).

decisions, of both government and opposition, to employ harsh means against what appear, by light of their particular projects of public order, as threats to the community's vital interests.

In such cases, genuine advocates of plausible conceptions of fairness can be found on both sides. This is made no less true by the fact that key actors on one or both sides might properly be classified as 'thugs'.[65] For example, the Chilean coup of 1973, the Salvadoran and Nicaraguan internal armed conflicts of the 1980s, and the attempted Venezuelan coup of 2002—all conflicts rooted in socio-economic polarisation—sharply divided the respective societies, including their liberal-democratic elements. Ethnic polarisation is, if anything, even more likely to pit sincerely held, but clashing, conceptions of fairness against one another in conflicts that are beyond the capacity of institutions to contain.[66]

Participants in unmediated social conflict are consequentialists, almost by necessity; political actors are expected to take responsibility, not exclusively for their own acts, but for the outcomes that befall their constituents. In such contexts, the cause of human dignity frequently appears to demand the violation of the rights of some as a means to protect or establish the rights of others. If there is a 'universal' intuition on this topic, it would seem to be that while many acts can be presumptively condemned as heinous, no acts are absolutely excluded where the most vital moral interests are perceived to be at stake.[67]

This is not to say that sadism, venality, bigotry and a plethora of other

[65] Indeed, it is no less true where demagogues are responsible for having exacerbated the polarisation, for the fact that the *other* side is in the grip of demagoguery presents genuine dilemmas for one's own side. Once convinced that the other side observes no limits, one can easily become convinced of the dire need for ruthless measures. One's reactive ruthlessness, in turn, may perversely serve to vindicate the fears initially conjured by the demagogues, so that both sides are trapped in a logic of escalating violence. This is one way to interpret the calamity of Yugoslavia in the 1990s.

[66] The Israeli–Palestinian conflict, though not an 'internal' conflict in the ordinary sense, comes to mind as an example of a violent confrontation as to which liberal internationalists from all over the world have taken up different sides, in vitriolic opposition even to one another.

Any use of illustrative examples has the serious pitfall that readers, depending on their own substantive political principles, will perceive different conflicts differently. Rest assured that the author has very strong loyalties of his own in regard to each of the conflicts cited here; the concession that informed persons of good faith and sound reason could support the opposite side of each is rather a grudging one.

[67] One need only mention the general complacency of Western populations, statesmen and even scholars about the deliberate incineration of hundreds of thousands of innocent people in Hamburg, Dresden, Tokyo, Hiroshima and Nagasaki. Even those who condemn the fire-bombings and atomic bombings generally feel compelled to engage seriously with the empirical question of whether these measures were necessary to prevent far worse harms. See, eg, Walzer, *Just and Unjust Wars*, above n 6, 251–68. Moreover, even condemnation of the acts seldom crosses the line to vilification of the actors; the scope for good-faith disagreement militates against attributing criminality to those who were in the unenviable position of having to make the decisions. (Of course, whereas 'civilised' folk may incinerate innocent civilians for weighty reasons, it is easily assumed from a distance that 'other' folk commit analogous acts for frivolous reasons.)

human vices do not play a major role in such practices around the world. But the typical focus on these human vices—especially evident in the current enthusiasm for retrospective and extraterritorial criminal prosecution of conflict participants who have employed ruthless means—distracts from the role that principled persons often play on both sides of violent conflicts. Even where leaders are cynical demagogues, their demagoguery operates precisely by mobilising the moral dispositions of constituents in support of decisive action. And while many of the worst atrocities are committed by thugs recruited for this purpose, in at least partial secrecy from those constituents—an implicit acknowledgement that they go beyond what even a wartime sensibility can abide—this is often because the constituents prefer not to know (and know that they prefer not to know) the details of what is done in pursuit of ends they endorse.[68]

Of course, this observation alone does not suffice to justify a pluralistic global order. The mere fact of intractable disagreement about the moral quality of political acts does not make the conduct in question any less wrongful (let alone any less harmful to its victims), and no moral immunities automatically attach to having thoughtful and decent reasons for acting on an egregious conception of justice. But the observation does have important implications for the design of a morally responsible approach to political difference: (1) the empirical intractability of the cir-

The increased stringency of *jus in bello* norms since the Second World War should not be taken to indicate any transcendence of consequentialism. International law continues to bar only those tactics anticipated to be unnecessary to legitimate military objectives, and conflicting assessments of necessity continue to reflect the parties' differential access to military technology. The collateral infliction of civilian losses is criminalised only where such losses figure to be 'clearly excessive in relation to the concrete and direct overall military advantage anticipated', *Statute of the International Criminal Court*, Art 8(2)(b)(iv). Moreover, notwithstanding the prohibitions of Articles 51–5 of Additional Protocol I to the Geneva Conventions (adopted 8 June 1977, entered into force 7 December 1978) 1125 UNTS 3, the major liberal war-fighting powers have refused to renounce belligerent reprisals against civilians, see E Benvenisti, 'Human Dignity in Combat: The Duty to Spare Enemy Civilians' (2006) 39 *Israel Law Review* 81, 103 n 84, and the International Court of Justice has been unwilling to rule out the legality of the use of nuclear weapons in the case of a dire threat to a state's survival, *Advisory Opinion on Legality of the Threat or Use of Nuclear Weapons* [1996] ICJ Rep 226, paras 95–7.

[68] The truth of this observation hides in plain sight. The Reagan Administration's conduct of the Cold War, after all, is associated in the public mind with 'moral clarity', rather than with that Administration's underwriting of armed factions whose ruthlessness (indeed, brutality) was known beyond cavil, such as the Salvadoran armed forces, the Nicaraguan *contras*, the Angolan UNITA rebels, Cambodian anti-Vietnamese insurgents operationally (as well as formally) conjoined to the genocidal Khmer Rouge, and the various unsavoury factions battling Soviet troops in Afghanistan. Whether the end justified the means in any or all of these cases is beyond the scope of this discussion; what matters is that a great many informed persons of good faith and sound reason thought so. And among those who thought otherwise, some proclaimed solidarity with opposing factions themselves known to employ ruthless means. Still others, while eschewing ruthless means in all of these cases, have accepted them, however reluctantly, in other cases.

cumstances of global pluralism, ie, a world made up of political communities dominated by incompatible conceptions of political morality; (2) the empirical possibility and moral respectability of a good-faith accommodation among bearers of incompatible conceptions of internal public order; (3) the practical peril of allowing powerful states (or particular constituencies within such states) selectively to attribute criminality to certain foreign officials whom they oppose for partisan reasons (because the target list is so rich), and who are not genuinely morally worse than, inter alia, other foreign officials whom those states may support; (4) the practical peril of conditioning reconciliation on prosecuting leaders for acts committed with a complicity that runs all the way down to the grass roots; (5) the practical peril of applying the label 'criminal' to foes whom one cannot wish away and with whom one must reach some kind of working arrangement; (6) the moral peril of affixing the stain of criminality for acts that most individuals, in truly analogous circumstances, would find themselves, even on the basis of considered moral judgement, committing or supporting (criminality properly implying not merely moral wrongfulness but deviance).

If deep political disagreement is endemic rather than aberrational, efforts to manage political conflict must accept a certain modesty of mission. A moralistic campaign to eradicate political ruthlessness will likely lead either to disillusionment or, far worse, to the licensing of a ruthlessness to end all ruthlessness. Attributions of outlawry to adverse regimes, in addition to hardening positions counterproductively (akin to the insistence that one will 'never negotiate with terrorists'), tend to place enforcement demands on international institutions that such institutions characteristically cannot bear, opening the door to unilateral exertions that can be rationalised as implementation of universal principles. Transnational criminal proceedings against foreign state actors, if directed at non-aberrational conduct, not only will be skewed by a political selectivity of prosecution, but may degenerate into festivals of self-righteousness, orchestrated not only to designate scapegoats for international dissensus, but also to reveal the fecklessness of those who counsel restraint and compromise in the face of a certified evil.[69]

[69] If my scholarship in this area can be said to have an immediate political purpose, it is to expose the latent kinship of certain human rights advocates with the neo-conservatives, whose practical positions they rarely embrace. But see F Tesón, 'Ending Tyranny in Iraq' (2005) 19 *Ethics & International Affairs* 1 (defending the 2003 Iraq invasion on human rights grounds); WM Reisman, 'Unilateral Actions', above n 45 (generally advocating the unilateral coercive implementation of the norms of a supposed human-rights-based international order).

In my view, a substantial element of human rights advocacy has lost its way, departing from the path that leads more reliably to peace. In generating demands that exceed the institutional capacities of the international system, the quest for a transcendent justice leads to a fork in the road, where one path leads to frustration and disillusionment and the other to alliance with the neoconservatives—who are, in essence, liberal internationalists who have become

A responsible approach to global order, therefore, is a pluralist approach. A commitment to pluralism in no way implies agnosticism about the wrongfulness of the other's conduct, nor need it assert that the conduct, albeit wrong 'for us', may be right 'for them'. Rather, pluralism (or more precisely, a qualified or 'bounded' pluralism) accords to the other, within a system of reciprocity, certain basic prerogatives and inviolabilities that withstand the other's wrongful, but non-aberrant, conduct.

Fidelity to such a system of respectful accommodation is a moral duty, insofar as that system is reasonably efficacious, compared with the foreseeable alternative, in preventing uncontrolled international conflict, limiting predation (often carried out in the name of humanitarianism) against poor and weak states, and providing the basis for international co-operation on matters of significant human concern. That fidelity also reflects a humility and restraint becoming of an outsider who lacks a stake appropriate to participation in an internal struggle. Even the best-intentioned outsiders face certain moral pitfalls. Our lack of familiarity and stake allows us: (a) to make judgements based on limited information, often packaged for us by partisans in the conflict; (b) to make judgements, supposedly in the interest of the whole, where our objectivity has been contaminated by identification with certain sectors of a foreign society at the expense of others; (c) to make judgements that leave others to bear the consequences of our decisions long after we have lost interest and moved on. Beyond this, as a matter of dignity, participants in a struggle over the basic direction of their own society should not, presumptively, have to suffer the coercive interference of those who will not have to live with the resulting conditions. (In principle, of course, deference should be reserved for those who speak authentically for the society, but this is typically what the conflict is *about*.)

Fundamental human concerns necessitate uniquely political decisions about the nature of the good society wherein the good life is pursued. The state—as opposed to non-territorial or micro-territorial communities rooted in sentimental attachment rather than potential for order-creation, and as opposed to an international community encompassing an unmanageable multiplicity of interests and values—represents the only community in the name of which the ineluctably contentious decisions needed to structure social life can be effectively made and enforced.[70]

disillusioned with the constraints of both broad multilateralism and deontological ethics. What I offer is a moral argument for adherence to international legal constraint that is unavailable to those who see international law merely as an instrument of transcendent justice.

[70] This is by no means to discount the impact on social conditions, and even on aspects of public order, of a wide range of international and sub-national (and even transnational) decision-making structures and processes. But such structures and processes cannot

Even in states where these decisions are not made democratically—by light of even the loosest of the standards that may be derived from any of the radically conflicting available conceptions of democracy[71]—the political independence of the territorial entity preserves for its population at least the object of democratic struggle, and therefore the possibility of eventually achieving what may plausibly be described as self-government.[72] Notwithstanding the inherent messiness and frequent nastiness of the processes by which these matters are worked out internally, the impositions of intermeddlers, themselves systematically prone to self-interestedness, arrogance or well-meaning short-sightedness, are rarely to be preferred. Human beings therefore have a morally important interest, albeit not always a paramount interest, in being part of a territorial political community that maintains the last word on its internal public order.

(5) The Legal Terms of a Bounded Pluralism

Sovereignty is the legal expression of the territorial political community's presumptive monopoly of the last word on internal public order. This entails more than merely the authority to give or withhold consent to international legal obligations. Although the point is often misunderstood, sovereign authority continues to exist alongside legal obligation with respect to the very same subject matter.

Sovereignty represents the political community's retention of ultimate authority within the territory, notwithstanding international legal obligations pertaining to the exercise of that authority.[73] Although local authorities' failures to implement obligations are breaches that require remedies and license appropriately limited countermeasures, breaches do not license external forces to take action within the territory without the consent of local authorities, and local officials may be immune from

undertake the most foundational decisions about public order without effectively establishing a super-state (as some hope or fear that the European Union will become) or a state-within-a-state (as in the case of the most fully autonomous regions and indigenous communities).

[71] I have addressed radically conflicting conceptions of democracy at length elsewhere. See, eg, Roth, *Governmental Illegitimacy*, above n 10, 75–120; BR Roth, 'Evaluating Democratic Progress' (1995) 9 *Ethics & International Affairs* 55; BR Roth, 'Retrieving Marx for the Human Rights Project' (2004) 17 *Leiden Journal of International Law* 31, 52–61; GH Fox and BR Roth, 'Democracy and International Law' (2001) 27 *Review of International Studies* 327, 343–8.

[72] The following words of Thomas Nagel make a similar point (though ironically, Nagel was speaking of global rather than—and at the expense of—state institutions): 'Unjust and illegitimate regimes are the necessary precursors of the progress toward legitimacy and democracy, because they create the centralized power that can then be contested, and perhaps turned in other directions without being destroyed.' T Nagel, 'The Problem of Global Justice' (2005) 33 *Philosophy and Public Affairs* 113, 146.

[73] 'International law . . . recognizes the power—though not the right—to break a treaty and abide the international consequences.' L Henkin, *Foreign Affairs and the Constitution* (New York, Foundation Press, 1972) 168.

personal liability in foreign courts for breaches committed within the scope of state authority. States do not typically renounce the capacity to put themselves out of compliance with international law; indeed, internal law may provide for a decision to override the dictates of international obligations, temporarily or permanently, based on a residual unilateral capacity to find the existence of emergency conditions or a fundamental change in circumstances, whether or not such findings preclude wrongfulness as a matter of international law. States anticipate that disagreements about norms will manifest themselves in contingencies, the details of which cannot be fully anticipated in the course of legal standard-setting. Without some assurance of the maintenance of the core legal capacity to resist impositions, states would be chilled in their willingness to subscribe to international obligations.

The international system licenses proportionate sanctions against states for adopting internal practices that breach obligations, but only in relatively rare cases—not ordinary human rights violations, but aberrant atrocities—are states deemed to have renounced, not only the practices themselves, but also the legal capacity to authorise them.[74] In still rarer cases will the international system approve recourse to armed intervention, either expressly through Security Council authorisation under Chapter VII or tacitly through acquiescence in unauthorised actions to forestall imminent humanitarian catastrophe.

Advocates of a 'transcendent justice' approach to international legal order find such negation of sovereign prerogative to be far too rare. And to a significant extent, they may be correct. The justification of the existing sovereign equality framework operates from the assumption that internal political conflict represents, in the largest number of cases, struggle among competing factions seeking, however ruthlessly, to apply their principled conceptions of public order to governance of the undivided whole. Yet internal political conflict has turned out, on too many occasions, to be a cover for something else: unlimited violence unleashed against civilian populations, either for reasons of ethno-nationalist ideology (eg, Rwanda, the former Yugoslavia) or as a by-product of efforts by wholly unprincipled armed gangs to usurp control of economic activity and natural resources (eg, Somalia, Liberia, Sierra Leone). Although the existing system has an available mechanism to address internal humanitarian crises as to which diverse elements of the international community can agree on the equities and the response—Chapter VII—and although

[74] See, eg, 'Judicial Decisions: International Military Tribunal (Nuremberg), Judgment and Sentences' (1947) 41 *AJIL* 172, 221 ('He who violates the laws of war cannot obtain immunity while acting in pursuance of the authority of the state if the state in authorizing action moves outside its competence under international law'). Although attributions of international criminal responsibility are no longer limited by the Nuremberg Tribunal's requirement of a nexus to interstate warfare, the threshold for the international criminalisation of state acts remains higher for purely internal conduct.

the system's failures to intervene are far less attributable to legal strictures than to an unwillingness of the powerful to invest blood and treasure in purely humanitarian pursuits, the inflexibilities of the existing system are genuinely problematic. Moreover, improved mechanisms of international criminal justice are needed to deny impunity to perpetrators of acts that, notwithstanding the colour of state authority, are beyond the pale of any plausible good-faith conception of public order.

Nonetheless, it is important not to move from a conceptually narrow (if empirically altogether too ample) class of cases in which the equities are starkly clear, to a sweeping rejection of strictures on the pursuit of moralistic causes. Whether or not (as conservative lawyers tend to say) 'hard cases make bad law', extreme cases surely invite bad 'dicta' (ie, broad elaborations of principle unnecessary to the outcome of the particular case). Although discrete reforms to the current system are needed, the system's underlying principles are sound. A broad licensing of cross-border exercises of power is less likely to further global justice than to open the door to arrogant (let alone self-interested) impositions, and to undermine the institutional basis for co-operation among the non-like-minded. The precise scope of exceptions to sovereign prerogative may properly be debated, but the exceptions should not be allowed to swallow the rule.

IV. CONCLUSION

For those who impute to the international legal order an inherent purpose to establish a universal justice that transcends the boundaries of territorial communities, the legal prerogatives associated with state sovereignty represent impediments to the global advance of legality. Sovereignty thus appears as the unconquered domain: a realm of lawlessness that must recede for international law to advance. This view, however, tends to neglect persistent and profound, albeit bounded, disagreement within the international community as to the requirements of justice. An alternative conception of international order predicates peace and co-operation on continued respect for each political unit's capacity to make and enforce the ineluctably contentious decisions needed to structure social life.

The international order's pluralism should never be confused with the 'gorgeous mosaic' pluralism of the liberal imagination, in which an overarching unity as to 'the right' renders inoffensive, and even enriching, the persistence of differences over 'the good'. A duty not to intervene in a foreign political community's internal conflict, so far as that duty extends, is a duty to respect patterns of coercion, and even violence, within a collectivity of which one is not a member. As long as profound disagreement about justice remains part of the human condition, an international pluralism, even in its ideal form, will at moments be a tense and even ugly pluralism, an accommodation among political communities dominated by incompatible positions on matters of justice and injustice, freedom and tyranny, and, ultimately, life and death.

Nonetheless, such pluralism is a moral, not merely a practical, imperative. Would-be reformers of international order must accept that internal struggles over competing conceptions of legitimate and just public order cannot always be contained by liberal constitutional solutions, and that recourse to ruthless means, while often objectively unjust, is a fact of political life that unbridled interventionism cannot eradicate—and may well exacerbate. Such reformers must acknowledge the unique stake of a territorial political community's members in the collective decisions that condition life in their society, and the inherent untrustworthiness of even well-intentioned and thoughtful (let alone self-interested and arrogant) outsiders poised to impose unilateral implementations of supposed universal standards. Moreover, such reformers must serve the moral interest in international coexistence and co-operation by strengthening, not weakening, the institutional basis for good-faith accommodation among the non-like-minded.

All of this can occur without any abandonment of moral judgement. Pluralism is not scepticism or relativism. To uphold limitations on transnational prosecution or forcible intervention is not to refrain from condemning or sanctioning breaches of legal obligations, just as to insist on consent-based methods for ascertaining states' legal obligations is not to abjure more wide-ranging standards for evaluating states' performance of their moral duties. A moral approach to international relations does not require—and properly conceived, does not permit—unleashing the strong to impose justice as they understand it.

7

Democracy without Sovereignty: The Global Vocation of Political Ethics†

ROBERT HOWSE* and KALYPSO NICOLAIDIS**

I. INTRODUCTION

IN THE *PYTHAGORAS*, Plato reminds his audience of how men were saved from annihilation by Prometheus who gave them the knowledge of fire and the arts—only to potentially fall victim of each other through incessant war. Zeus (as always!) cleaned up the mess by giving men a foundation for co-operation and for governing themselves. He entrusted Hermes with two gifts for men: *aidos* (respect, restraint, shame, reverence, awe) and *dike* (justice or rightfulness), 'in order to serve as the norm for cities and link men through ties of friendship'. These gifts were to be bestowed on all, not just on a small elite. Thus, for Plato, who explores in the *Pythagoras* the very foundations of experimental democracy in Athens, Zeus did not choose to give men formal laws or institutions, a list of permitted or banned actions, but a *relationship to law and polis.*[1] As Socrates tells his companion in Plato's later *Minos*, Zeus may have taught law-makers but he himself did not make law.

This chapter will therefore argue that as we embark on a new age of governance between all mankind, these Platonic lessons need to be revisited anew. In our view, if, in a localised context, a political ethics *à la Plato* must emphasise behavioural guidelines above specific institutions or strict rules of action, this is all the more the case in a context where *aidos* and *dike* must be pursued not only between men and women, but

† An initial version of this paper was presented at the NYU School of Law Conference on 'Legitimacy, Democracy and Justice in International Governance', 3–4 October 2002. We would like to thank the participants for their input, including Joseph Weiler and Robert Keohane. We would also like to thank Carolyn Deere, Matthew Eagleton Pierce and the members of the Oxford-WTO group for their feedback, as well as the participants in the conference which led to this volume.

* Robert Howse is Professor of Law at New York University Law School.

** Kalypso Nicolaïdis is Director of the European Studies Centre and Professor in International Relations at the University of Oxford.

[1] F Ost and L van Eynde, *Faust ou les Frontieres Du Savoir* (Belgium, Fonds national de la recherche scientifique, 2002).

between groups, nations and transnational associations. In the current, experimental stage of global governance, we believe that such an ethics ought to take central stage.

In this spirit, our essay challenges the notion that legitimate global governance should be conceived primarily in terms of the proper allocation or delegation of authority to global institutions. The interdependence of the local, national and global in today's world, as well as the connections between different realms of global governance (eg, trade and human rights, investment and environment), means that it is impossible to protect and promote democratic politics through a stable division of competences between local and national 'democratic' institutions and global institutions, or by restricting the mandate of particular global institutions to an agreed 'subject matter'. Instead, as we discuss below, we need to focus on the manner in which power is exercised by diverse agents in global sites of decision and deliberation, some highly institutionalised and others better characterised as informal networks.[2] Assessing and hopefully shaping the conduct of agents in global sites of governance in accordance with a political ethics of democracy offers considerable promise as an alternative—or perhaps complementary and mutually reinforcing—approach to legitimacy.

In this essay, we start by revisiting the principles of subsidiarity and supremacy in the EU context to argue that they should be understood as guiding principles of 'transnational democracy', ie, as a *horizontal* reading of sovereignty transfer—their import for the global level, in other words, is more heuristic than legalistic. Second, we make the general case for a global political ethics, by arguing that neither strict reliance on indirect accountability, in other words a limited reading of 'subsidiarity', nor simply granting 'supremacy' to international law, can 'buy' legitimacy at the global level. Third, we review the story of the General Agreement on Tariffs and Trade (GATT) and the World Trade Organization (WTO) in this light by focusing on both the illusion from below—technical expertise—and the illusion from above—constitutionalisation—that have underpinned their fifty-year history. We deal with these illusions by turning to architectural reform and its limits, before, finally, suggesting the outlines of the kind of transnational ethics we have in mind.

II. SOVEREIGNTY, SUBSIDIARITY AND SUPREMACY: THE HORIZONTAL READING OF EUROPEAN INTEGRATION

There is no denying the enigmatic spell sovereignty continues to have over our political imagination, including in the worlds of law and social

[2] A-M Slaughter, *A New World Order* (Princeton University Press, 2004).

science. The concept of sovereignty remains indispensable not only as the founding myth but also as the constitutive *language* of the modern international society of states; but it is at the same time deeply problematic and contested. The premise of this book is that sovereignty has become divided, shared, relocated, exploded, overlapping. In short: that we must give up once and for all, not the idea of sovereignty per se, but the fetishism of indivisibility which continues to plague international law and international relations. Indeed, our editors argue, international law has become partly 'verticalised', ie, that a vertical dimension has been added to the traditional 'horizontal' one defined around traditional state sovereignty and inter-state relations. The broad compact of norms and regimes that governs the actions of actors in the international system not only affects the formal allocation of authority with or away from sovereign nation-states, but perhaps more importantly how power is legitimised politically and how it is exercised and by whom. In this context, we argue that supremacy and subsidiarity are less *allocative* principles than *legimitising* norms. And under this reading, they function as guiding norms for political processes rather than institutional structures per se.

While the EU operates for this project as the *ontological avant-garde in the international system*, we must recognise that the capacity to transcend the aforementioned fetishism of indivisibility is shared to very different degrees among European peoples and their collective psyche. There is still a gulf between Rousseauist notions of supreme and exclusive authority within an exclusive territory and German federalism for instance. Thus, the case of the EU is illustrative precisely because, while this is where supremacy and subsidiarity are most formally entrenched, the practice associated with their adoption has been fluid and contested.

The EU case in particular encourages us to reconsider what we mean by 'verticality' and 'horizontality'. At least in the European version of federalism, verticality ought to be distinguished from hierarchy and the federal model from a federal state.[3] The fractal theory—of reproduction of similar patterns at different levels—is more relevant than the Russian doll vision of Europe. The EU system organises a dialogue between authorities rather than presenting a simple rule as to who prevails. This is why during the Convention debates, the formalisation of even the seemingly straightforward and entrenched principle of supremacy was contested—at least by the legally minded Brits (and here we say legally minded rather than sovereignty minded advisedly). Most fundamentally, to the prevailing notion of horizontal juxtaposition of sovereignty (which would be more traditional than the vertical transfer this book is

[3] K Nicolaidis and R Howse (eds), *The Federal Vision: Legitimacy and Levels of Governance in the US and the EU* (Oxford University Press, 2001).

concerned with), we must add a much deeper horizontal *transfer* of sovereignty associated in particular with the principle of mutual recognition.[4] Both notions of supremacy and subsidiarity can be seen as much as principles organising such horizontal transfer of sovereignty (even though through the verticalisation of rules) as principles of vertical allocation. That is because the EU can be characterised by the tension between the legal hierarchy of norms expressed through the principle of supremacy and the equality between its Member States coupled with the absence of an overarching political authority as with classic federal states. European law constrains states not only through allocating authority but in anchoring their behaviour towards each other, a logic described by Daniel Halberstam as stemming from the principle of loyalty.

Such a horizontal reading of subsidiarity and supremacy follows directly from the limits of the notion of sovereignty in a world where laws and actions within a polity increasingly have external effects. Supremacy and subsidiarity therefore can be defined in a dialectic way as complementary principles to deal with the fundamental conundrum of transnational democracy. Supremacy serves as a meta-norm of *conflict of law* between Member States such as to enhance the representation of foreigners inside the jurisdiction of every Member State, and to ask when and to what extent these interests should trump the domestic social contract. Subsidiarity, in turn, serves to mitigate the impact of foreign laws unaccountable to our own, and thus to circumscribe the domain within which this powerful logic of supremacy operates.

Many commentators view the supremacy debate as a process of constructive dialogue between the Community and national judges about the Union's evolving legal order—reminding the Court of Justice of the importance of protecting fundamental rights against potential infringements by the Union institutions, or of enforcing the limits to Union competences which are intended to safeguard national sovereignty.[5] But, whatever its constitutional nature, the principle of supremacy could not resolve the long-running *Kompetenz–Kompetenz* debate on the allocation of ultimate sovereignty, and the power of constitutional review, between the Union and its individual Member States. Supremacy exists *at the Union level*, but the whole point of the *Kompetenz–Kompetenz* debate is that the authority of those statements *at the national level* remains contested by certain domestic courts. Indeed, many legal scholars contest the existence

[4] See K Nicolaidis, 'Trusting the Poles? Constructing Europe through Mutual Recognition' (2007) 14 *Journal of European Public Policy* 682; See also, K Nicolaidis, 'Kir Forever? The Journey of a Political Scientist in the Landscape of Recognition', in M Maduro (ed), *The Past and Future of EU Law; The Classics of EU Law Revisited on the 50th Anniversary of the Rome Treaty* (Oxford, Hart Publishing, 2007).

[5] M Dougan, 'The Convention's Draft Constitutional Treaty: A "Tidying-Up Exercise" That Needs Some Tidying-Up of its Own' (2003) Federal Trust Constitutional Online Essay 27/03.

of a hierarchical relationship between the Community and the various national legal orders, and endow the principle of supremacy with a much more specific meaning, ie, as a device for settling concrete conflicts between Community and national law in cases where EU law has direct effect.[6]

This means in turn that the principle of supremacy is not unconditional. In certain situations, the imperative of disapplying national rules that are incompatible with provisions of Community law must be balanced against other equally fundamental principles of the Treaty system, such as the need for legal certainty and the protection of legitimate expectations. This conflict between supremacy as hierarchy and its reception into the national constitutional environment brings us back to the deep horizontal nature of the EU as organising the transfer of sovereignty between states rather than above states.

Similarly, as we argued in *The Federal Vision*, the norm of subsidiarity is less useful as a guide for the allocation of authority between the state and EU level, than as a multifaceted principle for rethinking European federalism in general. In other words, the practical success of subsidiarity in the EU depends in part on the capacity of EU actors to embrace this spirit of federal union which cannot be easily be subsumed in a vertical paradigm of centralisation–decentralisation and optimal allocation of powers. In terms of polity, the paradigm of federal union and horizontal sovereignty transfer calls for conceiving the EU as a *demoi-cracy* whereby identities and social bargains are shared and overlapping rather than merged and subsumed under a single umbrella.[7] In other words, *demoi-cracy* serves as a political philosophy principle to adjudicate the diversity between polities in the same way that supremacy and subsidiarity serve as legal principles to adjudicate conflicts of laws between states.

In sum, even in the EU context, a paradigm of legally framed vertical allocation of authority only takes us so far. Instead, we need to understand supremacy and subsidiarity as heuristics or boundary conditions for the dialogue between levels of governance, as a baseline for accountability for governance beyond the state. It is in terms of such a reading that we go on to explore the issue of power allocation at the global level.

III. FROM THE EU TO THE GLOBAL: THE FATE OF POLITICS

This diagnosis is all the more true at the global level. To come back to our initial question, how do or can allocative principles help achieve greater legitimacy for governance beyond the state without even an embryonic

[6] *Ibid.*

[7] N Nicolaidis, 'We the Peoples of Europe' (November/December 2004) *Foreign Affairs* 97–110.

polity such as the EU possesses? The classic response has been to describe how indirect accountability to domestic democratic polities has been refined recently along the lines of a delegation model.[8] But accountability to citizens through domestic representative institutions is burdened by problems of agency costs and information asymmetries,[9] and indeed it is precisely for this reason that we witness concern about a democratic deficit and a legitimacy crisis of global governance. Alternatively, many authors have tried to come up with imaginative proposals for reshaping global institutions at least partially along the lines of domestic institutions of representative democracy.[10]

The objections to both these lines are well rehearsed. Domestic institutions of representative democracy which aspire to the peaceful management of social conflict are far from an adequate source of legitimacy, even in the traditional domestic context. We know that these institutions are vulnerable to capture by the most powerful interests, to demagogical manipulation, to rational ignorance and indifference of the public, to biased time horizons, and the ebb and flow of fashion and electoral cycles. As Moravcsik argues, the fact that political outcomes often do not match the interests of the 'median voter' but that of the louder bullies in the ring provides a justification for non-majoritarian and 'apolitical' institutions of governance in domestic contexts (even if more democracy and better politics may be theoretically more satisfying answers to the imperfections of real-world representative democracy as we know it).[11] At the same time, partly due to globalisation and the increasing complexity, velocity and specialisation of the public function, executives and bureaucratic elites have been strengthened in domestic polities and the role of legislatures correspondingly diminished.

Beyond the domestic polity, the delegation of governance to actors who are insulated from the rough and tumble of daily democratic politics has often been defended on the grounds that the delegated issues are less salient in terms of citizen's preferences and more technical, while at the same time polities are hugely less homogeneous and more dispersed than at the national or sub-national level. More generally, as Sassen puts it, the

[8] R Keohane and R Grant, 'Accountability and Abuses of Power in World Politics' (2005) 99 *American Political Science Review* 29; D Held and M Koenig-Archibugi (eds), *Global Governance and Public Accountability* (London, Blackwell, 2005).

[9] R Howse, 'How to Begin to Think About the "Democratic Deficit"' at the WTO' in S Griller (ed), *International Economic Governance and Non-Economic Concerns: New Challenges for the International Legal Order,* European Community Studies Association of Austria (ECSA Austria), Publication Series 5 (Wien, New York, Springer-Verlag, 2003) 79–101. C Coglianese and K Nicolaidis, 'Securing Subsidiarity: Mechanisms for Allocating Authority in Tiered Regimes' in Nicolaidis and Howse, above n 3.

[10] I Clark, *Globalization and International Relations Theory* (Oxford University Press, 1999); D Held and A McGrew, *The Global Transformations* (Cambridge, Polity, 2000).

[11] A Moravcsik, 'Is there a "Democratic Deficit" in World Politics? A Framework for Analysis' (2004) 39 *Government and Opposition* 336.

national has been disassembled and state agendas denationalised: jurisdictional and territorial boundaries no longer match in any coherent way.[12] Such arguments are not easy to dismiss either on functional or normative grounds. In these circumstances, a reorientation towards the political ethics of democracy may be seen not simply as second-best ersatz for fully blown representative institutions at the global level, but as something that is perhaps ever more necessary for domestic governance as well.

In short, we suggest that instead of *reproducing* democratic institutions at the global level, we ought to take up the challenge of making the behaviour of agents who exercise power or authority in global sites conform to a political ethics, values and practices that exemplify the spirit and practice of democratic polity. In order to clarify what we mean by political ethics, we must start with the role of politics in the design of global governance.

The very notion of 'governance' and the *problematique* of legitimacy and justice that have become so prominent today rest on the increasing obsolescence of the traditional model of international 'politics' as inter-state diplomacy, ie, the international version of delegation and insulation.[13] Global governance comes into play not only through the legalisation of international co-operation but through its concurrent perception and contestation as a lasting system of rules and praxis autonomous from ad hoc bargains.[14] Today we can no longer ask *whether* but *to what extent* can indirect democracy and indirect accountability through the 'sovereign' state and its consent suffice to legitimise global governance. To the extent that it cannot, we enter the realm of global politics, or what we could call 'democratised governance'. Let us take one step back.

At a most general level, let us posit that modern governance systems rely on at least three sources of legitimacy: constitutional settlement, the politics of democracy, and technical expertise or effectiveness. If this is the case across issue areas, then, we would argue, not only will different *loci* of global governance need to rely on different balancing between these three sources, not only will such balancing evolve over time, but the legitimacy acquired on one ground will affect the others in complex and unpredictable ways. Legitimate global governance cannot be reduced to the imaginary test of a 'global opinion poll'. Rather, and with David Beetham, we would argue that legitimacy is not grounded in people's beliefs in the abstract but in the degree to which a set of power relations can be *justified in terms of* people's beliefs, values and expectations, even

12 S Sassen, *Territory, Authority, Rights: From Medieval to Global Assemblages* (Princeton University Press, 2006).

13 R Keohane and J Nye *Power and Interdependence* (3rd ed, New York, Longman, 1979; reprinted 2001).

14 See special issue on International Regimes, *International Organisation*, Fall 2002.

as either these beliefs and expectations or the capacity of the system to translate them into outcomes changes over time.[15] Sustained legitimacy therefore requires both consistency in purpose and flexibility in action. In this, we echo Ruggie's characterisation of political authority as 'a fusion of power with legitimate political purpose'.[16] Assessing the legitimacy of a given part of the global governance system therefore consists in asking how and to what extent the balance between the sources of legitimacy continues to support people's beliefs, values and expectations—bracketing for the moment the fundamental question as to who these peoples are and how their beliefs, values and expectations are to be measured. But how could such assessment operate outside of politics?

Let us zoom in on the governance of the global trading system. Here we argue that the governance of the trading system is currently off-balance. Historically, as it evolved over time from the GATT, managed by a low-key group of experts, to the semi-constitutionalised WTO, the space for politics in its midst has shrunk, while it should rather have expanded—a point conveyed by the self-styled anti-globalisers as they create new spaces for contestation in the street or on the Web. In their world, power and purpose are radically at odds, as the perceived powerlessness of the *citoyens du monde* engages with and 'democratises' at last the asymmetries in *state* bargaining power between the haves and the have-nots of globalisation.

In our schema, then, politics in the global governance of trade is threatened by two illusions, which are—as we see it—two illusions without a future. These illusions in turn both can be read as stemming from misreadings of the principles of supremacy and subsidiarity.

The first illusion—the illusion from below—is that conflicts over trade can be resolved by a technocratic insiders' network composed of trade law specialists, economists and scientists. Susan Strange has argued forcefully that global power has come to reside to a great extent in those holding key positions in 'the knowledge structure'—a claim bolstered with each stage of the rise of professional elites (dating back two centuries) and of the scientific revolution (genetics, risk assessment, etc). Reliance on the combination of trade law expertise and the scientific method (with its legitimacy-enhancing claim to consistency, reliability and transparency) becomes the basis for deriving 'truths' on which to pass judgment over domestic policies. The problem for many today is compounded by the 'privatisation' of decision-making by standards-setting bodies, international professional bodies and the like, which are

[15] D Beetham, *The Legitimation of Power* (London, Macmillan, 1991), see also Leonardo Martinez, 'Bottom-Up Legitimacy: Fusing Power and Purpose in the WTO' (Oxford University, mimeo, 2000).

[16] J Ruggie, 'International Regimes, Transactions, and Change: Embedded Liberalism in the Postwar Economic Order' (1982) 36 *International Organization* 382.

able to pre-empt public regulatory processes or substitute for them. Under the first illusion, therefore, subsidiarity has come to be captured by all those who are in a position to decide that somehow it is (scientifically, legally) right and proper to allocate authority to them or the likes of them.

But political space in the world of global trade is also increasingly threatened from above—witness the attempt to 'constitutionalise' the WTO as a form of higher law with 'supremacy', a set of authoritative rules placing beyond contestation a particular historical view of the appropriate limits of legitimate governmental action ('intervention') where there are effects on international trade, investment or intellectual property. As we have argued elsewhere, such hand-tying at the international level without extraordinary levels of democratic consent and a foundation in political and regulatory co-operation would only increase the WTO's unpopularity.[17]

Thus, while both some degree of expert management and some elements of constitutionalisation are (desirable) facts of life for the WTO, we cannot rely on emphasising either as the primary source of legitimacy. To be sure, both these 'apolitical' realms require democratic foundations as a *sine qua non*. But that would not be enough. While many of the conditions that may justify bypassing political processes obtain equally in the WTO and domestic contexts, it can be argued that it is precisely because more remote organisations such as the WTO (the actions of which nevertheless directly affect people's choices) lack a grounding in mutual trust and the identity bonds underpinning solidarity impulses at the domestic level that they need to be *more* democratic, *more* political than domestic institutions.

We need to spell out, of course, what we mean by democratic politics—a democratic politics appropriate to global governance, that is neither majoritarian nor solely representative, nor, even less, a deliberative free for all. By calling for the relevance of politics at the global level we mean to highlight the *limits* of a purely legalistic interpretation of the norms of 'subsidiarity' and 'supremacy' and the mix of technocratic and constitutional illusions associated with them, even in the EU context. We seek to stress the necessarily contested and *contestable* nature of issues at stake and the necessarily *controversial* and *unpredictable* nature of the solutions crafted on a day-to-day basis. We mean to stress the importance of power relationships in the regulation of globalisation and the desirability of systematically designing systems that can mitigate such asymmetries

[17] R Howse and N Nicolaidis, 'Legitimacy and Global Governance: Why a Constitution for the WTO Is a Step Too Far?' in Roger Porter et al (eds), *Equity, Efficiency and Legitimacy: The Multilateral System at the Millenium* (Washington DC, Brookings Institution Press, 2001); 'Enhancing WTO Legitimacy: Constitutionalization or Global Subsidiarity?' in M Verweij and T Josling (eds), *Deliberately Democratizing Multilateral Organization*, special issue of *Governance*, vol 16, no 1, January 2003.

without themselves becoming irrelevant. We also, and relatedly, believe that debates over legitimate global governance cannot bypass the question of justice beyond the state and that, in turn, such questions are eminently political.[18] Finally we wish to argue that architectural approaches to enhancing the legitimacy of global governance can only take us so far. For sure, there is room for tinkering with the formal structures of decision-making, but the heart of the matter is elsewhere, in the behaviour of the relevant actors and in the beliefs, values and expectations that inspire them—as well as ultimately, in the congruence with such values underpinning other levels of governance as well as individual citizens. Our focus must shift from the play's stage and set to the performances of the actors.

This leads us to sketch a political ethics for the age of globalisation. We have argued elsewhere that such a political ethics to a great extent already characterises an idealised version of the European Union, the very EU-topia which serves as the basis for narratives of projection from the EU to the global level.[19] And yet, at the EU level, just as with the global level, it has proven difficult for our political imaginations to move beyond the vertical logic of allocation of power towards a paradigm of horizontal mutual recognition.[20] A political ethics appropriate to the politics of globalisation will ultimately be tested on its capacity to legitimise global governance constraints on domestic political processes and socio-economic choices as well as on how each polity deals with 'the other' within, and on its capacity to speak to the fears of both current and future generations.

IV. DIAGNOSIS: FROM GATT TO WTO—THE SHIFTING BENCHMARK FOR POLITICS BEYOND THE STATE

A. Illusion From Below: Apogy and Obsolescence of Technocratic Management

The predecessor to the WTO, the GATT, notoriously came into being as the 'rump' of a failed grand design for governance of global trade—the stillborn ITO (International Trade Organisation). Like much of the Bretton

[18] R Foot, J Gaddis, and A Hurrell, (eds), *Order and Justice in International Relations* (Oxford University Press, 2002). K Nicolaidis and J Lacroix, 'Order and Justice Beyond the Nation-State: Europe's Competing Paradigms' in *Order and Justice in International Relations*.

[19] K Nicolaidis and R Howse, '"This is my EUtopia . . .": Narratives of Power' (2003) *Journal Of Common Market Studies*, Special Anniversary issue; and in JHH Weiler, J Peterson and I Begg (eds), *Integration in an Expanding European Union: Reassessing the Fundamentals.* (Oxford and Malden MA: Blackwell Publishing, 2003).

[20] Nicolaidis, 'Trusting the Poles' and 'Kir Forever?', above n 4.

Woods architecture (the World Bank, the IMF), the ITO would have, in some sense, transcended the classic model of a multilateral treaty, becoming a kind of regulatory agency on a global level.[21] The GATT, by contrast, consisted of little more than a framework for progressive negotiation of removal of tariffs or other border restrictions among a politico-administrative elite. The GATT established two general principles for governing these negotiations. These were 'most favoured nation' (MFN), which required that negotiated benefits be generalised to all the parties to the treaty, and 'national treatment', which required that internal policies of the parties not discriminate against imports (thus protecting against the undermining of negotiated concessions on border measures through protectionist domestic policies). The GATT itself contained no formal dispute-settlement procedures, only a general provision that allowed the parties as a whole to engage in dispute settlement (Article XXIII). Apart from the national treatment principle, the GATT contained a number of other provisions, which dealt in a subtle and ambiguous manner with domestic policies entailing controversial trade effects. Consider the language of the provisions on subsidies and on state-trading enterprises in this regard. Only one kind of trade policy instrument, quantitative restrictions (QRs: Article XI), was explicitly banned by the GATT, though this ban was subject to many exceptions.

Finally, the GATT was based on the notion that the parties preserved their sovereignty with regard to dealing with matters such as health, environment and public morals, regardless of any of the GATT treaty commitments (the Article XX exception), subject to the condition that such policies not constitute arbitrary or unjustified discrimination or a disguised restriction on international trade. The decision-making rule in the GATT, whether for treaty amendments, waivers or other matters (such as legally binding settlements of disputes) was consensus, *de jure* and *de facto*. The GATT Secretariat did not really have a legal basis in the treaty, but developed as a skeleton staff to administer the treaty and organise periodic negotiations on new concessions.

Thus described, the GATT fits very well with the liberal institutionalist theories of international co-operation characteristic of the international relations literature, especially in its international regime variant.[22] The GATT as an institution lacked any meaningful decision-making autonomy. Its function was to facilitate co-operation between the parties where such co-operation was mutually self-interested, by providing a loose structure to reduce the bargaining costs of mutually self-interested deals,

[21] On the post-war multilateral institutions as projections of the New Deal regulatory state, see A-M Slaughter, 'Regulating the World: Multilateralism, International Law, and the Projection of the New Deal Regulatory State' reprinted in R Howse (ed), *The World Trading System: Critical Perspectives on the World Economy*, vol I (London, Routledge, 1998) 50.

[22] R Keohane, *After Hegemony* (Princeton University Press, 1984).

to facilitate the flow and interpretation of information about compliance, and—through dispute settlement practice—to supplement decentralised monitoring and enforcement of the treaty. Through evolving practice, disputes increasingly were referred to panels of (mostly) trade diplomats, whose decisions were eventually supported by legal reasoning offered mostly by the Secretariat, but even this element of centralised monitoring of the bargain was balanced by the rule that, to be legally binding, the reports of the panels needed to be adopted by consensus of all the parties to the treaty, including the 'losing' party in the dispute.

If the notion of governance implies that an institution has some autonomous authority to make policy, articulate norms, stipulate priorities and resolve conflicts, the GATT had none, at least from a formal, juridical perspective. In this sense, understanding the power that it exercised in terms of a transfer of sovereignty is misguided.

Instead, from a neoliberal perspective the 'blueprint' of the GATT conformed well to the role of institutions in sustaining 'cooperation under anarchy'.[23] From a constructivist perspective, the GATT also became the site for what is a classic example of an epistemic community,[24] or network,[25] a technocratic elite, devoted to the telos of free trade, deeply engaged in setting agendas for negotiations, adjusting the bargain through treaty interpretations and on-going 'practice', and defining the 'norms' appropriate to a commitment to multilateral free trade.[26] Through the drafting of panel reports, the promulgation of various studies and documents bearing on the interpretation and modification of existing treaty provisions, the production of an Analytical Index summarising the results of previous dispute-settlement exercises, and through the management of the daily work of various committees and working groups, the GATT insider network arguably performed important governance functions, even in the absence of a formal decision-making authority allowing it to act without an explicit consensus of the parties on any matter other than the most trivial or mundane.

This insider network was particularly successful at not involving formal mechanisms of decision-making and accountability because of its diffuse nature—for the network not only consisted of professional

23 K Oye, *Cooperation under Anarchy* (Princeton University Press, 1985); R Axelrod and R Keohane 'Achieving Cooperation under Anarchy: Strategies and Institutions' (1985) 38 *World Politics* 226.

24 WJ Drake and K Nicolaidis, 'Ideas, Interests, And Institutionalization—Trade In Services And The Uruguay Round' (1992) 46 *International Organization* 37.

25 Slaughter, above n 2.

26 J Weiler, 'The Rule of Lawyers and the Ethos of Diplomats: Reflections on the Internal and External Legitimacy of Dispute Settlement' in Porter, above n 17, 334, 336–7; R Keohane and J Nye, 'The Club Model of Multilateral Cooperation and the World Trade Organization: Problems of Democratic Legitimacy' in Porter, *ibid*, 264ff.

employees within the GATT, but delegates from influential Member States of the GATT, domestic trade officials with strong ties to the GATT institution, and even pro-GATT academics and private practitioners.[27] The network was thus able to exercise its informal power across the dividing lines of diplomacy and technocracy, and in the interstices between the domestic and the international.

What united the insider network was the first source of legitimacy identified above, the shared recognition of its members of their 'expertise' about the GATT, the notion that they were applying rational bureaucratic and policy tools to the management of a regime that is beneficial to everyone. Normative conflicts, which underlay issues such as whether subsidies should be viewed as legitimate domestic public policies or cheating on the co-operative equilibrium of negotiated trade concessions, could be described by members of the insider network as 'system friction'[28] and 'interface' challenges,[29] implying that a solution could be engineered by technicians of competence and goodwill. This was plausible, because through much of the GATT's history, the politics of trade was low politics, and not grand Weberian politics entailing a choice between competing gods and demons, between fundamentally conflicting values. As Keohane and Nye remark:

> Politics takes place within the ground rules laid down by the regime, and generally is directed towards small advantages, favorable adjustments, or exceptions to the rules. Politics within the General Agreement on Tariffs and Trade (GATT) during much of the 1950s and 1960s conformed to this picture.[30]

In this context, national sovereignty was an instrumental feature of the system. There was unsurprisingly a solid political basis for the acceptance of the ground rules (such as national treatment) as a baseline for sorting legitimate domestic policies from 'cheating' on trade commitment.[31] The three decades following the post-war settlement were characterised in Ruggie's phrase by a basic transnational bargain over 'embedded liberalism'—the notion of multilateral trade liberalisation as facilitating the domestic, progressive welfare state but never trumping it.[32] Within broad agreement among the major players to this ecumenical conception

[27] Weiler, above n 26; R Howse, 'From Politics to Technocracy—And Back Again: The Fate of the Multilateral Trading Regime' (2002) *American Journal of International Law* 96; Nicolaidis and Howse, above n 19.

[28] S Ostry, *Who's on First? The Post-Cold War Trading System* (University of Chicago Press, 1997).

[29] J Jackson, *Sovereignty, WTO and Changing Fundamentals of International Law* (Cambridge University Press, 2006).

[30] R Keohane and J Nye, *Power and Interdependence: World Politics in Transition* (Boston, MA, Little Brown, 1977), 51.

[31] Howse and Nicolaidis, above n 17.

[32] Ruggie, above n 16.

of legitimate government, differences about whether specific domestic policy interventions constituted 'cheating at the margin' or even defection appeared manageable by diplomatic and technocratic techniques. It was not necessary to engage the underlying normative conflicts about the legitimate relationship between the state and the market, or to address issues of distributive justice (both intra-state and inter-state) and of relative gains.

We have discussed elsewhere the changes and stresses within domestic regimes and the global political economy that led to the pressure on, and the subsequent collapse of, the 'embedded liberalism' bargain in the 1970s and 1980s.[33] The ultimate result was the manifest failure of technocratic management[34] and a perceived need to negotiate new explicit *rules*, on issues that reflected basic normative conflict, such as subsidies, intellectual property rights, and food safety and other kinds of domestic risk regulation. Moreover, areas such as intellectual property rights and market access in regulated services industries raised issues of relative gains and distributive justice (most notably as between developed and developing countries). The strategy of the United States, along with other developed countries, in the Uruguay Round was to use their bargaining power to link the continuing ability of developing countries to benefit from the mutually self-interested GATT bargain to their acceptance of rules and commitments that were not clearly win–win by any means. It is sometimes suggested that this was in return for new commitments by developed countries to reduce protection on products of interest to developing countries, such as textiles and agricultural commodities. However, unlike the obligations on services and intellectual property, as well as technical regulations, the reduction of trade barriers on textiles, for example, was to be phased in over a very long period of time, with lots of scope for 'safeguards' and backtracking. Moreover, neoclassical trade theory would certainly view removal of trade barriers in the textiles and agricultural barriers as welfare-enhancing for the importing states, as well as offering new opportunities to developing country exporters. Conversely, in the area of intellectual property, and arguably too concerning some market access commitments for services and subsidies, the agreement resulted in net gain or loss across countries as well as within countries, which was one of the developments at the root of the ensuing legitimacy crisis.

[33] Howse and Nicolaidis, above n 17.

[34] See, eg, Robert Hudec's account of the increasing failure of the dispute-settlement system to induce compliance on issues of controversy, such as agricultural subsidies, in the 1980s: R Hudec, DL Kennedy and M Sgarbossa, 'A Statistical Profile of GATT Dispute Settlement Cases: 1948–1989' (1993) 2 *Minnesota Journal of Global Trade* 1.

B. Illusion from Above: The Move Towards Constitutional *Fuite en Avant*

It was these negotiations that resulted in the creation of the WTO and therewith a new architecture for multilateral trade relations.[35] The new agreements on services and intellectual property rights, subsidies and technical regulations (among other new treaties) were put under a single umbrella with the original GATT. This reflected the principle that 'membership' of the WTO, benefiting from any of these treaties, required accepting them all. Moreover, for all the main treaties, there would be compulsory jurisdiction for juridical dispute settlement, with the final arbiter an appellate court autonomous from the Secretariat, or the political and diplomatic organs of the WTO. Thus, subject to a negative consensus where *all* the states' parties blocked it, a ruling of the Appellate Body or an unappealed ruling of a panel (the tribunal of first instance) would be adopted automatically. Failure to comply with a ruling would result in authorised countermeasures for the winning party, and the meaning of compliance was also subject to arbitration.

As already noted, The GATT was an institution characterised by relatively few formal legal rules, and a large role for informal 'governance' by a technocratic network or epistemic community, as well as by low politics and a focus on mutually self-interested bargaining (with divergence of interests managed through linkage of concessions, ie, reciprocity). The WTO, by contrast, presents itself as system of many formal legal rules, a large number of which engage fundamental normative controversies and have distributive consequences that track in important ways existing imbalances in economic and political power among states. There is a centralised, juridical system of rule interpretation and enforcement, which further constrains the possibilities for managing and adjusting the 'bargain' through informal 'governance'. The WTO judiciary's interpretation of the rules can only be reversed by decision-making that as a matter of practice requires a consensus of the entire WTO membership (formally requiring at least a super-majority vote).

This contrast between the GATT and the WTO suggests a shift from an institution with strong, albeit informal, mechanisms for 'governance' to an 'ideal-type' of a multilateral treaty regime, ie, one where norms are specified in treaty rules that go from the general to the very detailed, with centralised mechanisms for treaty interpretation and enforcement (albeit with aggrieved states deputised as the enforcer)—characteristics longed for by international lawyers, but often not achieved. In such a context, there is still, of course, a role for day-to-day regime management by

[35] For a discussion on the origins and development of the constitutionalization debate, see D Cass, *The Constitutionalization of the World Trade Organisation; Legitimacy, Democracy, and Community in the International Trading System* (Oxford University Press, 2005).

officials, but 'governance' sounds much too grand, or grandiose, a description. Thus understood, the multilateral trading regime would seem, at first glance, to confound the kind of trajectory from classic treaty law to 'governance' that is suggested in the thematic statement introducing the agenda for this collection of essays. That is to say, the automatic application of fully specified treaty rules, often approved through domestic parliamentary processes, replaces the ongoing management and adjustment of the bargain by a technocratic policy elite at the global level.

One could argue, using the EU as an example, that treaty law with a central court is in fact a stage on the way to institutionalised formal 'governance' in the WTO; however, as we have explained elsewhere, this often favoured analogy is defective, in that the EU itself had political institutions of 'governance' right from the start, although the role of these institutions unquestionably deepened and strengthened in dialogue with the judiciary sketched in the first part of this chapter.[36] The regulation of trade at the global level has not yet established the kind of dialogue and division of labour between the judicial and political sphere that has characterised governance both in the domestic and the European contexts.

Nevertheless, 'governance' has been occurring within the WTO system, in both formal and informal ways. *Contra* the positivists, public law adjudication itself is a form of 'governance'—it has policy- and norm-creating and -expressing dimensions that go far beyond 'rule application'. The Appellate Body early on explicitly understood as part of its mandate the interpretation of treaty texts that balance different values and interests;[37] it has also not shied away from addressing the relationship of WTO law to other international legal regimes, biodiversity and the environment, which raises important issues of policy, and engages substantive normative choices all in the context of interpretation.[38] In *US—Shrimp* (especially the 21.5 implementation ruling)[39] the Appellate Body sent important messages about the relation of the WTO system to environmentalism in its acceptance that unilateral trade measures could be used in some circumstances to induce better protection of the global environmental commons. Similarly in the *EC—Asbestos*

[36] Howse and Nicolaidis, above n 17.

[37] Appellate Body Report, European Communities—Measures Concerning Meat and Meat Products (Hormones), WT/DS26/AB/R, adopted 13 February 1998, DSR 1998:I, 135.

[38] On the role of the judiciary in public law adjudication under conditions of value pluralism and normative conflict in the domestic context, see C Sunstein, *Legal Reasoning and Political Conflict* (Oxford University Press, 1996).

[39] Appellate Body Report, United States—Import Prohibition of Certain Shrimp and Shrimp Products Recourse to Article 21.5 of the DSU by Malaysia,WT/DS58/AB/RW, adopted 21 November 2001, DSR 2001:XIII, 6481.

case[40] the Appellate Body sent an important message on trade and health, by holding—contrary to the panel of first instance—that the health effects of different products cannot be taken into account in determining whether the GATT requires that they be treated the same in domestic regulation. In short, the supreme judicial authority in WTO has been drawing and redrawing its own line between acceptable and non-acceptable domestic regulation, a line broadly in keeping with an updated version of the embedded liberalism understanding—one where the domestic autonomy to be preserved is more regulatory rather than (micro- or macro-) economic policy.

Although based on a sound reading of the treaty texts, this is normative messaging that the insider network has not been too happy about. Yet because of the de facto judicial supremacy at the WTO (it takes a consensus effectively to reverse an Appellate Body interpretation), there is little they can do explicitly except to complain about 'judicial activism'. Indeed, the Appellate Body has gone so far as to assert judicial control over matters where responsibility has also been assigned to political or diplomatic organs or processes at the WTO (review of balance of payments restrictions and of regional trading arrangements). It has not shown any particular deference to the coexisting political or diplomatic processes in these areas; moreover, in a bold, *Marbury v Madison*-like stroke, the Appellate Body has assumed the competence to determine its own authority in relation to the other organs and branches within the WTO—*Kompetenz–Kompetenz*, as it were.[41]

In many ways, however, the insider network continues to practice covert 'governance'. One of the most significant phenomena in this respect is the management of the process of accession of new members to the WTO—which provides the occasion for the 'insider network' to communicate to the member-to-be or new member the 'meaning' of its commitment to the WTO. The same goes for 'technical assistance' to developing country members more generally. Generally, in these exercises the insider network presents itself as an authoritative guide to, and guardian of, WTO norms and policies.

Secondly, and relatedly, the insider network, which connects officials within national governments with those of other governments and in the Secretariat, operates to transmit messages about how WTO membership and rules constrain domestic policies directly into the domestic policy process itself. Typically, where there is a trade dimension to some domestic policy, a domestic trade official (usually connected to the insider

[40] Appellate Body Report, European Communities—Measures Affecting Asbestos and Asbestos-Containing Products, WT/DS135/AB/R, adopted 5 April 2001, DSR 2001:VII, 3243.

[41] Appellate Body Report, India—Quantitative Restrictions on Imports of Agricultural, Textile and Industrial Products, WT/DS90/AB/R, adopted 22 September 1999, DSR 1999:IV, 1763.

network) or external consultant (also likely to be so connected, or even recommended by the Secretariat) will weigh in on WTO consistency. The danger that a domestic policy may be anti-WTO, or lead to WTO dispute settlement, may well tip the balance against it in an inter-agency decision-making process. Many government decision-makers will never second-guess the view of their own trade officials or of insider-network authorised external consultants as to what is or is not compatible with the WTO—not only in terms of what can be justified under the current legal framework, but also where it might be desirable to press for reform or clarification of the law. Little attention is paid to the critical impact of 'filtering channels' between global rules and local acts.

Finally, at the global level, the insider network has a major role in shaping the shifting agenda trade rounds, with little high-level political input into the substance of the round outside a few salient meetings. This gives a fairly wide scope to the insider network for 'informal' governance through agenda setting, including the structuring and sequencing of certain negotiations.

Where, then, do we really see the primacy of politics—including contestation—in the WTO? To be sure, a great deal of the visible dealing and wheeling in the WTO happens in highly publicised and politicised moments of global public diplomacy—such as the signing or closing of trade rounds—where politicians increasingly pander to their respective national audiences. In between such events, formal 'governance' by the Appellate Body and informal 'governance' by the insider network (to some extent formal in as much as they still control much of the panel process), constitute the bulk of WTO activity. Democratic politics here is mostly reduced to the (limited) instances of indirect accountability.[42] Legitimacy is supposed to flow from the constitutional features of WTO law from above and technical expertise from below.

In the context of the Doha Round, the WTO has known a few moments of what we shall call transnational legal politics. In these moments, a political negotiation not primarily managed by the insider network, and inclusive of multiple constituencies representing diverse values and interests, has given direction to WTO law and policy outside of a formal treaty amendment process. The first such moment did not even happen at the WTO but rather in Montreal with the negotiation of the Biosafety Protocol, defining the relationship between trade and the regulation of genetically modified organisms (GMOs). Not all WTO members were signatories, but the Protocol, which engaged the attention of international civil society as well as many state actors, should play a large role in the application of the WTO rules to situations involving GMOs; the failure of

[42] Grant and Keohane, above n 8.

the panel in the *EC—Biotech* case[43] to take into consideration the Protocol represents old-style 'insider-network' governance, and had the ruling been appealed on this point, the Appellate Body would probably have reversed, given its openness to the consideration of environmental instruments in WTO interpretation, even where those instruments do not bind all WTO members.

Another moment of global politics was the negotiation of the Doha TRIPs Declaration, where the WTO membership agreed to a reading of the existing law, and indeed even to a manner of application of that law, that supported the ability of governments to limit intellectual property rights for purposes of affordable access to medicines. Again, multiple constituencies were engaged, from multinational pharmaceutical interests to health-and development-oriented non-governmental organisations. There have already been many efforts by legal scholars to characterise the TRIPs Declaration in terms of the standard categories of positive international law.

None exactly captures the distinctiveness of this moment, where the WTO system responded to normative conflict through a route quite different to that of informal insider regime management or formal legal change.[44] The TRIPs Declaration was not quite an authoritative, binding interpretation of a treaty, but merely a political statement of the delegates; it constituted normative guidance, legitimised by transnational democratic deliberation that rebalances the regime's mainstream attitude towards intellectual property protection within the parameters of existing treaty text (a text that allows for a number of possibilities for balancing, with profoundly different messages about the relation of different interests and values to one another). In essence, it was transnational legal politics, or what may constitute the first steps towards a democratised global governance.

IV. THE LIMITS OF ARCHITECTURAL REFORM

These observations concerning 'governance' in the WTO should suffice to make clear that, in addressing the relationship between governance and legitimacy, it is largely misguided to focus on the architecture of the WTO as an institution, either in terms of articulating the problem or its solution. Yet, in a wide variety of contemporary literature, there is an obsession with trying to define an architectural 'fix' to the legitimacy challenges surrounding WTO 'governance'. In our collaborative study of

43 Panel Report, European Communities—Measures Affecting the Approval and Marketing of Biotech Products (Biotech), WT/DS291/R, WT/DS292/R, WT/DS/293/R, adopted 29 September 2006.

44 P Lamy, *L'Europe en Premiere Ligne* (Paris, Le Seuil, 2002).

multi-level governance in the EU and US contexts,[45] we have drawn the conclusion that comprehensive architectural solutions to interrelationships between levels of governance and their interaction and legitimacy are largely a chimera.

These fixes remain in what might be called the formal sovereignty-based paradigm of governance, power and legitimation, as they are concerned not so much with the actual normative sources of legitimacy for outcomes, but with the transfer and allocation of sovereign powers or competences to authorities at the global level. Legitimacy problems are seen as fundamentally problems of dividing or allocating 'sovereignty.' Instead, it is better to conceive of multi-level governance as a dynamic process: performance art rather than architecture. One kind of architectural fix that is often suggested is a clear allocation or reallocation of competences or jurisdictions, as between the WTO and lower levels of governance or, horizontally, between the WTO and other international institutions, the International Labour Organization, for instance.[46]

As various of the contributions in *The Federal Vision* have shown, attempts to distribute exclusive or shared competences or jurisdictions to the level(s) of governance 'best' able to deal with the matter (howsoever defined) have been ineffective in addressing legitimacy, and particularly accountability concerns about multi-level governance. Because fixed competences do not capture well the interdependency of policy fields in modern government, the problem of legitimate governance is not really so much a problem of keeping each level within its own appropriate, jurisdiction but rather arises from the ongoing management of policy interdependency in concurrent fields of jurisdiction, ie, the management of the interrelationship of different levels of governance to one another in areas where both have some legitimate claim to be implicated. Moreover, democratic politics is characterised by cycles of centralisation and decentralisation, where citizens tend to view one level of governance or another as more salient in responding to their concerns. Changes in technology, prevailing beliefs, systemic characteristics and the more elusive politics of identity all contribute to influencing the political process that will determine not only levels of competence but above all the ways in which they interrelate. Effective and legitimate multi-level governance therefore requires, in as much as democracy and legitimacy are connected, a capacity to move back and forth between relative centralisation and relative decentralisation in various areas of interdependent policies.

45 Nicolaidis and Howse, *The Federal Vision*, above n 3, see 'The Federal Visions, Levels of Governance and Legitimacy' (introductory chapter).

46 Joel Trachtman has conceptualised the whole issue as a matter of allocating jurisdiction. See 'The World Trading System, the International Legal System and Multilevel Choice' (2006) 12 *European Law Journal* 469.

To shift this analysis to the WTO context, we can easily see that allocating to the WTO 'jurisdiction' over any subject matter of government decision-making is not what WTO rules are about in the first place. These rules place certain constraints or requirements on decision-making by governments that are deemed appropriate as part of sustaining a bargain on reciprocally liberalised trade. Even where the WTO has come closest to harmonised regulation, ie, intellectual property rights (IPRs), it could hardly be understood as operating an exclusive jurisdiction or competence. Instead, the IPR regimes provide criteria for national regimes to apply.

It can equally easily be shown that keeping the WTO 'out' of a certain area will not solve or avoid problems of legitimacy. Take the example of competition policy. There are good reasons to believe that the demands of global 'governance' with respect to competition policy ill fit the existing institutional capacities of the WTO.[47] However, if enough of the major players within the WTO believe that unilateral competition policies or anticompetitive practices by Member States are undermining a co-operative equilibrium with respect to bargained trade concessions, then to sustain the bargain it will need to be fortified with at least some rules about competition. Economists will argue that it usually makes sense to liberalise trade regardless of any agreed understanding with your trading partners about the appropriate parameters of competition policy or anticompetitive practices, and they will be right when the problem is viewed from the theory of competitive advantage. But comparative advantage is largely about unilateral trade liberalisation, and tells us nothing about the kinds of benchmarks that states may require to be able to identify cheating and defection, when what is involved is sustaining a bargain based on reciprocity, ie, a co-operative equilibrium under changing economic and social conditions, and today moreover without guidance or anchoring from an ecumenical policy paradigm such as that represented by the 'embedded liberalism' horizon.

On another front, most analysts in the insider network claim that labour rights ought to remain 'out' of the WTO, and are not a 'trade' issue. This claim has the effect of putting the burden of proof on the labour rights activists to prove that labour is something that should be 'in' the WTO. But labour is 'in' there already, to the extent that WTO rules already affect (i) the ability to use trade instruments to enforce or encourage compliance with international workers' rights, (ii) the available choices for worker adjustment to increased competition or (iii) wage inequality in individual Member States. The claim is that these effects do not merit explicit deliberation and action in the WTO because the WTO is

[47] Dan Tarullo and Merit Janow have persuasively argued along these lines. DK Tarullo, 'Competition Policy for Global Markets' (1999) 2 *Journal of International Economic Law* 445; M Janow, 'Competition Policy and the WTO' in J Bhagwati (ed), *The Uruguay Round and Beyond* (Ann Arbor, University of Michigan Press, 1998).

just 'a trade organisation, not a labour organisation'. It is as if a plumber were to come into our house, and in the course of fixing the drains in the kitchen, were to soil the floor, chip the woodwork, create an accident hazard and then deny any accountability with the notion that she was 'just plumbing' and had done a great job of fixing the drains—as for any problems created, they were someone else's responsibility, not being within the ambit of plumbing as a *techne*. Clearly, if plumbers kept talking that way, soon people would insist that the rules of plumbing had to *include* rules about not causing certain kinds of collateral damage. Here, how the plumbers interpret the existing rules about plumbing and the general norms of conduct that they consider appropriate in conducting that specialised activity will determine whether new rules of 'plumbing' have to be created.

One variant on the claim that labour should be outside the remit of the WTO is that there is another institution that 'deals with' labour, the International Labour Organization. By way of analogy, we might imagine the plumber saying that there are carpenters to deal with cabinets, cleaners to handle the stained floor, and doctors and hospitals to take care of slips and falls. But it begs the question of whether the better solution is to have plumbers who know to avoid these results while plumbing.

In the same way, formal institutional tinkering cannot help much in dealing with the 'spillage' of globalisation. If WTO treaty rules need to be interpreted and evolved through 'governance' that touches on a wide range of policy areas and human interests, and this governance cannot be 'jurisdictionally' circumscribed, contained or cabined off to other institutions in any kind of adequate ex ante manner, then we are faced squarely with how such governance can be legitimate. Clearly balancing values and the interests of multiple constituencies both inter-state and intra-state is going to be involved, so legitimacy will not fully come by any means from technical expertise. Democratic legitimacy may well be related to whether *agents* of governance conduct themselves in accordance with what we call a political ethics of governance—informed by norms such as inclusiveness, mutual respect, transparency, value pluralism, procedural justice and rational deliberation. It is to this political ethics that we now turn.

V. THE POLITICAL ETHICS OF GLOBAL SUBSIDIARITY

As an anchor for such a global political ethics, we come back to the spirit of subsidiarity, stripping the legal principle from its narrow meaning of allocation of power.[48] Instead we take it to mean that the transnational

[48] See Howse and Nicolaidis, above n 17, Nicolaidis and Howse, above n 3.

management of social conflict is more likely to be legitimate if addressed by the appropriate people in the appropriate 'space' of governance and in the appropriate way. Our argument, therefore, fits with cosmopolitan brands of international political theory which seek to identify political structures which may serve global norms of political and distributive justice while arguing that mere reliance on international institutions to do so is insufficient.[49] Instead we cannot consider which institutions are appropriate without considering which rights or *right processes* must be served by these institutions. As Caney argues, "institutions on their own are not guaranteed to produce benign policies . . . what is needed are certain political culture and certain character trait as well".[50] In short, the 'ethos of democracy' must remain about our intellectual freedom and the precious inclination anywhere and by anyone to question received wisdom and established political bargains as well as entrenched identities and interests.[51] Political structures are simply shells, more or less conducive to such democratic ethos.

In the era of globalisation, increases in exchanges without corresponding convergence in polities and domestic systems are bound to lead to increased friction. Whether an issue that requires 'governance' gets resolved through informal insider network 'governance', formal adjudication, or democratised governance and transnational legal politics, may vary depending on perceptions of what is at stake as well as the relative credibility of each alternative. We can imagine in the years ahead various kinds of competition and co-operation between these three kinds of 'spaces' for governance and the constellations of agents attached to them. Analysing such patterns will be more relevant to understanding WTO legitimacy than jurisdiction and boundary definition. Generally speaking, the political ethics we call for is already visible to some extent in formal adjudication and in transnational legal politics. Thus, while the transformation of insider network 'governance' by political ethics is unlikely to be rapid or easy, eventually the network will have to make itself open to this political ethics or it will simply continue to lose to other mechanisms of governance in the competition for legitimacy.

At least since Rousseau, the essence of democratic self-determination has been the notion that citizens can only be legitimately coerced by laws of their own making; this follows from the core democratic idea of political equality: the reflection in politics of the notion of the equal moral value of each individual. Thus, in order to characterise the spirit of a

[49] See S Caney, *Justice Beyond Borders, A Global Political Theory* (Oxford University Press, 2005); KA Appiah, *Cosmopolitanism—Ethics in a World of Strangers* (London, Allen Lane, Penguin, 2006).

[50] Caney, above n 49, 172.

[51] See D Campbell, *National Deconstruction: Violence, Identity and Justice in Bosnia* (Minneapolis, Minneapolis University Press, 1998), cited in Caney, above n 50.

transnational political ethics, we begin from a fundamental proposition, as obvious as it is often unstated: democracy as (qualified) majority rule implies that decisions be made by less than consensus: the question is what makes it legitimate for those who disagree—the dissenting minority, the losers with respect to a particular outcome—nevertheless to be subject to the outcome, even to be legitimately coerced by the laws and policies in question? What kinds of values and practices permit persons who disagree with or lose from particular outcomes nevertheless to view the outcomes in question as consistent with the political ideal of self-legislation or non-subordination?

A. Inclusiveness and Internalisation

Outcomes that result from the exclusion per se of the interests and values of individuals or groups from the decision-making process are likely to be inconsistent with the democratic ideal of political equality. In the WTO context, as we have already noted, such exclusion has often been justified by a formal conception of the allocation of authority between the WTO and other international organisations, or between the WTO and domestic polities. In the former case, interests and values affected or even jeopardised by trade liberalisation have been often excluded by the 'insider' community on the grounds that some other international organisation is 'responsible' for those concerns; at the same time, it has often been argued that social interests affected by trade liberalisation should seek voice through their own domestic government. Again, we have indicated why domestic politics may not be an adequate guarantee of inclusiveness.

Inclusiveness need not entail, however, the challenge of participation of every relevant group or its representatives in the various kinds of decision-making made at the WTO as a site of global governance. In a number of Appellate Body decisions, such as the *EC—Hormones*, the *US—Shrimp* and the *EC—Asbestos* cases, the Appellate Body has displayed some of this spirit of inclusiveness by showing awareness of the range and balance, and importance of the human values at stake, well beyond the interests of trade liberalisation. While the Appellate Body has displayed inclusiveness as participation by permitting submission of amicus briefs by non-governmental actors, thereby broadening the voices heard well beyond the insider community, the decisions mentioned show that inclusiveness need not always depend on participation, provided decision-makers have an ethics of inclusiveness in the way they are conscious of the full range of values and interests at stake in a given matter. Under an ethics consistent with the ideal of political equality, agents—be they judges, politicians or even activists—do not need to privilege those values and interests most characteristic of their own epistemic community.

Without formal mechanisms of participation, or minimal ones (eg, the possibility of observer status at WTO Ministerials), groups speaking for a range of values have recently been able to gain the ear of WTO delegates and negotiators; this has been notable in the case of TRIPs and the creation of the recent WTO instruments protecting access to affordable medicines; in the case of services, civil society groups have been able to sensitise delegates and negotiators as to how particular commitments under the General Agreement on Trade and Services (GATS) might affect the ability to ensure essential public services. This has been all the more remarkable because the delegations in question have often been from developing countries, whose governments have been typically known to be hostile to the direct involvement of civil society in the WTO. More generally, the creation of the NAMA 11 and G20 groups of developing countries and their push to be included in all big decisions is slowly changing the face of WTO negotiations, in part by increasing the confidence of these very countries and therefore their acceptance of other actors.

We may already be witnessing the albeit very early or limited effects on the global trend towards democratisation combined with generational change in influencing the values of those involved in the day-to-day governance processes of the WTO: one illustration is Faizel Ismail, the South African ambassador to the WTO, whose roots are in the progressive politics of the trade union movement in South Africa. In contrast, one sees the older elite-authoritarian values of an earlier generation of developing country policy elites in the decision of the previous Director General of the WTO, Suphachai Panitchpakdi to address the future governance challenges of the WTO by appointing a task force of elderly 'wise' gentlemen—the Sutherland Committee—tasked with consulting with no one in their deliberations as to the future of the Organization.

B. Review and Revision

In contrast to the Schmittean politics of friend/enemy, which gains its intensity from the possibility that one side will permanently suppress or annihilate the other in political struggle, a democratic political ethics will place a high value on opportunities to revisit and revise particular outcomes. This is not unrelated to inclusiveness in its connection to political equality. The possibility of review and revision allows 'losers' to have confidence that the fact that a particular outcome unfavourable to their values or interests does not indicate exclusion from or subordination in political life—they live to fight another day. Perhaps this is where the tension between our political ethics and the constitutionalist vision of the WTO is most visible, as the latter regards the *acquis* of each negotiating round as an irreversible 'progression' towards a global economic constitution.

This mindset has been seen in the attitude of a number of very significant developed countries to the meaning of the Doha Round as a development round. For many developing countries, calling the Round a development round had been seen as an opportunity to revisit and rebalance the Uruguay Round outcome, which was widely seen as unfair to developing countries; for the developed countries in question, new pro-development concessions are possible (based more or less on reciprocity—there is some openness to special and differential treatment), but there is the strong taboo that the main treaties of the Uruguay Round package cannot be 'opened up.' It is notable that even where review has been built into the WTO treaties themselves, such as with respect to services liberalisation, non-actionable subsidies and the need for safeguards with respect of service, such review processes have been long delayed or blocked. But such review processes were precisely put into the agreements in part at least to assure 'losers' that the matter would be reconsidered at a future point in time, in light of experience and changing perceptions. We believe that the trials and tribulations of the Doha Round, its likely closure on a minimalist and disappointing result, is due to no little extent to the betrayal of this spirit of return.

Here political ethics would point to an anti-architecture architecture: a consideration of political and legal mechanisms and devices that allow the membership collectively, but also individual members, to revisit and rebalance their rights and obligations. We fully admit that there may be some trade-off here with the value of the WTO system as a 'rules-based' system; however, we observe, with Jon Elster, that pre-commitment always involves tying someone *else's* hands, and thus is problematic from the point of view of democratic political equality and political ethics.[52]

C. Checks and Balances

The political ethics of democracy draw not only on the ideal of participation and self-determination *qua* Rousseau, but also the ideas of classical liberalism, *qua* Montesquieu and Madison, of which one of considerable importance is that of checks and balances, or separation of powers. Here, the thinkers of the eighteenth century understood that the functioning of the separation of powers depended not just on the actual architecture

[52] J Elster, *Ulysses Unbound: Studies in Rationality, Precommitment, and Constraints* (Cambridge University Press, 2002).

allocating competences but in the sense of each estate of its (limited) authority and legitimacy, its independent but at the same time non-hegemonic spirit. Because democracy can degenerate into faction, even majoritarian faction that menaces political equality, checks and balances are important as counterweight to any single institution or faction hegemonising decision-making to the exclusion or subordination of other interests and values.

Recently, the UN human rights institutions have begun to raise issues about decision-making in the WTO on behalf of constituencies and values traditionally excluded or marginalised there. This entails a certain spirit of contestation between institutions. International lawyers often regard tensions between institutions and regimes in international law as something negative—'fragmentation' or 'cacophony'—and many architectural proposals seek 'coherence'.[53] 'Coherence' can reflect the value of checks and balance if it means that outcomes should reflect in a balanced way the full range of values and interests at stake. But often 'coherence' is understood in the manner discussed above, as an attempt at enforcing a kind of 'watertight compartments' view of competences (the WTO is a 'trade' organisation not an 'aid' or a 'human rights' organisation and the latter have no business meddling in the former—they should stick to their own 'work'). Under the constitutionalisation school, our illusion from above, such coherence would be enforced, once and for all, through a system of rules brought outside of the political arena.

Attempts at co-operation, when not undertaken with the appropriate spirit of independence and contestation reflected in democratic political ethics, can result in co-optation, as happened when the WTO and the WHO secretariats 'co-operated' to write a study on trade and health; the WTO point of view, one quite narrow in terms of giving play to the value of human health in limiting trade liberalisation commitments, was more or less simply accepted by the WHO, which did not see its own expertise and distinctive constituencies as a basis for questioning or challenging the way that WTO law was interpreted and applied in health-related matters. Within the WTO, the outlook of the traditional trade policy elite has been opposed to any notion of a real separation of powers, or spirit of contestation between 'branches' of governance within the WTO. The notion of a 'member-driven organisation' has been used to attempt to suppress independence of spirit in the executive and judicial branches of the WTO, the Secretariat and the Appellate Body, respectively. In the former case, delegates have pressed for the rebuke of a secretariat official who made progressive-oriented comments on crucial issues concerning trade human rights and the environment. In the latter case, delegates

[53] See special issue of the *Michigan Journal of International Law* on *Diversity or Cacophony?: New Sources of Norms in International Law Symposium* (2004) 25 *Michigan Journal of International Law*.

attempted to intimidate the Appellate Body of the WTO into reversing its decision to allow amicus submissions from non-governmental actors.

D. Compromise and Compensation

Often, in democratic politics, the losers in particular debates and decisions are nevertheless able to accept the outcomes as legitimate, and consistent with a sense of their equal moral value as human beings, because this value is acknowledged through specific elements of compromise or mitigation, and/or some form of compensation. The more WTO outcomes in negotiation are characterised as 'constitutional'—ie, the 'right' rules—the less does the spirit of compromise and compensation, very typical of the 'embedded liberalism' of the original GATT, enter into the picture. Appropriate adjustment to trade liberalisation, once a central theme or preoccupation, has become peripheral in WTO negotiations. Apart from longer phase-in periods for developing countries in the case of some agreements, and the very generous 'safeguards' that developed countries managed to maintain in textiles and agriculture for those concentrated interests, the negotiation outcomes of the Uruguay Round displayed little sensitivity to needs for mitigation and compensation. Concepts such as 'aid for trade' have acquired some purchase in the current negotiations and promise to revive a spirit a compromise and compensation; but these ideas are all too easily blocked or watered-down by free-trade purists who balk at the notion of the WTO becoming an 'aid agency'. And aid for trade itself can become an instrument simply to enforce rather than compensate for outcomes of trade liberalisation. Domestic policy space for adjustment remains largely off of the table in the negotiations, inasmuch as it would require some retreat from the Uruguay Round outcomes or significant new flexibilities (eg, a new list of permitted non-actionable subsidies that facilitate adjustment).

VI. CONCLUSION: THE LEGITIMACY OF THE WTO CANNOT BE WON BY ARCHITECTURAL REFORM BUT DEMANDS A TRANSNATIONAL POLITICAL ETHICS

In the end, we argue, a genuine spirit of democracy at the global level calls for the fine-tuning of a transnational political ethics for our age of globalisation. Such ethics must start by speaking to the relationship between the universal and the local, the global and the regional. When considering the transfer from the EU to the global level of norms such as supremacy and subsidiarity, we have argued that we must distinguish between two aspects of the EU: on the one hand, the emergence of the EU as a political community which makes the export of its model a difficult proposition; and on the other hand, the insights linked to the fine-tuning of subsidiarity inside the EU that could inspire a model of global subsidiarity.

Such a model must itself be considered under the banner of transnationalism, contrasted on the one hand with sovereignty-centred law or legal nationalism, and on the other with supranational centred law or tradition constitutionalism, which both revolve around the trope of the state. Under a transnational paradigm, we recover the notion of horizontality as an organising principle but divorced from the notion of homogeneous and sovereign jurisdiction. It is fair to say, therefore, that such a transnational model of horizontal transfer of sovereignty raises normative concerns of its own. Legal transnationalism in the EU must first be understood in the spirit of Kantian cosmopolitan law as the consequence of greater accountability of a national system regarding how strangers to the jurisdiction are affected by its actions, thus addressing beyond the state one of the core challenge of democracy, eg, the disjunction between those deciding and those affected by political and legal decisions.

We have argued that global or transnational ethics must and can address such disjunction by incorporating other-regarding and minority-regarding consideration into decision-making and decision-shaping: including agents and values from outside one's circle; a commitment to returning to past outcomes on grounds not only of external change but also internal fallibility; incorporating checks and balances in the global management of economic exchange; and finally, taking seriously the need to compensate all those who for one reason or another tend to remain losers in our globalising world.

8

Subsidiarity, Fragmentation and Democracy: Towards the Demise of General International Law?

ANDREAS L PAULUS*

I. INTRODUCTION: UNIVERSAL INTERNATIONAL LAW AND ITS CRITICS

WHEN DEALING WITH the allocation of authority in the international realm, subsidiarity has become one of the key terms of reference. The more local and the more specialised an international norm is, the better its legitimacy, or its 'compliance pull'[1] for the states called upon to implement it. The very attempt to establish 'general international law' as a law binding on all states and other subjects of international law is called into question on two fronts: on the one hand, the age-old resistance to international regulation has found new supporters arguing that, in the absence of an international demos, international law suffers from an incurable 'democratic deficit' that severely limits its legitimacy, in particular when confronted with democratically mandated domestic majorities.[2] On the other hand, many international legal scholars maintain that international law has been deposed by new, issue-oriented international regulatory schemes, in particular regarding trade, but also human rights or the environment.[3]

* Professor of Public and International Law, University of Goettingen, Germany. I thank Mr Micha Comnick for his valuable research assistance.

[1] On the 'compliance pull' as expression of legitimacy see T Franck, *The Power of Legitimacy Among Nations* (Oxford, Clarendon Press, 1990) 43.

[2] See, eg, JL Goldsmith and EA Posner, *The Limits of International Law* (Oxford University Press, 2005) 205ff; C Hillgruber, 'Souveränität—Verteidigung eines Rechtsbegriffs' (2002) 57 *Juristenzeitung* 1072, 1079.

[3] G Teubner and A Fischer-Lescano, 'Regime-Collisions: The Vain Search for Legal Unity in the Fragmentation of Global Law' (2004) 25 *Michigan Journal of International Law* 999; P Zumbansen, 'Die vergangene Zukunft des Völkerrechts' (2001) 34 *Kritische Justiz* 46.

The relationship between the allocation of authority in international law, on the one hand, and democracy, on the other hand, seems to be a pretty simple one: democracy requires that decisions be taken as closely as possible to the citizen. This relationship implies that democracy resides in the city, or the nation, maybe even in private associations such as the club or the parish, but not in the international sphere or with international institutions, whether the European Union or the United Nations. It is not surprising, then, that the German Constitutional Court (Bundesverfassungsgericht, hereafter BVerfG), in its famous *Maastricht* decision, ruled that democracy is linked to the application of the principle of subsidiarity within the European Union.[4] In a recent interview with the German daily *Frankfurter Allgemeine Zeitung*, the President of the BVerfG emphasised that if the European Court of Justice did not better respect the principle of subsidiarity in the future, the BVerfG may again be called to intervene.[5] The 'democratic deficit' of international institutions, from the European Union to the United Nations and international law in general, is a rallying cry for those advocating national sovereignty as defence against the increasingly intrusive regulatory demands of globalisation.[6]

It is the purpose of the present contribution to this collection of essays to put this conventional wisdom on the allocation of authority in international law into question. Ruth Lapidoth (to whom the collection is dedicated), in her writings on the status of Jerusalem,[7] has shown herself to be an expert on the complexities of the 'allocation of authority' in the Holy City, and beyond. Ruth Lapidoth has also not failed to observe that the term 'sovereignty' has undergone great changes that render it quite malleable to functional considerations. Indeed, she has maintained that 'the diminished concept of sovereignty may assist in the quest for a compromise on Jerusalem'.[8] It appears fitting to follow her cue by pointing to

[4] 89 Entscheidungen des Bundesverfassungsgericht [Decisions of the (German) Federal Constitutional Court (hereinafter 'BVerfGE')] 155, English trans as *Brunner v European Union Treaty*, [1994] 1 CMLR 57, at 193 [Accordance of the German Act of Ratification of the Maastricht Treaty on European Union, [1992] 2 *German Federal Gazette* 1251, with the German Basic Law (Grundgesetz)].

[5] H-J Papier, 'Interview' *Frankfurter Allgemeine Zeitung* (Frankfurt, 24 July 2007), available at http://www.faz.net/s/Rub99C3EECA60D84C08AD6B3E60C4EA807F/Doc~EDBFB74C1D1114FE2AEA0917043918AE3~ATpl~Ecommon~Scontent.html (accessed 8 Aug 2007) (on the relations between the ECJ and the BVerfG in the light of the new Reform Treaty).

[6] See, eg, Goldsmith and Posner, above n 2, 205ff; Hillgruber, above n 2; see also U Haltern, *Was bedeutet Souveränität?* (Tübingen, Mohr, 2007) (describing the mythology of 'sovereignty'). For recent attempts to reinterpret sovereignty to fit into the modern development of international law, see C Warbrick and S Tierney (eds), *Towards an International Legal Community* (London, British Institute of International and Comparative Law, 2006); N Walker (ed), *Sovereignty in Transition* (Oxford, Hart Publishing, 2003).

[7] See, eg, R Lapidoth, 'The EU, Jerusalem and the Peace Process' in CD Classen et al (eds) *Liber amicorum Thomas Oppermann* (Berlin, Duncker, 2001) 267; R Lapidoth, 'Jerusalem—Some Jurisprudential Aspects' (1996) 45 *Catholic University Law Review* 661; more generally R Lapidoth, 'Israel and the Palestinians: Some Legal Issues' (2001) 76 *Die Friedens-Warte* 211, 223–7.

[8] Lapidoth, 'Jerusalem—Some Jurisprudential Aspects', above n 7, 684.

the relativity of other concepts such as 'subsidiarity' and 'democracy'. Yet, just as with 'sovereignty', these terms should not be disposed of altogether. Rather, the task is to present arguments that take due account of conceptual as well as factual complexities.

Democracy requires an agreement of the minority that it will abide by the decisions of the majority. In the strong version of the 'no demos'-thesis, democracy can only be exercised by a pre-existing people. In other words: no democracy without demos.[9] While criticising the German *Maastricht* decision for its apparent exclusion of a democracy beyond the state, its critics nevertheless agreed that democracy in an international or supranational setting requires modification of the state-model of democracy.[10] Thus, in a hypothetical example provided by Joseph Weiler, if Denmark were—heaven forbid—forced to join Germany, it would be of no solace to the Danish if they possessed their own elected representatives in the German Bundestag.[11] The acceptance of majority decisions presupposes a general agreement on the framework in which democratic decision-making can take place. In the absence of a global demos, international law has difficulty in commanding respect from democratically elected representatives of the nation-state or a local community. In other words, cosmopolitan ethics alone appears insufficient as a basis for the creation of rights and obligations that would overrule local or national democratic decisions.

Therefore, it should surprise no one that the 'democratic deficit' is held against international law, in particular when international law requires changes in national policies and laws that go beyond narrowly tailored functional regulation. Accordingly, international law does not possess any inherent authority because it does not relate to a more deeply seated community that goes beyond immediate self-interest. In the absence of a true international community, we should be sceptical if anyone cloaks their own more particular interests by employing the language of 'com-

[9] See J Isensee, 'Nachwort. Europa—die politische Erfindung eines Erdteils' in J Isensee (ed) *Europa als politische Idee und als rechtliche Form* (2nd edn, Berlin, Duncker & Humblot, 1994) 103, 133; P Kirchhof, 'Der deutsche Staat im Prozeß der Europäischen Integration' in J Isensee and P Kirchhof (eds) 7 *Handbuch des Staatsrechts* (CF Müller, Heidelberg, 1992) 855, paras 33, 39, 46, 52 *et passim*; cf the *Maastricht* decision of the German Constitutional Court, 89 BVerfGE 155, 186, which substitutes Kirchhof's and Isensee's 'never' by a 'not yet' and requires limits to European integration; see also 83 BVerfGE 37; 83 BVerfGE 60 (municipal right to vote of foreigners); partial English trans in DP Kommers, *The Constitutional Jurisprudence of the Federal Republic of Germany* (2d edn, Durham, NC and London, Duke University Press, 1997) 197–9.

[10] JHH Weiler, 'The State "über alles". Demos, Telos and the German Maastricht Decision' in O Due, M Lutter and J Schwarze (eds) *Festschrift für Ulrich Everling* (Nomos, Baden-Baden 1995) 1651, 1667, 1670–77. On the problem of multiple 'demoi' in the European Union, see also JHH Weiler, *The Constitution of Europe* (Cambridge University Press, 1999) 344. For a recent concession to the no demos-thesis, see JHH Weiler, 'The Geology of International Law' 64 *Zeitschrift für ausländisches öffentliches Recht und Völkerrecht* 547, 560: '[T]here is no convincing account of democracy without demos'.

[11] Weiler, 'The State "über alles"', above n 10, 1660, 1662.

munity' or pretends that 'humanity' could ever become such a community of morals and laws.[12] In the words of Proudhon, 'whoever says humanity wants to cheat'.[13] Thus, the authority of international law is limited to the reflection and co-ordination of immediate state interests. In cases of clashes between international and domestic law, the latter is supposed to prevail over domestic law emanating from the people's representatives.

A second criticism of 'general' international law deals with the increasing compartmentalisation of international society that requires specifically tailored solutions to common and indeed collective action problems of states. Thus, in a move 'from territoriality to functionality' (Niklas Luhmann),[14] legal regimes need to be *specific*, not general. Under this criticism, the lofty abstractness of classical international law leads it to oblivion. Rather, international law ought to become divided up into different issue areas: criminal law, trade law, human rights law, etc. 'General' international law has all but ceased to exist, or matter.[15] In the most elaborate version of this critique, Gunther Teubner and Andreas Fischer-Lescano have argued that legal systems establish themselves in acts of 'autopoiesis' (self-creation) without the need for a centralising and overarching system of law.[16] Accordingly, international law cannot constitute an overarching system of universal law because it lacks a subject in need of regulation.

Both of these critiques—the democratic and the functional-fragmentational critique—are related to the concept of 'subsidiarity' as a decentralising principle. In fact, they radicalise a 'subsidiarity' approach by asserting that there simply is no 'higher level' of decision-making than the nation-state or functional sub-systems of international law, respectively.[17] Whereas much of the democracy critique is rooted in traditional

[12] For diverse approaches on the notion of international community, see AL Paulus, *Die internationale Gemeinschaft im Völkerrecht* (München, CH Beck, 2001) 89–223.

[13] *Cf* M Koskenniemi, 'International Law in Europe: Between Tradition and Renewal' (2005) 16 *European Journal of International Law* 113, 116.

[14] N Luhmann, *Das Recht der Gesellschaft* (stw edn, Frankfurt am Main, Suhrkamp, 1995) 571ff; N Luhmann, *Die Gesellschaft der Gesellschaft* (Frankfurt/Main, Suhrkamp, 1997) 158–60.

[15] See, in particular, Teubner and Fischer-Lescano, 'Regime-Collisions', above n 3; G Teubner, '"Global Bukowina". Legal Pluralism in World Society' in G Teubner (ed) *Global Law Without a State* (Dartmouth, Aldershot, 1997) 3; similarly Zumbansen, 'Die vergangene Zukunft des VR', above n 3.

[16] Teubner and Fischer-Lescano, 'Regime-Collisions', above n 3, 1009, 1014, 1032 *et passim*. On autopoiesis generally, see G Teubner, *Recht als autopoietisches System* (Frankfurt am Main, Suhrkamp, 1989).

[17] For an argument as to the inapplicability of the principle of subsidiarity to a non-hierarchical international legal order, see U Fastenrath, 'Subsidiarität im Völkerrecht' in D Wyduckel (ed) *Subsidiarität als rechtliches und politisches Ordnungsprinzip in Kirche, Staat und Gesellschaft* (Berlin, Duncker and Humblot 2002) 475, 480. Only in the limitation of the local and personal scope of international regulation and in the 'margin of appreciation' of states in the implementation of international law could one see characteristics of subsidiarity. The term is used in this sense here too, namely as decision-making at the lowest and most specialised

sovereignty cloaked in the language of democracy, the fragmentational critique can point to the shift from the national to the functional level associated with the phenomenon of 'globalisation'. While national decision-making processes benefit from the democratic legitimacy of the decisions taken, international decisions are justified in a functional way, as a gain rather than loss of national decision-making power through the 'pooling' of pre-existing common interests of democratic sovereigns in a functionally limited issue area. In the absence of international community, functionalism reigns, but it is only skin-deep. In situations of conflict, the national sovereign must prevail because of its greater democratic legitimacy.[18]

Such a 'necessary' combination of democracy and subsidiarity is, however, too easy to be true. This contribution attempts to show that 'democracy' does not work in only one direction, ie, in favour of the national or sub-systemic level of decision-making. While it is certainly correct that the attachment of citizens to international decisions is much more limited than their attachment to national or local decisions, this is not the end of the matter. Subsidiarity does not only work in favour of the lower level, but may also require the lifting of authority to the higher level, if and to the extent that the higher level appears better suited to fulfil the task in question and guarantees the participation of those being subjected to the decision.[19] Thus, democracy may also be an argument in favour of, and not only against, regulation of matters of international concern by international law.

National democracies only represent the domestic electorate; subsystems, for all their autopoietic qualities, do have functional limitations that prohibit them from letting all relevant constituencies participate in their decision-making processes. Common tasks for the survival and well-being of humankind, from the protection of the environment to the non-proliferation of weapons of mass destruction,[20] require a minimum

level. However, subsidiarity in the narrower sense can also be applied to the vertical structures of public international law, see Fastenrath, *ibid*, 482.

[18] See, eg, U Haltern, 'Gemeinschaftsgrundrechte und Antiterrormaßnahmen der UNO' (2007) 62 *Juristenzeitung* 537 with regard to the anti-terror measures of the UN.

[19] See the wording of Art 5, para 2 TEC, OJ C 321 E/37 at 46: 'In areas which do not fall within its exclusive competence, the Community shall take action, *in accordance with the principle of subsidiarity*, only if and in so far as *the objectives of the proposed action cannot be sufficiently achieved by the Member States* and *can therefore, by reason of the scale or effects of the proposed action, be better achieved by the Community*' (our emphasis). See also C Calliess, *Subsidiaritäts- und Solidaritätsprinzip in der Europäischen Union* (Baden-Baden, 2nd edn, 1999) 32, 185 (solidarity as corrective for subsidiarity); SU Pieper, *Subsidiarität* (Heymanns, Köln, 1992) 72 (subsidiarity as expression of effectiveness).

[20] These considerations are usually framed as 'community interests', see B Simma, 'From Bilateralism to Community Interest in International Law' (1994 VI) 250 *Recueil des Cours* 217, 236–43. The present author prefers the term 'values' to interests because of the normative element contained in their assessment: see Paulus, *Internationale Gemeinschaft*, above n 11, 251–2. Cf the interchangeable use by L Henkin, *International Law: Politics and Values* (The

of central decision-making. In these cases, subsidiarity and democracy may point to central decision-making procedures rather than to individual decisions by decentralised actors.

This article proceeds in three steps: first, I shall deal with the democratic critique of both general international law and its fragmented equivalents that seek to bind international decisions to the democratic acceptance within nation states. Second, I shall look at the fragmentation critique of the international legal order that grounds international legitimacy in the self-ordering of functional issue areas. In the conclusion, we try to identify the contribution 'subsidiarity' can make to our discussion of both fragmentation and democracy.

II. SUBSIDIARITY AND THE 'DEMOCRATIC DEFICIT' OF INTERNATIONAL LAW

International institutions increasingly shape domestic decision-making, up to a point where national processes are losing much of their relevance. Moreover, the traditional means of international diplomacy do not fit the new circumstances. While, at least in democratic states, public decisions derive their legitimacy from democratically elected representatives of the people,[21] at the international level, the state is often represented by technical experts whose main interest lies in certain issue areas rather than the general interest. On the other hand, national parliaments prove more and more incapable of making decisions that reject regional or international regulation. For instance, most states do not have a real choice whether or not to participate in international regimes such as the World Trade Organization, both for political and for economic reasons. Democratic representation at the real loci of decision-making is becoming more and more remote. Market actors do not have—and in most cases do not need—democratic legitimacy, but they do increasingly influence international decision-making. 'Altruist' non-governmental organisations (NGOs) may claim the public interest for themselves, but they do not enjoy democratic legitimacy either. Certainly, all these non-state actors derive legitimacy from their expertise and sometimes benevolent motivation with regard to certain issue areas, and their contribution is often

Hague, Kluwer Law International, 1995) 97–108. Fastenrath, 'Subsidiarität im Völkerrecht', above n 17, 488 n 88, points out that the term 'values' connotes, at least in the German language, too much of a relationship with 'Wertphilosophie', arguing from an objective, not a subjective perspective on values. This, of course, is the opposite of what I intend to convey. Thus, the term 'community interests' will be used here.

[21] For the theory of the 'democratic chain of legitimation' for all holders of public office in German constitutional law, see, eg, 47 BVerfGE 253, 275; 52 BVerfGE 95, 130; 107 BVerfGE 59, 187; E-W Böckenförde, 'Demokratie als Verfassungsprinzip' in J Isensee and P Kirchhof (eds) 2 *Handbuch des Staatsrechts* (3d edn, Heidelberg, CF Müller, 2004) 429, 438, s 24 n 16.

indispensable for reaching effective and efficient decisions. But expertise and democracy are two different things. For example, environmental risks that a scientist may find acceptable because of potential benefits in the future may be unacceptable in the view of the general lay population. While most NGOs are certainly well-intentioned, this does not mean that the general public shares their views, whether on the treatment of refugees or regarding drastic measures for environmental conservation.

Hence, the inherent 'democratic deficit' of international decision-making appears, at first sight, as the major objection to the existence of a 'general' international law and to its capacity to contribute to the solution of common and/or collective problems in the contemporary world. Democracy in a meaningful sense of the term appears only possible within a nation-state or local setting, not on the world stage.

Even within Europe, there is much scepticism as to the prospects of a democratisation of the European Union. The BVerfG, in its *Maastricht* decision, rejected the idea of the transfer of the separation of powers and domestic democracy to a supranational body, in spite of the common value-system embraced by Europe, because it lacked the required social reality, in particular a common public opinion in which stable majorities could be formed around common projects.[22] While some have criticised the decision for its apparent exclusion of democratic processes at the European level,[23] even critics have agreed that the establishment of a supranational parliament alone does not suffice for multi-level democracy.[24]

In the United States, some of the opposition to the decisions of international bodies is also grounded in an apparent lack of democratic control over these institutions. Law without democracy, the argument goes, is not much more than an imposition that needs to be judged on the individual merits of the law in question, not on any inherent legitimacy of international law. In the words of professors Jack Goldsmith and Eric Posner:

> [W]e presume that domestic laws are good in a liberal democracy, where citizens have influence over the political process. The same cannot be said about international law. Much of the foundational rules of international law evolved long before liberal democracy became a common mode of political organization; more recent international law, it is generally agreed, almost always

[22] 89 BVerfGE, 155, 187, [1994] 1 CMLR 57, 88.

[23] Weiler, *Constitution of Europe*, above n 10, 345, speaking of the 'fallacy of the German Constitutional Court in its Maastricht decision: conceptualizing the European *demos* in the way that the German *demos* is conceptualized'. For a more extensive critique on these lines, see Weiler, 'The State "über alles"', above n 10, 1653–4 *et passim*, see also 1654–5, n 10 on Heller and Schmitt.

[24] Weiler, *Constitution of Europe*, above n 10, 269–70, 344ff; S Besson, 'Institutionalizing Global Demoi-cracy' in L Meyer (ed) *International Law, Justice and Legitimacy* (Cambridge University Press, forthcoming), embracing a pluralist theory of multiple *demoi* in a democratising European Union.

> reflects the interests of the powerful (and not always liberal) states rather than the interests of the world at large.[25]

And further they argue that international law:

> can have no democratic pedigree because there are no international institutions that reliably convert the world public's needs and interests into international law and that can change existing international law when the world public's needs and interests change.[26]

It is hardly surprising that the same authors reject a larger role for, as they call it, 'global governance schemes', let alone a world state.[27] A world state is indeed not a promising perspective, be it organised in a more or less democratic fashion or otherwise.[28] In a globalised world, which seems to exert a strong pull towards harmonisation, many people regard their national allegiance as the best conceivable defence of their peculiarity and cultural difference. Nevertheless, it appears that Posner and Goldsmith throw out the baby with the bathwater. Precisely these cultural, political and economic differences in the contemporary world demand a democratised international decision-making procedure complementing the existing democratic control mechanisms at the domestic stage. The reason is that, in a globalised society, different societies are so much linked with and dependent on each other that a limitation of democracy to the domestic level gives the stakeholders not more, but less influence on decisions affecting them.

Thus, the question does not consist of a choice between national democracy and international legality. Such a choice may occasionally impose itself upon political decision-makers, whether governmental, administrative or judicial, and one would indeed presume that, in such instances,

[25] Goldsmith and Posner, *Limits of International Law*, above n 2, 195.

[26] *Ibid*, 199.

[27] *Ibid*, 223: 'There are obvious objections to . . . quasi-world government or global democracy proposals. . . . The most obvious difficulty concerns the democratic deficit associated with ever-broadening governmental institutions. A related concern is that large-scale uniformity inherent in global governance schemes comes at the expense of too many unsatisfied individual preferences. Finally, there is the difficulty of human motivation and loyalty with respect to large, impersonal organizations' (citation omitted).

[28] Even Immanuel Kant was, for all his enthusiasm for a universal history towards an enlightened new world, rather sceptical regarding not only the prospects, but also the desirability of a Republican world state. See I Kant, 'Die Metaphysik der Sitten' in W Weischedel (ed) 4 *Werke in sechs Bänden* (Wissenschaftliche Buchgesellschaft, Darmstadt, 1798) 309, 474–5 s 61; I Kant, 'Zum ewigen Frieden: Ein philosophischer Entwurf' in W Weischedel (ed) 6 *Werke in sechs Bänden* (Wissenschaftliche Buchgesellschaft, Darmstadt 1983) 194, 208–13. But see, based on Kant's arguments, the federalising vision of O Höffe, *Demokratie im Zeitalter der Globalisierung* (München, Beck, 1999). Neo-Kantians go much beyond what Kant had envisaged, see, eg, FR Tesón, 'The Kantian Theory of International Law' (1992) 92 *Columbia Law Review* 53.

democracy prevails.[29] However, the processes of international law usually prevent this choice from presenting itself. Hardly any constitution admits of the direct applicability of international norms without a process of legislative and/or executive review. Rather, in most countries, important agreements, in particular multilateral, quasi-law-making treaties, require the assent of both executive branch and parliament. It is also hardly true—at least, I hope, not universally true[30]—that parliamentarians are unable to form an opinion on international agreements while being perfectly capable of assessing the desirability of often arcane domestic rules. Even when incorporating customary international law in their constitutions, states tend to do this only with broadly accepted customary rules or general principles of international law.[31] The danger of trespass into national law without implicit legislative or constitutional agreement is thus not negligible, but rather reduced.

Finally, if a potential clash between national preferences and international legality arises, domestic institutions may either follow the international stricture or strive for a modification of domestic law to meet their international obligations. Either states may achieve a modification of the international rule and thus free themselves from the charge of violating the law.[32] Or states need to go through the domestic legislation process to implement their international obligations. In this regard, states

[29] For a conspicuous example, see the recent *Waldschlösschen* case, in which the people of the German city of Dresden decided to build a bridge against the wishes of UNESCO, thus risking the status of the Elbe valley as a World Heritage Site under the UNESCO Convention concerning the Protection of the World Cultural and Natural Heritage of 16 Nov 1972 (1037 UNTS 153), see BVerfG, 2 BvR 695/07 of 29 May 2007, para 35, available at http://www.bverfg.de/entscheidungen/rk20070529_2bvr069507.html (accessed on 6 Aug 2007). The German court decided that a Convention that does not contain clear obligations binding on the federal State of Saxonia may well be overruled by a local referendum in spite of the risk of international sanctions.

[30] However, for an example of the incapacity of national parliaments to control international legislation, see, in the context of the implementation of European Union law, *European Arrest Warrant*, 113 BVerfGE 273; English press release no 64/2005 of 18 July 2005, available at http://www.bverfg.de/pressemitteilungen/bvg05-064en.html> (accessed on 6 Aug 2007).

[31] Thus, Article 25 of the German Basic Law only incorporates the 'general rules of public international law' ('allgemeine Regeln des Völkerrechts') into domestic law. For an overview, see I Pernice, in H Dreier (ed), *Grundgesetz-Kommentar* (2d edn, Tübingen, Mohr Siebeck, 2006) Article 25 MN 11–14. Whereas the common law generally recognises, in the words of Blackstone's Commentaries, international law 'as part of the law of the land' (4 W Blackstone Commentaries on the Law of England 1979, Book IV, ch V, at 67; on the respective case law, see I Brownlie, *Principles of International Law* (6th edn, Oxford University Press, 2003) 42ff), the US constitution does not mention customary international law, and its internal effect is in dispute to this day, see the diverging interpretations of *Sosa v Alvarez-Machain*, 542 US 692, 712 (2004) by CA Bradley, JL Goldsmith and DH Moore, '*Sosa*, Customary International Law, and the Continuing Relevance of *Erie*' (2007) 120 *Harvard Law Review* 869 and WS Dodge, 'Customary International Law and the Question of Legitimacy' (2007) 120 *Harvard Law Review Forum* 19.

[32] This is what Iceland achieved with regard to the extension of the Exclusive Economic Zone in the framework of the law of the sea after its defeat in *Fisheries Jurisdiction (United Kingdom v Iceland)* (Merits, Judgment) [1974] ICJ Rep 3; *Fisheries Jurisdiction (Federal Republic of Germany v Iceland)* (Merits, Judgment) [1974] ICJ Rep 175. The UN Convention on the Law of

have broad discretion as to how international obligations are implemented.[33] But, of course, this margin cannot be unlimited. Thus, the International Court of Justice (ICJ) rejected a US attempt to implement its obligation of consular information under the Vienna Convention on Consular Relations[34] pursuant to the LaGrand judgment[35] within the framework of the clemency process rather than by a judicially enforceable right.[36] Nevertheless, similar to subsidiarity, the margin of appreciation for the implementation of international law allows for some measure of accommodation rather than all-out confrontation.

The problem is much more complex, though. It is not so much international rules themselves, but rather their application and interpretation by international bodies that create the clash between domestic and international law. The further development of international law by these institutions can hardly be controlled by the constituency or the legislative body of a single state. In some instances, states may prefer to violate an international obligation rather than to modify their national legislation or jurisprudence in order to comply with international law. Thus, the Supreme Court of the United States recently denied domestic effect of key portions of the LaGrand and Avena judgments, arguing that the Court had misconstrued the adversarial criminal justice system.[37] The German BVerfG, in turn, treated both ICJ and the European Court of Human Rights as authoritative for the interpretation of international law, but preserved for itself the resolution of eventual conflicts with German constitutional law.[38] Similarly, regarding the barrier in the West Bank, the Israeli High Court of Justice has recognised the authority of the ICJ to interpret international law[39]—even in the case of a non-binding Advisory Opinion—but has strived to preserve its own prerogative to decide on the

the Sea of 30 Apr 1982, 1833 *UNTS* 3, Art 55ff followed the position of Iceland, however, so that the country got away with its non-compliance with the judgment. For details, see C Schulte, *Compliance with Decisions of the International Court of Justice* (Oxford University Press, 2004) 144–58.

[33] The European Court of Human Rights has developed an elaborate theory on the 'margin of appreciation' of domestic implementation of the European Convention on Human Rights, see *Lawless v Ireland*, Series A, no 1; *Kokkinakis v Greece*, Series A, no 260-A.

[34] Vienna Convention on Consular Relations, 24 Apr 1963, entry into force 19 Mar 1967, 596 *UNTS* 261.

[35] *LaGrand (Germany v US)* [2001] ICJ Rep 466.

[36] *Avena (Mexico v US)* [2004] ICJ Rep 12, 66 para 143.

[37] *Sanchez-Llamas v Oregon*, 126 SCt 2669 (2006) 2686–7. See also *Medellin v Texas*, 2008 WL 762533 (SCt 25 Mar 2008).

[38] For the interpretation of the European Convention on Human Rights by the European Court of Human Rights, see *Görgülü I*, 111 BVerfGE 307 (2004), official English trans available at http://www.bverfg.de/entscheidungen/rs20041014_2bvr148104e.html (accessed 6 Aug 2007) paras 35, 53, 62; for the implementation of ICJ decisions, see the Chamber decision in BVerfG, 2 BvR 2115/01 of 19 Sep 2006, 2 BvR 2115/01, available at http://www.bverfg.de/entscheidungen/rk20060919_2bvr211501.html (accessed 18 Mar 2007).

[39] See *Legal Consequences of the Construction of a Wall in the Occupied Palestinian Territory*, Advisory Opinion [2004] ICJ Rep 136.

domestic implementation of international law including the assessment of the relevant facts.[40]

While the German and Israeli courts did not put into question the international legal authority of international courts and tribunals as such, the US Supreme Court did not shy away from charging the ICJ with the wrong application of international law and maintained its own primacy with regard to the interpretation of the international legal obligations of the United States.[41] However, one reason for this difference may well lie in the different domestic laws to be applied: whereas the US Constitution maintains, in Article VI, that self-executing treaties are the 'law of the land', equal in rank to Congress legislation,[42] German constitutional law with regard to treaty law is essentially dualist in nature: only the transformation of international into domestic law renders it equal in rank to domestic legislation.[43] Thus, it appears sufficient to block the direct effect of an international decision in order to prevent modification of domestic laws by a new international legal rule. In Israel, in turn, the non-binding nature of the Advisory Opinion gave the Court additional leeway regarding its implementation, which may have played a role in its rejection of the treatment of facts by the ICJ.

All of these decisions, however, imply that it is the domestic legal order that ultimately determines how international law is to be implemented. Both democracy and subsidiarity considerations point into this direction. Whereas the US Supreme Court comes to this conclusion by rejecting the ICJ's interpretation of international law, the BVerfG and the Israeli Supreme Court modified the application of the international decision in the respective domestic legal orders rather than questioning the international legal authorities as such.

Indeed, if (and to the extent) the national court is nearer to the problem in question and enjoys better democratic legitimacy through the 'stakeholders' of the issue at hand, its 'gate-keeping'[44] against international decisions abstracting from social reality may not be a matter of concern.

[40] *Mara'abe v The Prime Minister of Israel*, HCJ 7957/04 (Judgment) 15 Sep 2005, para 74.

[41] *Sanchez-Llamas* and *Medellin*, above n 37.

[42] For the dominant doctrinal interpretation, see L Henkin, *Foreign Affairs and the US Constitution* (2d edn, Oxford, Clarendon Press, 1996) 198ff. While denying domestic effect to the ICJ interpretation of the VCCR, even the *Sanchez-Llamas* majority decision emphasises the importance of international treaty obligations, see Sanchez-Llamas, 126 SCt at 2687–8: 'Our holding in no way disparages the importance of the Vienna Convention. . . . It is no slight to the Convention to deny petitioners' claims under the same principles we would apply to an Act of Congress, or to the Constitution itself.'

[43] This is particularly relevant in the German *Waldschlösschen* case (above n 29) because the UNESCO Convention was not put to the German legislature for a vote previous to its ratification by the Federal President.

[44] The notion is from Kirchhof, 'Der deutsche Staat im Prozeß der Europäischen Integration', above n 8, para 183 n 65.

However, this implies that the international stakeholders are represented at the domestic level as well as they are represented internationally.

Alas, this is not always the case.[45] The critics of general international law seem to presume that 'democracy' leads to identical solutions whether it is exercised by a national of the US as the world superpower or by a Sudanese Darfurian. The interests of the latter are, however, neither represented by its government,[46] nor by the democratic governments of other countries that adopt decisions pursuant to the interests of their own population. To give another example, when the democratically elected Knesset in Israel makes decisions regarding the treatment of Palestinians in the West Bank, the decision will not be recognised as 'democratic' by the Palestinians in the Occupied Territories because they are not represented in the Knesset. The same is valid for the adjudication of claims: the Supreme Court of Israel may well be commended for its even-handedness in cases involving the occupied territories. However, as long as the Palestinians there are not represented on the bench (or on the judge-appointing body), they will not recognise the Israeli court's decisions as legitimate.

In other words, democratic legitimacy depends on the representation of the principal stakeholders. Any democratic legitimacy of decision-makers towards a certain population is not enough. Representation by a non-democratically elected government or NGO at the international level may be preferable to no representation at all, but is hardly equivalent to the representation by an elected government. A truly global democracy that would rely on a weighing of international votes according to the sizes of the respective population would fail to respect the inherent limitation of democracy, namely that it presupposes a consensus that the minority will accept the rule of the majority. To put it mildly, such an international consensus is internationally not forthcoming. It could lead to a directorate of some great powers (China, India, Russia, the United States, for example) to the exclusion of Europe, Africa or Latin America. While the current composition of the Security Council may be regarded unjust, its competences are limited to the maintenance of international peace and security[47] and do not extend to other matters.

One may regard the specific attention to one's fellow nationals rather than other humans elsewhere as the strong side of both nationalism and communitarianism. If one cares for everybody, one cares for nobody. But the inherent 'democratic deficit' of international decision-making will not,

[45] For a similar argument, see Besson, 'Institutionalizing Global Demoi-cracy', above n 24, and accompanying text.

[46] See the alleged crimes committed by their government against them: Report of the International Commission of Inquiry on Darfur to the Secretary General, UN Doc S/2005/60 (1 Feb 2005).

[47] UN Charter, Arts 24, 25, 39.

as conventional wisdom has it, go away when the final decision is made at the national or local level, as democratic as it may be. And this argument has not even yet taken account of the fact that refraining from a decision may be tantamount to taking one—in other words, both positive and negative decisions have consequences for stakeholders. For instance, when a majority of French and Dutch citizens rejected the European Constitutional Treaty, while the people of Luxembourg and Spain approved it, both the entry-into-force of the treaty and the preservation of the status quo were undemocratic with regard to parts of the European electorate. Therefore, the negotiation of a new Reform Treaty that preserves some of the basic features of the Constitutional Treaty appears to be the most 'democratic' solution, accommodating both sides of the debate.[48]

More and more decisions, both at the international and the domestic levels, affect a great number of people without regard to the boundaries of nation-states, and many tasks—from free trade to struggles against terrorism, climate change, global poverty and AIDS—cannot be realised at the national level only.[49] It is simply not good enough to point to national democratic processes as the solution to the problem of legitimacy. On the one hand, decisions taken, or not taken, at the domestic level affect not only the citizens of a single state, but of humanity at large, from the provision of AIDS medication to the waging of wars. On the other hand, international decisions have different effects on different national or international constituencies. Thus, the democratic deficit of international decisions cannot be balanced by domestic democratic processes alone.

Of course, in the current system of international law, representation goes through states. This two-level system is under threat from liberal ethicists and sovereigntists alike. While the latter reject any long-term international decision-making not subject to domestic ratification, the former demand the construction of something akin to a world democracy by introducing domestic constitutional processes in international decision-making.[50] Fortunately, for the reasons pointed out above,[51] none of them has been successful. Rather, what is required for the improvement of the legitimacy of international decisions is both a strengthening

[48] See Treaty of Lisbon amending the Treaty on European Union and the Treaty establishing the European Community, signed at Lisbon, 13 December 2007, Official Journal C306 of 17 December 2007.

[49] On these 'community interests', see Simma, 'From Bilateralism to Community Interest', above n 20.

[50] See, in particular, D Archibugi and D Held (eds), *Cosmopolitan Democracy: An Agenda for a New World Order* (Cambridge, Polity Press, 1995); D Held, *Democracy and the Global Order* (Cambridge, Polity Press, 1995). For a more moderate version, see Höffe, *Demokratie im Zeitalter der Globalisierung*, above n 27; Besson, 'Institutionalizing Global Demoi-cracy', above n 24.

[51] See above n 9, and accompanying text.

of the domestic representativeness of states as well as a more open, transparent process of decision-making at the international level that would allow for the interests of additional stakeholders to be taken into account in the decision-making process. By simply leaving decisions to the lowest possible level, however, be it democratically constituted or not, international decisions affecting the lives of many, if not all, human beings do not become inherently more democratic.

Thus, democracy may indeed constitute an argument in favour of leaving decisions at the lowest possible level. It does not, however, point against the attempt of construing multilateral institutions that are both capable of inter- and supranational decision-making, if the task in question requires an answer which goes beyond the purview of individual nation-states. Thus, the democratisation of global institutions, as limited it may be, is preferable to a simple throwing-up of arms and a return to domestic regulation. When global decisions are concerned, the democracy of domestic decisions alone is undemocratic when seen from the perspective of outsiders.

III. SUBSIDIARITY AND 'FRAGMENTATION'

The critique of international law from the standpoint of national democracy somewhat contradicts another experience of the contemporary lawyer: according to the European experience shaped by the process of European integration, the unity of the nation-state appears increasingly illusory. Accordingly, the international legal realm is characterised by a fragmentation into different issue areas. Although states are represented in the vast majority of decision-making bodies, whether at the WTO financial institutions, it may be more important whether a state representative regards herself as trade lawyer, environmental lawyer or human rights lawyer, than whether she represents the United Kingdom or Morocco. Of course, national procedures will counterbalance the impact of assigning specialists to international bodies by inter-agency and ministerial processes and the monitoring of their representatives. In addition, national governments and parliaments may be able to deny their assent to the results of any international agreement. Nevertheless, the more important an international agreement is, the less likely, or even feasible, its rejection becomes.[52] In addition, the domestic interest in any deal may outweigh any disadvantage incurred during the negotiation process. Thus, most states can hardly afford to withdraw from an international consensus on many issues. Some lawyers have thus concluded that globalisation is characterised by a shift from territorial borders to

[52] See Weiler, 'Geology of International Law', above n 10, 557.

functional boundaries.[53] Most issue areas such as trade, environment or human rights have left territorial boundaries behind and cannot be dealt with effectively at the national level only.

According to the proponents of autopoiesis, each sub-system of international law is itself capable of developing the relevant decision-making processes in a transparent and democratic fashion.[54] But this proposition presupposes an analysis of the proper identification of those affected by the decisions within a given issue area. Due to the uncertainty and fallibility of all consequential analysis, however, the effects of decisions in one sub-system on others will also be indeterminate and uncertain. Therefore, the presumption underlying the general competence of states—namely, that most decisions in the public sphere affect all citizens and must therefore be legitimised, directly or indirectly, by all of them—is also valid internationally, whether one deals with human rights, the environment, or trade and development. In turn, this demonstrates that the compartmentalisation of political decisions into issue areas carries considerable political and democratic costs.

Furthermore, general international law still provides the basic rules on international law-making and, at least subsidiarily, on their enforcement,[55] and the sub-systems often refer back to general international law on these matters. The legal regulations applied in the different issue areas, from internet regulation to the WTO, from environmental treaties to the International Criminal Tribunal for the Former Yugoslavia, stem from the very state or inter-state bodies that proponents of fragmentation have dismissed before as increasingly irrelevant. Thus, a trend from territorial to functional tasks will be followed by functional rather than territorial conflicts of norms. These conflicts, however, cannot be decided at the national level, but require international regulation. Hence the perceived need of some sort of international constitution as a repository of conflict rules between different issue areas.[56]

The parsimonious character of international law makes it quite malleable for the self-ordering of regimes, within certain limits. Inter-

[53] See, in particular, Luhmann, *Recht der Gesellschaft; Luhmann, Gesellschaft der Gesellschaft*, above n 14, and the radicalised version of Teubner and Fischer-Lescano, 'Regime-Collisions', above n 3. On this shift, see also AL Paulus, 'From Territoriality to Functionality? Towards a Legal Methodology of Globalization' in IF Dekker and WG Werner (eds) *Governance and International Legal Theory* (Leiden, Boston, MA, Martinus Nijhoff, 2004) 59; on the problem of the 'linkage' between these issue areas see DW Leebron, 'Linkages' (2002) 96 *American Journal of International Law* 5.

[54] On autopoiesis, see the contributions to G Teubner (ed), *Autopoietic Law: A New Approach to Law and Society* (Berlin/New York, de Gruyter, 1988).

[55] See B Simma and D Pulkowski, 'Of Planets and the Universe: Self-contained Regimes in International Law' (2006) 17 *European Journal of International Law* 483, 529 *et passim*.

[56] In this vein see JP Trachtman, 'The Constitutions of the WTO' (2006) 17 *European Journal of International Law* 623, 627; but see JL Dunoff, 'Constitutional Conceits: The WTO's "Constitution" and the Discipline of International Law' (2006) 17 *European Journal of International Law* 647, 674 (arguing that the WTO lacks the 'sociological legitimacy' required for a constitution).

national law grounds its obligations either in consent or in custom and recognises certain general principles, either internationally or as derived from domestic legal systems. One may dispute whether such an order fulfils HLA Hart's requirements for a modern legal system,[57] but it certainly provides enough leeway for the *leges speciales* of functionally differentiated regimes. The main problem does not lie in the international legal requirements for binding norms, but in the limitation of its law-making subjects to states. Yet this problem is not insuperable if one contemplates applying the same criteria—namely, the legally binding nature of formal commitments and of custom accompanied by a joint conviction regarding their legally binding nature—to the pronouncements of non-state actors. Moreover, non-state actors can only bind themselves. As soon as public interests are at stake, only public decision-making appears legitimate, because only public actors can claim to be representative of the whole of society independent of a specific issue area.

It is thus not surprising that the need for legitimation beyond one single sub-system leads to the acceptance of rules for the common ordering of the international realm, such as human rights or the protection of the global commons. Some of these rules will be more of a formal nature—how rules are to be made and to be interpreted—others will be substantive, setting material limits to the self-ordering of sub-systems.

Ultimately, of course, it is a matter of perspective whether one interprets the use of norms from other systems as an autonomous incorporation or as evidence for the existence of one common system. On the other hand, though, recognition of the same body of non-derogable norms beyond the fall-back rules of international law demonstrates the 'staying power' of an international *jus cogens* over and above the ordinary norms of specific legal regimes.[58] The main problem with the theory of the autopoietic character of the law of new legal regimes most likely relates to its lack of attention for questions of legitimacy—a legitimacy that each sub-system alone cannot provide.

To give an example: in the *Yahoo!* case,[59] a French court decided that Yahoo! had to block a website auctioning racist memorabilia from being accessed in France because its display there violated section R.645-2 of the

[57] HLA Hart, *The Concept of Law* (2nd edn, Oxford, Clarendon Press, 1994), 213ff, arguing that international law lacks the so-called 'secondary rules' to make it a complete system of law. But see JP Trachtman, 'The Constitutions of the WTO', above n 56, 627, arguing for 'tertiary' rules of allocation of rule-making authority.

[58] On *jus cogens*, see, recently, C Tomuschat and J-M Thouvenin (eds), *The Fundamental Rules of the International Legal Order* (Leiden, Boston, MA, Martinus Nijhoff, 2006); AL Paulus, '*Jus Cogens* in a Time of Hegemony and Fragmentation' (2005) 74 *Nordic Journal of International Law* 297 with further references.

[59] In France see, *LICRA et UEJF v Yahoo! Inc.*, Ordonnance Référé, TGI Paris, 20 Nov 2000, in English, available at http://www.lapres.net/yahen11.html (Daniel Lapres trans). For the quite fragmented US litigation drawing on questions of competence rather than substance, see *Yahoo! Inc v La Ligue Contre le Racisme et l'Antisemitisme*, 433 F3d 1199 (9th Cir, 12 Jan 2006 *en*

French Criminal Code. Should we allow such questions to be decided by the 'Web community', eg, the Internet Corporation for Assigned Names and Numbers (ICANN), because a regulation by a territorial state alone is not fully possible and the Internet should be regulated internationally rather than nationally? Or should we allow the French courts to order Yahoo! at least to take those steps to block territorial access that appear technically feasible (which would block access in France to about 90 per cent of users)? The result of the first solution would be a unified regulation mainly in the interest of most Internet service providers and of most customers. In the second case, 100 per cent efficiency cannot be reached (if one does not allow for a complete shutdown of the Internet in France, which no reasonable person would contemplate), but the majority of the French society which legitimises the outlawing of neo-Nazi propaganda would prevail over the interests of the global Internet community.

However, the solution on the basis of Internet self-ordering appears illegitimate. The eighty-year-old Holocaust victim is affected (and offended) by neo-Nazi propaganda on right-wing websites even if she does not use the Internet, but learns of the contents of the sites in her local newspaper. She is not represented, however, when the Internet community is allowed to regulate itself. Likewise, everybody, not only the potential Internet users, will be affected by the success of strategies to improve access to the Internet. This would require, in turn, that legitimate decisions need to include representatives of society as a whole—and leads, in the absence of representative international fora, to a preference for local or national decisions based on democratic legitimacy rather than for international decisions of unaccountable expert bodies. The best solution, however, would consist of a truly international regulation that takes account of the non-systemic concerns—ie, the integration of Internet regulation in the general international legal regime—which may include the delegation of competences to the most subsidiary and most special level.[60]

Because decisions made within many systems profoundly influence the fate of those not within the system, some general system of accountability and legitimacy appears necessary. At the very least, functional

banc). On this case, see also M Reimann, 'Introduction: The Yahoo! Case and Conflict of Laws in the Cyberage' (2003) 24 *Michigan Journal of International Law* 663 with further references.

[60] For a comment on the Tunis World summit of the Information Society 2005 on these lines, see KW Grewlich, 'Internet governance und "völkerrechtliche Konstitutionalisierung" nach dem Weltinfomrationsgipfel 2005 in Tunis' (2006) *Kommunikation und Recht* 156; for a summary of the international legal regulation, see F Mayer, 'Völkerrecht und Cyberspace: Entgrenztes Recht und entgrenzte Medien' in U Thiedeke (ed) *Soziologie des Cyberspace: Medien, Strukturen und Semantiken* (Wiesbaden, VS Verlag für Sozialwissenschaften, 2004) 491. But see JMEA Caral, 'Lessons from ICANN: Is Self-Regulation of the Internet Fundamentally Flawed?' (2004) 12 *International Journal of Law and Information Technology* 1 who argues in favour of self-regulation.

systems should be built by processes of a general nature—such as public international law treaties—and not by custom-designed special procedures. In other words, the move from territoriality to functionality should not be accompanied by a move from democracy to technocracy. But such sub-systems must include a minimum degree of public control over the private exercise of power.

In the end, decision-makers do not represent functional systems, but human beings, human beings who are not—or at least should not be—the objects, but the subjects of the system. Although each human being belongs to several functional associations, she is a whole, not a functionally disaggregated entity.[61] As such, she needs not only functional systems that serve her specific needs, but also a comprehensive system of representation which is able to weigh different interests against each other. Thus, states as representatives of the public appear to be not at all redundant. The disaggregated character of power in the European legal orders may sometimes appear to dissimulate the representative character of the democratic nation-state, but the discussion of the democratic deficit of European institutions brings the point home. As I have attempted to show above, this does not imply that legitimacy can be provided only at the domestic level. Parliamentary approval in nation-states is not equivalent to adequate international decision-making procedures. But the knowledge of international law-makers that they will have to justify the outcome before their domestic parliaments and the general public constitutes a healthy constraint on their decisions.

Thus, fragmentation does not do away with the need for the intervention by the general body politic. However, it makes the absence of a global public opinion, let alone a global democracy of a representative nature, even more glaring. If the analysis is correct and many global problems can only be solved at the world level, decisions should not be left to bureaucratic functionalists, but to representatives of broader constituencies.

IV. CONCLUSION: DEMOCRACY AND SUBSIDIARITY IN THE CONTEMPORARY INTERNATIONAL LEGAL ORDER

In conclusion, both processes appear necessary and legitimate—on the one hand, democratic processes within nation-states to ascertain the general acceptance of solutions taken at the international level; on the other hand, the technocratic expertise and international exchange of local views towards the solution of global problems. International regulation only appears acceptable for democratic states, however, when it meets at

[61] D von der Pfordten, *Rechtsethik* (Munich, Beck, 2001), 125.

least two conditions that may be described by the terms representation and subsidiarity:

1. The views of the relevant national and international constituencies must be taken into account—Albert Hirschman's famous element of 'voice' as opposed to the 'exit' towards other regimes.[62] Similar ideas are connected with models of 'deliberative democracy'.[63] However, it appears that these models are much more about deliberation than about rule by the demos—although the latter notion is what democracy originally meant.[64]
2. International regulation is necessary because nation-states cannot solve the problem at hand domestically. The development of a global public may complement such a development. International NGOs can help to bring about a more representative nature of international decisions. However, in the terminology used by Hauke Brunkhorst, as long as the global public remains 'weak' in the sense that it does not benefit from institutionalised 'channels' that ascertain its influence on the outcomes of global decision-making,[65] national processes of 'ratification' of global developments remain central.

Nevertheless, fragmentation is real, and reaffirmations of orthodoxy will be of little help. In spite of an ever-growing functional differentiation, issue areas are held together by a minimum of common values and decision-making procedures—in other words, by general international law which bases its legitimacy on decisions of, ideally democratic, national processes of decision-making. Linking international decisions to national democratic affirmation is not sufficient to guarantee international democratic legitimacy. Thus, both fragmentation and democracy may indeed favour subsidiarity in the sense of decision-making at lower and more specific levels instead of the level of general international law. But the other element of subsidiarity, namely the intervention from 'above' when a more parochial level is either incapable or not legitimated to take a decision alone, should be kept in mind, too. Subsidiarity thus may develop into a principle of international law as well as demo-

[62] See AO Hirschman, *Exit, Voice and Loyalty. Responses to Decline in Firms, Organizations and States* [1970] (Cambridge, MA, Harvard University Press, 1990). See also Weiler, *Constitution of Europe*, above n 10, 17.

[63] On 'deliberative democracy', see S Besson and JL Martí (eds), *Deliberative Democracy and Its Discontents* (Ashgate, Aldershot 2006); J Cohen and C Sabel, 'Directly-Deliberative Polyarchie' (1997) 3 *European Law Journal* 313; D Held, *Models of Democracy* (3d edn, Cambridge, Polity Press, 2006) 231–55; J Bohman and W Rehg (eds), *Deliberative Democracy* (Cambridge, MA and London, MIT Press, 1997).

[64] The Greek term δῆμος means 'people' and the term κρατία means 'rule'.

[65] H Brunkhorst, *Solidarität. Von der Bürgerfreundschaft zur globalen Rechtsgenossenschaft* (Frankfurt, Suhrkamp, 2002) 184ff, in English, H Brunkhorst, *Solidarity. From Civic Friendship to a Global Legal Community* (Cambridge, MA, MIT Press, 2005).

cracy[66]—but, in a time of globalisation, it will not lead to the removal of general international norms for international decision-making.

Of course, in the absence of a central global 'democracy', the problem of the (at least) bifurcated structure of the international community remains. It is exacerbated by the establishment of multiple fora within the international realm itself. These are mainly composed by experts, be they state or non-state actors, egoist or altruist.[67] The move from territoriality to functionality is in danger of becoming a move from nationalism to technocracy. 'Subsidiarity' should thus not become yet another heading for an argument in favour of the more parochial, more narrow-minded, more technocratic decision-making procedure. Instead, 'real' subsidiarity requires both the general and the special level, both the international and the domestic realms. Thus, this contribution suggests that 'subsidiarity' should be understood as a principle according to which decisions are taken at the lowest, and most specialised, possible level, but that allows, even requires, intervention from the general, international or rather global level.

This argument does not answer the question of how to establish anything like global democratic procedures. A global democracy remains elusive, in spite of numerous attempts to create a quasi-global parliamentary body, eg, a people's chamber at the UN General Assembly.[68] In the alternative, we should rather reflect on a political structure for the global realm that does not end up in a—democratic or autocratic or expertocratic—world state, but in an accommodation of the different levels of authoritative decision-making with a view to achieving a balance that may not be based on the utopia of genuine global majority voting but on less formalised, democratising but not necessarily fully democratic, procedures for the involvement of all stakeholders in global decision-making.[69] In the allocation of legal authority in such a multilevel system, subsidiarity may indeed constitute a guiding principle, but only if both of its aspects are taken into account—the decentralised

[66] See, famously, T Franck, 'The Emerging Right to Democratic Governance' (1992) 86 *American Journal of International Law* 46. For more detailed treatment, see GH Fox and BR Roth (eds), *Democratic Governance and International Law* (Cambridge University Press, 2000). But see also the healthy scepticism expressed by writers such as S Marks, 'The End of History? Reflections on Some International Legal Theses' (1997) 8 *European Journal of International Law* 449 and Weiler, 'Geology of International Law', above n 10, 552–3.

[67] See, in particular, A-M Slaughter, *A New World Order* (Princeton, NJ and Oxford, Princeton University Press, 2004).

[68] See, eg, T Franck, *Fairness of International Law and Institutions* (Oxford, Clarendon Press, 1995) 483, who does not, however, advocate a binding decision-making capacity.

[69] For such an attempt, see Besson, 'Institutionalizing Global Demoi-cracy', above n 24. For the problem of 'translation' of concepts tied to the state to an international environment, see N Walker, 'Postnational constitutionalism and the problem of translation' in JHH Weiler and M Wind (eds) *European Constitutionalism Beyond the State* (Cambridge University Press 2003) 27; Weiler, *Constitution of Europe*, above n 10, 270.

decision making *and* the need for global intervention where different nations, or issue areas, ought to be balanced.

Current international law meets some of those criteria, such as the establishment of special institutions, or the delegation of important functions in rule-making, rule-interpretation and rule-application to states, as well as a margin of appreciation for states in the execution of international rules.[70] Non-state actors may play an important role in that regard, but their own problems of transparency and accountability and their lack of democratic legitimacy prevent 'international civil society' from taking over the legitimising role of the state in international rule-making. Thus, a more representative nature of governments is rightly regarded as a central challenge for the international order. Democracy itself needs to be combined with subsidiarity: as much local—or special—democratic decision-making as is possible and acceptable from the view of the stakeholders, as much international, or global, intervention as may be necessary for achieving a maximum of democratic legitimacy and efficiency.

In her famous treatment of the intractable legal situation of the city of Jerusalem, Ruth Lapidoth has shown that complexity is not only a vice, but also a virtue of legal regulation. The same may be valid for the democratic legitimation of international law: it will require more than simply tying international decisions back to national democratic processes; but it is also not open to the easy solution of pointing to the autopoiesis of legal regimes legitimating themselves. Universal international law will remain with us, but so will the problem of its democratic credentials. It cannot be solved by local decision-making alone.

[70] For a description of those features in detail see Fastenrath, 'Subsidiarität im Völkerrecht', above n 17, 482ff.

III
Allocation of Authority among Judicial Bodies

9

Towards a Solange-*Method between International Courts and Tribunals?*

NIKOLAOS LAVRANOS*

I. INTRODUCTION

IN RECENT TIMES the issue of competing jurisdictions has received increasing attention from legal academia, induced, no doubt, by recent cases in which this issue has played a central role.[1] Two of the most famous competing jurisdiction cases are the *MOX plant* and *IJzeren Rijn* cases[2]—both of which concern the jurisdictional relationship between the European Court of Justice (ECJ) and other international arbitral tribunals. Another case that belongs to this category is the *Bosphorus* case, involving the ECJ and the European Court of Human Rights (ECHR).[3] This case is of particular importance because it touches

* Dr jur; LLM; Senior Advisor, Dutch Competition Authority; Senior Researcher University of Amsterdam, Law Faculty, Amsterdam Center for International Law. This contribution has been written within the framework of my research project 'Competing Jurisdiction between the ECJ and other International Courts and Tribunals' (2005–2009), sponsored by the Dutch Research Council NWO. I appreciate the comments of the Editors on an earlier draft version. The usual disclaimer applies.

[1] See, eg, Y Shany, *The Competing Jurisdiction of International Courts and Tribunals* (Oxford University Press, 2003); N Lavranos, 'Concurrence of Jurisdiction between the ECJ and other International Courts and Tribunals' (2005) 14 *European Environmental Law Review*, part I, September 2005, 213–25; part II, October 2005, 240–51; *ibid*, 'Das Rechtsprechungsmonopol des EuGH im Lichte der Proliferation internationaler Gerichte' (2007) 42 *Europarecht* 440.

[2] The MOX plant case consists of three different proceedings: (i) ECJ Case C-459/03 *Commission v Ireland* [2006] ECR I–4635; (ii) UNCLOS arbitral proceeding, http://www.pca-cpa.org/showpage.asp?pag_id=1148; and (iii) OSPAR arbitral proceeding, http://www.pca-cpa.org/showpage.asp?pag_id=1158.

The IJzeren Rijn arbitral tribunal decision is available at http://www.pca-cpa.org/showpage.asp?pag_id=1155.

See also: N Lavranos, 'The MOX Plant and IJzeren Rijn Disputes: Which Court is the Supreme Arbiter?' (2006) 19 *Leiden Journal of International Law* 223.

[3] *Bosphorus Hava v Ireland* (App no 45036/98) (Judgment) ECHR 30 May 2005, http://cmiskp.echr.coe.int/tkp197/search.asp?skin=hudoc-en.

on a long-standing and still unresolved matter, namely which court is the supreme court for the protection of fundamental rights in Europe.[4] Indeed, this issue surfaced when the ECJ brought fundamental rights protection within its jurisdiction.[5] Ever since then, it has been possible to detect a continuous interaction—some would say competition—between the ECJ and the ECHR. This competition has been informed, inter alia, by the still looming possibility that the EU itself would one day accede to the European Convention on Human Rights (EConvHR), thereby submitting the ECJ to the authority of the ECHR. However, the silent 'death' of the European Constitution and its 'resurrection' in the form of a 'reform treaty' leaves this question still unresolved.

Despite the impasse caused by the failure of EU Member States to adopt clear decisions on this matter, the European courts have not stood still, but rather found and used the *Solange*-method—a method developed by the German Constitutional Court (Bundesverfassungsgericht, hereafter BVerfG) to demarcate its 'reserve jurisdiction' vis-à-vis the ECJ—for the demarcation of the scopes of their respective jurisdictions.

At this point it is perhaps useful to explain what the term 'reserve jurisdiction' means. In short, 'reserve jurisdiction' means that a part of a jurisdiction is still retained by a court, despite the existence of an exclusive jurisdiction of another court. Moreover, it is important to appreciate that the BVerfG has never been prepared to give up its jurisdiction completely since the arrival of the ECJ on the European stage, notwithstanding the latter's assertion of supreme jurisdiction. Indeed, starting with its *Costa v ENEL*[6] and *Van Gend & Loos*[7] judgments, the ECJ has developed the concepts of direct effect and supremacy of EC law in national law, which, from the ECJ's point of view, also necessarily entailed the concepts of direct effect and supremacy of ECJ jurisprudence. The ECJ subsequently continued to expand its scope of jurisdiction to practically all fields of law, and has done so at the expense of the jurisdiction of national courts, including national constitutional courts.

Accordingly, in this chapter the '*Solange*-method' is thus defined as a tool for determining the scope of the 'reserve jurisdiction' of one court in relation to the existing jurisdiction of another court. Applying this

See N Lavranos, 'Das So-lange-Prinzip im Verhältnis von EGMR und EuGH'(2006) 41 *Europarecht* 79; A Haratsch, 'Die Solange-Rechtsprechung des Europäischen Gerichtshofs für Menschenrechte—Das Kooperationsverhältnis zwischen EGMR und EuGH' (2006) 66 *Zeitschrift für ausländisches öffentliches Recht und Völkerrecht* 927.

[4] See I Canor, 'Primus Inter Pares—Who is the Ultimate Guardian of Fundamental Rights in Europe?' (2000) 25 *European Law Review* 3.

[5] See ECJ Case 4/73 *Nold* [1974] ECR 491; Case 44/79 *Hauer* [1979] ECR 3727; see I Pernice, *Grundrechtsgehalte im Europäischen Gemeinschaftsrecht* (Baden-Baden, 1979).

[6] ECJ Case 6/64 *Costa v ENEL* [1964] ECR 585.

[7] ECJ Case 26/62 *Van Gend & Loos* [1963] ECR 1.

Solange-method results in refraining from exercising an existing jurisdiction of one court in favour of an existing jurisdiction of another court.

In the following section, the *Solange*-jurisprudence of the BVerfG will be briefly summarised. This will be followed by a discussion of the *Solange*-method approach of the ECHR. On that basis a comparative analysis showing the differences between both approaches will follow. All of this will then be summed up with some conclusions.

II. THE *SOLANGE*-JURISPRUDENCE OF THE BVERFG

For our purposes it suffices to focus on several key aspects of the BVerfG's *Solange*-jurisprudence.[8] In the first place, it should be noted that the development of this jurisprudence, which dates back to the BVerfG's first *Solange* judgment in 1974,[9] has not been linear, but rather has taken the form of waves: it has had its high and low points. The high points signify times in which the BVerfG was prepared to give up more of its 'reserve jurisdiction'; the low points indicate when the BVerfG assumed or reassumed more jurisdictional powers.

In the second place, it should be remembered that the *Solange*-method was introduced because the supremacy claim of the ECJ coupled with the expanding development of Community law collided with the protection of fundamental rights as guaranteed by the national constitutions of the Member States.

In particular, the BVerfG considered fundamental rights to be a 'no-go area' for the ECJ. As far as fundamental rights were concerned, the BVerfG kept, at all times, a 'reserve jurisdiction' in the sense that it considered itself always competent to exert its jurisdiction, despite the existence and use of ECJ jurisdiction (which, in the eyes of the ECJ is of an exclusive nature).

The *Solange I* case concerned the question of what domestic courts should do in case of a conflict between a provision of an EC Regulation and fundamental rights as protected by the German Constitution. The BVerfG held that as long as (*solange* is German for 'as long as') the integration process of the EC fails to incorporate an array of fundamental rights that meets the demands of the German Constitution and has not been duly approved by the German Parliament, a German court may, after requesting a preliminary ruling from the ECJ, request a ruling from the BVerfG as to the compatibility of the EC measure with the German

[8] See more extensively: N Lavranos, *Decisions of IOs in the European and Domestic Legal Orders of Selected EU Member States* (Groningen, Europa Law, 2004) 148–154.

[9] BVerfGE 37, 327 (Solange I), http://www.servat.unibe.ch/dfr/dfr_bvbd100.html.

Constitution.[10] In substance, the BVerfG concluded that in this case there was no conflict between the EC measure and the German Constitution.

In other words, the BVerfG found it necessary to emphasise that it did not consider the level of fundamental rights protection to be adequate, in particular because the EC did not possess a set of fundamental rights comparable to that existing in the German Constitution. Furthermore, since at that time fundamental rights had not been formally recognised at all in the jurisprudence of the ECJ, the BVerfG could not give up its jurisdiction regarding fundamental rights protection in favour of an exclusive ECJ jurisdiction.

That signal by the BVerfG was subsequently picked up by the ECJ, which started to develop a jurisprudence on fundamental rights protection.[11] In recognition of that development, the BVerfG did relinquish parts of its jurisdiction under certain conditions when it issued its second *Solange* judgment in 1986.[12] In this case the main issue was whether a judgment of the ECJ on the interpretation and application of EC law had to be considered final or whether it could still be reviewed by the BVerfG if a conflict with the fundamental rights as protected by the German Constitution could be established. In its *Solange II* judgment, the BVerfG held that as long as the case-law of the ECJ offers effective protection of fundamental rights against acts of public organs (ie, EC organs), which is comparable to the minimum level guaranteed by the German Constitution, the BVerfG would no longer exercise its jurisdiction in reviewing EC law measures.[13]

[10] *Ibid*, para 56: 'Solange der Integrationsprozeß der Gemeinschaft nicht so weit fortgeschritten ist, daß das Gemeinschaftsrecht auch einen von einem Parlament beschlossenen und in Geltung stehenden formulierten Katalog von Grundrechten enthält, der dem Grundrechtskatalog des Grundgesetzes adäquat ist, ist nach Einholung der in Art 177 des Vertrags geforderten Entscheidung des Europäischen Gerichtshofs die Vorlage eines Gerichts der Bundesrepublik Deutschland an das Bundesverfassungsgericht im Normenkontrollverfahren zulässig und geboten, wenn das Gericht die für es entscheidungserhebliche Vorschrift des Gemeinschaftsrechts in der vom Europäischen Gerichtshof gegebenen Auslegung für unanwendbar hält, weil und soweit sie mit einem der Grundrechte des Grundgesetzes kollidiert.'

[11] See, eg, ECJ Case 4/73 *Nold* [1974] ECR 449; Case 44/79 *Hauer* [1979] ECR 3727.

[12] BVerfGE 73, 339 (Solange II), http://www.servat.unibe.ch/dfr/dfr_bvbd100.html.

[13] *Ibid*, para 132: 'Solange die Europäischen Gemeinschaften, insbesondere die Rechtsprechung des Gerichtshofs der Gemeinschaften einen wirksamen Schutz der Grundrechte gegenüber der Hoheitsgewalt der Gemeinschaften generell gewährleisten, der dem vom Grundgesetz als unabdingbar gebotenen Grundrechtsschutz im wesentlichen gleichzuachten ist, zumal den Wesensgehalt der Grundrechte generell verbürgt, wird das Bundesverfassungsgericht seine Gerichtsbarkeit über die Anwendbarkeit von abgeleitetem Gemeinschaftsrecht, das als Rechtsgrundlage für ein Verhalten deutscher Gerichte und Behörden im Hoheitsbereich der Bundesrepublik Deutschland in Anspruch genommen wird, nicht mehr ausüben und dieses Recht mithin nicht mehr am Maßstab der Grundrechte des Grundgesetzes überprüfen; entsprechende Vorlagen nach Art. 100 Abs. 1 GG sind somit unzulässig.'

In other words, the BVerfG accepted that the interpretation of the ECJ regarding EC law is authoritative and final, and thus also binding on all German courts—including the BVerfG itself.

So, after *Solange II*, the relationship between the ECJ and the BVerfG was back on track. Indeed, the ECJ continued its approach of explicitly integrating fundamental rights into the Community legal order by issuing some bold judgments on the subject[14] (despite, or perhaps because, of the lack of a written catalogue of EC fundamental rights). However, it must be emphasised at the same time that the ECJ did not go as far as submitting itself to the jurisdiction of the ECHR when it rejected in its Opinion 2/94 the possibility of EC accession to the EConvHR.[15]

But in 1992 the Maastricht Treaty entered the European stage and introduced new tensions into the ECJ–BVerfG relationship. Although the Maastricht Treaty certified ECJ jurisprudence on fundamental rights protection, by explicitly referring in the EU Treaty to the fundamental rights as protected by the common constitutional traditions of the Member States and the EConvHR,[16] the other novel and far-reaching components of the Treaty—the EMU and the euro, common foreign and security policy, and police and justice cooperation—were too much for the BVerfG to swallow. Hence, in its *Solange III* judgment the BVerfG de facto overturned its *Solange II* jurisprudence by allowing for the non-application of EC law in Germany under certain conditions (the so-called *ausbrechender Gemeinschaftsakt*).[17]

So in its third *Solange* judgment on the Maastricht Treaty,[18] the BVerfG,

[14] See, eg, ECJ Case C-260/89 *ERT* [1991] ECR I–2925; ECJ Case 5/88 *Wachauf* [1989] ECR 2609; see generally: JHH Weiler, 'The Jurisprudence of Human Rights in The European Union, Integration and Disintegration, Values and Processes' *Jean Monnet Working Paper* 96/2, http://www.jeanmonnetprogram.org/papers/96/9602.html.

[15] ECJ Opinion 2/94 (Accession to EConvHR) [1996] ECR I–1759.

[16] See Treaty of the European Union (adopted 7 February 1992, entered into force 1 November 1993), Art 6, 46.

[17] In its BVerfGE 89, 155 (Maastricht Treaty, Solange III) decision, the BVerfG defined the conditions of 'ausbrechender Gemeinschaftsakt' as follows (at para 106):

> 'Würden etwa europäische Einrichtungen oder Organe den Unions-Vertrag in einer Weise handhaben oder fortbilden, die von dem Vertrag, wie er dem deutschen Zustimmungsgesetz zugrunde liegt, nicht mehr gedeckt wäre, so wären die daraus hervorgehenden Rechtsakte im deutschen Hoheitsbereich nicht verbindlich. Die deutschen Staatsorgane wären aus verfassungsrechtlichen Gründen gehindert, diese Rechtsakte in Deutschland anzuwenden. Dementsprechend prüft das Bundesverfassungsgericht, ob Rechtsakte der europäischen Einrichtungen und Organe sich in den Grenzen der ihnen eingeräumten Hoheitsrechte halten oder aus ihnen ausbrechen (vgl. BVerfGE 58, 1 [30 f.]; 75, 223 [235, 242]).'

> If European organs would apply and develop the EU Treaty in a way that is not covered anymore by the German Act ratifying the EU Treaty, then the measures resulting thereof would not be binding in Germany. The German organs would be prevented by reason of German Constitutional law to apply them. Accordingly, the BVerfG reviews whether the acts of European organs remain within the limits of the German ratification act or go beyond that. (translation by the author)

[18] BVerfGE 89, 155 (Maastricht Treaty) Solange III, http://www.servat.unibe.ch/dfr/dfr_bvbd100.html.

while allowing the ratification of the Maastricht Treaty by Germany, made clear that the future development of the EU required conditional approval by the BVerfG. Thus, the BVerfG reasserted its 'reserve jurisdiction' and signalled to the ECJ that it was prepared to question the doctrine of supremacy of EC law and, thus, the authority of the ECJ. In other words, the BVerfG challenged the ECJ's self-declared supremacy over national laws and institutions, whose impact largely depends on voluntary submission by national courts. At that time, the relationship between the BVerfG and the ECJ became frosty—to say the least.

The vigilant attitude taken by the BVerfG towards the ECJ was justified, at least from the perspective of the BVerfG (as well as large parts of German academia), by the position adopted by the ECJ and Court of First Instance (CFI) towards the EC 'banana regulation' and its WTO law inconsistency.[19] In short, German importers claimed that the EC banana regulation essentially disrupted all their import opportunities because the banana regulation made their imports from Central and South America much more expensive. This, the importers argued, constituted a violation of their fundamental property rights. Moreover, they claimed that the WTO law inconsistency of the banana regulation, which is an inconsistency of a lower norm (EC banana regulation) with a higher norm (EC Treaty, EConvHR), could not be accepted on the basis of the rule of law and the EConvHR. However, the ECJ/CFI were not prepared to review the compatibility of the EC banana regulation with WTO law or fundamental rights protected by the EConvHR and/or national constitutions.[20] Thus, the ECJ/CFI left the EC banana regulation intact.

Moreover, in parallel proceedings before the German courts, the importers claimed that this also constituted a violation of the German ratification act of the EC Treaty, and thus should be qualified as an 'ausbrechender Gemeinschaftsakt' within the meaning of *Solange III*.

But by the time the BVerfG was finally called upon by the Frankfurt Administrative court to disapply the banana regulation by qualifying it as 'ausbrechender Gemeinschaftsakt', the BVerfG had a different composition than it had back at the time of its *Solange III* ruling. The BVerfG now decided the time was ripe to offer the ECJ a 'peace treaty' by essentially giving up the concept of 'ausbrechender Gemeinschaftsakt'.[21] Thus, the

[19] For a detailed discussion, see: N Lavranos, 'Die Rechtswirkung von WTO panel reports im Europäischen Gemeinschaftsrecht sowie im deutschen Verfassungsrecht' (1999) 34 *Europarecht* 289.

[20] See, eg, N Lavranos, 'The Communitarization of WTO Dispute Settlement Reports: An Exception to the Rule of Law' (2005) 10 *European Foreign Affairs Review* 313.

[21] BVerfGE 102, 147 (bananas) Solange IV, http://www.servat.unibe.ch/dfr/dfr_bvbd100.html; see generally: I Pernice, 'Les bananes et les droits fondamentaux: La Cour Constitutionnelle Allemande fait le point' (2003) 3–4 *Cahier de Droit Europeen* 427; C Grewe, 'Le 'traite de paix' avec la Cour de Luxembourg: L'arret de la Cour Constitutionnelle Allemande du 7.6.2000 Relatif au Reglement du Marche de la Banana' (2001) 37 *Revue trimestrielle de droit européen* 1.

BVerfG held in its *Solange IV* judgment that it would review EC law measures only if it thought that the minimum level of fundamental rights protection was no longer being guaranteed by the EC organs on a general level.[22] So, even though the possibility of declaring an EC law measure as an *'ausbrechender Gemeinschaftsakt'* remains possible, the conditions for this are extremely difficult to meet. In effect, only an act of the EC that goes completely against basic fundamental rights on a general level—and not only in one or several specific cases—would meet those criteria.

So far it is hard to think of any such examples, although the complete lack of judicial review against UN sanctions implemented by the EC, as was argued by the CFI in its *Yusuf*[23] and *Kadi*[24] judgments, might meet those conditions.[25] However, it must be admitted that the CFI has gradually moved away from its initial position in its most recent case-law.[26] According to that case-law, judicial review is available in cases in which the EC Member States have submitted the names to the UN Sanctions Committee.

Be that as it may, the BVerfG moved back to its second *Solange* decision, thereby accepting the overall jurisdiction of the ECJ, while at the same

[22] In its decision on the EC banana regulation BVerfGE 102, 147 (bananas) Solange IV, the BVerfG defined the conditions as follows:

> 'Sonach sind auch nach der Entscheidung des Senats in BVerfGE 89, 155 Verfassungsbeschwerden und Vorlagen von Gerichten von vornherein unzulässig, wenn ihre Begründung nicht darlegt, dass die europäische Rechtsentwicklung einschließlich der Rechtsprechung des Europäischen Gerichtshofs nach Ergehen der Solange II–Entscheidung (BVerfGE 73, 339 <378 bis 381>) unter den erforderlichen Grundrechtsstandard abgesunken sei. Deshalb muss die Begründung der Vorlage eines nationalen Gerichts oder einer Verfassungsbeschwerde, *die eine Verletzung in Grundrechten des Grundgesetzes durch sekundäres Gemeinschaftsrecht geltend macht, im Einzelnen darlegen, dass der jeweils als unabdingbar gebotene Grundrechtsschutz generell nicht gewährleistet ist.* Dies erfordert eine Gegenüberstellung des Grundrechtsschutzes auf nationaler und auf Gemeinschaftsebene in der Art und Weise, wie das Bundesverfassungsgericht sie in BVerfGE 73, 339 (378 bis 381) geleistet hat.' [emphasis added]

> Thus even after the decision in Solange III, requests by national courts before the BVerfG are inadmissible if they do not argue that the required level of fundamental rights protection within the EC, including ECJ case-law, has fallen below the standard as determined in Solange II. Accordingly, a request must proof in detail that a violation of fundamental rights by secondary EC law measures is general and that the level of protection has fallen below the minimum level as determined by the German Constitution. (translation by the author)

The crucial condition is that a violation of fundamental rights by secondary EC law (such as the EC bananas regulation) must be specifically proven by showing that the absolute minimum level of fundamental rights is generally not guaranteed anymore.

[23] CFI Case T-306/01 *Yusuf* [2005] ECR II–3533.

[24] CFI Case T-315/01 *Kadi* [2005] ECR II–3649.

[25] See further: P Eeckhout, 'Community Terrorism Listings, Fundamental Rights and UN Security Council Resolutions—In Search of the Right Fit' (2007) 3 *European Constitutional Law Review* 183; N Lavranos, 'Judicial Review of UN Sanctions by the CFI' (2006) 11 *European Foreign Affairs Review* 471.

[26] CFI Case T–327/03 *Al Aqsa* (Judgment), 11 July 2007; CFI Case T–47/03 *Sison* (Judgment), 11 July 2007; CFI Case T–228/02 *Organisation des Modjahedines du peuple d'Iran* [2006] ECR II–4665; CFI case T–253/02 *Ayadi* [2006] ECR II–2139.

time limiting its own 'reserve jurisdiction' to a minimum. This coincided with other developments conducive to the ECJ–BVerfG relationship: the (unadopted) European Constitution contained an explicit provision facilitating the accession of the Union to the EConvHR.[27] In addition, the Charter of Fundamental Rights was to obtain full legal force under the Constitution. In other words, the European Constitution was designed to enhance—on a formal legal basis and by binding effect— fundamental rights protection by both the Strasbourg and Luxembourg courts, thus significantly reducing the need for national courts to watch over the compatibility of EC law with national fundamental rights protection.

However, this honeymoon did not last for long: the ECJ soon trespassed on another 'holy ground' of Member States' law, namely criminal law. While Member States had accepted that criminal law was an important and necessary component of the EU, as illustrated by its third pillar (Justice and Home Affairs, renamed Police and Justice Cooperation), they clearly did not intend to bring criminal law into the first pillar (the Community) and delegate to the EC the competence to impose criminal law obligations with supranational force (ie, endowed with supremacy over the national laws of the Member States). However, the ECJ apparently thought otherwise and rendered ground-breaking judgments in *Pupino*[28] and *Commission v Council*[29] regarding the criminal enforcement of environmental law. As a result, criminal law has entered the Community legal order. When this development is combined with the continuous stream of far-reaching legislation in the third pillar, it can be seen that EU law has had a forceful impact on national competencies in criminal law issues, which increasingly affects individuals directly. Hence, when the BVerfG got the opportunity to decide on the German law implementing the European Arrest Warrant (EAW),[30] it is perhaps not surprising that it returned to its *Solange*-formula as developed in its Maastricht judgment. This case concerned the issue of constitutionality of the German Act implementing the EAW, which was adopted within the third pillar as an EU Framework Decision. The crucial novelty of the EAW is the automatic binding force that is given to arrest orders from any EU Member State and their automatic mutual recognition. In other words, a Member State that is requested to arrest and transfer a citizen

[27] Draft Treaty Establishing a Constitution for Europe, art I–9.

[28] ECJ Case C–105/03 *Pupino* [2005] ECR I–5285. See E Spaventa, 'Opening Pandora's Box: Some Reflections on the Constitutional Effects of the Decision in Pupino' (2007) 3 *European Constitutional Law Review* 5.

[29] ECJ Case C–176/03 *Commission v Council* [2005] ECR I–7879; see also: J Prinssen, 'Doctrinal Legal Effects of EU criminal law: A Transfer of EC Law Doctrines?' in N Lavranos and D Obradovic (eds), *Interface between EU Law and National Law* (Groningen, Europa Law, 2007) 313–31.

[30] BVerfGE 113, 273 (European Arrest Warrant), http://www.servat.unibe.ch/dfr/dfr_bvbd100.html; see generally: F Schorkopf (ed), *Der Europäische Haftbefehl vor dem Bundesverfassungsgericht* (Tübingen, Mohr Siebeck, 2006).

(including own nationals) to another EU Member State is no longer able to review that decision. The BVerfG, however, held that despite the current level of fundamental rights protection guaranteed by the ECJ, the ECHR and in the other EU Member States, this could not affect or exclude the possibility of judicial review in individual cases as guaranteed by the German Constitution.[31] Accordingly, the 'reserve jurisdiction' of German courts, and ultimately of the BVerfG, in this matter remains intact.

In other words, the BVerfG continues to exercise its jurisdiction regarding third-pillar measures irrespective of the existence of any (limited) ECJ jurisdiction in this area. Hence, in policy areas that inevitably affect fundamental rights in a substantial way, such as in matters of police and judicial co-operation (third-pillar), the BVerfG is not yet prepared to limit its jurisdiction in the same way as it did regarding first-pillar cases. Accordingly, one can now distinguish between a rather limited BVerfG 'reserve jurisdiction' in first-pillar cases and a rather broad 'reserve jurisdiction' in third-pillar cases.

In sum, it can be concluded that the *Solange*-method has been used by the BVerfG in a flexible way in order to allow it to accommodate its jurisdictional relationship with the ECJ according to developments in the ECJ case-law, as well as developments on the more general European political scene. Accordingly, the *Solange*-method enables the BVerfG to limit its jurisdiction in favour of the jurisdiction of the ECJ depending on the existing level of fundamental rights protection at the European level. In short, a high level of fundamental rights protection means limited interference from the BVerfG, while a low level of fundamental rights protection means more interference from the BVerfG. But this flexibility should not be misunderstood as implying at any time a complete renunciation of jurisdiction, since the BVerfG has always kept its 'reserve jurisdiction'.

[31] *Ibid*, para 118: 'Der Gesetzgeber wird die Gründe für die Unzulässigkeit der Auslieferung Deutscher neu zu fassen haben und die Einzelfallentscheidung über die Auslieferung als abwägenden Vorgang der Rechtsanwendung ausgestalten. Das primäre Unionsrecht thematisiert zwar mit Art. 6 EU die Frage der Homogenität der Strukturen zwischen den Mitgliedstaaten. Die bloße Existenz dieser Vorschrift, eines die Strukturprinzipien absichernden Sanktionsmechanismus (Art 7 EU), und eines gesamteuropäischen Standards des Menschenrechtsschutzes durch die Europäische Konvention zum Schutze der Menschenrechte und Grundfreiheiten rechtfertigen aber nicht die Annahme, dass die rechtsstaatlichen Strukturen unter den Mitgliedstaaten der Europäischen Union materiell synchronisiert sind und eine entsprechende nationale Einzelfallprüfung deshalb überflüssig ist. Insoweit kann durch das Inkraftsetzen eines strikten Grundsatzes der gegenseitigen Anerkennung und der damit verbundenen weitgehenden gegenseitigen Vertrauensbekundung der Staaten untereinander die verfassungsrechtliche Gewährleistung der Grundrechte nicht eingeschränkt werden' (vgl. dazu auch Europäischer Gerichtshof für Menschenrechte, – Waite und Kennedy, NJW 1999, S 1173 <1175>; – Matthews, NJW 1999, S 3107 <3108>).

III. THE *SOLANGE*-METHOD OF THE ECHR

From the outset it must be realised that the legal framework of the relationship between the ECJ and the ECHR is rather peculiar. On the one hand, the ECHR has exclusive competence to adjudicate on the correct implementation of the EConvHR in the Contracting Parties, thus being the highest court for the protection of fundamental rights in Europe. On the other hand, as the previous section illustrated, the ECJ has—over time and due to the pressure from the BVerfG—developed a jurisprudence on fundamental rights, thereby usurping substantial parts of the task of the ECHR—at least as far as EU Member States are concerned.[32]

Indeed, since the 1990s, the ECJ has systematically incorporated the EConvHR into the Community legal order, thereby attaching to the EConvHR as applied by the ECJ some EC law characteristics, in particular supremacy over the domestic legal order of the EU Member States.[33] In other words, whereas the EConvHR and the ECHR jurisprudence did not enjoy direct effect and supremacy in most EU Member States, the ECJ has modified that situation. In general, this 'communitarisation' of the EConvHR has had an amplifying effect for the protection of fundamental rights in Europe, and thus should be welcomed.

But the result of this 'communitarisation' has also been that we now have two 'supreme' European Courts that consider themselves competent to adjudicate on fundamental rights protection within the EU Member States.[34] Since both courts are not formally bound by each other's decisions, divergent or even conflicting judgments are possible—to the potential detriment of the individual whose rights may need protection, and in any case to the detriment of legal certainty and consistency. Hence, the ECJ and the ECHR now have concurrent or even 'competing' jurisdictions over cases involving fundamental rights protection.[35] Although, in the large majority of cases that have been brought before the ECJ to date, the ECJ has applied the relevant ECHR case-law, this has not always been the case.[36]

[32] See N Lavranos, above n 8.

[33] See, eg, ECJ Case C–60/00 *Carpenter* [2002] ECR I–6279; Case C–413/99 *Baumbast* [2002] ECR I–7091.

[34] S Douglas-Scott, 'A Tale of Two Courts: Luxembourg and Strasbourg and the Growing European Human Rights Acquis' (2006) 43 *Common Market Law Review* 629.

[35] See, eg, C Dippel, *Die Kompetenzabgrenzung in der Rechtsprechung von EGMR und EuGH*, Diss, Berlin 2004, http://edoc.hu-berlin.de/dissertationen/dippel-carsten-2004–06–08/HTML/front.html.

[36] See D Spielmann, 'Human Rights Case Law in the Strasbourg and Luxembourg Courts: Conflicts, Inconsistencies and Complementarities', in Ph Alston (ed), *The EU and Human Rights* (Oxford University Press, 1999) 757–80. Examples in which the ECJ explicitly refused to apply ECHR-jurisprudence are Case C–17/98 *Emesa Sugar* [2000] ECR I–665 and Case C–94/00 *Roquette Frères* [2002] ECR I–9011.

The ECHR reacted to the ECJ's parallel annexation of parts of its competence by declaring itself competent to indirectly review EC law measures, ie, measures adopted by EConvHR Contracting Parties, which are also EC Member States, for the purpose of implementing their EC law obligations.[37] The ECHR thus signalled that acts of international organisations (such as the EC/EU) to which Contracting Parties have transferred competences remain within its jurisdiction and are thus reviewable.[38] But it was only with its *Bosphorus* judgment that the ECHR clarified more explicitly how far it would go (or rather not go) in reviewing EC acts and ECJ judgments.[39]

The *Bosphorus* case concerned the implementation of UN sanctions against former Yugoslavia. Bosphorus was leasing an aeroplane from the state-owned Yugoslav airline JAT. Due to UN sanctions, which were implemented by an EC Regulation, the Bosphorus aeroplane was

[37] ECHR, Case of *Cantoni v France* (Judgment), 15 November 1996; Case of *Matthews v UK* (Judgment), 18 February 1999, all available at http://cmiskp.EHRConv.coe.int/tkp197/search.asp?skin=hudoc-en.

[38] In *Matthews, ibid*, the ECHR stated: '32. The Court observes that acts of the EC as such cannot be challenged before the Court because the EC is not a Contracting Party. The Convention does not exclude the transfer of competences to international organisations provided that Convention rights continue to be 'secured'. Member States' responsibility therefore continues even after such a transfer.' In case of *Bosphorus* v *Ireland* (Judgment), 30 June 2005, the ECHR stated in the same vein that:

> '152. The Convention does not, on the one hand, prohibit Contracting Parties from transferring sovereign power to an international (including a supranational) organisation in order to pursue co-operation in certain fields of activity (the *M & Co* decision, at p 144 and *Matthews* at § 32, both cited above). Moreover, even as the holder of such transferred sovereign power, that organisation is not itself held responsible under the Convention for proceedings before, or decisions of, its organs as long as it is not a Contracting Party (see *CFDT v European Communities*, no 8030/77, Commission decision of 10 July 1978, DR 13, p 231; *Dufay v European Communities*, no 13539/88, Commission decision of 19 January 1989; the above-cited *M & Co* case, at p 144 and the above-cited *Matthews* judgment, at § 32).
>
> 153. On the other hand, it has also been accepted that a Contracting Party is responsible under Article 1 of the Convention for all acts and omissions of its organs regardless of whether the act or omission in question was a consequence of domestic law or of the necessity to comply with international legal obligations. Article 1 makes no distinction as to the type of rule or measure concerned and does not exclude any part of a Contracting Party's 'jurisdiction' from scrutiny under the Convention (*United Communist Party of Turkey and Others v Turkey* judgment of 30 January 1998, Reports, 1998-I, § 29).
>
> 154. In reconciling both these positions and thereby establishing the extent to which State action can be justified by its compliance with obligations flowing from its membership of an international organisation to which it has transferred part of its sovereignty, the Court has recognised that absolving Contracting States completely from their Convention responsibility in the areas covered by such a transfer would be incompatible with the purpose and object of the Convention: the guarantees of the Convention could be limited or excluded at will thereby depriving it of its peremptory character and undermining the practical and effective nature of its safeguards (*M & Co* at p 145 and *Waite and Kennedy*, at § 67). The State is considered to retain Convention liability in respect of treaty commitments subsequent to the entry into force of the Convention (*mutatis mutandis*, the above-cited *Matthews v the United Kingdom* judgment, at §§ 29 and 32–34, and *Prince Hans-Adam II of Liechtenstein v Germany* [GC], no 42527/98, § 47, EHR CONV 2001-VIII).'

[39] ECHR *Bosphorus Hava v Ireland*, above n 3.

impounded by the Irish authorities. Bosphorus started proceedings against those measures which in the end reached the ECJ. The ECJ ruled that the measures were acceptable in order to attain the objectives of the UN sanctions.[40] Following that ruling, Bosphorus started proceedings against Ireland before the ECHR, claiming that the measure violated its fundamental rights as protected by Article 1 of Protocol 1 to the EConvHR, which protects the right to property. The ECHR was thus called upon to review in effect the EC measure and the *Bosphorus* judgment of the ECJ.

The ECHR repeated the position it had already adopted in *Matthews* that EC law measures could be reviewed—indirectly—and that EU Member States could not hide behind an international organisation.

However, the ECHR shied away from actually performing that review. Instead, the ECHR explicitly applied the *Solange*-method for the first time vis-à-vis the ECJ.

In a first step, the ECHR held that the level of fundamental rights protection, including the available procedures for obtaining judicial review before the ECJ, within the EC is equivalent to, though not identical with, the EConvHR level.[41] Consequently, a presumption of sufficient fundamental rights protection within the EC exists.

[40] ECJ Case C–84/95 *Bosphorus* [1996] ECR I–3953.

[41] ECHR, *Bosphorus*, above n 3:

'155. In the Court's view, State action taken in compliance with such legal obligations is justified *as long as* the relevant organisation is considered to protect fundamental rights, as regards both the substantive guarantees offered and the mechanisms controlling their observance, in a manner which can be considered at least equivalent to that for which the Convention provides (see the above-cited *M & Co* decision, at 145, an approach with which the parties and the European Commission agreed). By 'equivalent' the Court means 'comparable': any requirement that the organisation's protection be 'identical' could run counter to the interest of international co-operation pursued (paragraph 150 above). However, any such finding of equivalence could not be final and would be susceptible to review in the light of any relevant change in fundamental rights' protection.

156. If such equivalent protection is considered to be provided by the organisation, the presumption will be that a State has not departed from the requirements of the Convention when it does no more than implement legal obligations flowing from its membership of the organisation.

However, any such presumption can be rebutted if, in the circumstances of a particular case, it is considered that the protection of Convention rights was manifestly deficient. In such cases, the interest of international co-operation would be outweighed by the Convention's role as a 'constitutional instrument of European public order' in the field of human rights (*Loizidou v Turkey (preliminary objections)*, judgment of 23 March 1995, Series A no 310, § 75).

[. . .]

165. In such circumstances, the Court finds that the protection of fundamental rights by EC law can be considered to be, and to have been at the relevant time, 'equivalent' (within the meaning of paragraph 155 above) to that of the Convention system. Consequently, the presumption arises that Ireland did not depart from the requirements of the Convention when it implemented legal obligations flowing from its membership of the EC (see paragraph 156).'

In a second step, the ECHR explicitly held that *as long as* that fundamental rights protection is 'not manifestly deficient' in a specific case, the ECHR would not exercise its jurisdiction.[42] In other words, the ECHR will, in principle, refrain from reviewing EC law measures unless a specific case reveals a 'manifestly deficient' protection of fundamental rights within the EC.[43] Only in such a situation would the ECHR review EC law measures. Unfortunately, the ECHR did not define what 'manifestly deficient' actually means or when that threshold would be reached.[44] So, unlike the BVerfG, the ECHR applies a vague *Solange*-method. Perhaps a future case will provide an opportunity for the ECHR to shed some more light on what exactly 'manifestly deficient' means.

However, some indication of when the threshold of 'manifestly deficient' is met came recently, from a not so surprising corner, namely from Advocate General Mengozzi when he delivered his Opinion in the *SEGI* case.[45] In this case, SEGI, a group supposedly linked to the ETA terrorist group in Spain, faced sanctions imposed by 'autonomous' EU measures (ie, measures not emanating from the UN, but adopted independently by the EU). These measures were based on the second and third pillars of the EU Treaty, thereby excluding to a large extent any possibility of judicial review. Although the ECJ did not render a judgment in favour of SEGI,[46] Advocate General Mengozzi forcefully and bluntly emphasised that:

> In particular, from the point of view of observance of the obligations undertaken by the Member States when they signed the EHR Conv, it is entirely improbable that the European Court of Human Rights would extend to the third pillar of the Union the presumption of equivalence in the protection of the fundamental rights that it has established between the EHR Conv and Community law, or the 'first pillar' of the Union, and which leads that Court to carry out only a 'marginal' review of the compatibility of acts adopted by the Community institutions with the EHR Conv. On the other hand, it is highly likely that, in the course of a full examination of the compatibility of

[42] *Ibid*.

[43] Thus, the ECHR concluded that: '166. The Court has had regard to the nature of the interference, to the general interest pursued by the impoundment and by the sanctions regime and to the ruling of the ECJ (in the light of the opinion of the Advocate General), a ruling with which the Supreme Court was obliged to and did comply. It considers it clear that there was no dysfunction of the mechanisms of control of the observance of Convention rights.

In the Court's view, therefore, it cannot be said that the protection of the applicant's Convention rights was manifestly deficient with the consequence that the relevant presumption of Convention compliance by the respondent State has not been rebutted.'

[44] See, eg, C Costello, 'The Bosphorus Ruling of the European Court of Human Rights: Fundamental Rights and Blurred Boundaries in Europe' (2006) 6 *Human Rights Law Review* 87.

[45] Opinion of AG Mengozzi in joined cases Case C–354/04 P *Gestoras Pro Amnistía et al* and C–355/04 P *Segi et al*, [2007] ECR I–1579.

[46] ECJ joined cases Case C–354/04 P *Gestoras Pro Amnistía et al* and C–355/04 P *Segi et al*, [2007] ECR I–1657, para 86.

> acts adopted by the institutions under Title VI of the EU Treaty with the EHR Conv, the European Court of Human Rights will in future rule that the Member States of the Union have infringed the provisions of that Convention, or at least Articles 6(1) and/or 13.[47]

The author could not agree more with this statement.

In sum, it can be concluded that after the *Bosphorus* judgment of the ECHR, it has become more difficult to convince the ECHR to review measures adopted by the Member States for the purpose of implementing EC/EU law obligations. This means that a final forum has been effectively closed off for individuals who wish to obtain judicial review—albeit indirectly—regarding the compatibility of EC measures with fundamental rights as enshrined in the EConvHR.

IV. ANALYSIS

This analysis consists of two parts. The first part focuses on the institutional aspects regarding the relationship between the ECJ and the ECHR. The second part focuses on the question as to what this relationship and the application of the *Solange*-method actually mean for individuals and their right to obtain effective judicial review before the ECJ and the ECHR.

A. Institutional Aspects of the *Solange*-Method

Similar to the *vertical relationship* between the BVerfG and the ECJ, the *Solange*-method is used by the ECHR in order to determine the scope of its 'reserve jurisdiction' vis-à-vis its *horizontal relationship* with the ECJ. In this context, it is important to remember that the ECJ has so far only once fully submitted itself—in its *Schmidberger* ruling—to the ECHR by giving the EConvHR supremacy over primary EC law, thereby accepting an ultimate 'reserve jurisdiction' of the ECHR.[48] In the *Schmidberger* case, the ECJ accepted Austria's argument that the restriction of the free movement of goods between Austria and other EC Member States caused by demonstrations on the Brenner motorway was justified by the fundamental right of freedom to associate and freedom of expression as enshrined in the EConvHR. In other words, the ECJ gave primacy to the EConvHR even over primary EC law, ie, the EC Treaty and the four internal market freedoms.

[47] Opinion of AG Mengozzi, above n 45.

[48] ECJ Case C–112/00 *Schmidberger* [2003] ECR I–5659; see G Gonzales, 'EC Fundamental Freedoms v Human Rights' (2004) 31 *Legal Issues of Economic Integration* 219.

Nonetheless, like the BVerfG, the ECHR has made it clear that it continues to retain its jurisdiction to indirectly review EC law measures. In other words, EU Member States must be aware of their continued obligations flowing from the EConvHR when adopting or implementing EC/EU law measures. Of course, this is only an indirect way of fundamental rights protection, and is less effective than the direct review that would be exercised if the EC/EU were to eventually accede to the EConvHR.

Moreover, it is also important to note that whereas the BVerfG requires a deficiency on a general basis in the system of fundamental rights protection by the EC/ECJ, the ECHR looks at it on a case-by-case basis. Since a 'manifestly deficient' situation is more likely to occur in a specific case rather than on a general level, the chance that the ECHR's *Solange*-method could be applied is much higher than the BVerfG's *Solange*-method.

At the same time, however, the rather vague conditions of 'manifest deficiency' that the ECHR introduced in its *Bosphorus* judgment illustrate that the ECHR seems to be not too eager actually to review ECJ rulings. Here we enter the world of high judicial politics and mutual respect among European top judges. Rather than potentially criticising one another, a practice that might potentially undermine the authority of all relevant courts, the judges use a more subtle way of letting each institution reign over their 'kingdoms' without external interference—except in very extreme cases. In this way, both European courts reaffirm their scope of jurisdiction, while at the same time agreeing informally to follow and respect each other's decisions.

Indeed, one could qualify the *Solange*-method as an example of judicial comity, which can be considered as a solution to the more general development of jurisdictional competition between international courts that is currently taking place, due to the continued proliferation of international courts and tribunals.[49] The issue of proliferation of international courts and tribunals and the consequences that flow from it are hotly debated at this moment.[50] In short, the crucial question is whether this proliferation leads to more unity of international law, thereby leading towards a constitutionalisation of international law[51] or whether it leads to a fragmentation of international law,[52] due to the lack of co-ordination between the various international courts and tribunals.

It is submitted that while an institutionalisation or even constitution-

[49] Y Shany, above n 1.

[50] See for a detailed discussion: N Lavranos, 'Jurisdictional Competition between the ECJ and other International Courts and Tribunals' (2007) *European Law Reporter* 156.

[51] See the contributions in the special issue of the *Leiden Journal of International Law* 2006, issue 3.

[52] See P-M Dupuy, 'A Doctrinal Debate in the Globalisation Era: On the 'Fragmentation' of International law' (2007) *European Journal of Legal Studies*, issue 1, http://www.ejls.eu/.

alisation of international law is currently taking place, at the same the danger of a fragmentation of international law is real.[53] Consequently, the question of how to deal with the negative consequences associated with jurisdictional competition, in particular conflicting rulings on the same issue of law, must be addressed.

From the analysis above it can be concluded that the *Solange*-method can help to reduce the chance of conflicting or diverging rulings, and thus the potential for fragmentation of fundamental rights in Europe is contained. Similarly, a wider application of the *Solange*-method by all international courts and tribunals could equally reduce the risk of fragmentation of international law.

B. The Solange-*Method and Individual Right of Judicial Review*

However, the positive effect of the *Solange*-method as discussed above for the distribution of the jurisdictional competence between the ECJ and the ECHR comes along with a negative effect for individuals and their rights to effective judicial review of governmental acts. Just like in the case of the *Solange*-method as used by the BVerfG in the banana episode, in which individuals were practically unable to challenge the constitutionality of EC law measures before German courts, individuals are essentially unable to subject EC law measures to indirect review by the ECHR. Of course, it remains to be seen how the ECHR will define the conditions of 'manifest deficiency', but as it stands now it seems very difficult to prove that the fundamental rights protection or procedures for judicial review under the Community legal order are 'manifestly deficient'. This would only be the case if the level of fundamental rights protection within the EC would fall below the absolute minimum of the EConvHR standard.

One example that could meet the 'manifestly deficient'-standard, however, could be the lack of judicial review against EU third pillar measures. As the statement of Advocate General Mengozzi quoted above illustrates, an almost complete absence of access to judicial review cannot be considered to be in conformity with the EConvHR and the relevant ECHR jurisprudence. This is especially so in cases emanating from Member States that have not opted for the possibility of allowing their national courts to request preliminary rulings from the ECJ on third pillar issues.[54] Indeed, quite a large number of Member States have either

[53] *Ibid.*

[54] See generally: S Peers, 'Salvation Outside the Church: Judicial Protection in the Third Pillar after the Pupino and Segi Judgments' (2007) 44 *Common Market Law Review* 883.

limited that possibility to their highest courts or have excluded that possibility altogether.[55]

So, in the areas governed substantively by EU third pillar measures, which could affect individuals' rights very dramatically, the possibility of judicial review might be the most limited within the European legal order. It is exactly for this reason that the BVerfG reasserted its reserve jurisdiction in its *EAW judgment* in order to avoid a lacuna in the system of judicial review.[56]

In sum, it can be concluded that the *Solange*-method as applied by the ECHR can be a useful tool for the distribution of the jurisdiction between the ECJ and the ECHR in an effective way. However, it comes with a high price tag of limiting or even fully excluding the possibilities of individuals to obtain judicial review before the ECHR, in particular of EC law measures implemented by Member States. This is notwithstanding the fact that the EC and EU are increasingly adopting measures that affect individuals to growing extent. One could indeed describe this as an asymmetric development in which the institutional architecture is reconfigured at the expense of the individual rights.

Of course, individuals continue to be able to enforce their fundamental rights before the ECJ, but since the EC/EU is still not formally party to the EConvHR, the ECJ is formally not bound by the EConvHR and ECHR jurisprudence. But individuals have effectively lost—except in 'manifestly deficient' cases—their last instance to appeal before the ECHR as far as European law measures are concerned.

V. CONCLUDING REMARKS

With its *Bosphorus* judgment, the ECHR has introduced and applied the *Solange*-method in order to demarcate its jurisdiction vis-à-vis the jurisdiction of the ECJ. Accordingly, based on the *Solange*-method, the ECHR will not exercise its jurisdiction anymore to review—indirectly—EC law measures as long as the level of fundamental rights protection within the EU is not manifestly deficient.

In other words, the ECHR retains a 'reserve jurisdiction' concerning the fundamental rights protection. Indeed, since the question of which court is the supreme fundamental rights court in Europe remains still unresolved, it is quite likely that the ECHR will need to resort to the *Solange*-method more frequently, thus developing and refining it further.

[55] Sixteen Member States have chosen to allow all courts and tribunals to refer preliminary questions to the ECJ, whereas Spain has limited the power to refer questions to its final courts. The remaining ten Member States have not yet accepted the jurisdiction of the ECJ at all in the third pillar. See for the most recent overview: http://eur-lex.europa.eu.LexUriServ/LexUriServ.do?uri=OJ:C:2008:069:0001:0001:EN:PDF.

For instance, one can expect that EU third pillar measures will be challenged more often before the ECHR. The first attempt of doing so, however, initiated by the above-mentioned SEGI group failed, because the ECHR argued that SEGI was targeted as a group and not the individual members by the EU sanctions.[57]

While the benefits of the *Solange*-method for the configuration of the jurisdictional architecture between the top European courts are obvious and should be welcomed for reducing the possibility of divergent or conflicting rulings regarding the EConvHR, one should not lose sight of the individuals and their possibilities of obtaining effective judicial review. Moreover, one gets the impression that the increasing workload of both the ECJ and ECHR could very well be another important reason for limiting the access to European Courts in general. The 14th Protocol to the EConvHR is evidence of how access of individuals to the ECHR is further limited.[58]

In my view, this is a dangerous development which could eventually undermine the authority of European Courts and their ability to effectively protect individual fundamental rights.

[56] See the discussion above at n 30.

[57] See case of *Segi v 15 EU Member States* (App no 6422/02) ECHR 23 May 2002 The ECHR held that:

> In any event, concrete measures such as those which have been adopted or might be in the future would be subject to the form of judicial review established in each legal order concerned, whether international or national. That is true more specifically of measures which might give rise to disputes under Articles 10 and 11 of the Convention. The same applies to Community acts such as the above-mentioned Council Regulation (EC) no. 2580/2001 (subject to review by the Court of Justice of the European Communities), other international instruments binding the member States or even any decisions that may have been taken by domestic courts which have referred to the common positions. Moreover, the applicants have not adduced any evidence to show that any particular measures have been taken against them pursuant to Common Position 2001/931/CFSP. The mere fact that the names of two of the applicants (Segi and Gestoras Pro-Amnistía) appear in the list referred to in that provision as 'groups or entities involved in terrorist acts' may be embarrassing, but the link is much too tenuous to justify application of the Convention. The reference in question, which is limited to Article 4 of the common position, does not amount to the indictment of the 'groups or entities' listed and still less to establishment of their guilt. In the final analysis, the applicant associations are only concerned by the improved cooperation between member States on the basis of their existing powers and they must accordingly be distinguished from the persons presumed to be actually involved in terrorism who are referred to in Articles 2 and 3 of the common position.
>
> With more particular regard to Article 8 of the Convention, pleaded by the applicants who are natural persons, the Court notes that their names do not appear in the list annexed to Common Position 2001/931/CFSP.
>
> Consequently, the Court considers that the situation complained of does not give the applicant associations, and *a fortiori* their spokespersons, the status of victims of a violation of the Convention within the meaning of Article 34 of the Convention.
>
> It follows that the applications must be declared inadmissible, pursuant to Article 34 and Article 35 §§ 1, 3 and 4 of the Convention.

[58] Protocol No 14 to the Convention for the Protection of Human Rights and Fundamental Freedoms, amending the control system of the Convention, http://conventions.coe.int/treaty/en/Treaties/Html/194.htm.

Fortunately, the development of the relationship between the ECJ and the ECHR is closely watched and followed by national courts, in particular national constitutional courts. As the BVerfG made clear in its *EAW judgment*, if serious situations of lack of judicial review actually arise, the BVerfG will step in and seize its 'reserve jurisdiction' to the extent necessary in order to restore the rule of law.

Besides, on a more general level, the application of the *Solange*-method for the purpose of organising the jurisdictional relationship between the two permanent, highly respected, European courts can be of great significance for tackling the problems associated with the proliferation of international courts and tribunals in general.

Indeed, if the *Solange*-method would be applied by all international courts and tribunals in case of jurisdictional overlap, the risk of diverging or conflicting judgments could be effectively minimized thus reducing the danger of a fragmentation of the international (including European) legal order.

Of course, the *Solange*-method is a 'voluntary restraint instrument' whose application solely depends on the attitude and readiness of each and every court and tribunal. Nonetheless, one could argue that the *Solange*-method and for that matter judicial comity in general is part of the legal duty of each and every court to deliver justice. In doing so, taking due account of the existing jurisdiction of another court and subsequently drawing the conclusion of not exercising its own jurisdiction if the jurisdiction of another court is more appropriate, is of course a task that all courts and tribunals should perform.[59]

Indeed, justice is part of the rule of law, which is the most fundamental principle that underpins the belief in supranational and international co-operation and its advantages for the individuals. Without a firm place of the rule of law at the supra- and international level, the shift in sovereignty that we currently perceive in so many different facets will have little benefits for the individual.

[59] See generally on this point: E-U Petersmann, 'Multilevel Judicial Governance of International Trade requires a Common conception of Rule of Law and Justice' (2007) 10 *Journal of International Economic Law* 529, advance access published on 30 July 2007, http://jiel.oxfordjournals.org/cgi/content/abstract/jgm019v1. It is submitted that this is not confined to international trade but applies equally to all areas of international law.

10

Exercise in Constitutional Tolerance? When Public International Law Meets Private International Law: Bosphorus *Revisited*

IRIS CANOR*

'Mirror, mirror, on the wall, who in this land is fairest of all?'
Jacob and Wilhelm Grimm, *Snow-White* (1812)

I. INTRODUCTION

SOME TEN YEARS ago, at the start of my academic career, still enjoying a mixture of enthusiasm and naïvety, I published an article criticising the European Court of Justice's (ECJ) decision in the *Bosphorus* case.[1] Being a strong believer in human rights I criticised the ECJ for taking the easy way by insisting that impounding property of innocent third-party individuals was necessary for effective implementation of UN sanctions against the Federal Republic of Yugoslavia in the early 1990s, which were aimed at ending the armed conflict in the

* Senior Lecturer, School of Law, Academic Studies, College of Management; Adjunct Lecturer, Europa-Institut, University of Saarland, Germany.

[1] The case concerns two aircraft belonging to a company residing in the Former Republic of Yugoslavia (FRY) which were leased to the applicant—Bosphorus Hava Yollari Turizm (Bosphorus), a Turkish airline charter company. The aircraft were brought to Ireland in order to have maintenance work performed on them, and one of them was impounded on the authorisation of the Irish Minister of Transport on the basis of EC Regulation that implemented the UN sanctions regime against the FRY. Bosphorus went before the Irish High Court claiming that the Minister's decision had infringed its right to respect for property. On appeal by the Irish Minister of Transport, the Irish Supreme Court asked for a preliminary ruling from the ECJ, Case C–94/95 *Bosphorus Hava Yollari Turizm ve Ticaret AS v Minster for Transport, Ireland* [1996] ECR I–3953.

region.[2] I argued that while the ECJ could have ruled that the EC had correctly transposed the UN sanctions into the EC legal system, the discretion of the implementing national authorities which decided to seize the property was nevertheless exercised in an excessive and disproportionate manner.

A decade later, the European Court of Human Rights (ECHR) was called upon to rule on the same issue between the same parties and upheld the decision of the ECJ.[3] Paradoxically, though still being passionate about the protection of human rights, I will argue below that the fact that the case was brought before another court, namely the ECHR, institutionally justifies the detrimental effect on the protection of human rights when the different point of perception of the ECHR is taken into account.[4]

The ECHR presumed that the ECJ complied with human rights and gave preference to concerns relating to the need to promote international co-operation. In a world of overlapping international and supranational jurisdictions, I will argue, the main burden to properly protect human rights rests on the shoulders of the court first seized with the matter. The scope of manoeuvre of the court secondly seized should be much more limited, and the possibility to diverge from the ruling of the first court should be restricted to the most serious violations of human rights classifiable as severe threats to public order.[5] In all other circumstances the second court should exercise restraint for the sake of ensuring better judicial co-operation.

Put differently, in the following pages I will attempt to examine the relationship between the ECJ and the ECHR. As this is a long road much travelled[6] (and, following the ECHR's *Bosphorus* decision, has regained its

[2] I Canor, 'Can Two Walk Together, Except They Be Agreed?' The Relationship Between International Law and European Law: The Incorporation of United Nations Sanctions against Yugoslavia into the European Community Law through the Perspective of the European Court of Justice' (1998) 35 *Common Market Law Review* 137. For further criticism see N Burrows, 'Caught in the Cross-Fire' (1997) 22 *European Law Review* 170; E Drewniak, 'The Bosphorus Case: The Balancing of Property Rights in the European Community and the Public Interest in Ending the War in Bosnia' (1997) 20 *Fordham International Law Journal* 1007.

[3] *Case of Bosphorus Hava Yollari Turizm ve Ticaret Anonim Sirketi v Ireland*, Application No 45036/98, 30 June 2005 (hereafter *Bosphorus*).

[4] For a different view see S Peers, 'Limited Responsibility of European Union Member States for Actions within the Scope of Community Law, Judgment of 30 June 2005, *Bosphorus Airways v Ireland*, Application No 45036/98' (2006) 2 *European Constitutional Law Review* 443.

[5] For a recent discussion of the term public order see R de Lange, 'The European Public Order, Constitutional Principles and Fundamental Rights' (2007) 1 *Erasmus Law Review* 3.

[6] To mention just few: T Tridimas, *The General Principles of EU Law* (2nd ed, Oxford University Press, 2007) 342; S Douglas-Scott, 'A Tale of Two Courts: Luxembourg, Strasbourg and the Growing European Human Rights *Acquis*' (2006) 43 *Common Market Law Review* 629; C Rieder, 'Protecting Human Rights within the European Union: Who is better Qualified to Do the Job, The European Court of Justice or the European Court of Human Rights?' (2005) 20 *Tulane European and Civil Law Forum* 73; I Canor, '*Primus Inter Pares*. Who is the Ultimate Guardian of Fundamental Rights in Europe' (2000) 25 *European Law Review* 3.

popularity),[7] I will try to contribute to the existing literature on two, relatively limited, points. First, I will try to take a critical look at the binary ECHR–ECJ relationship and explore whether it should be governed by the principle of comity (as is often argued by those who deal with overlapping international jurisdictions). I will examine the pros and cons of whether one can argue that the ECHR has treated the ECJ in a manner that coincides with Hillel's interpretation of the comity principle, namely: 'that which is hateful unto thee do not do unto thy neighbour', both from the advocates' and the critics' perspective. Moreover, I will suggest that this flexible, vague, undefined and elastic notion of comity is not capable of setting clear guidelines for the way in which international courts and tribunals should treat their counterparts.

Second, and alternatively, I will try to establish that there are lessons to be learnt from the discipline of private international law when attempting to tackle the way in which international judicial bodies should correspond with each other and to delineate the optimal construction of their relationship. I will show that international judicial bodies do not simply constitute an international judicial system, but all belong to an 'international regime complex' in which promotion of coherence is not the only, not even the principal, principle which they follow while adjudicating a case. In particular, I will concentrate on the relationship between the ECHR and the ECJ and argue that they constitute an intertwined pluralistic regime. I will then maintain that the best way to preserve this pluralistic character while safeguarding a certain coherence of the system is to borrow from the principles of private international law. Finally, I will illustrate this argument by focusing on the specific problem that the ECHR was facing, namely how to deal with a prior decision rendered by another international court on the same case. As a solution I will propose that the second court could draw inspiration from the common rules concerning recognition of foreign judgments.[8]

[7] Peers, above n 4; K Kuhnert, 'Bosphorus Double Standards in European Human Rights Protection?' (2006) 2 *Utrecht Law Review* 177; C Lebeck, 'The European Court of Human Rights on the Relations between ECHR and EC-law: the Limits of Constitutionalism of Public International Law' (2007) 62 *Zeitschrift für öffentliches Recht* 195; C Costello, 'The Bosphorus Ruling of the European Court of Human Rights: Fundamental Rights and Blurred Boundaries in Europe' (2006) 6 *Human Rights Law Review* 87; S Douglas-Scott, 'Case Note' (2006) 43 *Common Market Law Review* 243; C Eckes, 'Does the European Court of Human Rights Proved Protection from the European Community?—The Case of Bosphorus Airways' (2007) 13 *European Public Law* 47; A Hinarejos Parga, 'Bosphorus v Ireland and the Protection of Fundamental Rights in Europe' (2006) 31 *European Law Review* 251; J Phelps, 'Reflections on Bosphorus and Human Rights in Europe' (2006) 81 *Tulane Law Review* 251.

[8] The question whether the injection of rules stemming from the discipline of private international law might also fit *mutatis mutandis* to other international jurisdictions confronted with the same problem is a separate question which will only be touched upon scarcely and which falls beyond the scope of this article.

II. COMITY

A. Preliminary Remarks

The phenomenon of overlapping international jurisdictions is a by-product and a side effect of the currently increasing density of international regimes and the increasing multiplication of legal instruments regulating distinct issues. This implies increasing overlap across regulatory rules, and confusion regarding which international and bilateral treaties covers a certain issue.[9] The consequence of this multiplicity is that 'today it is perfectly natural for an individual simultaneously to have several loyalties not merely to different persons and institutions but to different systems of law'.[10]

Discussing this phenomenon, which is often referred to as 'global governance', has become by now almost 'mission impossible', given the vast and diverging literature on every aspect of this subject: its definition,[11] its origins,[12] its containment and its future.[13] For the purpose of this chapter it will suffice to say that I side with those who define the international sphere—with its states, sub-states, supranational and trans-national actors as building blocks, and the myriad of agreements connecting these actors—as a complex system, ie, a system with a large number of elements or agents capable of interacting with each other and with their environment. Their organisation in different types of regimes may be generalised as: 'overlapping regimes', 'nested regimes' and 'parallel regimes'.[14]

[9] C Tomushat, 'International Law: Ensuring the Survival of Mankind on the Eve of a New Century. General Course on Public International Law' (1999) 281 *Recueil des Cours Académie de Droit International de La Haye* 9, 306; B Simma, 'Self-Contained Regimes' (1985) 16 *Netherlands Journal of International Law* 111.

[10] K Schiemann, 'Europe and the Loss of Sovereignty' (2007) 56 *International and Comparative Law Quarterly* 475, 476.

[11] Among the different definitions offered to this term, this article will refer to it in the sense of fragmented fields of functional specialisation, which are often identified as special 'in the sense that rules of general international law are assumed to be modifies or even excluded in their administration', M Koskenniemi, 'Report of the Study Group of the International Law Commission, Fragmentation of International Law: Difficulties Arising from the Diversification and Expansion of International Law' (13 April 2006) UN Doc A/CN.4/L.682.

[12] Many and varied reasons are offered as an explanations to this phenomenon. It is argued that sometimes states join international agreements which are intended only as a starting point to be followed up by subsequent agreements among them or across issues. Others argue that sometimes sub-groups of states desire different or deeper co-operation than the whole, thus they break off to tackle co-operation within a specific issue, or in a specific region.

[13] A Lindroos and M Mehling, 'Dispelling the Chimera of "Self-Contained Regimes": International Law and the WTO' (2005) 17 *European Journal of International Law* 857.

[14] KJ Alter and S Meunier, 'The Politics of International Regime Complexity', available at http://ssrn.com/abstract=996889. On the definition of 'international regimes' see SD Krasner, 'Structural Causes and Regime Consequences: Regimes as Intervening Variables' in S Krasner (ed), *International Regimes* (Ithaca, NY, Cornell University Press, 1983)

As noted above, most of these regimes create not only political institutions but set up also judicial bodies for dispute settlements.[15] Yet, these courts and tribunals with their differing scopes of jurisdiction are guided by a diverse choice of legal rules on which law they should apply to a case. The common typology concerning the applicable law is as follows: rules allowing the application of all international law norms; rules that permit the application of all international law norms, but establish a normative hierarchy and prefer certain rules over the others; and rules allowing for the application of some parts of international law only, contracting out of the remaining international law norms.[16] Needless to mention, even when superiority rules (or choice-of-law rules) are formulated for a certain regime in a given treaty, they are often vague and subject to conflicting interpretations.

This ongoing development of norms lacking clear hierarchy and the absence of an overriding mechanism to officially regulate possible conflicts are characteristic of the 'international regime complex'. This complexity cannot be straightforwardly explained by simply invoking the traditional Kelsenian or Hartian notion of legal order as a hierarchical structure of norms organised in social and political authority. Moreover, the overlapping effect creates a competitive environment, which provokes destabilisation, causes incoherence and aggravates unpredictability. This has given rise to the fear of 'fragmentation' of international law, and has stimulated a lively scholarly debate that culminated in the International Law Commission (ILC) setting up a study group on the issue.[17] Admittedly some authors have attempted to formulate the hierarchical dimension of international law and to describe it as a layered system,[18] but such endeavours are controversial.[19] Furthermore, this

[15] B Kingsbury, 'Is the Proliferation of International Courts and Tribunals a Systematic Problem?' (1999) 31 *New York University Journal of International Law and Politics* 679; G Guillaume, 'Editorial Comments on the Proliferation of International Courts, Advantages and Risks of Proliferation: A Blueprint for Action' (2004) 2 *Journal of International Criminal Justice* 300; C Brown, 'The Proliferation of International Courts and Tribunals: Finding Your Way Through the Maze' (2002) 3 *Melbourne Journal of International Law* 453.

[16] H Hestermeyer, 'Where Unity Is at Risk: When International Tribunals Proliferate' in D König et al (eds), *International Law Today: New Challenges and the Need for Reform?* (Heidelberg, Springer, 2008). For a slightly different but mostly comparable division of the relevant international judicial bodies see JG Merrills, 'The Mosaic of International Dispute Settlement Procedures: Complementary or Contradictory?' (2007) LIV *Netherlands International Law Review* 361, 371.

[17] 'Fragmentation of International Law', above n 11.

[18] B Fasbender, 'The Meaning of International Constitutional Law' in N Tsagourias (ed), *Transnational Constitutionalism: International and European Perspectives* (Cambridge University Press, 2007) 307; E de Wet, 'The Emergence of International and Regional Value Systems as a Manifestation of the Emerging International Constitutional Order' (2006) 19 *Leiden Journal of International Law* 611; E-U Petersmann, 'How to Constitutionalize International Law and Foreign Policy for the Benefit of Civil Society' (1998) 20 *Michigan Journal of International Law* 1; E-U Petersmann, 'Constitutionalism and International Adjudication: How to Constitutionalize the UN Dispute Settlement System?' (1999) 31 *New York University Journal of International Law and Politics* 753.

[19] P Weil, 'Towards Relative Normativity in International Law' (1983) 77 *American Journal of International Law* 413.

'break up' of international law could be perceived as a welcome phenomenon that is pluralistic and hybrid in nature.

Be that as it may, most writers, despite their genuine attempt to formulate some 'hard law' rules of conduct for international overlapping jurisdictions, eventually, perhaps regretfully and disappointedly, fall back on the recurring theme of comity.[20] Accordingly, they contend that international courts and tribunals seized with a dispute should generally defer to already existing jurisprudence of other international courts and tribunals, unless overriding considerations mandate otherwise. They further suggest that adjudicating cases anew which have already been decided by other tribunals should be viewed as inconsistent with judicial propriety. They invoke the notion of collegiate respect as an operative principle in the context of choice between substantive rules. Thus, the seized forum is obliged to duly defer to jurisprudence developed by other judicial bodies in their respective area of specialisation or under general international law, whenever a similar or correlative legal question is litigated.

Indeed, comity has become the darling of the majority of academic commentators. It seems that never has the rule of comity been so popular, despite its ambivalent reception in the courts.[21] However, what has grown into a leitmotif for the academic sector dealing with this branch of public international law[22] is considered to be 'old news' for private international law scholars.[23] Moreover, some private international researchers

[20] See, eg, R Higgins, 'A Babel of Judicial Voices? Ruminations from the Bench' (2006) 55 *International and Comparative Law Quarterly* 791, 804: 'We must read each other's judgments; We must have respect for each other's judicial work; We must try to preserve unity among us unless context really prevent this.'

[21] But see Judge Wilkey, *Laker Airways Ltd v Sabena, Belgium World Airlines*, 731 F2d 909 (DC Cir 1984): 'Comity serves our international system like the mortar which cements together a brick house. No one would willingly permit the mortar to crumble or to be chipped away for fear of compromising the entire structure. . . . The central percept of comity teaches that, when possible, the decisions of foreign tribunals should be given effect in domestic courts, since recognition fosters international cooperation and encourages reciprocity, thereby promoting predictability and stability through satisfaction of mutual expectations.'

[22] 'In their intercourse with one another, States do observe not only legally binding rules and such rules as have the character of usages, but also rules of politeness, convenience, and goodwill. Such rules of international conduct are no rules of law, but of comity. The Comity of Nations is certainly not a source of International Law, as it is distinctly the contrast of the Law of Nations. But there can be no doubt that many a rule which formerly was a rule of International Comity only, is nowadays a rule of International Law. And it is certainly to be expected that this development will go on in future also, and that thereby many a rule of present International Comity will in future become one of International Law', R Jennings and A Watts (eds) 1 *Oppenheim's International Law* (9th ed, London, Longman, 1992) 25.

[23] J Story, *Commentaries on The Conflict of Law* (Boston: Hilliard, Gray and Co, 1834) s 38; HE Yntema, 'The Comity Doctrine' (1966) 65 *Michigan Law Review* 9; L Collins, 'Comity in Modern Private Law' in J Fawcett (ed), *Reform and Development of Private International Law—Essays in Honor of Sir Peter North* (Oxford University Press, 2002) 89; AF Lowenfeld, 'Harold Maier, Comity and the Foreign Relations Restatement' (2006) 39 *Vanderbilt Journal of Transnational Law* 1415; S Weber Waller, 'The Twilight of Comity' (1999–2000) 38 *Columbia Journal of Transnational Law* 563.

and lawyers are highly critical of the notion of comity. They treat it condescendingly and object to suggestions that national courts should base their relationship with one another thereupon. Comity is defined by them as a blend of legal policies and high international politics,[24] entailing too much discretion. They argue that comity lacks the necessary precision, and does not provide judges with clear and sharp guidelines concerning the limits of their jurisdiction.

Clearly the ECHR and the ECJ form part of this broad phenomenon of 'judicial regime complex'. Admittedly, they make up just a tiny fraction of the whole phenomenon and they bear their own unique affinities. Nevertheless, it will be interesting to examine them as a test case and inquire whether one can say that they manage to satisfy this mandate of relating to each other on the basis of the principle of comity.

B. Finding Your Way Through the Maze[25]—Two Possible Readings of the *Melchers* Decision in the Light of the Principle of Comity

The (hi)story of the relationship between the ECHR and the ECJ is well known and needs almost no repetition.[26] After a certain period of uncertainty, both national courts in Europe and the ECHR eventually expressed trust in the potential adjudication of human rights by their counterpart—the ECJ—without the need for a guiding hand from above or below. Such confidence was, so it seemed, so great that the ECHR was willing to participate in a system of courts which could be best described as 'separate but equal'.[27] The ECHR and the ECJ occupied separate 'legal territories' in the sense that the ECHR regarded as inadmissible applications against states for alleged violations committed while implementing mandatory EC legislation—while acting within the EC's 'legal territory'.

The prerequisites for such co-operation were first developed by the German Constitutional Court and were nicknamed the *Solange* model,[28] which was then followed by the European Commission of Human Rights

[24] HG Maier, 'Interest Balancing and Extraterritorial Jurisdiction' (1983) 31 *American Journal of Comparative Law* 579, 589.

[25] By analogy from C Brown, 'The Proliferation of International Courts and Tribunals: Finding Your Way Through the Maze' (2002) 3 *Melbourne Journal of International Law* 453.

[26] For an excellent evaluation of the case-law see L Scheeck, 'The Relationship between the European Courts and Integration through Human Rights' (2005) 65 *Zeitschrift für ausländisches öffentliches Recht und Völkerrecht* 837.

[27] Canor, above n 6.

[28] More accurately it should be nicknamed 'the *Solange II* model', BverfGE 73, 339 (Solange II) available at: www.servat.unibe.ch/dfr/dfr_bvbd100.html. N Lavranos, 'Das So-lange-Prinzip im Verhältnis von EGMR un EuGH' (2006) 41 *Europarecht* 79; N Lavranos, 'Towards a Solange-Model between International Courts and Tribunals' This Volume; A Haratsch, 'Die Solange-Rechtsprechung des Europäischen Gerichtshofs für Menschenrechte—Das Kooperationsverhöltnis zwischen EGMR und EuGH' (2006) 66 *Zeitschrift für ausländisches öffentliches Recht und Völkerrecht* 927. For the implementation of this model to the context of the

(ECommHR) in the *Melchers* decision. There, the ECommHR decided that:

> . . . the transfer of powers to an international organization is not incompatible with the Convention . . . as long as the relevant organization is considered to protect fundamental rights, as regards both *substantive guarantees offered and the mechanisms controlling their observance*, in a manner to which can be considered *at least equivalent* to that for which the Convention provides.[29]

Thus, the *Solange* model preconditions the ECHR co-operation with the ECJ on the *generally comparable* level of human rights protection by the Community.

Submitting a dispute concerning violation of human rights as a result of the application of EC law to any court other than the ECJ would then entail the dismissal of the application as inadmissible, given the ECHR's lack of jurisdiction *rationae materiae* over the case.[30] The ECommHR considered the ECHR as incompetent to examine the compatibility of EC acts with human rights[31] and waived ECHR jurisdiction on the matter.[32] Clearly, the underling assumption is that had the two courts (or the ECommHR and the ECJ) reviewed the same case they might have reached conflicting results;[33] however, according to the ECommHR, the

implementation of international law into the EC law see P Ecckhout, 'Community Terrorism Listings, Fundamental Rights, and UN Security Council Resolutions, In Search of the Right Fit' (2007) 3 *European Constitutional Law Review* 183. For an analysis of recent attitude of the French Constitutional Court towards EC law, see JH Reestman and LFM Besselink, 'Constitutional Identity and the European Courts' (2007) 3 *European Constitutional Law Review* 177.

29 *M & Co v Federal Republic of Germany*, Application No 13258/87, 64 DR 138 (1990); available at http://cmiskp.echr.coe.int.

30 C Banner and A Thomson, 'Human Rights Review of State Acts Performed in Compliance with EC Law—Bosphorus Airways v Ireland' (2005) 6 *European Human Rights Law Review* 649, 651. Recently, the German Constitutional Court has repeated this view, BVerfGE 102, 147 (bananas) Solange IV, available at www.servat.unibe.bh/dfr/dft_bvbd100.html; A Peters, 'The Bananas Decision 2000 of the German Federal Constitutional Court: Towards Reconciliation with the ECJ as regards Fundamental Rights Protection in Europe' (2000) 43 *German Yearbook of International Law* 276; CU Schmid, 'All Bark and No Bite: Notes on the Federal Constitutional Court's "Banana Decision"' (2001) 7 *European Law Journal* 95; F Hoffmeister, 'Case Note—National German Courts Bundesverfassungsgericht: Alcan' (2001) 38 *Common Market Law Review* 791.

31 There are those who consider that the Commission's decision should not be interpreted too restrictively, J-P Jacqué, 'Communauté Européenne et Convention Européenne des Droits de l'homme', in *L'Europe et le droit, Mélanges en hommage à Jean Boulois* (Paris 1991) 339.

32 Frowein suggests that as far as the application of the model by the German Constitutional Court is concerned, the German Constitutional Court's jurisdiction on the matter continued to exist only it agreed not to exercise it as long as the present condition as to the protection of fundamental rights by the ECJ prevails, JA Frowein, 'Solange II' (1998) 25 *Common Market Law Review* 201, 203. See also W-H Roth, 'The Application of Community Law in West Germany: 1980–1990' (1991) 28 *Common Market Law Review* 137.

33 For a view according to which if all courts and tribunals will be presented with *all* international law binding between the parties, it will mean that although they may have

review of EC law as such does not fall under the scope of the Convention.[34]

The question is whether the *Melchers* decision is a genuine expression of the principle of comity? The answer depends on the definition of this principle. To the extent that the principle of comity relates primarily to political considerations, namely the obligation of a judicial body to avoid offending foreign nations or international organisations or foreign courts, one could interpret the ECommHR's decision along the lines of the principle of comity. In the absence of a clear procedural division of competences between the two judicial systems, the ECHR suspended final decision on which court was competent to uphold human rights standards by waiving its own jurisdiction. In doing so, it set the ground for establishing a constructive dialogue with the ECJ, creating voluntarily what was termed by Slaughter a 'community of courts'.[35]

Indeed, the relations between the ECHR and the ECJ are a classical case of overlapping jurisdictions in which an attempt to identify by way of interpretation the more specialised jurisdiction could have been futile, as it would have not been possible to determine a priori which court would be in a better position to address the matter at hand. Under these circumstances, a self-limiting approach, helped to prevent unnecessary litigation, contradictory or conflicting results, fortuitous outcomes and polarisation of the system. The *Melchers* decision transformed the relationship between the two jurisdictions into a veritable horizontal model in the sense that each had different functions, which were to be performed within each court's own allocated sphere. They still had overlapping functions in the sense that both were competent interpret the same legal rules, namely the European Convention of Human Rights and European Community law, but they were separate in the sense that the exact same case based on the same facts between the same parties could not as a matter of fact be brought before both courts. An actual conflict within such a model remained hence only theoretical, and actual jurisdictional disputes were avoided.

Within such a community of courts a discourse between the courts takes place. Each of the courts serves as a supervisor of the other, without

jurisdiction to examine different claims, in so doing they would apply *the same law*, hence in theory no conflict should arise, see J Pauwelyn, 'Bridging Fragmentation and Unity: International Law as a Universe of Inter-Connected Island' (2004) 25 *Michigan Journal of International Law* 915.

[34] Attention should be drawn to the fact that the ECHR did not satisfy itself with declaring the case as inadmissible *rationae personae*, having no competence as regards the Community as such, but went further to declare that it lacks jurisdiction *rationae materiae*. See the discussion at *Behrami and al v France*, Application No 71412/01, 2 May 2007, para 143–52, available at http://cmiskp.echr.coe.int.

[35] A-M Slaughter, 'A Global Community of Courts' (2003) 44 *Harvard International Law Journal* 191, 204.

being endowed with specific decision-making power. Each court asserts its respective claims through a dialogue of incremental decisions, thereby signalling to the other court opposition or co-operation. More generally, each of the courts participates in a dialogue within a constitutional–supranational–international framework. The ECHR has cited ECJ decisions it concurred with or distanced itself from them in the appropriate instances; the ECJ has paid full respect towards the ECHR. Indeed, there is a growing volume of cases before the Court of First Instance (CFI) and the ECJ in which ECHR jurisprudence is cited and used.[36]

Admittedly, some commentators have sharply criticised the *Melchers* decision and the ECommHR's failure to formulate a proper test for what constitutes the required general guarantee of fundamental rights. They regretted the reduction of the ECHR's power of review in this context to one with mostly symbolic political significance. Yet exactly this effect of the decision provoked many to hail it as evidence of co-operative institutional relationship between the two courts. They argued that a direct conflict between the courts had been successfully avoided. The exercise of judicial self-restraint on behalf of the ECHR organs was applauded as an exercise of comity by the ECommHR towards the ECJ.[37]

Put differently, it could be maintained that the tacit competing supremacy claims served to create an atmosphere of co-operation between the two courts, under which each court had an incentive to strive to respect the position and traditions of the other. Hence the ECommHR set the platform for creating what could have been perceived as an ever-lasting mutual confidence between the courts.

Yet, to the extent that comity is a principle under which judicial decisions reflect the systemic value of reciprocal tolerance and goodwill, it might be said, relying on the wisdom of hindsight, that the *Melchers* decision was not really based on the principle of comity. Although the relationships between these two jurisdictions were often presented as a token of successful implementation of mutual respect, in reality serious disputes over the distribution of powers were lurking below the surface, and tensions remained. Hence, the motivation for opting for the Melchers solution was not provoked by mutual esteem but more by institutional suspicion.

As Scheeck has thoroughly demonstrated, the risks of actual conflict between the legal systems provided incentives for each party to strive towards harmonious interpretation of the law.[38] These fears of 'mutually assured destruction' that accompanied the courts' rulings could be summarised, in a nutshell, by referring to the realisation of the ECHR that

[36] Tridimas, above n 6, 343.

[37] Y Shany, *The Competing Jurisdictions of International Courts and Tribunals* (Oxford University Press, 2004) 265.

[38] Scheeck, above n 26.

it could benefit from the supremacy of Community law as a tool for enforcing Convention law in national courts, and its realisation that without the support of the ECJ it might find itself fully subject to the discretion of the national legal systems.[39] The ECJ, on its behalf, explicitly recognised the European Convention on Human Rights as part of the legal basis on which the European Community was founded.[40] Although it was unwilling to accept neither the ECHR's authority nor primacy,[41] it also realised that, notwithstanding the notion of supremacy, without referring to the Convention it lacked the necessary legitimacy for the unlimited and wholehearted implementation of Community law by national jurisdictions. Hence, the restraint expressed in the *Melchers* decision was not necessarily exercised due to goodwill and good faith but was, perhaps, more reflective of strategic considerations.

C. Upstairs, Downstairs?—Two Possible Readings of the *Bosphorus* case in the Light of the Principle of Comity

The jurisdictional division between the two international courts continued for quite some time during which the ECHR strictly kept within its boundaries, limiting its review powers over Community law to a unique situation in which the ECJ entertained no jurisdiction over the matter.[42] It might have been supposed that the two systems had managed to find their equilibrium and that they would continue onwards as a genuine network of a community of courts. However, in the *Bosphorus* case, the ECHR reshuffled the cards and challenged the established peaceful coexistence.

One possible way of reading the *Bosphorus* case relies on the diagnosis according to which the case clearly departs from the *Solange*-model in some important aspects. First, the ECHR newly asserts its jurisdiction *ratione materiae* in cases that fall within the scope of Community law.

[39] M Hartwig, 'Much Ado about Human Rights: The Federal Constitutional Court Confronts the European Court of Human Rights' (2005) 6 *German Law Journal*, available at www.germanlawjournal.com/article.php?id=600; JA Frowein, 'The Binding Force of ECHR Judgments and its Limits' in S Breitenmoser et al (eds), *Human Rights, Democracy and the Rule of Law, Liber amicorum Luzius Wildhaber* (Baden-Baden, Nomos Verlagsgesellschaft, 2007) 261.

[40] As opposed to the concern which the ECJ expressed when it was dealing with other potential overlapping jurisdictions concerning the manifest risk to the jurisdictional order laid down in the treaties and the probable advert effect of the autonomy of the Community legal system. See Case C–459/03 *Commission v Ireland* (not yet reported) para 154 (30 May 2006), available at http://curia.europa.eu.

[41] FG Jacobs, 'European Community Law and the European Convention on Human Rights' in D Curtin and T Heukels (eds) *Institutional Dynamics of European Integration, Essays in Honour of HG Schermers* (Dordrecht, Martinus Nijhoff Publishers, 1994) 561.

[42] *Matthews v United Kingdom*, Application No 24833/94, 18 February 1999, available at http://cmiskp.echr.coe.int; Canor, above n 6.

Thus, the Court clearly acknowledges its jurisdiction to review the compatibility with the Convention of measures enacted by the Member States when implementing EC regulations, even if the latter leave no room for their discretion. In doing so, the ECHR clearly departs from the decision given in *Melchers* [43] insofar as the 'territorial' division between the courts ceases to exist.

This jurisdictional matter is not a trifling issue. Often in international law the question of jurisdiction is resolved by states, which in general have to consent to the jurisdiction of an international tribunal. However, instances in which the courts themselves are left to define their scope of jurisdiction (as was undertaken by the ECHR in *Bosphorus*) are quite rare. Clearly the issue of jurisdiction is not trivial, since it determines whether a court can entertain a case and whether its jurisdiction might result in a possible trespass into the jurisdiction of another court. In the latter case, the two courts run the risk of not only interpreting the same rule of international law differently, but also of deciding the very same factual case differently. This entails not only the danger of jeopardising the unity of international law, but also of undermining the moral foundation of the two legal systems.

Second, turning to the substance, the ECHR ostensibly repeated the *Melchers* criterion stipulating that state action taken in compliance with its international legal obligations creates a presumption that it is justified if the relevant organisation offered protection of fundamental rights which was *at least equivalent* to that provided by the Convention. It also repeated the observation that protection must be equivalent insofar as both substantive guarantees and the mechanisms controlling their observance are concerned. However, in the *Melchers* decision the ECommHR clearly found that the ECJ's role in reviewing EC acts for compatibility with fundamental rights provided in itself an equivalent protection. Hence, it was mainly interested in the control mechanism offered by the EC legal order. In the *Bosphorus* case, however, the ECHR placed more emphasis on the substantive review, refining the equivalency-test by adding that 'any such presumption can be rebutted if, in the circumstances of a *particular case*, it is considered that the protection of Convention rights was *manifestly deficient*'.[44] Hence, the operation of the 'equivalent protec-

[43] See the joint concurring opinion of Judges Rozakis, Tulkens, Traja, Botoucharova, Zagrebelsky and Garlicki: 'Thus, the Court clearly acknowledges its jurisdiction to review the compatibility with the Convention of a domestic measure adopted on the basis of a European Community Regulation and, in so doing, departs from the decision given in *M & Co v the Federal Republic of Germany*', *Bosphorus*, para 1.

[44] *Bosphorus*, para 156. See also the description offered by the former president of the ECHR Judge Luizius Wildhaber, to the essential difference between the two approaches: 'Whereas the German Constitutional Court requires for the presumption of equivalence to be rebutted that a general or large-scale drop in the EU-standards by established, under the Bosphorus jurisprudence the presumption can be rebutted on a case by case basis. Hence the fact that

tion' doctrine in *Bosphorus* can be regarded as being in sharp contrast with the earlier jurisprudence. This is because the manifest deficiency approach facilitates a deep and specific inquiry into the level of protection of fundamental rights provided by the EU and the ECJ in individual cases.

Yet, there is an alternative way of reading the *Bosphorus* case, according to which it should not be perceived as a distinctive break with the past, but merely an implementation and continuation of the *Solange*-rule.[45] Hence, there are commentators who recognise *Bosphorus* to be

> suggestive of a desired relationship of comity, or even cooperation, between the Courts . . . [in which] the Court of Human Rights avoids 'piercing the corporate veil' of the EU and finding its Member States responsible for a violation unless there is no other way out.[46]

Such commentators interpret the decision as explicitly confirming the 'equivalent protection' test. They of course realise that while the *Solange*-doctrine requires that the standard of protection of fundamental rights in the EU should be generally lower for the presumption of equivalence to be rebutted, the *Bosphorus*-doctrine focuses on each individual case and allows the presumption of equivalence to be rebutted on a case-by-case basis. However, they assume that the ECHR does not intend to apply the ruling in a robust manner, and hence does not perceive it as a substantive break with the past. Such an assumption concerning the limited eagerness on the part of the ECHR to review ECJ decisions can be presupposed given the scarce judicial review carried out by the ECHR concerning the specific facts of the case in *Bosphorus*—a case in which the applicant remained an unfortunate victim whose rights were not aptly protected. The deference expressed by the ECHR and its general assessment of the facts of the case may drive the point home according to which the ECHR was only playing with different formulations but basically did not deviate from the *Melchers* decision. To the extent that this observation is an accurate reflection of the prevailing ties between the courts, it may be said that the decision is just another phase in the cordial dialogue conducted between the courts.

contrary to the situation under German law, applications challenging in Strasbourg the domestic implementation of Community law are in principle not inadmissible *ratione materiae*.' L Wildhaber, 'The Coordination of the Protection of Fundamental Rights in Europe, Address by the President of the European Court of Human Rights' (2005) 6–7 *Council of Europe*, available at http://www.echr.coe.int.

[45] AH Parga, 'Bosphorus v Ireland and the Protection of Fundamental Rights in Europe' (2006) 31 *European Law Review* 251, 258: '. . . the outcome of the two-tier test in *Bosphorus* shows a "green light" to the way the Community is protecting human rights at present . . . '

[46] S Douglas-Scott, 'Bosphorus Hava Yollari Turizm Ve Ticaret Anonim Dirketi v Ireland, application No. 45036/98, judgment of the European Court of Human Rights (Grand Chamber) of 30 June 2005, (2006) 42 EHRR 1' (2006) 43 *Common Market Law* 243, 249.

Can one argue that the *Bosphorus* case implies that the ECHR expresses comity towards the ECJ? Again the answer depends on the way in which comity is defined. On the one hand the decision can still be seen as corresponding to the principle of comity. The mere fact that the ECHR politely criticises the ECJ[47] should not imply that it was showing disrespect. Quite the contrary, the ECHR was taking an intensive, deep, serious and dignifying look at the European legal system,[48] treated the ECJ as an equal, and supported it in carrying out its role. Hence, one could argue that the ECHR re-examined the appropriate limits of deference due to the ECJ and reaffirmed these on the basis of a relative broad discretionary leeway. By choosing the equivalence standard, the ECHR implied that the ECJ should provide 'comparable' protection of human rights and not 'identical' protection, since the latter approach would run counter to the interest of international co-operation which the impugned act pursued. It could be said that the *Bosphorus* case sets the minimum benchmark needed to enable the two courts to work together in a way that promotes the delivery of justice under the rule of law.

Clearly the ECHR believes that creating unanimity on all perplexing problems derived from the European Convention on Human Rights is unachievable. Yet, it also adheres to the view that it will resolve disagreements in an authoritative manner only in extreme circumstances. Otherwise it will adhere to the principle of subsidiarity. This has led many to debate the question of whether the ECHR has provided the ECJ with a more extensive margin of appreciation than that afforded to other Contracting Parties, and, therefore, whether it has created a double standard for the protection of human rights in Europe. Be that as it may, the ruling clearly suggests tolerance on behalf of the ECHR to the ECJ's possible different standard of respect for human rights. In this sense, both courts can be perceived to be part of one veritable European system and the ruling can be regarded as an act of courtesy.

On the other hand, the *Bosphorus* case can be perceived as planting the seed for greater control of the ECHR over the EU in the future, and harbingering a substantial change in the legal discourse that is ultimately designed to subordinate the ECJ to its superior authority. The ECHR reclaimed the exclusive jurisdiction it granted the ECJ, notwithstanding the fact that nothing in the behaviour of the ECJ was patently offensive towards the ECHR-jurisdiction or public policy and might have justified such a ruling. As for the substance, the ECHR has probably understood that the future of European human rights law lies in the European Community's domestic law. Therefore, it might have felt pressure to make EU law embrace even more closely the processes and institutions of

[47] Concerning, eg, access of individuals to the ECJ, *Bosphorus*, para 162.

[48] *Bosphorus*, paras 72–99.

the rules of the European Convention on Human Rights. Just as the Member States are accustomed to daily 'soft EU intervention in their domestic affairs', the ECHR decided that the EU will need to get accustomed to a possible similar intervention on its behalf.

It is the first time the ECHR directly dealt with EU-related issues falling within the scope of jurisdiction of the ECJ, thereby tilting the hierarchical balance in favour of its own court. In other words, the ECHR has placed itself in the position of a supervisor overseeing the legal activities of the Community. This might be interpreted as a certain token of arrogance, since the ECHR appears to be of the opinion that in cases where the ECJ will not arrive at a sufficient protection of human rights, the interest of institutional co-operation should be outweighed by the Convention's role as a 'constitutional instrument of European public order'.[49] In this sense, the relationship between the courts after *Bosphorus* has become more of a vertical one, with the ECHR sitting at the apex of the judicial hierarchy. To the extent that the *Bosphorus* case can be perceived by the ECJ as threatening its supremacy, it might jeopardise the amicable relations between the courts and therefore cannot be seen as an exercise of comity.

In sum, the contribution of the doctrine of comity to the analysis of the ECHR/ECJ regime seems insignificant. Given the prevalent confusion over the scope of the term comity, the principal criticism might be that it does not lead to an accurate analysis of legal issues. It is an expression of unexplained authority, imprecise meaning, uncertain function, which lacks articulated workable guidelines for its application. I believe that we can do better. We can formulate more precise rules that will give more accurate guidelines to judges aiming to further the normative agenda for the international project of making judicial globalisation work. Such rules can be derived from the discipline of private international law—a discipline that is recommended as a softer alternative to hard hierarchical constitutional choices.[50]

III. TOWARDS DETAILED RULES DERIVED FROM PRIVATE INTERNATIONAL LAW

A. Preliminary Remarks

As is well known, private international law is a field of law designed to address cross-border relationships. The rules of private international law

[49] *Loizidou v Turkey*, Application No 15318/89, 23 March 1995, para 93.

[50] See in general, C Joerges, 'The Challenges of Europeanization in the Realm of Private Law: A Plea for a New Legal Discipline' *EUI Working Paper Law* No 2004/12, available at www.ieu.it.

are meta-rules (ie, rules to decide which rules should be applied). Thus, choice-of-law rules are Hart's secondary rules, and more precisely a category of 'rules of recognition'.[51]

Nevertheless, there are those who maintain that rules stemming from the sphere of private international law are not applicable to the international level as they are created by autonomous, sovereign states which do not belong to a single system. As these jurists support the view that international law constitutes a system of law, they argue that 'the relations between international courts and tribunals are different than those found between the courts of different states'. Hence they conclude that:

> international judicial bodies belong to a single legal system and are responsible for promoting its coherence as much as possible. No similar considerations can be found to apply in relation to the putative need of regulating the jurisdictions of different national courts belonging to different legal systems.[52]

I, however, will try to establish that rules of private international law are appropriate for assisting in regulating the overlap between international jurisdictions. Although I agree that international courts and tribunals belong to a universal system, it is, in my opinion, a complex system which is based on tensions, paradoxes, inconsistencies and mainly on the notion of pluralism. As will be shown in the following discussion, rules of private international law manage to find a balance between the aspiration to advance systemic network sensitivity between courts and preserving the autonomy, distinctiveness and uniqueness of juridical bodies. Naturally, these trans-boundary rules should be modified in order to fit better into the international sphere.

I will now turn to explaining this notion of a complex system with regard to the relationship between the ECHR and the ECJ, and will subsequently demonstrate how the rules of private international law represent appropriate guidelines for courts that are part of such a complex system.

B. Pluralism

The ECHR legal order and European Community legal system should be perceived as intertwined pluralistic regimes. This is true if we follow Twining's definition of pluralism, according to which pluralism implies: 'legal systems co-existing in the same geographical space'.[53] This is also true if we follow Maduro's definition, according to which pluralism prevails when one legal order must respect the identity of the other legal

[51] HLA Hart, *The Concept of Law* (Oxford University Press, 1997).
[52] Shany, above n 37, 127.
[53] W Twining, *Globalization and Legal Theory* (London, Butterworths, 2000) 83.

order and that no formal hierarchy exists among the applicable legal orders.[54] Hence already after the *Melchers* decision, when neither the ECJ nor the ECHR could have assumed the supremacy of their own legal orders, Europe could have been perceived as being an intertwined pluralistic regime.

However, the *Bosphorus* case transformed Europe into a pluralistic legal system in a different, more complex sense. Since *Bosphorus*, not only has Europe become pluralistic in the sense that there are contradictory legal mechanisms which apply to a single factual situation,[55] and not only are there two autonomous legal orders which coexist, but it has also become pluralistic in the sense that each of the legal regimes is claiming ultimate legal authority.[56] It is precisely this existence of competing plausible claims to ultimate legal authority from two different sources—the supranational and the international—that distinguishes European legal pluralism from classical legal pluralism.[57] The EC proclaims its autonomous legal order for which the Member States have limited their sovereign rights, albeit in limited fields. The Convention regime, while lacking formal authority over domestic courts, has increasingly come to be perceived as a regime with a supranational constitutional court, whose authority as the ultimate arbiter of European human rights disputes has largely been accepted.[58]

In the *Bosphorus* case, the ECHR aimed to establish its hierarchical superiority towards the ECJ concerning the way in which it will interpret the Convention. However, this decision does not bind the ECJ, which is an independent judicial body and free to rule differently. The ECJ still regards European law as interpreted by it, as the highest source of law within the EU. Despite the fact that the Convention is conceived as part of European general principles of law, it will not be able to trump obligations stemming from the EC Treaty.[59] Moreover, it was recently demon-

[54] MP Maduro, 'Conceptual Law: Europe's Constitutional Pluralism in Action' in N Walker (ed), *Sovereignty in Transition* (Oxford, Hart Publishing, 2003) 521, 526.

[55] NW Barber, 'Legal Pluralism and the European Union' (2006) 12 *European Law Journal* 306, 324.

[56] N Walker, 'Sovereignty and Differentiated Integration in the European Union' in Z Bankowski and A Scott (eds), *The European Union and its Order: The Legal Theory of European Integration* (Oxford, Blackwell, 1999) 59.

[57] M Avbelj, 'The EU and the Many Faces of Legal Pluralism, Toward a Coherent or Uniform EU Legal Order?' (2006) 2 *Croatian Yearbook of European Law and Policy* 377. While Avbelj refers to pluralism in Europe between the Member States' legal systems and the European Union legal order, I refer to the relationship between the European Community legal order and the European Convention of Human Rights legal system.

[58] RB Ahdieh, 'Between Dialogue and Decree: International Review of National Courts' (2004) 79 *New York University Law Review* 2029.

[59] The formal reason is that the EC is not a party to the European Convention on Human Rights. But see K Lenaerts, 'The Court of Justice of the European Communities and the European Court of Human Rights—An Old Couple in a New Setting' in *La Cour de Justice des Communautés Européennes 1952–2002: Bilan et Perspectives* (Bruxelles, Bruylant, 2004) 89, 103,

strated that although the EC courts acknowledge the possibility that they might be bound by the rulings of another tribunal, they have never accepted this in an actual case.[60] The ECJ considers the EU as a closed system, which opens itself to legal acts from the outside only after the thorough control of the ECJ.[61] Therefore, if the ECHR and the ECJ make inconsistent claims, there is no authoritative rule of hierarchy and each supremacy claim contains an implicit negation of the other. In both cases these rules are presented as duties resting on the courts: each court claims that it is compelled to give precedence to the different sources of law. Put differently, each court follows a different rule of choice of laws. Each court claims ultimate legal authority vis-à-vis the other.

In the absence of authoritative hierarchy and lacking a commanding rule that will reconcile these potential diverse legal orders,[62] the relationships between these two regimes might be described as closely related to MacCormick's model of heterarchy.[63] According to this model, mutual recognition of the autonomous existence of both systems, which are, however, subordinated to the overall rules and principles of international law, should provide a solution to a case where two equally plausible claims of legal orders to ultimate legal authority conflict. As opposed to the hierarchical models, the heterarchical approaches recognise that both legal orders have equally plausible claims to ultimate legal authority within their respected fields.[64]

In the era following the *Bosphorus* case we may speak of overlapping courts which have genuine de facto overlapping jurisdictions. This overlap transcends the legal norms (as had already been effected by the *Melchers* decision) and enters the very core of the respective jurisdictions.

who argues that when applying the EU's Charter of Fundamental Rights the ECJ is already bound by the interpretation given by the ECHR to corresponding rights guaranteed by the European Convention on Human Rights.

[60] M Bronckers, 'The Relationship of the EC Courts with other International Tribunals: Non-Committal, Respectful or Submissive?' (2007) 44 *Common Market Law Review* 601.

[61] M Nettesheim, 'UN Sanctions against Individuals—A Challenge to the Architecture of European Union Governance' (2007) 44 *Common Market Law Review* 567, 582.

[62] An attempt was made to perceive certain provisions of the Vienna Convention on the law of Treaties as such rules, 'Fragmentation of International Law', above n 11, para 487. But see, Higgins, above n 20, 800; Hestermeyer, above n 16.

[63] N MacCormick, 'Judicial Pluralism and the Risk of Constitutional Conflict' in N MacCormick (ed) *Questioning Sovereignty: Law, State and Nation in the European Commonwealth* (Oxford University Press, 1999) 97.

[64] See also N Krisch, 'The Open Architecture of European Human Rights Law' *LSE Law, Society and Economy Working Papers* 11/2007, available at www.lse.ac.uk/collections/law/wps/wps.htm: '[a pluralistic order] in which the relationships of the constituent parts are governed not by legal rules but primarily by politics, often judicial politics . . . In a pluralistic order, we do not find a common set of norms at the top . . . that would allow to resolve conflicts . . . but at least the norms on which the argument centers are shared and unity constitutes a common regulative ideal'; E Cannizzaro, 'The European Constitutional Framework: Re-reading Eric Stein's Thoughts from a Bridge on the 50th Anniversary of the Treaty of Rome' (2007) 55 *American Journal of Comparative Law* 767.

Both courts will readily decide the same matter on the same facts between the same parties. Hence, the possibility of conflicting decisions has become much more imminent. As mentioned above, when facing the question of how to settle conflicts which might arise in such a heterarchical regime, I would suggest that one might turn to rules of conflict of laws between states for inspiration. I will now turn to elaborate on this point.

C. Rules of Private International Law

The study of private international law deals with a class of relationships pertaining to multiple states or nationalities. Since most cross-border relationships are extremely complex, private international law has to resolve serious problems caused by the complexity of these relationships. Thus, complexity should be regarded as the most essential and inevitable feature of the study of private international law.[65]

Its complexity is reinforced by the fact that it affects not only the private parties' interests but also the welfare of the multiplicity of states involved in the conflict. Indeed, it was traditionally difficult to precisely situate private international law between private law on the one hand and public international law on the other.[66] Acknowledging its international law aspects, which focus on the interests of states or governments, it is often argued that each state has an incentive to control this relationship, yet they all operate within one universal network. Indeed, in the modern world, every country with a developed legal system has its own set of conflict-of-law rules which form part of its private law. Yet, while at first sight it may seem as if private international law permits courts and states to take discretionary, myopic and selfish actions, following such an approach might be detrimental to all states in the global system and undermine the purpose of the rules themselves. Given the intensification of the study of the phenomenon of globalisation, theories emphasising collaboration and mutual assistance increasingly influence the discipline of private international law.[67] Due to the international nature of the circumstances and the legal problems involved

[65] K Kagami, 'The Systematic Choice of Legal Rules for Private International Law: An Economic Approach' in J Basedow and T Kono (eds), *An Economic Analysis of Private International Law* (Tübingen, Mohr Siebeck, 2006) 15, 17.

[66] I Mills, 'The Private History of International Law' (2006) 55 *International and Comparative Law Quarterly* 1; R Wai, 'Transnational Liftoff and Juridical Touchdown: The Regulatory Function of Private International Law in an Era of Globalization' (2002) 40 *Columbia Journal of Transnational Law* 209; R Michaels, 'Two Economists, Three Opinions? Economic Models for Private International Law—Cross Border Torts as Example', in J Basedow and T Kono (eds), *An Economic Analysis of Private International Law* (Tübingen, Mohr Siebeck, 2006) 15, 17.

[67] L Brilmayer, *Conflict of Laws* (Boston, Little, Brown, 1995) 169; LD Kramer, 'Rethinking Choice of Law' (1990) 90 *Columbia Law Review* 277.

whenever private international laws are invoked, international co-operation is of particular importance to private international law.

Indeed, as demonstrated by Slaughter, national judges handling transnational commercial disputes no longer think of themselves as operating within separate, self-contained, isolated spheres, but rather feel that they belong to a global community of courts.[68] They have adjusted many principles of private international law to accommodate this new common judicial enterprise. Emphasis is thus placed on the international aspects of the discipline of private international law. What is more, the doctrines of reciprocity and comity have been modified so as to accommodate not only the principle that courts are equal but distinct, but also the notion that many courts act under the presumption of an integrated system. The judges concerned also inject ideas of legal pluralism while applying rules of private international law. Hence, though applied by sovereign states, the philosophy lurking behind private international law is now one of systemic co-operation. Therefore, the view according to which national courts are perceived as part of an unseen integrated network already finds expression within the discipline of private international law.

Following similar reasoning, Teubner observes that the global society, which is a society without an apex or a centre,[69] has called for the creation of an 'inter-systemic conflicts law', derived from collisions between the traditional private international law of distinct nations and also from what he described as 'collisions between distinct global social sectors'. Similar views were expressed by Berman.[70] Admittedly, both scholars soften the territorial-sovereign bias which is attributed to some doctrines of private international law, and adjust some of the policies to be more compatible with a pluralistic system of law. However, their starting point is that the principles of private international law can serve as a basis to manage pluralist legal systems.

Broadly speaking, private international law sketches the three classic legal topics which need to be decided by overlapping competing jurisdictions acting within a global and pluralistic world: jurisdiction, choice of law, and judgment recognition and enforcement. The rules of private international law essentially consist of a mixture of formal and procedural aspects of law to which are added a pinch of substantive examination, which can mainly be found in the public policy doctrine. Private

[68] Slaughter, above n 35, 204; C Baudenbacher, 'Judicial Globalization: New Developments or Old Wine in New Bottles?' (2003) 38 *Texas International Law Journal* 505.

[69] A Fischer-Lescano and G Teubner, 'Regime-Collisions: The Vain Search for Legal Unity in the Fragmentation of Global Law' (2004) 25 *Michigan Journal of International Law* 999.

[70] PS Berman, 'Towards a Cosmopolitan Vision of Conflict of Laws: Redefining Governmental Interests in a Global Era' (2005) 153 *University of Pennsylvania Law Review* 1819; PS Berman, 'A Pluralist Approach to International Law' (2007) 32 *Yale Journal of International Law* 301, 316; PS Berman, 'Global Legal Pluralism' (2007) 80 *Southern California Law Review* 1155.

international law rules thus manage to integrate the perception of law as effective, certain and coercive with the prospect of strengthening legitimacy and attaining justice. This fits well into the specific contours of the overlapping European regimes, since, as noted above, the ECHR expressed the view in the *Bosphorus* case that it would add a touch of substantive examination to the procedural assessment carried out by the *Melchers* decision.[71]

It falls beyond the scope of this chapter to further develop *in abstracto* a comprehensive private international law theory that would relate to all fields of law and to all international courts. Clearly, private international law is not made of one tissue and therefore one should pick and choose the appropriate mixture of rules which will suit the international global level and the different regimes within it. Yet, given the different nuances of private international law, it seems that recourse to their inherent flexibility is the best way to deal with these complex overlapping regimes. Below, I will examine the precise blend of procedural and substantive rules that will best fit the unique relationship between the ECJ and the ECHR. Given the intimacy between the two legal systems, their familiarity with one another, their mutual dependence and collegial relationship, which appears to reflect a vote of confidence in one another, one should arguably opt for private international law rules tailored for legal systems that are accustomed to expressing full trust in each other, while not being fully harmonised.

D. Recognition of Foreign Judgments

Despite the fact that those who are willing to rely on rules of private international law for regulating international overlapping jurisdictions often content themselves mainly with the jurisdictional aspect of the rule of *res judicata*,[72] I suggest that lessons can be drawn from the rules of private international law concerning recognition of foreign judgments.[73] The dialogue involved in considering recognition can help bridge gaps between communities that can lead to a broader political compromise. Although the problem of drawing a line can be formidable in this context,

[71] See also Concurring Opinion of Judge Ress, *Bosphorus*, para 3: 'It is undisputed that the level of control extends to both procedural and substantive violations of the Convention guarantees.'

[72] E-U Petersmann, 'Justice as Conflict Resolution: Proliferation, Fragmentation, and Decentralization of Dispute Settlement in International Trade' (2006) 27 *University of Pennsylvania Journal of International Economic Law* 273, 352; Shany refers not only to the doctrine of *res judicata* but also to doctrines of *forum non convenience, lis alibi pendens*, Shany, above n 37, 128–255.

[73] SL Stevens, 'Commanding International Judicial Respect: Reciprocity and the Recognition and Enforcement of Foreign Judgments' (2002) 26 *Hastings International and Comparative Law Review* 115, 117. See also Shany, above n 37, 166.

the basic inquiry into the rules of recognition of foreign judgments seeks to bring disparate communities into dialogue with each other and pave the way for functioning co-operation without imposing uniformity. It is not necessary for a court wishing to recognise foreign judgments to agree with another court's substantive norms or even for them to acknowledge each other's legitimacy or claims to authority in order to recognise each other's legal judgments, at least in the main run of cases. Communities generally recognise and enforce each other's judgments, even when the judgment reflects a normative commitment that differs from the one accepted in the recognising community. Indeed, such negotiation of difference could actually provide a foundation for political compromise on the broader question of supremacy.

As a matter of fact, the rules concerning recognition of foreign judgments play the same role as the complementarity principle, according to which, in the case of two legal communities claiming jurisdiction over a single actor, one community agrees not to assert its jurisdiction as long as the other community takes action.[74] The result of such a policy, Burke-White argues,

> may be a virtuous circle, in which the [International Criminal] Court welcomes [other] . . . judicial efforts and stimulates the exercise of domestic jurisdiction through the threat of international intervention.[75]

This is a hybrid mechanism because one community does not hierarchically impose a solution on the other, but it does assert influence on the other's domestic processes through its mere presence as a potential jurisdictional actor in the future.

However, contrary to the complementarity principle, rules dealing with recognition of foreign judgments are more detailed and can be more easily fine-tuned to complex situations. At the risk of generalisation, rules

[74] The complementary principle is closely associated with the International Criminal Court. Art 17 of the Rome Statute of the International Criminal Court, (1998) reads: '. . . the Court shall determine that a case is inadmissible where: (a) The case is being investigated or prosecuted by a State which has jurisdiction over it, unless the State is unwilling or unable genuinely to carry out the investigation or prosecution . . . ' It means that domestic courts remain the primary institutions for prosecuting international crimes, in the sense that a case can be brought before the International Criminal Court only if a state with jurisdiction is unwilling or unable genuinely to investigate or prosecute the case. The basic idea is to maintain State sovereignty under which it is the duty of every State to exercise its criminal jurisdiction over those responsible for international crimes, to enhance the national jurisdiction over core crimes prohibited in the Statue, and to perfect a national legal system so as to meet the needs of investigating and prosecuting persons who committed the international crimes listed in the Statute. The principle of complementarity has impact mainly on a State's procedural law, and the way it implements international substantive criminal law and its exercise of jurisdiction.

[75] WW Burke-White, 'Protective Complementarity: The International Criminal Courts' in 'The Rome System of Justice' University of Pennsylvania Law School, Public Law Working Paper No 07/08, 5, available at http://lsr.nellco.org/upenn/wps/papers/144.

of recognition of foreign judgments consist of a relatively scarce review of the penumbra of the judgment, namely checking on the validity of jurisdictional title of the court rendering the original judgment, procedural requirements of due process and limited substantive review of public policy. Assuming the first judgment meets these minimal standards, the second court seized with the same case will opt to recognise the foreign judgment and strive to treat it as conclusive regarding the matters which it decided. Put differently, both the rules concerning complementarity and the rules concerning recognition of foreign judgments accord precedence and deference to the court first seized with the matter. Only in exceptional and rare circumstances will the second court refuse recognition and prefer to adjudicate the matter de novo.

As Berman demonstrates, a pluralist vision of judgment recognition requires judges to see themselves as part of an international network of normative communities and the parties before them as potentially affiliated with many such communities. Those various communities might legitimately seek to impose their norms on such affiliated parties. Thus, when faced with a recognition decision regarding a foreign judgment, courts should not necessarily assume that their own local public policies trump the dictates of the foreign judgment. Instead, courts must undertake a nuanced inquiry as to whether the affiliations of the parties render the original judgment legitimate. Although the local policies of the forum country are not irrelevant, those policies should be weighed against the overall interest in creating an interlocking system of international adjudication.[76] This is even true if the judgment under consideration would be considered illegal under the laws of the recognising state, unless it violates the recognising state's public policy.[77]

It is maintained that the *Bosphorus* reasoning is based on the same rationale. The ECHR expressed an explicit reluctance to review the ECJ's decisions anew, given its wish to advance the interest of the Member States' co-operation in international organisations.[78] In this sense, the ECHR recognises that the dictates of international co-operation may sometimes override human rights considerations. Indeed, not enough attention has been paid in the literature analysing the *Bosphorus* case to this wider goal of the ECHR.[79] Dealing with the nitty-gritty normative

[76] Berman, above n 70.

[77] Indeed, if one of these days the ECHR will state that it will not refuse to recognise the ECJ's judgment even when it violates its public policy we will be able to say that we reached the highest legal integration possible. In the American judgment *Baker v General Motors*, 522 US 222, 233 (1998) the Supreme Court of the United States made it clear that there is no public policy exception to the full faith and credit due judgments.

[78] *Bosphorus*, para 155.

[79] The ECHR, specifically distinguishes its previous ruling in *Pellegrini v Italy* (App No 30882/96) ECHR 20 July 2001, on the ground that the responsibility of a Contracting State is not comparable to compliance with a legal obligation emanating from an international organisation to which Contracting Parties have transferred part of their sovereignty, Bosphorus, para 157. But see, Lebeck, above n 7, 218.

aspects of possible deflection of the ECJ from the minimum standards set by the ECHR and the possibility of creating a double standard in European human rights protection changed the focus of the justification put forward by the ECHR for not subjecting the EC system fully to its jurisdiction. The main reason underlying this stance has become to encourage the creation of an interwoven system of co-operation between overlapping international jurisdictions. The ECHR aimed to spread the philosophy according to which, in the era of globalisation, it is not only states that can no longer pursue their interests single-handedly; specialised international organisations also need to co-operate nowadays with other international bodies. Hence, the ECHR emphasise the importance of ensuring the functioning of such networks which are based on active interaction and do not represent isolated jurisdictional 'islands'. The ECHR has been concerned to uphold these objectives even at the expense of human rights considerations, giving more weight to state interests in co-operating in international organisations than to individuals' interests.[80]

Therefore, the deviation by the ECHR from its previous line of reasoning—according to which the two international judicial bodies act on the basis of parallel jurisdiction between which dichotomies prevail—can still be perceived as evidence of the close relationship between the courts and their mutual confidence in each other's candid attempt to protect human rights. By establishing a strong presumption that the ECJ's ruling had complied with the Convention, the ECHR shifted the burden of proof to the party who wishes to depart from the first judgment, thereby signalling to the ECJ that it will rarely interfere with its decisions. In the *Bosphorus* case itself, the ECHR retained its self-restraint and devoted only little effort to examining whether the presumption was rebutted in the circumstances of the case, while reducing its substantive reviewing powers to a bare minimum. As mentioned earlier, the same philosophy is often mirrored in the rules concerning recognition of foreign judgments, where concerns for the facilitation of the free movement of judgments would be frustrated if the court in the recognising state were to carry out a detailed review of the judgment granted.

[80] Similarly in the case of *Waite and Kennedy v Germany* (Application No 26083/94) ECHR 18 February 1999, the Court approves the transfer of competences from Contracting Parties to international organizations as long as individuals have ' . . . available to them reasonable alternative means to protect effectively their rights under the Convention'. The applicants contended that their right of access to a court under art 6(1) of the ECHR had been violated. The ECHR noted that the applicants did have access to a means of legal process, and the limitation on the right of access did not impair the essence of their right to a court. However, it seems that the ECHR appeared to be favouring a shift towards considering the specific facts of the case, but its position was far from clear.

E. Recognition of Foreign Judgments—*Bosphorus* as a Case Study

Although the *Bosphorus* case does not overtly use the discourse of private international law and the language of rules of recognition of foreign judgments, it is possible to explain this case in terms borrowed from private international law.

Review of Jurisdiction

As for the jurisdictional title of the ECJ, the ECHR, while departing from the prevailing practice concerning recognition of foreign judgments, excluded jurisdictional review of the ECJ. It is for the ECJ to define its jurisdiction and competences, and the ECHR will not coerce its own rules concerning the aptness of these definitions. This approach, which is similar to the one prevailing between the Member States, is apparently based on the close relationship between the two legal regimes and their strong mutual confidence in each other's courts.

Procedural Review

Procedural impropriety or unfair procedure is a widely accepted motive to resist recognition of a foreign judgment. The extent of such a review also depends on the trust between the legal systems. It seems that the ECHR paved the way to a position according to which only grossly excessive violations of procedural rights of the individuals will justify withholding ECJ judgments by the ECHR.

In *Bosphorus*, the ECHR specifically examined the issue of access of individuals to the ECJ. Although the right of access to the courts is not expressly guaranteed by Article 6 of the EConvHR, which is entitled 'Right to a Fair Trial',[81] decisions by the ECHR have made it clear that denial of access to national courts may amount to a breach of Article 6. The EU legal system likewise has a duty to remove potential lacunae regarding to access to courts.[82] The right of access to a court is not

[81] Art 6(1) provides that 'In the determination of his civil rights and obligations or any criminal charge against him, everyone is entitled to a fair and public hearing within a reasonable time by an independent and impartial tribunal established by law.' The ECJ, on its behalf, found that the right to a fair trial, which is incorporated in art 6(1) of the Convention forms part of the so-called European Community procedural public policy, Case C–7/98 *Krombach v Bamberski* [2000] ECR I–1935.

[82] Recently, in Case T–333/02 *Gestoras Pro Amnistía et al v Council*, unpublished and Case T–338/02, *Segi et al v Council* [2004] ECR II–1647, the Court of First Instance ruled that it was manifestly outside the judicial powers of the EU courts to adjudicate a claim for damages based on the inclusion in a least of terrorist suspects in an annex to a Common Position. In the appeal proceedings, Advocate General Mengozzi took a different position according to which: 'if in a case such as that of the appellants there is genuinely no effective judicial remedy, this would not only be an extremely serious and flagrant inconsistency of the system

absolute and may be subject to restrictions, provided that these pursue a legitimate aim and are proportionate in nature. While, in *Bosphorus,* the ECHR acknowledged that the access of individuals to the ECJ is limited, it nevertheless found that their rights are well protected, and avoided declaring the system procedurally deficient.[83] Accordingly, as a rule, essential procedural errors will be accepted unless they seriously contradict ECHR rulings and hence violate the European public order.

Substantive Review—Ordre Public

In the *Bosphorus* case, the ECHR insists that it will perform a substantive case-by-case examination of the ECJ's ruling; however, it will only interfere if the standard of protection of human rights applied by the ECJ is manifestly deficient compared to the standard offered by the ECHR. Making such a determination requires consideration of when normative differences are 'legitimate' or 'acceptable' and when they are so different that they cannot be recognised. This can be compared to rules according to which only judgments that run manifestly contrary to the public policy of the normative system within which the addressed court is operating will not be recognised.[84] Indeed the ECHR introduces into the *Bosphorus* decision an assumption that deflections might occur and that the ECJ as an EU domestic institution should provide a corrective mechanism. Only in the extreme cases in which the ECJ proves too weak to address these challenges will the ECHR step in, pushing for a particular substantive outcome. To the extent that the ECJ takes human rights seriously while taking into account decisions of the ECHR, there would be a strong presumption that its ruling is compatible with European public policy, and therefore the ECHR should not interfere with it.[85] For the ECHR

within the Union but also a situation which, . . . exposes the Member States of the Union to censure by the European Court of Human Rights' (Opinion of Advocate General Mengozzi, Gestoras Pro Amnistía, Case C–354/04 *P, and Segi,* Case C–355/04 P, 26 October 2006, not yet reported, para 57, available at http://curia.europa.eu). The ECJ, in an act of judicial law making reinterpreted art 35 TEU, according to which it ought to be admissible to make a Common Position which, on the basis of its content, has a scope going beyond that assigned by the EU Treaty to that kind of act, subject to review by the ECJ, Case C–354/04 P, *Gestoras Pro Amnistía et al,* 27 February 2007, not yet reported, paras 49–57, available at http://curia.europa.eu.

[83] *Bosphorus,* paras 162–4.

[84] See in general, HP Meidanis, 'Public Policy and Ordre Public in the Private International Law and the EC/EU: Traditional Positions of the Member States and Modern Trends' (2005) 30 *European Law Review* 95.

[85] See Concurring Opinion Judge Ress, *Bosphorus,* para 3: 'In other cases concerning new questions of interpretation or application of a Convention right, it may be that the ECJ would decide in a way which the ECHR would not be prepared to follow in future cases, but in such cases it would be difficult to say that the deficiency was already manifest . . . I am convinced that it is only in exceptional cases that the protection will be found to have been manifestly deficient.'

not to recognise the ECJ's judgment, it will not suffice to point to a discrepancy between the legal rule applied by the ECJ and that which would have been applied by the ECHR. Just as recourse to public policy can be envisaged only where recognition would be at variance to an unacceptable degree with the legal order of the legal system addressed inasmuch as it infringes a fundamental principle, the infringement by the ECJ would have to constitute a manifest breach of a rule of law or of a right recognised as fundamental in order. Therefore, only extremely erroneous interpretations or implementations of the European Convention would justify overruling the judgment of the ECJ.

By awarding primacy to rules of private international law, a result that obliges the ECHR to interfere in every case in which it considers the ECJ did not adequately protect human rights as offered by the Convention can be avoided. A breach of the Convention would of course be identified by the ECHR. However, adding private international law principles to the human rights examination would mean that identifying such a breach would still leave open the question whether this breach must always lead to judicial intervention. Therefore, only flagrant breaches amounting to a violation of the public order will command interference.[86] In other words, human rights concerns could be sometimes overridden by other interests, in particular the desire to uphold international co-operation.

By following this track, the ECHR made it possible to acknowledge the political sovereignty of EC law while legitimising its own decisions that criticise it. In this way, the ECHR could, for example, articulate a particular concept of rights, while recognising that the manner in which these rights are implemented is subject to various alternative conceptions. Such a solution permits social tensions and conflicts to be carried out in the jurisdictional arena. Clearly, deference to other normative communities will have long-term reciprocal benefits and will contribute to a more tolerant, jurisgenerative European order.

IV. CONCLUSION

Despite asserting anew its jurisdiction on deciding matters that fall within the sole jurisdiction of the ECJ, the ECHR, even after the *Bosphorus* decision, still maintains that the ECJ is more apt to deal with the interpretation and validity of Community acts. Therefore, parties to a dispute which evolve around Community law should not turn to the ECHR and seek its ruling prior to submitting the case to the ECJ. This resembles closely the rules concerning the exhaustion of local remedies.

[86] I am borrowing the hybrid human rights/private international law approach from JJ Fawcett, 'The Impact of Article 6(1) of the ECHR on Private International Law' (2007) 56 *International Comparative Law Quarterly* 1, 36, yet I am applying it differently.

Therefore, the ECHR is attempting to eliminate competition between the courts and to reduce the negative effects of forum shopping at least in the initial phase. It believes that by determining the propriety of the exercise of jurisdiction, it is the ECJ that should have the initial jurisdiction over EC law.

Yet again, the *Bosphorus* decision has been understood by many as a unilateral attempt on behalf of the ECHR to re-establish its superiority over the ECJ as it retains the task of being the final arbitrator on human rights issues. Post *Bosphorus*, they would claim, it is more obvious that the ECHR sits in a superior position compared to that of the ECJ. Accordingly, the *Bosphorus* decision, according to them, amounts to a 'de facto annexation' of the EU to the Convention, and just like a formal accession, it decides the struggle for supremacy in favour of the ECHR.

However, in this chapter I have tried to demonstrate that, as a matter of fact, an opposite result was achieved. Just as is the case between parallel, independent cross-border jurisdictions which aim to enhance their co-operation, when it comes to recognition of foreign judgments, the first jurisdiction in time carries more impetus and, in fact, superiority. Therefore the second court in time will often acknowledge the first judgment, even if it was erroneous, and will, almost as a rule, incorporate the first ruling into its own legal system.

To paraphrase Slaughter and Burke-White, it seems that the ECHR is backstopping EU law.[87] The ECHR will operate only in case where the ECJ completely fails to act as a first-line means of protection. To the extent that this is the correct way to read the *Bosphorus* decision, the relationship between the courts could be then described as substantively complementary,[88] or integrative comity.[89] Post *Bosphorus*, the ECHR is taking the whole system one step further by providing a second line of defence when EU institutions have substantively failed, not because they were unwilling but because they were as a matter of fact unable to avert the deflection from the standard of protection of human rights.

This is a desirable outcome in a globalised world, in which countries are increasingly obliged to co-operate with each other and in which courts have a role to play in facilitating and reinforcing such co-operation.

[87] In the meaning attributed to that notion by A-M Slaughter and WW Burke-White, 'The Future of International Law Is Domestic (or, The European Way of Law)' (2006) 47 *Harvard International Law Journal* 327.

[88] A Clapham, 'On Complementarity: Human Rights in the European Legal Orders' (2000) 21 *Human Rights Law Journal* 8.

[89] MW Lien, 'The Cooperative and Integrative Models of International Judicial Comity: Two Illustrations Using Transnational Discovery and Breard Scenarios' (2001) 50 *Catholic University Law Review* 591.

11

Domestic Courts and Sovereignty

AMICHAI COHEN*

I. INTRODUCTION

IN RECENT YEARS, the world has witnessed the emergence of an increasing number of *transnational* courts.[1] I use this term to describe, in the main, courts possessing, or claiming to possess, jurisdiction that is not based on the ancient principle of territorial jurisdiction and its several classic exceptions,[2] but rather on some form of universal jurisdiction. First and foremost amongst these bodies are international courts and tribunals. For instance, though international criminal courts and tribunals have been in existence since before the middle of the twentieth century,[3] their number and substantive jurisdiction have markedly grown since the 1990s. The second form of transnational adjudication is that of national courts, which refer to the principle of universal jurisdiction when asserting jurisdiction over cases that occurred in other countries.

In this chapter, I seek to assess the effect that the emergence of transnational courts has had on the jurisprudence of domestic courts and

* Lecturer, Ono Academic College, Israel. I wish to thank Eyal Benvenisti, Tomer Broude, Iris Canor, Stuart A Cohen and Yuval Shany, as well as the participants of the conference for comments on earlier versions of this article.

[1] I use here the term 'transnational' as opposed to international courts in order to emphasise that their jurisdiction is not limited, as in the traditional sense, to nations. It also extends to the adjudication of private persons, either as defendants or claimants. Transnational courts or tribunals are also not necessarily international, and certainly not 'supranational'. They can be foreign domestic courts that apply universal jurisdiction. Note, then, that the term domestic courts may refer to both the courts in the countries where the facts occurred, and to the courts of other nations asserting universal jurisdiction. In order to avoid confusion I shall use the term *domestic courts* where referring to the former, and *national courts* when referring to the latter.

[2] Traditionally, the jurisdiction of courts was limited to acts occurring in the area of the state in which the court operated. The exceptions were the protective principle, and the nationality principle. See, eg, Restatement (Third) of the Foreign Relations Law of the United States (1987) ss 402–41.

[3] For a history of the evolution of international criminal tribunals see GJ Bass, *Stay the Hand of Vengeance: The Politics of War Crimes Tribunals* (Princeton University Press, 2000).

national judges.[4] I shall attempt to examine this question from both a predictive perspective (ie, the possible effect) and an actual perspective (ie, what in fact occurs). Naturally, since the rise of transnational jurisdiction is a fairly recent phenomenon, the article will predominantly be concerned with the predictive perspective.

My claim is that the main effect of transnational courts is to reinforce the decision-making power of domestic courts, and not, as is sometimes believed, to limit national decision-making powers. I shall attempt to show that domestic courts use the *potential* power of international law in order to strengthen their own position, and redefine the term *domestic sovereignty*.

Many scholars consider the term 'sovereignty' to be in tension, and perhaps even in conflict, with the supremacy of transnational courts, globalisation and international co-operation. Scholars who support sovereignty tend to claim that increased globalisation impedes the sovereignty of states. They contend that international law and international co-operation should continue to be based on the consent of states, and consider international adjudication to undermine this goal.[5] On the other hand, academics supportive of international co-operation, international law and globalisation tend to see this approach as the alternative to the outdated system of sovereignty, which represents an archaic conception of the role of the nation-state in the formation of international law and international relations.

For some time now, scholars of international law and international relations have disputed this dichotomy. Chayes and Chayes, in their seminal 1998 book, *The New Sovereignty*, claimed that

> sovereignty no longer consists in the freedom of states to act independently, in their perceived self-interest, but in membership, in reasonably good standing in the regimes that make up the substance of international life.[6]

Hence, on the descriptive level, sovereignty is a prerequisite to international co-operation not an obstacle thereto. It defines a political entity that is able to co-operate with similar entities. It draws the borders of legitimate co-operation, and allocates decision-making powers among those institutions that approve such co-operation. Sovereignty, in short, is what enables international co-operation to exist.[7]

[4] I use the terms domestic courts, national courts, national judges interchangeably when referring to courts and judges which form a part of national judicial systems.

[5] Eg, JL Goldsmith and EA Posner, *The Limits of International Law* (Oxford University Press, 2005) 161 (discussing the Dispute Settlement Body (DSB) of the World Trade Organization and forecasting it would succeed only if its decisions were compatible with states' interests).

[6] A Chayes and AH Chayes, *The New Sovereignty: Compliance with International Regulatory Agreements* (Cambridge, MA, Harvard University Press, 1998) 27.

[7] Kenneth Anderson described a continuum of seven stages from 'pure' sovereignty to international democracy. See K Anderson 'Book Review: Squaring the Circle? Reconciling

In this chapter I suggest that these ideas can be developed further. I argue that in order to co-operate with and enforce international law, domestic courts and national judges use terms usually associated with sovereignty. They do so, however, not in order to assert *independence* from international law, but rather in order to justify *adherence* to it. This way they strengthen their position domestically, and have far more effect on national decision making. I will further claim that the emerging system of international law enforcement by international tribunals encourages such strategic behaviour on the part of domestic courts. In other words, the modern system of transnational adjudication supports the independence of domestic courts, and creates incentives for national judges to enforce international law domestically.

Part II of this chapter analyses the traditional way domestic courts implemented international law, and the reasons for their (usually negative) attitudes towards it. Part III will deal with the way transnational courts change what domestic courts do. Part IV attempts to tie the analysis to the growing debate over the effects of international decision-making on domestic sovereignty. My basic claim in this part is that domestic courts use sovereignty, and other terms connected with it, in order to enhance international co-operation.

A note of caution is required. Although my claims are general, I adduce examples from a limited number of jurisdictions, mainly Israel, the United States and (in small part) from Europe. Naturally, in order to verify whether my claims are of a universal nature, more comprehensive research needs to be undertaken.

II. TENDENCIES OF DOMESTIC COURTS TOWARDS INTERNATIONAL LAW

A. A Historical Perspective

How do domestic courts react when confronted with an international norm that contradicts the policy of their own government or their previous jurisdictions? Do they enforce it? Or do they ignore it?

Before attempting to answer these questions, I would like to emphasise one point: courts are supposed to enforce the law, including international law, to the extent that it applies in the domestic sphere in accordance with constitutional law.[8] Therefore, the starting point for any discussion of the

Sovereignty and Global Governance through Global Government Networks' (2005) 118 *Harvard Law Review* 256. Anderson's description is more about the ideals, and less about the cooperation of states.

[8] The point here is, of course, that constitutional law is not always clear on the subject of incorporation of international law. Hence, domestic courts are left with much discretion as to the actual application of international law in their domestic system.

subject should be that unless otherwise proved, the presumption is that national courts should apply international law as a matter of national law.[9] To put the matter slightly differently, there are certainly issues or cases in which courts would not be willing to come into conflict with their own government on any basis. However, on these issues in which courts are willing to contradict their governments based on *domestic* laws, there is a need to explain why they would not be willing to do the same based on *international* law. This need for explanation is further strengthened by looking at some of the other factors that influence the decision-making of courts.

A first factor derives from the fact that one of the main tasks of judges sitting on supreme or constitutional courts is to protect individual rights against governmental attempts to curtail them—a goal that converges with the declared intention of important parts of international law, such as international human rights law, or humanitarian law. In addition, one of the most important attributes of the modern national court is its independence vis-à-vis its domestic government. Many courts are known for their willingness to clash with governments over matters of civil rights or adequate administrative procedures. This is especially true with regard to courts of liberal-democratic countries, which are the central focus of the analysis in this article. Yet a third factor is the growing tendency of judges to interact with judges of foreign countries, and to be aware of international and comparative law.

Surveys of how national courts actually behave[10] have shown that courts usually avoid implementing international law when it contradicts important policies of their own governments.[11] Domestic courts adopt in such cases a series of techniques in order to avoid the need to implement international law. One such technique is the American 'non-self-executing treaty' doctrine, according to which many of the international treaties that are signed by the United States, and approved by the Senate, cannot be implemented by US courts because their nature requires domestic implementing legislation.[12] Other techniques are the 'non-justiciabil-

[9] Of course, as will be explained later, some national courts consistently interpret their domestic national constitutional order in a way which limits the realm of international law which should be applied domestically.

[10] The main work on the subject is E Benvenisti 'Judicial Misgivings Regarding the Application of International Law: An Analysis of Attitudes of National Courts' (1993) 4 *European Journal of International Law* 159.

[11] Recently, others have suggested some other roles for domestic courts with regard to the implementation of international law. See, eg, MA Waters, 'Mediating Norms and Identity: The Role of Transnational Judicial Dialogue in Creating and Enforcing International Law' (2005) 93 *Georgetown Law Journal* 487 (claiming that national judges have a role of mediating between international law and domestic values). Benvenisti's basic conclusions, however, remain unchallenged as to probative evidence of past behaviour of national courts.

[12] For a historical survey and support for it see JC Yoo, 'Globalism and the Constitution: Treaties, Non-Self-Execution, and the Original Understanding' (1999) 99 *Columbia Law Review* 1955; For a critical approach see C-M Vasquez, 'Response: Laughing at Treaties' (1999) 99 *Columbia Law Review* 2154.

ity' and 'act of state' doctrines.[13] A further important avoidance technique is the judge-made doctrine of dualism, according to which courts in England, and in countries affected by these courts, have refused to adjudicate any claim based on a treaty that the state has not incorporated into its domestic law.[14] In short: domestic courts attempt to avoid implementing international law in a way that will cause a clash, based on international law, with their governments.

B. Why Do National Courts Avoid Implementing International Law?

There are several possible explanations for the dissonance between what international lawyers expect from domestic courts—with relation to international law implementation—and what they actually do. The traditional explanation given by courts has been that foreign policy is a matter for the executive. Accordingly, courts should not get involved in matters relating to foreign policy and national security.[15] Since much, though certainly not all, of foreign policy and national security is manifested in international law, from an institutional point of view the result is that it is the executive branch that should properly interpret and implement international law.[16] Recent trends in the substance and scope of international co-operation make this claim very problematic, however. International law now deals with almost every issue covered by domestic law, from environmental matters to the proper use of police forces. It makes very little sense to place all these matters outside the scope of judicial review. Another possible explanation is that domestic courts, despite their frequent criticism of the executive and legislative branches, still see themselves as strongly associated with national governments. When the interests of their own governments are balanced against those

[13] Of course, act of state or non-justiciability in the narrow sense may be a stipulation of international law. According to this narrow use of the doctrine, courts do not criticise the acts of foreign governments in their own territories. This might be seen as a measure of respect to the sovereignty of other nations. However, courts have extended this doctrine to include cases in which foreign governments violated international law. See *Banco Nacional de Cuba v Sabbatino* 376 US 398 (1964). But see the later view adopted by British courts, eg, *Kuwait Airways Incorporation v Iraqi Air Company* [2002] UKHL 19 (Decision) 16 May 2002. See generally: L Henkin, *International Law: Politics and Values* (Dordrecht, Martinus Nijhoff, 1995) 74–5.

[14] For a description of these mechanisms see MN Shaw, *International Law* (5th edn, Cambridge University Press, 2003) ch 4.

[15] This is true especially with regard to treaties, in many common law countries (including the UK and Israel) where treaties are not implemented by courts unless incorporated by domestic statutes. See, eg, Shaw, *ibid*, 135. See also *Youngstown Sheet & Tube Co v Sawyer (steel seizure cases)* 343 US 579, 634–5 (1952).

[16] See, eg, JG Ku and JC Yoo '*Hamdan v Rumsfeld:* The Functional Case for Foreign Affairs Deference to the Executive Branch' (2006) 23 *Constitutional Commentary* 101.

of other governments, they identify with their own government, and not with some virtual community of international lawyers or international courts. A third explanation is that national judges, while sometimes willing to clash with elected officials of government on grounds derived from domestic laws or constitutions, possess sound democratic arguments for not doing so where international law is concerned. International law, according to this claim, lacks the legitimacy of domestic laws because of its different origin and unique process of formation.[17]

A final explanation, promoted by Benvenisti, derives from game-theory.[18] National courts, he claims, find themselves in a prisoner's dilemma when considering whether to impose international law on their own governments. In order not to put their own state at a disadvantage vis-à-vis other states, national courts must assume that all national courts would impose international law on their governments. However, because of the lack of any hierarchical institution compelling national courts to act in this way, national judges may fear other judges in other parts of the world will refrain from imposing international law on their governments. Under these circumstances, rational national judges may also refrain from imposing international law on their own government, since to do so would place that government at a disadvantage.[19]

This explanation captures the anxiety of courts in enforcing international law in two ways. First, as Benvenisti emphasises, domestic courts do not *want* to disadvantage their governments on the international plane. Perhaps more important are the domestic problems for national courts created by the absence of enforcement mechanisms that might have compelled judiciaries in other countries to impose international law on their governments. Domestic courts can hardly justify, internally, the enforcement of international law on their own government, when it is clear that other governments are not likely to comply with the same law. This exacerbates the criticism that any court that intervenes in government policy is likely to face—ie, that the court is acting contrary to the wishes of democratically elected government. (One writer has termed

[17] This is basically John Yoo's claim in a series of articles he wrote about international law in US law. See, eg, Yoo, above n 12.

[18] See Benvenisti, above n 10, see also E Benvenisti, 'Exit and Voice in the Age of Globalization' (1999) 98 *Michigan Law Review* 167.

[19] An excellent example of this mechanism is the jurisprudence of the European Court of Justice (ECJ) with regard to the direct effect of the General Agreement on Tariffs and Trade (GATT) and other World Trade Organization (WTO) agreements. The ECJ (which I treat here as similar to domestic courts in its incentives relating to international law) decided that as the GATT and WTO agreements do not have direct effect in the member states Case 21–24/72 *International Fruit Company v Produktschap voor Groenten en Fruit* [1972] ECR 1219, and later: Case C–149/96 *Portugal v Council* [1999] ECR I-8395 (stating that: 'the lack of reciprocity in that regard in the part of the community's trading partners, in relations to the WTO agreements . . . may lead to disuniform application of the WTO rules', para 45 of the Portugal decision).

this a 'counter-majoritarian nightmare'.[20]) Hence, the problem is not only whether to enforce the law, but rather how to justify its enforcement.

The upshot of all these explanations, from a historical perspective, is that supporters of the application of international law in domestic courts have not been able to rely on domestic courts to enforce international law where it mattered most—against important policies of their own governments. From the point of view of international law this is troubling. This is because domestic courts are the institutions most capable of effectively enforcing international law. Indeed, no international system can operate without the co-operation of a domestic system; no international law can be enforced without the co-operation of domestic courts.

In the next part I will assess some solutions offered to the non-implementation of international law by domestic courts.

III. POSSIBLE SOLUTIONS TO THE NON-IMPLEMENTATION OF INTERNATIONAL LAW BY DOMESTIC COURTS

A. Hierarchical Courts

One obvious way to overcome the tendencies of domestic courts to avoid implementing international agreements is to create hierarchical institutions that actually force states to obey international law. Some claim that a prominent example for such a court is the European Court of Justice (ECJ).[21] The decisions of the ECJ, its direct control over domestic courts through the preliminary decision mechanism, and its willingness to declare the direct effect and superiority of Community law over Member States' laws, have brought about the almost universal adherence to European Community laws by the domestic courts of European Member States.[22] It has been claimed that the European Court of Human Rights (ECHR) stands in a relationship of hierarchical superiority to

[20] 'Monism is in some way the fulfillment of the worst counter-majoritarian nightmare . . . Monism rejects the belief that legal authority in a democracy can only be derived from the domestic democratic process. By applying international over municipal sources, judges appear to be not only acting politically and independently of the other branches, but doing so at the expense of our legal sovereignty', J Turley, 'Dualistic Values in an Age of International Legisprudence' (1993) 44 *Hastings Law Journal* 185, 205.

[21] JHH Weiler 'Quiet Revolution—The European Court of Justice and its Interlocutors' (1994) 26 *Comparative Political Studies* 510. For a review of the different approaches to the relationship between the ECJ and national courts of member states, see K Alter, 'Explaining National Court Acceptance of European Court Jurisprudence: A Critical Evaluation of Theories of Legal Integration' in A-M Slaughter et al (eds), *The European Court and National Courts—Doctrine and Jurisprudence* (Oxford, Hart Publishing, 1998) 227.

[22] LR Helfer and A-M Slaughter, 'Toward a Theory of Effective Supranational Adjudication' (1997) 107 *Yale Law Journal* 273.

domestic courts in Europe.[23] I hesitate to adopt this position. As I will briefly show below, the ECHR's relationship with domestic courts is more complex.[24]

Outside Europe, however, success has been quite limited. Empirical evaluation shows that the level of state compliance with decisions of the International Court of Justice (ICJ) is not very high.[25] Even rarer, as I will show immediately, have been instances in which domestic courts enforced decisions of the ICJ when these clashed with important policies of their own government. Although domestic judges have occasionally cited ICJ decisions in order to justify their policy choices, complete adherence has not been observed.[26] Compliance with decisions of the Inter-American Court of Human Rights, and other institutions with even less power, adheres to the same pattern.[27]

B. Anne-Marie Slaughter and Transnational Judicial Networks

If hierarchy is not a global solution, perhaps international co-operation in the implementation of international law may be a result of a more horizontal process—whereby domestic and national courts *co-operate* in the invocation and implementation of international law.

Such suggestions have taken centre stage in many writings. A prominent example is Anne-Marie Slaughter's work. Slaughter has made transjudicial co-operation one of the centrepieces of her celebrated book *A New World Order*.[28] Slaughter emphasises that national judges are a part of the growing (trans)governmental network. In this view, domestic

[23] See, eg, MW Janis et al, *European Human Rights Law: Text and Material* (Oxford University Press, 1995) 428 (claiming that 'the convention enables the European Court of Human Rights to exercise a form of quasi-constitutional supervision over the exercise of state power'); A Drzemczewski 'Principal Characteristics of the New ECHR Control Mechanism, as Established by Protocol No 11' (1992) 15 *Human Rights Law Journal* 81 (claiming that 'The Convention's achievements have been quite staggering, the case-law of the European Commission and the Court of Human Rights exerting an ever deeper influence on the Laws and Social Realities of State Parties' (82)).

[24] In order to appeal to the ECHR one has to exhaust domestic remedies. Furthermore, the ECHR has adopted a very significant jurisprudence of margin of appreciation which allows it not to intervene in many cases.

[25] T Ginsburg and R McAdams 'Adjudicating in Anarchy: An Expressive Theory of International Dispute Resolution' (2004) 45 *William and Mary Law Review* 1229.

[26] Mark Weisburd puts the matter bluntly: 'There appear to be no cases in which a domestic court has seen itself as obliged to enforce decisions of the ICJ or of its predecessor, the Permanent Court of International Justice (PCIJ).' AM Weisburd 'International Judicial Decisions, Domestic Courts, and the Foreign Affairs Power' (2004–5) *Cato Supreme Court Review* 289, 299.

[27] EA Posner and JC Yoo, 'Judicial Independence in International Tribunals' (2005) 93 *California Law Review* 1 (claiming that the Inter-American Court of Human Rights has a 5 per cent compliance rate).

[28] A-M Slaughter, *A New World Order* (Princeton University Press, 2004).

courts are handing down an increasing number of decisions in which they rely on the constitutional thought of other nations.[29] Slaughter's theory is a complex one, and I cannot do it justice in just a few sentences.[30] It is based on the premise that modern states are best described as 'disaggregated states', each consisting of several different, even rival components (eg, courts, legislature and different administrative agencies).[31] In the globalising world each of these different components creates its own transnational governmental network with similar institutions in other countries.[32] The result is that these global networks, which trade information, find solutions, and even enforce them, govern much of our world. According to Slaughter, judges—especially those of higher courts (in the hierarchical sense)—constitute an especially formidable transnational network.[33] For one thing, judges easily create transnational networks, and are willing to meet with judges from other countries and learn from their experience. One common attribute of almost all democracies is the independence of the judicial system. Hence, there exist no institutional limitations on the ability of the judges to meet and exchange views with their overseas counterparts (thus, they do not need the clearance of their respective foreign offices in order to meet with judges from other countries, etc). Second, judicial decisions move easily across borders. Because court decisions, especially those of high courts, emphasise an analytical approach,[34] their logic is readily understood in other countries. On the normative level, Slaughter applauds such a transnational judicial network. She believes that a better world will be created by more international co-operation, and that judges should, and can, contribute to this end.

Slaughter's description of transnational *judicial* networks,[35] as well as her specific examples and cases, seem to be problematic both descriptively and as an explanatory mechanism. Slaughter's account of how judges exchange views might be accurate, but it is unclear how much foreign decisions actually have an effect on the outcome of the case, even when they are cited. It seems that judges use foreign decisions as rhetorical tools when those decisions support their own positions, and

[29] Slaughter, *ibid*, 69. See also: A-M Slaughter 'Court to Court' (1999) 92 *American Journal of Internationa Law* 708.

[30] For a review of *A New World Order* with some sharp criticisms, see Anderson, above n 7

[31] Slaughter, above n 28, 12.

[32] *Ibid*, 14.

[33] *Ibid*, ch 2, 65.

[34] *Ibid*, 77.

[35] Slaughter's description of transnational *administrative* networks seems to be correct both intuitively and according to the evidence she brings. Indeed, administrators co-operate transnationally at a level that is much higher than anything the world has hitherto witnessed. For a review on administrative co-operation, see, eg, A Cohen, 'Bureaucratic Internalization: Domestic Governmental Agencies and the Legitimization of International Law' (2005) 36 *Georgetown Journal of International Law* 1079.

not as something they necessarily learn from.[36] Where Slaughter does show actual reliance it is usually in the context of the European Community, where (as I have already noted) a different system exists. Moreover, much of what Slaughter claims relates to co-operation between judges from different countries, not to the implementation of international law, which is what we are looking for. In other words: all that Slaughter's conclusions show is that judges use comparative law, not that they implement international law. Thus, not too much emphasis need be placed on the fact that in several recent cases the justices of the US Supreme Court have cited decisions of foreign courts or of international tribunals.[37] At most, they did so as a source for indicating how the world thinks about a subject, not out of an obligation to international law.

It is also not very clear exactly how networks operate between judges. As discussed in other works on transnational networks, networks support co-operation across borders for several reasons: networks create trust, and offer a forum for co-ordination and discussions. Networks also create certain sanctions, though only on a very limited basis.

Applying these criteria to transnational *judicial* networks would mean that judges would tend to co-ordinate their thinking when they meet.[38] Supposedly, judges who defect from the common consensus would suffer some level of condemnation by other members of the group.

Slaughter puts up these claims, but her description of the actual operation of transjudicial network is somewhat deficient. While judges certainly meet, the nature of the judicial profession, in contrast to scientific work, for example, does not motivate team work. Certainly, judges see cases coming from other countries, but their day-to-day function does not *require* transnational co-operation. There is no database which factually examines how many judges actually attend international meetings, but it seems that these meetings are quite exclusive, and are attended only by judges at the apex of their own judicial systems. And sanctions surely have a very limited effect on judges who are used to

[36] Eg, HG Cohen, 'Supremacy and Diplomacy: The International Law of the US Supreme Court' (2005) 24 *Berkeley Journal of International Law* 101 (claiming that: '[The court] also appears to be far more comfortable with foreign and international law as persuasive authority or as an interpretive device—which it can choose to apply, than as a rule of decision by which it would be bound. The Court is eager to engage international and foreign law, but only on its own terms.'). Anderson, above n 7, correctly points out that most of Slaughter's evidence of cases where judges learn from judges in other countries are focused on Western, usually more liberal, judges using Western, usually liberal judgments.

[37] *Lawrence v Texas* 539 US 558, 576 (2003) (the court cited the ECHR in support of its position that states should not be allowed to prohibit same-sex sexual conduct); *Atkins v Virginia* 536 US 394 n 21 (2002) (the court mentioned that there is widespread international opposition to imposing the death penalty on the mentally retarded); *Roper v Simmons* 120 S Ct 1183, 1200 (2005) (the court cited the position of many states in support of its decision that capital punishment should not be imposed for crimes committed by minors).

[38] Slaughter puts much emphasis on the meetings of judges, especially constitutional judges, from different countries. See, eg, Slaughter, above n 28, 96.

political pressures, who have incentives for voicing independent views, and who also have a domestic community to satisfy.

No doubt there are more international decisions, and of course, there are more national decisions that mention international law than used to be in the past. We can also see a somewhat more elaborate system of cross-fertilisation between different judicial and legal systems.[39] But which mechanism generates these phenomena? Why do judges respect some transnational courts, and not others? It seems to me that the transnational networks mechanism does not provide a satisfactory mechanism for this operation.

IV. TRANSNATIONAL COURTS AND DOMESTIC COURTS—THE EFFECT

Hierarchical courts and transnational judicial networks thus provide, at best, a partial solution to the problem of non-implementation of international law. Transnational adjudication, performed by courts assuming transnational jurisdiction as described above, provides a third solution to this problem of non-implementation.

A. What is Special about Transnational Courts?

Since the beginning of the 1990s there has been a steady growth in the number, power and jurisdiction of courts with transnational jurisdiction. Transnational courts have been in operation ever since the beginning of the twentieth century, and certainly since the middle of that century. However, their jurisdiction, power and geographical area of control were for long very limited. Such was the case with respect to the European courts (the ECJ for the European Community and later the European Union; and the ECHR), the military tribunals after the Second World War (in Nuremberg and Tokyo—which operated only in the years immediately following the war) and the dispute settlement system of the General Agreement on Tariffs and Trade (GATT) (whose decisions had to be approved through consensus by all GATT contracting parties).

Since the 1990s this situation has changed dramatically. Firstly, many new tribunals have emerged in recent years. Several war crimes tribunals have been created by the United Nations Security Council (UNSC) and by

[39] Although there is evidence that such cross-fertilisation has always been occurring. See, eg, A Watson, 'Legal Change: Sources of Law and Legal Culture' (1983) 131 *University of Pennsylvania Law Review* 1121, 1125 (claiming that 'Borrowing from another system is the most common form of legal change').

special agreements.[40] In 2003 a permanent International Criminal Court with very wide jurisdiction began to operate.[41] Slaughter and Helfer list 27 permanent international courts and tribunals.[42] Approximately half of these have been created since the end of the 1980s. Secondly, the role of existing courts became wider, and they were granted more powers. Hence the formation of the World Trade Organization, which replaced the GATT system, was coupled with the lifting of many of the restraints from its dispute settlement system.[43] Thirdly, the re-emergence of the UNSC as a dominant force in international politics seemed to suggest that decisions of international tribunals which lacked enforcement mechanisms, might not be so easily ignored in the future.

It is sometimes claimed that the revolution in the international judicial system is best seen in the emergence of courts that possess superiority over domestic courts. These are sometimes called *supranational courts* as they can override the domestic judicial system and directly deal with citizens.[44] As I mentioned before, however, that superiority in this sense is greatly overstated. It is mostly evident in Europe,[45] and there is little evidence of its existence elsewhere.[46]

Another model of jurisdiction of courts is what might be called 'complementary jurisdiction' where transnational (ie, either international or domestic courts of other countries) use their jurisdiction only if the domestic court does not do so. For example, the statute of the International Criminal Court includes a specific provision investing the court with jurisdiction even where the case has already been tried on the national level, if the proceedings in the domestic court were 'intended to shield the person concerned from criminal responsibility' or 'were not

[40] There are currently two international criminal tribunals, and four more hybrid courts (mix of international and domestic judges).

[41] Rome Statute of the International Criminal Court (hereafter 'the Rome Statute') (adopted 17 July 1998, entered into force 1 July 2002) (1998) 37 ILM 999.

[42] A-M Slaughter and L Helfer, 'Why States Create International Tribunals: A Response to Professors Posner and Yoo' (2005) 95 *California Law Review* 899.

[43] See generally JH Jackson, *The World Trading System: Law and Policy of International Economics Relations* (2nd ed, Cambridge, MA, MIT Press, 1997) ch 4, 107–37.

[44] Eg, Helfer and Slaughter, above n 22.

[45] It is quite common to exclude European courts from evaluation of international tribunals, due to the unique nature of the European Community, and the history and foundation of the European Court of Human Rights. Eg. Posner and Yoo, above n 27.

[46] Recently, several works have surveyed the scope and effectiveness of the new international courts. Two of the more important were published in 2005 in the *California Law Review*. In the first, Eric Posner and John Yoo studied the effectiveness of international tribunals. Their conclusion was that there is a negative correlation between the independence of an international tribunal and its effectiveness. The more an international tribunal is independent, the less is its effectiveness. Posner and Yoo, above n 27. Anne-Marie Slaughter and Laurence Helfer responded to this article and claimed that Posner and Yoo used flawed information and statistics, and failed to prove their position. Slaughter and Helfer claim that effectiveness of international courts is built on many factors, among them the type of agreement, the actual states that participate in the international agreement, the overall structure of the agreement, etc. Slaughter and Helfer, above n 42.

conducted independently or impartially in accordance with norms of due process recognized by international law'.[47] The same is true with regard to domestic courts applying universal jurisdiction. The American Terror Victim Protection Act specifies that US courts may entertain a tort litigation based on acts against international law only if the court with territorial jurisdiction does not adjudicate the case.[48]

This description of formal jurisdiction, however, does not reflect the full extent of the effect of transnational courts with complimentary jurisdiction. In order to understand their actual role one has to return the problems that impede the universal application of international law.

B. How Transnational Courts Can Change the Judicial Landscape

What is the effect of these transnational courts? And wherein lies their power?

If we accept Benvenisti's main explanatory mechanism for avoidance of international law by domestic courts—the prisoner's dilemma involved in the enforcement of international law *obligation*—it is easier for us to understand the effects of transnational courts and tribunals. These courts do not offer a classic hierarchical judicial system, but something completely different: they alter the incentives of domestic courts, and the environments in which they operate. First, these courts clearly change the equilibrium governing the way domestic courts view each other. Because transnational tribunals have authority to act only when domestic courts do not, it becomes more likely that domestic courts would adjudicate the cases they have before them, and apply international law in the course of this adjudication. If courts really avoid implementing international law because they are anxious about whether other courts would act likewise, then the solution to these avoidance dynamics is a credible mechanism that would convince domestic courts of the likelihood that courts in other countries would also enforce international law. International courts and tribunals are a form of tit-for-tat, or a way to enforce commitments, without causing the nations involved to collide publicly. International courts create an enforcement mechanism that allows national courts to co-operate, because they lessen the chances that other national courts, in other countries, would defect.[49]

[47] Rome Statute, Art 20.

[48] 18 USC s 1350.

[49] It is also clear why international courts have become stronger in areas of human rights and humanitarian law. It is exactly in these areas that reciprocity has lost its tit-for-tat effect. The major enforcement mechanism of international law, in the absence of any judicial enforcement, was reciprocity. States knew that their violations of international law would generate similar behaviour on the part of other states. Human rights, however, were always impossible to enforce by threats of reciprocity, and humanitarian law becomes less and less

Transnational courts change the way domestic courts work not only because they provide the small marginal enforcement mechanism required. They also contribute to the emergence of judicial enforcement by creating a point of *equilibrium* to which all domestic courts can refer. One major problem of international law is its lack of clarity.[50] Even when domestic courts do wish to enforce international law on their respective governments, they are hard put to discern what it actually says. The language of treaties and conventions, not to mention custom, is rarely clear and unambiguous, often intentionally so. When domestic courts interpret such documents they create differing interpretations of international law. One example of such a process is the way Israel interpreted the Fourth Geneva Convention[51] during the first 30 years of its occupation of the territories, a period when the Israeli Supreme Court was in fact almost the only court in the world attempting to interpret the convention in any way. The results of this experiment in judicial enforcement of international law are very illuminating. In almost every case that came before it, the Israeli Supreme Court interpreted the Fourth Geneva Convention in a way that coincided with Israeli interests and with the practices of the Israel Defense Forces (IDF), even when such interpretations made little sense according to accepted interpretive principles of international law.[52] This way of interpretation is not of course unique to Israel. The basic intuition of all courts is to adopt the following strategy: the court should use the mode of interpretation least likely to conflict with the practices of the state.[53]

However, if international law interpretation is to become more widespread, and especially if there exist international tribunals that interpret international law in a specific way, the adoption of such a strategy becomes difficult. Once a competent international tribunal hands down a judicial interpretation, it becomes a point of departure for domestic courts. Although domestic courts can certainly adopt different interpretations, they have now to provide some justification for doing so. Once again this situation may be explained in game theory terms: the interpretation of the international tribunal usually supplies the equilibrium point. Domestic courts may depart from it, but their awareness that any such departure is unstable, because it is likely to be rejected elsewhere in the world, leads them to avoid taking that course of action very often.

appropriate for the working of the reciprocity mechanism, as modern-day conflicts become less symmetric, and more internal. Moreover, as international trade grows more complex, and more states join the international trade regime, reciprocity looses its effect in that area too.

[50] TM Franck, *The Power of Legitimacy Among Nations* (Oxford University Press, 1990) 30–35.

[51] Geneva Convention Relative to the Protection of Civilians in Time of War (adopted 12 August 1949, entered into force 21 October 1950) 75 UNTS 287.

[52] D Kretzmer, *The Occupation of Justice: The Supreme Court of Israel and the Occupied Territories* (Albany, State University of New York Press, 2002).

[53] See the discussion above text next to n 15.

Moreover, transnational courts offer domestic courts a *justification* for enforcing international law, principally by making the prospect of enforcement more likely in other countries, too. The presence of such courts, even if their jurisdiction is limited, creates a possibility of intervention by these courts. The position of the domestic court, if it wishes to enforce the norms based on international law, becomes much stronger. It becomes harder to raise claims based on inequality so that no other country would enforce this norm. Of course, not all domestic judges prefer international law, but for those who do, enforcing international law becomes much easier.

In addition there are at least two reasons to assume that the propensity of national judges to use norms based on international law is becoming stronger. The first is that transnational tribunals shape global public opinion. Non-governmental organisations (NGOs), academics and the media view decisions of transnational courts as representing the correct interpretation of international law. The members of these professions usually *do* form transnational networks, and naturally have allies within the state, and across national borders. Hence, the effect of transnational courts' decisions on the opinions of national judges is not achieved by pressure from the outside, but rather by affecting the views of domestic public opinion-makers, especially those who possess the most extensive transnational connections. As many observers have noted, judges take into their consideration the position of public opinion, especially of elite groups, at least to some degree. International law, as was described by Harold Koh, has to go through a process of internalisation in order to be enforced. This process of internalisation includes not only legal adoption, but also political and social adoption of international norms. NGOs, academics and media play a crucial role in the process of political and social acceptance of international norms.[54]

Joseph Weiler, analysing the development of European Community law before 1990, has pointed out another reason for the tendency of domestic courts to accept *European Community* law.[55] By extension, it may be claimed that there is a tendency of domestic courts to resort more to *international law* now that a larger number of transnational tribunals exist. Weiler showed that the reason national courts in Europe co-operated with the ECJ was in part due to the fact that the implementation of European law gave those courts more power vis-à-vis their own governments. It became much easier for them to overturn political decisions, laws and regulations. The same may be true with regard to domestic courts that use international law. These courts may credibly claim that a particular decision, unless passed of the courts' own volition, will be foisted on

[54] HH Koh, 'Why Do Nations Obey International Law?' (1997) 106 *Yale Law Journal* 2599.
[55] JHH Weiler, 'The Transformation of Europe' (1991) 100 *Yale Law Journal* 2403.

them by international tribunals. There are reasons to assume that the state prefers international law to be enforced by a domestic court rather than by an international tribunal that has no reason to show respect for domestic interests.[56]

It should be noted that these explanations are not necessarily based on the transnational tribunal *exercising* its jurisdiction. Domestic courts need only show the possibility of such international intervention in order to attain the described authority. The explanations above are not based on actual international intervention, but on the threat of such an intervention having an effect on domestic court. The level of credibility of the threat can be arguable. But the danger of such intervention, whatever the chances are of its happening, is what may give domestic courts the legitimacy to enforce international norms.

C. Israel, the United States and the United Kingdom: Three Examples of Acceptance Through Transnational Pressure—How Domestic Courts Deal with the Problem

My claim thus far has been that the appearance and strengthening of transnational tribunals would have the effect of increasing the enforcement of international law by domestic courts. This, I suggested, is true even when it is unlikely that the transnational court will actually enforce international law against the relevant state. The effectiveness of international law is enhanced by the mere existence of transnational courts, even when they do not actually enforce their decisions. If this is correct, domestic courts would be more willing to confront their own governments when the matter involves something that is within the power and authority of a transnational tribunal, as described above, than when no such jurisdiction exists.

This is, of course, a far-reaching claim, and much more extensive research is required in this area. However, it can be substantiated to some degree by reference to three examples, provided by the Israeli and US Supreme Courts, and the British House of Lords. Even when it is borne in mind that these cases might be of limited value, their thrust is clear. Although all courts had no qualms about ignoring international law in general, even against clear decisions of the ICJ, each changed its attitude when cases within the jurisdiction of an international court were involved

[56] It is possible to claim that the truth is that governments prefer international decision because domestic courts have superior enforcement capabilities, and hence international decisions are less likely to have an effect in reality. It seems to me that the reputation costs of losing a case in a transnational court are much higher than any possible gains in terms of non-enforcement in specific cases.

(1) The Israeli Supreme Court

Israel's Supreme Court has come into direct confrontation with the ICJ over the last few years. The clash was occasioned by a case centring on the Israeli-built barrier (alternatively termed a wall, or fence) intended to separate Israel from parts of the territories inhabited by Palestinians.[57] The barrier is built along the 'green line', with varying degrees of incursions into the territories at various points.[58] In its first major decision on the issue (handed down in 2004), the Israeli Supreme Court declared the barrier and its alignment to be based on security considerations, and not on political ones. Hence, the court approved the expropriation of lands needed for the construction of the barrier. On the other hand, the court disapproved of the specific route taken by the barrier, as proposed by the government, which was considered to infringe upon the rights of individual Palestinians in a manner disproportionate to the expected security gain. As a result, the court ordered the government to redraw the barrier's alignment in a way likely to cause less harm to Palestinians.[59] The Israeli Supreme Court decision was handed down less than ten days before the ICJ released its advisory opinion on the legality of the construction of the barrier.[60] This decision adopted the opposite view. It claimed that the construction of the barrier was indeed politically motivated, and hence, among other reasons, forbidden by international law. It also claimed that the barrier could not be justified on the premise that it protects Israeli settlers in the territories, since these settlements are themselves illegal. The ICJ also emphasised the negative impact of what it termed 'the wall' on the lives of Palestinians in the territories.[61]

In a later decision, handed down in 2005, the Israeli court responded to the ICJ's decision.[62] While nominally showing respect for the opinion, the Israeli court rejected the ICJ's position that the construction of the barrier was political, and defended its own view that the motives behind its construction were related to security. The Israeli Supreme Court added that its decision must not be taken to imply any rejection of a normative rule of international law, as applied by the ICJ, only of its factual positions. I think this claim is at best arguable. However, the fact remains

[57] The exact term, of course, reflects the political views of the user. The UN General Assembly in its decision used the term 'separation wall'. Israeli spokespersons usually use the term 'fence'. Some scholars use the term 'barrier', which is supposedly more neutral.

[58] See, eg, 'B'Tselem: The Separation Barrier', available at http://www.btselem.org/english/Separation_Barrier/Statistics.asp (accessed 19 September 2007).

[59] HCJ 2046/04 *Beit Surik Village Council v Government of Israel* 58(5) PD 807.

[60] *Legal Consequences of the Construction of a Wall in the Occupied Palestinian Territory*, Advisory Opinion (2004) 43 ILM 1009 (9 July 2004).

[61] For a more detailed view of the decision, see, eg, Y Shany, 'Capacities and Inadequacies: A Look at the Two Separation Barrier Cases' (2005) 38 *Israel Law Review* 230, and see generally the whole issue, no 38.

[62] HCJ 7957/04 *Mara'abe v Prime Minister of Israel* (Judgment) 15 September 2005.

that the Israeli Supreme Court flatly and expressly rejected the position of the ICJ.

It is important to compare these cases with those in which the domestic court confronted the possibility that a transnational tribunal might oversee its authority. So far the Israeli Supreme Court has changed course in several cases where it thought that an international tribunal might be willing to intervene. Thus, in a famous 1999 decision, the court altered its previous jurisprudence and declared certain interrogation techniques of Israel's General Security Service to be prohibited.[63] As Amnon Reichman has shown, this specific decision was definitely influenced by the Supreme Court's realisation that courts in other countries are willing to enforce the prohibition on torture by using universal jurisdiction.[64]

After 2000, and the eruption of the second *intifada,* the Israeli Supreme Court similarly imposed certain prohibitions and limitations on IDF actions in the territories. Of the several decisions which illustrate that policy, three warrant specific mention. First, the court adopted an almost complete ban on deportations and very strict restrictions on the transfer of population from one part of the territories to another.[65] Second, the court prohibited completely any use of civilians in assistance to the armed effort.[66] In a further decision the court ordered the army, in the midst of a military operation, to allow medical assistance and food to people in the Rafah refugee camps.[67] In all these decisions the Israeli court adopted its position based on international law. More importantly, in all these cases the international law involved is international humanitarian law, a branch of international law strongly associated with transnational adjudication.

Of course, the court did not ban all actions of the military that may have been in conflict with international law. On the contrary, it sometimes approved military action, most controversially so when sanctioning the policy of targeted killings.[68] The latter decision is interesting because although the court allowed the policy of targeted killing to proceed in principle, it set limits on the use of this policy based on the principle of proportionality.[69] Specifically, the Court ruled that targeted killings may be used only if the possible damage to the civilian population would be

[63] HCJ 5100/94 *The Public Committee against Torture v Government of Israel* 53(4) PD 817.

[64] A Reichman, 'When We Sit to Judge, We Are Being Judged' (2001) 9 *Cardozo Journal of International and Comparative Law* 41.

[65] HCJ 7015/02 *Ajuri et al v IDF Commander in the West Bank* (Judgement) 3 September 2002, see E Benvenisti, 'Scrutiny: Ajuri et al' (2003) 9(4) *European Public Law* 481.

[66] HCJ 3799/02 *Adalah—The Legal Center for Arab Minority Rights in Israel v GOC Central Command* (Judgment) 23 June 2005.

[67] HCJ 4764/04 *Physicians for Human Rights v Commander of IDF in Gaza* 58(5) PD 385.

[68] HCJ 769/02 *Public Committee against Torture in Israel v Government of Israel* (Judgment) 14 December 2006.

[69] For a more detailed description of the court's requirements, see A Cohen and Y Shany, 'A Development of Modest Proportions' (2007) 5 *Journal of International Criminal Justice* 310.

proportional to the gains from the operation. The use of proportionality in this case deserves attention: proportionality is a term recognised by international tribunals, although one that is very difficult to apply.[70] On the other hand, it provides a means for courts to allow intervention in specific operations and review actions. The court has therefore used proportionality to tighten its grip on military operations. Once again, we see that international law is used in a way that strengthens the position of domestic courts.

It is important to note that not all of these actions were based on international law. On the contrary, the interrogation techniques decision[71] consciously avoids being based on international law, and focuses almost exclusively on Israeli law. As I will point out later, I do not think this is insignificant. The court purposely chose *not* to base its decision on international law. The end result, however, is that the Israeli Supreme Court applied international humanitarian law in precisely those areas in which transnational judicial organs have been most active.[72]

(2) The United States Supreme Court

Similar phenomena can be detected in the US Supreme Court. Like the Israeli Supreme Court, the US court directly clashed with the ICJ in one specific instance: cases involving 'consular notification'. According to the Vienna Convention on Consular Relations,[73] when a foreign national is arrested, the detaining state must give notification to the detained person's home country consul. The US, although party to this agreement, has notoriously disregarded the 'consular notification' obligation, principally because the persons responsible for enforcing the relevant law are local and state police officers, with little knowledge of or interest in the obligations of the US as laid down in the Vienna Convention. Famously, the Supreme Court refused to intervene in state cases, even when a foreign national was sentenced to death without being allowed to see his country's consul.[74] The court arrived at this position notwithstanding two

[70] The sole exception is the discussion of proportionality in the case of *Kuperškić*, ICTY (Judgment) 14 January 2000, para 524. Even in this case, there were other reasons for criminal liability.

[71] Above n 63.

[72] I do not claim that there are no international judicial organs dealing with international trade law (of course there are) and that human rights issues are not discussed in national courts of countries other the ones in which violations of human rights occurred (they are). My claim is that strong transnational adjudication, based on the principle of complementary jurisdiction, is evident mainly in cases of war crimes (ie, grave violations of international humanitarian law) or grave violations of human rights. In other cases there is no credible threat of transnational courts substituting the jurisdiction of domestic courts, except *perhaps* in Europe.

[73] Vienna Convention on Consular Relations (adopted 24 April 1963, entered into force 19 March 1967) Art 36, para (1)–(2), 21 UST 77, 100–01, 596 UNTS 261, 292–3.

[74] *Breard v Greene*, 523 US 371, 375 (1998) (per curiam).

clear ICJ decisions that specifically prohibited the US from executing such persons.[75] The Supreme Court stressed that it is not bound by ICJ decisions. Lower courts, when faced with a growing number of cases, have consistently managed to avoid any enforcement of the Vienna Convention in accordance with the decisions of the ICJ.[76] There is not even one known case where any court accepted the claim that failure to notify suspects of their rights would disqualify their confessions.

Cases involving the Guantánamo prisoners, on the other hand, reveal the existence of an entirely different strain at work in the US federal system.[77] In these cases the Supreme Court, again faced with the clear divergence of US policy from international law, cited American law in order to overrule the decision of the government to bar habeas corpus claims on the part of Guantánamo prisoners.

An even more interesting case is the *Hamdan* case.[78] In this case the US Supreme Court declared that the military commissions created by the President to judge persons connected with Al-Qaeda lack the power to proceed because their structure and procedure violate relevant US laws. Specifically it is interesting to note that the court declared that one of the reasons that the military commissions should not be allowed to proceed is because they violate the Geneva Conventions. The court decided that Common Article 3 of the Geneva Conventions requires due-process rights which the military commissions do not provide.[79] Most interesting in this case is that the court, in order to understand the proper meaning of the terms of the laws of war, refers both to the interpretation adopted by the official commentary of the International Committee of the Red Cross,[80] and, and even more importantly, to the jurisprudence of the international criminal tribunal in Nuremberg.[81]

[75] The ICJ handed two decisions specifically prohibiting the United States from executing foreign nationals convicted in committing murder (*Case concerning Avena and other Mexican Nationals* (Mexico v US) 2004 ICJ 128 (3 March 2004); *LaGrand Case* (FRG v US), 2001 ICJ 104, para 91 (June 27 2001)). The US Supreme Court rejected this decision in the Breard case (above n 74). In a recent case the court once again refused to deal with the issue (*Jose Ernesto Medellin v Dretke* 544 US (2005)).

[76] AN Bishop, 'The Unenforceable Rights to Consular Notification and Action in the United States: What Changed Since the LaGrand Case?' (2002) 25 *Houston Journal of International Law* 1.

[77] *Hamdi v Rumsfeld* 542 US 507 (2004).

[78] *Hamdan v Rumsfeld* 548 US (2006); 126 S Ct 2749 (2006).

[79] Specifically the court concluded that the provisions in the military commission violate the Common Article 3 requirements according to which persons accused of war crimes should be tried before 'regularly constituted court affording all the judicial guarantees which are recognized as indispensable by civilized peoples'.

[80] Part IV(D)(iii) to the opinion of Justice Stevens, learning from the ICRC commentary to the Geneva Conventions that Common Article 3 applies to all non-international armed conflicts, including those which are not internal.

[81] Part III to the opinion of Justice Stevens (using the jurisprudence of the Nuremberg court to prove that conspiracy to commit a crime is usually not a war crime).

This is not to argue that the US Supreme Court actually arrived at a specific decision because it feared the interference of the International Criminal Court.[82] What the case does suggest, however, is that the emergence of International Criminal Tribunals provided the judges of the US Supreme Court with a greater degree of certainty that their clash with their government could be justified, because of the perceived potential of the International Criminal Court to intervene as well as the support of public opinion.

(3) The United Kingdom House of Lords

British courts have also been under pressure from transnational tribunals, especially the ECHR. The way in which they have begun to respond is most strikingly illustrated by the recent decision of the House of Lords in the *Al-Skeini* case.[83]

Arising out of the UK's presence in Iraq following the 2003 Iraq war, the *Al-Skeini* case concerns an appeal to the UK courts against a decision on the part of the British government not to investigate illegalities in the death of several Iraqi nationals. It is clear to all justices and courts that the shadow of the ECHR looms over this case. The appellants clearly state that if denied redress in UK courts, they would turn to Strasbourg. Hence, the House of Lords in its own judgment, clearly states that it is aware of the possibility that an appeal against its decision could be lodged with the ECHR.

The major question in *Al-Skeini* is the jurisdiction of the UK's Human Rights Act (1998), which purported to implement the European Convention on Human Rights. It is clear to the House of Lords that the ECHR's jurisprudence dictates that the Convention applies at least towards one of the applicants,[84] because he was in the custody of UK forces at the time of his death. Hence, his death should be investigated. The government's contention was that the Human Rights Act has a different, more limited jurisdiction, and that it therefore covers only conduct occurring within the territory of the UK. The majority of the court decided, however, that interpretation of the jurisdictional clause of the British statute should be

[82] See text above next to n 56. It is not probable that the prosecutor of the ICC would decide in the near future to prosecute a case against the United States or Israel, which are both not Member States of the ICC. Even if the legal obstacles to such a case could be overcome, the political ramifications would be enormous. See, eg, DF Orentilcher, 'Unilateral Multilateralism: United States Policy Toward the International Criminal Court' (2004) 36 *Cornell Journal of International Law* 415.

[83] *Al-Skeini v Secretary of State for Defence* (Decision) 13 June 2007.

[84] The relevant case is the *Banković* case [*Banković v Belgium and others*, (2001) 11 BHRC 435, 445–50, paras 65–70], according to which the conventions covers all acts taken in territories controlled by a Member State of the convention.

decided according to the jurisprudence of the Strasbourg Court, perhaps even contrary to the plain meaning of the Act.

Courts do not always set down the full policy considerations behind their decisions. *Al-Skeini* is a striking decision because it makes very clear that the court uses the possibility of a case going to the ECHR in order to widen the scope of its own jurisdiction. The court explicitly interprets the national law in a way that would be commensurate with the interpretation of the ECHR. It is also evident that the main motivation behind the decision is the possibility that the case might be dealt with by the transnational tribunal. The House of Lords uses this possibility as a leverage to increase its own jurisdiction and authority.

I propose that it is possible to discern a pattern here, which suggests—although it cannot of course be proven—the process that domestic courts are going through. When the ICJ gives a ruling, courts do not feel obligated to comply. But the solution to the question of implementing international law in courts is not to enforce it by a superior court. What we are witnessing here is a system of enforced independence and sovereignty. Domestic courts are implementing international law because they can now build on the possibility of it being heard in an international court. They can justify their decision, to themselves, as not having been borne out of international pressure, but the opposite. They can build on domestic and international support, and they may assume that they do not put their own country at a disadvantage.[85] The current system of *transnational* tribunals allows domestic courts to assert sovereignty. To put matters another way, they can control actions of governments with the *help* of international courts, but not with their *interference.* This situation provides domestic courts with a reason, a justification and an incentive to take on the implementation of international law. What is also important to note is that both in the US case of Hamdi and in the Israeli case of the Public Committee against Torture, international law was not evident as the basis of the decision. In deciding to overrule the decision of the government, the court clearly attempts to base its decision on domestic laws, which are considered more legitimate. International law remained in the background, yet ever-present. Decisions of domestic courts do not have to be based on international law, nor even to cite it, in order to better implement it. The central point is that the judicial result is compatible with international law.

The next part of this paper explores the wider context of this change in judicial attitude.

[85] See above text next to n 49, and the footnote, for a detailed discussion of this point.

V. THE NEW MEANING OF SOVEREIGNTY

A. International Law vs Domestic Sovereignty?

Some scholars maintain that the emergence of strong international tribunals undermines the concept of domestic sovereignty. It is a common enough position that international organisations, and especially international courts, create a zero-sum game with sovereignty. One either supports domestic sovereignty or is in favour of enhanced international control. There are two sides to this coin, of course. One is represented by supporters of domestic sovereignty; the other by advocates of greater levels of international co-operation.

'It is well past the point when the unrestrained and uncritical acceptance of Globalist slogans can be allowed to proceed' writes John Bolton, formerly US permanent representative to the UN,

> the costs to the United States—impaired constitutional autonomy, reduced popular sovereignty . . . and limitations on our domestic and international policy solutions—are far too great . . .[86]

On a different occasion he warned that

> [the ICC is] an organization that runs contrary to fundamental American precepts and basic constitutional principles of popular sovereignty, checks and balances, and national independence.[87]

Hence, Bolton contrasts global legalisation with sovereignty and claims that international courts force states to act against their interests and impinge their right to sovereign independence. Although his statements might be more straightforward than those of others, Bolton is surely not alone in voicing such views.[88]

On the other side of the debate, there are those who claim that sovereignty should be curtailed in order to allow international co-operation to evolve. According to some scholars, claims of sovereignty hinder international co-operation and globalisation.[89] Since the middle of the

[86] JR Bolton, 'Should We Take Global Governance Seriously?' (2000) 1 *Chicago Journal of International Law* 205, 221.

[87] JR Bolton, *American Justice and the International Criminal Court*, Remarks at the American Enterprise Institute (3 November 2003), available at http://www.state.gov/t/us/rm/25818.htm.

[88] For other, perhaps less blunt statements, though with practically the same conclusions, see, eg, EA Young, 'The Trouble with Global Constitutionalism' (2003) 38 *Texas International Law Journal* 527, 542.

[89] Louis Henkin famously claimed that: 'Sovereignty has also grown a mythology of state grandeur and aggrandizement that misconceives the concept and clouds what is authentic and worthy in it, a mythology that is often empty and sometimes destructive of human values . . . away with the 'S' word!' [March–May 1993] *Newsletter of the ASIL* 1, 6–7.

twentieth century many international lawyers have directed their efforts towards criticising and limiting the concept of state sovereignty, which they portray as the major barrier to the international protection of human rights. Sovereignty represents the vices of the old world, and its supporters are opposed to the adoption of more humane universal standards.

Contrary to this dichotomy, I suggest that the relationship between international co-operation and sovereignty is more complex. Sovereignty has never meant the total autonomy of the nation state. As Stephan Krasner once claimed:

> Rulers have always operated in a transnational environment; autarky has rarely been an option; regulation and monitoring of transborder flows have always been problematic. The difficulties for states have become more acute in some areas, but less in others.[90]

Sovereignty has always been a term used by states and rulers to define their role in this world of co-operation. It has rarely been the practice of states to operate alone, and it is not so now. States were always coerced to take actions by other states, by international institutions, and by the needs of an economy that in order to evolve has always required some measure of compromise on certain state interests, in order to achieve greater utilities. Sovereignty in the international law sense was an attempt to find the correct division of authority and power between international institutions and domestic ones.[91] Hence, sovereignty as a legal and political term does not always reflect a position adversarial to international co-operation. On the contrary, it was a term that allowed states to co-operate internationally.

This is not to deny that globalisation weakens the national state. Of course it does. But the equation that more international law and organisations means less domestic sovereignty is not always correct.[92] In fact, in some areas states are strengthened by international organisations, not weakened by them (as is illustrated by the example of Luxembourg, a small state that became part of a larger international organisation, the EU). Moreover, the judiciary constitutes one of the main networks in which international co-operation leads to the strengthening of domestic sovereignty. This, indeed, is one of the meanings of the new legal sovereignty. This term does not imply that courts can decide on domestic

[90] SD Krasner, *Sovereignty: Organized Hypocrisy* (Princeton University Press, 1999) 223.

[91] JP Trachtman, 'Reflections on the Nature of the State: Sovereignty, Power and Responsibility' (1994) 20 *Canada-United States Law Journal* 399.

[92] Slaughter's theory of transnational networks is all about the displacement of the traditional state with a new 'disaggregated state' where international co-operation between epistemic communities and similarly minded bureaucrats is what moves the world. Slaughter, *A New World Order*, above n 28, 12, 15. As I have already pointed out, I do not think Slaughter's claim is particularly convincing with regard to judicial transnational networks.

policy entirely independent of any international law or opinion—which in fact was anyway rarely the case in the past. Rather, it signifies that it is now *the domestic court* which takes the final decisions about policy, and not some international organisation or network. Moreover, it does so—at least in part—in consideration of international law, rather than national politics. Hence, the emergence of transnational jurisdiction does not signify annulment of domestic sovereignty. It is more a shift of domestic decision-making from national governments to courts. Courts now represent domestic decision-making in certain aspects of foreign relations.

As I have already explained, when faced with the emergence of transnational tribunals domestic courts assume more responsibility, and hence strengthen their position. Indeed, if we are to adopt Joseph Weiler's position,[93] courts can be quite pleased to have a justification for enforcing international law and thereby change their governments' policies. By so doing, they measurably augment their own domestic status and power.

Whether this shift is to be considered a positive one, and what its normative implications might be, are questions that of course have to be approached from two different perspectives: one that supports the implementation of international law, and the other that favours the independence of state decision-making

B. An International Perspective

From an international perspective, the implementation of international law by domestic courts possesses one dominant disadvantage: it introduces the dangers of anarchy. After all, were every state to be allowed to implement international law independently, without the existence of hierarchical institutions, international law might evolve into many international laws. Every state would adopt its own jurisprudence of what international law really is. If certainty and a unified body of international law are required, then a supremacy-based system must be developed.

Despite this disadvantage, implementation of international law by domestic courts has some clear *advantages* that in my opinion outweigh the disadvantage discussed above. For one thing, in the current state of international politics states are unlikely to agree to a court in possession of real supremacy.[94] A system that empowers domestic courts to implement international law is far preferable to having no system at all.

But even were a truly supranational system possible, we might still wish to see international law being implemented by domestic courts. This is because outside coercion can hardly be considered conducive to the

[93] That of Joseph Weiler, above n 21.

[94] Once again, the success of the concept of supremacy in Europe is due, I think, to the unique characteristics of the states forming the European Community.

true acceptance of international law by citizens of the state or its institutions. As Harold Koh explained, in order for international law to be effective, it must be internalised through domestic institutions, politics and law.[95] For example, one of the ingenious achievements of the European Community, and possibly the major reason that led to its success, was that it delegated enforcement to domestic courts. Hence domestic courts became agents of the implementation of European law within the country, and the success of the European law became their interest.[96] If one supports the real implementation of international law, domestic institutions implementing international law must be strengthened.

C. A Domestic Perspective

As pointed out above, the emerging system of transnational tribunals accords precedence to domestic courts. This fuels anxiety amongst opponents, as well as supporters, of a stronger international system. This is because the processes that I have described imply that national courts can use international law in order to overcome and oppose the policies of the elected domestic government. Hence, the specific anxiety is that national *courts* are getting stronger than national *governments*. This, it is claimed, runs contrary to democratic principles and traditional divisions of power.

Several observations need to be made with regard to these claims. Firstly, criticism about the power of national courts is almost as old as their existence. Governments have always claimed that national courts wield too much power over elected institutions. Secondly, from the point of view that supports national independence, situations in which decisions are made by national courts are far preferable to those in which they are made by international tribunals. Thirdly, national governments profit from judicial review. It gives them legitimacy, by portraying them as institutions acting in accordance with legal and moral norms, and not in response to some narrow national interests. Moreover, transnational tribunals already exist. Supporters of national independence and sovereignty would therefore do well not to attempt to fight the unavoidable, but to work at strengthening the national judicial system. Finally, and most important, is the observation about the legal basis of the commitment to international law. Given that there is some moral or contractual obligation to follow international law, it is the role of the judge to enforce this rule. After all, governments undertake the initial commitments, not courts.

[95] See, eg, HH Koh, 'Bringing International Law Home' (1998) 35 *Houston Law Review* 623.

[96] AS Sweet, *The Judicial Construction of Europe* (Oxford University Press, 2004); Also Weiler above n 55.

In addition to these observations, there is a further reason why implementation of international law by domestic courts should be viewed positively, from a domestic perspective. The democratic system allows courts to enjoy a certain amount of trust. Precisely because they are not subjected to constant elections every four years, they are considered to be keepers of higher values and guardians of the constitution. They prevent day-to-day politics from intruding into the area of what Bruce Ackerman has termed 'higher politics'.[97] Discourse about international law and its application within a state, especially where human rights and humanitarian law are involved, should take place in the sphere of higher politics. Indeed, a court might overturn a specific governmental decision. When such a judgement is deemed truly harmful to national interests, the government will overturn it. Necessarily, any such process would require deliberate action, and involve considerable public discussion and argument. But this is so much the better. After all, where human rights are involved, public discussion and argument are exactly what is desired.

D. A Compound Perspective

As already mentioned, Anne-Marie Slaughter views the 'new world order' as one in which the term national sovereignty loses its importance. The world is built around a web of transnational networks. My own view is that even if this description is correct with respect to governments at large, it does not reflect how domestic courts behave in practice.

I contend that domestic courts retain a very important position in 'the new world order'. They become the branch of government that actually safeguards sovereignty. Contrary to Slaughter, I claim that it is not transnational judicial networks which matter, but rather the emergence of transnational tribunals. Courts can gain sovereignty, and become the true representative of the state. If Slaughter is correct, than courts are actually the *only* true representatives of national sovereignty. They are the bodies that combine international law and co-operation with domestic values. Precisely because they are able to retain their independence, courts are agents of the internalisation of international law. The future of international law in the democratic world relies on the success of these agents, not on the creation of hierarchical institutions. If courts could internalise international law, as they did in Europe, then there exists a chance that the project of international law might succeed. As institutions in possession of both national and international legitimacy, domestic courts can combine these legal systems.

[97] BA Ackerman, *We the People*, vol 1: *Foundations* (Cambridge, MA, Harvard University Press, 1990).

The success of this project depends on the existence of an independent judiciary. In the absence of an independent national judicial system, no domestic court can force the government to act in accordance with its international obligations. Hence, the model that we have outlined here works only in those states that possess what we consider to be an independent judiciary. Without independence of courts, the internalisation of international law cannot succeed.

Hence, the main project of international law should be the strengthening of domestic courts. Ultimately, it is on the independence of those bodies that the success of international law depends.

IV
Allocations of Authority in Specific Normative Contexts

12

Regionalism, Economic Interdependence, Approximation of Laws and their Impact on Sovereignty, National Identity, and Legitimacy: The Euro-Med *Case*

GUY HARPAZ*

I. INTRODUCTION

IN RECENT YEARS the EU has offered its neighbouring Mediterranean countries enhanced trade and political relations. In return, it expects them, inter alia, to align their national legislation, regulatory practices and standards, to an extent yet to be determined,

* Jean Monnet Lecturer, Law Faculty and the Department of International Relations, Hebrew University of Jerusalem and President of the Israeli Association for the Study of European Integration. The article was first presented in the Conference 'Sovereignty, Supremacy, Subsidiarity: The Shifting Allocation of Authority in International Law', Hebrew University, Jerusalem, 19 June 2006. I would like to express my gratitude for the helpful comments made by Yuval Shany, Tomer Broude, Michal Gal, Lior Herman and Moshe Hirsch on prior drafts, for the instructive research assistance of Alon Unfus, Carmel Shenkar and Asaf Shamis, and for the insightfil remarks expressed by participants at the Conference. I am also grateful for the generous support given by the EU under the aegis of the Jean Monnet Action, by the Leonard Davis Institute for International Relations of the Hebrew University of Jerusalem and by the University Institute for Diplomacy and Regional Co-operation, Tel Aviv University. The usual caveat applies. For legal analysis of approximation of laws, see G Harpaz, 'When East Meets West—Approximation of Laws in the Euro-Mediterranean Context' (2006) 43 *Common Market Law Review* 1. For an international relations' analysis, see G Harpaz, 'EU-Med Approximation of Laws: A Realist Perspective' (2007) 9/3 *European Journal of Law Reform* (forthcoming). For a more focused analysis of the interface between approximation of laws and sovereignty, see G Harpaz, 'Approximation of Laws to the EU *Acquis*, Extraterritorial Europeanization and the Erosion of National Sovereignty', paper submitted to the International Joint Conference of the Czech Association of European Studies and the Israeli Association for the Study of European Integration 'Integrating with Europe' (forthcoming).

with its *acquis communautaire*.[1] Such a legislative move may bring these countries much benefit,[2] and yet it may prove to be challenging, complex, problematic and disadvantageous in terms of erosion of sovereignty, national identity and legitimacy. This chapter is devoted to an analysis of these potential repercussions. The analysis focuses on Israeli–EU relations, yet some of its findings may be found to be applicable, *mutatis mutandis*, to other countries in the Mediterranean region and elsewhere that are facing legislative pressures from the EU or major trading nations with which they have asymmetric economic, trade and political relations.

II. APPROXIMATION OF LAWS

Harmonisation of laws may be defined as the process of making different domestic laws, regulations, principles and government policies the same or substantially similar.[3] In the course of this process, features of different legal systems are reconciled.[4]

Legislative convergence can be a mutual, co-operative process under which countries attempt to bridge legal differences (commonly termed harmonisation of laws). Alternatively, it may constitute a one-way process, whereby one country adopts the laws of another (commonly termed approximation of laws, or legal transplant).[5]

The EU is a fine example of regional integration under which extensive co-operative harmonisation of laws has continuously been performed. In the EU this process has gone beyond merely reducing legislative differences and adopting common legislative instruments, to enter the realm of harmonising Member States' policies, regulatory schemes and institutions. Harmonisation of laws within the EU may thus be seen as a co-operative process of creating a quasi-federal European legal system, which contributes, in turn, to the positive integration of the internal market, and consequently to socio-political integration.[6]

[1] G Harpaz, 'When East Meets West—Approximation of Laws in the Euro-Mediterranean Context' (2006) 43 *Common Market Law Review* 1.

[2] *Ibid.*

[3] G Mayeda, 'Developing Disharmony? The SPS and TBT Agreements and the Impact of Harmonization on Developing Countries' (2004) 7 *Journal of International Economic Law* 737; D Leebron, 'Claims for Harmonization: A Theoretical Framework' (1996) 27 *Canadian Business Law Journal* 63.

[4] M Boodman, 'The Myth of Harmonization of Laws' (1991) 39 *American Journal of Comparative Law* 699, 703.

[5] A Watson, *Legal Transplants—An Approach to Comparative Law* (London, University of Georgia Press, 1974); O Kahn-Freund, 'On Uses and Misuses of Comparative Law' (1974) 37 *MLR* 1; A Watson, 'Legal Transplants and Law Reform' (1980) 92 *LQR* 79; D Berkowitz, K Pistor and JF Richard, 'The Transplant Effect' (2003) 51 *American Journal of Comparative Law* 163; W Twining, 'Diffusion and Globalization Discourse' (2006) 47 *Harvard Journal of International Law* 507.

[6] DM Walker, *The Oxford Companion to Law* (Oxford, Clarendon Press, 1980) 72.

This legislative process is, however, rather different in the Euro-Med context. As demonstrated below, it constitutes a one-way process under which the Community's Mediterranean neighbours are expected to bring their legislation closer to that of the EU, and not vice versa.

III. APPROXIMATION OF LAWS IN THE EURO-MEDITERRANEAN CONTEXT

Bilateral relations between the EU and its neighbours in the Middle East and North Africa are governed by Association Agreements (the Euro-Med Association Agreements). Under the Euro-Med Association Agreements, the EU and the Mediterranean countries granted one another preferential economic, commercial and technological status. The core of each Euro-Med Association Agreement is a bilateral free trade agreement relating to industrial goods. A legal framework for liberalisation of trade in agricultural goods, of services and of movement of capital is also provided for.

Each and every Euro-Med Association Agreement provides a general legal basis for the approximation of laws between the two respective parties. The EU-Israel Association Agreement, for example, includes a provision that stipulates that '[t]he Parties shall use their best endeavours to approximate their respective legislations in order to facilitate the implementation of this Agreement'.[7] The general call for approximation of laws provided for under Euro-Med Association Agreements is supported by more specific provisions scattered throughout these Agreements. The EU-Israel Association Agreement, for example, calls for approximation of laws in specific sectors, such as intellectual property,[8] agriculture,[9] standards,[10] financial services[11] and combating drug-trafficking[12] and money laundering.[13] Similar legal arrangements for approximation of laws can also be found in the EU-Algeria Association Agreements[14] and EU-Tunisia Association Agreement.[15]

[7] See Art 55 of the EU-Israel Association Agreement, EU-Israel Association Agreement (1995) Euro-Mediterranean Agreement establishing an association between the European Communities and their Member States, on the one part, and the State of Israel, on the other part, Official Journal L 147, 21 June 2000, 0003–0171.

[8] See, eg, Art 39, EU-Israel Association Agreement.

[9] See, eg, Art 46, EU-Israel Association Agreement.

[10] See, eg, Art 47, EU-Israel Association Agreement.

[11] See, eg, Art 48, EU-Israel Association Agreement.

[12] See, eg, Art 56, EU-Israel Association Agreement.

[13] See, eg, Art 56, EU-Israel Association Agreement.

[14] See, eg, Arts 56 and 57, the EC-Algerian Association Agreement, available at http://ec.europa.eu/external_relations/algeria/docs/assoc_art.pdf (accessed 12 July 2007).

[15] See, eg example, Arts 51–3, the EC-Tunisian Association Agreement, available at http://trade.ec.europa.eu/doclib/docs/2006/march/tradoc_127986.pdf (accessed 12 July 2007).

The European Neighbourhood Policy (ENP),[16] launched in 2003 in order to upgrade relations between the EU and its neighbours in North Africa, the Middle East and Eastern Europe, intensified legislative pressure from the EU:

> In return for concrete progress demonstrating shared values and effective implementation of political, economic and institutional reforms, including aligning legislation with the *acquis*, the EU's neighbours should benefit from the prospect of closer economic integration with the EU.[17]

The various Action Plans,[18] signed under the aegis of the ENP with the neighbouring countries, increase the pressures upon these states to approximate their laws to those of the EU.[19] Recent EU official statements,[20] working papers and reports,[21] issued under the ENP, all

[16] For analysis, see G Harpaz, 'The Europe Neighborhood Policy and its Impact on the Israeli-European Union-United States Triangle' (2005) 6 *San Diego International Law Journal* 295; A Magen, 'The Shadow of Enlargement: Can European Neighbourhood Policy Achieve Compliance?' (2006) 12 *Columbia Journal of European Journal* 495.

[17] Communication from the Commission to the Council and the European Parliament, Wider Europe-Neighbourhood: A New Framework for Relations with our Eastern and Southern Neighbours, COM(2003) 104 final (2003), 10.

[18] Action Plans, based on the Strategy Report and the relevant Country Report, provided a specific outline of reciprocal social, political and economic commitments between the EU and the relevant neighbouring state, covering political dialogue, economic and social development policy, trade, and justice and home affairs.

[19] For the text of the Actions Plans, see http://ec.europa.eu/world/enp/documents_en.htm (accessed 6 June 2007). See, eg, Section I (Introduction) of the EU-Israel Action Plan (2005), available at http://ec.europa.eu/world/enp/documents_en.htm (accessed 6 June 2007). The Action Plan with Israel was endorsed by the Commission, by the Government of Israel and by the EC-Israel Association Council. The EU-Israel Action Plan, which involves 'a significant measure of economic integration and a deepening of political co-operation', is aimed at the fulfilment of the 1994 Essen Declaration in which the EU announced its willingness to establish special relations with Israel. More specifically, the EU-Israeli Action Plan provides for enhanced political dialogue and co-operation, increased economic integration, enhanced co-operation in justice and home affairs, greater integration of Israel to EU programmes and schemes, and improved people-to-people interactions. See also Section I of the EU-Jordan Action Plan, available at http://ec.europa.eu/world/enp/documents_en.htm (2004) (accessed 6 June 2007); Section I of the EU-Morocco Action Plan, available at http://ec.europa.eu/world/enp/documents_en.htm (2004) (accessed 6 June 2007); EU-Lebanon Action Plan, 1–3, 10, available at http://ec.europa.eu/world/enp/pdf/lebanon_enp_ap_final_en.pdf (2004) (accessed 6 June 2007); EU-Palestinian Authority Action Plan, 1, available at http://ec.europa.eu/world/enp/pdf/action_plans/pa_enp_ap_final_en.pdf (2004) (accessed 6 June 2007).

[20] See, eg, D Hübner, 'The Essential Role of the Community Conditionality in the Triumph of Democracy and Market Economy', Conference on European Strategies for Promoting Democracy in Postcommunist Countries, Vienna, 21 January 2006, SPEECH/06/27, available at http://europa.eu/rapid/pressReleasesAction.do?reference=SPEECH/06/27&format=HTML&aged=0&language=EN&guiLanguage=en.

[21] Commission of the European Communities Staff Working Document (2006) accompanying the Communication from the Commission to the Council and to the European Parliament on Strengthening the European Neighbourhood Policy, Overall Assessment, Brussels 4 December 2006 SEC(2006) 1504/2, available at http://ec.europa.eu/world/enp/documents_en.htm 5; Commission of the European Communities Staff Working Document (2006) accompanying the Communication from the Commission to the Council and to the

recognise, albeit in vaguer terms,[22] the link between the offer of enhanced trade and investment relations and legislative and regulatory convergence with the EU.[23]

It must be emphasised that the EU is not the only entity exerting legislative pressures on the non-EU Mediterranean countries. The United States, the World Trade Organization (WTO), as well as other international organisations and non-governmental organisations (NGOs), supported by global market forces, all place such pressures on the legal systems of these countries.[24]

The legislative pressure exerted by the EU has not gone unnoticed by the non-EU Mediterranean countries. Let us take, for example, the case of Israel. Since the conclusion of the EU-Israel Association Agreement in 1995, Israel has moved in the direction of EU legislation in certain areas, including standards,[25] competition law,[26] environmental law,[27] animal protection[28] and money-laundering legislation.[29]

European Parliament on Strengthening the European Neighbourhood Policy, Sectoral Progress Report, Brussels 4 December, 2006 SEC(2006) 1512/2, available at http://ec.europa.eu/world/enp/documents_en.htm, 2–4; Commission of the European Communities Staff Working Document (2006) accompanying the Communication from the Commission to the Council and to the European Parliament on Strengthening the European Neighbourhood Policy, ENP Progress Report, Ukraine, Brussels, 4 December, 2006 SEC (2006) 1505/2, available at http://ec.europa.eu/world/enp/documents_en.htm, 10–14; Commission of the European Communities Staff Working Document (2006) accompanying the Communication from the Commission to the Council and to the European Parliament on Strengthening the European Neighbourhood Policy, ENP Progress Report, Israel, Brussels, 29 November, SEC(2006) 1507/2, available at http://ec.europa.eu/world/enp/documents_ en.htm, 3.

22 Magen, above n 16, 526–8, who analyses the gradual softening of EU linkage between approximation of laws and economic integration under the ENP.

23 Commission of the European Communities Communication from the Commission to the Council and to the European Parliament on Strengthening the European Neighbourhood Policy, Brussels, 4 December 2006, COM(2006) 726 final, available at http://ec.europa.eu/world/enp/documents_en.htm, 4–5 (accessed 6 June 2007): 'Deeper Economic Integration with our ENP partners will be central to the success and credibility of the policy. From the outset, a key premise of the ENP was that economic integration should go beyond free trade in goods and services to also include "behind the border" issues: addressing non-tariff barriers and progressively achieving comprehensive convergence in trade and regulatory areas (such as technical norms and standards, sanitary and phytosanitary rules, competition policy, enterprise competitiveness, innovation and industrial policy, research cooperation, intellectual property rights, trade facilitation customs measures and administrative capacity in the area of rules of origin, good governance in the tax area, company law, public procurement and financial services). The objective would ultimately be that our partners share a common regulatory basis and similar degree of market access.'

24 A Reich, 'Globalization and Law: The Future Impact of International Law on Israel's Commercial Law' (2001) 17 *Bar-Ilan Legal Studies* 17, 27–29 [in Hebrew].

25 H Hadar, *The European Union and its Activities in Product Certification, Standardization and Accreditation* (Tel-Aviv, Shaba, 2002) [in Hebrew].

26 See M Gal, 'Size Does Matter: The Effects of Market Size on Optimal Competition Policy' (2001) 74 *University of Southern California Law Review* 1437, 1477.

27 See O Perez, 'The WTO and the Environment: Lessons for the State of Israel' (2003), available at http://www.biu.ac.il/law/unger/working_papers/3–02.doc (accessed 1 August 2007).

28 G Harpaz and R Frid, 'Case Note—The Israeli Supreme Court Judgment on Force-Feeding of Geese' (2004) 10 *International Trade Law and Regulation* N-2–3.

29 See Explanatory Notes of the 2000 money laundering legislation, Number 2809, 1999, 420,

It is submitted that any further implementation of the concept of approximation of laws in the EU-Med context could change the nature of the prevailing legal regimes of the non-EU Mediterranean countries, including that of Israel, and bring them closer than ever to that of the EU *acquis*. Such consequences may bring these countries much benefit in terms of trade and economy, among other things.[30] Yet, as described below, there may also be problematic repercussions in terms of erosion of sovereignty, national identity and legitimacy.

IV. APPROXIMATION OF LAWS AND SOVEREIGNTY

A. The Concept of Sovereignty

The concept of sovereignty has always puzzled philosophers, political scientists, jurists, historians and theorists in international relations.[31] Scholars analyse and qualify this concept through its own contestable elements: legal versus political sovereignty, external versus internal sovereignty, indivisible versus divisible sovereignty, and governmental versus popular sovereignty.[32]

Sovereignty relates to the state's general independence from and legal impermeability in relation to foreign powers, its exclusive jurisdiction and supremacy of governmental powers over its territory and inhabitants, a monopoly over fundamental political decisions, as well as over legislative, executive and judiciary powers, and the right to determine its political, cultural and socio-economic identities, both current and future.[33]

Lake perceived sovereignty as a type of authority relationship.[34] Inter-

at 422. For analysis, see L Herman, 'World Money Laundering and Israel' (2002) 117 *The Israeli Tax Quarterly* 7 [in Hebrew].

30 Harpaz, above n 1.

31 N Walker, *Sovereignty in Transition* (Oxford, Hart Publishing, 2003); DA Lake, 'The New Sovereignty in International Relations' (2003) 5 *International Studies Review* 303; H Spruyt, *The Sovereign State and its Competitors: An Analysis of Systems Change* (Princeton University Press, 1994); TL Ilgen (ed), *Reconfigured Sovereignty—Multilayer Governance in the Global Age* (Aldershot, Ashgate, 2003); A Osiander, 'Sovereignty, International Relations, and the Westphalian Myth' (2001) 55 *International Organization* 251; J Bartelson, 'The Concept of Sovereignty Revisited' (2006) 17 *European Journal of International Law* 463; D Sarooshi, 'Sovereignty, Economic Autonomy, the United States, and the International Trading System: Representations of a Relationship' (2004) 15 *European Journal of International Law* 651.

32 Sarooshi, above n 31, 653, analysing the works of Besson. See also J Ruggie, 'Continuity and Transformation in the World Polity: Toward a Neorealist Synthesis' in RO Keohance (ed), *Neorealism and its Critics* (New York, Columbia University Press, 1986) 131, 143 and Lake, above n 31, 304–05.

33 See H Steinberger, 'Sovereignty' in R Bernhardt (ed), 4 *Encyclopedia of Public International Law* (Amsterdam, Elsevier, 2000) 500, 502, 507 and 515.

34 See Lake, above n 31, 304–05.

nally, it defines the highest authority within a state, while externally it serves as a social concept, as it entails the recognition by other similarly recognised states that the sovereign state is 'one of them'.

Krasner identified four different meanings of the term sovereignty, namely interdependence, domestic, Westphalian and international legal sovereignty. According to his analysis, interdependence sovereignty refers to the ability of states to control movement across their borders.[35] Domestic sovereignty denotes authority structures within states and the ability of these structures to effectively regulate conduct.[36] Westphalian sovereignty is the enjoyment by the sovereign state of a monopoly over authoritative decision-making, to the exclusion of external sources of authority, operating in an environment of non-intervention in one's internal affairs.[37] International legal sovereignty refers to mutual recognition: juridical independent territorial entities are capable of entering into voluntary contractual agreements, each operating on a free and equal footing,[38] none of which entities 'is entitled to command, none is required to obey'.[39]

Under classical Realism, sovereignty is understood as a practical matter, resulting from the Treaty of Westphalia (1648), denoting the existence of the supreme authority of the state over a certain territory.[40] Under Realism, the aforesaid external characteristic of sovereignty constitutes anarchy in international relations.[41]*Per contra*, under Constructivism, sovereignty, in both its internal and external elements, is a socially constructed trait that is not exogenous to the international system, but a social fact that is produced, and reproduced, through the practices of states and by other social norms, practices and entities.[42]

The pressures exerted by the EU on the non-Mediterranean countries to approximate their laws to the EU's *acquis*, policies and regulatory schemes may not match the aforesaid classic perception of sovereignty. The analysis conducted below will demonstrate that the adoption by Mediterranean countries of EU norms, regulatory practices and standards

[35] According to some, the technological progress of globalisation has reduced the costs of transportation. Since states cannot regulate trans-border movements, sovereignty is being eroded, SD Krasner, 'Abiding Sovereignty' (2001) 22 *International Political Science Review* 231.

[36] Different aspects of domestic sovereignty can involve the recognition of a given authority structure, or the level of control officials can actually exercise. Thus, the loss of interdependence sovereignty would also imply some loss of domestic sovereignty, Krasner, above n 35, 231–2.

[37] Krasner, above n 35, 232–3.

[38] Krasner, above n 35, 233.

[39] KN Waltz, *Theory of International Politics* (Reading, MA, Addison-Wesley, 1979), analysed by Lake, above n 31, 305.

[40] Lake, above n 31, 305–6.

[41] Lake, above n 31, 305; H Bull, *The Anarchical Society: A Study of Order in World Politics* (New York, Columbia University Press, 1977).

[42] Lake, above n 31, 305–8.

may erode these countries' legislative, bureaucratic, judicial and political autonomy. These repercussions will be examined in turn.

Nonetheless, such examination will not provide us with a comprehensive picture. An argument may be made, based on the literature of the economic interdependence school of thought, that regional integration, the conclusion of free trader agreements and the resultant approximation of laws is voluntary conduct, pursued by the Mediterranean countries as an exercise of their sovereignty for their own commercial and political benefit.[43] This section will attempt to address this argument.

B. Approximation of Laws and the Erosion of Legislative and Judicial Autonomy

The EU's expectation that its norms be adopted, as provided by the various Association Agreements, and reiterated under the ENP, renders it more difficult for the neighbouring countries to pursue an autonomous legislative agenda. As a result of these European legislative pressures, none of these countries can any longer fully determine its national legislative destiny.[44]

Such consequences are incompatible with the aforementioned concept of interdependence sovereignty. Adopting the EU *acquis* may result in a more liberalised EU-Med trading environment, facilitating easier movement of goods, services, capital and persons. Consequently, non-EU Mediterranean countries can no longer control movements across their borders, in the same manner in which they did prior to the adoption of European norms.[45] Similarly, such legislative course of action is in conflict with the concept of domestic sovereignty, because approximation of laws erodes the ability of the non-EU Mediterranean countries to regulate

[43] Approximation of laws may prove to be highly beneficial for the international trade of the Mediterranean countries, because it may reduce information costs, allow traders to utilise economies of scales, and render the international trading arena fairer, more predictable and less costly, thereby facilitating and intensifying international trade, and attracting more foreign investment. See Leebron, above n 3; D Geradin and N Petit, 'Competition Policy and the Euro-Mediterranean Partnership' (2003) 8 *European Foreign Affairs Review* 153, 173; Reich, above n 24.

[44] Take, for example, Israel and its sector of financial services. As demonstrated by Herman, an EU-Israeli free-trade area in services would promote the approximation of legislation by the former. Israel must harmonise appropriate European legislation, practices and standards, in order to be in conformity with the Single Market framework. Approximation should also be used as a tool to tackle issues such as state aid and competition policy, to ensure that European services suppliers are not discriminated against vis-à-vis their Israeli counterparts. See L Herman, 'Two for Tango: European Union Free Trade Areas in Services and Israel' (2005) 42 Working Paper, The Helmut Kohl Institute for European Studies, The Hebrew University of Jerusalem.

[45] See above n 35.

domestic conduct effectively.[46] Likewise, the adoption of European norms is not in harmony with the concept of Westphalian sovereignty, as it compromises the monopoly of the neighbouring countries over authoritative decision-making within their territories.

The move towards approximation of laws may also be out of line with the principle of non-intervention in sovereign's internal affairs.[47] As long ago as the eighteenth century, Wolff wrote that

> to interfere in the government of another, in whatever way indeed that may be done is opposed to the natural liberty of nations, by virtue of which one is altogether independent of the will of other nations in its action.[48]

Any attempt on the part of the EU to induce the adoption of its laws is precisely the action that Wolff warned against.

Finally, aligning one's laws with the *acquis* is incompatible with international legal sovereignty, because, as demonstrated above and below, such a course of action is not pursued on an equal footing within the EU.[49]

These consequences with regard to legislative erosion may also pose great challenges for the judiciaries of the neighbouring countries. As analysed above, one of the traditional manifestations of sovereignty is the state's monopoly over judicial powers and the ability of the domestic judiciary to independently develop the domestic legal system. Can such a form of domestic sovereignty be maintained in the face of legislative requirements to approximate one's laws to those of an external economic power?

Admittedly, approximation of laws results in the adoption of foreign laws into the municipal legal system, requiring the national judiciary to construe domestic legal provisions. Such a process is certainly not unique. Similar processes take place under public international law whereby states incorporate international obligations into their domestic legal systems. In the latter scenario there are no objections regarding the erosion of judicial autonomy. Why should there thus be any such objection on the grounds of approximation of laws to those of the *acquis*?

It is submitted that the adoption of European norms by the legal systems of the neighbouring countries may still result in some erosion of the autonomy of these countries' judiciaries. These legal systems will encompass a growing body of European norms, and that might induce

[46] Different aspects of domestic sovereignty can involve the recognition of a given authority structure, or the level of control officials can actually exercise. Thus, the loss of interdependence sovereignty would also imply some loss of domestic sovereignty, see Krasner, above n 35, 231–2.

[47] See Krasner, above n 35, 232–3.

[48] Quoted and analysed in Krasner, above n 35, 232.

[49] Krasner, above n 35, 233.

their judiciaries, when interpreting 'imported' European norms, to take into account the judicial pronouncements of the European Court of Justice (ECJ) on such European norms as are adopted into their legal systems.

Such an expectation is not purely speculative. The creation of the European Economic Area (EEA) between the EU and Norway, Iceland and Liechtenstein supports that prediction. Following that occurrence, those countries adopted virtually all of the EU commercial *acquis*. The experience gained from the EEA teaches us about the profound impact that the EEA has had on the national judiciaries of Norway, Iceland and Liechtenstein, the latter being increasingly influenced by the EU jurisprudence pertaining to EU norms.[50] Admittedly, the EEA includes provisions that called upon the judiciaries of the EFTA countries to take into account the case-law enunciated by the ECJ regarding these norms.[51] *De jure* these provisions are not present in the EU-Med context. Yet *de facto* a similar such impact on the judiciaries of the neighbouring countries may take place, as is evident at times in the Israeli case-law pertaining to certain provisions of the Israeli competition legislation that were 'cut and pasted' from the EU *acquis*.[52]

C. Approximation of Laws and the Erosion of Executive-Bureaucratic Autonomy

Approximation of laws on the part of the non-EU neighbouring countries also narrows their scope for executive-bureaucratic manoeuvres, because they can no longer employ trade instruments, standards and regulatory practices, as they were accustomed to prior to the process of approximation of laws.

Such consequences are incompatible with the aforesaid concept of interdependence sovereignty. The adoption of EU trading norms, and the resultant more liberalised trading environment may, for example, erode the neighbouring countries' ability to control movement across their borders, as they did prior to the adoption of European norms. Furthermore, such legislative pressures are not in harmony with the concept of domestic sovereignty. The need to adopt European norms erodes these countries' ability to effectively regulate domestic conduct in the manner

[50] For analysis, see Baudenbacher, 'The EFTA Court—An Example of the Judicialisation of International Economic Law' (2003) 28 *European Law Review* 880.

[51] For the EFTA countries' experience in that regard, see Baudenbacher, *ibid*.

[52] See, eg, Decision of 14 March 2005 in case 2616/03 *Isracard Inc v Howard Reis et al*, para 17, not yet published, as analysed by M Gal, 'The 'Cut and Paste' of Article 82 of the EC Treaty in Israel: Conditions for a Successful Transplant' (2007) 9 *European Journal of Law Reform* (n 67). One may, however, argue that the experience gained in the process of European integration was that the convergence of national laws actually empowered national judges vis-à-vis other national branches of governance.

they please. This is also not in line with traditional notions of Westphalian sovereignty, as the latter places authority over relations between rulers and ruled entirely in the hands of national governments, while domestic policies are not subject to challenge by external actors.[53]

D. Approximation of Laws and the Erosion of Political Autonomy

It is nowadays very difficult for small economies, like those of the EU's neighbours, to thrive in economic terms without joining a regional economic bloc. Approximation of laws to the *acquis* and the resultant enhanced integration of the Mediterranean markets to the Internal Market may further increase the neighbouring countries' dependence on European markets, while such an increase may impose further restrictions on their political autonomy.

Thus, approximation of laws, regulatory practices and standards may result in further integration of the markets of the neighbouring countries to that of the Internal Market, and such consequences will lead to their increased dependence on European markets, resulting, ultimately, in less political independence for them. Thus, indirectly, and in the long run, approximation of laws may erode their political autonomy.

Let us take again the example of Israel. Israel is gradually appreciating the importance of the EU as a global and regional economic player, and the fact that its growing economic dependence on the EU requires it to be more attuned to the political demands of Brussels.[54]

Such gradual change in Israeli perceptions is evident in the willingness of Israel to adopt a EU-sponsored resolution of the EU-Israeli dispute over the legal treatment of products exported to the EU from the territories which have been under Israel's control since the Six Day War (1967).[55] It is also reflected in the EU-Israel Action Plan, signed under the aegis of the ENP,[56] and in Israel's willingness to allow EU involvement in the monitoring of the Palestinian-Egyptian crossing point at Rafah.

[53] Krasner, above n 35, 237.

[54] G Harpaz, 'The Dispute over the Treatment of Products Exported to the European Union from the Golan Heights, East Jerusalem, the West Bank and the Gaza Strip—The Limits of Power and the Limits of the Law' (2004) 38 *Journal of World Trade* 1049.

[55] For the trade implications of that dispute, see C Hauswald, 'Problems under the EC-Israel Association Agreement: The Export of Goods Produced in the West Bank and the Gaza Strip under the EC-Israel Association Agreement' (2003) 14 *European Journal of International Law* 591; M Hirsch, 'Rules of Origin as Foreign Policy Instruments?' (2003) 26 *Fordham International Law Journal* 572.

[56] See EU-Israel Action Plan (2005), above n 19, Art 2.1: Under the Action Plan, Israel undertook far-reaching political commitments vis-à-vis the EU. It undertook, for example, to work 'together with the EU . . . with the aim of reaching a comprehensive settlement of the Israeli/Palestinian conflict and a permanent two-state solution with Israel and the Palestinian state living side by side in peace and security . . .', and to minimize 'the impact of security and counter-terrorism measures on the civilian population'.

The previous sub-sections attempted to demonstrate that the adoption of EU norms into the legal systems of the non-EU Mediterranean countries is a manifestation of the constraints placed on their sovereignty. Some may argue that such an adoption reflects an expression of sovereignty, and not a limitation on it. This argument will be addressed below.

E. Approximation of Laws and the Erosion of Sovereignty in an Era of Regionalisation and Globalisation

An argument may be made, based on the literature of the economic interdependence school of thought, that regional integration, the conclusion of free trade agreements and the resultant approximation of laws is a voluntary conduct, pursued by the Mediterranean countries for their own commercial and political benefit.[57]

Thus, for example, approximation of Israel's trade laws to those of the EU is a product of Israel's choice, and as such, its interdependence with the EU and the adoption of EU norms becomes not a constraint on its sovereignty, but rather an expression of such sovereignty. Tying Israel's hands is not an infringement of sovereignty, but a manifestation of it.[58]

It is my opinion that although such a line of argument may be sustained, when examined from a purely formal perspective, realities on the ground are far more nuanced. The dependence theory teaches us that in a situation of differences in the relative powers of the co-operating entities, and resultant economic dependence, dependence, like the adoption of external norms, cannot be perceived as an independent choice.[59]

Admittedly the same can be said of the EU Member States themselves with regard to their approximation of laws. Nonetheless, such erosion of sovereignty may be justified, in the EU context, on the grounds that the accession of any given country to the EU is a voluntary act performed by an independent, well-informed, consenting state, co-operating with other consenting states to advance mutual interests and visions, under the aegis of a legislative-partnership process in which they have a 'voice'.[60]

[57] See above n 43.

[58] See Lake, above n 31, 307, analysing RO Keohane, *After Hegemony: Cooperation and Discord in the World Political Economy* (Princeton University Press, 1984) and R Gilpin, *US Power and the Multinational Corporation: The Political Economy of Foreign Direct Investment* (New York, Basic Books, 1975).

[59] J Galtung, 'A Structural Theory of Imperialism' (1971) 8 *Journal of Peace Research* 81, as analysed by Lake, see above n 31, at 307.

[60] This argument applies with added force to the smaller Member States, as the legislative procedures in the Council of Ministers grant them at times a strong voice relative to their size. On the other hand it may be argued that the acceding countries are forced to accept the *acquis en bloc* with virtually no voice in the accession procedures.

The same cannot be said either in the EU-Mediterranean context, in general, or in the EU-Israeli context, in particular. Formally, the call for approximation of laws was couched in reciprocal terms in the various Euro-Med Association Agreements. Nonetheless, given the clear economic asymmetry between the EU and the neighbouring countries, the heterogeneity of the neighbouring countries and the EU's external aspirations, the EU does not perceive approximation of laws as a co-operative process among equal states, as it had been perceived in the context of the Internal Market.[61] Rather it is a paternalistic, one-way process, under which the Mediterranean neighbours are required to bring their legislation closer to that of the EU.[62]

Moreover, such a process may be seen as part of the larger process of external Europeanisation:[63]

> External Europeanization is . . . qualitatively different from intra-EU processes in that, unlike Member States who participate in the creation of the rules they are expected to comply with, the extraterritorialization of EU rules involves one-sided alignment by third countries that are excluded from the EU rule-making institutions.[64]

As Westbrook contends, when a sovereign imposes itself upon people outside its established borders, expands and creates new subjects, we may speak of imperialism.[65] The ENP's campaign for approximation of laws may be perceived in such a manner, because it amounts to 'highly intrusive demands on national sovereignty through formally depoliticized and legalized language'.[66]

The Middle East is one of the principal areas for such intrusive, external Europeanisation. This region is afflicted by structural, social, political and economic problems, which hamper the development of democratic values, the protection of human rights, prosperity and ulti-

[61] Yet an argument may be made that newly acceding Member States had to accept the *acquis en bloc* during a process in which they virtually had no voice.

[62] See Geradin and Petit, above n 43. The area of competition law is a case in point, see *ibid*, 167: there is a high expectation on the part of the EU, in particular in the area of competition law, where the EU expects the neighbouring countries' deep convergence of competition rules and regulatory practices.

[63] JS Nye, Jr, *Soft Power—The Means to Success in World Politics* (New York, Public Affairs, 2004) 75–83; RG Whitman, *From Civilian Power to Superpower? The International Identity of the European Union* (London, Macmillan, 1998); E Aoun, 'European Foreign Policy and the Arab-Israeli Dispute: Much Ado about Nothing?' (2003) 8 *European Foreign Affairs Review* 289, 299.

[64] See Magen, above n 16, 498.

[65] DA Westrbrook, 'Theorizing the Diffusion of Law: Conceptual Difficulties, Unstable Imaginations, and the Effort to Think Gracefully Nonetheless' (2006) 47 *Harvard Journal of International Law* 489, 496.

[66] A Magen, 'Building Democratic Peace in the Eastern Mediterranean: An Inevitably Ambitious Agenda' (2004) 9 Working Paper, Stanford Institute for International Studies 27.

mately the peaceful resolution of conflicts in the Middle East.[67] Europe is concerned with the prevailing state of affairs in the Middle East, fearing that political extremism, terrorism, socio-economic unrest, narcotics trafficking and illegal immigration in the neighbouring countries may spill over into the EU.[68] After all, as the former French Foreign Minister, H de Charette has noted, 'When violence returns to the Middle East, sooner or later it will show up in Paris.'[69]

Europe too had to face significant political, economic and social problems in the aftermath of the Second World War. The EEC, and then the EC and the EU, served as efficient instruments that enabled Europe to extricate itself from its own problems, and thereby to achieve stability. The EU believes that it can draw on its own experience to assist in resolving the structural problems in the non-EU Mediterranean countries. To that end, the EU is striving to 'export' its successful model of integration to other parts of the world, including, in particular, the Middle East.[70]

To advance effective regional involvement, as it wishes to do, the EU cannot rely on hard-power instruments, because it suffers from what may be termed a hard-power deficit.[71] Consequently, and in addition to building economic strength, the EU is attempting to position itself, as Duchêne predicted as early as 1972, as a civil, normative power.[72] The EU is trying to translate its ever-growing economic leverage into a diplomatic tool and for that purpose it relies on economic and normative, soft-power

[67] These include, according to the EU, deficits in governance, marginalisation of women, poor implementation of international human rights conventions, insufficient independence of legal and judicial systems, low status of non-governmental organisations, unevenly dispensed education, authoritarianism and poor economic and social performance, Commission of the European Communities (2003) Communication from the Commission to the Council and the European Parliament, Reinvigorating EU Actions on Human Rights and Democratisation with Mediterranean Partners, Strategic Guidelines, Brussels 21.05.2003 Com(2003) 294 final, 4.

[68] F Tanner, 'North Africa: Partnership, Exceptionalism and Neglect' in R Dannreuther (ed), *European Union Foreign and Security Policy—Towards a Neighbourhood Strategy* (London, Routledge, 2004) 135; N Tocci, 'Does the ENP Respond to the EU's Post Enlargement Challenges?' (2005) XL/1 *The International Spectator* 21; N Tocci, 'The Widening Gap between Rhetoric and Reality in the EU Policy towards the Israeli-Palestinian Conflict' (2005) 217 CEPS Working Document, available at http://www.ceps.be/Default.php (accessed 5 February 2007), 24.

[69] R Dannreuther, 'The Middle East—Towards a Substantive European Role in the Middle East Peace Process' in R Dannreuther (ed), *European Union Foreign and Security Policy—Towards a Neighbourhood Strategy* (London, Routledge, 2004) 151, 152.

[70] P Bilgin, 'Whose "Middle East"? Geopolitical Inventions and Practices of Security' (2004) 18 *International Relations* 25, 34; R Prodi, Speech by Romano Prodi, former President of the European Commission, on 'Europe and Peace' at the University of Ulster (Derry) 1 April 2004, available at http://europa-eu-un.org/articles/fi/article_3372_fi.htm.

[71] R Kagan, 'Why the United States and Europe See the World Differently' (2002) 113 *Policy Review* 7, 7–8.

[72] F Duchêne, 'Europe's Role in the World Peace', in R Mayne (ed), *Europe Tomorrow: Sixteen Europeans Look Ahead* (London, Fontana, 1971); Kagan, above n 71; Aoun, above n 63, 299.

instruments,[73] in order to expand its political, economic and normative influence both regionally and globally.[74]

Such EU civil involvement in the neighbouring countries has attracted much scholarly attention. Some have described it as a diluted enlargement policy,[75] others as extraterritorial Europeanisation,[76] others as external European governance.[77] The EU neighbourhood policies may thus be seen as a form of EU external governance, which consists of selective extension of its legal boundaries (norms, rules and policies), while precluding the opening of its institutional boundaries (through fully fledged membership).[78]

One of the methods used by the EU to gain such regional and global influence is approximation of laws. European countries can no longer shift armadas around the globe as they did in the past, and the days of European military-backed colonialism are gone, hopefully not to return. The EU can, on the other hand, attempt to export its legal regime, through approximation of laws, to its neighbours and beyond, thereby gaining economic influence and consequently political and normative influence. Hence the EU perceives legal, socio-economic and political reforms in the Mediterranean countries, on the one hand, and economic prosperity and the resolution of the Middle East conflict, on the other hand, as intertwined. [79] Put differently, European military colonialism is 'out'; soft, enlightened, legal colonialism is 'in'.

A quid pro quo is thus postulated. In return for its willingness to open its economic gates, under the aegis of the ENP, the EU expects its neighbours to adopt its basic values.[80] Such adoption requires the pursuance of reforms, and these reforms entail the approximation of laws and regulatory practices to the EU *acquis*.[81] The call for approximation of laws is thus utilised as one component of the EU's external strategy of positive conditionality.[82]

[73] Nye, above n 63, 75–83.

[74] For general survey, see HA Fernandez and R Youngs (eds), *The Euro-Mediterranean Partnership: Assessing the First Decade* (Madrid, FRIDE, 2005).

[75] J Kelley, 'New Wine in Old Wineskins: Promoting Political Reforms through the New European Neighbourhhod Policy' (2006) 44 *Journal of Common Market Studies* 29, 41.

[76] Magen, above n 16.

[77] S Lavenex, 'EU External Governance in 'Wider Europe'' (2004) 11 *Journal of European Public Policy* 680.

[78] *Ibid*.

[79] See Magen, above n 66, 115.

[80] Namely peace, the rule of law, democracy, the protection of human rights and a free market economy.

[81] For a theoretical analysis of the attempts of the West to 'export' Western values, see by analogy, A Etzioni, 'A Self-restrained Approach to Nation Building by Foreign Powers' (2004) 80 *International Affairs* 1, 1.

[82] For the use of positive conditionality, see N Tocci, 'The Widening Gap between Rhetoric and Reality in the EU Policy towards the Israeli-Palestinian Conflict' (2005) 217 CEPS Working Document, appears in http://www.ceps.be/Default.php (accessed 5 February 2007).

Thus the undertaking by the Mediterranean countries, including Israel, to approximate their laws to those of the EU cannot be seen as a pure exercise of their unfettered sovereignty. Rather it can be seen as their reaction, albeit a beneficial one, to EU pressures, an exercise of limited and qualified sovereignty, constrained by the forces of regionalisation.

V. APPROXIMATION OF LAWS, NATIONAL IDENTITY AND PARTICULARISM

It is further argued that the transplant of EU norms into the legal systems of the neighbouring countries may create problems in practical and normative terms, given the socio-cultural differences that exist between the EU and these countries.

Admittedly there are some scholars, belonging to the 'transferist' camp, who contend that legal norms can be effectively transplanted into any socio-economic and political context. The leading advocate of such a theory is Watson.[83] He contends that the law develops by transplantation rather than by creation *ex nihilo*. Based on an analysis of various legal norms and systems, including the Ten Commandments and Roman law, Watson reached the conclusion that the law may develop far from social realities, and that it may be successfully borrowed by other countries whose socio-economic, political and geographic circumstances are very different from those of the donor country. According to Watson, the law is by and large autonomous and distinct from the contextual culture and social environment in which it operates.[84] It is the scientific creation of a clever, law-making elite, the latter being concerned with professional solutions to technical-legal problems, and not with social norms or social change.[85] The legal elite treats the law, its means of creation and its sources, as autonomous, and almost sacrosanct. As such, a good law, embodying a good idea, is easily transferable and adaptable to local use by clever professionals in the importing country, irrespective of any socio-cultural differences that may exist between the exporting country and the importing country.

With all due respect, it is my opinion that such a formal, legalistic treatment of the law is unwarranted. Law and society are not two autonomous institutions, but are inextricably linked.

It was Montesquieu who argued that 'the political and civil laws of each nation should be so closely tailored to the people for whom they are

[83] See above n 5.

[84] Watson, above n 5, as analysed by W Ewald, 'Comparative Jurisprudence (II): The Logic of Legal Transplants' (1995) 43 *American Journal of Comparative Law* 489, 501–3.

[85] As analysed by I Markovits, 'Exporting Law Reform—But Will It Travel?' (2004) 37 *Cornell International Law Journal* 95.

made', and that the law is therefore not necessarily transferable: as civil laws depend on political laws because they are made for one society, it would be well if, when one wants to transfer a civil law from one nation to another, one examines beforehand whether they both have the same institutions and the same political right.[86] Otherwise, 'it would be pure chance if the laws of one nation could meet the needs of another'.[87] This approach, which places heavy emphasis on the interface between law and society, was later supported by Savigny (1814)[88] and by numerous contemporary scholars, including Kahn-Freund, Small, Friedman, Ewald and Legrand, who together formed the 'culturalist' camp.[89]

According to these scholars, the law is a culturally determined artefact and cannot therefore be severed from the socio-economic circumstances in which it was originally formulated.[90] A legal rule is an incorporative cultural form, encoding social experience. Just as culture is a source of identity, so are rules, which collectively serve as an instrument that reflects and shapes socio-political identity.[91] Culture derives from historical experience, as do the forms that culture embraces, such as the law.[92] The law changes in response to changes external to it, reflecting the power relations of society, the working of market forces, the ideology of possessive individualism, the cunning of *Weltgeist*, the self-interest of the elite, or the political ideology of the age.[93] As Friedman wrote with respect to US law, the law does not act

> . . . as a kingdom unto itself, not as a set of rules and concepts, not as a province of lawyers alone, but as a mirror of society. It takes nothing as historical accident, nothing as autonomous, everything as relative and moulded by economy and society.[94]

Legislation is, after all, one manifestation of a society's DNA. Different social attributes, including endowments, technologies, preferences, institutions and coalition formation, may legitimately lead to different national legislative and regulatory choices.[95] Legal divergence may thus

[86] Montesquieu (1748), Book XXIX, ch 13.

[87] *Ibid*.

[88] FK von Savigny, *Of the Vocation of our Age for Legislation and Jurisprudence* (Haywood trans, 1814).

[89] Kahn-Freund, above n 5; G Small, 'Towards a Theory of Contextual Transplants' (2005) 19 *Emory International Law Review* 1431; L Friedman, *A History of American Law* (1985); P Legrand, 'The Impossibility of Legal Transplants' (1997) 4 *Maastricht Journal of European and Comparative Law* 111.

[90] Small, above n 89.

[91] Legrand, above n 89.

[92] *Ibid*, 56–57.

[93] Ewald, above n 84, 490.

[94] Friedman, above n 89.

[95] Leebron, above n 3, 92–3.

be perceived as a natural barrier that is inherent in the existence of sovereign, socio-political jurisdictions.[96]

The concept of law operating independently from society must therefore be abandoned.[97] In any event, it must be remembered that the object of diffusion of law, examined from the perspective of the 'donor', in our case the EU, extends beyond legal doctrine to include modes of thought, ideology, procedures, norms and institutions.[98] In the same vein, when examined from the perspective of the receiving country, the law depends on interpretation, the latter being based on normative assumptions that are themselves historically and culturally conditioned.[99]

The law should thus be seen, as the 'culturalists' perceive it, as mirroring society. The law embodies, as the US Supreme Court Chief Justice Oliver Wendell Holmes noted, 'the story of a nation's development through many centuries and it cannot be dealt with as if it contained only the axioms and corollaries of a book of mathematics'.[100]

As a corollary, any attempt to transplant legislation into a foreign socio-economic environment may prove to be problematic in terms of legitimacy, social receptiveness and effectiveness.[101] Law addressees are embedded in their specific legal system and hence law reform requires the co-operation of citizens in order to be effective.[102] Where the law develops internally through a process of trial and error, innovation and correction, and with the participation of the users of the law and the legal profession, legal institutions tend to be highly effective, but where foreign law is imposed and legal evolution is external, legal institutions tend to be very weak.[103] The transfer of legal norms into different socio-economic and institutional contexts may create a 'transplant effect', the mismatch between pre-existing conditions and institutions and the transplanted law, which would ultimately weaken the effectiveness and legitimacy of the imported legislation.[104]

A society with a strong sense of the legitimacy of any properly enacted legal norm will give greater effect to the new law than a society where the legitimacy of law is weak.[105] Law reforms that are inconsistent with

[96] Boodman, above n 4, 717.

[97] Legrand, above n 89.

[98] Twining, above n 5, 512.

[99] Legrand, above n 89.

[100] From the first of 12 Lowell Lectures delivered by Oliver Wendell Holmes Jr on 23 November 1880, which were the basis for the Common Law.

[101] For support, see Small, above n 89, 1431–3; Kahn-Freund, above n 5, 27.

[102] Markovits, above n 85, 99 and 110.

[103] Berkowitz, Pistor and Richard, above n 5.

[104] Berkowitz, Pistor and Richard, above n 5, 171.

[105] J Miller, 'A Typology of Legal Transplants: Using Sociology, Legal History and Argentine Examples to Explain the Transplant Process' (2003) 51 *American Journal of Comparative Law* 839, 844.

deeply held moral and political beliefs may contradict fundamental cultural gut reactions and might ultimately be rejected.[106]

Given this interface between national particularism and legal differences, it may thus be argued that the campaign for approximation of laws can be legitimately and effectively conducted where a significant degree of historic, social, cultural and economic commonality exists.[107] The importation of legal norms to the Mediterranean countries should to a significant extent reflect the socio-political environment in which they are to be absorbed.

Is this the case with the EU and the societies of the Mediterranean countries? Such a question lies beyond the scope of this chapter. Suffice to say that the societies of the non-EU Mediterranean countries do not in all respects share a common normative, cultural, socio-economic, geo-political apparatus with European society/societies. Israeli society is a fine case in point.[108]

Consequently, EU legal norms may not at all times neatly fit the legal systems of the non-EU Mediterranean countries.[109] It may thus be argued that those cultural and social differences between the EU and these countries ought to be reflected in the respective legal environments in which the EU and these countries operate, and not in a sweeping adoption of EU legal norms.

The proponents of approximation of laws to those of the EU may take issue with that line of argument, contending that the EU Member States

106 Markovits, above n 85, 99 and 110.

107 As, for example, in the early days of the EEC. But see the works of Watson who provides numerous examples to the contrary, see above n 5.

108 For a comparison between the EU and Israel, placing emphasis on the social differences between the two, see A Tovias and R Del Sarto, 'Caught Between Europe and the Orient: Israel and the ENP' (2001) 36/4 *The International Spectator* 91; A Bardi and L Sagiv, 'The EU and Israel: Comparison of Cultures and Implications', in K Boehnke (ed), *Israel and Europe—A Complex Relationship* (2003). But as Tovias recently argued, EU enlargement to the East, the massive immigration of Russian Jews to Israel, globalisation and technological progress have transformed to some extent the Israeli society and it macro-economic persona according to European patterns, see A Tovias, 'Spontaneous v Legal Approximation: The Europeanization of Israel' (2007) 9/3 *European Journal of Law Reform* (n 85). See also Gal, above n 52. Indeed, strong cultural affinity to Europe is evident at times in Israeli daily life, while European culture affects Israeli mores. Many Israelis maintain strong cultural ties with Europe and feel strong cultural and ideological affinity with, and admiration for, it. Israel is indeed heavily involved in European cultural and sporting events and tournaments, such as football, basketball and the Eurovision contest. Israelis are avid aficionados of European culture, while European films, music and theatre are well known and admired by the Israeli public. Europe (particularly Paris and London), has long been Israel's preferred tourist destination, and numerous European languages are learned by many Israelis. These close cultural ties are fostered by several cultural European institutes, situated in Israel. The EU *acquis* might therefore be nowadays more suitable for transplantation into the Israeli socio-economic and geopolitical landscape than it was few years ago.

109 See, eg, D Keridis, 'Europe and Israel: What Went Wrong?' (2004), The Begin–Sadat Centre for Strategic Studies, Bar-Ilan University. Keridis refers to the erosion of the dominance of Israel's European elite and to the rise of Oriental Jews.

have made significant progress towards harmonisation of laws *inter se*, despite significant social differences. Israel and Tunisia, for example, are not the only countries that had to adjust their legislation. The United Kingdom, France and Germany, for example, have had to undergo the same process. Israel or Tunisia are no more 'special' than these countries. Thus if France has aligned its legislation with the *acquis*, why can't Israel and Tunis pursue the same course of action?[110]

It is submitted, however, that the latter proposition is not entirely convincing. As Krasner demonstrates, the current status of the EU has emerged over a period of time out of complex negotiations designed to deal with specific issues rather than some effort to conform to a set of rules and norms.[111] France, in our example, approximates its laws to those of other EU Member States through the use of, inter alia, EU directives, adopted by the Council of Ministers, where it has certain voting rights, and where decision-making is largely intergovernmental.[112] France has therefore some voice in, and hence influence over, the EU legislation process. Moreover, EU directives are, to a certain extent, sensitive to national sovereignty, diverse national interests and endowments.[113] The process of EU integration may thus be seen as a partnership of independent states, in which, in our example, France is a partner.[114]

The process of approximating the laws in the Euro-Med context is, on the other hand, as analysed above, a paternalistic, one-sided one, in which the EU attempts to export European norms to the socio-legal systems of its neighbours, and where these neighbours, despite the EU's latest assertions,[115] have virtually no official voice in the legislative process of legal norms pertaining to them.[116]

Thus this inability of the non-EU Mediterranean countries to fully determine their own national legislative destiny may result in their failure to ascribe sufficient pride of place to their national history, identity

[110] Tovias, above n 108.

[111] Krasner, above n 35, 244. It is submitted, however, that this contention is not entirely applicable to the acceding Member States who are called to accept the *acquis en bloc*.

[112] For the discussion of the Council's voting requirements see P Craig and G de Burca, *EU Law Text, Cases and Materials* (3rd ed, Oxford University Press, 2003), 153–7. See Art 94 of the Treaty Establishing the European Community, which provides the legal basis for approximation of laws for the effective functioning of the Internal Market.

[113] See Craig and De Burca, *ibid*, 114–15.

[114] See, eg, N Nugent, 'Cyprus and the European Union: The Significance of its Smallness, both as an Applicant and as a Member' (2006) 28 *Journal of European Integration* 51.

[115] See European Neighbourhood Policy, Strategy Paper (2004): 'Joint ownership of the process, based on awareness of shared values and common interests is essential. The EU does not seek to impose priorities or conditions on its partners. The Action Plans depend, for their success, on the clear recognition of mutual interest. There can be no question of asking partners to accept pre-determined set of priorities.'

[116] R Aliboni, 'The Geopolitical Implications of the European Neighbourhood Policy' (2005) 10 *European Foreign Affairs Review* 1.

and particular socio-economic, geopolitical, cultural and religious characteristics.

A caveat must, however, be attached to my conclusion that the law should reflect society and that EU legal norms fail at times to meet that requirement vis-à-vis the non-EU Mediterranean societies. The law should indeed reflect the society in which it operates. But this must not be its sole task. The law can also constitute, shape and improve the social infrastructure of any given nation. The law can and should not only be reflective but also transformative, serving as an engine for reform. After all, and as Hiller argues, transplanted laws carry with them so much imperceptible and incommensurable cultural 'baggage' that the receiving country will inevitably experience far more internal cultural change than it either realised, intended or would have intended.[117]

These should not always be seen as negative consequences. Take, for example, the case of Israel. In recent years Israeli law has played a prominent reforming role, conceiving new and better ways in which Israeli society perceives a range of issues, including gender rights, minority rights and Palestinian rights.[118] This dramatic enhancement of the role of Israeli law was seen to be part of a gradual change in Israeli law and Israeli legal education, termed by Mautner 'the rise of norms and fall of formalism'.[119] The argument can thus be made that if Israeli law played a reformative role in sensitive issues such as Palestinian rights, it can also play an activist role in advancing, for example, superior EU environmental norms. Similar arguments may be raised with respect to other non-EU Mediterranean countries.

The conclusion of the last two sections is that the alignment of the laws of non-EU Mediterranean countries with those of the EU may raise difficulties in terms of loss of sovereignty and national identity. Such alignment may also prove to be problematic in terms of legitimacy.

VI. APPROXIMATION OF LAWS AND LEGITIMACY

A. The Concept of International Legitimacy

The concept of legitimacy may be seen as a normative belief that a rule or

[117] JA Hiller, 'Language, Law, Sports and Culture: The Transferability or Non-Transferability of Words, Lifestyles, and Attitudes through Law' (1978) 12 *Valparaiso University Law Review* 433, 434.

[118] See, eg, AM Gross, 'Challenges to Compulsory Heterosexuality: Recognition and Non-Recognition of Same-Sex Couples in Israeli Law' in R Wintemute and M Andenas (eds), *Legal Recognition of Same-Sex Partnerships: A Study of National, European and International Law* (Oxford, Hart Publishing, 2001) 391–414; G Harpaz, 'The Israeli Supreme Court in Search of Universal Legitimacy' (2006) 65 *CLJ* 7.

[119] M Mautner, *The Decline of Formalism and the Rise of Values in Israeli Law* (Tel-Aviv, Maagale Daat, 1993) [in Hebrew].

institution should be obeyed, not due to coercion or self-interest, but due to its inherent normative strength,[120] being perceived as desirable, proper or appropriate within a socially constructed system of norms, values, beliefs and definitions.[121] As Max Weber contended:

> But custom, personal advantage, purely effectual or ideal motives of solidarity do not form a sufficiently reliable basis for a given domination. In addition, there is normally a further element, a belief in legitimacy. Experience shows that in no instance does domination voluntarily limit itself to the appeal to material or effectual or ideal motives as a basis for its continuance. . . . Every such system attempts to establish and to cultivate the belief in its legitimacy.[122]

In Hurd's opinion, legitimacy contributes to compliance by providing an internal reason for an actor to follow a rule. When the rule is perceived by that actor as legitimate, compliance is no longer motivated by a fear of sanctions or a by a calculation of self-interest, but by an internal sense of moral obligation.[123] According to this line of thinking, more theorists of international law who belong to the sociological camp are concerned with the interface between legitimacy and compliance.[124] Yet aggressive legislative pressures applied by the EU may be perceived in Israel, for the reasons analysed below, as illegitimate.

B. The EU as an Illegitimate Internal and External Power?

The EU's institutional apparatus and legislative process are not free of vices, leading many scholars to conclude that the EU suffers, internally, from democratic, legitimacy and community deficits.[125] The adoption by the non-EU Mediterranean countries of legislation that is the end-product of such institutional and legislative design may thus be seen as illegitimate.

Yet the EU's legitimacy problems are not confined to the internal sphere. Due to reasons that lie far beyond the scope of this chapter, the EU is perceived by many scholars as an illegitimate external actor.[126] Such

[120] J Steffek, 'The Legitimation of International Governance: A Discourse Approach' (2003) 9 *European Journal of International Relations* 249, 252; T Franck, *The Power of Legitimacy among Nations* (New York, Oxford University Press, 1990); I Hurd, 'Legitimacy and Authority in International Politics' (1999) 53 *International Organization* 379, 379, 381 and 387.

[121] M Suchman, 'Managing Legitimacy: Strategic and Institutional Approaches' (1995) 20 *Academy of Management Review* 571, 574.

[122] M Weber, *Economy and Society* (Berkeley, University of California Press, 1978) 213.

[123] See Hurd, above n 120, 387.

[124] See the analysis of M Hirsch, 'Compliance with International Norms in the Age of Globalization: Two Theoretical Perspectives' in E Benvenisti and M Hirsch (eds), *The Impact of International Law on International Cooperation* (Cambridge University Press, 2004).

[125] A Etzioni, 'The Community Deficit' (2007) 45 *Journal of Common Market Studies* 23.

[126] G Harpaz, 'Normative Power Europe and the Problem of a Legitimacy Deficit: An Israeli Perspective' (2007) 12 *European Foreign Affairs Review* 89.

narrative erodes the legitimacy of the EU, thereby making it very difficult for it to position itself as a normative power, in general, and as norm-exporter, in particular.[127]

C. Approximation of Laws and the (Non-) Participatory Democracy

The proximity between the policy-maker and the recipient of legal norms constitutes a sign of healthy governance. That fact was recognised by ancient Greek philosophers,[128] by the Church,[129] and in more recent times by the EU itself, under the aegis of the General Principle of Subsidiarity.[130] A prerequisite for an effective law is, after all, the existence of legal cultures and institutions which are receptive to the law, supported by local constituencies with a strong interest in the law:[131]

> Making decisions on a more local basis has both substantive and procedural value. The substantive value derives from the ability of a more local population to implement choices which . . . better reflect its preferences, resources and technologies. . . . The procedural value of localism is one of participation, of having a more meaningful say over the policies that affect one's life, and to maintain more direct influence over one's government and governmental officials. [132]

These propositions are also applicable to our context. The adoption by Mediterranean countries of provisions enacted in Brussels will distance their citizens from the legislative process, thereby running contrary to the aforesaid principle.

The analysis conducted so far indicates that approximation of laws by the non-EU Mediterranean countries may have problematic repercussions in terms of sovereignty, national identity and legitimacy. These may result in internal opposition in these countries to the importation of EU norms.

D. Social Opposition

The European legislative campaign, which can be conceptualised in terms of Constructivist theories of international relations,[133] includes certain

[127] *Ibid.*

[128] Aristotle, *The Politics of Aristotle* (Ernest Barker trans, 1957) 68–76.

[129] Poorley, 'Limit and Possibility: An Augustinian Counsel to Authority' in K Paffenroth and K Hughes (eds), *Augustine and Liberal Education* (Aldershot, Ashgate, 2000) 14, 14–161.

[130] Art 5 of the EC Treaty, as analysed by A Estella De Noriega, *The EU Principle of Subsidiarity and its Critique* (Oxford University Press, 2002).

[131] Mayeda, above n 3, 745.

[132] See Leebron, above n 3, 104.

[133] Constructivism is first and foremost a sociological theory. Contrary to Realism, which

components of social engineering and nation-building. The pursuit of such policies by foreign powers is likely to create internal opposition. After all, these policies may at times seek to overcome prevailing social forces and long-established moral and social cultures, societal structures and traditions, and attempt to undo deeply ingrained cultural and psychological predispositions, strong emotional ties and religious beliefs.[134]

Given the traditional atmosphere of suspicion and scepticism towards Europe that prevails at times in the non-EU Mediterranean countries, the potential social opposition to European legislative pressures may be particularly conspicuous.[135] In such an environment, an assertive 'exportation' of European legal norms may be perceived in these countries as intellectual parochialism, conventionalism, paternalism and even as neo-imperialism.[136]

Thus the EU campaign of approximation of laws, in itself, and when examined in its wider context, namely the attempt to pursue wide-scale reforms in the Mediterranean countries, is likely to encounter significant challenges, complications, and opposition stemming from the external intervention involved, and the loss of sovereignty and legitimacy entailed.

It must be emphasised, however, that such a course of action does not carry merely negative implications in legitimacy terms. Positive spill-overs may also occur.

E. Positive Spillovers

Miller provides a typology of the reasons why an importing country would seek legal transplants; these include cost-saving,[137] externally dictated,[138] entrepreneurial[139] and legitimacy-generated motives.[140]

The latter motive may at times apply to the non-EU Mediterranean countries. The executive branches of these countries lack, in certain important areas, the required management and workforce to face the

focuses on the material world, Constructivism claims, according to Adler, that the manner in which the material world shapes and is shaped by human action and interaction depends on dynamic normative and epistemic interpretation of the material world. See E Adler, 'Seizing the Middle Grounds: Constructivism in World Politics' (1997) 3 *European Journal of International Relations* 322.

134 Etzioni, above n 81, 4.

135 For general analysis, see EW Said, *Orientalism* (New York, Pantheon Books, 1978).

136 See by analogy, Boodman, above n 4, 721–3.

137 Transplant saves time and costly experimentation.

138 Countries forced to accept legislative pressure exerted by a foreign entity as a prerequisite for doing business.

139 Individuals and groups reap benefits from investing their energies in learning and encouraging local adoption of foreign legal norms.

140 Enjoying the prestige of the foreign model, see Miller, above n 105.

legislative challenges stemming from complex global and regional realities.[141] In a few instances such a state of affairs has already caused delays in implementing international obligations, and led to the inclusion of certain countries in various 'blacklists'.[142] Approximating these countries' laws to those of the EU may assist in addressing that challenge, by providing policy-makers with ready-made,[143] high-quality legislation,[144] which would afford it better protection from domestic rent-seekers.[145]

Israel is an indicative example of the potential positive contribution that approximation of laws with the *acquis* may have in legitimacy terms. Israel has in recent years adopted a more co-operative stance towards the United Nations,[146] and is attempting to join the OECD,[147] to enhance its relations with NATO[148] and with the European Union. Approximation of laws and resultant enhanced credibility in European and international forums can assist Israel in that respect.[149]

VII. SUMMARY AND CONCLUSIONS

The European Union has in recent years offered its neighbouring Mediterranean countries enhanced trade, economic and political relations. In return it expects them to align their national legislation, to an extent yet to be determined, with its *acquis communautaire*. This legislative course of action may bring abundant trade, economic and other benefits to the Mediterranean countries, and yet, as analysed in this chapter, it

[141] The area of anti-dumping legislation is one case in point.

[142] The area of money laundering is only one case in point. Lebanon and Israel were initially included in the 'blacklist' of the FATF, see Herman, above n 29.

[143] Boodmand, above n 4, 718: Jurisdictions that do not want to devote resources to lengthy law-reform projects can 'free ride' upon the law-reform project of other jurisdictions.

[144] *Ibid*.

[145] See A Nov, 'Wider Europe: The EU State Aid Regime and its Opportunity for the Southern Mediterranean Countries', a paper presented at the Sixth Mediterranean Social and Political Research Meeting, Montecatini Terme, 16–20 March 2005, at 7–8: '. . . it may be beneficial for a country that provides tax incentives to FDI as a result of political pressure, to relinquish its sovereignty and be bound by a global or regional regime that will require that country to abstain from providing tax incentives.'

[146] But compare with Y Shany, 'Capacities and Inadequacies: A Look at the Two Separation Barrier Cases' (2005) 38 *Israel Law Review* 230, 234–5.

[147] D Catarivas and L Herman, 'Israel's Accession to the OECD', in G Harpaz (ed), 11 *Newsletter of the Israeli Association for the Study of European Integration* (Ramat-Gan, Israeli Association for the Study of European Integration, 2004) 51.

[148] U Arad and T Steiner, 'Israel and the Euro-Atlantic Community: An Israeli Perspective' in *Israel and the Euro-Atlantic Community, Project Report*, the Atlantic Forum for Israel (2004) 1, 1.

[149] See Geradin and Petit, above n 43, at 174 for the application of this argument in the area of competition law.

may prove to be challenging, complex, problematic and disadvantageous, in terms of sovereignty, national identity and legitimacy.

Given these positive and negative repercussions, the question arises: how should the non-EU Mediterranean countries confront the European legislative pressures? It is submitted that these countries cannot and should not dismiss the EU's call for approximation of laws. The classical Westphalian paradigm of international law as a horizontal model, based upon principles of sovereignty, formal equality of states, non-intervention in domestic affairs and state consent, no longer represents twenty-first-century trade, economic, social and political realities. The days in which sovereignty was perceived in such a manner are nearly over, if not already a thing of the past.[150]

This state of affairs applies also to Israel. Evolving global and regional realities, Israel's dependence on European markets, and the EU move towards more assertive treatment of countries that do not abide by international norms, render the resistance to European legislative pressures ill-advised. The possibility that Israel 'shall dwell alone and shall not be reckoned among the nations' does not represent a viable option. Israel needs regional economic backing. The implementation of the ENP in general, and approximating Israel's laws with those of the EU in particular, may in fact partially satisfy that need. Regional co-operation carries with it membership fees, and approximating Israel's laws with those of the EU, and the resultant erosion of its sovereignty, is part of that cost.

The non-EU Mediterranean countries should thus adjust their perceptions of sovereignty to fit modern realities and their trade, socio-economic and geopolitical situation. Sovereignty must not be seen by them as absolute, rigid, and indivisible, but as qualified, flexible, dynamic, relative and divisible, subject to continuous changes.[151]

Yet in light of the above analysed challenges, problems and disadvantages in terms of sovereignty, national identity and legitimacy, these countries should not blindly place their faith in the concept of approximation of laws with the *acquis*. Instead they should treat it cautiously: 'Blind without history, jurisprudence without comparative understanding can scarcely rise above the level of provincial casuistry and empirical craft.'[152] In other words, the non-EU Mediterranean countries should strive to secure the benefits of European regionalisation, without

[150] Westbrook, above n 65, 503–04.

[151] As Barkin and Cronin argue, sovereignty is a social construct, and like all social institutions, its location is neither fixed not constant, but is subject to changing interpretation, which alters, in turn, the environment in which states treat one another, S Barkin and B Cronin, 'The State and the Nation: Changing Norms and Rules of Sovereignty in International Relations' (1994) 48 *International Organization* 107, 109 and 128. See also the works of Sarooshi, Lake and Bartelson, all referred to in n 31 above.

[152] Yntema (1945), in E Rabel, *The Conflicts of Laws*, XIII.

having to sustain disproportionate losses in terms of national sovereignty, legislative supremacy and their ability to determine their own national destiny and collective identity.

According to the econometric analysis conducted by Berkowitz, Pistor and Richard of numerous cases of legal transplant, a good legal reform strategy should be to carefully choose the legal rules whose meaning can be understood and whose purpose is appreciated by domestic law-makers, law-enforcers and economic agents, who are the ultimate consumers of the law. Legal reforms must ensure that there is domestic demand for the new norm and the foreign supply of that norm may match.[153] The non-EU Mediterranean countries should adopt that cautious and selective course of action.

The *à la carte* nature of the ENP may serve that purpose. It would, in principle, allow the non-EU countries to choose to adopt some of internal market's regimes, consistent with their own interests and social values (eg, proposed liberalisation in trading of services in the case of Israel), while rejecting, in principle, other components that might harm those interests and values (eg, the legal obligation to permit free movement of persons in the case of Israel).

In addition, the imported EU norms should be adapted to the climate of the non-EU Mediterranean countries. The above-mentioned econometric analysis of Berkowitz *et al* establishes that a legal transplant increases its own receptivity by making significant adaptations to local pre-existing formal and informal legal order.[154] For the law to be effective, a demand for it must exist. If the transplanted law is adapted to domestic conditions, then the law will be used. If the law is not so adapted, or is imposed via colonisation, and the population is not familiar with it, a 'transplant effect' may be expected. The initial demand for the law will be weak, while the legal order will function less effectively.[155]

The non-EU Mediterranean countries should thus avoid the unnecessary 'cut and paste' of EU norms, attempting instead to adjust these norms to their own particular socio-economic landscape. Lord Denning's view may be pertinent in our context too:

> . . . just as with an English oak, so with the English common law. You cannot transplant it to the African continent and expect it to retain the tough character which it has in England. It will flourish indeed but it needs careful tending.[156]

Other instruments should be employed to temper the adverse effects

[153] Berkowitz, Pistor and Richard, above n 5, 192.
[154] *Ibid.*
[155] *Ibid*, 167 and 174.
[156] *Nyali, Ltd v Attorney-General* [1956] 1 QB 16.

stemming from approximation of laws. The principle of subsidiarity may be one of them. This requires, in the EU context, that the EU refrain from action where the goals of the proposed action could be better achieved on a lower level, such as that of the Member States. The adoption of such a principle in the Euro-Med context should be examined. Under it, the neighbouring countries should align their legislation with that of the EU only if and insofar as the objective of the proposed legislative action cannot be sufficiently achieved by their domestic laws, and can therefore be better achieved by adopting EU legislation.

A cost–benefit analysis may also prove to be useful in that regard. Any proposed area for approximation of laws must be examined on an ad hoc basis, weighing the trade and other advantages embodied in such a move, as manifested on the regional and global fronts, against the likely costs in terms of loss of national sovereignty, identity and legitimacy. Only where such an ad hoc, nuanced examination indicates that a distinctive overall advantage is likely to result from aligning one's legislation, should the neighbouring countries approximate their laws to those of the EU.

Academia, think-tanks and industry should contribute to that analysis. Additional guidance should be sought from the experience of countries that have acceded to the EU, and that have had to align their statute books with that of the EU. Israel, like other Mediterranean countries with strong relations with the United States, should seek to profit from the particular experience of those acceding European countries that maintain strong trade and social links with both the European Union and the United States.[157]

The analysis conducted in this chapter has focused on the implications and repercussions of approximation of laws by the non-EU Mediterranean countries with the EU *acquis* (with special emphasis on the Israeli perspective). Yet many of the findings of this chapter may be applicable, *mutatis mutandis*, to other countries facing pressure to approximate their laws to those of trading powers with which they have asymmetric economic, trade and political relations. Further research is thus called for in order to determine the precise degree of such applicability.

[157] See B Hoekman, 'From Euro-Med Partnership to European Neighborhood: Deeper Integration *à la carte* and Economic Development' (2005) 103 Working Paper, The Egyptian Center for Economic Studies, July 2005, 5, available at http://www.ycsg.yale.edu/focus/gta/from_euro_med.pdf, 30: Mechanism involving voluntary exchange of information and peer review may be a precondition for governments to identify where formal approximation of laws to those of the *acquis* may prove to be beneficial. Such voluntary co-operation may help improve domestic policies and performance. It can also generate information on the size and distribution of costs and benefits of the status quo and reduce uncertainties stemming from the call to change that status quo through approximation of laws.

13

Conflicting Obligations in International Investment Law: Investment Tribunals' Perspective

MOSHE HIRSCH*

I. INTRODUCTION

THE RAPID PROLIFERATION of international investment agreements, the increasing number of treaties in other branches of international law, and the considerable increase in investor–state arbitrations[1] enhance the prospects for conflicts between investment and non-investment obligations. This chapter focuses on these conflicts but it is noteworthy that the interrelationships between international investment and non-investment obligations are not necessarily contradictory ('relationships of conflicts').[2] Legal rules derived from several spheres of international law often complement and reinforce one other.[3] Thus, international investment tribunals may (and are even encouraged to do so by the International Law Commission) harmonise overlapping

* Arnold Brecht Chair in European Law, Faculty of Law and Department of International Relations, Hebrew University of Jerusalem; Principal Research Fellow, Centre for Energy, Petroleum, Mineral Law and Policy, Faculty of Law, University of Dundee.

[1] For quantitative data on investor–state cases, see UNCTAD, Latest Developments in Investor–State Dispute Settlement, International Investment Agreements Monitor No 4 (2006) UNCTAD/WEB/ITE/IIA/2006/11, available at

[2] The International Law Commission (ILC) Study Group on the Fragmentation of International Law defines *relationships of conflict* as cases in which 'two norms that are both valid and applicable point to incompatible decisions so that a choice must be made between them'. ILC, Report of the ILC on the Work of its 58th Session: Conclusion 2, Conclusions of the work of the Study Group on the Fragmentation of International Law: Difficulties Arising from the Diversification and Expansion of International Law (2006) UN Doc A/61/10, para 251 (hereafter 'Conclusions of the ILC Fragmentation Report').

[3] On relationships of interpretation, see Conclusion 2, Conclusions of the ILC Fragmentation Report, *ibid*.

rules of international law, and interpret the provisions of international investment treaties in light of non-investment treaties.[4]

This chapter briefly examines the rules developed by investment tribunals that addressed arguments regarding inconsistent obligations, and analyses the factors that influenced these tribunals to adopt a reluctant approach to non-investment instruments. Finally, the chapter considers some ongoing trends in investment tribunal proceedings and discusses their likely implications for the future jurisprudence of investment tribunals in this sphere.

II. CONFLICTING OBLIGATIONS

Obligations arising from an investment contract or an international investment treaty may contradict obligations arising from other branches of international law, most prominently legal duties prescribed in environmental and human rights treaties. Arguments regarding inconsistent obligations are brought by different parties and arise at different stages of international litigation. On the governmental side, Canada argued in the *Myers* case[5] that its investment obligations (under Chapter 11 of the North American Free Trade Agreement (NAFTA)) were inconsistent with its other international obligations, including the Basel Convention on the Control of Transboundary Movement of Hazardous Wastes and their Disposal,[6] and that this treaty prevailed over its Chapter 11 obligations.[7] Similarly, Egypt contended in the *SPP* case[8] that the entry into force of the UNESCO Convention for the Protection of the World Cultural and Natural Heritage required it to cancel the permit issued to the foreign investor regarding the Pyramids Oasis Project.[9]

On the other side of state–investor relations, foreign investors have also invoked non-investment treaties to buttress their claims against host states. Thus, in the *Biloune* case, the investor argued that the government of Ghana had breached both the investment agreement and international human rights instruments, claiming damages for both violations.[10] Similarly, the Channel Tunnel Group argued in the *Euro-Tunnel* case that the obligations of the United Kingdom and France, as set out in the 1986

[4] See Conclusion 4, Conclusions of the ILC Fragmentation Report, *ibid.*

[5] *SD Myers v Canada* (2001) 40 ILM 1408.

[6] This global Convention prohibits the export and import of hazardous waste from and to states that are not contracting states unless such movement is subject to bilateral, multilateral or regional agreement. Arts 4(5) and 11, Basel Convention on the Control of Transboundary Movement of Hazardous Wastes and their Disposal (adopted 22 March 1989, entered into force 5 May 1992) 28 ILM 657.

[7] *Myers v Canada,* above n 5, para 150.

[8] *SPP (ME) v Egypt* (1994) 19 Yearbook Commercial Arbitration 51.

[9] *Ibid,* para 150.

[10] *Biloune v Ghana* (1993) 95 ILR 183.

Concession Agreement, should be read in conjunction with the European Convention on Human Rights and its First Protocol regarding peaceful enjoyment of possessions.[11]

Non-governmental organisations (NGOs) also invoke non-investment instruments, and the *amicus* briefs they submit to international investment tribunals often cite human rights and environmental treaties. Thus, for example, in an ongoing NAFTA litigation between Glamis and the United States,[12] the Quechan tribe is arguing that the territory upon which the investor (Glamis) would have dug its mine is located within the tribe's sacred areas, and that the US measures (which allegedly constitute expropriation) are justified under international treaties. The Quechan people are contending that their indigenous rights, which are threatened by possible approval of the Glamis claim, are protected, inter alia, by the 1966 International Covenant on Civil and Political Rights, the 1972 UNESCO World Heritage Convention, the 1989 ILO Convention concerning Indigenous and Tribal Peoples, and the Inter-American Convention on Human Rights.[13]

Non-investment treaties are invoked not only during the litigation stage that focuses on the determination of liability but also in the subsequent stage that addresses the determination of remedies. For example, in the *Santa Elena* case,[14] the tribunal was asked by Costa Rica to rule on the impact of its international obligation to preserve the ecological site (in which the confiscated property was located) upon the amount of compensation to be paid to the investors.[15] In *Siemens v Argentina*,[16] Argentina invoked the jurisprudence of the European Court of Human Rights (ECHR) to reduce the amount of compensation for property deprivations that were motivated by social objectives.[17]

III. INVESTMENT TRIBUNALS' MISGIVINGS

Investment tribunals that encounter complex questions regarding inconsistent obligations may search for guidance in the rules developed

[11] *Channel Tunnel Group v Governments of the United Kingdom and France* (Partial Award) (2007) paras 107, 110, available at http://www.pca-cpa.org/upload/files/ET_PAen.pdf.

[12] On this dispute, see J Wallace 'Corporate Nationality, Investment Protection Agreements, and Challenges to Domestic Natural Resources Law: The Implications of Glamis Gold's NAFTA Chapter 11 Claim' (2005) 17 *Georgetown International Environmental Law Review* 365.

[13] *Glamis Gold Ltd v United States of America*, Non-Party Submission: Submission of the Quechan Indian Nation, Nature of the Cultural Resources and Sacred Places at Issue in Claim, 8–9, available at http://www.naftaclaims.com/Disputes/USA/Glamis/Glamis-Amicus-Quechan-01-19-08-05.pdf.

[14] *Santa Elena v Costa Rica* (2000) 15 ICSID Review 169.

[15] *Ibid*, paras 71–2.

[16] *Siemens v Argentina* (2005), available at http://www.iisd.org/pdf/2005/investment_investsd_april27_2005.pdf.

[17] *Ibid*, para 346.

in general international law regulating inconsistencies among international legal rules. As noted by the ILC Fragmentation Report, these rules include, inter alia, principles of normative hierarchy, and methods for determining what rules should prevail, or at least, what consequences follow from a breach of the requirements of one regime by deferring to another.[18]

A. General International Law on Conflicting Obligations

Under general international law, international norms that are considered as *jus cogens* (peremptory norms) prevail over all other inconsistent rules of international law.[19] Article 53 of the 1969 Vienna Convention on the Law of Treaties (VCLT) further establishes that such a conflicting treaty is void.[20] The primacy of some fundamental international human rights over investment obligations may be invoked, for example, by investors with regard to their right to property, as well as regarding their right to fair trial (to the extent that these are recognised as peremptory norms).

Allegations regarding a conflict between these fundamental human rights and international treaties were seriously considered by the European Court of First Instance in the *Kadi* case.[21]

Unless peremptory rules of international law are involved, Article 103 of the United Nations Charter provides that the Charter's provisions prevail over other incompatible treaties.[22] The special status of the UN Charter's provisions was affirmed by the International Court of Justice's decision in the *Lockerbie* case regarding the relationship between Article 25 of the Charter and the 1971 Montreal Convention for the Suppression of Unlawful Acts Against the Safety of Civil Aviation.[23] In *Kadi* and other cases, the European Court of First Instance has also accepted the primacy

[18] M Koskenniemi, Report of the Study Group of the International Law Commission, Fragmentation of International Law: Difficulties Arising from the Diversification and Expansion of International Law (13 April 2006) UN Doc A/CN4/L682, para 194 (hereafter 'Koskenniemi Report on Fragmentation of International Law').

[19] Art 53 of the VCLT, 8 ILM 679 (1969). See also Conclusions 32–3, Conclusions of the ILC Fragmentation Report, above n 2; See also, D Shelton 'Normative Hierarchy in International Law' (2006) 100 *American Journal of International Law* 291, 297–319.

[20] Art 53 of the VCLT provides as follows: 'A treaty is void if, at the time of its conclusion, it conflicts with a peremptory norm of general international law.' VCLT, above n 19. For an extensive analysis of this article, see A Orakhelashvili, *Peremptory Norms in International Law* (Oxford University Press, 2006) 133–204.

[21] Case T–315/01 *Kadi v Council of the European Union* [2005] ECR II–3649.

[22] See also Art 30(1) of the VCLT, above n 19. On Art 103 of the UN Charter, see Conclusions 34 of the Conclusions of the ILC Fragmentation Report, above n 2.

[23] *Case Concerning Questions of Interpretation and Application of the 1971 Montreal Convention Arising from the Aerial Incident at Lockerbie* (*Libyan Arab Jamahiriya v United Kingdom*), Request for the Indication of Provisional Measures (Order of 14 April) 1992 ICJ Rep 3.

of the UN Charter's provision over legal obligations arising from treaties establishing the European Union.[24]

Where rules of *jus cogens* or the UN Charter provisions are not involved, other rules of international law regulate interactions among inconsistent international legal rules. If different international rules arise from customary and treaty law, generally, treaty and custom have equal weight,[25] and inconsistencies are regulated by three interrelated principles: (i) *lex specialis derogat generali*, ie, a specific rule prevails over general one; (ii) *lex posterior derogate priori*, ie, a later rule prevails over a prior one; (iii) respecting the parties' intentions, ie, where the parties intend to replace a rule deriving from one source of international law with another rule included in another source of law (eg, replace a customary rule with a treaty rule), the rule preferred by the parties will prevail.[26] Similar regulatory principles apply where the inconsistent rules are included in the *same source* of international law. Thus, where rules emanating from two (or more) treaties are incompatible, the specific treaty trumps the general one.[27] Additional rules regarding the relationships between conflicting *treaties* are elaborated in Article 30 of the VCLT.

The trigger for the application of the above regulatory rules necessitates a prior determination that the rules deriving from different treaties or sources of international law are inconsistent. Such a determination depends to a significant extent on the interpretation given to the international rules involved, and whether or not these rules are reconcilable. A more moderate approach avoids establishing hierarchical order for different legal rules by means of harmonious interpretation of the relevant treaties. Such an approach, which strives to interpret one treaty rule in light of other treaty or international customary rules, is consistent with Article 31(3) of the VCLT.[28]

[24] *Kadi*, above n 21, para 224. See also Case T–253/02 *Ayadi v Council of the European Union*, para 116, available at http://curia.europa.eu/jurisp/cgi-bin/form.pl?lang=en&Submit=Submit&docj=docj&docop=docop&numaff=T-253%2F02&datefs=&datefe=&nomusuel=&domaine=&mots=&resmax=100; *Yusuf v Council and Commission of the European Union*, para 231, available at http://eur-lex.europa.eu/LexUriServ/LexUriServ.do?uri=CELEX:62001A0306:EN:HTML, para 231.

[25] LF Damrosch et al, *International Law* (4th ed, St Paul, Minnesota, West, 2001) 119.

[26] Conclusions 5, 10 and 24 of the Conclusions of the ILC Fragmentation Report, above n 25; Damrosch et al, above n 2, 109.

[27] R Reuter, *Introduction to the Law of Treaties* (London, Kegan Paul, 1995) 132–3.

[28] Conclusion 4, Conclusions of the ILC Fragmentation Report, above n 2, states in this respect: '*The principle of harmonization*. It is a generally accepted principle that when several norms bear on a single issue they should, to the extent possible, be interpreted so as to give rise to a single set of compatible obligations.' See also Conclusion 9 of this Report. On this method of interpretation, see C McLachlan, 'The Principle of Systematic Integration and Article 31(3)(c) of the Vienna Convention' (2005) 54 *International and Comparative Law Quarterly* 279.

B. Reluctant Tribunals

An analysis of the jurisprudence of investment tribunals reveals that while these tribunals often incorporate in their decisions rules of general international law on state responsibility and treaty law, they are generally reluctant to rely on general principles regarding inconsistent obligations arising from non-investment instruments. Thus, for example, while investment tribunals often cite various provisions of the VCLT, they have so far not invoked Article 53 of this Convention which deals with peremptory norms, or Article 30 regarding inconsistent treaties.[29] This practical disregard may appear even more puzzling in light of the fact that contemporary international investment law does not include a coherent body of rules in this sphere.

Investment tribunals have approached arguments regarding inconsistencies between the investment agreement and non-investment law in a very cautious (and even suspicious) manner. Thus far, no investment tribunal has absolved a party that encountered inconsistent obligations from its investment obligations, or reduced the amount of compensation due to be paid to the injured party in such cases.[30]

International investment tribunals faced with arguments regarding conflicting obligations have not attempted to develop systematic rules to address such questions. Rather, they addressed such questions sporadically, providing specific answers to the particular questions that arose in each case. Below, we will briefly examine the principles arising from the scattered jurisprudence of investment tribunals in this emerging field.[31]

In general, investment tribunals that addressed arguments regarding inconsistent obligations agreed to examine the non-investment treaty's provisions. This examination sought to discover whether or not the investment obligation indeed contradicted non-investment instruments, and if so, which obligation prevailed. For example, this approach was adopted by the tribunals in the *Myers*[32] and *SPP* cases.[33]

[29] The very recent arbitral *Sempra* award addresses the relationships between the provisions of bilateral investment treaties and the rules of general international law regarding 'necessity' (under the ILC rules on State Responsibility), implicitly refers to the *lex specialis* principle; *Sempra v Argentina*, para 378, available at http://www.investmentclaims.com/decisions/Sempra_Energy-Award.pdf.

[30] For a criticism of this approach of investment tribunals, see M Sornarajah, *The Clash of Globalizations and the International Law on Foreign Investment* (Ottawa, The Norman Paterson School of International Affairs, 2002) available at http://www.carleton.ca/ctpl/pdf/papers/sornarajah.pdf.

[31] For a detailed examination of investment tribunals' jurisprudence in this field, see M Hirsch 'Interactions between Investment and Non-Investment Obligations in International Investment Law', in C Schreuer et al (eds), *Oxford Handbook of International Law on Foreign Investment* (Oxford University Press, forthcoming).

[32] *Myers v Canada*, above n 5, paras 205–9, 213–15.

[33] See, eg, the statement of the SPP tribunal regarding the relevance of the 1972 UNESCO Convention: 'Nor is there any question that the UNESCO Convention is relevant . . .'. *SPP v Egypt*, above n 8, para 78.

An examination of investment tribunal jurisprudence indicates that this approach is not undertaken in two exceptional cases: where the non-investment instruments are essentially invoked to expand the tribunal's substantive jurisdiction and with regard to the host state's obligations following *expropriation* of property. In these exceptional cases, discussed below, investment tribunals have categorically refused to examine the relevant non-investment treaties.

As to the substantive jurisdiction of investment tribunals, the arbitral tribunal in the *Biloune* case stated that it lacked jurisdiction to address violations of human rights treaties as an independent cause of action.[34] Similarly, the *Euro-Tunnel* tribunal emphasised that its jurisdiction was limited to claims related to rights and obligations of the parties under the Concession Agreement and the relevant treaty.[35]

Investment tribunals have also declined to examine the non-investment obligations in the context of the obligation to compensate for the expropriation of property and to set the level of compensation. The *Santa Elena* tribunal categorically stated that the source of the environmental obligation that motivated the expropriation, whether domestic or international, did not alter the government's duty to compensate the investor. Similarly, the host state's international obligations do not affect the amount of compensation.[36] A similar approach regarding the measure of compensation following expropriation also arose from the *Siemens* case, in which the tribunal refused to take into account the jurisprudence of the ECHR and observed that the 'margin of appreciation' afforded to states by the ECHR is not part of customary international law or the relevant bilateral investment treaty.[37]

Some other tribunals that were ready to examine the non-investment instruments eventually rejected arguments of inconsistent obligations because of the findings they reached regarding the real motivation of the party that breached the agreement. Such tribunals checked not only the non-investment instrument, but also whether the evidence supported the contention that the latter instruments genuinely motivated the party to deviate from its investment obligations. Where the tribunal found that the real motivation was not related to the non-investment instrument (but rather, for example, to deliberate discrimination against foreigners), the

[34] The tribunal explained: 'This Tribunal's competence is limited to commercial disputes arising under a contract entered into in the context of Ghana's Investment Code. As noted, the Government agreed to arbitrate only disputes "in respect of" the foreign investment. Thus, other matters—however compelling the claim or wrongful the alleged act—are outside this Tribunal's jurisdiction.' *Biloune v Ghana*, above n 10, 213.

[35] The tribunal, however, drew a distinction between the issue of jurisdiction and questions relating to the applicable law. The above refusal to examine non-investment obligations related to the issue of jurisdiction. *The Channel Tunnel Group Limited v Governments of the United Kingdom and the French Republic*, above n 11, paras 151–3.

[36] *Santa Eelena v Costa Rica*, above n 14, para 71.

[37] *Siemens v Argentina*, above n 16, para 354.

reliance on the non-investment treaty was rejected. This position clearly arises from the *Myers* case, [38] and a similar approach is also revealed by the *SPP*[39] and *International Bank of Washington*[40] cases.

The de facto refusal of investment tribunals to accept arguments regarding inconsistent non-investment obligations also relates to the question of whether the non-investment treaty was voluntarily undertaken by the party that invoked it. The tribunal in the *SPP* case rejected Egypt's argument regarding the UNESCO Convention and emphasised that the relevant obligation had not been externally imposed on the government of Egypt, but rather resulted from Egypt's voluntary activities.[41]

An additional reason that led the SPP tribunal to reject Egypt's argument regarding inconsistent obligations lies in the temporal sequence of obligations. The *SPP* tribunal scrutinised the chronological order of the inconsistent obligations involved and concluded that Egypt's obligation under the UNESCO Convention entered into force *after* the investment obligations were undertaken vis-à-vis the investor.[42] The chronological order of obligations is significant because of the information available to the parties (regarding the legal obligations) at the time when the investment obligation is undertaken.[43]

The restrained approach of investment tribunals to non-investment instruments is also revealed from their rulings regarding cases in which a genuine and unavoidable inconsistency between the investment and non-investment obligations exists. In such cases, the discretion of a party that encounters inconsistent obligations is limited. As the *Myers* tribunal

[38] Following a review of the evidence, the *Myers* tribunal concluded that Canada's policy was shaped to a great extent by the desire to protect and promote the market share of enterprises that would carry out the destruction of polychlorinated biphenyl (PCB) waste in Canada, and that were owned by Canadian nationals. The tribunal stated that the relevant Canadian measures favoured Canadian nationals over non-nationals. *Myers v Canada*, above n 5, paras 193, 195.

[39] The tribunal's analysis of the facts regarding Egypt's choice of sites to be protected under the UNESCO Conventions seems to trace the genuine intentions of Egypt. See *SPP v Egypt*, above n 8, para 154.

[40] The tribunal in this case also dealt with conservation measures (regarding forestry but not arising from international treaty). The crucial question in this case was whether the forestry decrees issued by the Dominican Republic's agencies amounted to expropriatory action. As in the *Myers* case, the tribunal carefully examined the facts regarding the host state's intention and concluded that the relevant 'regulations were aimed at a genuine concern with forestry conservation, and not discriminatory in application'. *International Bank of Washington v OPIC*, (1972) 11 ILM 1216, 1227. The tribunal concluded that the government's conservation measures were not expropriatory actions.

[41] *SPP v Egypt*, above n 8, para 154.

[42] The tribunal stated in this respect: 'The Tribunal's determination that the Claimants' activities on the Pyramids Plateau would have become internationally unlawful in 1979, but not before that date, has significant consequences in other respects which are discussed below'. *SPP V Egypt*, above n 8, para 157.

[43] The significance of the information available to the parties at the time the investment is made relates to the principle of fair and equitable treatment in BITs. See the analysis in Hirsch, above n 31, Section IV(4).

ruled, the party that is legally bound to comply with the non-investment obligation must choose the alternative that is the least inconsistent with its investment obligations.[44]

IV. DISINTEGRATIVE APPROACH: ROOTS AND OUTCOMES

As discussed above, the jurisprudence of investment tribunals reveals both integrative and disintegrative approaches, with a strong tendency towards the latter.[45] While these tribunals often incorporate rules of general international law regarding state responsibility and treaty law, they are generally reluctant to draw upon the rules of international law regarding conflicting obligations (eg, Articles 53 and 30 of the VCLT). This disintegrative inclination is particularly prominent with regard to rules derived from more specialised branches of international law, such as human rights and environmental treaties. This section seeks to discuss some possible explanations for the latter disintegrative approach, and to emphasise some structural features of international investment law and tribunals.

A. The **inter partes** *model and public interests*

Generally, international tribunals fulfil two principal functions in the international legal system: settling disputes between the particular rival parties and developing legal rules to guide future behaviour. Tribunals in different spheres emphasise different roles, and their inclination in that regard often influences their decisions. Tribunals that accord significant weight to their law-making role are more likely to take into account wider public policy considerations (eg, human rights and environmental protection) and seek a due balance between the competing principles. On the other hand, tribunals that emphasise their role in settling the dispute between the particular parties (the '*inter partes* model') are less likely to grant significant weight to broader policy issues that are reflected in such general treaties.

Most investment tribunals incline to adopt the '*inter partes* model' (which is prevalent in commercial arbitration) and grant precedence to

[44] *Myers v Canada*, above n 5, para 215. It is interesting to note that the tribunal stated in that regard that this rule is consistent with case-law arising out of the WTO agreements; para 221.

[45] On integrative and disintegrative approaches within international investment law (discussing parallel contract and treaty claims arising from the same investment disputes), see Y Shany, 'Contract Claims v Treaty Claims: Mapping Conflicts between ICSID Decisions on Multisourced Investment Claims' (2005) 99 *American Journal of International Law* 835, 844–5.

their role as settlers of disputes between the particular parties.[46] This tendency is revealed, inter alia, in the recent string of inconsistent decisions rendered by investment tribunals regarding the defence of 'necessity' (under rules of state responsibility) arising out of essentially identical events (the economic crisis in Argentina in 2001–2002) and based on the same legal instruments.[47] Although the recent decision in the *Enron* case (rendered in May 2007)[48] contradicted the *LG&E* award (rendered in October 2006),[49] the *Enron* tribunal did not attempt to distinguish its reasoning from the *LG&E* decision (even though one arbitrator was a member of both tribunals).[50] In light of this prevalent *inter partes* conception, most investment adjudicators are inclined to focus on the particular facts of the dispute and on the particular legal instruments—mainly the contract between the investor and the host state, as well as the investment treaty.

B. Ad hoc tribunals and limited jurisdiction

The jurisdiction of most investment tribunals in recent years is based on bilateral treaties (and in some cases on trilateral agreements, such as NAFTA)[51] and the adjudicators are nominated on an ad hoc basis. Thus, investment arbitrators are more likely to perceive their role as adjudicators selected to settle a particular dispute between the specific parties rather than as global or regional judges. This common perception

[46] See, eg, T Walde, 'The Present State of Research Carried Out by the English-Speaking Section of the Centre for Studies and Research' (2007) *Hague Academy Report on International Investment Law* 75–6; G Van Harten *Investment Treaty Arbitration and Public Law* (Oxford University Press, 2007) 5–6, 58.

[47] On these conflicting decisions regarding Art XI of the United States–Argentina bilateral investment treaty and Art 25 of the International Law Commission Rules on State Responsibility, see SW Schill, 'German Constitutional Court Rules on Necessity in Argentine Bondholder Case' (2007) 11 *ASIL Insight* Issue 20, 31 July; A Reinisch, 'Necessity in International Investment Arbitration—An Unnecessary Split of Opinions in Recent ICSID Cases? Comments on *CMS v Argentina* and *LG&E v Argentina*' (2007) 8 *Journal of World Investment and Trade* 191; AK Bjorklund, 'Emergency Exceptions to International Obligations in the Realm of Foreign Investment: The State of Necessity and Force Majeure as Circumstances Precluding Wrongfulness' in C Schreuer et al (eds), *Oxford Handbook of International Law on Foreign Investment* (Oxford University Press, forthcoming).

[48] *Enron v Argentina*, paras 288–345, available at http://ita.law.uvic.ca/documents/Enron-Award.pdf. This decision largely followed the CMS award; *CMS Gas Transmission v Argentina*, paras 304–94, available at http://www.worldbank.org/icsid/cases/CMS_Award.pdf.

[49] *LG&E International v Argentina (Decision on Liability)*, paras 201–66, available at http://www.worldbank.org/icsid/cases/pdf/09_LGE_Liability_e.pdf.

[50] 'Enron Wins $106 Million (US) in Financial Crisis Claim against Argentina', *Investment Treaty News*, 27 May 2007.

[51] The major exception is the Energy Charter Treaty, 34 ILM 360 (1995). On the investment provisions of the Energy Charter Treaty, see T Walde, 'International Investment Under the 1994 Energy Charter Treaty' (1995) 29 *Journal of World Trade* 5; T Walde (ed), *The Energy Charter Treaty: An East–West Gateway for Investment and Trade* (The Hague, Kluwer, 1996).

of an investment adjudicator's role tends to undervalue the public interests involved in investment disputes.

Furthermore, a significant deviation from the provisions of the investment treaty from which the jurisdiction of investment tribunals derives may lead to allegations (by losing parties) that the tribunals exceeded their authority, which is a common ground for the annulment of international arbitral awards.[52] This fact may explain why investment tribunals that have dealt with arguments regarding non-investment treaties in the context of their jurisdiction, have categorically refused to consider such non-investment instruments.[53]

C. Transparency and public participation

One of the significant factors influencing the character of investment tribunals such as *inter partes* or public dispute-settlement mechanisms relates to the exposure of their proceedings to the public, as well as the participation of public interest groups in the legal proceedings. In general, investment arbitration proceedings are not open to the public: tribunals do not disclose copies of written pleading and other documents submitted to them, and oral hearings are closed to the public.[54] The prevailing atmosphere of confidentiality in most investment arbitral proceedings tends to intensify the adjudicators' perception that their principal role is settling the particular dispute between the specific parties, and to diminish the weight given by the tribunals to broader public interests that are often reflected in non-investment treaties.[55]

D. Law-making by states and investment tribunals

The disinclination of investment tribunals to strike a meaningful balance

[52] See, eg, Art 52(d) of the Convention on the Settlement of Investment Disputes between States and Nationals of other States (adopted 18 March 1965, entered into force 14 October 1966) 575 UNTS 159. On this ground for annulment of arbitral awards, see C Schreuer, *The ICSID Convention: a Commentary* (Cambridge University Press, 2001); M Hirsch, *The Arbitration Mechanism of the International Center for the Settlement of Investment Disputes* (The Hague, Kluwer-Nijhoff, 1993) 33–5.

[53] See the positions undertaken by the investment tribunals in *Biloune v Ghana* and the *Euro-Tunnel case* in Section II above.

[54] As noted by Knahr and Reinisch, the most restrictive rules are included in UNCITRAL Arbitration rules, ICSID tribunals handle confidentiality issues rather restrictively, and access to documents is easier in the context of NAFTA Chapter 11 proceedings. For a detailed analysis of the arbitration rules of UNCITRAL, ICSID and NAFTA, see C Knahr and A Reinisch 'Transparency versus Confidentiality in International Investment Arbitration—The Biwater Gauff Compromise' (2007) 6 *International Courts and Tribunals* 97, 98–103; J Delaney and DB Magraw 'Procedural Transparency' in C Schreuer et al (eds), *Oxford Handbook of International Law on Foreign Investment* (Oxford University Press, forthcoming).

[55] On recent changes in this sphere, see Section IV.

between investment and non-investment interests also relates to the law-making role of states and tribunals in international investment law. In general, tribunals are more likely to be active in creating new law (through interpretation) in spheres in which the legislators are relatively passive.[56] Contemporary international investment law is dominated by rules included in treaties,[57] and states quite often conclude new investment treaties with new provisions responding to the changing circumstances.[58] Thus, for example, the recent US and Canadian model bilateral investment treaties (BITs) include specific provisions regarding investment and environment.[59] Similarly, the latter states seek, in response to public pressure, to include new provisions in investment treaties that enhance procedural transparency.[60] The inclination of states to respond to recent changes by amending their investment treaties is also noticeable with regard to Most-Favoured Nation (MFN) clauses in the recent US investment treaties[61] (responding to the investment awards regarding the application of the MFN clause to dispute-settlement procedures).[62]

In light of the active law-making role undertaken by states in the sphere of international investment law (prominently, with regard to the relationships between investment and environmental protection),

[56] For a sociological explanation of this trend, see M Hirsch 'The Sociology of International Law' (2005) 55 *University of Toronto Law Journal* 891, at 919–21.

[57] See, eg, C Schreuer, 'Diversity and Harmonization of Treaty Interpretation in Investment Arbitration' (2006) 3 *Transnational Dispute Management* 1; JW Salacuse and HJ Braker, 'The Treatification of International Investment Law' (2006) 3 *Transnational Dispute Management* (No 3).

[58] Furthermore, the Parties to NAFTA are authorised to issue interpretations that bind the panels. Art 1131(2) NAFTA, 32 ILM 289 (1993).

[59] Art 12(2) of the 2004 US Model Bilateral Investment Treaty provides as follows: 'Nothing in this Treaty shall be construed to prevent a Party from adopting, maintaining, or enforcing any measure otherwise consistent with this Treaty that it considers appropriate to ensure that investment activity in its territory is undertaken in a manner sensitive to environmental concerns.' Treaty Between the Government of the United States of America and the Government of [Country] Concerning the Encouragement and Reciprocal Protection of Investment, 2004, available at http://www.ustr.gov/assets/Trade_Sectors/Investment/Model_BIT/asset_upload_file847_6897.pdf; See, for also, Art 10.11 of the Dominican Republic – Central America – United States Free Trade Agreement, available at http://www.ustr.gov/assets/Trade_Agreements/Bilateral/CAFTA/CAFTA-DR_Final_Texts/asset_upload_file328_4718.pdf; Art 11 and Art 1 of Annex III of the Canadian Model BIT. Model BIT. Agreement Between Canada and __ for the Promotion and Protection of Investments, available at http://www.sice.oas.org/investment/NatLeg/Can/2004-FIPA-model-en.pdf.

[60] On recent BITs' provisions regarding transparency, see Section IV below. See also D Vis-Dunbar, 'Czech Republic and Hungary Opposed to Canada's Investor–State Transparency Demands' *Investment Treaty News*, 27 April 2007.

[61] The recent US treaties with Peru and Columbia include a footnote to the MFN clause, stating that the clause does not apply to dispute-resolution mechanisms. FB Diaz, Peru–US Trade and Investment Pact Moving Towards Approval by US Senate and House, *Investment Treaty News* (30 October 2007).

[62] See, eg, *Maffezini v Spain*, 124 *ILR* 58 (2003); *Plama Consortium v Bulgaria*, (Decision on Jurisdiction) 44 ILM 721 (2005).

investment arbitrators are more passive in regulating the interactions between investment and non-investment obligations

E. Global rifts and bilateral solutions

The emphasis that investment tribunals place on the *inter partes* elements of the disputes is also related to the bilateral (or trilateral) nature of most rules of investment law,[63] and to looming global tensions regarding the formation of global law in this sphere. International investment law comprises a relatively small number of global rules, few of which are customary norms,[64] and the major attempt to establish a comprehensive Multilateral Agreement on Investment (MAI) failed in 1998.[65] Following the breakdown of the MAI negotiations, efforts to establish multilateral rules in this sphere shifted to the World Trade Organization (WTO). Although the 1996 WTO Singapore Ministerial Declaration established a working group to examine the relationship between trade and investment,[66] the WTO members agreed in summer 2004 that this topic should be dropped from the Doha Development Agenda.[67] The lack of dense global rules in this field is explained by various factors, prominently among them disagreements between developing and developed states, as well as the opposition of environmental and human rights NGOs.[68]

Widespread controversies between developing and developed states regarding the content of international investment rules reached their peak during the 1960s and 1970s, a period that also marked an ideological

[63] Schreuer, *Diversity and Harmonization of Treaty Interpretation*, above n 57. As noted above, the major exception to the bilateral/ trilateral pattern is the Energy Charter Treaty.

[64] See, eg, Salacuse, above n 57; *Case Concerning Ahmadou Sadio Diallo* (*Republic of Guinea v Democratic Republic of The Congo*) (Preliminary Objections) para 88, available at http://www.icj-cij.org/docket/files/103/13856.pdf; M Sornarajah, *The International Law on Foreign Investment* (2nd ed, Cambridge University Press, 2004) 89.

[65] The efforts to conclude the Multilateral Agreement on Investment were undertaken by the OECD states but an essential part of the OECD strategy was that developing states would be invited to accede to the MAI, and that those who seek to attract foreign investments would find themselves unable to afford not to join the agreement. MJ Trebilcock and R Howse, *The Regulation of International Trade* (3rd ed, London, Routledge, 2005) 459–60. On the MAI, see also M Matsushita et al, *The World Trade Organization: Law, Practice And Policy* (New York, Oxford University Press, 2006) 833–5; AB Zampetti and P Sauve, 'International Investment' in AT Guzman and AO Sykes (eds), *Research Handbook in International Economic Law* (Boston, MA, Elgar, 2007) 211, 249–51.

[66] Art 20, Ministerial Declaration (18 December 1996) WT/MIN(96)/DEC, available at http://www.wto.org/english/thewto_e/minist_e/min96_e/wtodec_e.htm.

[67] Art g, Decision Adopted by the General Council (1 August 2004) WT/L/579, 2 August 2004, available at http://www.wto.org/english/tratop_e/dda_e/ddadraft_31jul04_e.pdf. See also Trebilcock and Howse, above n 65, 460–1.

[68] See, eg, Trebilcock and Howse, above n 65, 457–61; Matsushita *et al*, above n 65, 836–8; Zampetti and Sauve, above n 65, 249–51; 'WTO: Members Decide on Way Forward in Doha Round' (December 2003) 7 *Bridges Weekly Trade News Digest* 43, 17.

divide.[69] This rift still reverberates in contemporary international investment law, particularly in regard to the highly sensitive issues of expropriations and compensation for expropriations. Consequently, investment arbitrators tend to adopt a depoliticising strategy by sticking to the specific provisions set out in the particular bilateral or trilateral treaty, while avoiding the more controversial non-investment treaties.

The tendency of investment tribunals to evade widely debated issues is prominent in the case-law regarding measures of compensation. Several questions related to expropriation of investors' property (particularly the standard of compensation) were among the most divisive issues in international law during the 1960s and 1970s. This controversy marked the sharpest divide between developing and developed states, as well as numerous scholars of international law.[70] At the height of the debate, the UN General Assembly adopted the resolutions on the New International Economic Order,[71] which were backed by a majority of developing states and by virtually no developed countries.[72] These resolutions were intended to constitute a global challenge to existing international economic relations.[73] The debate has considerably receded, the ideological overtones have largely been silenced,[74] but its divisive effects still linger.

In light of the history of tension regarding the standard of compensation, it is not surprising that arguments raised by host states seeking to reduce the amount of compensation for expropriation because of the application of environmental treaties or human rights treaties were categorically rejected by investment tribunals.[75] Focusing on the narrower rules of the particular investment instruments enables the tribunals to avoid the hotly debated issues in international law and the echoes of the past North–South polarisation in international investment law. It is interesting to note that the WTO dispute-settlement panels have also largely avoided directly addressing claims under the 1994 WTO

[69] AF Lowenfeld, *International Economic Law* (Oxford University Press, 2002) 378–80, 403–15.

[70] See, eg, Lowenfeld, *ibid*, 387; RD Bishop, J Crawford and VM Reisman, *Foreign Investment Disputes: Cases, Materials and Commentary* (The Hague, Kluwer, 2005) 1298–325; M Pellonpaa, and M Fitzmaurice, 'Taking of Property in the Practice of the Iran–US Claims Tribunal' (1988) 14 *Netherlands Yearbook of International Law* 53, 166, 176; O Schachter, 'Compensation for Expropriation' (1984) 79 *American Journal of International Law* 121.

[71] See Declaration on the Establishment of a New International Economic Order, UNGA Res 3201 (S-VI) (1 May 1974), available at http://daccess-ods.un.org/TMP/9190966.html; Charter of Economic Rights and Duties of States, UNGA Res 3281 (XXIV) (12 December 1974), available at http://daccessdds.un.org/doc/RESOLUTION/GEN/NR0/738/83/IMG/NR073883.pdf?OpenElement; Lowenfeld, above n 69, 410–14.

[72] T Walde, 'Remedies and Compensation in International Investment Law' (July 2005) Paper submitted to ILA Committee on International Law of Foreign Investment, 44–6. On the status of these General Assembly Resolutions, see *Texaco v Libya* (1978) 17 ILM 1, 148–53.

[73] A Cassese, *International Law* (2nd ed, Oxford, Oxford University Press, 2005) 509.

[74] Cassese, *ibid*, 44–5, 508–9.

[75] See the discussion in Section II on the *Santa Elena* and *Siemens* cases.

Agreement on Trade Related Investment Measures (TRIMs) by choosing to consider the related claims of violation of the national treatment obligation under the (less controversial) General Agreement on Tariffs and Trade (GATT).[76]

F. Asymmetric Features and Conceptual Divide

As noted above, while investment tribunals have not hesitated to draw upon the rules of general international law regarding treaties and state responsibility, they have been reluctant to rely on international law rules regulating conflicts between international legal rules (*jus cogens*, etc). The reason for the discrepancy between international investment and those parts of general international law lies, inter alia, in the distinctive features and concepts that underlie these branches of international law. The above-mentioned international law rules regulating inconsistencies may be considered as neutral regarding the involved branches of international law (eg, environment and investment) or as according preference to fundamental human rights (via the concept of *jus cogens*) and rules regarding international peace and security (via Article 103 of the UN Charter). Investment tribunals, on the other hand, strive to advance the basic goal of international investment treaties, primarily increasing the flow of foreign investments, often by granting private investors enhanced protection.[77]

The basic features of international investment law are fundamentally different from most branches of international law. While the underlying assumption of inter-state relations under public international law is sovereign equality, the legal relationships between host states and foreign investors are clearly asymmetric. Host states are in an a priori superior position in regard to their capacity to influence the content of the domestic law and the relevant norms of international law (particularly with regard to treaties).[78] These structural differences have led investment tribunals to grant precedence to contractual or consensual rules that have been agreed upon by host states and investors. Following the contractual stage, and during most stages of the implementation of the investment agreement, the superior position of the host state regarding influence upon the content of both domestic and international law is glaring. Consequently, investment tribunals are inclined to level the

[76] Trebilcock and Howse, above n 65, at 456–7.

[77] Thus, for example, BITs are interpreted according to their objects and purposes (under Art 31 of the VCLT). Since investment treaties aim to promote foreign investment, this principle of interpretation often leads investment tribunals to interpret investment treaties in favour of the investor. Schreuer, above n 57, 2.

[78] See, eg, Hirsch, above n 52, 133–4; Wälde, above n 46, 76–9.

normative field and emphasise the obligations included in the investment agreement and the circumstances prevailing at this critical stage (such as the information available to both parties in this phase).[79]

The emphasis placed by investment tribunals on the vulnerability of the foreign investors and the need to protect them is well illustrated in two related arbitral awards regarding the relevance of the jurisprudence of the ECHR to investment relations. In the *TECMED* case, the arbitral tribunal considered whether the decision undertaken by the Mexican agency (that was considered expropriation) was reasonable and proportional with respect to its goals. The tribunal emphasised the weakness of the foreign investors, as the latter had reduced or no participation in the taking of decisions that affect them (partly because they are not entitled to exercise political rights reserved for the nationals of host states).[80] The tribunal also discussed the particular vulnerability of foreign investors to bearing an excessive share of the burden involved in the realisation of public aims, and cited with approval the judgment of the ECHR in *James v UK*:

> Especially as regards a taking of property effected in the context of a social reform, there may well be good grounds for drawing a distinction between nationals and non-nationals as far as compensation is concerned. . . . non-nationals are more vulnerable to domestic legislation: . . . although a taking of property must always be effected in the public interest, different considerations may apply to nationals and non-nationals and there may well be legitimate reason for requiring nationals to bear a greater burden in the public interest than non-nationals.[81]

This citation of the jurisprudence of the ECHR was discussed by the arbitral tribunal in the *Siemens* case. The government of Argentina argued that when a state expropriates for social or economic reasons, the regular 'fair market standard' does not apply because otherwise it would limit the sovereignty of the country to introduce reforms. Argentina relied here on the above citation of the ECHR in the *TECMED* case as an example to follow in terms of considering the purpose and proportionality of the measure taken vis-à-vis the private investor.[82] The *Siemens* tribunal rejected this argument and explained, inter alia, that 'Article I of the First Protocol to the European Convention on Human Rights permits a

[79] The significance of the information known to the parties at that time is relevant to the interpretation of the 'fair and equitable treatment' principle in BITs. Hirsch, above n 31, s 3(d).

[80] *TECMED v Mexico* (2004) 43 ILM 133, para 122.

[81] [1986] *European Court of Human Rights* 2 (21 February 1986), para 50. On the European Court of Human Rights jurisprudence on the protection of property, see A Mowbray, *European Convention on Human Rights* (Oxford University Press, 2007) 895–955.

[82] *Siemens v The Argentine Republic*, above n 16, para 354.

margin of appreciation not found in customary international law or the Treaty.'[83]

Thus, while the *TECMED* tribunal cited the jurisprudence of the ECHR in order to emphasise the weakness of foreign investors, the *Siemens* tribunal refused to accept the jurisprudence of the same court, emphasising the inconsistency between the European Convention's rules regarding the special measure of discretion available to the host state (under the 'margin of appreciation' doctrine)[84] and international investment law.[85]

V. CONTEMPORARY TRENDS AND FUTURE CHANGES?

The preceding section discusses some factors explaining the current reluctant approach of investment tribunals vis-à-vis non-investment instruments. This explanation should not lead to the conclusion that the above-discussed factors are likely to stand still and that no changes are expected to take place in this legal sphere. Some ongoing developments indicate that the existing attitude of investment tribunals to non-investment law may well change somewhat in the future.

As discussed above, one of the significant factors influencing investment tribunals not to accord significant weight to non-investment instruments relates to the extent of the exposure of these tribunals to the public, as well as the involvement of public interest groups in the legal proceedings. In general, it seems that increasing public transparency and participation of NGOs in investment proceedings is likely to exert further pressure on investment arbitrators to accord a greater weight to broader public interests. The latter public interests, such as environmental and human rights protection, are often reflected in non-investment treaties.

The current trend to enhance the transparency of investment tribunal

[83] *Ibid*, para 354. On the margin of appreciation doctrine under the European Convention on Human Rights, see Mowbray, above n 81, 629–33; JG Merrills, *The Development of International Law by the European Court of Human Rights* (2nd ed, Manchester University Press, 1993) 150–76.

[84] On the margin of appreciation doctrine in international and European law, see Y Shany, 'Toward a General Margin of Appreciation Doctrine in International Law?' (2006) 16 *European Journal of International Law* 907; E Benvenisti, 'Margin of Appreciation, Consensus, and Universal Standards' (1999) 31 *New York University Journal of International Law and Politics* 843. Several other international tribunals employed similar or equivalent principles. See, eg, Advisory Opinion of the Inter-American Court of Human Rights on Proposed Amendments to the Naturalization Provision of the Constitution of Costa Rica (1984), paras 57–8, available at http://www.corteidh.or.cr/serieaing/A_4_ING.html, and Decision of the UN Human Rights Committee in Communication No 547/1993, *Apirana Mahuika v New Zealand*, Communication No 547/1993, para 9.4, available at http://www1.umn.edu/humanrts/undocs/547-1993.html.

[85] See also the *Myers* award in which the tribunal drew on WTO law in order to narrow the measure of discretion available to host states in cases of inconsistent treaties. *Myers v Canada*, above n 5, para 221.

proceedings to the public[86] is manifested in several instruments, arbitral decisions and state practice. The recent changes of the International Centre for Settlement of Investment Disputes (ICSID) Arbitration Rules (taking effect in April 2006) included the revised Article 37(2) which grants the tribunal the authority (after consulting the parties) to allow non-disputing parties to submit *amicus* briefs.[87] Indeed, several NGOs have already utilised this rule and presented written submissions to ICSID tribunals.[88]

As to public access to NAFTA documents, the NAFTA Trade Commission published in July 2001 a Note of Interpretation, stating that 'nothing in the NAFTA precludes the Parties from providing public access to documents submitted to, or issued by, a Chapter Eleven tribunal'.[89] In addition, the parties to the NAFTA pronounced that they agree to make available to the public all documents submitted or issued by a Chapter Eleven Tribunal.[90] Furthermore, the NAFTA Trade Commission issued a declaration, in October 2003, stating that 'No provision of the [NAFTA] . . . limits a Tribunal's discretion to accept written submissions from a person or entity that is not a disputing party',[91] and recom-

[86] On this trend, see, eg, Knahr and Reinisch, above n 54, 97; JE Vinuales, 'Amicus Intervention in Investor–State Arbitration' (2007) 61(4) *Dispute Settlement Journal* 72.

[87] Art 37(2) of the ICSID Arbitration Rules provides as follows:

> (2) After consulting both parties, the Tribunal may allow a person or entity that is not a party to the dispute (in this Rule called the "non-disputing party") to file a written submission with the Tribunal regarding a matter within the scope of the dispute. In determining whether to allow such a filing, the Tribunal shall consider, among other things, the extent to which: (a) the non-disputing party submission would assist the Tribunal in the determination of a factual or legal issue related to the proceeding by bringing a perspective, particular knowledge or insight that is different from that of the disputing parties; (b) the non-disputing party submission would address a matter within the scope of the dispute; (c) the non-disputing party has a significant interest in the proceeding. The Tribunal shall ensure that the non-disputing party submission does not disrupt the proceeding or unduly burden or unfairly prejudice either party, and that both parties are given an opportunity to present their observations on the non-disputing party submission. (ICSID Rules of Procedure for Arbitration Proceedings, available at http://www.worldbank.org/icsid/basicdoc/partF. htm)

On these rules, see K Tienhaara, 'Third Party Participation in Investment-Environment Disputes: Recent Developments' (2007) 16 *Review of European Community and International Environmental Law* 230.

[88] See L Cotula, Briefing 5, International Arbitration (International Institute for Environment and Development), available at http://www.iied.org/pubs/pdf/full/17016IIED.pdf.

[89] Notes of Interpretation of Certain Chapter 11 Provision (NAFTA Free Trade Commission, July 31, 2001), available at http://www.naftaclaims.com/files/NAFTA_Comm_1105_Transparency.pdf. On this Note, see M Kinnear, 'Transparency and Third Party Participation in Investor–State Dispute Settlement' (2005), available at http://www.oecd.org/dataoecd/6/25/36979626.pdf, 4.

[90] *Ibid.*

[91] NAFTA Free Trade Commission, Statement of the Free Trade Commission on Non-Disputing Party Participation, available at http://www.dfait-maeci.gc.ca/nafta-alena/nondisputing-en.pdf.

mended procedures for tribunals to accept and rule on petitions for *amicus* briefs.[92] The parties to the *Methanex* dispute agreed to allow public observation of the tribunal hearings through closed-circuit television.[93]

The link between public participation in investment proceedings and the public interests involved was emphasised by the *Methanex* tribunal in its ruling to accept written *amicus* briefs:

> There is an undoubtedly public interest in this arbitration. The substantive issues extend far beyond those raised by the usual transnational arbitration between commercial parties. This is not merely because one of the Disputing Parties is a state . . . The public interest in this arbitration arises from its subject matter.[94]

On the other hand, a proposal to revise the UNCITRAL arbitration rules that would expressly extend confidentiality to the very existence of arbitral proceedings themselves (as well as any materials brought before the tribunal) met fierce opposition from several NGOs.[95]

The trend of increasing transparency of investment arbitral proceedings to the public and participation of NGOs is also manifested in new bilateral investment treaties, prominently those concluded by the US and Canada.[96] Thus, for example, the recent investment chapter included in the 2005 Free Trade Agreement between the US and Central American countries and the Dominican Republic provides that third parties may make oral and written submissions to the tribunal and that the latter has the authority to accept *amicus curiae* submissions from non-disputing parties.[97] This treaty also explicitly states that most arbitral documents will be freely available and oral hearings will be open to the public.[98]

The recent procedural decision rendered by the *Biwater* tribunal (of September 2006) highlights the competing interests regarding trans-

[92] *Ibid.*

[93] SE Gaines, 'International Decisions: *Methanex v US*' (2006) 100 *American Journal of International Law* 683, n 33.

[94] *Methanex v United States*, Decision of the Tribunal on Petitions from Third Persons to Intervene as 'Amici Curiae', para 49, available at http://www.iisd.org/pdf/methanex_tribunal_first_amicus_decision.pdf.

[95] D Vis-Dunbar, 'NGOs Call for Transparency as UNCITRAL Governments Meet in Vienna' (2007) *Investment Treaty News*, 7 September; Center for International Environmental Law and International Institute for Sustainable Development, Revising the UNCITRAL Arbitration Rules to Address State Arbitrations, February 2007, available at http://www.iisd.org/pdf/2007/investment_revising_uncitral_arbitration.pdf. For a background of this proposal, see J Paulsson and G Petrochilos, Revision of The UNCITRAL Arbitration Rules (2006) 8–9, 78–9, available at http://www.uncitral.org/pdf/english/news/arbrules_report.pdf.

[96] See, eg, Vis-Dunbar, above n 60.

[97] Art 10.20(2)–(3) of the Dominican Republic – Central America – United States Free Trade Agreement, available at http://www.ustr.gov/assets/Trade_Agreements/Bilateral/CAFTA/CAFTA-DR_Final_Texts/asset_upload_file328_4718.pdf.

[98] *Ibid*, Art 10.21.

parency, as well as the general trend in investment arbitration. The *Biwater* tribunal was careful to indicate that, against the need for transparency in treaty proceedings, there is a need for procedural integrity of the arbitral proceedings.[99] The tribunal explained that in light of the accepted need for greater transparency in treaty proceedings,[100] the public nature of the particular investment dispute and the interests in transparency of public information, any restrictions on transparency 'must be carefully and narrowly delimited'.[101] As to the current trends in investment arbitration, the tribunal stated that 'Without doubt, there is now a marked tendency towards transparency in treaty arbitration.'[102]

The above brief examination of contemporary practice of states and tribunals indicates that a process of increasing transparency of investment tribunals' proceedings is taking place. The growing public scrutiny of investment arbitral proceedings is likely to exert growing pressure (inter alia by NGOs) on international investment tribunals to accord greater weight to public interests, including those reflected in non-investment international treaties.

VI. CONCLUDING REMARKS

Investment tribunals increasingly encounter arguments regarding conflicts between investment and non-investment obligations. As discussed above, these tribunals have generally been reluctant to accord a significant role to rules emanating from non-investment instruments. Thus far, no investment tribunal has absolved a party that encountered inconsistent obligations from its investment obligations or reduced the amount of compensation due to be paid to the injured party in such cases. Nevertheless, the law in this field is in a formative stage and investment tribunals have not laid down a comprehensive body of rules to regulate interactions between overlapping and conflicting obligations.

The restrained approach undertaken by investment tribunals vis-à-vis non-investment instruments may be explained by various factors, and Section III presents several explanations for this tendency. It seems that certain institutional, historic and conceptual features that characterise current international investment adjudication and law account for the cautious attitude of investment tribunals in this field. Thus, for example, it is clear that the *inter partes* model (which characterises international commercial arbitration) is prevalent among most investment adjudi-

[99] *Biwater Gauff v United Republic of Tanzania* (Procedural Order), para 112, available at http://www.worldbank.org/icsid/cases/arb0522_procedural_order3.pdf.
[100] *Ibid*, para 133.
[101] *Ibid*, para 147.
[102] *Ibid*, para 114.

cators, and that it influences their tendency not to grant a significant weight to public interests. Similarly, the considerable tensions that existed in the past between developing and developed states regarding the content of global investment standards lead investment tribunals to stick to the less controversial rules included in the particular investment treaties. In addition, the asymmetric relations between host states and foreign investors (and the vulnerability of the latter) lead investment tribunals to grant precedence to the contractual or consensual rules that have been agreed upon by host states and investors.

These explanations, however, should not lead to the conclusion that the current approach of investment tribunals will remain the same in the future. On the contrary, as the discussion in Section IV indicates, the ongoing process of increasing transparency of tribunal proceedings is likely to exert more pressure on tribunals to accord greater weight to broader public interests, including those reflected in non-investment instruments (such as environmental and human rights treaties).

14

Multi-level Accountability: A Case Study of Accountability in the Aftermath of the Srebrenica Massacre

ANDRÉ NOLLKAEMPER*

I. INTRODUCTION

THE QUEST FOR accountability after the Srebrenica massacre in 1995[1] offers an apposite example of a situation that in modern political science terminology may be called 'multi-level accountability'. This term refers to a situation in which accountability extends over multiple levels of government, straddling the boundary between the national and international levels.[2] In the case of Srebrenica, the accountability of the main actors, including individual perpetrators,[3] Serbia,[4] the United Nations[5] and its Member States,[6] has indeed extended to national and international levels.

Although multi-level accountability is certainly not a new phenomenon, it seems that the number of situations that may be characterised by the term is on the rise. This may be a consequence of, on the one hand, the increasing interconnections between the international and the

* André Nollkaemper is Professor if Public International Law and Director of the Amsterdam Center for International Law, the Netherlands.

[1] The qualification 'genocide' was used by the ICJ in its judgment in *Application of the Convention on the Prevention and Punishment of the Crime of Genocide (Bosnia and Herzegovina v Serbia and Montenegro)*, available at http://www.icj-cij.org/docket/index.php?p1=3&p2=3&k=f4&case=91&code=bhy&p3=4, para 297. An excellent factual account of the events at Srebrenica remains D Rohde, *Endgame: The Betrayal and Fall of Srebrenica, Europe's Worst Massacre since World War II* (New York, Farrar, Straus and Giroux, 1997).

[2] The term 'multi-level accountability' is used for instance by M Bovens, 'New Forms of Accountability and EU-Governance' (2007) 5 *Comparative European Politics* 104.

[3] See s IVA.

[4] See s IVB.

[5] See s IVC.

[6] *Ibid.*

[7] See generally JE Nijman and A Nollkaemper (eds), *New Perspectives on the Divide between National and International Law* (Oxford University Press, 2007).

domestic sphere[7] and, on the other hand, an increasing concern with accountability to international law, both at the international and domestic level.

Compared to the situation where accountability is confined to either the international or the domestic sphere, multi-level accountability may offer benefits to those seeking accountability. In theory at least, accountability at one level may fill gaps that exist at other levels. In that respect, accountability at national and international levels may be complementary. The fact that in the early years after the events at Srebrenica, no reliable prosecution was to be expected at the national level could in part be remedied at the international level via the International Criminal Tribunal for the Former Yugoslavia (ICTY).[8] The fact that the ICTY later could not handle enough cases could be remedied by transferring cases back to the domestic level.[9] Likewise, the fact that the UN could not be sued at the international level for its failure to protect the safe haven of Srebrenica could perhaps be partially remedied by suing contributing Member States, notably the Netherlands, at the domestic level.[10] Finally, the fact that the UN was not able to accept a meaningful form of political responsibility might perhaps be compensated for in part by the resignation of a Dutch government over the matter.[11]

These and other possible forms of complementarity are, however, surrounded by much uncertainty. Is it really true that the ICTY could provide what could not be provided at the domestic level in terms of accountability, and could it satisfy the expectations of the victims? Is it really true that the accountability of the UN or a Member State in a domestic court could fill the gap left by the lack of remedies at the international level? Can domestic accountability mechanisms that often primarily serve domestic audiences be relevant to audiences in other states or at the international level? Moreover, might the potential benefits not easily turn into blame-shifting and buck-passing?[12] Courts or other

[8] The ICTY was already established before the events in Srebrenica by UNSC Res 827 (25 May 1993) UN Doc S/RES/827. The prosecutor has brought a number of indictments directly relating to the genocide in Srebrenica (though not all accused have been charged with genocide), including: *Prosecutor v Karadžić/Mladić* ICTY-IT-95-5/18, *Prosecutor v Krstić* ICTY-IT-98-33, *Prosecutor v Obrenović* ICTY-IT-01-43, *Prosecutor v Blagojević et al* ICTY-IT-02-53, *Prosecutor v Popović* ICTY-IT-05-88, *Prosecutor v Blagojević and Jokic* ICTY-IT-02-60, *Prosecutor v Erdemović* ICTY-IT-96-22, *Prosecutor v Milošević* ICTY-IT-02-54, *Prosecutor v Momir Nikolić* ICTY-IT-02–60/1, *Prosecutor v Drago Nikolić* ICTY-IT-02-63, *Prosecutor v Pandurević and Trbić* ICTY-IT-05-86, *Prosecutor v Milorad Trbić* ICTY-IT-05-88/1, and *Prosecutor v Zdravko Tolimir* ICTY-IT-05-88/2.

[9] The Security Council established the completion strategy in UNSC Res 1503 (28 August 2003) UN Doc S/RES/1593. See discussion in D Raab, 'Evaluating the ICTY and its Completion Strategy Efforts to Achieve Accountability for War Crimes and their Tribunals' (2005) 3 *Journal of International Criminal Justice* 82.

[10] See s IVB.

[11] *Ibid*

[12] See generally C Hood, 'The Risk Game and the Blame Game' (2002) 37 *Government and Opposition* 15.

institutions may easily be inclined to defer judgment to other levels—from the international to the domestic level and vice versa. This seems to have happened in the case of Srebrenica. More than 12 years after the events, victims are still continuing their search for satisfactory forms of accountability, moving back and forth between international and domestic procedures.

Indeed, the phenomenon of multi-level accountability raises fundamental questions as to the possibility of interplay between international and national accountability mechanisms and their power to provide accountability for events that straddle the boundaries between them. It is against that background that I will examine certain aspects of the concept and applications of multi-level accountability in the aftermath of the Srebrenica massacre. The aim of the chapter is to clarify what we know and do not know about multi-level accountability, and how it can or cannot help provide accountability for events that are not confined to any single state.

The main argument that I will develop is that, in many situations, neither the international nor the domestic level is sufficient, though the levels are to some extent complementary. The powers of international accountability mechanisms to achieve effects at the domestic level and vice versa remain limited. While international and domestic procedures may complement each other, they are not perfect substitutes.[13]

I will first discuss the concept of accountability and its relevance to international law (section II). In section III I will discuss the complications that may arise from the fact that accountability may extend to different actors, in particular individuals, states and international organisations. In section IV, the core of this chapter, I will review the complementary nature (or lack thereof) of the relations between accountability procedures at international and domestic levels. Section V contains brief conclusions.

II. THE CONCEPT OF ACCOUNTABILITY

In examining the quest for accountability after Srebrenica, it is proper to make use of the concept of accountability rather than the concept of 'responsibility'—a much more established term in international law terminology. I use the term 'accountability' to refer to a process in which an actor explains her conduct and gives information to a forum, and in

[13] This argument has been made in general terms by EA Posner and AO Sykes, 'An Economic Analysis of State and Individual Responsibility Under International Law' (2007) 9 *American Law and Economics Review* 1, 24.

[14] M Bovens, 'Analysing and Assessing Public Accountability. A Conceptual Framework' (*EUROGOV) No* C-06-01, available at http://www.connex-network.org/eurogov/pdf/egp-

which, subsequently, the forum may render judgment on the basis of prior established rules, and impose some form of sanctions (formal or informal) on the actor.[14]

Accountability, like responsibility, is essentially a retrospective process. It consists of giving an account of prior conduct. Often, it may take a more prospective form and extend, for example, to standard-setting. For instance, the UN Secretary General's report into Srebrenica and the consequences drawn therefrom essentially constitute a forward-looking exercise.[15] However, I take it as my starting point that while such prospective effects may be important, they are not a proper substitute for ex post facto accountability.

The established rules on the basis of which judgment will be passed will mostly be legal rules. It is in that respect that the term 'legal accountability' may be appropriate[16] and that international responsibility can properly be considered one form of accountability.

However, in a case such as Srebrenica, it may be too narrow to confine accountability processes to judgments based on legal rules. Law cannot have a claim to exclusivity as a benchmark for accountability. Political accountability, democratic accountability, administrative accountability and other forms of accountability that are not necessarily based on law can all play their part.[17] Political accountability, a term referring to accountability of holders of political authority through political processes,[18] is certainly not confined to assessment on the basis of law. Political accountability may be related to a breach of an (international) obligation, but that is not usually a decisive criterion, and indeed there may well be political accountability for acts that are perfectly lawful. It is noteworthy that both in the debate in the UN on accountability and in the debates surrounding the resignation of the Dutch government, questions of legal wrongfulness played only a marginal role.[19] The same is true for administrative accountability, a term referring to a process of an administrative nature, such as the resignation of civil servants or disciplinary penalties. An example is the resignation of a Dutch commander following the Srebrenica inquiry.[20] Like political accountability, administrative

connex-C-06-01.pdf, 9. See also A Benz, C Harlow and Y Papadopoulos, 'Introduction' (2007) 13 *European Law Journal* 441, 444.

[15] Report of the Secretary-General pursuant to General Assembly Resolution 53/35, 'The Fall of Srebrenica' (1999) UN Doc A/54/549.

[16] Although the term legal accountability is often used to refer to the nature of the process (notably accountability before the courts) rather than to the basis of the passing of judgments; see, eg, Bovens, above n 14, 16.

[17] For an overview of the various forms of accountability, only some of which are based on legal rules, see RW Grant and RO Keohane, 'Accountability and Abuses of Power in World Politics' (2005) 99 *American Political Science Review* 29.

[18] *Ibid.*

[19] See s IVC.

[20] See, eg, 'Dutch General Joins Srebrenica Exodus', *BBC News* (17 April 2002) available at http://news.bbc.co.uk/2/hi/europe/1935484.stm.

accountability may be related to an alleged breach of (international) law, but this does not appear to be a common occurrence. Yet, if our concern is with accountability for the events in Srebrenica, it may be an unduly narrow approach to exclude a priori such non-legal forms of accountability.

The concept of accountability encompasses international responsibility (since it may be based on legal standards) but at the same time it is more extensive, transcending the set of secondary principles that determine the conditions and consequences of an internationally wrongful act. International responsibility (whether in its application to individuals, states or international organisations) certainly covers a major part of the accountability processes after Srebrenica, but by no means exhausts such accountability.

There are multiple reasons for using a concept of accountability rather than the narrower concept of international responsibility. First, international responsibility is not frequently invoked. In fact, the aftermath of Srebrenica is rather atypical in that the responsibility of individuals, states and the United Nations was invoked with regard to a single set of events. In the large majority of cases, this does not happen, making it implausible that international responsibility would exhaust the need for accountability. In particular for international organisations, the rise of accountability concerns seems to be caused by the fact that invocation of responsibility is exceedingly rare (and that moreover it is nearly impossible to find a judicial forum to litigate claims against international organisations).[21]

Second, the concept of accountability has the benefit that it can be used with regard to actors that cannot easily be subjected to international responsibility. Indeed, it is not surprising that the term accountability has mostly been used in connection with actors whose actions are not readily subject to international responsibility, such as multinational corporations[22] or armed opposition groups.[23] In the case of Srebrenica, this broader conceptual power of accountability seems particularly relevant for collective entities that may otherwise escape any form of accountability, notably the Bosnian Serb Republic.[24]

[21] IF Dekker, 'Making Sense of Accountability in International Institutional Law' (2005) 36 *Netherlands Yearbook of International Law* 83.

[22] See, eg, E Oshionebo, 'The UN Global Compact and Accountability of Transnational Corporations: Separating Myth from Realities' (2007) 19 *Florida Journal of International Law* 1, and F MacLeay, 'Corporate Codes of Conduct and the Human Rights Accountability of Transnational Corporations: a Small Piece of a Larger Puzzle' in JG Frynas and S Pegg (eds), *Transnational Corporations and Human Rights* (Oxford University Press, 2006).

[23] L Zegveld, *The Accountability of Armed Opposition Groups in International Law* (Cambridge University Press, 2002). See also SR Ratner and JS Abrams, *Accountability for Human Rights Atrocities in International Law: Beyond the Nuremberg Legacy* (Oxford University Press, 2001).

[24] In its judgment in the Genocide case (above n 1), the ICJ made several references to the role of the Bosnian Serb forces in the genocide; see, eg, para 294. In para 388, the Court stated

Finally, the use of the concept of accountability reflects the emergence of increasing numbers of procedures in which subjects are held to account with respect to international (legal) standards, without such accountability qualifying as a determination of international responsibility. Examples are non-compliance procedures under international environmental agreements, or reporting and review procedures under human rights treaties.[25] Such procedures entail neither formal invocation nor formal determinations of responsibility, yet it is hard to say that they do not provide some form of accountability under international law.

Indeed, in the aftermath of Srebrenica, there appeared a wide variety of accountability processes that cannot all be classified in terms of international responsibility, but that may nonetheless be relevant to the accountability that is eventually being sought by the victims. These included early resolutions by the UN General Assembly and the Security Council, the aforementioned report of the UN Secretary General and the General Assembly's response to that report. Political forms of accountability at the national level were also detectable as well as domestic judicial procedures that are normally not relevant to the determination of international responsibility.[26]

It thus follows that accountability encompasses international responsibility, but it is broader in scope. There can be accountability without any invocation of responsibility or without any breach of an obligation of the type that engages responsibility. The international responsibility of individuals, states and international organisations captures only a small fraction of accountability processes in international law. Indeed, accountability is both a response to the limited role of international responsibility in practice, and to the conceptual limitations of international responsibility.[27]

While the various forms of accountability (legal, political, administrative, etc) may all be important and contribute to the same ends, they are not always interchangeable. This depends in large part on the needs and perceptions of the persons seeking accountability. If a victim seeks compensation, political accountability may have little to offer. The situation may be different if the aim is closure or prevention. It should be

that 'The functions of the VRS officers, including General Mladić, were however to act on behalf of the Bosnian Serb authorities, in particular the Republika Srpska, not on behalf of the FRY; they exercised elements of the public authority of the Republika Srpska.' However, on the international level formal responsibility of the Republika Srpska obviously was not an option. In 2004, the government of the Republika Srpska acknowledged the crimes committed by Bosnian Serb forces; see International Justice Tribune, 21 June 2004, http://www.justicetribune.com/index.php?page=v2_article&id=2679.

[25] See generally G Ulfstein, T Marauhn and A Zimmermann (eds), *Making Treaties Work: Human Rights, Environment and Arms Control* (Cambridge University Press, 2007).

[26] See s IV.

[27] J Brunnee, 'International Legal Accountability through the Lens of the Law of State Responsibility' (2005) 36 *Netherlands Yearbook of International Law* 21.

recalled that accountability in principle retains a relational aspect. The fact that an actor is accountable to some forum reflects the broadly accepted, though not undisputed, view that accountability is relational: accountability does not exist in isolation, but in relation to some 'significant other'[28] and it may be rendered towards states (in the case of Srebrenica above all towards the state of Bosnia and Herzegovina); against individual victims, but also, perhaps, against the international community. The phenomenon of overlapping audiences (or 'many eyes')[29] is relevant, because each subject to whom accountability is owed may have different hopes and demands, posing different requirements for accountability processes. Gardner wrote that 'who is to receive the explanation affects what suffices as a rational explanation'.[30] For instance, a procedure within the UN may settle the question of accountability for the General Assembly, but not for the individual victims. As a consequence, actors who are called to account must satisfy multiple forums with different preferences.[31]

While, as noted above, some victims' needs (notably compensation) can only be served by particular forms of accountability, it seems useful to consider the various forms of accountability together. Aims such as prevention, upholding of the rule of law, providing a public record of what had happened, and closure may be achieved by several forms of accountability. Clearly, legal responsibility is not the only incentive for actors to take preventive measures, nor the only means of providing a full record, and certainly not the only means of obtaining closure.

For these reasons it would also be wrong to say that accountability not involving legally binding determinations of responsibility, would not be governed by (or not of interest to) international law. In domestic law, ministerial responsibility is not a matter of liability, yet it is certainly governed by (constitutional) law and of interest for the maintenance of the rule of law. This is not much different for international accountability mechanisms. Even when they do not result in a formal determination of responsibility or an imposition of remedies, they may well be subjected to and constitute part of the system of international law. In particular they can contribute to the aims of international law.

[28] Bovens, above n 14. Note that it has been said that the modern law of state responsibility would no longer be of a correlative nature, but would rather be of an objective nature in the sense that responsibility can arise regardless of legal injury. See A Pellet, 'Remarques sur une révolution inachevée. Le projet d'árticles de la CDI sur la responsabilité des Etats' (1996) 42 *Annuaire Français de Droit International* 7–32. J Gardner, 'The Mark of Responsibility' (2003) 23 *Oxford Journal of Legal Studies* 157, 164–5 more generally critiques the notion of accountability as a relational concept.

[29] Bovens, above n 14, 15.

[30] Gardner, above n 28, 157.

[31] Y Papadopoulos, 'Problems of Democratic Accountability in Network and Multilevel Governance' (2007) 13 *European Law Journal*, 469, 480.

III. THE PLURALITY OF ACCOUNTABLE ACTORS

A distinct feature of accountability processes in the aftermath of Srebrenica is that accountability extends to multiple actors, notably individuals, states, and the UN and its Member States. The Bosnian Serb Republic should also be considered as part of this group of accountable actors. Some victims sought the accountability of individual perpetrators, others of the collective entities situated behind the perpetrators, and still others sought the accountability of the international community for letting the perpetrators commit their crimes. These disparate quests reflected the fact that while there is no denying that the massacre was committed by individuals, it might not have happened were it not for the collective entity of which they were a part, or for the failure of the international community to intervene.

The multiplicity of actors involved in processes of accountability such as this raises what has been called the 'problems of many-hands'.[32] It may lead to the paradox of shared responsibility: 'as the responsibility for any given instance of conduct is scattered among more people, the discrete responsibility of every individual diminishes proportionately'.[33] It may also lead to blame-shifting games between actors.[34] Such factors may complicate attempts to seek accountability at the international and domestic levels, since it may be necessary to proceed against different actors at different levels, multiplying accountability processes.

If we confine ourselves to international responsibility as a narrow form of international accountability, in formal legal terms, the situation is relatively straightforward. Each actor is responsible for its own acts: responsibility of an actor does not presume, or of itself imply, the responsibility of another actor. Hence, the responsibility of the individual perpetrators for the events in Srebrenica is not contingent upon, nor does it imply or exclude, responsibility of the state of which they were an organ.[35] The converse is also true.[36] Neither could individuals or states claim that their responsibility was somehow diminished or otherwise affected by the fact that the UN should have acted. Similarly the UN, or its Member States, could not claim that it should not be responsible because the individual perpetrators or states were the real culprits. At

[32] Bovens, above n 14, 18.

[33] M Bovens, *The Quest for Responsibility: Accountability and Citizenship in Complex Organizations* (Cambridge University Press, 1998) 46; Papadopoulos, above n 31, 473.

[34] Hood, above n 12.

[35] Compare Art 35(4) of the Statute of the International Criminal Court, stating that no provision in this Statute relating to individual criminal responsibility shall affect the responsibility of states under international law.

[36] Compare Art 58 of the Articles on the Responsibility of States for Internationally Wrongful Acts, contained in the Annex of UN Doc A/Res/56/83 of 28 January 2002 (stating

most, questions of compensation may be influenced by the fact that one actor may not have caused the full extent of injury.

However, the International Court of Justice (ICJ)'s judgment in the Genocide Case has made clear that responsibility of one subject need not be fully autonomous from that of other subjects.[37] The ICJ held there that a state is responsible for genocide where

> a person or group whose acts are legally attributable to the State, commits any of the acts proscribed by Article III of the [Genocide] Convention.[38]

Thus it would seem that criminal responsibility for genocide becomes a prerequisite for state responsibility.[39] Findings on individual responsibility may thus be relevant to state responsibility. This may also explain why the court relied so heavily upon the case-law of the ICTY in discussing the nature of the events that took place in Bosnia.[40]

It seems that even though the basis of the two forms of responsibility is separate, any claims, eg, for compensation against a state for its involvement in genocide, whether at the international or domestic level, may be supported by earlier findings that agents of that state were guilty of genocide.[41] While international courts may accord most weight to determinations made by other courts at the international level, it seems that domestic processes can also be relevant.[42] In this respect there is some interdependence between different levels of responsibility (but the same may be true for the broader phenomenon of accountability)

The ICJ did make clear, however, that this finding did not mean that the exercise of its judicial function—deciding on a claim on state responsibility—was contingent upon the exercise of criminal jurisdiction by a national or international tribunal.[43] The court held that holding otherwise 'could entail that there would be no legal recourse available under the Convention in some readily conceivable circumstances', namely when genocide has allegedly been committed by the leaders of a state and

that 'These articles are without prejudice to any question of the individual responsibility under international law of any person acting on behalf of a State'). In its judgment in the *Genocide Case* (above n 1), the Court referred to the duality of responsibility that continued to be 'a constant feature of international law', para 173.

[37] *Genocide Case*, above n 1.

[38] *Genocide Case*, above n 1, para 179.

[39] P Gaeta, 'On What Conditions Can a State Be Held Responsible for Genocide?' (2007) 18 *European Journal of International Law* 631, 644.

[40] *Ibid*, 646.

[41] *Ibid*.

[42] See ICJ, *Armed Activities on the Territory of the Congo (Democratic Republic of the Congo v Uganda)*, Judgment (2005), para 61 (attributing evidentiary weight to the findings of the Judicial Commission of Inquiry into Allegations of Illegal Exploitation of Natural Resources and Other Forms of Wealth in the Democratic Republic of the Congo set up by the Ugandan Government).

[43] *Genocide Case*, above n 1, para 182.

> they have not been brought to trial because, for instance, they are still very much in control of the powers of the State . . . and there is no international penal tribunal able to exercise jurisdiction over the alleged crimes.[44]

Thus it made clear that in procedural terms, accountability processes against a state and against individuals remain separate in that the determination of responsibility of one actor is not a formal condition for responsibility of another actor.

IV. MULTI-LEVEL ACCOUNTABILITY

Multi-level accountability is a corollary of the phenomenon of multi-level governance—a term that emphasises the fact that an increasing number of areas are governed by an increasing number of layers: local, national, regional, global, but also public and private.[45] If governance is indeed distributed across multiple interacting layers, then accountability mechanisms should also straddle the different layers. For instance, where domestic institutions give effect to international policies or obligations ('distributed administration'),[46] they may be accountable to an international forum. International institutions may also carry out some form of supervision over these domestic institutions .[47]

The term multi-level accountability may suggest the existence of some organised and invented process. However, while in some legal systems, notably the EU, one can identify some formalised connections between international and domestic accountability mechanisms (courts, parliaments, ombudsmen), in the general international legal order the process is largely unorganised[48] (although even under international law there are some examples where domestic accountability processes are defined and formalised).[49]

Multi-level accountability is a proper term for characterizing accountability processes in the aftermath of Srebrenica. In view of the international nature of the wrongs that were at issue, the international level

[44] *Genocide Case*, above n 41.

[45] See eg I Bache and M Flinders (eds), *Multi-level Governance* (Oxford University Press, 2004), and C Harlow and R Rawlings, 'Promoting Accountability in Multilevel Governance: A Network Approach' (2007) 13 *European Law Journal*, 542.

[46] B Kingsbury, N Krisch and R Stewart, 'The Emergence of Global Administrative Law' (2005) 68 *Law and Contemporary Problems* 15, 21.

[47] See, eg, Ulfstein et al, above n 25.

[48] Examples are the obligation to provide remedies for human rights violations, eg, under Art 13 of the European Convention on Human Rights, the local remedies rule and the principle of complementarity in the ICC Statute.

[49] One may characterise accountability processes in the international legal order in terms of a 'fatalistic worldview', where the availability and outcome of processes is hard to predict and may at times have the appearance of a lottery; see for this term C Hood, *The Art of the State* (Oxford University Press, 2000) 11–12.

(eg, the ICTY, ICJ and UN General Assembly) was the obvious level for considering questions of accountability.[50] But the events obviously also had a strong domestic component, and questions of accountability were considered by domestic courts, both in criminal cases and in civil claims, and by national parliaments. Apparently, neither accountability processes at the international nor those available at the domestic level were capable of providing full accountability (and relief) for those seeking it. Although genocide is an essentially international crime, the quest for accountability relied heavily on domestic processes, which could indeed provide forms of accountability outside the reach of the international level. Nevertheless, the domestic level was unable to provide full accountability by itself.

These patterns of generating the accountability of implicated actors will subsequently be reviewed for selected forms of accountability for individuals, states and the international community. While the discussion by no means aims to cover the entire spectrum of accountability processes, and in particular does not engage in the larger doctrinal debate on transitional justice, each of the forms of accountability discussed below demonstrates the limitations of international processes to provide accountability of the key actors towards the victims of the genocide.

A. Individuals

Much has been made of the argument that international courts and domestic courts, charged with making determinations of responsibility of individuals, fulfil complementary functions. On the one hand, it has been said that international courts such as the ICTY fulfil the function of a domestic court when the domestic justice system is unable or unwilling to act, as appeared to be the case immediately after the genocide. In that case the ICTY was able to adopt the function that the domestic courts in Serbia, Bosnia and Herzegovina or any other state should have fulfilled.[51] On the other hand, it is said that domestic courts adjudicating international crimes—such as the war crimes court of Bosnia and Herzegovina—can be seen as agents of a larger 'community of courts' and serve goals similar to those of international courts.[52]

[50] A Pellet, 'Internationalized courts: better than nothing . . .', in CPR Romano, A Nollkaemper and JK Kleffner (eds), *Internationalized Criminal Courts and Tribunals* (Oxford University Press, 2004) 437, 439, (arguing that because of international crimes defy boundaries and threaten the foundations of the international legal order, they should only be prosecuted at international level).

[51] This is what A-M Slaughter and W Burke-White, in 'The Future of International Law is Domestic (Or, The European Way of Law)' in Nijman and Nollkaemper, above n 7, 122, call the 'backstopping' function of international courts.

[52] See for the concept of a 'community of courts', W Burke-White, 'A Community of Courts: Toward a System of International Criminal Law Enforcement' (2002) 24 *Michigan Journal of International Law* 1.

However, these arguments capture only part of a complex reality and may conceal the fact that prosecution at the international and domestic levels may well serve different objectives. The international and domestic accountability processes for individual responsibility cannot be considered as perfect substitutes. While the need for accountability could be satisfied at the international and national levels, neither is in itself adequate or interchangeable with the other.[53]

This conclusion is supported by considering the multiple aims that accountability processes for individual responsibility after Srebrenica might fulfil. A first aim might be said to be that by corroborating victims' experiences and insisting on the wrongfulness of the perpetrator's actions, prosecution would serve justice for the individual victim and provide an occasion for catharsis.[54]

Second, accountability processes could break the cycle of violence and thus lead to benefits for the domestic society at large. Retribution might satisfy the victims' desires for vengeance and prevent vigilante justice. Trials break the cycle of impunity that nurtured the human rights violations and contribute to specific and general prevention by deterring individuals and society at large. Not only does this establish the foundations for the rule of law for the future; it also places past lawlessness, the characteristic of the pre-transition period, in the dock.[55]

Third, by providing a public forum for the judicial confirmation of the facts, trials could establish truth and provide a record of past events, serving public education and, assuming that lessons are learnt, preventing reoccurrence. A common historic account is also a prerequisite for reconciliation and could serve as a weapon against revisionism and 'inoculat[e] the populace against lapses into oppressive behaviour'.[56]

Moreover, trials may contribute to the public's faith in the government. By putting the perpetrators on trial, the successor regime can strengthen its legitimacy by distinguishing itself from the previous regime responsible for the atrocities; otherwise the successors might appear to be collab-

[53] See generally on the functions of criminal trials, in particular in situations of transitional justice: NJ Kritz, 'Coming to Terms with Atrocities: a Review of Accountability Mechanisms for Mass Violations of Human Rights'(1996) 59 *Law and Contemporary Problems* 127; S Landsman, 'Alternative Responses to Serious Human Rights Abuses: Of Prosecution and Truth Commissions' (1996) 59 *Law and Contemporary Problems* 81; and MJ Aukerman, 'Extraordinary Evil, Ordinary Crime: a Framework for Understanding Transitional Justice' (2002) 15 *Harvard Human Rights Journal* 39.

[54] NJ Kritz, 'Coming to Terms with Atrocities: A Review of Accountability Mechanisms for Mass Violations of Human Rights' (1996) 59 *Law and Contemporary Problems* 127, 128.

[55] L Huyse, 'Justice after Transition: On the Choices Successor Elites Make in Dealing with the Past' in NJ Kritz (ed), *Transitional Justice: How Emerging Democracies Reckon with Former Regimes* (Washington DC, United States Institute of Peace Press, 1995).

[56] S Landsman, 'Alternative Responses to Serious Human Rights Abuses: Of Prosecution and Truth Commissions' (1996) 59 *Law and Contemporary Problems* 81, 83.

orators.[57] A trial can also be an important first step in rebuilding the domestic judiciary and criminal justice system.[58]

Each of these objectives arguably could best be fulfilled at the domestic level. However, that option was not readily available for a variety of reasons, at least not immediately after the genocide. Hence attention was focused on international processes. However, while international procedures could, in the aftermath of the Srebrenica genocide, fulfil some of these objectives, clearly these were not sufficient and indeed their operative objectives were not identical. The ICTY was established with a view to protecting international peace and security; after all that was the justification for its establishment by the Security Council. It was perhaps also intended to serve as a guardian of international law and to radiate a message of deterrence that transcended the borders of the state in which the events took place.[59] These objectives certainly are not the primary objectives of domestic trials and may indeed be largely beyond their reach.

On the other hand, trials in the ICTY could not fully achieve the aims of criminal accountability at the domestic level. The deterrent effect of international prosecutions for would-be perpetrators remains uncertain.[60] Also, if international trials help re-establish the public's confidence in the rule of law, that may be true for the international enforcement of the rule of law, but it is less plausible that international trials will inspire confidence in the ability of domestic courts to uphold the rule of law. On the contrary, international courts send the message that the domestic legal order is too weak to deal with gross violations of the rule of law. The fact that international actors, not the state itself, are condemning the state's past also impedes collective learning from the past as a tool against reoccurrence. Neither do insulated and distant courts help in rebuilding the domestic judiciary and the national criminal justice system. Finally, the type of justice done at the international level may be perceived as differing from the national standards and requirements of justice, with the consequence that in the eyes of the affected state and its citizens no real justice is done.[61]

[57] J Sarkin and E Daly, 'Too Few Answers: Reconciliation in Transitional Societies' (2004) 35 *Columbia Human Rights Law Review* 661, 670.

[58] Kritz, above n 54, 133.

[59] See the third preambular paragraph of the Rome Statute of the International Criminal Court (1998) 'Recognizing that such grave crimes threaten the peace, security and well-being of the world.' See also D Zolo, 'Peace through Criminal Law?' (2004) 2 *Journal of International Criminal Justice* 727 and TJ Farer, 'Restraining the Barbarians: Can International Criminal Law Help?' (2000) 22 *Human Rights Quarterly* 90, 116–17.

[60] MA Drumbl, 'Collective Violence and Individual Punishment: The Criminality of Mass Atrocity' (2005) *Northwestern University Law Review*, available at SSRN, http://ssrn.com/abstract=530182, 575–576; I Tallgren, 'The Sense and Sensibility of International Criminal Law' (2002) 13 *European Journal of Iinternational Law* 561, 594.

[61] See on the different impact of domestic and international trials JE Alvarez, 'Crimes of State/Crimes of Hate: Lessons from Rwanda' (1999) 24 *Yale Journal of International Law* 365, 402–3, 466.

The fact that international trials are less able to achieve the positive effects of domestic trials on the society concerned is not a temporary problem that can be easily overcome. International courts have a unique set of ambitions. While they may wish to serve as a proxy for domestic courts,[62] their power and capacity in that respect is limited. That is not only because of the sheer number of international crimes,[63] but also because grave doubts exist as to the capacity of international tribunals, far removed from any national society, to have a significant deterrent effect. The justification of international tribunals thus may be found in different areas, such as the protection of international peace and security[64] and the expressive dimensions of punishment, which are principally distinct from the aims sought in the domestic domain.[65]

In conclusion of this discussion of individual accountability, accountability processes at the international level can be said to be rather imperfect substitutes for domestic processes. The ICTY was structurally limited in achieving specific accountability aims for victims, and was designed to serve more ambiguous aims at the international level. To a limited extent international procedures might supplement domestic procedures, as is, for instance, manifested in the role of the ICTY in supporting the power of domestic prosecutions.[66] In such situations the international level can help produce accountability outcomes that seem to fall beyond the aims of the international community.

B. States

Accountability mechanisms at the international and domestic level have some, albeit limited, power to supplement each other also with regard to states.[67] As far as legal accountability is concerned, the domestic level seemed less appropriate for various reasons. Certainly in Serbia (and Serbia and Montenegro) there may have been serious problems relating to access to the courts and their independence. Thus it was unlikely that victims (whether individuals, collectivities or the state) would find

[62] RD Sloane 'The Expressive Capacity of International Punishment' (2007) 43 *Stanford Journal of International Law*, available at SSRN, http://ssrn.com/abstract=900641, 12 and Slaughter and Burke-White, above n 51.

[63] Sloane, above n 62, 13.

[64] Above n 59.

[65] Sloane, above n 62, 3–4. On the need to develop independent rationales for punishment in international criminal law (independent from domestic law) see also Drumbl, above n 59, and Tallgren, above note 59.

[66] WM Burke-White, 'The Domestic Influence of International Criminal Tribunals: The International Criminal Tribunal for the Former Yugoslavia and the Creation of the State Court of Bosnia and Herzegovina' University of Penn Law School, Public Law Research Paper No 07–44 (22 October 2007), available at SSRN, http://ssrn.com/abstract=1023923.

[67] I confine the analysis to Serbia's accountability.

proper relief there. In the courts of Bosnia and Herzegovina, claims against Serbia would have to deal with problems of jurisdiction, immunity and enforcement. And perhaps most significantly, individual claims in local courts could hardly deal with the collective nature of the problem.[68] Individual claims would not do justice to the larger interests involved, and mass claims seem to be an unlikely option.

Therefore, procedures at the international level, most notably the procedure between Bosnia and Herzegovina, on the one hand, and Serbia, on the other, might have been regarded as an important supplement to the legal options available at the domestic level. Of course, that procedure did not primarily seek to provide redress analogous to what could have been granted at the domestic level. First and foremost it sought to provide interstate redress and perhaps, though less likely, to uphold the international legal order, and in that respect, to protect the interests of the international community.[69] Still, it should be recalled that Bosnia and Herzegovina did not only seek redress for its own injuries by bringing a claim against Serbia before the ICJ: it also acted there as *parens patriae* for its citizens.[70]

However, the procedure before the ICJ was, in several respects, a weak vehicle for providing accountability and serving the interests of Bosnia and Herzegovina, and in particular the interests of the injured individual victims. This is because the court had to overcome some notable barriers. The first one was whether Serbia, as a state, could be held responsible for genocide at all. The answer to that question in general international law surely should be in the affirmative, but the court was limited in the scope of its jurisdiction and could not address Serbia's possible responsibility under a customary law prohibition of genocide. It therefore had to find, not entirely convincingly, that the Genocide Convention also prohibited states from committing genocide.[71] Overcoming this barrier proved irrel-

[68] C Tomuschat, 'Individual Reparation Claims in Instances of Grave Human Rights Violations: The Position under General International Law' in A Randelzhofer and C Tomuschat (eds), *State Responsibility and the Individual: Reparation in Instances of Grave Violations of Human Rights* (The Hague, Martinus Nijhoff, 1999).

[69] It remains an odd situation that the responsibility of the state, which in several respects will be the locus of power in regard to the events, remains in the hands of one injured state, that has to overcome all sorts of political pressure to maintain the case, rather than, as in the case of individual responsibility, in the hands of the international community. See A Nollkaemper, 'Concurrence Between Individual Responsibility and State Responsibility in International Law' (2003) 52 *International and Comparative Law Quarterly* 615, 627.

[70] In the oral pleadings, Bosnia and Herzegovina required the Court to adjudge and declare inter alia that 'that Serbia and Montenegro must redress the consequences of its international wrongful acts and, as a result of the international responsibility incurred for the above violations of the Convention on the Prevention and Punishment of the Crime of Genocide, must pay, and Bosnia and Herzegovina is entitled to receive, in its own right and as *parens patriae* for its citizens, full compensation for the damages and losses caused', *Genocide Case,* above n 1, para 66.

[71] *Genocide Case,* above n 1, para 166–7. See the critique of this conclusion by *Gaeta,* above n 39.

evant, however, as the ICJ subsequently could not find, based on the facts, that Serbia actually had committed genocide. Serbia was only to be found in breach of the obligation to prevent genocide, an obligation much more clearly imposed upon states.

The question then became whether the ICJ could deliver remedies that Bosnia—but perhaps even more importantly, the individual victims—may have hoped for. Bosnia on this point had only requested a declaration—in itself an indication that an interstate procedure may not be the best option to protect the interests of individual victims. The court nonetheless proceeded to consider the remedy of compensation, but eventually concluded that it could not be provided because the requirement of causality was not satisfied[72] (though, arguably, a different outcome might well have been possible).[73] It is to be recalled that even if the court had ordered compensation, such compensation would not necessarily have reached the individual victims. Whether the conclusion that a mere finding of a breach of the obligation of prevention could satisfy the quest for accountability by Bosnia and Herzegovina and the individual victims remains a matter of speculation.

In that situation it is perhaps no surprise that attempts to find some form of accountability for the state of Serbia have continued to surface at the domestic level.[74] But the drawbacks indicated above (access, jurisdiction, independence, enforcement, difficulty to deal with the collective nature) remain intact. It appears, therefore, that neither the international nor the domestic level can provide proper legal accountability for the state(s) involved. In this respect the aftermath of Srebrenica serves as an example of a situation where the international legal system produced an outcome that sacrifices the interests of the individual to protect that of the collective.[75]

There remained the possibility that some form of political accountability could supplement legal accountability (in the form of state responsibility), and perhaps even fulfil similar functions. Indeed, the question may be asked whether there is a significant difference between a declaration by the ICJ, or another form of satisfaction, and accountability rendered through a political mechanism. However, here we encounter the fundamental problem that political accountability (accountability through the political processes) is not well developed at the international level, and perhaps, given the structure of the international community, is

[72] *Ibid*, para 462.

[73] A Gattini, 'Breach of the Obligation to Prevent and Reparation Thereof in the ICJ's Genocide Judgment' (2007) 18 *European Journal of International Law* 711.

[74] See, eg, '2 Bosnian Muslims sue Serbia over alleged police torture, human rights group says' *Associated Press* (Belgrade, 1 August 2007), International News.

[75] LC Backer, 'The Fuhrer Principle of International Law: Individual Responsibility and Collective Punishment' (2003) 21 *Penn State International Law Review* 509, 555.

[76] J Ferejohn, 'Accountability in a Global Context' IILJ Working Paper 2007/5, available at http://www.iilj.org/working%20papers/documents/2007-5.Ferejohn.web_000.pdf, 21–4.

not likely to become well developed.[76] Though the General Assembly and the Security Council pronounced repeatedly on the Srebrenica genocide, it seems that these mechanisms could hardly be qualified as capable of rendering accountability. The more fundamental problem here may be that political accountability requires some form of political process that is mostly absent at the international level. Other forms of accountability nonetheless may have played some role, such as supervisory accountability, peer accountability and public reputational accountability.[77] Whether these would have meaning for the victims of Srebrenica who were in search of accountability remains uncertain and would seem to require further consideration and research.

C. The International Community

Quite a different set of questions presented itself with regard to the accountability of the UN, and the individual troop-contributing states, that sought to protect Srebrenica. It is now widely accepted that the United Nations had its share of responsibility: it set up a safe area that it subsequently failed to protect.[78]

However, as will be indicated further below, at the UN level it was difficult, if not impossible, to find some meaningful form of accountability. In this situation, the question became whether international institutions could be accountable to a domestic forum or, in a less far-reaching proposition, whether domestic mechanisms can help to provide for accountability for acts or omissions at the international level.

The case for examining the contribution of domestic procedures to accountability in the international legal order or vice versa is compelling. The Srebrenica genocide illustrates that the transfer of powers to international institutions creates accountability gaps. Even though states may have consented to a transfer of powers (and in that respect may have granted international institutions some form of legitimacy), the exercise of such powers may move far beyond the initial consent and thus call for additional processes of accountability. At the international level, only very partial procedures of that nature exist. Although the principles of responsibility of international institutions are relatively well established, they are little used in practice, in part because of a shortage of procedures where the responsibility of international organisations can formally be invoked.

As a general proposition, accountability processes at the domestic level

[77] Grant and Keohane, above n 17, 8–9.

[78] Srebrenica was declared a safe area by UNSC Res 819 (6 April 1993) UN Doc S/RES/819. See for an assessment of the causes of the failure to protect the safe area: 'The Fall of Srebrenica', above n 15, para 467 and following.

then may fill gaps left open at the international level. One even may construe domestic processes as part of an interlocking or interdependent system of accountability in which the distinction between 'the' international and 'the' domestic level is not that relevant, but in which both domestic and international accountability contribute to accountability. However, while the examples given below suggest that domestic accountability processes are perceived as alternatives to, or as being able to supplement, international processes that stakeholders consider to be incomplete or otherwise unsatisfactory, the case of Srebrenica also illustrates (comparable to the situation with accountability of individuals and states) that the international and domestic alternatives are no perfect substitutes.

(1) Political Accountability

The search for accountability for the Srebrenica genocide focused first on political accountability. After four years of initial non-accountability, the failure of the UN triggered some form of accountability processes at the international level. The General Assembly requested the Secretary General to report on the role of the UN in Srebrenica.[79] The Secretary General subsequently accounted in his 1999 report on Srebrenica for the full facts and accepted responsibility, though not in legal terms. The main thrust of the report, as well as its reception in the General Assembly, was forward looking. It aimed to renew the practice of peace-keeping with a view to prevent recurrences in the future.[80]

The fundamental question was, and still is, whether the acceptance of a share of (non-legal) responsibility combined with forward-looking measures was sufficient, in terms of retrospective accountability. Can such responsibility accepted by a UN Secretary General, for the UN as a whole, in a report addressed to the General Assembly, ever be accepted as a meaningful form of accountability towards individual victims who probably do not feel part of the international community that the UN believes to represent? Is there an accountability relationship between the UN and individual victims? These questions may lend themselves to empirical research, but prima facie it seems doubtful that even if the UN Secretary General would have accepted a greater share of responsibility, that would have satisfied the 'accountability needs' of the individuals who felt betrayed by an organisation which promised to protect them but did not deliver.

The fact that the quest for accountability continued afterwards and moved to the domestic level also suggests that the acceptance of some

[79] UNGA Res 53/35 (13 January 1998) UN Doc A/RES/53/35, para 18.
[80] 'Fall of Srebrenica', above n 15, para 5.

responsibility by the UN did not bring an end to the quest for accountability. As a result, accountability questions were also raised in domestic institutions of the troop-contributing states: this has happened in France[81] and in particular in the Netherlands. The Netherlands was the main troop-contributing state, and a significant part of the failure of the UN to protect Srebrenica was in fact the failure of DutchBat to provide the protection that it was expected to provide, at least to the local population.[82]

The Srebrenica affair caused an unprecedented sequence of events in Dutch parliamentary history. The role of DutchBat and the involvement of the Netherlands in the peace-keeping operation was the subject of a major political and public debate. It led to several large inquiries. After the authoritative report by the Netherlands Institute for War Documentation, published in 2000,[83] the government resigned.[84] As yet this appears to be the only time a government has resigned in relation to a failed UN operation.

One can approach the issue of political responsibility in the Netherlands from several perspectives. On the one hand, the government may have resigned for its own failures, for instance for accepting the mandate (that perhaps was not sufficiently robust) in the first place or for not taking a stronger position when Srebrenica threatened to be overtaken and no air support was forthcoming. On the other hand, the resignation might be interpreted as a manifestation of a larger responsibility. Significantly, one of the reasons advanced by the then Dutch Prime Minister Kok was that the government needed to assume responsibility because there was no meaningful way in which the international community, or the United Nations, could assume responsibility. Prime Minister Kok said:

> The 'international community' is faceless and cannot express its responsibility to the victims and survivors of Srebrenica. I can, and I do so now.[85]

The exact meaning of this statement remains a matter of some uncertainty. Did Prime Minister Kok assume his (or the Government's) share of responsibility for the failure of the UN to act? Or did he assume

[81] Rapport d'Information sur les événements de Srebrenica, 22 November 2001, available at http://www.assemblee-nationale.fr/legislatures/11/pdf/rap-info/i3413-01.pdf.

[82] See for an assessment the report by the Netherlands Institute for War Documentation (NIOD, Srebrenica—a 'safe' area Reconstruction, background, consequences and analyses of the fall of a Safe Area), available at http://193.173.80.81/srebrenica/, in particular ch 7.16.

[83] NIOD, *ibid.*

[84] See Statement by Prime Minister Wim Kok on the government's resignation, made to the House of Representatives of the States General, available at http://minaz.nl/english/News/Speeches/2002/04/Statement_by_Prime_Minister_Wim_Kok_on_the_governments_resignation.

[85] *Ibid.*

the full responsibility of the UN, which itself could not do so? Either way, this statement is a rare reflection on the inherent and essential limitations of the possibilities of the international community, of the UN, to render account to local or domestic communities. It also hints at the need for domestic communities to step into its place. Because there is no proper mechanism for political accountability at the international level, accountability is channelled to one actor at the domestic level.

In terms of the terminology introduced in section I, this is an example of political accountability, resulting in the resignation of a government. The role of law in the entire process seems to have been negligible. Although a legal analysis might have been made, the overall debate was of a political nature and there is no indication in the debate that the government would have had to resign because of a breach of international law. This form of political accountability is in no way contingent on violations of international law. Nonetheless, in view of repeated statements by the victims that what they were looking for was some form of acknowledgement and recognition of the role of the UN (or the contributing states), in theory such a process might well have been relevant. Indeed, this episode indicates that alternative normative modes exist which have consequences that may overlap with or supplement legal accountability.

The question remains, however, to whom any accountability taken at domestic level was directed and by whom it was received? In a narrow sense, the forum of the accountability process was the Dutch Parliament; in a broader sense, perhaps Dutch society. Could it also have significance beyond that—for victims, for Bosnia, or perhaps for the international community? That all seems rather doubtful. It seems that the true meaning of the accountability process following Srebrenica was rather one of catharsis or closure, as it allowed for a conclusion of the painful political and public debate. This was largely a Dutch objective. Indeed, in the absence of similar procedures at the international level that reach the communities involved, it may well be that such catharsis can only be effected at lower levels of individual states.

(2) Legal Accountability

On a separate note, we also have seen the legal accountability move from the international to the domestic level. In 2002, relatives of persons who were killed in the 1995 Srebrenica massacre brought a claim in a Netherlands court. They alleged that the Netherlands, which had provided troops to the UN operation, were responsible vis-à-vis the victims and their relatives for failing to provide an adequate level of protection in the 'safe haven' of Srebrenica.[86] In 2007, a further suit by a larger group of plaintiffs followed.[87]

Both groups of plaintiffs had laid their claims before the United Nations. But in both cases it was soon clear that the UN would not accept any legal liability for the events and would invoke immunity if it were sued in a domestic court.[88] Given that the procedure at the domestic level against the UN stood little chance of success due to the latter's immunity, and that no proper procedure is available at international level, the question became whether a procedure against the main troop-contributing state could fill the gap. It remains to be seen what will become of the claims, which at the time of writing are pending in the district court in The Hague. But at this provisional stage, some general observations can be made.

There seem to be two main bases for the claims against the Netherlands. On the one hand, the Netherlands may be held responsible for their own acts or omissions relating to the exercise of control over the acts or omissions of DutchBat.[89] On the other hand, responsibility of a Member State may be based on the fact that it participated in a UN action and the UN subsequently failed to provide relief.[90] The responsibility then would be a subsidiary responsibility, triggered by the impossibility of finding relief at the international level. It is to be acknowledged that both type of claims face considerable hurdles, even more so after the already infamous judgment of the European Court of Human Rights (ECHR) in *Behrami*.[91]

[86] See 'Families of Srebrenica Massacre Victims to Sue Dutch Government', *Agence France Presse* (Eng) (10 July 2005) available at http://web.lexis-nexis.com/professional/. *Nuhanovic v State of the Netherlands* (pending) Case No 265615.

[87] See 'UN and the Netherlands are Sued over Srebrenica killings', *International Herald Tribune* (4 June 2007), available at http://www.iht.com/articles/2007/06/04/news/serbs.php. *Mothers of Srebrenica v State of the Netherlands* (pending) Case No 295247.

[88] In the case referred to in n 86 a suit against the UN was indeed brought in courts in the Netherlands. The UN indicated that it would invoke immunity. See 'UN Says it has Immunity from Suit by Survivors of Srebenica Massacre in Bosnia', *Associated Press Worldstream* (9 June 2007).

[89] Art 5 of the draft ILC Articles on Responsibility provides: 'The conduct of an organ of a State or an organ or agent of an international organization that is placed at the disposal of another international organization shall be considered under international law an act of the latter organization if the organization exercises effective control over that conduct' (UN Doc A/CN4/L86 (2004), p 2). Also joint attribution might be considered; see Second Report on Responsibility of International Organizations by Giorgio Gaja, para 42 (UN Doc A/CN4/541 (2004)).

[90] *Bosphorus Hava Yollari Turizm v Ireland* (App No 45036/98) ECHR 30 June 2005, para 156.

[91] *Behrami and Behrami v France* (App No 78166/01) ECHR 2 May 2007 (para 149 stating that: 'Since operations established by UNSC Resolutions under Chapter VII of the UN Charter are fundamental to the mission of the UN to secure international peace and security and since they rely for their effectiveness on support from member states, the Convention cannot be interpreted in a manner which would subject the acts and omissions of Contracting Parties which are covered by UNSC Resolutions and occur prior to or in the course of such missions, to the scrutiny of the Court.')

If a court were to judge the claims on their merits, it is clear that it would be far removed from a fully international accountability process at the UN level. Not only would the responsible actor no longer be the UN but a Member State, but the claims and remedies would also be coloured by the specific domestic context. Generally speaking, domestic courts that determine a violation of a rule of international law proceed to apply domestic principles of responsibility and thereby engage in a process of translating international into domestic principles of reparation. For the victims, however, that distinction may be less relevant—in their search for accountability, the stakeholders value real outcomes more than the dichotomies between the international and the domestic arena.

V. CONCLUSIONS

The concept of multi-level accountability may contribute in several respects to our understanding of accountability processes in regard to violations of international law. The case-study of the aftermath of the Srebrenica massacre demonstrates that multi-level governance and multi-level accountability are not hierarchical phenomena. Whereas the classic understanding, in international law is one of hierarchical relations (international, national, local), multi-level accountability is premised on the idea of levels that are not hierarchically ordered but are intertwined in a more complex manner.

In many situations, neither the international nor the domestic level can function independently. While international and domestic procedures are substitutes for each other, clearly they are not perfect substitutes. Thus they do not create what has been called 'redundancy', whereby overlapping accountability mechanisms reduce the centrality of any of them.[92] Rather, they provide an example of what Scott calls an interdependence model,[93] in which accountability at one level may be supplemented by accountability at other levels, and in which, moreover, one form of accountability (eg, legal accountability) can be supplemented by other forms of accountability (eg, political) and in which accountability of one actor (eg, the state) can be supplemented by accountability of other actors. In all these respects, one can speak of an interdependency of accountability.

While most of the accountability processes examined in this chapter form part of legal accountability, the debate over the accountability of the UN demonstrates that accountability processes based on legal standards and conducted through legal procedures do not cover the full spectrum

[92] C Scott, 'Accountability in the Regulatory State' (2000) 27 *Journal of Legal Studies* 52.
[93] Scott, *ibid*, 38; Harlow and Rawlings, above n 45, 544.

of accountability options. Indeed, viewed from the quest for accountability of the injured parties, it may be fruitful to consider these different mechanisms—international procedures, domestic constitutional procedures and domestic tort law—as part of the same complex, and, by and large, as pursuing similar aims. International responsibility provides only a partial view of the rich environment in which inter-state strands, or even strands involving international organisations, have come to be embedded. Diverse modes of international accountability have evolved around them, and international law should not neglect that complex environment.

A question that has been insufficiently researched is whether political accountability can be considered, in certain cases, as a substitute for legal accountability. Because there may be obstacles for using one form (eg, because of the immunity of international organisations that hinder a determination of their legal responsibility), political accountability may be the only option. However, it is also to be recognised that at the international level political accountability remains rather problematic due to the absence of properly functioning political arenas, whereas political accountability at the domestic level may be relevant to the state in question, but lacks the power to provide accountability across borders.

15

Territorial Administration by Non-territorial Sovereigns

MALCOLM N SHAW QC*

I. INTRODUCTION

THE CONCEPT OF sovereignty plays a critical role in the structure of international law, composed as it is primarily of states possessing comprehensive international legal personality and equality in formal juridical terms.[1] If statehood (and territorial sovereignty as its operating principle) is the primary and most important model of an entity existing within the framework of international law and the one possessed of the most extensive collection of rights and duties consequent upon international legal personality, it is clearly not the only one, and indeed to focus exclusively upon that model would be to misunderstand the international system. The question addressed in this chapter is the extent to which that model is inadequate in the light of modern experience and the need to refocus our conception of the relationship between the international community, the state and territory. Indeed, it is one of the arguments of this chapter that this relationship has become more distant than in the past.

Sovereignty in international law, or external sovereignty, refers to 'legal authority which is not in law dependent on any other earthly authority'.[2] Judge Huber in the *Island of Palmas* case put it as follows:

> Sovereignty in the relations between States signifies independence. Independence in regard to a portion of the globe is the right to exercise therein, to the exclusion of any other State, the functions of a State.[3]

* The Sir Robert Jennings Professor of International Law, University of Leicester.

[1] See, eg, I Brownlie, *Principles of Public International Law* (6th edn, Oxford University Press, 2003) 287.

[2] R Jennings and A Watts (eds), *Oppenheim's International Law* (9th edn, London, Longmans, 1992) 122.

[3] *Island of Palmas Case* (1928) 2 RIAA 829, 838 (1928).

That means that each state as a matter of definition possesses a spatial dimension within which no other state may act and with regard to which the state exercises a range of competences as recognised in international law.

A fundamental element of sovereignty consists of the relationship of the state to its territory, whether the title to territory itself or the competence to acquire one way or another additional territory. The concept of territorial sovereignty is concerned with the nature of the authority exercised by the state over its territory. Territory forms the spatial framework for the existence and exercise of sovereign rights. Territorial sovereignty is, therefore, centred upon the rights and powers coincident upon territory in the geographical sense. As such it has provided the basis for modern international law. Territorial sovereignty must exist before one can talk of a state.

Maine wrote that

> if sovereignty had not been associated with the proprietorship of a limited portion of the earth, had not, in other words, become territorial, three parts of the Grotian theory would have been incapable of application.[4]

Judge Huber regarded the principle of the exclusive competence of the state in regard to its own territory as the point of departure in settling most questions that concern international relations,[5] while Jennings referred to the 'mission and purpose of traditional international law' as being the delimitation of the exercise of sovereign power on a territorial basis.[6] Brierly emphasised that sovereignty referred not to a relation of persons to persons, nor to the independence of the state itself, but to the characteristics of rights over territory and was a convenient way of contrasting 'the fullest rights over territory known to the law' with certain minor territorial rights, eg, leases and servitudes.[7] In other words, the notion of territorial sovereignty is the basis of international law and comprises a key element of its substance and it focuses upon the notion of rights and duties, being the pinnacle of a structure of such attributes.

Territorial sovereignty has a positive aspect, ie, the exclusive competence of the state within its territory, and a negative aspect, ie, the obligation to protect the rights of other states, and characterises a particular kind of link between state and land recognised by international law. The collection of competences associated with the concept of territorial sovereignty may be seen as derived ultimately from the norms of

[4] H Maine, *Ancient Law* (1861) 66.

[5] *Island of Palmas*, above n 3, 838.

[6] RY Jennings, *The Acquisition of Territory in International Law* (Manchester University Press, 1963) 2.

[7] JL Brierly, *The Law of Nations* (6th edn, Oxford University Press, 1963) 162.

the international legal order itself. But this should not be understood as detracting from the important social and psychological role played by the state in the life of a community. Sovereignty in international law reflects the need for security and stability, but it also constitutes, in Alvarez's words, 'an institution, an international social function of a psychological character'.[8] Territorial sovereignty is the answer provided by international law as regards the needs for security, stability and identity felt by a particular population within a certain area

Holsti has summed up the meaning of sovereignty in the following way:

> Sovereignty is a foundational institution of international relations because it is the critical component of the *birth, maintenance,* and *death* of states. . . . Sovereignty helps create states; it helps maintain their integrity when under threat from within or without; and it helps guarantee their continuation and prevents their death. . . . Sovereignty defines the limits of a legal realm. Jurisdiction exists only within a specified territory and extends no further. . . . The external aspect of sovereignty is that the state has constitutional independence. It is not legally subject to any external authority.[9]

However, sovereignty in international law is not absolute in the way that sovereignty internally could be. Sovereignty, and territorial sovereignty, derives from international law and is thus subject to it and to the way in which it evolves. It is limited by the need to accept the sovereignty of other states and by the obligations imposed on states from time to time by the rules of international law, and it has long been accepted that such norms need not be consensual in order to be binding.[10] Indeed, the Draft Declaration on Rights and Duties of States proclaimed in 1949 that 'the States of the world form a community governed by international law'.[11] Further, recent approaches to sovereignty have treated the concept in a variable or relative context, rather than focusing on any attributes that are deemed absolute.[12]

Holsti has written that:

> Sovereignty is a distinct legal or juridical status. A state is either sovereign or it is not. It cannot be partly sovereign or have 'eroded' sovereignty no matter

[8] *Corfu Channel* case, [1949] ICJ Rep 4, 43.

[9] KJ Holsti, *Taming the Sovereigns* (Cambridge University Press, 2004) 113 (emphasis in original).

[10] See, eg, *Oppenheim's International Law,* above n 2, 29

[11] UNGA Res 375 (IV) (6 December 1949). Para 1 of the Preamble.

[12] See, eg, H Spruyt, *The Sovereign State and Its Competitors* (Princeton University Press, 1994); J Bartelson, *A Genealogy of Sovereignty* (Cambridge University Press, 1995); TL Ilgen (ed), *Reconfigured Sovereignty* (Aldershot, Ashgate, 2003); N Walker (ed), *Sovereignty in Transition* (Oxford, Hart Publishing, 2003); and J Bartelson, 'The Concept of Sovereignty Revisited' (2006) 17 *European Journal of International Law* 463.

> how weak or ineffective it may be. . . . It is an absolute category and not a variable. Interpretations of the term, as well as sovereignty practices, change with time, but its foundational principles have remained essentially intact. . . . This is not to deny all sorts of anomalies, of which there are quite a few, but not enough to constitute a pattern or regular practice.[13]

However, the range of what Holsti terms anomalies is increasing and the absolute nature of sovereignty is decreasing in the light of the needs of the international community, such that traditional descriptions of sovereignty in bold absolute terms require rethinking. Lapidoth has pointed out that the concept of sovereignty 'is one of the most controversial notions in constitutional law and international law, as well as in political science and international relations'. It has been linked to the idea of absolute political authority and has been used or abused to justify totalitarianism and expansionist regimes and to glorify the state.[14] On the other hand, there is an inherent flexibility in the notion of sovereignty in the context of functional competence that may enable the circle to be squared.[15]

The challenges to the absolutist approach to sovereignty are many and varied.[16] On the one hand the rise of other international legal persons as characterised by international law has clearly impacted upon the exclusivity of states within the international system. International organisations, both global and regional, play an increasing role in the conduct of international relations. They can enter into agreements with states, create rights and duties for other legal persons, establish and enforce binding norms of international law and are increasingly important in the multiplying mechanisms for dispute resolution.[17] Across a range of areas, states have surrendered elements of their sovereign power to such organisations in the belief that this may prove a more effective method of achieving aims no longer adequately attainable by themselves alone. Non-governmental organisations and multinational enterprises flourish and function now on the international scene in a manner inconceivable in earlier decades and with increasing effect. Individuals are now the repositories of rights and duties directly under international law and may enforce their international rights through international mechanisms[18] and

[13] Holsti, above n 9, 114.

[14] R Lapidoth, *Autonomy* (Washington, US Institute of Peace Press, 1997) 41.

[15] See *ibid*, ch 6 and generally.

[16] See, eg, A-M Slaughter, 'Sovereignty and Power in a Networked World Order' (2004) 40 *Stanford Journal of International Law* 283.

[17] See, eg, MN Shaw, *International Law* (5th edn, Cambridge University Press 2003) ch 23.

[18] See, eg, the Optional Protocol to the International Covenant on Political and Civil Rights (adopted 16 December 1966); International Convention on the Elimination of All Forms of Racial Discrimination (adopted 21 December 1965, entered into force 4 January 1969) Art 14.

be prosecuted through international courts.[19] Certain groups may benefit from the application of international law norms[20] and may even have the right to independence in certain circumstances.[21] On the other hand, in the face of challenges of an international nature and increasing awareness of global interdependence, states through processes of co-operation with other states and entities have constrained their own exercise of sovereignty in areas such as human rights and humanitarian law, the environment and international trade, and thereby permitted other states to impact upon matters heretofore recognised as subject to exclusive domestic jurisdiction.

Sovereignty, therefore, is not the iconic talisman of the classic period of international law. While in most cases critical issues do not arise as to how to deal with asymmetries between sovereignty and actual control and administration, in some situations such problems may arise and these require careful consideration of the circumstances and thus the allocation of rights and responsibilities in each particular case. In other words, in order to deal with many of the most critical situations in international relations, an exclusive focus upon sovereignty is simply not sufficient, and indeed as the concept of sovereignty is undoubtedly evolving, the range and manner of methodologies of actual control and administration of territory has perhaps been insufficiently examined.

II. ADMINISTRATIVE CONTROL BY THIRD PARTIES

A. General

Consideration of a number of situations in which effective control is exercised by other than the territorial sovereign will be undertaken briefly in order to demonstrate the increasing range of examples in which the absolute territorial sovereignty model has been superseded, at least for a time, in the light of the perceived inadequacy of that mechanism and in order to illustrate some of the problems that may ensue. First, however, some of the reasons that have impelled such approaches should be noted. Such a disjunction between control and sovereignty may arise as a consequence of the inability of the international community, or the major powers, to agree upon or recognise the allocation of sovereignty or

[19] See the Statute of the Yugoslav Tribunal (adopted 25 May 1993 by UNSC Res 827); the Statute of the Rwanda Tribunal (adopted 8 November 1994 by UNSC Res 955); Statute of the International Criminal Court (adopted 17 July 1998) 2187 UNTS 90.

[20] See, eg, A Cassese, *Self-Determination of Peoples* (Cambridge University Press, 1998), and G Simpson, 'The Diffusion of Sovereignty: Self-Determination in the Post-Colonial Age' (1996) 32 *Stanford Journal of International Law* 255; and see for indigenous peoples, P Thornberry, *Indigenous Peoples* (Manchester University Press, 2002).

[21] In the case of colonial territories, see, eg, Cassese, above n 20.

because that is the solution agreed upon for reasons deriving from idealism or power balance considerations either on a permanent or a temporary basis, or because the existing political system in a territorial unit has collapsed and the existing and recognised sovereign power is unable to maintain order or prevent egregious violations of human rights.[22]

Further, the actual mechanisms of such administration may vary from military to civilian control and the mix of applicable law may be different from one situation to another. Military officials tend to feel more at home with the minimalist approach of traditional occupation law with its stress on military necessity, while international organisation officials focus more upon international norms relating to human rights and development.[23] Similarly, accountability issues may be dealt with in various ways, whether exclusively within the territory concerned or involving military or civilian elements within the occupying or administering power or involving the responsibility and authority of organs of international organisations, such as the Security Council or the Secretary General.

It should be noted in passing that states may agree to restrict the range of rights they possess by virtue of territorial sovereignty. The UK and France, for example, have agreed to permit each other's frontier control officers to work in specified parts of one another's territory, thus allowing for the application and enforcement of the laws of one state in the territory of the other,[24] while Annex I(b) and (c) of the 1994 Israel–Jordan Peace Treaty recognises the areas of Naharayim/Baqura and Zofar/ Al-Ghamr as under Jordanian sovereignty but subject to a special regime permitting extensive Israeli jurisdiction.

Classical international law has long accepted the existence of entities of more limited personality, including states. Several states, for example, were rendered subject to special operating conditions. Switzerland (1815), Belgium (1831)[25] and Austria (1955), for example, were recognised as guaranteed and neutral states by virtue of international agreements.[26] Again, certain states entered into protectorate agreements or arrangements whereby one state took over certain sovereign powers from another, usually the conduct of foreign affairs and national defence.[27]

[22] See, eg, R Wilde, 'From Danzig to East Timor and Beyond: The Role of International Territorial Administration' (2001) 95 *American Journal of International Law* 583, discussing the categories of 'sovereignty' and 'governance' problems.

[23] See S Ratner, 'Foreign Occupation and International Territorial Administration: The Challenges of Convergence' (2005) 16 *European Journal of International Law* 695, 702–3.

[24] See the Protocol Concerning Frontier Controls and Policing, Co-operation in Criminal Justice, Public Safety and Mutual Assistance Relating to the Channel Fixed Link, 1991 and the Protocol of 29 May 2000 and the Channel Tunnel (International Arrangements) Order 1993.

[25] This ceased after the First World War.

[26] See, eg, *Oppenheim's International Law*, above n 2, 319ff.

[27] *Ibid*, 266ff. See, eg, Tunisia under French protection and Morocco partly under French and partly under Spanish protection, see MF Lindley, *The Acquisition and Government of Backward*

However, not all protectorate arrangements fell into the same pattern. The 'colonial protectorate' as applied in Africa in the nineteenth century was essentially little more than a colonising device.[28] These examples, however, operated by recognising de jure the sovereignty in question, while de facto restricting some of the consequences thereof.

B. Control of Territory by Another State

(1) In a Situation of Unallocated Sovereignty

After the end of the First World War and the collapse of the German, Austro-Hungarian, Russian and Ottoman empires, a system for dealing with the colonies of the defeated powers that did not involve annexation was developed. These territories, no longer under the sovereignty of the former powers, were to be governed according to the principle that 'the well-being and the development of such peoples form a sacred trust of civilisation' which would be implemented by entrusting the tutelage of the peoples of such territories to 'advanced nations'. These arrangements were to be exercised by these 'advanced nations' as mandatories on behalf of the League of Nations to which they reported and were accountable.[29] The mandatory power exercised a full range of administrative and legislative control over the territory, but not the expanse of competences and authorities consequent upon ownership. While it was clear that sovereignty over the territory did not pass to the mandatory power,[30] it was less clear where sovereignty did reside. Various possibilities were canvassed, ranging from the Council of the League to the

Territories in International Law (Longman, Green, 1926), and Persian Gulf States under British protection, see HM Al-Baharna, *The Arabian Gulf States: Their Legal and Political Status and Their International Problems* (2nd edn, Beirut: Librairie du Liban, 1978), and the Malay States, see AP Rubin, *International Personality of the Malay Peninsula* (Kuala Lumpur: Penerbit Universiti Malaya, 1974).

[28] See *Land and Maritime Boundary (Cameroon v Nigeria)*, [2002] ICJ Rep paras 205 and 207. See also MN Shaw, 'The Acquisition of Territory in Nineteenth Century Africa: Some Thoughts' in PM Dupuy et al (eds), *Festschrift for Christian Tomuschat* (Kehl, NP Engel Verlag, 2006) 1029.

[29] Covenant of the League of Nations (adopted 28 April 1919) Art 22. See also the *International Status of South West Africa* [1950] ICJ Rep 128, 132; the *Namibia* case [1971] ICJ Rep 16, 28–9 and *Cameroon v Nigeria* [2002] ICJ Rep para 212. See also J Crawford, *The Creation of States in International Law* (2nd edn, Oxford University Press, 2006) ch 13; HD Hall, *Mandates, Dependencies and Trusteeship* (London, Stevens, 1948) and *Oppenheim's International Law*, above n 2, 295ff.

[30] Note that an assertion by South Africa of sovereignty over its mandated territory of South West Africa in a boundary agreement with Portugal of 22 June 1926 was withdrawn after objections from the League of Nations' Permanent Mandates Commission, see Crawford, above n 29, 568. Judge McNair in his separate opinion in the *Status of South West Africa* case noted that sovereignty over a mandated territory was 'in abeyance' to be revived if and when the inhabitants of the territory obtained recognition as an independent State, [1950] ICJ Rep 150.

principal allied powers and from the League to the inhabitants of the territory.[31] What was accepted was that such territories possessed 'an international status'.[32]

The mandate system was transformed into the United Nations trusteeship system after the conclusion of the Second World War and the demise of the League, together with territories taken from the defeated states as a result of that conflict.[33] Although there was no obligation upon mandatory powers to transfer mandated territories into trust territories, all but South Africa in respect of South West Africa did so. In the latter case, the International Court held that the mandate arrangements simply continued. Indeed, what is also of importance in this context is that the Court held that the League's supervisory competence with regard to mandated territories was inherited by the United Nations with regard to trust territories.[34]

With regard to trust territories, the obligation to safeguard and advance the interests of the inhabitants was deemed paramount, while one of the objectives of the system was to promote the progressive development of the territories 'towards self-government or independence' in the light of the 'freely expressed wishes of the people concerned'.[35] Indeed, the International Court made it clear that the principle of self-determination was applicable to mandate and trust territories,[36]

Mandatory and trusteeship powers possessed wide-ranging competence in the legislative and administrative field, subject to the requirement to the supervision of the League of Nations and then the UN General Assembly,[37] but this did not include the capacity to modify the international status of the territory concerned. This capacity rested with the power acting with the consent of the international organisation.[38] While the trust power could administer the territory concerned together with a neighbouring territory, it could not alter unilaterally international boundaries nor otherwise dispose of the territory.

[31] Crawford, above n 29, fn 6. See also Q Wright, 'Sovereignty of the Mandates' (1923) 17 *American Journal of International Law* 691 and id, *Mandates under the League of Nations* (Chicago University Press, 1930).

[32] *International Status of South West Africa* [1950] ICJ Rep 132. Duncan Hall noted that 'twenty years of inconclusive speculation among international lawyers as to where sovereignty was really lodged did not really help matters', above n 29, 73.

[33] UN Charter, Art 77.

[34] *International Status of South West Africa* [1950] ICJ Rep 137, 140 and 143–4.

[35] UN Charter, Art 76.

[36] See the *Namibia* case [1971] ICJ Rep 6, 31 and the *Western Sahara* case [1975] ICJ Rep 12, 31–3.

[37] Strategic trust territories were subject to a slightly different regime under the supervision of the Security Council, See, eg, M Whiteman, *Digest of International Law* vol I (Washington, Government Printing Office, 1963) 769–839.

[38] *International Status of South West Africa* [1950] ICJ Rep 143–4.

(2) In a Situation Where the Recognised Sovereign Was Deprived by Force of Control

(i) Traditional Occupation The capture by force of the territory of another state and the establishment of control raises immediately in international law the status of belligerent occupation with a range of consequential applicable norms. Such rules were essentially predicated upon the expectation of a relatively short period of occupation of the territory of the defeated enemy, and this coloured the nature of the relevant provisions. The occupying state was entitled to exercise a variety of powers, focused upon the establishment and preservation of order, but such powers were carefully constrained. The fundamental principle, however, was that the capture and control of such territories could not of themselves transfer sovereignty from the defeated to the victorious power.[39] Thus the process of occupation in law involved the regulation of control by the occupying power notwithstanding the continuation of the existing sovereign title with a view to resolving the dispute by a peace agreement with the minimum of disruption to the lives of the occupied population.

Territory is deemed occupied, according to Article 42 of the Hague Regulations attached to the 1907 Hague Convention IV on the Laws and Customs of War on Land and accepted as part of customary international law,[40] 'when it is actually placed under the authority of the hostile army', while 'the occupation extends only to the territory where such authority has been established and can be exercised'. This has recently been underlined by the International Court in *Democratic Republic of Congo v Uganda*, where it was further noted that:

> In order to reach a conclusion as to whether a State, the military forces of which are present on the territory of another State as a result of an intervention, is an 'occupying Power' in the meaning of the term as understood in the *jus in bello*, the Court must examine whether there is sufficient evidence to demonstrate that the said authority was in fact established and exercised by the intervening State in the areas in question.

[39] See, eg, E Benvenisti, *The International Law of Occupation* (Princeton University Press, revised paperback printing 2004) 5–6, and UK Ministry of Defence, *The Manual of the Law of Armed Conflict* (Oxford University Press, 2004) 278. Note the special situation of the administration of Germany by the Four Allied Powers in 1945, see Crawford, above n 29, 452–4; ID Hendry and MC Wood, *The Legal Status of Germany* (Cambridge, Grotius Publications, 1987) and ME Bathurst and JL Simpson, *Germany and the North Atlantic Community* (London, Stevens, 1972).

[40] See, eg, Judgment of the International Military Tribunal of Nuremberg, 30 September and 1 October 1946, 65; *Legality of the Threat of Use of Nuclear Weapons* [1996] ICJ Rep 256; *Legal Consequences of the Construction of a Wall in the Occupied Palestinian Territory* [2004] ICJ Rep __ para 89 and *Democratic Republic of Congo v Uganda* [2005] ICJ Rep 116, para 219. See also the Eritrea–Ethiopia Claims Commission, Partial Award, Central Front, Ethiopia's Claim 2, The Hague, 28 April 2004 at para 16.

The mere presence of occupying forces was not sufficient; there was a need to substitute their own authority for that of the Congolese Government. Any justification given by Uganda for its occupation would be of no relevance nor would it be relevant whether or not a structured military administration of the territory occupied had been established.[41]

In other words, the test is purely pragmatic with no necessary implication as to title. It matters not to the application of the law that there may be a genuine dispute as to the repository of sovereignty with regard to any particular territory. Accordingly, for example, the Israeli Supreme Court (sitting as the High Court of Justice) has affirmed that Israel holds the areas of Judea and Samaria in belligerent occupation.[42]

The law of belligerent occupation is further contained in the Fourth Geneva Convention on the Protection of Civilian Persons in Time of War 1949. Article 2, paragraph 2, provides that the Convention is to apply

> to all cases of partial or total occupation of the territory of the High Contracting Party, even if the said occupation meets with no armed resistance.

The International Court has taken the position that the Convention 'is applicable in any occupied territory in the event of an armed conflict arising between two or more High Contracting Parties' so that with regard to the Israel/Palestine territories question

> the Convention is applicable in the Palestinian territories which before the conflict lay to the east of the Green Line and which, during that conflict, were occupied by Israel, there being no need for any enquiry into the precise legal status of those territories.[43]

The Eritrea–Ethiopia Claims Commission has pointed out that:

> These protections [provided by international humanitarian law] should not be cast into doubt because the belligerents dispute the status of territory. . . . respecting international protections in such situations does not prejudice the status of the territory.[44]

[41] *Democratic Republic of Congo v Uganda* [2005] ICJ Rep, para 173. See also the *UK Manual of the Law of Armed Conflict*, above n 39, 275.

[42] See HCJ 2056/04 *Beit Sourik Village Council v Government of Israel and Others* (Judgment) 30 June 2004, President A Barak, para 1, and HCJ 7957/04 *Mara'abe v Prime Minister of Israel* (Judgment) 15 September 2005, President A Barak, para 14.

[43] *Legal Consequences of the Construction of a Wall*, above n 40, para 101. It should be noted that Israel has long asserted that it applies the humanitarian parts of the Convention to the occupied territories, See, eg, M Shamgar, 'The Observance of International Law in the Administered Territories' (1977) *Israel Yearbook on Human Rights* 262, and T Meron, 'West Bank and Gaza' (1979) *Israel Yearbook on Human Rights* 108. See also *Mara'abe v The Prime Minister of Israel*, above n 42, President A Barak, para 14.

[44] Partial Award, Central Front, Ethiopia's Claim 2, The Hague, 28 April 2004, para 28.

Further, the Commission emphasised that:

> neither text [the Hague Regulations and the Fourth Geneva Convention] suggests that only territory the title of which is clear and uncontested can be occupied territory.[45]

Article 4 of Protocol I to the Geneva Conventions 1977 reinforces the fundamental approach that:

> The application of the Conventions and of this Protocol, as well as the conclusion of the agreements provided for therein, shall not affect the legal status of the Parties to the conflict. Neither the occupation of a territory nor the application of the Conventions and this Protocol shall affect the legal status of the territory in question.

In the case of an occupied territory under the traditional law, the rights and duties of the occupying power are tightly circumscribed. Article 43 of the Hague Regulations[46] provides that:

> The authority of the legitimate power having in fact passed into the hands of the occupant, the latter shall take all the measures in his power to restore and ensure, as far as possible, public order and safety [l'ordre et la vie publics], while respecting, unless absolutely prevented, the law in force in the country.

Accordingly, the structure of an occupation under international law is predicated upon the regulation of the actual exercise of power and not its legitimacy, the upholding of public order and the maintenance of the local legal system. The focus was upon minimalist interference with the pre-existing framework, while ensuring public order.[47] Military necessity constitutes the key to the regulation of the exercise of power by the occupant as balanced by humanitarian considerations, although the precise contours of that relationship are controversial. In the difficult balance between military necessity and humanitarian concern, the twin poles of traditional occupation law, a key rule is played by the principle of proportionality and this may provide the test by which military necessity may be deemed acceptable in the light of the terms of the law of occupation as a whole.[48]

[45] *Ibid*, para 29.

[46] Described by Benvenisti as 'a sort of miniconstitution for the occupation administration', above n 39, 9. See also M Sassoli, 'Legislation and Maintenance of Public Order and Civil Life by Occupying Powers' (2005) 16 *European Journal of International Law* 661, 663ff.

[47] See, eg, the occupation of areas of France in the Franco-Prussian war, see DA Graber, *The Development of the Law of Belligerent Occupation 1863–1914* (New York, Columbia University Press, 1949) 268.

[48] See, eg, R Higgins, *Problems and Process* (Oxford University Press, 1994) 219; JG Gardam, 'Proportionality and Force in International Law' (1993) 87 *American Journal of International Law* 391 and the Judgment of President Barak in *Beit Sourik*, above n 42, para 36ff.

Article 23(g) of the Hague Regulations prohibits the destruction or seizure of enemy property, unless imperatively demanded by the necessities of war. Article 46, a key provision, insists that the family honour and rights, the lives of persons, and private property, as well as religious convictions and practice, must be respected, while private property cannot be confiscated. Requisitions in kind and services must be restricted to the needs of the army of occupation,[49] while any taxes or other money contributions levied in the occupied territories shall be for the expense of the administration of the territory in question or for the needs of the army. Article 50 of the Hague Regulations states that no general penalty, pecuniary or otherwise, shall be inflicted on the population on accounts of acts of individuals for which they cannot be regarded as jointly and severally responsible. Article 55 emphasises that the occupying power is to be regarded

> only as administrator and usufructuary of public buildings, real estate, forests and agricultural estates belonging to the hostile State, and situated in the occupied country. It must safeguard the capital of these properties, and administer them in accordance with the rules of usufruct.

This pattern was replicated and reinforced in the provisions of the Fourth Geneva Convention.[50] Article 27 provides that persons in the hands of the occupying power are entitled in all circumstances to respect for their persons, their honour, their family rights, their religious convictions and practices, and their manners and customs. They are to be humanely treated at all times, although the parties to the conflict may take such measures of control and security in regard to them as may be necessary as a result of the war.[51] Article 47 provides that the benefits of the Convention are not to be taken away by any change introduced by the occupying power, up to and including annexation of the whole or part of the occupied territory, while Article 49 prohibits individual or mass forcible transfers, as well as deportations of protection persons from the occupied territory, although evacuation of an area may be undertaken if the security of the population of imperative military reasons so demand. Further, the occupying power shall not deport or transfer parts of its own civilian population into the territory it occupies. The destruction of private or public property is prohibited, except where rendered absolutely necessary by military operations.[52] Article 54 provides that the

[49] Hague Regulations, Art 52.

[50] The Eritrea–Ethiopia Claims Commission in its Partial Award, Central Front, Ethiopia's Claim 2, The Hague, 28 April 2004, paras 15 and 16, takes the position that the Convention is part of customary international law. See also Partial Award, Central Front, Eritrea's Claims 2, 4, 6, 7, 8 and 22, The Hague, 28 April 2004, paras 21 and 22.

[51] See also Arts 29, 31, 32, 33 and 34.

[52] Art 53.

occupying power may not alter the status of public officials or judges in the occupied territories or in any way apply sanctions to or discriminate against them, although it retains the right to remove public officials from office, eg, for refusing obedience to the occupying power.[53] The penal laws of the occupied territory shall remain in force with the exception that they may be repealed or suspended where they constitute a threat to the security of the occupying power or an obstacle to the application of the Convention itself.[54]

Thus, to summarise, the traditional international law on occupation[55] seeks (i) to prevent any unilateral change in the pre-existing sovereignty position; (ii) to emphasise the temporary nature of the occupation; (iii) to permit the occupying power to restore and maintain public order and public life; (iv) to constrain the activities of the occupier to the minimum necessary consistent with the need to upkeep public order; and (v) to maintain its own stance as interpreted in the light of military necessity and oblige the occupier to treat the population of the area in question with humanity and dignity. However, the application of the relevant principles becomes ever more complex the longer the occupation goes on and the predominant assumption of the temporary control of the territory pending a peace settlement weakens or disappears.[56] Problems will arise in a period of rapid social, economic and political changes taking place both within the territory in question and outside where this is impacting upon the population under occupation, particularly where the legal and political system of the territory is anchored in a different time and cultural framework and is thus unable to deal with the evolving situation. The rules traditionally provided by the law of occupation are predicated upon the temporary and minimally interfering nature of the occupation, not upon any perceived need to bring the social, economic and political system of the territory up to date and reform inappropriate laws, practices or procedures. The Israeli Supreme Court put it this way:

> Life does not stand still, and no administration, whether an occupation administration or another, can fulfil its duties with respect to the population if it refrains from legislating and from adapting the legal situation to the exigencies of modern times.[57]

Roberts has written that the argument that in a prolonged occupation,

[53] See *UK Manual of the Law of Armed Conflict*, above n 39, 283.

[54] Art 64.

[55] See generally Graber, above n 47, and A Roberts, 'What Is a Military Occupation?' (1984) 55 *British Year Book of International Law* 249.

[56] See A Roberts, 'Prolonged Military Occupation: The Israeli-Occupied Territories Since 1967' (1990) 84 *American Journal of International Law* 44, especially 47.

[57] *The Christian Society for the Sacred Places v Minister of Defence*, 26 (1) PD 574, 582 (1971) as cited in Benvenisti, above n 39, 146.

new and sometimes long-term measures have to be taken in response to new problems is 'powerful', while raising the problem of how to assess the changing needs of the population.[58] Coupled with the unfortunate fact that many military occupiers have in the recent past simply refused to accept and apply the rules of belligerent occupation with regard to the territory they control,[59] it is clear that the traditional rules are under some pressure

(ii) Traditional Occupation Plus—The Application of International Human Rights Law The question of the application of treaties generally to occupied territory has long been an issue,[60] with particular resonance for international human rights law. In recent years, the issue has been faced as a consequence of the evolving range of such rights, the increasing penetration of international human rights law into domestic legal system, and the changes in the nature of occupation governance. Human rights has long been seen by the international community as relevant to armed conflicts, ironic as this may seem,[61] and where the parties are subject to a particular human rights regime implemented by a judicial mechanism this becomes clear and evident.[62] The UK Manual of the Law of Armed Conflict, for example, concludes that:

> Where the occupying power is a party to the European Convention on Human Rights the standards of that Convention may, depending on the circumstances, be applicable in the occupied territories.[63]

One particular issue of more general issue before the English courts concerns the relationship between human rights law and Security Council resolutions, and the House of Lords has taken the position that the European Human Rights Convention provisions concerning liberty and security of persons must give way to the provisions of Security Council resolution 1546 permitting the post-occupation multinational

[58] Roberts, above n 56, 94.

[59] See, eg, the Moroccan occupation of Western Sahara since 1974, the Indonesian occupation of East Timor from 1975 to 1999, territories occupied by Eritrea and Ethiopia since the conflict of 1998, the occupation of part of the Democratic Republic of Congo by Uganda and Rwanda, and the occupation of Northern Cyprus by Turkey since 1974.

[60] See, eg, Roberts, above n 56, 70, and T Meron, 'Applicability of Multilateral Conventions to Occupied Territories', (1978) 72 *American Journal of International Law* 542.

[61] See, eg, UNGA Res 2444 (XXIII) (19 December 1968).

[62] See, eg, *Cyprus v Turkey* (Judgement) ECHR 10 May 2001.

[63] *UK Manual of the Law of Armed Conflict*, above n 39, 282. See also as to the application of the European Convention of Human Rights to the British occupation of and subsequent presence in southern Iraq, the decisions of the House of Lords in *Al-Skeini v Secretary of State for Defence* [2007] UKHL 26 and *Al-Jedda v Secretary of State for Defence* [2007] UKHL 58. See also *Coard v United States*, Report No 109/99, 29 September 1999, for the view expressed by the Inter-American Commission on Human Rights that the US was bound by relevant rules of humanitarian law and human rights law in the Grenada intervention.

force in Iraq to intern people for imperative reasons of security as a consequence of the operations of Article 103 of the Charter, whereby Charter obligations prevail over obligations under any other international agreement.[64]

More generally, the International Court has discussed the relationship between international humanitarian law and international human rights law. In its advisory opinion on the Legality of the Threat of Use of Nuclear Weapons, the court emphasised that

> the protection of the International Covenant of Civil and Political Rights does not cease in times of war, except by operation of Article 4 of the Covenant whereby certain provisions may be derogated from in a time of national emergency

and in such cases the matter will fall to be determined by the applicable *lex specialis,* ie, international humanitarian law.[65] The court returned to this matter in its advisory opinion on Legal Consequences of the Construction of a Wall in the Occupied Palestinian Territory, where it declared more generally that:

> the protection offered by human rights conventions does not cease in case of armed conflict, save through the effect of provisions for derogation of the kind found in Article 4 of the International Covenant on Civil and Political Rights.[66]

As to the relationship between international humanitarian law and human rights law, the court noted that there were three possible situations. First, some rights might be exclusively matters of humanitarian law, some rights might be exclusively matters of human rights law and some matters may concern both branches of international law.[67] It was essentially a question of interpretation of the particular instrument in question. In particular, the jurisdiction of states, while primarily territorial, may sometimes be exercised outside the national territory and in such a situation the International Covenant and other relevant human rights treaties had to be applied by state parties.[68] In reaching this conclusion, the court clearly relied, albeit implicitly, upon the evolution of the jurisprudence of the European Court of Human Rights (ECHR) with

[64] *Al Jedda v Secretary of State for Defence* [2007] UKHL 58 at para 26ff.

[65] [1966] ICJ Rep 239.

[66] [2004] ICJ Rep, para 106.

[67] *Ibid.*

[68] *Ibid*, paras 109, 112 and 113. This was a matter of interpretation of the Covenant and of the practice of the Human Rights Committee established thereunder, *ibid.* See also *Banković v Belgium*, decision of 12 Dec 2001, with regard to a similar statement concerning the European Convention on Human Rights.

regard to the meaning of 'jurisdiction' contained in Article 1 of the European Convention,[69] as well as the practice of the UN human rights organs and the general principle of state responsibility for the acts of its organs which would obviously include members of its armed forces.[70] The court interestingly referred to the prolonged occupation question, observing in this human rights context, although specifically dealing with the International Covenant on Economic, Social and Cultural Rights, that 'the territories occupied by Israel have for over 37 years been subject to its territorial jurisdiction as the occupying Power' and then noting that

> In the exercise of the powers available to it *on this basis*, Israel is bound by the provisions of the International Covenant on Economic, Social and Cultural Rights.[71]

The court returned to the question of the relationship between international humanitarian law and international human rights law in *Democratic Republic of Congo v Uganda*, and reaffirmed that:

> international human rights instruments are applicable 'in respect of acts done by a State in the exercise of its jurisdiction outside its own territory', particularly in occupied territories.[72]

A series of international human rights instruments was listed as being applicable with regard to the Congo situation, including the International Covenants on Human Rights, the Convention on the Rights of the Child, and the African Charter on Human and Peoples' Rights.[73] It was concluded that Uganda was responsible for various violations of international human rights law and international humanitarian law, including those committed by virtue of failing to comply with its obligations as an occupying power.[74] Reference was also made to the violation of Article 47 of the Hague Regulations and Article 33 of the Fourth Geneva Convention and of the African Charter on Human and Peoples' Rights with regard to the exploitation of the natural resources of Congo.[75]

Accordingly, it is now accepted that the law applicable in occupation

[69] See, eg, *Loizidou v Turkey* (Judgment) ECHR 18 December 1996; *Cyprus v Turkey* (Judgment) 10 May 2001; *Ilaşcu v Moldova and Russia* (Judgment) 8 July 2004 and *Asanidze v Georgia* (Judgment) 8 April 2004.

[70] See, eg, *Difference Relating to Immunity from Legal Process of a Special Rapporteur* [1999] ICJ Rep 87 and *Democratic Republic of Congo v Uganda* [2005] ICJ Rep, paras 213–4. See also the International Law Commission's Articles on State Responsibility, 2001, A/56/10, Art 4; and UNGA Res 56/83 (12 December 2001).

[71] *Legal Consequences of the Construction of a Wall*, above n 40, para 112 (emphasis added).

[72] [2005] ICJ Rep, para 216.

[73] *Ibid*, paras 217–18.

[74] *Ibid*, paras 219–20.

[75] *Ibid*, paras 245–50.

situations includes multilateral human rights instruments to which the occupying power is a party. This means inevitably not only that the organs and agents of the occupying power must act in conformity with the provisions of such instruments, but also that the population is entitled to the benefit of their application, and as such it must follow that laws and practices already in operation in the territory prior to the occupation that do not meet these human rights standards must be modified. Thus, the application of human rights law in these situations impacts upon the powers and duties of the occupier and affects the traditional attempts to balance military necessity and humanity in any occupation.

(iii) Occupation Mutating—Israel, the Palestinian Territories and the Palestinian Authority A fascinating example of the slow mutation of occupation into the envisaged establishment of a new and recognised sovereign is provided by the situation in what is termed the Palestinian Territories, ie, the West Bank of the Jordan River and the Gaza Strip, captured respectively from Jordan and Egypt in 1967.[76]

Under the Declaration on Principles on Interim Self-Government Arrangements signed by Israel and the Palestine Liberation Organisation (PLO) on 13 September 1993 (following an exchange of letters whereby the PLO recognised Israel's right to exist and Israel recognised the PLO as the representative of the Palestinian people), a transitional period of up to five years of Palestinian interim self-government in the West Bank and the Gaza Strip was posited and a transfer of certain powers and responsibilities to the newly created Palestinian institutions provided for. This took place by virtue of the Cairo Agreement of 4 May 1994 on the Gaza Strip and Jericho; an Agreement on Preparatory Transfer of Powers and Responsibilities of 29 August 1994, passing powers to the Palestinian Authority in the areas of education, social welfare, tourism health and taxation; a protocol of 27 August 1995 transferring powers in the areas of labour, trade and industry, gas and gasoline, insurance, postal services, statistics, agriculture and local government; the Interim Agreement of 28 September 1995 incorporating and superseding earlier agreements; an agreement on a Temporary International Presence in Hebron of 9 May 1996; the Hebron Protocol of 17 January 1997; the Wye River Memorandum of 23 October 1998; and the Sharm el-Sheikh Agreement of 4 September 1999.

The withdrawal of Israeli forces and citizens and facilities from the

[76] See, eg, Crawford, above n 29, 442ff; A Shapira and M Tabory (eds), *New Political Entities in Public and Private International Law* (The Hague, Kluwer, 1999); E Benvenisti, 'The Status of the Palestinian Authority' in E Cotran and C Mallat (eds), *Arab-Israeli Accords: Legal Perspectives* (Boston, MA, Kluwer Law, 1996); E Benvenisti, 'The Israeli–Palestinian Declaration of Principles: A Framework for Future Settlement' (1993) 4 *European Journal of International Law* 542; and P Malanczuk, 'Some Basic Aspects of the Agreements Between Israel and the PLO from the Perspective of International Law', (1996) 7 *European Journal of International Law* 485.

Gaza Strip in August and September 2005 (and from four northern West Bank settlements) needs also to be noted. Although Israel continues to control maritime, airspace and most land access to the Gaza Strip, an agreement was signed in November 2005 providing for the reopening of the Rafah border crossing between Gaza and Egypt under joint Palestinian Authority and Egyptian control with monitoring provided by the European Union.

The effect of these agreements was to establish a territorial and personal jurisdictional patchwork of powers and responsibilities pending a final status solution. In particular, the following points should be noted. First, the agreements deal with the gradual shift from full belligerent occupation of the territories by Israel to an agreed 'final status' depending upon the wishes and consent of the parties. Second, the territorial framework for the exercise of powers by the Palestinian authorities was described as 'West Bank and Gaza territory', ie, with the omission of the definite article, thereby leaving open the possibility that some areas may not fall under Palestinian jurisdiction in the interim period.[77] Thus redeployment matters covered in the agreements do not cover areas which are 'issues that will be negotiated in the final status negotiations', such as Jerusalem, settlements, specified military locations, Palestinian refugees, borders, foreign relations and Israelis.[78] Third, an additional exception to redeployment is constituted by 'Israel's overall responsibility for Israelis and borders'.[79] Fourth, Israeli forces are to be redeployed to 'specified military locations' to be determined by Israel.[80] Fifth, powers and responsibilities not transferred to the Palestinian Council were reserved to Israel.[81] Sixth, following the redeployment of Israeli forces, Palestinian jurisdiction covered two areas. Area A comprised the cities of Jenin, Nablus, Tulkarem, Kalkilya, Ramallah, Bethlehem and Jericho, containing some 26 per cent of the Palestinian population in which the Palestinian Council, elected in January 1996, was given full responsibility for internal security and public order as well as full responsibility for civil affairs. The city of Hebron was rendered subject to special arrangements set out in the Interim Agreement and the 1997 Protocol. Area B comprised the Palestinian towns and villages in the West Bank, containing some 70 per cent of the Palestinian population, where the Palestinian Council assumed full civil authority and responsibility for public order, while

[77] See Israeli–Palestinian Interim Agreement on the West Bank and the Gaza Strip (28 September 1995) Art XI.2. To be contrasted with references in the Gaza–Jericho agreement which referred to 'withdrawal from *the* Gaza Strip and Jericho', Arts V and VI of the Declaration of Principles on Interim Self-Government Arrangements (13 September 1993) (hereafter 'Declaration of Principles') (emphasis added).

[78] Interim Agreement, Art XVII.

[79] *Ibid*, Art XIII.2b(8).

[80] *Ibid*, Art XI.2(f).

[81] Declaration of Principles, Art VII (5).

Israel retained overriding security responsibility to safeguard its citizens and combat terrorism. A third area, C, comprised the largely unpopulated areas of the West Bank deemed of strategic value to Israel together with Jewish settlements. In these areas, Israel retained full responsibility for security and public order and civil responsibilities related to the territory, such as planning and archaeology; the Palestinian Council has civil responsibility for all other civil spheres. The first and second phases of the redeployment were completed in March 2000, at which point some 40 per cent of the West Bank, comprising some 98 per cent of the Palestinian population, was under full Palestinian civilian control and full or partial security control.

In this situation, it is necessary to emphasise two points. First, that the Palestinian Authority emerging out these agreements is not identical to the PLO, recognised by the international community and by Israel as the representative of the Palestinian people, but is rather an entity deriving its legitimacy and powers from the agreements.[82] Secondly, the effect of these agreements is not to terminate as such the status of belligerent occupation. Indeed, Article XXXI (7) of the Interim Agreement specifically states that neither side shall initiate or take any step that will change the status of the West Bank and Gaza pending the outcome of negotiations, while Article XXXI (8) provides that the status of these areas will be preserved during the interim period. Thus both Israeli annexation and a unilateral declaration of Palestinian independence are precluded.[83]

In principle, therefore, Israel remains the occupying power and retains its international powers and responsibilities. Those powers and responsibilities transferred to the Palestinian Authority may be seen as an exercise in delegation and the creation of an autonomous zone coupled with certain self-imposed constraints upon Israeli action. However, this does leave a grey area where actions are undertaken by Palestinian forces free from Israeli control and thus to some extent, but only to some extent, free from its jurisdiction. To that extent, and bearing in mind the nature of the agreements between Israel and the PLO, a rather curious occupation regime has emerged with a clear co-occupation element.

(iv) Occupation Plus Plus—The Case of Iraq 2003–4: A New Model Occupation? In the letter from the Permanent Representatives of the UK and the USA to the Security Council on 8 May 2003, following the military operations commenced against Iraq on 20 March 2003, the two states concerned noted that:

[82] See, eg, Crawford, above n 29, 444–5 and OM Dajani, 'Stalled Between Seasons: The International Legal Status of Palestine During the Interim Period' (1997) 26 *Denver Journal of International Law and Policy* 27.

[83] See, eg, J Singer, 'The Oslo Peace Process: A View from Within', in *New Political Entities*, above n 76, 17, 49.

> The States participating in the Coalition will strictly abide by their obligations under international law, including those relating to the essential humanitarian needs of the people of Iraq

and informed the Council of the creation of the Coalition Provisional Authority 'to exercise powers of government temporarily'.[84] On 22 May 2003, the Security Council adopted resolution 1483 (2003), described by Benvenisti as 'a rare and significant event in the history of the troubled law on occupations'.[85] Essentially this resolution both affirmed the position of the UK and US as occupying powers in Iraq under international law and placed a range of other powers and responsibilities upon them over and above the law relating to occupation.[86] This was accepted by the occupying powers. CPA Regulation No 1 (16 May 2003) declared that the Authority was

> vested with all executive, legislative and judicial authority necessary to achieve its objectives, to be exercised under relevant UN Security Council resolutions, including Resolution 1483 (2003), and the laws and usages of war,

while CPA Memorandum No 3 on Criminal Procedures specifically stated that the CPA was acting 'consistent with the Fourth Geneva Convention of 1949 Relative to the Treatment of Civilians in Time of War' and that the provisions therein set out 'give effect to the requirements of international humanitarian law' (section 1(2)). The formal status of occupation ended on 28 June 2004 with the formal handover of authority to the Iraqi Interim Government, as recognised in Security Council resolution 1546.

Resolution 1483 recognised in the preamble

> the specific authorities, responsibilities and obligations under applicable international law of these States [UK and US] as occupying powers under unified command (the 'Authority')

thereby according UN acceptance of the concept of occupation both generally and particularly with regard to the Iraq situation. The resolution also noted that other states 'not occupying powers are working now or in the future may work under the Authority', thus rendering such states subject to the rules and principles contained both in occupation law

[84] S/2003/538.

[85] See E Benvenisti, 'Water Conflicts During the Occupation of Iraq' (2003) 97 *American Journal of International Law* 860 and *ibid*, 'The Security Council and the Law on Occupation: Resolution 1483 on Iraq in Historical Perspective' (2003) 1 *IDF Law Review* 19, 20.

[86] See generally, 'Iraq: Law of Occupation', House of Commons Research Paper 03/51, 2 June 2003; Benvenisti, *ibid*; M Hmoud, 'The Use of Force Against Iraq: Occupation and Security Council resolution 1483' (2004) 36 *Cornell International Law Journal* 435; D Scheffer, 'Beyond Occupation Law' (2003) 97 *American Journal of International Law* 842; GH Fox, 'The Occupation of Iraq' (2005) 36 *Georgia Journal of International Law* 195.

and under the resolution. What is particularly interesting is the extent to which the resolution expands the range of the competence of the occupying powers (and other relevant states) beyond those flowing from the traditional law of occupation.[87]

The following provisions are particularly relevant. Operative paragraph 4

> calls upon the Authority [which includes states not being occupying powers themselves], consistent with the Charter of the United Nations and other relevant international law, to promote the welfare of the Iraqi people through the effective administration of the territory, including . . . the creation of conditions in which the Iraqi people can freely determine their own political future.

Paragraph 22 noted 'the relevance of the establishment of an internationally recognised, representative government of Iraq'. Paragraph 8 calls upon the Secretary General to appoint a Special Representative for Iraq whose independent responsibilities were to include 'in coordination with the Authority', assisting the people of Iraq across a range of activities, including

> working intensively with the Authority, the people of Iraq and others to advance efforts to restore and establish national and local institutions for representative governance . . . promoting the protection of human rights . . . [and] . . . encouraging international efforts to promote legal and judicial reform.[88]

Such provisions clearly go beyond the minimalist competences in such matters in the traditional law of occupation. In addition to requiring the occupying powers in the form of the Authority to effectively administer the territory for the welfare of the population and create the framework for democratic expression, the Authority was also obliged to act, with others, to create national and local representative institutions and an internationally recognised representative government. Further, the Authority, in co-ordination with the Special Representative, was required to promote human rights and legal and judicial reform.[89]

This approach may also be linked with the unique provisions in the resolution for international monitoring. Paragraph 8, as noted, called for the appointment of a Special Representative for Iraq with substantial

[87] Operative para 5 'calls on all concerned to comply fully with their obligations under international law, including in particular the Geneva Conventions of 1949 and the Hague Regulations of 1907'.

[88] Para 8(a), (b), (c), (d), (e), (g) and (i). Para 9 provides the support of the Council for the 'formation, by the people of Iraq with the help of the Authority and working with the Special Representative, of an Iraqi interim administration as a traditional administration run by Iraqis, until an internationally recognised, representative government is established by the people of Iraq and assumes the responsibilities of the Authority'.

[89] See for criticism of this, Hmoud, above n 86, 448–9.

co-ordinating responsibilities, reporting to the Council, while an International Advisory and Monitoring Board[90] of the Development Fund for Iraq was established with the duty to approve the appointment of independent public accountants to audit the Development Fund and all export sales of petroleum, petroleum products and natural gas.[91] Further, the Secretary General was asked to continue or commence the exercise, in co-ordination with the Authority, of responsibilities for a six-month period in order to terminate the UN oil-for-food programme and after this period to transfer the administration of any remaining activity under the programme to the Authority.[92] The Secretary General was also requested to transfer as soon as possible to the Development Fund for Iraq $1 billion from funds held pursuant to resolutions 778 (1992) and 986 (1995).[93]

Thus, both in the range of competences exercisable by the occupying powers, particularly in the human rights, welfare and economic fields,[94] and by the establishment of various monitoring mechanisms, resolution 1483 marks a highly significant step in the evolution of the law of occupation, and a consequential shift in the traditional balance between military necessity and humanitarian considerations. In addition, the aims of the occupation and the methodology of seeking to achieve them are markedly different. In traditional occupations, the aim of the occupation was simply to hold on to the territory with minimal cost to the occupier and the occupied pending a peace settlement which almost invariably involved the return of the territory to the dispossessed sovereign. In Iraq, the aim of the occupation was to ensure that the previous regime could not return to power and that the whole political, social, economic and legal system be totally transformed. Therefore, even the approach of the traditional occupation as supplemented by human rights law has been overtaken in this major exercise in societal reordering as internationally mandated.

As Crawford has written, the broad responsibilities laid down in resolution 1483 'would be difficult to satisfy if the general obligations of

[90] The membership of the Board was to include duly qualified representatives of the Secretary General, of the Managing Director of the International Monetary Fund, of the Director General of the Arab Fund for Social and Economic Development and of the President of the World Bank.

[91] Paras 12, 20.

[92] Para 16.

[93] Para 17.

[94] Note, eg, the new laws adopted by the Authority with regard to foreign investments (CPA Order No 39, 19 September 2003), securities markets (CPA Order No 74, 18 April 2004), copyright law (CPA Order No 83, 1 May 2004) and anti-money-laundering legislation (CPA Order No 93, 3 June 2004), as well as those establishing a property claims commission (CPA Regulation No 12, 23 June 2004) and banning former members of the Ba'ath Party from public-sector employment (CPA Order No 1, 16 May 2003).

an occupying power were observed'.[95] The key question, therefore, is on what basis did this new model occupation framework arise? Since there was in the Iraq case clearly no consent by the population to such arrangements, the only answer can be with regard to the Chapter VII powers of the Security Council.

III. CONTROL OF TERRITORY BY AN INTERNATIONAL AUTHORITY

A. As a Mechanism to Pass Sovereignty or Territorial Control to the Recognised Sovereign

In a number of situations and for various reasons spreading over a century, the international community has assumed control of a territory.[96] Such international administration has sometimes been in order to act as a procedural device whereby sovereignty would pass with as little disruption as possible from the recognised sovereign or effective controller of the territory to a recipient recognised by the international community as the correct and appropriate beneficiary. These are cases where there is little or no serious dispute as to the ultimate destination of title to the territory in question, but considerable difficulties in practice with regards to the process of transmission itself.[97]

B. Within States

A number of examples may be noted here of the use of international administration as a methodology to pass control from one entity to the

[95] Crawford, above n 29, 563. See also V Lowe, 'The Iraq Crisis: What Now?' (2003) 52 *International and Comparative Law Quarterly* 859

[96] See, eg, S Chesterman, *You, The People: The United Nations, Territorial Administration and State-building* (Oxford University Press, 2004); R Caplan, *A New Trusteeship? The International Administration of War-torn Territories* (Adephi Paper No 341, Oxford University Press, 2002); M Ydit, *Internationalised Territories* (Leyden, Sythoff, 1961); SR Ratner, 'Foreign Occupation', above n 23; R Wilde, 'From Danzig to East Timor and Beyond', above n 22; *ibid*, 'The Complex Role of the Legal Adviser When International Organisations Administer Territory' (2001) 95 *Proceedings of the American Society of International Law* 251; *ibid*, 'Representing International Territorial Administration: A Critique of Some Approaches' (2004) 15 *European Journal of International Law* 71; *ibid*, 'The United Nations as Government: The Tensions of an Ambivalent Role' (2003) 97 *Proceedings of the American Society of International Law* 212; MJ Matheson, 'United Nations Governance of Postconflict Societies' (2001) 95 *American Journal of International Law* 76.

[97] This chapter does not deal with the supervisory responsibility of the League of Nations or the United Nations with regard to mandate and trust territories respectively, nor the failed arrangements with regard to Jerusalem or Trieste, see generally Ydit, above n 96, chs 3 and 4, 231–72 and 273–315.

recognised sovereign within a state where there was no dispute as to the territorial sovereignty of the state in question.

The area of Eastern Slavonia within Croatia was controlled by insurgent Serb forces from the outbreak of the armed conflict over the future of Yugoslavia. An agreement was signed on 12 November 1995 between Croatia and the Serb forces providing for a period of UN administration pending reincorporation into Croatia, and the United Nations Transitional Administration in Eastern Slavonia (UNTAES) came into existence.[98] Security Council resolution 1037 (1996) laid down the mandate of UNTAES as the peaceful reintegration of the area[99] into the Republic of Croatia including demilitarisation, the return of refugees and displaced persons, the reconstruction of the region, and the organisation of free and fair elections. The resolution also stressed the importance of full respect for human rights and fundamental freedoms in the territory.[100] The employment, educational and health sectors were integrated, social and security was essentially achieved, and the political rights of the local Serbs guaranteed by a Croatian letter of intent by autumn 1997; the mandate ended on 15 January 1998.[101]

Mostar was a city divided into Croat and Bosniak (Muslim) sectors, within Bosnia and Herzegovina. In the face of the deep inability to reach any kind of agreement, the two parties signed a Memorandum of Understanding on 6 April 1994 in Geneva empowering the European Union to administer Mostar until a more permanent solution could be reached.[102] A Memorandum of Understanding signed on 5 July 1994 by the states of the European Union, the Western European Union who supplied the police force, the Republic of Bosnia and Herzegovina, the Federation of Bosnia and Herzegovina and local Mostar administrators laid down the legal framework for the EU administration of Mostar. The EU administration was accorded legislative and executive powers,[103] organised, inter alia, the spending of reconstruction funds, and secured the parties' agreement to an Interim Statute regulating the city's governance on 7

[98] Croatia–local Serbian Community: Basic Agreement on the Region of Eastern Slavonia, Baranja and Western Sirmium, (1996) 35 *International Legal Materials* 184. See also M Bothe, 'The Peace Process in Eastern Slavonia' (December 1996–January 1996) *International Peacekeeping* 6, and JP Klein, 'The United Nations and Administration of Territory: Lessons from the Front Line, The United Nations Transitional Administration in Eastern Slavonia (UNTAES)' (2003) 97 *Proceedings of the American Society of International Law* 205.

[99] Eastern Slavonia, Baranja and Western Sirmium.

[100] See also UNSC Res1043 (31 January 1996), UNSC Res 1079 (15 November 1996), UNSC Res 1120 (14 July 1997) and UNSC Res 1145 (19 December 1997).

[101] See Klein, above n 98, 207–9.

[102] See, eg, International Crisis Group, *Reunifying Mostar: Opportunities for Progress*, April 2000, and *ibid, Building Bridges in Mostar*, November 2003.

[103] Note that Art 7(1) of the Memorandum stipulated that the EU administration had to exercise its authority in conformity with the overall principle of subsidiarity, taking due account of the views and wishes of the local parties and population.

February 1996, which has had in practice little success.[104] At the date agreed in the July 1994 Memorandum of Understanding of 22 July 1996, the responsibilities of the EU administration were transferred to a Special Envoy of the European Union in the city of Mostar.[105] From January 1997, these responsibilities passed to the Office of the High Representative in Bosnia and Herzegovina and a regional office was opened in the city. A Statute of the City of Mostar was adopted on 28 January 2004.

The area of Brčko within Bosnia and Herzegovina was disputed between the Serbs and the Bosniaks and the issue remained unresolved at the Dayton peace conference in 1995.[106] Article V of Annex 2 of the Dayton Peace Agreement provided for binding arbitration 'of the disputed portion of the Inter-Entity Boundary Line in the Brčko area'. The tribunal's first award was published on 14 February 1997.[107] Noting that the Republika Srpska had failed to implement its obligations under the Dayton accords to permit the return of refugees and allow free movement in that part of Brčko under its control, the tribunal authorised the establishment for one year of 'interim international supervision of Dayton implementation in the Brčko area'. The Supervisor was given a specific mandate including the phased and orderly return of refugees and displaced persons, enhancement of democratic government and a multi-ethnic administration of the town of Brčko, ensuring freedom of movement, the establishment of normal democratic policing function and the promotion of economic revitalisation. The Supervisor (and Deputy High Representative) was empowered to issue binding orders and regulations in furtherance of his mandate.

This mandate was reaffirmed and strengthened in the Tribunal's supplemental award of 15 March 1998, in which it was ruled, inter alia, that the Supervisor should have the same powers as those conferred on the High Representative of Bosnia and Herzegovina, including the authority to sack any public official who obstructed the implementation of the Dayton agreement, and to strengthen democratic institutions and revive the economy in the Brčko area.[108] A final award was issued on 5 March 1999 (and Annex published on 18 August 1999). This established a special district for the pre-war Brčko *Opstina,* under the exclusive sovereignty of Bosnia and Herzegovina, with the territory belonging to the two

[104] The principles of which had already been agreed at the Dayton conference and included as an Annex to the Dayton Agreement 1995. See International Crisis Group, *Building Bridges,* above n 102, 1 and 3.

[105] See EU Joint Action of 15 July 1996, 96/442/CFSP.

[106] See, eg, International Crisis Group, *Brčko Arbitration,* August 1996; *ibid, Brčko: A Comprehensive Solution,* February 1999 and *ibid, Bosnia's Brčko: Getting On and Getting Out,* June 2003, 4. See also PC Farrand, 'Lessons from Brčko: Necessary Components for Future Internationally Supervised Territories' (2001) 15 *Emory International Law Review* 529.

[107] See (1997) 36 *International Legal Materials* 396.

[108] Award, 272.

entities (Republika Srpska and the Federation of Bosnia and Herzegovina). The demilitarised district was to be self-governing with a single, unitary, multi-ethnic and democratic government and a unified and multi-ethnic police force and independent judiciary, with extensive powers reserved to the Supervisor, including the right to select voting mechanisms, dissolve existing municipal assemblies, disband and reconstitute municipal governments, appoint initially members of the judiciary and prosecutorial services, appoint the first chief of police, have the final word on the budget, and to transfer publicly owned property to the administration of the district and to privatise it in accordance with Bosnian law.[109] This was described in an International Crisis Group report as creating 'a fully fledged if small scale international trusteeship'.[110] The High Representative of Bosnia issued a Decision on the Establishment of the Brčko District of Bosnia and Herzegovina on 8 March 2000 formally creating the District as a special unit of local self-government under Bosnian sovereignty.[111] A Statute was declared to be in force and an interim government appointed pending elections by orders of the Supervisor on that same date.[112]

C. As Between a Third Party Controlling Administration and a Recognised Sovereign

A second category is where an international authority is introduced as a method of transmitting power between a third-party-controlled administration, often of controversial legitimacy, and an entity recognised internationally as the beneficiary of sovereign title, in circumstances where direct action is not politically feasible. Several examples may be given here.

(1) Leticia

In 1932, Peruvian irregular forces captured the Colombian town and district of Leticia in violation of the treaty between the states of 24 March 1922 that ceded the territory to Colombia.[113] Following the involvement of the League of Nations, the parties concluded an agreement on 25 May 1933 under which the territory was entrusted to a special League of Nations Commission, acting in the name and at the expense of Colombia,

[109] Annex of the Final Award. See also *Bosnia's Brčko*, above n 106, 9–11.
[110] *Bosnia's Brčko*, above n 106, 9. See also (2000) 39 *International Legal Materials* 879.
[111] See www.ohr.int. See also the Report from the Supervisor of Brčko to the Peace Implementation Council of 18 March 2004, available at www.ohr.int.
[112] *Bosnia's Brčko*, above n 106, 13.
[113] See, eg, Ydit, above n 96, 59ff; L Woolsey, 'The Leticia Dispute between Colombia and Peru' (1935) 29 *American Journal of International Law* 94; and Wilde, above n 22, 587.

for a period of one year pending a resolution of the dispute. In the event the parties reached an agreement on 24 May 1934, and the territory was handed over by the Commission to the Colombian authorities. The short period of League administration essentially enabled Colombia to regain control, while maintaining a critical symbolic presence in the territory during this period,[114] and allowed Peru a measure of face-saving as well as providing a point of pressure to encourage Colombia to come to a comprehensive border settlement.

(2) Libya

The Peace Treaty with Italy in 1947 authorised the Allied Powers to determine the future status of the former Italian colony of Libya. The question was passed on to the UN General Assembly, which appointed a UN Commissioner for Libya with the aim of preparing the territory for independence.[115] The territory was administered by the two Administering Powers (UK and France) in co-operation with the UN Commissioner, and the territory became independent on 24 December 1951.[116]

(3) West Irian

West Irian (West New Guinea) was a Dutch colony which remained under Dutch control after the rest of the Dutch East Indies came to independence as Indonesia, and its future was disputed between the two states.[117] Ultimately, it was agreed that the Netherlands would transfer administration of the territory to a UN Temporary Executive Authority (UNTEA) under the jurisdiction of the Secretary General, which would pass control to Indonesia.[118] UNTEA was to have full authority to administer the territory in accordance with the agreement, including the power to legislate and to replace Dutch officials with non-Indonesian ones. The costs of the administration were shared between the two states. Control over the territory was established on 1 October 1962 and transferred to Indonesia after 1 May 1963.

[114] Eg, it provided troops for the Commission and its flag flew alongside that of the League, Ydit, above n 96, 61.

[115] See UNGA Res 289 (21 November 1949). See also Ydit, above n 96, 68–9; Crawford, above n 29, 554–5; and A Pelt, *Libyan Independence and the United Nations: A Case of Planned Decolonisation* (New Haven, Yale University Press, 1970).

[116] Ydit, above n 96, 69.

[117] See, eg, Crawford, above n 29, 555 and DW Bowett, *United Nations Forces* (London, Stevens, 1964) 255–61.

[118] Indonesia–Netherlands Agreement of 15 August 1962. See also UNGA Res 1752 (XVII) (21 September 1962).

(4) Namibia

In October 1966, the General Assembly resolved that since South Africa had failed to fulfil its obligations, its mandate over South West Africa (Namibia) was therefore terminated and the territory was to come under the direct authority of the United Nations.[119] The UN Council for Namibia was established as the legal administering authority over the territory pending independence.[120] Decree No 1 of the Council declared null and void permits or licenses issued by South Africa with regard to the exploitation of natural resources in the territory and forbade such activities.[121] The Council also issued travel documents, but was refused entry into the territory. It remained essentially ineffective. SWAPO (the South West Africa People's Organisation) was recognised in 1973 as the representative of the Namibian people with regard to the 'international territory of Namibia'.[122] In 1978, South Africa accepted the proposals negotiated by the five Western contact powers for Namibian independence involving elections supervised by a UN Transitional Assistance Group and peacekeeping forces.[123] After some difficulties,[124] Namibia obtained its independence and was admitted to the United Nations on 23 April 1990.[125]

(5) East Timor

One of the major examples of UN territorial administration in this context has taken place with regard to East Timor. Portugal evacuated its colony in 1975 amidst domestic upheavals, and Indonesia took control and pur-

[119] See UNGA Res General Assembly resolution 2145 (XXI) (27 October 1966). See also J Dugard, *The South West Africa/Namibia Dispute* (Berkeley, University of California Press, 1973) and S Slonim, *South West Africa and the United Nations* (Baltimore, Johns Hopkins University Press, 1973). See also LL Herman, 'The Legal Status of Namibia and of the United Nations Council for Namibia' (1975) 13 *Canadian Yearbook of International Law* 306.

[120] See UNGA Res 2248 (XXII) (19 May 1967), S-9/2, 1978, 33/182 (C).

[121] 27 September 1974. See also UNGA Res 35/227/I (6 March 1981) and 43/29 (22 November 1988). This decree was described by the UN Commissioner for Namibia as a 'new and strange concept', A/AC.131/81, 18 July 1980.

[122] UNGA Res 3111 (XVIII) (12 December 1973). See also UNSC Res (24 January 1969), UNSC Res 269 (12 August 1969), UNSC Res 276 (30 January 1970) and the *Namibia case* (Advisory opinion) [1971] ICJ Rep 16, approved in UNSC Res 301 (20 October 1971).

[123] (1978) 17 *International Legal Materials* 762–9. See UNSC Res (29 September 1978). See also VP Fortna, 'United Nations Transition Assistance Group in Namibia', in WJ Durch (ed), *The Evolution of UN Peacekeeping* (New York, St Martin's Press, 1994) 353.

[124] See, eg, S/14459, S/14460/Rev 1, S/14461 and S/14462.

[125] Note also the role of the UN with regard to Western Sahara. The UN Mission for a Referendum in Western Sahara (MINURSO) was established in Security Council resolution 690 (1991) to implement a peace plan proposed by the Secretary General (S/21360 and S/22464). MINURSO has been mandated to monitor the ceasefire, oversee the exchange of prisoners and organise a referendum. To date no such referendum has been held. MINORSO's mandate was extended in Security Council resolution 1675 (2006).

ported to annex it shortly thereafter.[126] The Security Council reaffirmed the right of the territory to self-determination and called upon Indonesia to withdraw its forces.[127] Eventually in 1999 Portugal and Indonesia agreed to a popular consultation under UN auspices.[128] This was supported by the Security Council[129] and a UN Mission in East Timor (UNAMET) was established.[130] The referendum rejected Indonesia's proposal of autonomy status, and violence by pro-Indonesian militias ensued.[131] As a result, the Security Council adopted resolution 1264 (1999) condemning the violations of human rights and humanitarian law, and acting under Chapter VII of the Charter, a multinational force (INTERFET) was authorised. This force, under Australian command, began to deploy on 20 September 1999. In resolution 1272 (1999), the Security Council established the UN Transitional Administration in East Timor (UNTAET) with a wide-ranging mandate to administer the territory.[132] By Regulation No 1 adopted on 27 November 1999, all legislative and executive authority with respect to East Timor, including the administration of the judiciary, was vested in UNTAET and exercised by the Transitional Administrator. This Administrator was given the competence further to appoint any person to perform functions in the civil administration in the territory, including the judiciary, or remove such person and to issue regulations and directives.

UNTAET was further to administer all immovable and movable property of the Republic of Indonesia or its organs and agencies in the territory of East Timor. All persons undertaking public duties or holding public office were to observe internationally recognised human rights standards.[133] The applicable law was stated to be the pre-25 October

[126] See, eg, Crawford, above n 29, 560ff; C Stahn, 'The United Nations Transitional Administrations in Kosovo and East Timor: A First Analysis' (2001) 5 *Max Planck Yearbook of United Nations Law* 105; H Strohmeyer, 'Collapse and Reconstruction of a Judicial System: The United Nations Missions in Kosovo and East Timor' (2001) 95 *American Journal of International Law* 46; M Ruffert, 'The Administration of Kosovo and East Timor by the International Community' (2001) 50 *International and Comparative Law Quarterly* 613; RS Clark, 'East Timor, Indonesia and the International Community' 14 (2000) *Temple International and Comparative Law Journal* 75; J Dunn (ed), *International Law and the Question of East Timor* (Leiden, CIIR, 1995); R Goy, 'L'indépendence du Timor Oriental' (1999) 45 *Annuaire Français de Droit International* 203; and JM Sorel, 'Timor Oriental: Un résumé de l'histoire de droit international' (2000) 104 *Revue Générale de Droit International Public* 37.

[127] See UNSC Res 384 (22 December 197) and 389 (22 April 1976). See also the *East Timor* case [1995] ICJ Rep 90, 96–7.

[128] See S/1999/513.

[129] UNSC Res 1236 (7 May 1999).

[130] UNSC Res 1246 (11 June 1999). See also S/1999/595.

[131] Under the direction, it seems, of the Indonesian military, see UNAMET's analysis, S/1999/976, Annex, para 1.

[132] See also S/1999/24. Note the heavy reliance of UNTAET on the experience of the UN in Kosovo, see Chesterman, above n 96, 63.

[133] In particular, the Universal Declaration on Human Rights (adopted 10 December 1948); the International Covenants on Human Rights (adopted 16 December 1966); the Convention on the Elimination of All Forms of Racial Discrimination (adopted 21 December 1965); the

1999[134] local law insofar as it did not conflict with human rights standards, the fulfilment of the mandate of UNTAET under resolution 1272 or any regulation or directive issued by the Transitional Administrator and until replaced by UNTAET Regulations or subsequent legislation of democratically elected institutions of East Timor.[135] UNTAET also set up a National Consultative Council as a mechanism for transition to self-government[136] and signed an agreement with Australia on behalf of the territory to continue the application of the Australian–Indonesian Treaty on the Timor Gap.[137] UNTAET adopted a number of Regulations covering a number of important issues, including the introduction of the dollar as the currency in the territory[138] and the creation of central fiscal authorities.[139]

East Timor became an independent state in 2002 and was admitted as a member of the United Nations on 27 September that year.[140]

B. As a Mechanism to Realise or Sustain a Recognised Settlement

Elements of international administration in one form or another may also be introduced as an important constituent of reaching and maintaining a settlement of a dispute where there are significant and often irreconcilable internal tensions.

The Free City of Danzig was established by the Treaty of Versailles as a compromise in order to ensure Poland's access to the sea, although the population was German. Germany renounced its rights over the territory in favour of the Principal Allied and Associated Powers,[141] who created the Free City as a unit under the protection of the League of Nations and under therefore neither German nor Polish sovereignty.[142] The Free City

Convention on the Elimination of All Forms of Discrimination Against Women (adopted 18 December 1979); the Convention Against Torture (adopted 10 December 1984) and the International Convention on the Rights of the Child (adopted 20 November 1989) Section 2, Regulation No 1.

135 The date of adoption of resolution 1272.

136 UNTAET Regulation 1999/1, s 3. Note the dispute as to whether the local law was Indonesian law or Portuguese law, see S de Bertodano, 'East Timor—Justice Denied' (2004) 2 *Journal of International Criminal Justice* 910; H Strohlmeyer, 'Policing the Peace: Post-Conflict Judicial Reconstruction in East Timor' (2001) 24 *University of South Wales Law Journal* 171, cf *Prosecutor v Armando Dos Santos*, Case No 16/2001 of the East Timor Court of Appeal, 15 July 2003, available at http://jsmp.minihub.org//judgmentspdf/courtofappeal/Ct_ofApp-dos_Santos_English22703.pdf.

137 Regulation No 2, 1999. See also S/2000/53.

138 See Crawford, above n 29, 562.

139 UNTAET Regulation No 2000/7.

139 UNTAET Regulation No 2000/1.

140 UNSC Res (23 May 2002) and UNGA Res (20 September 2002).

141 Art 100. See, eg, Crawford, above n 29, 236–41; Chesterman, above n 96, 20–21 and H Hannum, *Autonomy, Sovereignty and Self-Determination* (Philadelphia, University of Pennsylvania Press, 1990) 375–9.

142 Art 102.

possessed extensive domestic powers, but its Constitution was guaranteed by the League, which could intervene to implement it.[143] The League also appointed a High Commissioner.[144] The foreign relations of the Free City were undertaken by Poland, by virtue of an international agreement between Danzig and Poland of 9 November 1920.[145] The arrangement collapsed with the outbreak of the Second World War.[146]

In another relevant case, following Vietnamese intervention and an ensuing and vicious civil war, agreements on a comprehensive settlement of the Cambodia conflict were signed on 2 October 1991.[147] The Comprehensive Settlement Agreement created a Supreme National Council as the 'unique legitimate body and source of authority in which, throughout the transitional period, the sovereignty, independence and unity of Cambodia are enshrined'.[148] The Supreme National Council in turn transferred to the United Nations 'all powers necessary to ensure implementation of this Agreement'.[149] The United Nations was invited in particular to set up the UN Transitional Authority in Cambodia (UNTAC) with civilian and military components under the direct responsibility of the UN Secretary General and with the mandate specified in the Agreement.[150] The mandate in question called for the establishment of a neutral political environment conducive to free and fair general elections, with the requirement for such UN control over a wide range of governmental organs, including those dealing with foreign affairs, defence, finance and information, as was necessary to ensure their strict neutrality.[151] There were also provisions concerning the relationship between UNTAC and the Supreme National Council, so that, for example, the former had to follow the advice of the latter if it was acting unanimously (or if Prince

[143] Art 103. See *Treatment of Polish Nationals in the Danzig Territory*, PCIJ Reports, Series A/B, No 44, 21 (1932) and *Consistency of Certain Danzig Legislative Decrees with the Constitution of the Free City*, PCIJ Reports, Series A/B, No 65, 13 (1935).

[144] However, this did not prevent the Free City from introducing anti-Semitic legislation, following the Nuremberg laws of 1936 in Germany, see Crawford, above n 29, 241, n 211.

[145] See Art 104 of the Versailles Treaty and *Jurisdiction of the Courts of Danzig*, PCIJ Reports, Series B, No 15, 17 (1928). The nature of the arrangement was discussed by the Permanent Court in *Free City of Danzig and the ILO*, PCIJ Reports, Series B, No 18, 13 (1930).

[146] Cf. the position with regard to the Memel Territory in the inter-War period. This was transferred by the Principal Allied and Associated Powers from Germany to Lithuania after the end of the First World War in order to provide that state with a port. However, in view of the fact that the population involved was German, a special regime was established, under Lithuanian sovereignty, with legislative, judicial, administrative and financial autonomy with the limits prescribed by the Statute. See Art 99 of the Versailles Treaty and the Convention Concerning the Territory of Memel 1924 with annexed Statute. See also Crawford, above n 29, 237–8; Lapidoth, above n 14, 77–85 and Hannum, above n 141, 379 –84.

[147] See, eg, SR Ratner, 'The Cambodia Settlement Agreements' (1993) 87 *American Journal of International Law* 1; MW Doyle, *UN Peacekeeping in Cambodia: UNTAC's Civil Mandate* (Boulder, Lynne Rienner, 1995); and Chesterman, above n 96, 74–5.

[148] Art 3. See also to this effect, UNSC Res 668 (20 September 1990).

[149] Art 6.

[150] Art 2.

[151] Art 6.

Sihanouk as the President of the Council provided the advice on its behalf) and if such advice was consistent with the objectives of the Agreement as determined by the head of UNTAC, the Secretary General's Special Representative.[152]

UNTAC was formally established by the Security Council in resolution 745 (1992) for a period not exceeding eighteen months with elections to be held in May 1993.[153] The mandate laid down for UNTAC, unlike that relating to UNTEA in West Irian three decades earlier,[154] was detailed and specific. The provisions concerning civil administration were thorough. The Special Representative was given power, for example, to issue binding directives to a wide range of government agencies and to introduce UN officials with unrestricted access to information and administrative operations, and to remove or reassign existing officials. UNTAC took control of the civil police and other law-enforcement systems and was competent to act against activities deemed inconsistent with a comprehensive political settlement. The mission consisted essentially of seven distinct components: human rights, electoral, military, civil administration, civilian police, repatriation and rehabilitation. Although with only a relatively short duration, UNTAC was the first comprehensive effort by the UN to assume significant elements of control and administration concerning a state.

Bosnia and Herzegovina provides a further example of this usage of international control powers. Recognised as an independent state, the degree of international control over basic governmental functions is nonetheless high. Unlike other situations, however, this international control has been diffuse rather than focused and centralised, involving different agencies. The military component consisted of the NATO-led implementation force, IFOR,[155] and from 20 December 1996 a stabilisation force, SFOR,[156] replaced on 2 December 2004 by the European Union's EUFOR.[157] The civilian components consisted of UN Mission (UNMIBH), based on a UN International Police Task Force and a UN civilian office,

[152] See Annex I of the Agreement, Sec A, para 2 (a), (d) and (e).

[153] Such elections were duly held and certified by the UN Special Representative as free and fair, see Chesterman, above n 96, 74. See also UNSC Res (4 November 1993) noting the conclusion of UNTAC's mission. However, a coup followed in 1997 and flawed elections the following year: *ibid*, 75 and International Crisis Group, *Back from the Brink: Cambodian Democracy Gets a Second Chance* (January 1999).

[154] Which simply gave the head of UNTEA 'full authority under the direction of the Secretary General to administer the territory', Art V of the Agreement on West New Guinea. See, eg, Ratner, above n 147, 15.

[155] UNSC Res 1031 (15 December 1995). IFOR took over from the UN Protection Force (UNPROFOR), established by UNSC Res 743 (21 February 1992) and see also UNSC Res 749 (7 April 1992), 757 (30 May 1992), 758 (8 June 1992), 770 (13 August 1992) and 776 (14 September 1992).

[156] UNSC Res 1088 (12 December 1996).

[157] UNSC Res 1575 (22 November 2004). See also UNSC Res 1551 (9 July 2004) and 1639 (21 November 2005).

and the High Representative. The High Representative, whose mandate terminated on 31 December 2002, to be replaced by an EU Police Mission,[158] was responsible for the 'interpretation of this Agreement on the civilian implementation of the peace settlement',[159] and in particular, played a steadily enlarging role in the areas of the police, judicial system, human rights, co-ordination of humanitarian relief and refugees, landmine clearance, and elections.[160]

The establishment of the post of High Representative arose out of the end of the Bosnian war with the signing of the Dayton Peace Agreement in 1995. Bosnia and Herzegovina was established as a state consisting of two units (or Entities) each with significant autonomy (Republika Srpska and the Federation of Bosnia and Herzegovina). The Dayton Agreement provided for the designation of a High Representative[161] as 'the final authority in theatre'. The High Representative was to monitor the implementation of the peace settlement, promote the full compliance of the parties with the civilian aspects of the peace settlement, co-ordinate the activities of the civilian organisations and agencies in Bosnia and Herzegovina to ensure the effective implementation of the settlement, and facilitate the resolution of difficulties in implementation.[162] The High Representative is nominated by the Steering Board of the Peace Implementation Council,[163] a group of 55 countries and international organisations that sponsor and direct the peace implementation process, and this nomination is then endorsed by the Security Council.

The relatively modest powers of the High Representative under Annex 10 were subsequently enlarged in practice by the Peace Implementation Council in the decisions it took at the Bonn Summit of December 1997. In particular, paragraph XI of the Bonn Conclusions recognised the competence of the High Representative to adopt binding decisions with regard to interim measures when the parties are unable to reach agreement, remaining in force until the Presidency or Council of Ministers has adopted a decision consistent with the Peace Agreement on the issue concerned and

> other measures to ensure implementation of the Peace Agreement throughout Bosnia and Herzegovina and its Entities, as well as the smooth running of the common institutions.

158 UNSC Res 1423 (12 July 2002). See also the final report of the Secretary General on the mission, S/2002/1314.

159 Art V, Annex 10.

160 See, eg, Chesterman, above n 96, 77.

161 See Annex 10 of the Dayton Peace Agreement. See also R Caplan, 'International Authority and State Building: The Case of Bosnia and Herzegovina' (2004) 10 *Global Governance* 53; International Crisis Group, *Bosnia: Reshaping the International Machinery*, November 2001.

162 Art II, Annex 10. Note, the High Representative has no authority over IFOR and is unable to interfere in the conduct of military operations, Art II (9).

163 See www.ohr.int/ohr-info/gen-info/#pic.

Such measures could include, for example, actions against persons found by the High Representative to be in violation of legal commitments made under the terms of the implementation of the Peace Agreement.[164]

In this context, the High Representative has taken a wide-ranging number of decisions, from imposing the Law on Citizenship of Bosnia and Herzegovina in December 1997[165] and imposing the Law on the Flag of Bosnia and Herzegovina in February 1998[166] to enacting the Law on Changes and Amendments to the Election Law in January 2006 to mark the ongoing process of transferring High Representative powers to the domestic authorities in the light of the improving situation.[167] In addition, a number of persons were removed from public office. From March 1998 to mid-2003, over 100 elected officials were so removed, including a former prime minister of the Federation of Bosnia and Herzegovina, a president of Republika Srpska and a member of the Bosnian presidency.[168] More recently, the ban on removals from office has been lifted in a number of cases with regard to specific individuals.[169] Decisions were also adopted limiting removals from public office. For example, on 28 November 2005, a decision was issued lifting the ban except with regard to certain positions of a defence, security or intelligence nature,[170] and on 4 April 2006 a decision was adopted which permitted those banned from public office by a decision of the High Representative to apply for and hold a position in a public enterprise or institution not covered by civil service laws but supported by public funding.[171] In view of the improving situation, the Steering Board of the Peace Implementation Council announced on 24 June 2005 its intention to continue the process of transferring responsibilities to the Bosnian authorities and to replace the High Representative with an EU Special Representative, something that would require a Security Council resolution.[172]

[164] www.ohr.int/pic/default.asp?content_id=5182. This competence has been regularly affirmed by the Security Council, See, eg, UNSC Res 1247 (18 June 1999), 1395 (27 February 2000), 1357 (21 June 2001), 1396 (5 March 2002) and 1491 (11 July 2003).

[165] www.ohr,int/statemattersdec/default.asp?content_id=343.

[166] www.ohr,int/statemattersdec/default.asp?content_id=344.

[167] www.ohr,int/statemattersdec/default.asp?content_id=36465.

[168] See Chesterman, above n 96, 130–1 and the lists by year contained on the High Representative's website: www.ohr.int/decisions/removalssdec.

[169] See, eg, that on Milandan Pesic, www.ohr.int/decisions/removalssdec/default.asp?content_id=36467, 30 January 2006; on Svetozar Radulovic, www.ohr.int/decisions/removalssdec/default.asp?content_id=36515, 30 January 2006 and on Zelijko Jangic, www.ohr.int/decisions/removalssdec/default.asp?content_id=36513, 30 January 2006.

[170] Decision of 28 November 2005, www.ohr.int/decisions/removalssdec/default.asp?content_id=36075.

[171] Decision of 4 April 2006, www.ohr.int/decisions/removalssdec/default.asp?content_id=36919. The decision does not apply to any elected, executive, advisory, security or managerial civil servant position, Art 4.

[172] www.ohr.int/pic/default.asp?content_id=3491. Note that the EU's General Affairs Council appointed the High Representative as the EU's Special Representative in March 2002, See, eg, Council Joint Action 2004/569/CFSP; Council Joint Action 2005/825/CFSP and Council Joint Action 2006/49/CFSP.

C. As a Mechanism to Promote a Settlement Where Sovereignty Is Disputed

(1) The Saar

International administration of territory as a way of a holding operation pending the reaching of a new settlement is not new. Under the Versailles Treaty of 1919, France was authorised to exploit the coalmines in the Saar territory of Germany for a period of 15 years.[173] Germany renounced 'in favour of the League of Nations, in the capacity of trustee, the government of the territory'.[174] The question of ultimate sovereignty over the territory remained unclear, but the better view is that it resided with Germany.[175] The League of Nations administered the territory for the 15-year period through a Governing Commission appointed by the League of Nations Council. After the end of this period, a plebiscite was held in which the population voted to return to German administration. It is interesting to note that both union with France and a continuation of international administration were possible outcomes of the process under the Versailles Treaty.[176]

(2) Kosovo

The Serbian province of Kosovo, with its 90 per cent ethnic Albanian population, had been the site of increasing domestic unrest since the ending of its autonomous status in 1989.[177] Security Council resolution 1160 (1998) called for an 'enhanced status for Kosovo' including 'a substantially greater degree of autonomy'. Talks held at Rambouillet failed[178]

[173] See, eg, Ydit, above n 96, 44–7; Chesterman, above n 96, 18–20; Crawford, above n 29, 233–4 and Wilde, 'From Danzig to East Timor', above n 22, 589.

[174] Versailles Treaty, Art 49.

[175] See Crawford, above n 29, 233 n 172, cf Ydit, above n 96, 44.

[176] Note that the League had the responsibility of settling disputes between the Free City of Danzig (where local powers were split between the city and Poland, while Poland was responsible for its foreign relations) and Poland over the interpretation of their respective powers and of guaranteeing the status of the city by the competence to approve or not of constitutional amendments, see Arts 102–4 of the Versailles Treaty and Crawford, above n 29, 236–41.

[177] See C Tomuschat (ed), *Kosovo and the International Community: A Legal Assessment* (The Hague, Kluwer Lane International, 2002); Crawford, above n 29, 557–60; Chesterman, above n 96, 79–83; Strohmeyer, above n 126; B Knoll, 'From Benchmarking to Final Status? Kosovo and the Problem of an International Administration's Open-Ended Mandate' (2005) 16 *European Journal of International Law* 637; *Kosovo: KFOR and Reconstruction* (1999) House of Commons Research Paper 99/66; A Yannis, 'The UN as Government in Kosovo' (2004) 10 *Global Governance* 67; International Crisis Group, *Kosovo: Towards Final Status*, January 2005; *ibid*, *Kosovo: The Challenge of Transition*, February 2006; A Zimmermann and C Stahn, 'Yugoslav Territory, United Nations Trusteeship or Sovereign State? Reflections on the Current and Future Legal Status of Kosovo' (2001) 70 *Nordic Journal of International Law* 423.

[178] See S/1999/648.

and internal repression led to increasing flows of refugees. NATO operations commenced on 24 March 1999[179] and concluded on 9 June that year with the signing of a military-technical agreement between the NATO-led international security force (termed KFOR) and the Federal Republic of Yugoslavia, as a consequence of which Yugoslav forces withdrew from Kosovo and KFOR was deployed.[180] The following day, Security Council resolution 1244 (1999)[181] was adopted under Chapter VII.

This resolution reaffirmed 'the commitment of all Member States to the sovereignty and territorial integrity of the Federal Republic of Yugoslavia', but deprived this of all but symbolic meaning by authorising Member States and relevant international organisations to establish both an 'international security presence' and an 'international civil presence' in Kosovo with extensive powers. The former was to be endowed with all necessary means to fulfil its responsibilities, which included establishing a secure environment for the return of refugees and displaced persons, the operation of the international civil presence, the establishment of a transitional administration, the delivery of humanitarian aid, and ensuring public safety and order until the international civil presence could take responsibility. The international civil presence was granted responsibilities, including promoting 'the establishment, pending a final settlement, of substantial autonomy and self-government'; performing basic civilian administrative functions; organising the development of provisional institutions for democratic and autonomous self-government, pending a political settlement; and protecting and promoting human rights.[182]

The authority vested in the UN Interim Administration Mission (UNMIK), as this international civil authority was termed, by resolution 1244 became exercisable by the Special Representative of the UN Secretary General, who was made responsible for the four main components as defined with the participation of other international organisa-

[179] Questions as to the legitimacy of the use of force in Kosovo are not addressed in this chapter. See, eg, C Gray, *International Law and the Use of Force* (Oxford University Press, 2000) 31; B Simma, 'NATO, the UN and the Use of Force: Legal Aspects' (1999) 10 *European Journal of International Law* 1; KA Annan, *The Question of Intervention: Statements by the Secretary-General* (New York, United Nations Department of Public Information, 1999); 'NATO's Kosovo Intervention', various writers, (1999) 93 *American Journal of International Law* 824–62; D Kritsiotis, 'The Kosovo Crisis and NATO's Application of Armed Force Against the Federal Republic of Yugoslavia' (2000) 49 *International and Comparative Law Quarterly* 330; P Hilpod, 'Humanitarian Intervention: Is There a Need for a Legal Reappraisal?' (2001) 12 *European Journal of International Law* 437; and 'Kosovo: House of Commons Foreign Affairs Committee 4th Report, June 2000' various memoranda (2000) 49 *International and Comparative Law Quarterly* 876–943.

[180] S/1999/672, annex.

[181] Prefigured in Art 1(2) of the Agreement. KFOR deployment occurred two days after the resolution was adopted.

[182] Paras 10 and 11.

tions, so that while the UN is concerned with civil administration, the OSCE (Organisation for Security and Co-operation in Europe) deals with institution-building matters, the UNHCR (UN High Commissioner for Refugees) with humanitarian matters and the European Union with reconstruction issues. [183]

Annex 1 of the resolution provided for an immediate and verifiable end to violence and repression in Kosovo; the withdrawal of the military, police and paramilitary forces of the Federal Republic of Yugoslavia; establishment of an interim administration to be decided by the Security Council; the safe and free return of all refugees; a political process providing for substantial self-government; the demilitarisation of the Kosovo Liberation Army (KLA); and a comprehensive approach to the economic development of the crisis region. It also called for, crucially, the

> deployment in Kosovo of effective international civil and security presences, endorsed and adopted by the United Nations, capable of guaranteeing the achievement of the common objectives.

Annex 2 reaffirmed these principles, noting in paragraph 3 that there needed to be agreement on the

> deployment in Kosovo under United Nations auspices of effective international civil and security presences, acting as may be decided under Chapter VII of the Charter, capable of guaranteeing the achievement of common objectives.

Paragraph 4 noted that

> The international security presence with substantial North Atlantic Treaty Organisation participation must be deployed under unified command and control and authorised to establish a safe environment for all people in Kosovo and to facilitate the safe return to their homes of all displaced persons and refugees.

The very extensive nature of the competence of UNMIK was early signalled. Section 1.1 of the first Regulation issued by UNMIK in 1999 stated that:

> All legislative and executive authority with respect to Kosovo, including the administration of the judiciary is vested in UNMIK and is exercised by the Special Representative of the Secretary General[184]

[183] See S/1999/779, Report of the UN Secretary General, 12 July 1999. These components became known as the Four Pillars, with Pillar I being police and justice under the direct leadership of the UN; Pillar II being civil administration under the direct leadership of the UN; Pillar III being democratisation and institution building led by the OSCE and Pillar IV being reconstruction and economic development led by the EU.

[184] UNMIK/REG/1991/1, S/1999/987, P 14.

while section 1.2 provided that the Special Representative could appoint any person to perform functions in the civil administration in Kosovo, including the judiciary, or remove such person in accordance with the applicable law.[185] Section 3 of this Regulation provided that the laws applicable in Kosovo prior to 24 March 1999 would continue to apply insofar as they did not conflict with internationally recognised human rights standards, the fulfilment of the mandate given to UNMIK under resolution 1244 or any Regulation issued by UNMIK.[186] Section 4 provided for the issuance of legislation in the form of regulations, while section 6 provided that UNMIK was to administer all property of the Federal Republic of Yugoslavia or Republic of Serbia in Kosovo. Regulation 1999/3 established a customs system for Kosovo,[187] while Regulation 1999/4 introduced the deutschmark as a permitted currency in the territory. It is also worth noting Regulation 2005/16, which regulates the movement into and out of Kosovo.

On 15 May 2001, the Special Representative signed the Constitutional Framework for Provisional Self-Government under which responsibilities were transferred to Provisional Institutions of Self-Government.[188] Article 1.1 of Chapter I of the Constitutional Framework defined Kosovo as 'an entity under interim international administration', while the responsibilities transferred to the Provisional Institutions[189] were to be within the limits of resolution 1244.[190] The powers reserved exclusively to the Special Representative included full authority to ensure that the rights and interests of the communities were fully protected; dissolving the assembly and calling for new elections; final authority with regard to the budget and monetary policy; exercising final authority regarding the

185 As amended in UNMIK/REG/2000/54.

186 This was repealed in UNMIK/REG/1999/25. The law in force in Kosovo was stated in UNMIK/REG/1999/24 to be (a) Regulations promulgated by the Special Representative and subsidiary instruments issued thereunder and (b) the law in force in Kosovo on 22 March 1989. This was reaffirmed in UNMIK/REG/2000/59, which noted that if a court or body or person required to implement a provision of the law determines that a subject matter or a situation is not covered by these law, then the law in force in Kosovo after 22 March 1989 shall be applied exceptionally, provided that it is non-discriminatory and complies with international human rights conventions as listed in s 1.3. S 1.3 provided that all persons exercising public functions shall observe internationally recognised human rights standards as reflected in particular in the Universal Declaration, the International Covenants on Human Rights, the European Convention on Human Rights, the Racial Discrimination Convention, the Women's Discrimination Convention, the Torture Convention and the Rights of the Child Convention. S 3 also substituted a sentence of a term of imprisonment for the death sentence applicable under the law in force as at 22 March 1989.

187 Amended by UNMIK/REG/2005/11.

188 UNMIK/REG/2001/9. Note that amendments with regard to the executive branch of the Provisional Institutions were adopted in UNMIK/REG/2001/19 and UNMIK/REG/2005/16.

189 Ch 5.

190 Preamble, para 6 and ch 2 (a).

appointment, removal from office and disciplining of judges and prosecutors;[191] exercising powers and responsibilities of an international nature in the legal field; exercising authority over law-enforcement institutions; exercising control and authority over the management of the administration and financing of civil security; concluding agreements with states and international organisations in all matters within the scope of resolution 1244; external relations; and customs matter.[192]

Further, Chapter 12 emphasised that the exercise of the responsibilities of the Provisional Institutions under the Constitutional Framework

> shall not affect or diminish the authority of the SRSG [Special Representative] to ensure full implementation of UNSCR 1244 (1999), including overseeing the Provisional Institutions of Self-Government, its officials and agencies, and taking appropriate measures whenever their actions are inconsistent with UNSCR 1244 (1999) of this Constitutional Framework

while Chapter 14.3 provides that the Special Representative on his own initiative may effect amendments to the Constitutional Framework.[193]

The international community is currently discussing the future of Kosovo and there is no doubt that the independence of the territory is one strong possibility. Although, the UN embarked upon a 'standards before status' approach,[194] the Security Council appointed former Finnish President Ahtisaari in November 2005 as a special envoy to start a political process to determine the final status of the territory.[195]

[191] As to which, see also UNMIK/REG/1999/7 and UNMIK/REG/2000/57.

[192] Ch 8.

[193] In addition, ch 6 underlines that the Kosovo police service functions under the authority of the Special Representative and under the supervision of UNMIK Police, while ch 13 notes that nothing in the Constitutional Framework is to affect the authority of KFOR.

[194] See, eg, Security Council Presidential Statement of 30 April 2004, SC/8082. See also B Knoll, 'From Benchmarking to Final Status? Kosovo and the Problem of an International Administration's Open-Ended Mandate' (2005) 16 *European Journal of International Law* 637; BS Brown, 'Human Rights, Sovereignty and the Final Status of Kosovo' (2005) 80 *Chicago Kent law Review* 235; and International Crisis Group Reports of January 2005 and February 2006, above n 177.

[195] SG/A/955, 15 November 2005. See also the Eide Report of 7 October 2005, S/2005/635. This process has started with moves for decentralisation focusing on local finance, the creation of new municipalities and cross-boundary co-operation, see UN press release of 3 May 2006, www.un.org/apps/news/story.asp?NewsID=18337. The Ahtisaari Plan was presented to the UN Security Council on 26 March 2007, S/ 2007/168, but has since become mired in disputes between Western states and Russia and Serbia as to its application, See, eg, *Kosovo: No Good Alternatives to the Ahtisaari Plan*, International Crisis Group Report, 14 May 2007 and *Breaking the Kosovo Stalemate: Europe's Responsibility*, International Crisis Group Report, 21 August 2007. Kosovo declared independence on 17 February 2008.

IV. THEMATIC CONCLUSIONS

A. Why Does the Administration of Territory by Non-Sovereign Situations Arise?

The administration of territory by (third party) non-sovereigns arises essentially because of a breakdown of either international or internal peace and security. The situation constitutes an exception to the norm of administration and control by the territorial sovereign and poses a problem to international law, focused as it is upon the rights and responsibilities of sovereign states. The fundamentals of the legal system cope, in theory, easily with traditional occupations, since these are predicated upon temporary and relatively minimal societal control by the forces of one state of the territory of another pending a peace settlement. Problems have arisen in practice where the occupation is prolonged, and tensions have therefore arisen between the traditional rules and the need to take account of the needs of the local population in an evolving society. Beyond that, the interposition of organised international administration, although not a new phenomenon, has recently assumed a higher profile and this has brought new problems to the fore.

Territory may be administered by an entity, whether state or international organisation or other arrangement, for a number of reasons. First, as a consequence of armed conflict whether legal or illegal. Second, as an attempt to facilitate the transmission of control and/or sovereignty from one international entity to another. Third, as an attempt to resolve difficulties of governance within a state, flowing usually from a civil war or outside intervention or a mix of the two. Such administrations may result, therefore, in the creation of a new or restored independent state, in the integration of the territory into an existing state whether the previous sovereign or a third party, or in a new internal constitutional arrangement. Methodologies and aims may differ, of course, depending on the circumstances. The traditional occupation regime, for example, is focused upon the preservation of order and minimalist control by the occupying power so as to prevent annexation and to protect the local population pending a formal peace treaty, while some international administrations are created with a proactive mission. Globalisation, both in the form of the immediate and dramatic impact of crisis situations upon the international community and in the form of the spread of international law standards, particularly those relating to human rights, has increased pressures for international action to resolve or mitigate or minimise such crises, and the device of international administration now forms part of the mechanisms readily to hand.

B. The Source of Authority

In the case of occupations of territory by (third-party) states, authority will flow from the factual situation itself, ie, from the establishment of actual control resulting from the use of force, whether legal or illegal, and the consequential application of international humanitarian law. It is by its very nature non-consensual and the views of the local population fall outside of this equation, except that in the light of the development of human rights law and the principle of self-determination, it is impossible to ignore the wishes of the local population in terms, at least, of the resolution of the particular dispute.

In the case of administration of territory by an international organisation, authority will flow from the constitutional norms of the organisation in question and from the nature and scope of any relevant international agreements. Often the international organisation in question will be the UN Security Council, which has the power to adopt decisions under Chapter VII of the Charter, which is binding upon all members of the UN. Such resolutions have laid down the basic principles of governance and have been complemented by legislative activity within the territory. As far as the authority of the Security Council itself to undertake such enterprises is concerned, it is now beyond dispute that the Security Council can deal with questions of the administration and even disposition of territory.[196] Although the normal and natural basis for this is Chapter VII action, it is possible for an international administration to be established on the basis of Chapter VI's peaceful settlement provisions.[197]

The fount of authority will vary from situation to situation. In the case of Cambodia, UNTAC derived its power from a UN resolution after the Supreme National Council, established by the Comprehensive Settlement Agreement, had transferred to the UN 'all powers necessary' to implement the agreement, which also contained provisions concerning the relationship between the Supreme National Council and UNTAC. The mandate for UNTAES, UNTAET and UNMIK derived from Security Council resolutions,[198] that for the EU administration of Mostar from an

[196] See, eg, Crawford, above n 29, 563, and Zimmermann and Stahn, above n 177, 438. Whether there is a limit to what the Council can do as a matter of principle in the context of particular threats to or breaches of international peace and security is beyond the scope of this chapter.

[197] See, eg, UNTAC and Cambodia, see above

[198] Note the argument that the Federal Republic of Yugoslavia was not a member of the UN at the relevant time, see Zimmermann and Stahn, above n 177, 438–40. See UNGA Res 47/1 (22 December 1992) and 55/12 (1 November 2000); UNSC Res 757 (30 May 1992) and 777 (19 September 1992) and the UN Legal Opinion of 29 September 1992, A/47/485. However, the FRY did at that time maintain that it was such a member and the doctrine of estoppel would no doubt apply to constrain any subsequent denial with regard specifically to Kosovo. In any event, the FRY gave its consent to the Kosovo arrangements in the Military and Technical Agreement of 9 June 1999.

agreement between the EU and other relevant parties, that for the administration of Brcko from a series of arbitration awards based upon the Dayton Peace Agreement, while that of the High Representative in Bosnia and Herzegovina from the Dayton Peace Agreement as substantively enhanced in practice by the decision of the Peace Implementation Council. The situation in Iraq from 2003 to 2004 marks a confluence of two sources of authority: the traditional law of occupation plus the extended mandate provided by the Security Council. In each case, the range of powers granted to the particular administration will depend primarily upon the terms of the mandate, however sourced and subsequent practice, so that, for example, while UNTAES exercised executive power and little legislative power, both UNMIK and UNTAET exercised significant legislative power, as did the Authority in Iraq between the commencement of military operations and the formal ending of occupation in June 2004.

Where there is more than one source of authority, issues often arise as to priority and conflicting or inconsistent requirements. Insofar as hierarchical questions are raised, it is clear that a Security Council resolution under Chapter VII will be superior to the rules of belligerent occupation where this is relevant. This follows from the Iraq situation between 2003 and 2004 where the proactive requirements of resolution 1483 were clearly intended to operate notwithstanding the law of occupation to the contrary and from the terms of resolution 1244 concerning Kosovo where the range of powers granted to UNMIK far exceeded the limits imposed by traditional occupation law and included the authority to reorganise governmental institutions of all kinds. However, this cannot be taken to mean that in such situations the rules of international humanitarian law were totally superseded. The correct position must rather be that international humanitarian law is applied subject to any particular norms being necessarily replaced by clear provisions to that effect contained in a binding Security Council resolution.

Where there is one source of authority, interpretational problems will tend to arise in the context of the exercise of legislative or executive power. For example, it may be argued that it is far from clear that the authority of the High Representative, as it has evolved, can be firmly grounded upon the Dayton agreement. Perhaps some element of reinterpretation of the agreement has taken place by the relevant parties as a matter of subsequent practice as reflected in the Conclusions of the Bonn Summit of 1997 or consensual activity by the Bosnian government and constituent Entities. Further, in the case of UNMIK, it could be maintained that its legislative competence derived, in the absence of an explicit provision, implicitly by way of a broad understanding of the resolution as expressed in its first Regulation. However one characterises the precise nature of such legislative enactments (usually termed Regulations or

Orders),[199] legal questions do arise as to their interpretation in the context of the mandating instruments and accountability.

The issue of the termination of the authority of the third-party administration is an important one. In the case of occupation, termination occurs upon a peace treaty between the parties concerned or other internationally recognised formal withdrawal of effective control over the territory or where the ousted sovereign is able to regain control,[200] but otherwise the position is rather unclear, appearing to focus upon the exercise of actual control without defining what that means, a point raised with regard to the Gaza Strip. In the case of international administration, the date of termination may be specified, as in the case of UNTAC (Cambodia) where the mission was authorised to operate for a period of up to 18 months, or dependent upon the completion of a particular defined task, as in the cases of Libya, West Irian and East Timor, or rather more open-ended with objectives less clearly specified, as in Bosnia and Kosovo. In the latter situation, it is then up to the mission concerned (and ultimately the Security Council) to determine when its aim has been achieved.

C. Applicable Law

Unlike the situation that exists with regard to the source of authority, the position as to the applicable law as it affects occupation and international administration situations shows elements of convergence. In the case of traditional occupations, the occupying power is to retain the existing framework as far as possible, consistent with the maintenance of public order and the needs of military necessity. However, evolving international law has made international human rights law as well as humanitarian law applicable in addition to the pre-existing local law. How far the introduction of the former impacts upon the presumption upon minimal interference with the local law is unclear, but that it does have an impact is beyond dispute. One further issue concerns the application of the domestic law. Officials, including armed forces personnel, are subject to their own local law to the extent that governmental activities are concerned. Thus in English law, soldiers are subject

[199] See, eg, Ruffert, above n 126, and E De Wet, 'The Direct Administration of Territories by the United Nations and its Member States in the Post Cold War Era: Legal Bases and Implications for National Law' (2004) 8 *Max Planck Yearbook of United Nations Law* 291.

[200] HP Gasser suggests also *debellatio*, but this probably unlikely, D Fleck, *The Handbook of Humanitarian Law in Armed Conflicts* (Oxford University Press, 1995) 251. Art 6 of the Fourth Geneva Convention provides merely that the application of the Convention shall cease one year after the general close of military operations, although the occupying power will be bound by a number of key provisions to the extent that the power exercises the functions of government in the territory.

to English criminal law wherever they are, as if they are in the jurisdiction.[201] This will include legislative provisions concerning war crimes, crimes against humanity and genocide and will include the provisions of the European Convention on Human Rights as incorporated by the Human Rights Act 1998 in certain situations.[202]

In the case of the international administration of territory, the applicable law will usually be specified in an enactment by the mission in question. To the local law will usually be added the legislative acts of the mission authorities, as in the case of Kosovo and East Timor, for example, and priority will be accorded to the latter, as indeed was the case with Namibia. Sometimes the provisions of the local law will be deemed to apply to the extent that they are consistent with the international administration's decrees. In Kosovo, the applicable local law was redefined from that in being at the date of the relevant Security Council resolution to that in force on 22 March 1989 due to the introduction after that date of discriminatory laws. Priority is given to the Regulations of UNMIK and the application of international human rights provisions is established. A further question is whether international humanitarian law also applies. Until relatively recently, international organisations were ambivalent as to the application of humanitarian law to their mission.[203] On 6 August 1999 the Secretary General issued a statement confirming that the principles and rules of international humanitarian law apply to UN forces when in situations of armed conflict they are actively engaged as combatants.[204] However, this statement does not appear to cover forces not operating under UN command and control, so many questions remain,[205] although it should be pointed out that the states supplying forces for international administration duties are bound by humanitarian law.

Other issues of priority with regard to the established applicable law that are raised include the position with regard to any conflict between

[201] See s 70 of the Army Act 1955 as amended and Lord Bingham, *R v Boyd* [2002] UKHL 31 at paras 4–5. See also the International Criminal Court Act 2001.

[202] See the decision of the House of Lords in *Al-Skeini v Secretary of State for Defence* [2007] UKHL 26. Currently the situation in English law is that persons held in British military detention facilities benefit from the application of the European Human Rights Convention, but that the Convention would not apply outside of the UK where British forces are simply on patrol in areas not within their effective overall control as per the Convention case law, See, eg, *Cyprus v Turkey* (Judgment) ECHR 10 May 2001; *Banković v Belgium* (Judgment) 12 December 2001and *Issa v Turkey* (Judgment) 16 November 2004.

[203] See, eg, L Green, *The Contemporary Law of Armed Conflict* (2nd edn, Manchester, Manchester University Press, 2000), ch 20 and C Greenwood, 'International Humanitarian Law and United Nations Military Operations' (1998) 1 *Yearbook of International Humanitarian Law* 3. See also the resolutions of the Institut de Droit International stating that humanitarian law applied to the UN, (1971) 54 (II) *Annuaire de l'Institut de Droit International* 465 and (1975) 56 *Annuaire de l'Institut de Droit International* 540

[204] ST/SGB/1999/13.

[205] See Ratner, 'Foreign Occupation', above n 23, 705–6.

the provisions of humanitarian law and human rights law conflict, for example, with regard to the detention of persons and by extension between a Security Council mandate and human rights. With regard to the latter, the recent English Court of Appeal case of *Al-Jedda v Secretary of State for Defence* came to the conclusion that in such a situation priority lies with the Security Council in view of Article 103 of the Charter providing for the superiority of Charter obligations over those arising from other international instruments.[206]

D. Accountability Issues

In the case of occupations, occupying forces are subject to their own domestic law, which will usually contain international humanitarian law principles, either by direct legislative action incorporating the Geneva Conventions and other pertinent agreements or by way of international customary law, such as the Hague Regulations, deemed part of the internal law, as well as relevant public law principles. Together with relevant human rights provisions, a framework for accountability thus exists. Internationally, the existence of, for example, the International Committee of the Red Cross and other non-governmental organisations, and the operations of various international organisations will or may constitute sources of pressure for the accountability of those violating the law in occupied territories. Further, the Security Council or the International Court of Justice may adopt relevant binding measures.

In the case of international administrations of territory, the matter is more complex. UN missions will be subject to a measure of UN control, being accountable in principle to the Secretary General and Security Council,[207] but in practice this may be seen as operating in a less than efficacious manner. Officials and forces on UN mission will remain subject to accountability under their own domestic legal systems, but accountability within the territory being administered is likely to prove problematic. This issue has received much attention in Kosovo in view of the wide immunities conferred on UNMIK and KFOR in Regulation 47/2000, thereby depriving the local courts of jurisdiction with regard to such personnel and their property and assets. In Bosnia, the High Representative has often asserted that certain executive decisions are not subject to domestic review as they were adopted pursuant to an international mandate and in the light of his position as a 'final authority' under the Dayton Agreement, and this has been accepted by the Consti-

[206] [2006] EWCA Civ 327.

[207] See, eg, SR Ratner, *The New UN Peacekeeping: Building Peace in Lands of Conflict After the Cold War,* (New York, St Martin's Press, 1995) 41–50.

tutional Court of Bosnia and Herzegovina.[208] An Ombudsman has been established and ways to rendering enforceable the European Convention on Human Rights in the territory are being investigated, although complications exist in view of the uncertain status of the territory in international law and for the purposes of identifying the state or states within whose jurisdiction the territory may be deemed to fall in view of the lack of control exercised by Serbia and Montenegro (the former Federal Republic of Yugoslavia). Further, the ECHR held in *Behrami v France* that both KFOR and UNMIK were operating under the valid and binding authority of Chapter VII of the UN Security Council and that any impugned action would therefore be attributable to the United Nations, which benefited from an international legal personality separate from that of its member states. Since the UN was not a member of the European Convention system, the ECHRwould not have jurisdiction with regard to a complaint against a state or states acting in Kosovo within the framework of either or both KFOR and UNMIK.[209]

While UNMIK has recently signed an agreement to implement the Framework Convention for the Protection of National Minorities of the Council of Europe and for the extension of the right of the European Committee for the Prevention of Torture and Inhuman or Degrading Treatment or Punishment to visit places of detention coming under the authority of the interim civil administration in Kosovo, such an agreement with regard to KFOR has not been reached.

E. Sovereignty and Third-Party Administration

In the light of the extensive developments taking place with regard both to traditional occupations and to international administration of territory, the question may finally be asked as to the place of sovereignty in the changed world. Sovereignty remains as a totemic symbol. No entity seeking sovereignty will willingly settle for less; no state will willingly forego its sovereign status. Compromises will usually be made on the exercise of sovereignty in specific areas in order to maximise particular benefits, especially economic ones, as the evolution of international trade law demonstrates, or indeed to further human rights, but no surrender of the very existence of that status can easily be achieved. However, the problems arise not where states exist without existential challenge or where aspirant candidates encounter no opposition, but in the troubled region of significant breakdown in civil society, whether internal or international, whether actual or potential. In such instances, mechanisms

[208] See, eg, *Milorad Bilbija et al*, AP-953/05, decision of the Constitutional Court of Bosnia and Herzegovina, 8 July 2006, http://www.esiweb.org/pdf/esi_news_id_113a.pdf.

[209] Judgment of 2 May 2007.

will be sought to resolve or cope with the crises in question and it is here that recourse to the nature of sovereignty is of little assistance in practice. The suspension, or by-passing, or sovereignty may in certain situations be the best way to move forward. As the scope of international law increases to cover an ever broader range of persons and issues, so the legal advantages of formal sovereign status tend to fade. Effective control, which is in any event a component of territorial title, may be the best way in which to resolve an actual or threatened breakdown of peace and security pending a final settlement acceptable to all, and functional administrative operations may constitute a perfectly acceptable alternative to a highly contested sovereignty, at least as an interim or transitional measure. Of course, there may be circumstances where an administrative arrangement involving less than full sovereignty may in any event be the optimum solution with elements of divided control by overlapping authorities. The goal will tend to be sovereignty, but reality may interpose an alternative solution, and if it works, that will be its own justification.

Index

Milton Keynes UK
Ingram Content Group UK Ltd.
UKHW021049180224
437976UK00003B/8/J

9 781841 137971